Notable American Novelists

Revised Edition

MAGILL'S CHOICE

Notable American Novelists

Revised Edition

Volume 1

James Agee — Ernest J. Gaines

1 – 504

edited by

Carl Rollyson

Baruch College, City University of New York

SALEM PRESS, INC.

Pasadena, California Hackensack, New Jersey

Cover photo: ©iStockphoto.com/Stefan Klein

Some essays in these volumes originally appeared in *Critical Survey of Long Fiction, Revised Edition,* 2000. New material has been added.

∞ The paper used in these volumes conforms to the American National Standard for Permanence of Paper for Printed Library Materials, Z39.48-1992 (R1997).

Library of Congress Cataloging-in-Publication Data

Notable American novelists / edited by Carl Rollyson.
p. cm. — (Magill's choice)
Includes bibliographical references and index.
ISBN 978-1-58765-393-3 (set : alk. paper) — ISBN 978-1-58765-394-0 (vol. 1 : alk. paper) — ISBN 978-1-58765-395-7 (vol. 2 : alk. paper) — ISBN 978-1-58765-396-4 (vol. 3 : alk. paper) 1. Novelists, American—Biography—Dictionaries. 2. American fiction—Bio-bibliography—Dictionaries. 3. American fiction—Dictionaries. I. Rollyson, Carl E. (Carl Edmund)

PS371.N68 2007
813.009'0003—dc22
[B]

2007018542

First printing

PRINTED IN CANADA

Contents—Volume 1

Publisher's Note

This three-volume contribution to the Magill's Choice series is the first revision of Salem Press's *Notable American Novelists* (2000), which had biographical and analytical essays on 120 of the best-known American writers of long fiction from the nineteenth and twentieth centuries. This new edition includes all the original essays and adds 25 other important writers, including 9 Canadians, for a total of 145 essays. All these essays have been updated, as necessary, to cover developments through early 2007. In selecting the authors covered here, every effort has been made to choose the novelists whose works are most often studied in North American high school and undergraduate literature courses.

Among the frequently studied authors covered in *Notable American Novelists, Revised Edition* are such nineteenth century giants as James Fenimore Cooper, Nathaniel Hawthorne, Herman Melville, and Mark Twain and such towering twentieth century writers as Ernest Hemingway, William Faulkner, Sinclair Lewis, Toni Morrison, Katherine Anne Porter, and John Steinbeck. Other major writers covered here include E. L. Doctorow, Joseph Heller, John Irving, Norman Mailer, Vladimir Nabokov, Joyce Carol Oates, Thomas Pynchon, John Updike, and Kurt Vonnegut, as well as such popular writers as Stephen King, Larry McMurtry, James Michener, and Anne Rice. The Canadian authors added to this edition are Margaret Atwood, Morley Callaghan, Robertson Davies, Frederick Philip Grove, Margaret Laurence, Hugh MacLennan, Mordecai Richler, Sinclair Ross, and Ethel Wilson. Other notable additions to this set include Toni Cade Bambara, John Grisham, Rolando Hinojosa, and Robert Penn Warren.

The range of genres and styles covered in *Notable American Novelists, Revised Edition* encompasses the naturalism of Theodore Dreiser and Frank Norris, the metafiction of John Barth, and the nonfiction novel of Truman Capote. Beat writers Jack Kerouac and William Burroughs are included, as are a number of writers from such disparate genres as science fiction and mystery and detective fiction. Among the notable science fiction writers covered are Isaac Asimov, Ray Bradbury, Marion Zimmer Bradley, Octavia E. Butler, Samuel R. Delany, Philip K. Dick, and Ursula K. Le Guin. Mystery writers include Raymond Chandler, Dashiell Hammett, Elmore Leonard, and Ross Macdonald.

The wide diversity of the American experience is also well represented here. Among the African American writers covered are Arna Bontemps, James Baldwin, Toni Cade Bambara, Ralph Ellison, Ishmael Reed, Alice Walker, and Richard Wright. Hispanic authors include Rudolfo Anaya, Oscar Hijuelos, and Rolando Hinojosa. Native American novelists include Louise Erdrich, Barbara Kingsolver, and Leslie Marmon Silko. Jewish writers include Saul Bellow, Bernard Malamud, Chaim Potok, Philip Roth, and Isaac Bashevis Singer. Asian American writers are represented by novelist Amy Tan.

How to Use This Book

Essays are arranged alphabetically by authors' names. Each essay begins with standard reference data: the dates and places of the author's birth and death and a list of the author's principal works of long fiction, with first publication dates. The balance of each essay is divided into the following subheaded sections:

- **Other literary forms** briefly describes the literary genres other than long fiction in which the author has worked.
- **Achievements** summarizes the author's central contribution to the field of long fiction and notes the authors' major honors and awards.
- **Biography** provides a sketch of the author's life.
- **Analysis** examines the author's long fictional works in detail, illuminating characteristic themes and techniques. This section is subdivided into sections subheaded with the titles of selected works representing the author's most important and most representative novels.
- **Other major works** is a categorized list of the titles and dates of works by the author in genres other than long fiction, such as plays, poetry, short fiction, and nonfiction.
- **Bibliography** is an annotated list of books and articles useful for further study. Every author bibliography in this revised edition has been updated to include an average of at least two new citations.

All articles are signed by their principal writers and, where applicable, by their updating contributors.

Three helpful reference features are included at the end of volume 3: a glossary titled "Terms and Techniques," a time line of the authors' birth dates, and a general index. A list of contributing scholars, with their affiliations, appears at the beginning of volume 1.

List of Contributors

Michael Adams
City University of New York, Graduate Center

Timothy Dow Adams
West Virginia University

Terry L. Andrews
Rutgers University

Karen L. Arnold
Independent Scholar

Marilyn Arnold
Independent Scholar

Linda C. Badley
Independent Scholar

Dan Barnett
Butte College

Kate Begnal
Utah State University

Alvin K. Benson
Utah Valley State College

Jacquelyn Benton
Metropolitan State College of Denver

Margaret Boe Birns
New York University

Nicholas Birns
New School University

Mary A. Blackmon
Hardin-Simmons University

B. Diane Blackwood
Independent Scholar

Bernadette Lynn Bosky
Independent Scholar

William Boyle
Independent Scholar

Harold Branam
Savanna State University

Carl Brucker
Arkansas Tech University

Domenic Bruni
Oklahoma State University

Hallman B. Bryant
Clemson University

Karen Carmean
Converse College

Thomas Cassidy
South Carolina State University

Allan Chavkin
Southwest Texas State University

John L. Cobbs
Independent Scholar

Robin Payne Cohen
Southwest Texas State University

David W. Cole
University of Wisconsin Colleges

David Conde
Metropolitan State College of Denver

David Cowart
University of South Carolina

Carol I. Croxton
University of Southern Colorado

Clark Davis
Northeast Louisiana University

J. Madison Davis
Pennsylvania State University

Bill Delaney
Independent Scholar

Lloyd N. Dendinger
University of South Alabama

Richard H. Dillman
Independent Scholar

David C. Dougherty
Loyola College

Stefan Dziemianowicz
Independent Scholar

Grace Eckley
Independent Scholar

Wilton Eckley
Colorado School of Mines

Bruce L. Edwards, Jr.
Bowling Green State University

Robert P. Ellis
Independent Scholar

Ann Willardson Engar
Independent Scholar

Grace Farrell
Butler University

Howard Faulkner
University of Kansas

John H. Ferres
Michigan State University

Richard A. Fine
Independent Scholar

Edward Fiorelli
St. John's University, New York

June M. Frazer
Western Illinois University

Miriam Fuchs
Independent Scholar

Kelly Fuller
Claremont Graduate University

Honora Rankine Galloway
Independent Scholar

Ann D. Garbett
Averett University

Marshall Bruce Gentry
University of Indianapolis

Craig Gilbert
Portland State University

James R. Giles
Northern Illinois University

L. H. Goldman
Independent Scholar

Charles A. Gramlich
Xavier University of Louisiana

Jay L. Halio
University of Delaware

David Mike Hamilton
Independent Scholar

John P. Harrington
Independent Scholar

June Harris
University of Arizona South

Peter B. Heller
Manhattan College

Terry Heller
Coe College

Allen Hibbard
Middle Tennessee State University

Arthur D. Hlavaty
Independent Scholar

James L. Hodge
Bowdoin College

Nika Hoffman
Crossroads School

William Hoffman
Independent Scholar

Watson Holloway
Brunswick College

Gregory D. Horn
Southwest Virginia Community College

Pierre L. Horn
Wright State University

Linda Howe
Independent Scholar

E. D. Huntley
Appalachian State University

Julie Husband
State University of New York at Buffalo

Clarence O. Johnson
Independent Scholar

Theresa M. Kanoza
Lincoln Land Community College

Deborah Kaplan
Independent Scholar

Anna B. Katona
Independent Scholar

Steven G. Kellman
University of Texas, San Antonio

Sue L. Kimball
Methodist College

Anne Mills King
Prince George's Community College

James Reynolds Kinzey
Independent Scholar

Marilyn Kongslie
Independent Scholar

Brooks Landon
University of Iowa

Ralph L. Langenheim, Jr.
University of Illinois, Urbana-Champaign

Donald F. Larsson
Mankato State University

Norman Lavers
Arkansas State University

Henry J. Lindborg
Marian College

Robert Emmet Long
Independent Scholar

Philip A. Luther
Independent Scholar

Joanne McCarthy
Independent Scholar

James C. MacDonald
Humber College

Fred B. McEwen
Waynesburg College

Edythe M. McGovern
West Los Angeles College

Dennis Q. McInerny
Holy Apostles College

Bryant Mangum
Independent Scholar

Patricia Marks
Valdosta State College

Bruce K. Martin
Drake University

Charles E. May
California State University, Long Beach

Laurence W. Mazzeno
Alvernia College

Jaime Armin Mejía
Southwest Texas State University

Ray Mescallado
Independent Scholar

P. Andrew Miller
Independent Scholar

Joseph R. Millichap
Western Kentucky College

Kathleen N. Monahan
Saint Peter's College

Robert A. Morace
Daemen College

Charmaine Allmon Mosby
Western Kentucky University

Roark Mulligan
Christopher Newport University

John M. Muste
Ohio State University

William Nelles
University of Massachusetts, Dartmouth

Stella A. Nesanovich
McNeese State University

John Nizalowski
Mesa State College

Jim O'Loughlin
Behrend College, Pennsylvania State University

James Norman O'Neill
Independent Scholar

Lisa Paddock
Independent Scholar

Donald Palumbo
Northern Michigan University

Robert J. Paradowski
Rochester Institute of Technology

John G. Parks
Miami University

David B. Parsell
Furman University

William E. Pemberton
University of Wisconsin, La Crosse

Alice Hall Petry
Rhode Island School of Design

Victoria Price
Independent Scholar

Karen Priest
Lama University at Orange

Catherine Rambo
Independent Scholar

Edward C. Reilly
Arkansas State University

Rosemary M. Canfield Reisman
Charleston Southern University

Martha E. Rhynes
Independent Scholar

Carl Rollyson
Baruch College, City University of New York

Arthur M. Saltzman
Missouri Southern State College

Joan Corey Semonella
Independent Scholar

Walter Shear
Pittsburgh State University

Frank W. Shelton
Limestone College

T. A. Shippey
St. Louis University

R. Baird Shuman
University of Illinois, Urbana-Champaign

Charles L. P. Silet
Iowa State University

Linda Simon
Independent Scholar

Jamie Sondra Sindell
Onondaga Community College

Rebecca G. Smith
Independent Scholar

Roger Smith
Independent Scholar

Traci S. Smrcka
Hardin-Simmons University

Katherine Snipes
Independent Scholar

Joshua Stein
University of California, Riverside

Karen F. Stein
University of Rhode Island

J. David Stevens
Seton Hall University

William B. Stone
Independent Scholar

Gerald H. Strauss
Bloomsburg University

W. J. Stuckey
Purdue University

Mary Ellen Stumpf
Independent Scholar

Peter Swirski
University of Hong Kong

Philip A. Tapley
Louisiana College

Judith K. Taylor
Northern Kentucky University

Thomas J. Taylor
Independent Scholar

Richard Tuerk
Texas A&M University, Commerce

Nancy Walker
Vanderbilt University

Gary P. Walton
Northern Kentucky University

Bernice Larson Webb
University of Southwestern Louisiana

Judith Weise
State University of New York, Potsdam

Craig Werner
University of Wisconsin

John T. West III
Northwest Arkansas Community College

Dexter Westrum
Ottawa University

Bruce Wiebe
Independent Scholar

Albert Wilhelm
Tennessee Technological University

Thomas Willard
University of Arizona

Donna Glee Williams
North Carolina Center for the Advancement of Technology

Judith Barton Williamson
Sauk Valley Community College

Chester L. Wolford
Behrend University, Pennsylvania State University

Jennifer L. Wyatt
Civic Memorial High School

Complete List of Contents

Contents—Volume 1

Contents—Volume 2

Contents—Volume 3

Notable American Novelists

Revised Edition

James Agee

Born: Knoxville, Tennessee; November 27, 1909
Died: New York, New York; May 16, 1955

Principal long fiction • *The Morning Watch,* 1951; *A Death in the Family,* 1957.

Other literary forms • James Agee's earliest published book, *Permit Me Voyage* (1934), was a collection of poems, his second a nonfiction account of Alabama sharecroppers during the Great Depression. He and photographer Walker Evans lived with their subjects for eight weeks in 1936 on a *Fortune* magazine assignment, with a number of critics hailing the resulting book, *Let Us Now Praise Famous Men* (1941), as Agee's masterpiece. From 1941 through 1948, Agee wrote film reviews and feature articles for *Time* and *The Nation*; thereafter, he worked on film scripts in Hollywood, his most notable screenplay being his 1952 adaptation of C. S. Forester's novel *The African Queen* (1935). He also wrote an esteemed television script on Abraham Lincoln for the *Omnibus* series in 1952. *Letters of James Agee to Father Flye* (1962) contains his thirty-year correspondence with an Episcopalian priest who had been his teacher.

Achievements • The prestigious Yale Series of Younger Poets sponsored Agee's first book, Archibald MacLeish contributing its introduction. Agee went on to gain an unusual degree of literary fame for a man who published only three books, two of them slim ones, in his lifetime. Sometimes accused of wasting his talent on magazine and film "hack" work, Agee lavished the same painstaking attention on film reviews as on his carefully crafted books. His film work was highly prized by director John Huston, and their collaboration on *The African Queen* resulted in a film classic. His greatest fame developed posthumously, however, when his novel *A Death in the Family* won a 1958 Pulitzer Prize. Three years later, Tad Mosel's dramatization of the novel, *All the Way Home* (1960), earned another Pulitzer. The continued popularity of Agee's work attests his vast human sympathy, his unusual lyrical gift, and his ability to evoke the tension and tenderness of family life in both fiction and nonfiction.

Biography • Born in Knoxville, Tennessee, on November 27, 1909, James Rufus Agee was the son of Hugh James Agee, from a Tennessee mountain family, and Laura Whitman Tyler, the well-educated and highly religious daughter of a businessman. His father sang mountain ballads to him, while his mother passed on to him her love of drama and music. Hugh Agee's death in an automobile accident in the spring of 1916 profoundly influenced young Rufus, as he was called in the family.

Agee received a first-rate education at St. Andrew's School, near Sewanee, Tennessee, where he developed a lifelong friendship with Father James Harold Flye; at Phillips Exeter Academy, Exeter, New Hampshire; and at Harvard College, where in his senior year he edited the *Harvard Advocate.* Upon his graduation in 1932, he went immediately to work for *Fortune* and later its sister publication, *Time.* Over a sixteen-year period, he did a variety of staff work, reviewing, and feature stories while living in the New York metropolitan area.

Library of Congress

After 1950, Agee spent considerable time in California working mostly with John Huston, but his health deteriorated. Highly disciplined as a writer, Agee exerted less successful control over his living habits, with chronic insomnia and alcohol contributing to a succession of heart attacks beginning early in 1951. Agee married three times and had a son by his second wife and three more children by his third, Mia Fritsch, who survived him. He succumbed to a fatal heart attack in a New York taxicab on May 16, 1955, at the age of forty-five.

Analysis • Neither James Agee's novella *The Morning Watch* nor his novel *A Death in the Family* offers much in the way of plot. The former covers a few hours of a boy's Good Friday morning at an Episcopalian boys' school, the latter a few days encompassing the death and funeral of a young husband and father. His fiction develops a remarkable lyric intensity, however, and dramatizes with sensitivity the consciousness of children. He presents the minutiae of life as experienced by his characters at times of maximum awareness and thereby lifts them out of the category of mere realistic detail into the realm of spiritual discovery.

Even a cursory glance at the facts of Agee's life reveals how autobiographically based his fiction is. There is no reason to doubt that St. Andrew's, where he spent the years from ten to sixteen, supplies the framework for *The Morning Watch*, or that Agee's own family, seen at the time of Hugh Agee's fatal accident, furnishes the building blocks of the more ambitious *A Death in the Family*. At the same time, Agee permitted himself artistic freedom in selecting, altering, and arranging the facts of raw experience. It is clear that his literary appropriation of his childhood owes much to reflection and interpretation in the light of maturity.

Agee was a writer who stayed close to home in his work. His fiction displays no trace of the two-thirds of his life spent mainly in New England, New York, and California. As is so often the case with southern writers, Agee's work is imbued with a sense of his origins, of folk traditions viewed in their own right and in competition with the emerging urban culture. The South, with its insistence on the primacy of personal and familial relationships, was in his bones. In keeping to his earliest and most vividly felt years, Agee created a convincing context in which experiences of universal significance can unfold.

The Morning Watch • At the beginning of *The Morning Watch*, a preadolescent boy and several of his classmates are awakened in the wee hours of Good Friday morning to spend their assigned time in an overnight vigil in the school chapel as part of the Maundy Thursday-Good Friday devotions. Anyone who has experienced a period of religious scrupulosity in childhood will respond to Agee's presentation of Richard. While his friends fumble and curse in the darkness, Richard prepares for adoration. After arriving in the chapel before the veiled monstrance, he strives to pray worthily despite the almost inevitable distractions of potentially sinful thoughts, the dangers of spiritual pride, and the torture of the hard kneeling board. Richard wonders whether he can make a virtue of his discomfort: To what extent is it proper for him to suffer along with the crucified Savior? Agee brings Richard intensely alive and conveys the power and the puzzlement of mighty spiritual claims at this stage of life.

The narrative also develops from the start Richard's sense of his relationships with the other boys, most of whom, he realizes, lack his delicate spiritual antennae. After the stint in the chapel is over, he and two classmates do not return to the dormitory as expected but decide on an early morning swim. Their adventure is presented in a heavily symbolic way. Richard dives into deep water at their swimming hole, stays down so long that his friends begin to worry, and emerges before his lungs give out. The boys torture and kill a snake, with Richard (who, like Agee himself, cannot bear to kill) finishing off the job. He debates in his mind whether the snake is poisonous and whether to wash the slime from his hand, deciding finally in the negative. He carries back to the school a locust shell he has found on the way. The snake, which seemingly cannot be killed, suggests both ineradicable evil and, in its victimization, Christ; the locust shell, which he holds next to his heart, seems to represent suffering in a purer form. Richard's dive into the water and subsequent resurfacing obviously symbolize his own "death" and "resurrection" in this Christian Holy Week.

Some critics have noted the influence of James Joyce on this novella. Certainly Richard resembles in certain ways the young protagonists of some of Joyce's *Dubliners* (1914) stories as well as Stephen Dedalus in *A Portrait of the Artist as a Young Man* (1916). Attracted by religious mysteries and artifacts, Richard wishes to appropriate them for his own purposes. He senses the conflict of religion with the world, evinces distaste for the practices of the latter, and hopes to fashion a life that blends the best of both. Although Richard's appropriation of religious rite and doctrine is less consciously the artist's than is that of Stephen Dedalus, the reader senses that his individualistic spirituality will almost inevitably bring him into a Joycean conflict with conservative religious practice.

A Death in the Family • Because *The Morning Watch*, despite its provocatively ambiguous conflict between the world and the spirit, is somewhat labored and precious, and because Agee's short stories were few and insignificant, his reputation as an important American novelist rests primarily on one book that he did not quite complete before his early death, *A Death in the Family*. As he left it, the story begins at the supper table of the Follet household in Knoxville, Tennessee, in about 1915, and ends just after Jay Follet's funeral on the third day following. Agee had written a short descriptive essay, "Knoxville: Summer 1915" (which makes an appropriate preface to the novel), and six additional sections, which together make up about one-fifth the length of the narrative.

Although all the six scenes (as they will be termed here) pertain to times prior to that of the main story, it remains unclear where Agee intended to place them, or whether he would have used stream-of-consciousness flashbacks, a story-within-a-story technique, or perhaps another method suggested by his cinematic experience to incorporate them. Surely he intended to use them, for they illuminate and enrich the death story despite the absence of any formal linkage among them or collectively to the narrative. The editorial decision to print three of them after each of the first two parts of the three-part narrative seems as logical as any other way under the circumstances.

The novel has no single protagonist. Jay Follet, strong, tall, and taciturn, is described most specifically, at one point being compared to President Abraham Lincoln, though apparently more handsome. Last seen alive one-third of the way through the narrative, he appears in five of the six scenes and remains the main object of the other characters' thoughts in the last two parts of the narrative. At various stages, each important family member reflects on him: his wife Mary, son Rufus, brother Ralph, Mary's parents, Joel and Catherine, Mary's aunt Hannah and her brother Andrew, and even Jay's and Mary's three-year-old daughter, also named Catherine. Agee employs Rufus and Mary as a focus most frequently. No point of view outside the family circle intrudes, and, except on two occasions when the six-year-old Rufus interacts with neighborhood children outside, attention is focused on family members exclusively. Throughout the novel, Agee juxtaposes the tensions and tendernesses of domestic life. The reader is constantly made to feel not only how much the family members love one another but also how abrasive they can be. Recognizing that a family does not succeed automatically, Agee portrays a continual struggle against external divisive pressures and selfishness within.

Jay and Mary's marriage has withstood a number of strains. First of all, their origins differ greatly. Mary's people are the citified, well-educated Lynches; the Follets are Tennessee mountain folk. The couple's ability to harmonize their differences is exemplified in the second of the six scenes. Rufus notes that when singing together, his father interprets music flexibly, "like a darky," while his mother sings true and clear but according to the book. Rufus particularly admires his father's sense of rhythm. Sometimes, the boy observes, his mother tries to sing Jay's way and he hers, but they soon give up and return to what is natural.

Jay's father, who indirectly causes Jay's death, is one point of difference. Mary's antipathy to him is known to all the Follets, but even Jay realizes that his likable father is weak of character. When Jay's brother calls and informs him that their father is very ill, Jay wastes no time in preparing to go to him, despite his suspicion that the unreliable Ralph has greatly exaggerated the danger. It is on his return trip, after learning that his father is all right, that a mechanical defect in Jay's car causes the crash that kills him instantly.

Jay's drinking problem, a Follet weakness, has also distressed his wife, and Jay has vowed to kill himself if he ever gets drunk again. In one of the scenes, Rufus, aware that whiskey is a sore point between his parents, accompanies his father when he stops at a tavern, and it appears that he has overcome his habit of excess, but his reputation has spread. Both the man who finds Jay's body and the children who later taunt Rufus on the street corner attribute his accident to drunken driving, and Mary has to fight off the temptation to consider the possibility.

Religion is another divisive issue. Jay does not appear to be a denominational Christian, while Mary is, like Agee's own mother, a fervent Episcopalian. The men on both sides of the family are either skeptics or thoroughgoing unbelievers. A devotee of Thomas Hardy's fiction, Mary's father, Joel, has little use for piety or what he calls "churchiness." Although he originally disapproved of Mary's marriage to Jay, he has come to terms with Jay, whom he views as a counterweight to Mary's religiosity. Mary's brother Andrew carries on open warfare with the Christian God. When he first hears of Jay's accident, Mary senses that he is mentally rehearsing a speech about the folly of belief in a benevolent deity. Even young Rufus is a budding skeptic. Told that God has let his father "go to sleep," he ferrets out the details and concludes that the concussion he has heard about, "not God," has put his father to sleep. When he hears that his father will wake up at the Final Judgment, he wonders what good that is. The women accept the inscrutable as God's will, but the men take an agnostic stance and fear the influence of the Church. Father Jackson, the most unpleasant person in the novel, ministers to Mary in her bereavement. Rufus quickly decides that the priest's power is malevolent and that, were his real father present, the false father would not be allowed into his home.

Some hours after the confirmation of Jay's death, Mary feels his presence in the room, and though Andrew and Joel will not concede any kind of spiritual visitation, they acknowledge that they too felt "something." Later, Andrew tells Rufus of an event he considers "miraculous": the settling of a butterfly on Jay's coffin in the grave and the creature's subsequent flight, high into the sunlight. The men's unbelief, then, is not positivistic; they recognize the possibility of a realm beyond the natural order, but they bitterly oppose the certified spiritual agent, Father Jackson, as too self-assured and quick to condemn.

To counter the estrangements brought on by cultural and religious conflicts in the family, reconciliations dot the narrative. Rufus senses periodic estrangements from his father and then joyful feelings of unity. Jay frequently feels lonely, even homesick. Crossing the river between Knoxville and his old home, he feels restored. To go home is impracticable, bound up with a vanished childhood. In one of the scenes, the family visits Rufus's great-great-grandmother. It is a long, winding journey into the hills and into the past. It is apparent that none of the younger generations of Follets has gone to see the old woman in a long time. Rufus, who has never been there, comes home in a way impossible to his father. The old woman, more than one hundred years old, barely acknowledges any of her numerous offspring, but she clasps Rufus, the fifth-generation descendant, who is joyful to her. On other occasions, Jay, by imaginative identification with Rufus, can feel as if he is his "own self" again.

Mary also feels alternate waves of friendship with, and estrangement from, her father. He, in turn, has a wife with whom communication is difficult because of her deafness. When Catherine cannot hear her husband, she seldom asks him to repeat himself, as if fearful of exasperating him. In this way, she is insulated from his unbelief. Although they talk little, they communicate by gestures and physical closeness. Agee shows him taking her elbow to help her over a curb and carefully steering her up the street toward their home. Rufus and his father are usually silent on their walks; they communicate by sitting together on a favorite rock and watching passersby.

Much of the talk following Jay's death is irritable and nerve-shattering. Andrew dwells thoughtlessly on the one-chance-in-a-million nature of Jay's accident, for which his father rebukes him. Mary begs Andrew to have mercy and then hysterically begs his forgiveness, upon which her aunt censures her for unwarranted humility. Both Mary and Andrew are enduring crises, however, and are hardly responsible for what they say. She is resisting the temptation to despair of God's mercy; he is trying to come to terms with a possibly meaningless universe. Andrew communicates best with services; throughout the hours of distress, he is unfailingly helpful.

The truest communication exists between Jay and Mary. When he is not silent, he can be sullen or wrathful. As he prepares to set forth on his journey to his father's, Mary dreads the "fury and profanity" she can expect if, for example, the car will not start, but this sometimes harsh husband stops in the bedroom to recompose their bed so it will look comfortable and inviting when she returns to it. She disapproves of his drinking strong coffee, but she makes it very strong on this occasion because she knows he will appreciate it. By dozens of such unobtrusive deeds, Jay and Mary express their love, which prevails over the numerous adverse circumstances and personal weaknesses that threaten it.

Long before he began work on *A Death in the Family*, Agee expressed his intention to base a literary work on his father's death. The eventual novel is thus deeply meditated and very personal. At the same time, it attains universality by means of its painstaking precision. In the Follets can be seen any family that has striven to harmonize potentially divisive differences or has answered courageously a sudden tragedy. As in loving families generally, the tensions do not disappear. At the end, Andrew, for the first time in his life, invites Rufus to walk with him. Sensing the negative feelings in his uncle, Rufus nevertheless is afraid to ask him about them. Walking home with this man who can never replicate his father but who will fill as much of the void as possible, Rufus comes to terms with his father's death in the silence that in Agee's fiction communicates beyond the power of words. In this reconstruction of his own most momentous childhood experience, Agee portrays the most difficult reconciliation of all.

Robert P. Ellis

Other major works

SHORT FICTION: "A Mother's Tale," 1952; *Four Early Stories by James Agee*, 1964; *The Collected Short Prose of James Agee*, 1968.

SCREENPLAYS: *The Red Badge of Courage*, 1951 (based on Stephen Crane's novel); *The African Queen*, 1952 (based on C. S. Forester's novel); *The Bride Comes to Yellow Sky*, 1952 (based on Crane's short story); *Noa Noa*, 1953; *White Mane*, 1953; *Green Magic*, 1955; *The Night of the Hunter*, 1955; *Agee on Film: Five Film Scripts*, 1960.

POETRY: *Permit Me Voyage*, 1934; *The Collected Poems of James Agee*, 1968.

NONFICTION: *Let Us Now Praise Famous Men*, 1941; *Agee on Film: Reviews and Comments*, 1958; *Letters of James Agee to Father Flye*, 1962; *James Agee: Selected Journalism*, 1985; *Brooklyn Is: Southeast of the Island, Travel Notes*, 2005 (wr. 1939).

Bibliography

Barson, Alfred. *A Way of Seeing: A Critical Study of James Agee*. Amherst: University of Massachusetts Press, 1972. A revisionist view of Agee, whose earliest critics thought that his talents were dissipated by his diverse interests but who judged him to have been improving at the time of his death. Barson inverts this thesis, stating that Agee's finished work should not be so slighted and that his powers were declining when he died. Contains notes and an index. Should not be confused with *A Way of Seeing: Photographs of New York*, a collection of photographs by Helen Levitt with an essay by Agee.

Bergreen, Laurence. *James Agee: A Life*. New York: E. P. Dutton, 1984. This is one of the best biographies of Agee, thorough and well researched. Its critical analyses are cogent and thoughtful. Bergreen's writing style is appealing. Contains illustrations, notes, bibliography of Agee's writings, bibliography of works about him, and index.

Hughes, William. *James Agee, Omnibus, and Mr. Lincoln: The Culture of Liberalism and the Challenge of Television, 1952-1953.* Lanham, Md.: Scarecrow Press, 2004. Study of Agee's involvement in the early 1950's television production of a drama on Abraham Lincoln.

Kramer, Victor A. *Agee and Actuality: Artistic Vision in His Work.* Troy, N.Y.: Whitston, 1991. Kramer delves into the aesthetics of Agee's writing. This study is valuable for identifying controlling themes that pervade the author's writing.

____________. *A Consciousness of Technique in "Let Us Now Praise Famous Men": With Thirty-one Newly Selected Photographs.* Albany, N.Y.: Whitston, 2001. A reconsideration of Agee's nonfiction work *Let Us Now Praise Famous Men.*

____________. *James Agee.* Boston: Twayne, 1975. Although this well-written book is dated, it remains one of the more valuable sources available to the nonspecialist, useful for its analyses, its bibliography, and its chronology of the author's life.

Lofaro, Michael A., ed. *James Agee: Reconsiderations.* Knoxville: University of Tennessee Press, 1992. The nine essays in this slim volume are carefully considered. Mary Moss's bibliography of secondary sources is especially well crafted and eminently useful, as are penetrating essays by Linda Wagner-Martin and Victor A. Kramer.

Madden, David, and Jeffrey J. Folks, eds. *Remembering James Agee.* 2d ed. Baton Rouge: Louisiana State University Press, 1997. The twenty-two essays in this book touch on every important aspect of Agee's life and work. They range from the reminiscences of Father Flye to those of his third wife, Mia Agee. The interpretive essays on his fiction and films are particularly illuminating, as are the essays on his life as a reporter and writer for *Fortune* and *Time.*

Neuman, Alma. "Thoughts of Jim: A Memoir of Frenchtown and James Agee." *Shenandoah* 33 (1981-1982). A perceptive family assessment by Agee's second wife.

Spiegel, Alan. *James Agee and the Legend of Himself.* Columbia: University of Missouri Press, 1998. In this critical study of Agee's writing, Spiegel offers especially sound insights into the role that childhood reminiscence plays in the author's fiction and into the uses that Agee makes of nostalgia. The hundred pages on *Let Us Now Praise Famous Men* represent one of the best interpretations of this important early work. Teachers will appreciate the section titled "Agee in the Classroom."

Louisa May Alcott

Born: Germantown, Pennsylvania; November 29, 1832
Died: Boston, Massachusetts; March 6, 1888

Principal long fiction • *Moods*, 1864 (revised, 1881); *Little Women*, 1868; *Little Women, Part 2*, 1869 (also known as *Good Wives*, 1953); *An Old-Fashioned Girl*, 1870; *Little Men*, 1871; *Work: A Study of Experience*, 1873; *Eight Cousins*, 1875; *Rose in Bloom*, 1876; *A Modern Mephistopheles*, 1877; *Under the Lilacs*, 1878; *Jack and Jill*, 1880; *Jo's Boys, and How They Turned Out*, 1886.

Other literary forms • In addition to her novels, Louisa May Alcott wrote a collection of fairy tales, *Flower Fables* (1854); several short-story collections, notably *Aunt Jo's Scrap-Bag* (1872-1882, 6 volumes), *A Garland for Girls* (1887), and *Lulu's Library* (1895); a nonfiction work, *Hospital Sketches* (1863); a collection of plays, *Comic Tragedies Written by "Jo and Meg" and Acted by the "Little Women"* (1893); a few poems; and some articles and reviews for major periodicals. Surviving letters and journal entries were edited and published in 1889 by Ednah D. Cheney.

Achievements • Alcott first gained the recognition of a popular audience and then acceptance by the critics as a serious writer, becoming a giant in the subgenre of adolescent girls' novels and the family story. She was unique in having moral lessons exemplified by her characters' actions, thus avoiding the sermonizing of her contemporaries. Her heroes and heroines are flawed humans often trying to overcome their weaknesses. Much of the time, Alcott managed to avoid making her novels a vehicle to promote social or political issues, which was a fairly common practice of the day. She was a master of character development, and, despite adverse scholarly criticism and changing literary tastes among readers, her novels endure for what they offer in timeless values: the importance of a strong family life and honest, hard work.

Biography • Louisa May Alcott was the second daughter of Abby May and Amos Bronson Alcott, a leader in the Transcendentalist movement headed by Ralph Waldo Emerson. When it became evident that Bronson Alcott would not be a reliable provider for the family, Louisa perceived it as her mission in life to support the family. The death of her younger sister and the marriage of her older sister, Anna, were traumatic experiences, and partly to fill the void left by their absence, partly to seek some purpose in life and to participate in the Civil War in the only way open to women, Alcott became an army nurse in Washington, D.C. After six weeks, she contracted typhoid fever, from which she never fully recovered, due to the effects of mercury poisoning from her medication. These experiences are recorded in *Hospital Sketches*, the work that would establish her as a serious writer.

Alcott had also begun writing gothic thrillers, which brought in money for the family but did not enhance her literary reputation. Her first novel appeared in 1864. In 1865, Alcott toured Europe, and soon after her return, she became editor of the children's magazine *Merry's Museum*. About that time, the editor Thomas Niles urged

Alcott to write a novel for girls, resulting in *Little Women*, an overnight success. After her father suffered a stroke in 1882, Alcott moved him to Boston, and she continued to try to write. Sensing by this time that she would not regain her health, she adopted her nephew, John Sewell Pratt, who would become heir to her royalties and manage her affairs after her death. Louisa May Alcott died on March 6, 1888, two days after the death of her father. The two are buried in the Sleepy Hollow Cemetery, Concord, Massachusetts.

Analysis • Versatility characterizes the canon of Louisa May Alcott, which includes children's literature, adult novels, gothic thrillers, autobiography, short stories, poetry, and drama. Although Alcott's works for children may be distinguished from those of other writers of children's stories in some important ways, they nonetheless fit into the broader context of American literature of the time. What set Alcott's children's novels apart from the rest was her careful avoidance of the overt didacticism and sermonizing that characterized many others. A code of proper behavior is implicit, but it is detected in situations in the novels rather than showcased by authorial intrusion. In the juvenile novels, excepting the March family works, Alcott wrote less from her own experiences, and she was more prone to rewrite earlier works. The most enduring of Alcott's collection are the girls' novels and the family stories, which continue to be read because of the vitality of the characters—how they deal with life situations and challenges with humor, even fun—and the way Alcott uses detail to present simple, honest lives. Although criticism of Alcott's work in the late twentieth century found the children's novels to be overly sentimental, readers of the day enjoyed them.

The works for adults portray a less simplistic view of life than do the children's stories. Readers meet people with boring, unhappy, or even sordid lives, lives that would not be deemed suitable for those works that earned Alcott the epithet "children's friend." Alcott's skill in building character, in using dialogue, and in exploring social issues of the day is evident.

Moods • *Moods,* Alcott's first and favorite novel, was published in 1864. Having been advised to cut its length by about half, Alcott submitted a text predictably unsatisfactory both to her and to her critics. Nearly twenty years later, a new edition was published with some deletions and the restoration of former chapters. The basic story remained the same: The heroine, Sylvia Yule, is dominated by mood swings. Governed more by feelings than by reason, she is prone to making misguided judgments in love. She loves Adam Warwick, a model of strength, intellect, and manliness, but she learns, too late, that he uses others to serve his own purposes and then shuns them. After Adam leaves Sylvia, his best friend, Geoffrey Moor, becomes a true friend to Sylvia, but he mistakes the friendship for love. He is totally unlike Adam: slight of build, sweet, and tranquil. Sylvia decides to marry him because he is a "safe" choice, not because she loves him. When Sylvia finally confesses to Geoffrey her love for Adam, Geoffrey leaves for one year to see if his absence will help her learn to love him. The plan works, but on his way back to claim her love, Adam, Geoffrey's traveling companion, is drowned. Though saddened, Sylvia and Geoffrey are reunited, wiser and more cognizant of the value of their mutual love. In the 1864 edition of the book, Sylvia develops tuberculosis, and when Geoffrey returns, he nurses her through her terminal illness, before she dies in his arms. In the 1881 edition, in which Sylvia falls ill but recovers and accepts Geoffrey's love, Alcott focuses more clearly on the theme of moods rather than of marriage, and plot and characterization are more even.

Little Women • Although Louisa May Alcott was already an established author upon the publication of *Little Women*, it was that novel that brought her an enduring reputation. The novel was written quickly; the original manuscript was completed in six weeks. Because the public clamored for a sequel revealing how the sisters married, Alcott obliged with *Little Women, Part 2* (later published as *Good Wives*) one year later. The two were subsequently published as a single novel. *Little Women* is based on the fictionalized life of the Alcott sisters at their house in Concord. The plot is episodic, devoting at least one chapter to each sister. The overall theme is the sisters' quest to face the challenges of life and to overcome those "burdens" so that they may develop into "little women." The chief burden of Meg, the eldest, is vanity. Jo, like her mother, has a temper that she must learn to control if she is to become a "little woman." Beth, thirteen, is already so nearly perfect that her burden is simply to overcome her shyness. Amy is the proverbial spoiled baby in the family, and she must try to overcome her impracticality and thoughtlessness.

When the sisters are not sharing intimacies and producing dramatic productions for entertainment, they interact with the next-door neighbors, Mr. Lawrence and his orphaned grandson Laurie. Laurie is wealthy in material things but longs to have family; he often enjoys the March girls' activities vicariously, from a window. Mrs. March, affectionately called Marmee, is a central character in the novel. The girls know that they can confide in their mother about anything, and at any time. She is strong, wise, and loving, clearly the anchor of the family. Mr. March is a clergyman who has gone to serve in the Civil War and so is absent during the course of the novel. The story ends with the engagement of Meg, the eldest sister; with Jo's decision to become a writer and to leave her tomboyish childhood for a mature relationship; and with Amy's betrothal to Laurie. Beth, tragically, dies of a terminal illness. *Little Women* was an overnight success, and the public eagerly awaited the sequel, provided in *Little Women, Part 2*.

Little Women, Part 2 • The sequel to *Little Women* was released in January of 1869. *Little Women, Part 2* begins with Meg's wedding day; she settles into a conventional marriage in which her husband is the breadwinner and she is the docile, dependent wife. They have two children, Daisy and Demi-John. For a time, Alcott allows Jo to be happy being single and to enjoy her liberty. After she has married Amy off to Laurie in another conventional romantic marriage, she bows to the wishes of her readers and has Jo marry Professor Bhaer, the kindly older man about whom Jo became serious in *Little Women*. Jo is able to maintain a degree of freedom and to pursue intellectual interests in a way that conventional marriages of the day would not have allowed. Together, they operate the Plumfield School, whose pedagogy parallels the philosophy of Alcott's father in his Temple School; thus, the success of Plumfield is a tribute to Bronson Alcott.

An Old-Fashioned Girl • Alcott's 1870 novel, *An Old-Fashioned Girl*, was not as commercially successful as were the March family books. The theme of this book is that wealth in itself does not bring happiness. Polly Milton pays an extended visit to her wealthy friend Fanny Shaw, only to realize that this very "new-fashioned" family is not much of a family at all: Brother Tom is left uncared for by everyone except his grandmother, who is also ignored by the rest of the family; Maud, the six-year-old sister, is a petty, ill-tempered child. The father gives himself wholly to his work; the mother neglects the household largely because of a self-proclaimed invalidism. Fanny herself is lazy and shallow. Polly Milton's family, on the other hand, though poor, is noble. The Reverend Milton is a country parson who provides for his family's needs and has a loving and happy family. Mrs. Milton, like Marmee of *Little Women*, is a wise and caring confidante who dresses Polly appropriately for her age and who teaches respect and charity by word and deed. She is an able seamstress and cook; she operates the household economically and within their means. Polly helps improve the Shaw family, and she returns unspoiled to her loving family. She becomes a music teacher so that she can send her brother to college. Polly is not perfect, however; her flaw is vanity. As a working woman without a fashionable wardrobe, she does not enjoy full social acceptance.

Polly seeks proper marriages for the Shaw children. A reversal of financial circumstances in the Shaw family forces Fanny to learn from the Miltons how to make do with little, but it is a blessing because both Tom and Fanny become better people. By the end of the novel, marriages have been planned for all except Maud, who remains a happy spinster.

Little Men • *Little Men*, published in 1871, employs the episodic technique of earlier novels to continue the story that *Little Women* began. The focus is on Professor and Jo March Bhaer and their students at Plumfield. Jo has a son Rob and a lovable baby boy, Teddy; Daisy and Demi, Meg's twins, are now old enough to be students at the school, as is Bess, Laurie and Amy's daughter. Professor Bhaer's nephews, Emil and Franz, are senior students. Other students include the stock characters Stuffy Cole, Dolly Pettingill, Jack Ford, Billy Ward, and Dick Brown. Four other students are more fully developed: Tommy Bangs, an arsonist; Nat Blake, who loves music and tells lies; Nan, who wanted to be a boy and becomes a physician; and Dan Kean, a troublemaker who threatens to upset the reputation the Bhaers have gained for success in reforming wayward students. The children are rarely seen in the classroom, carrying out Bronson Alcott's Temple School principle of cultivating healthy bodies and spirits as well as developing the intellect. Corporal punishment of students is not practiced, and the school is coeducational. Under the guidance of the long-suffering Professor Bhaer and the now-motherly Jo, the school is like a magnet that draws its former charges back to its stable shelter.

Work • Some critics consider *Work* to be Alcott's most successful novel for adults. Christie Devon, an orphan, leaves home to seek independence. She goes through a number of jobs quickly—a chapter is given to each one, in episodic fashion—before she meets Rachel, a "fallen" woman whom she befriends. When Rachel's past is discovered, she is fired from her job, as is Christie for remaining her friend. Christie becomes increasingly poor, hungry, lonely, and depressed, to the point of contemplating suicide. Rachel comes along in time and takes Christie to a washerwoman who introduces her to the Reverend Thomas Power. He arranges for Christie to live with the widow Sterling and her son David, a florist. Christie tries to make David heroic, which he is not, but in time they are married, just before David goes off to war. He is killed, and Christie goes to live with David's family and has a child. Rachel turns out to be David's sister-in-law. The novel focuses on the loneliness and frustration of women in situations such as these. Like Alcott, they find salvation in hard work, and though financial recompense is paltry, it is not deemed beneath their dignity. More than in her other novels, Alcott realistically portrays relationships between men and women.

Eight Cousins • Alcott published *Eight Cousins* in 1875. She does not resort to the episodic technique of earlier novels as she focuses clearly on the character Rose Campbell, also the heroine of the sequel to *Eight Cousins, Rose in Bloom*. A ward of her Uncle Alex, the orphaned heir Rose comes to live with her relatives. Her six aunts all have strong opinions about Rose's education, but her schooling merely crams Rose full of useless facts; she is not really educated. Finally, Uncle Alex takes over her education and provides her with "freedom, rest, and care," echoing Bronson Alcott's educational philosophy. Rose is in frequent contact with her seven male cousins, to whom she becomes a confidante. She submits to Uncle Alex's wholesome regimen, but she has her ears pierced despite his disapproval, and she admires what is fashionable even though she chooses the outfits her uncle suggests. The central theme of the novel is a woman's education. It prescribes physical exercise, housework, and mastery of some kind of trade. It allows courses that were nontraditional for women at the time the novel appeared and rests on practical experience rather than reading of books, although reading is respected. Although the novel clearly has in mind a treatment of various social issues, it succeeds nevertheless because of Alcott's development of the children and the humor with which she views the foibles of the adult characters.

A Modern Mephistopheles • In 1876, Alcott's publisher requested a novel to be published anonymously in the No Name series of works by popular writers. She chose a manuscript she had written ten years earlier that had been deemed sensational. A revised version enabled Alcott to write in the gothic mode without compromising her reputation as a children's writer. Furthermore, she had been impressed with Johann Wolfgang von Goethe's *Faust* (1808, 1833), and the parallels to Goethe's masterpiece are obvious. Just when Felix Canaris, a rejected but aspiring poet, is contemplating suicide, Jasper Helwyze comes along, rescues Felix, and befriends him, promising to make him successful. Within a year, Felix has indeed succeeded. He falls in love with Olivia, a former love who had rejected Jasper, but Gladys, an orphan protégé of Olivia, also falls in love with Felix.

Completely under Jasper's influence, Felix is forced to marry Gladys instead of Olivia. Jasper harasses the young couple in various ways. As they look forward to life with a child, Jasper forces Felix to reveal his secret to Gladys: He has no real talent—Jasper has been writing the successful poetry. Gladys does not reject Felix, but after going into premature labor, she and the baby both die. Before her death, she implores Felix and Jasper to forgive each other. Thus, Felix is freed from his bondage to Jasper and goes on to live a worthwhile life; Jasper has a stroke. Alcott's novel is not simply a rewritten *Faust*; a dominant theme in the novel is the power of women, both wives and mothers, to save men from themselves, an idea of high interest to the readers of the day. There is a great deal of foreshadowing, partly because of its parallels to *Faust.* Alcott explores the darker side of human nature in a way that she could not, or would not, do in her works for children.

Jack and Jill • *Jack and Jill*'s episodic plot may be explained by the fact that it was first serialized in the *St. Nicholas* magazine in 1879 and 1880, although several of Alcott's other novels also employed this technique. Alcott called it a "village story," and Harmony Village is her fictionalized Concord. Jack and Frank are modeled after Anna Alcott's sons, and Ed is based on Ellsworth Devens, a Concord friend. Jack and Jill are recovering from a serious sliding accident, and the novel concerns the way the other Harmony Village children are inspired by the near tragedy to improve their ways, both physically and morally. Like Beth of *Little Women*, Ed is almost too good to be true, foreshadowing his early death. This novel, like *Little Men*, is an educational novel.

Jo's Boys, and How They Turned Out • In 1886, Alcott brought closure to the March family novels with a final story portraying the changes that have occurred within the previous ten years. Mr. Lawrence, the kind next-door neighbor of *Little Women*, endows a college next door to the Plumfield School of *Little Women, Part 2* and *Little Men.* Meg notes the absence of the beloved Marmee, Beth, and her late husband John. Readers learn that Demi has gone into the publishing business; Daisy is a "little woman" who marries Nat Blake, and Nan becomes a doctor. Nat completes his musical education in Germany; Emil becomes a ship's officer who takes charge of a lifeboat when the captain becomes ill; Dan Kean, who decided to seek his fortune in the West, kills a man in self-defense when a crooked card game goes sour. It is remembering and upholding the honor of Plumfield that guides these young men. The one character who cannot return to the inner circle of the March family is the "bad boy," Dan. He does come back to Plumfield after he is wounded while working with Native Americans in the West, but he is not allowed to marry Beth, the daughter of Amy March and Laurie Lawrence. Feminism is the main focus of the novel; all of the young women succeed in careers that were denied the title characters in *Little Women.*

Victoria Price

Other major works

SHORT FICTION: *Flower Fables*, 1854; *On Picket Duty, and Other Tales*, 1864; *Morning-Glories, and Other Stories*, 1867; *Aunt Jo's Scrap-Bag*, 1872-1882 (6 volumes); *Silver Pitchers: And Independence, a Centennial Love Story*, 1876; *Spinning-Wheel Stories*, 1884; *A Garland for Girls*, 1887; *Lulu's Library*, 1895; *From Jo March's Attic: Stories of Intrigue and Suspense*, 1993; *Louisa May Alcott Unmasked: Collected Thrillers*, 1995; *The Early Stories of Louisa May Alcott, 1852-1860*, 2000.

PLAYS: *Comic Tragedies Written by "Jo" and "Meg" and Acted by the "Little Women,"* 1893.

POETRY: *The Poems of Louisa May Alcott,* 2000.

NONFICTION: *Hospital Sketches,* 1863 (essays); *Life, Letters, and Journals,* 1889 (Ednah D. Cheney, editor); *The Journals of Louisa May Alcott,* 1989 (Joel Myerson and Daniel Shealy, editors); *The Sketches of Louisa May Alcott,* 2001.

Bibliography

Alcott, Louisa May. *A Double Life: Newly Discovered Thrillers of Louisa May Alcott.* Edited by Madeleine B. Stern. Boston: Little, Brown, 1988. This book contains tales of mystery and melodrama that were published anonymously in weeklies before Alcott wrote her tales of social realism. These stories reveal a side of Alcott that is little known by the general public.

____________. *Louisa May Alcott: Selected Fiction.* Edited by Daniel Shealy, Madeleine B. Stern, and Joel Myerson. Boston: Little, Brown, 1990. A collection of stories that cover the romances Alcott wrote during her teens and the thrillers and Gothic novels she wrote before turning to realism. In these stories, Alcott's rebellious spirit is reflected as a supporter of abolition and women's rights.

Anthony, Katharine S. *Louisa May Alcott.* New York: Alfred A. Knopf, 1938. Reprint. Westport, Conn.: Greenwood Press, 1977. Reveals the social influence of Alcott's writing as she kept alive the ideals of the Victorian period. Anthony's biography discusses the misrepresentation of Alcott by the literary world, which consistently categorizes her as a children's writer. Includes an excellent bibliography on Alcott and her entire family.

Delamar, Gloria T. *Louisa May Alcott and "Little Women."* Jefferson, N.C.: McFarland, 1990. Unlike other Alcott biographers, Delamar includes reviews and critical analyses of Alcott's work, ratings given to *Little Women,* her showing in polls, and her commemoration with a postage stamp.

Eiselein, Gregory, and Anne K. Phillips, eds. *The Louisa May Alcott Encyclopedia.* Westport, Conn.: Greenwood Press, 2001. General reference source with entries on Alcott's works, characters, and details of her life.

Elbert, Sarah. *A Hunger for Home: Louisa May Alcott and "Little Women."* Philadelphia: Temple University Press, 1984. A feminist study of Alcott, this critical biography analyzes the connections between Alcott's family life and her work, and places Alcott squarely within the reform tradition of the nineteenth century and the debate over the proper role of women.

Lyon Clark, Beverly, ed. *Louisa May Alcott: The Contemporary Reviews.* New York: Cambridge University Press, 2004. Comprehensive collection of reviews of Alcott's books published at the time of their original appearance. Exceptionally useful for assessing contemporary criticism of her work.

Meigs, Cornelia. *Invincible Louisa.* Boston: Little, Brown, 1933. This biography emphasizes Alcott's work with young people and her belief that children must have the opportunity to earn independence. Meigs also discusses Alcott's assistance to soldiers during the Civil War and her trip to Europe. Contains a fine chronology of Alcott's life.

Showalter, Elaine. *Sister's Choice: Traditions and Change in American Women's Writing.* Oxford, England: Clarendon Press, 1991. Chapter 3 discusses the wide variance in feminist critical reception of Alcott's *Little Women:* Some feel that bowing to pressures of the time kept her from fulfilling her literary promise; others see the novel as an excellent study of the dilemma of a literary woman writing in that age.

Stern, Madeleine B. *Louisa May Alcott.* Norman: University of Oklahoma Press, 1950. Considered the standard biography of Alcott, it provides a readable account of the author's life and an excellent bibliography.

____________. *Louisa May Alcott: From Blood and Thunder to Hearth and Home.* Boston: Northeastern University Press, 1998. In evaluating Alcott's literary reputation, Stern concludes that the author was more than just the "children's friend."

____________, ed. *L. M. Alcott: Signature of Reform.* Boston: Northeastern University Press, 2002. Examination of Alcott's interest in reform movements by the author of the standard biography of Alcott.

Strickland, Charles. *Victorian Domesticity: Families in the Life and Art of Louisa May Alcott.* University: University of Alabama Press, 1985. Like the work by Elbert above, Strickland's study surveys the range of Alcott's ideas about domestic life and considers Alcott's literary treatment of women, families, and children within the various fictional forms in which she chose to work.

Rudolfo A. Anaya

Born: Pastura, New Mexico; October 30, 1937

Principal long fiction • *Bless Me, Ultima,* 1972; *Heart of Aztlán,* 1976; *Tortuga,* 1979; *The Legend of La Llorona,* 1984; *Lord of the Dawn: The Legend of Quetzalcóatl,* 1987; *Alburquerque,* 1992; *Zia Summer,* 1995; *Jalamanta: A Message from the Desert,* 1996; *Rio Grande Fall,* 1996; *Shaman Winter,* 1999; *Jemez Spring,* 2005.

Other literary forms • In addition to his novels, Rudolfo Anaya has written short stories, children's literature, essays, plays, and poetry. His early short stories are collected in *The Silence of the Llano* (1982). *The Farolitos of Christmas,* first published in 1987, is a children's short story; it was published again as an illustrated edition in 1995. Anaya's essay output is largely a result of his many lectures offered around the United States. An important exception, however, is *A Chicano in China* (1986), which is a daily account of a visit to China in 1984. *The Anaya Reader* (1995) is a collection of short stories, essays, a poem, and plays, including *Who Killed Don José?* (pr. 1987).

Achievements • Anaya became one of the foremost Chicano novelists of the twentieth century. He came to the forefront of the literary field as the Chicano movement of the late 1960's began to strengthen its vision during the early 1970's. His first novel, *Bless Me, Ultima,* won the Premio Quinto Sol literary award in 1972. The recognition of his work brought him into the center of an important discussion on the issues of the history, culture, and identity of the Chicano. Anaya answered the challenge of his new role as a force in the evolution of Chicano letters by publishing *Heart of Aztlán,* a novel that represents a search for the Chicano soul in the barrios of Albuquerque, New Mexico. Aztlán, the legendary homeland of the Aztecs and the term used as a symbol of unity during the Chicano movement, is a key term in Chicano history. With *Heart of Aztlán* the term also becomes important in literature.

Alburquerque won the International Association of Poets, Playwrights, Editors, Essayists, and Novelists (PEN) Center West Award for fiction. Anaya's work in children's literature has also been recognized nationally. The 1995 illustrated edition of The Farolitos of Christmas, a warm tale of family love and a traditional Christmas, received the Southwest Texas State University Tomás Rivera Mexican American Children's Book Award.

Biography • Rudolfo Anaya was born in the little town of Pastura in eastern New Mexico. His family moved to Santa Rosa, New Mexico, while he was still a child. His experience during those early years in the countryside served as the material for his first novel, *Bless Me, Ultima.* Later, Anaya's family moved to Albuquerque, where he attended high school. *Heart of Aztlán* takes Albuquerque as its setting. As a sophomore in high school, the author experienced a serious spinal injury in a swimming accident. The pain and suffering caused by this injury are reflected in *Tortuga,* his third novel, which uses the ordeal of pain as part of the hero's search for universal understanding.

Anaya attended the University of New Mexico as an undergraduate and graduate student, eventually earning master's degrees in both literature and counseling. It was at the university that he began to write. His poetry and early novels dealt with major questions about his own existence, beliefs, and identity. He ended that phase of his life by burning all of the manuscripts of his work. After college he took a teaching job and married; his wife was a great source of encouragement and an excellent editor.

Anaya began writing *Bless Me, Ultima* during the 1960's. He struggled with the work until, in one of his creative moments, Ultima appeared to him in a vision. She became the strongest character of the novel, as well as the spiritual mentor for both the protagonist and the novelist. Finding a publisher was not easy. After dozens of rejection letters from major publishers, Anaya turned to Quinto Sol Publications, a small Chicano press in Berkeley, California. The publishers not only accepted the work for publication but also awarded to him the Premio Quinto Sol for writing the best Chicano novel published in 1972. Anaya went on to become an internationally known storyteller and writer, as well as a mentor to young and old seeking to practice the craft of writing. He also became a committed advocate of Chicano self-definition and a major voice in the process of bringing cultures together for mutual enrichment.

Analysis • Anaya's works project a Magical Realism that blends contemporary life with the hidden manifestations of humanity and cultural identity. In his books, the principal characters struggle with the sometimes contradictory notions of Chicano identity tied both to an Aztec and Spanish past and to the English-speaking world of the present. Most of Anaya's developed characters are influenced by that duality. The struggle caused by these contesting notions elevates the Chicano human condition to that of every person. Anaya's first three novels, *Bless Me, Ultima, Heart of Aztlán,* and *Tortuga,* best exemplify these themes and characterizations.

Bless Me, Ultima • *Bless Me, Ultima* is Anaya's first novel of a trilogy, which also includes *Heart of Aztlán* and *Tortuga. Bless Me, Ultima* is a psychological and magical portrait of a child's quest for identity. In this classic work, Antonio, the protagonist, is subjected to competing realities that he must master in order to grow up. These realities are interwoven with symbolic characters and places, the most powerful of which are Ultima, a *curandera* (healer) who evokes the timeless past of a pre-Columbian world, and a golden carp that swims the river waters of the supernatural and offers a redeeming future.

Antonio is born in Pastura, a very small village on the eastern New Mexican plain. Later his family moves to a village across the river from the small town of Guadalupe, where Antonio spends his childhood. His father is a cattleman, and his mother is from a farming family. They represent the initial manifestation of the divided world into which Antonio is born and a challenge he must resolve in order to find himself. Antonio's father wants him to become a horseman of the plain, like his ancestors before him. His mother wants Antonio to become a priest to a farming community, which is the honored tradition. The parents' wishes are symptoms of a deeper spiritual challenge facing Antonio, involving his Roman Catholic beliefs and those associated with the magical world of the pre-Columbian past. Ultima, the *curandera* and a creature of both worlds, is a magical character who guides Antonio through the ordeal of understanding and dealing with these challenges. She is there to supervise his birth; she comes to stay with the family in Guadalupe when Antonio is seven. On several occasions, Antonio is a witness to her power in life-and-death battles.

Antonio's adventure takes him beyond the divided world of the farmer and the horseman and beyond the Catholic ritual and its depictions of good and evil. With Ultima's help, he is able to bridge these opposites and channel them into a new cosmic vision of nature, represented by the river, which stands in the middle of his two worlds, and the golden carp, which points to a new spiritual covenant. The novel ends with the killing of Ultima's owl by one of her enemies. Because the owl carries her spiritual presence, Ultima dies as well. However, her work is completed before her death: Antonio can now choose his own destiny.

Heart of Aztlán • *Heart of Aztlán*, Anaya's second novel of the trilogy, is, like *Bless Me, Ultima*, a psychological and magical portrait of a quest for Chicano identity and empowerment. It is the story of the Chávez family, who leave the country to search for a better life in the city, only to discover that their destiny lies in a past believed abandoned and lost. The story focuses on two characters, Clemente Chávez, the father, and Jason, one of the sons. Jason best depicts the adjustments the family has to make to everyday life in the city. However, it is Clemente who undergoes a magical rebirth, which brings to the community a new awareness of its destiny and a new will to fight for its birthright.

The novel begins with the Chávez family selling the last of their land and leaving the small town of Guadalupe for a new life in Albuquerque. They go to live in Barelas, a barrio on the west side of the city where many other immigrants reside. The Chávezes soon learn, as the other people of the barrio have discovered, that their lives do not belong to them. They are controlled by industrial interests, represented by the railroad and a union that has compromised the workers. They are manipulated by politicians through Mannie García, "el super," who delivers the community vote.

Michael Mouchette

In Barelas, Clemente also begins to lose the battle for control of his household, especially his daughters, who have no regard for his insistence on the tradition of respect and obedience to the head of the family. The situation worsens when Clemente loses his job in the railroad yard during a futile strike. He becomes an alcoholic, and in his despair he attempts suicide. Crispín, a magical character who represents eternal wisdom, comes to his aid and shows him the way to a new life. With Crispín's help, Clemente solves the riddle of a magical stone in the possession of "la India," a sorceress who symbolically guards the entryway to the heart of Aztlán, the source of empowerment for the Chicano.

Clemente's rebirth takes the form of a journey to the magical mountain lake that is at the center of Aztlán and of Chicano being. Reborn, Clemente returns to his community to lead the movement for social and economic justice in a redeeming and unifying struggle for life and for the destiny of a people. The novel ends with Clemente taking a hammer to the Santa Fe water tower in the railroad yard, a symbol of industrial might, before coming home to lead a powerful march on his former employers.

Tortuga • *Tortuga*, the third novel of the trilogy, is a tale of a journey to self-realization and supernatural awareness. In the story, Benjie Chávez, the protagonist, undergoes a symbolic rebirth in order to take the place of Crispín, the keeper of Chicano wisdom, who upon his death will pass his position to Benjie. At the end of *Heart of Aztlán*, Benjie was wounded by his brother Jason's rival, fell from the railyard water tower, and was paralyzed. He was transported to the Crippled Children and Orphans Hospital in the south for rehabilitation. His entry into the hospital was also a symbolic entry into a world of supernatural transformation.

The hospital sits at the foot of a mountain called Tortuga (which means turtle), from which flow mineral springs with healing waters. Benjie is also given the name Tortuga after he is fitted with a body cast that makes him look like a turtle. What follows is a painful ordeal, both physically and psychologically, as the protagonist is exposed to every kind of human suffering and deformity that can possibly afflict children. Not even this, however, prepares him for the visit to the ward of the "vegetables," the immobile children who cannot breathe without the help of an iron lung. There Tortuga meets Salomón, also a vegetable, but one with supernatural insight into the human condition. Salomón enters Tortuga's psyche and guides him on the path to spiritual renewal.

Salomón compares Tortuga's challenge with the terrible ordeal newly born turtles undergo as they dash to the sea. Most of them do not survive, because other creatures lie in wait to devour them. Tortuga must endure the turtle's dash in order to arrive at his true destiny, which is called "the path of the sun." Tortuga experiences a near-death ordeal, which includes a climactic moment when Danny, an important character, pushes him into a swimming pool, where he would have drowned if others had not rushed to his aid. Tortuga survives his symbolic turtle dash to the sea. The vegetables are not so lucky; one night Danny succeeds in turning off the power to their ward. With the iron lungs turned off, they all die. The end of novel and Tortuga's rehabilitation also bring the news that Crispín, the magical helper of Tortuga's neighborhood, has died. The news of Crispín's death arrives along with his blue guitar, a symbol of universal knowledge, which is now Benjie's.

The trilogy that ends with this novel, along with Anaya's literary production as a whole, reflects a search for the meaning of existence as expressed in Chicano life. This search is often a journey that takes the protagonists into the past and the present and into the physical and mythical landscapes of the urban and rural worlds of the Southwest, revealing the relationship of these worlds to the social and political power structure of mainstream America.

David Conde

Other major works

SHORT FICTION: *The Silence of the Llano*, 1982; *Serafina's Stories*, 2004; *The Man Who Could Fly, and Other Stories*, 2006.

PLAYS: *The Season of La Llorona*, pr. 1979; *Who Killed Don José?*, pr. 1987; *Billy the Kid*, pb. 1995.

SCREENPLAY: *Bilingualism: Promise for Tomorrow*, 1976.

POETRY: *The Adventures of Juan Chicaspatas*, 1985 (epic poem); *Elegy on the Death of Cesar Chávez*, 2000 (juvenile).

NONFICTION: *A Chicano in China*, 1986; *Conversations with Rudolfo Anaya*, 1998.

CHILDREN'S LITERATURE: *The Farolitos of Christmas: A New Mexico Christmas Story*, 1987 (1995; illustrated edition); *Maya's Children: The Story of La Llorona*, 1997; *Farolitos for Abuelo*, 1998; *My Land Sings: Stories from the Rio Grande*, 1999; *Roadrunner's Dance*, 2000; *The Santero's Miracle: A Bilingual Story*, 2004 (illustrated by Amy Cordova, Spanish translation by Enrique Lamadrid).

EDITED TEXTS: *Voices from the Rio Grande*, 1976; *Cuentos Chicanos: A Short Story Anthology*, 1980 (with Antonio Márquez); *A Ceremony of Brotherhood, 1680-1980*, 1981 (with Simon Ortiz); *Voces: An Anthology of Nuevo Mexicano Writers*, 1987; *Aztlán: Essays on the Chicano Homeland*, 1989; *Tierra: Contemporary Short Fiction of New Mexico*, 1989.

MISCELLANEOUS: *The Anaya Reader*, 1995.

Bibliography

Augenbraum, Harold, and Margarite Fernández Olmos, eds. *The Latino Reader: An American Literary Tradition from 1542 to the Present*. Boston: Houghton Mifflin, 1997. Survey of Latino literature that is useful in placing Anaya's writings in historical context.

Baeza, Abelardo. *Man of Aztlan: A Biography of Rudolfo Anaya*. Austin, Tex.: Eakin Press, 2001. This concise biography offers a fresh look at the man behind the classic novels. Includes bibliographical references.

Clements, William. "The Way to Individuation in Anaya's *Bless Me, Ultima*." *Midwest Quarterly* 23 (Winter, 1982). Applies the theories of Carl Jung to the novel.

Dasenbrock, Reed. "Forms of Biculturalism in Southwestern Literature: The Work of Rudolfo Anaya and Leslie Marmon Silko." *Genre* 21 (Fall, 1988). Focuses on the treatment of storytelling.

Dick, Bruce, and Silvio Sirias, eds. *Conversations with Rudolfo Anaya*. Jackson: University Press of Mississippi, 1998. For students and general readers, this book is designed to present Anaya's point of view and philosophy. Includes index.

Elias, Edward. "*Tortuga:* A Novel of Archetypal Structure." *The Bilingual Review/La Revista Bilingüe* 9 (January, 1982). Employs the archetypal approach to reveal Anaya's art.

Fernández Olmos, Margarite. *Rudolfo A. Anaya: A Critical Companion*. Westport, Conn.: Greenwood Press, 1999. Part of the publisher's series of reference books on popular contemporary writers for students, this volume provides detailed plot summaries and analyses of Anaya's novels, along with character portraits, a biography of Anaya, and an extensive bibliography. Includes bibliographical references and an index.

González-T., César A., ed. *Rudolfo A. Anaya: Focus on Criticism*. La Jolla, Calif.: Lalo Press, 1990. Mainly for specialists. The author is an eminent scholar and critic of Anaya. Contains select bibliography and index.

González-T., César A., and Phyllis S. Morgan. *A Sense of Place: Rudolfo A. Anaya, an An-*

notated Bio-bibliography. Berkeley: University of California Press, 2000. Substantial, annotated bibliography on Anaya that also includes maps by Ronald L. Stauber.

Klein, Dianne. "Coming of Age in Novels by Rudolfo Anaya and Sandra Cisneros." *The English Journal* 81 (September, 1992). Focuses on initiation into adulthood. An insightful comparative study.

Martínez, Julio, and Francisco A. Lomelí. *Chicano Literature: A Readers' Guide.* New York: Greenwood Press, 1985. A good starting point for determining Anaya's place in Chicano literature. Includes biographical essays on Anaya and other Chicano authors.

Taylor, Paul Beekman. "Chicano Secrecy in the Fiction of Rudolfo A. Anaya." *Journal of the Southwest* 39, no. 2 (1997): 239-265. Exploration of an interesting motif in Anaya's fiction.

Vasallo, Paul, ed. *The Magic of Words: Rudolfo Anaya and His Writings.* Albuquerque: University of New Mexico Press, 1982. Provides an excellent reading and discussion of Anaya's early literary work.

Sherwood Anderson

Born: Camden, Ohio; September 13, 1876
Died: Colón, Panama Canal Zone; March 8, 1941

Principal long fiction • *Windy McPherson's Son,* 1916; *Marching Men,* 1917; *Winesburg, Ohio,* 1919; *Poor White,* 1920; *Many Marriages,* 1923; *Dark Laughter,* 1925; *Beyond Desire,* 1932; *Kit Brandon,* 1936.

Other literary forms • In addition to *Winesburg, Ohio,* which some critics regard as a collection of loosely related short stories, Sherwood Anderson produced three volumes of short stories: *The Triumph of the Egg* (1921); *Horses and Men* (1923); and *Death in the Woods, and Other Stories* (1933). He published two books of prose poems, *Mid-American Chants* (1918) and *A New Testament* (1927). *Plays: Winesburg and Others* was published in 1937. Anderson's autobiographical writings, among his most interesting prose works, include *A Story Teller's Story* (1924), *Tar: A Midwest Childhood* (1926), and the posthumously published *Sherwood Anderson's Memoirs* (1942). All three are such a mixture of fact and fiction that they are sometimes listed as fiction rather than autobiography. Anderson also brought out in book form several volumes of journalistic pieces, many of which had appeared originally in his newspapers: *Sherwood Anderson's Notebook* (1926), *Perhaps Women* (1931), *No Swank* (1934), *Puzzled America* (1935), and *Home Town* (1940). *The Modern Writer* (1925) is a collection of lectures.

Achievements • Anderson was not a greatly gifted novelist; in fact, it might be argued that he was not by nature a novelist at all. He was a brilliant and original writer of tales. His early reputation, which brought him the homage of writers such as James Joyce, Ford Madox Ford, Gertrude Stein, Ernest Hemingway, and F. Scott Fitzgerald, was established by the stories published in *Winesburg, Ohio, The Triumph of the Egg,* and *Horses and Men.* Anderson had published two novels before *Winesburg, Ohio* and was to publish five more afterward, but none of these achieved the critical success of his short pieces.

Anderson's difficulties with the novel are understandable when one sees that his great gift was for rendering moments of intense consciousness—"epiphanies," as James Joyce called them—for which the short story or the tale is the perfect vehicle. The novel form requires a more objective sense of a world outside the individual consciousness as well as the ability to move characters through change and development and to deal to some extent with the effect of character on character. The best parts of Anderson's novels are those scenes in which he deals, as in the short stories, with a minor character trapped by his own eccentric nature in a hostile world.

Another serious limitation to Anderson's talent as a novelist was his inclination to preach, to see himself as a prophet and reformer and to make sweeping generalizations that are as embarrassing as they are inartistic. Even in *Poor White,* probably his best novel, his characters run to types and become, finally, representative figures in a social allegory. In his worst novels, the characters are caricatures whose absurdity is not perceived by their author. Anderson's style, which could at times work brilliantly, became excessively mannered, a kind of self-parody, which was a sure sign that he had lost his grip on the talent that had produced his best and earlier work.

Library of Congress

Winesburg, Ohio is without doubt Anderson's great achievement. It is a collection of tales striving to become a novel; indeed, most critics regard it as a novel, a new form of the novel, which, though perhaps first suggested by Edgar Lee Masters's *Spoon River Anthology* (1915), took on its own expressive form and became the model for later works such as Hemingway's *In Our Time* (1924) and William Faulkner's *The Unvanquished* (1938). A few of the Winesburg stories, such as "Godliness," are marred by a tendency to generalization, but on the whole they assume the coherence and solidity of such masterpieces as Mark Twain's *Adventures of Huckleberry Finn* (1884) and Stephen Crane's *The Red Badge of Courage* (1895), which bristle with implications not only about the life of their times but also about the present. If Anderson had published only *Winesburg, Ohio,* he would be remembered and ranked as an important minor American novelist.

Biography • Sherwood Anderson was born September 13, 1876, in Camden, Ohio, to Irwin and Emma Anderson. When he was eight years old, his family moved to Clyde, Ohio, where Anderson spent his most impressionable years. In later life, Anderson remembered Clyde as an ideal place for a boy to grow up; it became a symbol of the lost innocence of an earlier America. Many of his best stories have a fictionalized Clyde as their setting, and his memory of it shaped his vision of the American past and became a measure of the inadequacies of the industrialized, increasingly mechanized America of city apartments and bloodless sophistication.

Anderson's family was poor. Irwin Anderson, a harness maker, was thrown out of work by industrialization and periods of economic instability. Thus he was forced to work at various odd jobs, such as house painter and paper hanger. Anderson's mother took in washing, while Sherwood and his brother did odd jobs to help support the family. In his autobiographical accounts of growing up, *A Story Teller's Story, Tar,* and *Memoirs,* Anderson expresses his humiliation at his impoverished childhood and his resentment toward his father for the inability to support his family. Anderson was particularly bitter about the hardship inflicted on his mother, to whom he was deeply attached. He held his father accountable for his mother's early death, and in *Windy McPherson's Son* one may see in the portrait of the father Anderson's view of his own father as a braggart and a fool whose drunkenness and irresponsibility caused the death of his wife. In time, Anderson's attitude toward his father softened; he came to see that his own gifts as a storyteller were derived from his father, who was a gifted yarn spinner. Even more important in Anderson's development as a writer was the sympathy awakened in him by his father's failures. A braggart and a liar, Irwin Anderson nevertheless had romantic aspirations to shine in the eyes of the world; his pathetic attempts to amount to something made him grotesque by the standards of the world. An underlying tenderness for his father grew stronger as Sherwood Anderson grew older, enabling him to sympathize with those people in life who become the victims of the wrong kinds of dreams and aspirations. The portrayal of the narrator's father in "The Egg" is one example of Anderson's eventual compassion for such individuals.

Anderson's young manhood, however, was marked by a rejection of his father and a worship of progress and business success. He eagerly embraced the current version of the American Dream as exemplified in the Horatio Alger stories: the poor boy who becomes rich. Anderson's own career followed that pattern with remarkable fidelity. He took any odd job that would pay, whether it was selling papers or running errands, and earned himself the nickname "Jobby." After a brief stint in the army during the Spanish-American War and a year at the Wittenburg Academy completing his high school education, Anderson started in advertising in Chicago and moved up the financial ladder from one position to the next until he became the owner of a paint factory in Elyria, Ohio, the success of which depended upon his skill in writing advertising letters about his barn paint.

Anderson's personal life also developed in a traditional way. In 1904 he married a young woman from a middle-class family, had three children, and associated with the "best" people in Elyria. Around 1911, however, contradictory impulses at work in Anderson precipitated a breakdown. He worked hard at the paint factory and at night spent increasing amounts of time in an attic room writing fiction. The strain eventually took its toll, aided by the pressures of conflicting values: Anderson wanted business and financial success, yet, deep down, he believed in something very different. One day, without warning, he walked out of his paint factory and was later found wandering about the streets in Cleveland, dazed and unable to give his name and address. After a short stay in the hospital, Anderson returned to Elyria, closed out his affairs, and moved to Chicago.

Anderson later told the story of his departure from the paint factory and each time he told it, the details were different. Whatever the exact truth, the important fact appears to be that his breakdown was the result of serious strain between the kind of life he was leading and the kind of life something in him was urging him to live. Rex Burbank in *Sherwood Anderson* (1964) remarks that the breakdown was moral as well as psychological; it might be called spiritual as well, for it had to do with feelings too vague to be attached to questions of right and wrong. Anderson, in his best work, was something of a mystic, a "Corn Belt mystic" one detractor called him, and his mystical sense was to be the principal source of his gift as a fiction writer, as well as his chief liability as a novelist.

Anderson's life after he left the paint factory in Elyria was a mixture of successes and failures. He wandered from Chicago to New York to New Orleans and finally to Marion, Virginia, in 1927, where he built a house and became the publisher of two local newspapers. His first marriage had ended in divorce shortly after he moved to Chicago; he married three more times, his last to Eleanor Copenhaver, a Virginian. Anderson's financial status was always somewhat precarious. His reputation had been established early among eastern intellectuals who were attracted to what they saw as Anderson's primitivism, a quality he learned to cultivate. Except for *Dark Laughter*, however, which was something of a best-seller, none of his books was very successful financially, and he was forced to lecture and to do journalistic writing. His most serious problem, though, was the waning of his creative powers and his inability after 1923 to equal any of his earlier successes. During his later years, before his final and happiest marriage, Anderson often was close to a breakdown.

During his years in Virginia and under the influence of his fourth wife, Anderson increasingly became interested in social problems. He visited factories, wrote about labor strife, and lent his name to liberal causes. His deepest commitment, however, was not to politics but to his own somewhat vague ideal of brotherhood, which he continued to espouse. In 1941, while on a goodwill tour to South America for the State Department, he died of peritonitis.

Analysis • All novelists are to some extent autobiographical, but Sherwood Anderson is more so than most; indeed, all of Anderson's novels seem to arise out of the one great moment of his life, when he walked out of the paint factory and left behind the prosperous middle-class life of Elyria. In his imagination, his defection from material success took on great significance and became not only the common paradigm for his protagonists but also the basis for his message to the modern world. Industrialization and mechanization, money making, advertising, rising in the world, respectability—all of which Anderson himself had hankered after or had sought to encourage in others—became in his fiction the target of criticism. This is not to accuse him of insincerity, but only to point out the extent of his revulsion and the way in which he made his own personal experience into a mythological history of his region and even of the modern world. Anderson's heroes invariably renounce materialism and economic individualism and their attendant social and moral conventions and seek a more spiritual, more vital existence.

Windy McPherson's Son • Anderson's first published novel, *Windy McPherson's Son*, though set in Caxton, Iowa, is clearly based on Anderson's boyhood in Clyde, Ohio, and his later years in Elyria and Chicago. Sam McPherson is a fictionalized version of "Jobby" Anderson, with his talent for money-making schemes; his father, like Anderson's own, is a braggart and liar who frequently disgraces his hardworking wife and ambitious son in front of the townspeople of Caxton. After his mother's death, Sam leaves Caxton and takes his talent for money making to Chicago, where in effect he takes over management of an arms manufacturing plant. Sam becomes rich and marries the boss's daughter, but, instead of finding satisfaction in his wealth and position, he discovers that he is dissatisfied with business success and his childless marriage. He walks out of the business, abandons his wife, and wanders through the country attempting to find meaning in existence. After discovering that "American men and women have not learned to be clean and noble and natural, like their forests and their wide, clean plains," Sam returns to his wife Sue, bringing with him three children he has adopted. Out of some sense of responsibility, he allows himself to be led back into the darkened house from which he had fled, a curious and unsatisfactory "happy" ending.

Marching Men • *Marching Men*, Anderson's second novel, repeats the same basic pattern: success, revolt, search, revelation, elevation—but in a less convincing way. The setting is Coal Creek, a Pennsylvania mining town. The hero is Beaut McGregor, who rebels against the miners' passive acceptance of their squalid existence and escapes to Chicago, where he becomes rich. McGregor continues to despise the miners of Coal Creek until he returns for his mother's funeral; then, he has an awakening, a sudden illumination that gives him a spiritual insight that alters his existence. He sees the miners as men marching "up out of the smoke," and that insight and the marching metaphor become the inspiration for McGregor's transformation. Back in Chicago, he becomes the leader of a new movement called the "marching men," an organization as vague and diffuse as its aim: to find "the secret of order in the midst of disorder," in order that "the thresh of feet should come finally to sing a great song, carrying the message of a powerful brotherhood into the ears and brains of the marchers." A great march takes place in Chicago on Labor Day, and though the marching of the men makes its power felt when the day is over, it is clear that the movement, whatever its temporary success, has no future. The marchers disperse in roving gangs, and an "aristocratic" opponent of the movement muses on its success and failure, wondering whether in deliberately turning away from the success of business and embracing the ultimate failure of the marching men, Beaut McGregor did not achieve a higher form of success.

Though a failure as a novel, *Marching Men* is interesting as Anderson's attempt to give expression to his own kind of achievement and as a place to experiment with concepts successfully handled later in *Winesburg, Ohio.* Anderson had given up success in the business world for a precarious career as a writer; he saw himself as a prophet preaching ideals of brotherhood that had nothing to do with political movements or social programs, but that expressed a mystical yearning for order and unity. The metaphor of the marching men was intended to express this vague ideal. The quest for order and brotherhood was a theme to which Anderson was to return in his next novel, *Winesburg, Ohio,* where he found the form best suited to its expression. The format of *Marching Men,* with its lack of convincing motivation and realistic development, exposed the inadequacy of Anderson's marching metaphor for sustaining a full-length realistic novel.

Winesburg, Ohio • *Winesburg, Ohio* is Anderson's masterpiece, a collection of interrelated stories that are less like chapters than like the sections of a long poem; within these pieces, however, there is what might be called a submerged novel, the story of George Willard's growth and maturation. Willard appears in many of the stories, sometimes as a main character, but often as an observer or listener to the tales of other characters. There is the story of Alice Hindeman, who refuses to elope with Ned Curry because she does not want to burden him and eventually runs naked out into the rain. There is also Wing Biddlebaum in "Hands" and Elmer Cowley of "Queer," who desperately try to be normal but only succeed in being stranger than ever. There is the Reverend Curtis Hartman, who spies through a chink in his study window the naked figure of Kate Swift and ends by having a spiritual insight: Christ manifest in the body of a naked woman. These minor characters raise an important critical question: What bearing have they on the submerged *Bildungsroman?*

In five stories, beginning with "Nobody Knows" and ending with "Sophistication" and including "The Thinker," "An Awakening," and "The Teacher," George Willard moves from a lustful relationship with Louise Trunion to a feeling of respectful communion with Helen White, discovering the ultimate reverence for life which Anderson describes as the only thing that makes life possible in the modern world. The discovery was one Anderson himself had made in the early years of his newfound freedom in Chicago, following his escape from the paint factory. In "An Awakening," the pivotal story in the submerged novel, George is made to undergo a mystical experience in which he feels himself in tune with a powerful force swinging through the universe; at the same time, he feels that all of the men and women of his town are his brothers and sisters and wishes to call them out and take them by the hand, including, presumably, the so-called grotesques of the other stories.

The precise relationship of these other stories to those that constitute the growth and maturation of George Willard is a matter of continual critical conjecture, for *Winesburg, Ohio* is the kind of book that does not give up its meanings easily, partly because the kind of meaning the book has can only be suggested, but also because Anderson's way of suggesting is so indirect, at times even vatic. Anderson was possibly influenced by the French post-Impressionist painters such as Paul Cézanne and Paul Gauguin, whose works he had seen in Chicago, and his interest in rendering subjective states indirectly might well parallel theirs. Whether such influences were in fact exerted is arguable. What is clear, however, is that Anderson was by temperament an oral storyteller and that he depended upon tone, colloquial language, and folk psychology rather than the more formal structures of the novelist. In *Winesburg, Ohio* he was also a poet, working by suggestion and indirection, a method that produces intellectual and narrative gaps that the reader is obliged to cross under his or her own power.

One of the chief critical issues of *Winesburg, Ohio* is the nature of Anderson's characters. In an introductory story, "The Book of the Grotesque" (an early title for the novel), Anderson supplied a definition of a grotesque as one who took a single idea and attempted to live by it, but such a definition, while it can be applied to some characters such as Doctor Parcival of "The Philosopher," hardly fits others at all. In an introduction to the Viking edition of *Winesburg, Ohio* (1960), Malcolm Cowley suggested that the problem of the Winesburg characters was an inability to communicate with one another. Jarvis Thurston's article in *Accent* (1956), "Anderson and 'Winesburg': Mysticism and Craft," offers a more compelling view; the Winesburg characters, Thurston says, are all spiritual questers, and their often violent behavior is symptomatic, not of their inability to communicate, but of a blockage of the spiritual quest. Only George Willard succeeds in that quest, when he undergoes, in "An Awakening," a transcendent experience. Burbank, however, in *Sherwood Anderson*, emphasizes the difference between Willard and the other characters of *Winesburg, Ohio* in this way: They are all "arrested" in a state of loneliness and social isolation. George, on the other hand, because he has heard the stories of the grotesques and has absorbed their lives, has managed to break out of a meaningless existence into a meaningful one. Burbank calls George "an artist of life."

Whatever view one takes of Anderson's characters, it is clear that no simple explanation will suffice, especially not the old writer's, though some critics think of him as Anderson's spokesman. Indeed, the prospect of a single idea summarizing and explaining all of the characters seems ironic in the light of the old writer's assertion that such simplemindedness produces grotesques. *Winesburg, Ohio* has its own kind of unity, but it has its own kind of complexity as well. It is a book of contradictory impulses that stands conventional judgment on its head; at times it is funny and often at the same time profoundly sad. It is a book in praise of the emotions, but, at the same time, it is aware of the dangers of emotional excess.

Winesburg, Ohio was well received by reviewers and even had a moderate financial success. It also confirmed, in the minds of eastern critics such as Van Wyck Brooks and Waldo Frank, Anderson's authentic American genius. He was seen as part of that native American tradition that came down through Abraham Lincoln, Walt Whitman, and Mark Twain, expressing the essential nature of American life, its strengths, its weaknesses, and its conflicts.

Winesburg, Ohio has not been without its detractors. From a certain point of view, the antics of a character such as Alice Hindeman dashing naked into the rain are ridiculous, and Anderson's style at times slips into the mode of the fancy writer of slick fiction; even his mysticism can be ridiculed if one sees it as Lionel Trilling does in *The Liberal Imagination* (1950) as a form picking a quarrel with respectable society. Despite its faults, however, *Winesburg, Ohio* still lives—vital, intriguing, moving. It remains a modern American classic, expressing in its eccentric way a certain quality of American life that is all but inexpressible.

Poor White • Anderson's next novel was to be a more traditional sort of work with a hero and a heroine and a "happy" ending that included the requisite embrace, though the hero and the embrace were anything but popularly traditional. Hugh McVey, the protagonist of *Poor White*, is the son of a tramp, born on the muddy banks of the Mississippi and content to live there in a dreamy, sensual existence until taken up by a New England woman who does her best to civilize him. Hugh is tall and lanky, rather like Lincoln in appearance if more like Huck Finn in temperament. When Sarah Shepard, the New England woman, leaves Missouri, Hugh goes east to the town of Bidwell, Ohio, where he becomes the town's telegrapher, and then, out of boredom, begins inventing laborsaving machinery. Being naïve and something of a social outcast, Hugh is unaware of the changes his inventions make in Bidwell. He thinks he is making life easier for the laborers, but opportunists in the town get hold of Hugh's inventions; the factories they bring into being exploit both Hugh and the farm laborers, who, without work in the fields, have swarmed into the new factories, slaving long hours for low pay. Inadvertently, Hugh has succeeded in corrupting the lives of the very people he had set out to help.

Clearly, the story of Hugh's "rise" from a dreamy loafer into a rich inventor and the changes that take place in Bidwell from a sleepy farm community into a bustling factory town are meant to tell the story of mid-America's transformation from a primitive, frontier society of hardworking, God-fearing people to an urban society that differentiates between the rich and the poor, the exploiters and the exploited, the slick new city types and the country-bred factory hands. It is meant to be a pathetic story. In welcoming industry and mechanization—and for the best of reasons—America has managed to stamp out and stifle the older, more primitive but vital life of the frontier. Hugh's "love" affair is less clearly and convincingly done. He marries, is separated from, and then reunited with the daughter of the rich farmer who exploits him. This part of the novel attempts to make a statement, presumably, about emotional life in the new industrial period, but it seems contrived and mechanical compared with the chapters dealing with Hugh's rise.

Poor White, then, is not an entirely successful novel. There are too many flat statements and not enough scenes; the character of Hugh McVey—part Lincoln, part Finn, part Henry Ford—seems at times too mechanical. Although *Poor White* has its moments; it is an ambitious attempt to deal fictionally with the changes in American life that Anderson himself had experienced in his journey from poor boy to businessman to writer. It is by common assent his best novel after *Winesburg, Ohio.*

Many Marriages* and *Dark Laughter • After *Poor White,* Anderson's career as a novelist seriously declined. He continued to write and to publish novels: *Many Marriages* in 1923, and in 1925, *Dark Laughter,* which became a best-seller. Both novels, however, betray what Anderson himself condemned in other writers: the tendency to oversimplify the psychological complexities of human nature. Both novels are anti-Puritan tracts, attacking sexual repression, which writers and popular critics of the day singled out as the source of so much modern unhappiness. In *Many Marriages,* John Webster, a washing machine manufacturer who has found true sexual fulfillment with his secretary, decides to liberate his militantly virginal daughter by appearing naked before her and lecturing her and her mother on the need to free their sexual impulses. *Dark Laughter* retells the story of Anderson's escape from the paint factory by inventing an improbable hero who gives up his career as a journalist and goes back to the town in which he grew up. There he becomes the gardener and then the lover of the factory owner's wife, an experience meant to suggest the interrelation of physical and spiritual love.

Both *Many Marriages* and *Dark Laughter* suffer from Anderson's inability to think through the implications of his theme and to dramatize it effectively with developed characters and situations. The same limitations are reflected in his last two published novels, *Beyond Desire,* a novel about labor unions and strikes, which is badly confused and poorly written, and *Kit Brandon,* the story of a young woman who is the daughter-in-law of a bootlegger. The weaknesses of these last four novels show that Anderson's talent was not essentially novelistic. His real strengths lay in rendering an insight or an illumination and in bodying forth, often in a sudden and shocking way, an unexplained and unexplainable revelation: Wash Williams smashing his respectable mother-in-law with a chair, or the Reverend Curtis Hartman rushing out into the night to tell George Willard that he had seen Christ manifest in the body of a naked woman. Both of these scenes are from *Winesburg, Ohio,* a book that by its structure did not oblige Anderson to develop or explain his grotesque characters and their sudden and violent gestures. In *Many Marriages* and *Dark Laughter,* scenes of nakedness and sexual awakening are made ridiculous by Anderson's attempt to explain and develop what is better left evocative.

After his death in 1941, Anderson was praised by writers such as Thomas Wolfe and Faulkner for the contribution he had made to their development and to the development of modern American fiction. Though he was limited and deeply flawed as a novelist, he ranks with Twain, Crane, and Hemingway as an important influence in the development of American prose style, and he deserves to be remembered as the author of *Winesburg, Ohio* and a number of hauntingly evocative short stories.

W. J. Stuckey

Other major works

SHORT FICTION: *The Triumph of the Egg,* 1921; *Horses and Men,* 1923; *Death in the Woods, and Other Stories,* 1933; *The Sherwood Anderson Reader,* 1947.

PLAYS: *Plays: Winesburg and Others,* pb. 1937.

POETRY: *Mid-American Chants,* 1918; *A New Testament,* 1927.

NONFICTION: *A Story Teller's Story*, 1924; *The Modern Writer*, 1925; *Sherwood Anderson's Notebook*, 1926; *Tar: A Midwest Childhood*, 1926; *Hello Towns!*, 1929; *Perhaps Women*, 1931; *No Swank*, 1934; *Puzzled America*, 1935; *Home Town*, 1940; *Sherwood Anderson's Memoirs*, 1942; *The Letters of Sherwood Anderson*, 1953; *Sherwood Anderson: Selected Letters*, 1984; *Letters to Bab: Sherwood Anderson to Marietta D. Finley, 1916-1933*, 1985.

Bibliography

Anderson, David D. *Sherwood Anderson: An Introduction and Interpretation*. New York: Holt, Rinehart and Winston, 1967. This critical biography argues that all Anderson's work, not just *Winesburg, Ohio*, must be considered when attempting to understand Anderson's career and his place in the literary canon.

Appel, Paul P. *Homage to Sherwood Anderson: 1876-1941*. Mamaroneck, N.Y.: Paul P. Appel, 1970. A collection of essays originally published in homage to Anderson after his death in 1941. Among the contributors are Theodore Dreiser, Gertrude Stein, Thomas Wolfe, Henry Miller, and William Saroyan. Also includes Anderson's previously unpublished letters and his essay "The Modern Writer," which had been issued as a limited edition in 1925.

Bassett, John E. *Sherwood Anderson: An American Career*. Selinsgrove, Pa.: Susquehanna University Press, 2006. A biography of Anderson that focuses on his nonfictional and journalistic writing and takes a look at how he coped with cultural changes during his time.

Campbell, Hilbert H. "The 'Shadow People': Feodor Sologub and Sherwood Anderson's *Winesburg, Ohio*." *Studies in Short Fiction* 33 (Winter, 1996): 51-58. Discusses parallels between some of Sologub's stories in *The Old House and Other Tales* and the stories in *Winesburg, Ohio*. Suggests that the Sologub stories influenced Anderson. Cites parallels to Sologub's tales in such Anderson stories as "Tandy," "Loneliness," and "The Book of the Grotesque."

Campbell, Hilbert H., and Charles E. Modlin, eds. *Sherwood Anderson: Centennial Studies*. Troy, N.Y.: Whitston, 1976. Written for Anderson's centenary, these eleven previously unpublished essays were solicited by the editors. Some of the essays explore Anderson's relationship with other artists, including Edgar Lee Masters, Henry Adams, Alfred Stieglitz, and J. J. Lankes.

Papinchak, Robert Allen. *Sherwood Anderson: A Study of the Short Fiction*. New York: Twayne, 1992. An introduction to Anderson's short stories that examines his search for an appropriate form and his experimentations with form in the stories in *Winesburg, Ohio*, as well as those that appeared before and after that highly influential book. Deals with Anderson's belief that the most authentic history of life is a history of moments when we truly live, as well as his creation of the grotesque as an American type that also reflects a new social reality. Includes comments from Anderson's essays, letters, and notebooks, as well as brief commentaries by five other critics.

Rideout, Walter B., ed. *Sherwood Anderson: A Collection of Critical Essays*. Englewood Cliffs, N.J.: Prentice-Hall, 1974. Treats Anderson from a variety of perspectives: as prophet, storyteller, and maker of American myths.

Small, Judy Jo. *A Reader's Guide to the Short Stories of Sherwood Anderson*. New York: G. K. Hall, 1994. Provides commentary on every story in *Winesburg, Ohio*, *The Triumph of the Egg*, *Horses and Men*, and *Death in the Woods*. Small summarizes the interpretations of other critics and supplies historical and biographical background, accounts of how the stories were written, the period in which they were published, and their reception. Ideally suited for students and general readers.

Townsend, Kim. *Sherwood Anderson.* Boston: Houghton Mifflin, 1987. In this biography of Sherwood Anderson, Townsend focuses, in part, on how Anderson's life appears in his writing. Supplemented by twenty-six photographs and a useful bibliography of Anderson's work.

White, Ray Lewis, ed. *The Achievement of Sherwood Anderson: Essays in Criticism.* Chapel Hill: University of North Carolina Press, 1966. This collection of essays treats an important variety of subjects, including isolation, Freudianism, and socialism in Anderson's texts, as well as his development as an artist.

Isaac Asimov

Born: Petrovichi, Soviet Union (now in Russia); January 2, 1920
Died: New York, New York; April 6, 1992

Principal long fiction • *Pebble in the Sky,* 1950; *Foundation,* 1951; *The Stars Like Dust,* 1951; The Currents of Space, 1952; *Foundation and Empire,* 1952; *Second Foundation,* 1953; *The Caves of Steel,* 1954; *The End of Eternity,* 1955; *The Naked Sun,* 1957; *The Death-Dealers,* 1958 (also known as *A Whiff of Death*); *Fantastic Voyage,* 1966; *The Gods Themselves,* 1972; *Murder at the ABA: A Puzzle in Four Days and Sixty Scenes,* 1976; *Foundation's Edge,* 1982; *The Robots of Dawn,* 1983; *Foundation and Earth,* 1985; *Robots and Empire,* 1985; *Fantastic Voyage II: Destination Brain,* 1987; *Azazel,* 1988; *Prelude to Foundation,* 1988; *Nemesis,* 1989; *Robot Dreams,* 1989; *Robot Visions,* 1990; *Nightfall,* 1991 (with Robert Silverberg); *The Ugly Little Boy,* 1992 (with Silverberg); *Forward the Foundation,* 1993; *The Positronic Man,* 1993 (with Silverberg).

Other literary forms • Isaac Asimov was an unusually prolific author with more than five hundred published books in his bibliography, including fiction, autobiographies, edited anthologies of fiction, and nonfiction works ranging in subject from the Bible to science, history, and humor; only the most famous, "principal" novels are listed above. Asimov also wrote regular articles on science and literature and lent his name to a science-fiction magazine for which he wrote a monthly article. He wrote three autobiographies. *In Memory Yet Green* (1979) covers his life from 1920 to 1954. *In Joy Still Felt* (1980) continues from 1954 to 1978, and *I, Asimov: A Memoir* (1994) spans his life in more anecdotal form. *Yours, Isaac Asimov* (1995) is a posthumous collection of excerpts from letters written by Asimov and edited by his brother Stanley.

Achievements • Asimov was widely known as one of "the big three" science-fiction writers, the other two being Robert Heinlein and Arthur C. Clarke. In addition to obtaining a doctorate in biochemistry from Columbia University, Asimov was awarded fourteen honorary doctoral degrees from various universities. He won seven Hugo Awards (for achievements in science fiction) in various categories. He was awarded the Nebula Award (awarded by the Science Fiction Writers of America) in 1972 for *The Gods Themselves* and again in 1977 for the novelette "The Bicentennial Man" (later expanded by Robert Silverberg to *The Positronic Man*). Ten years later, in 1987, Asimov received the Nebula Grand Master Award, the eighth to be given. All seven of the previous awards had been given to science-fiction authors who were still living and had begun publication before Asimov. Earlier, the American Chemical Society had given him the James T. Grady Award in 1965, and he had received the Westinghouse Science Writing Award in 1967. Asimov wrote on a huge number of subjects, and he has at least one book numbered in each of the ten Dewey Decimal Library System's major classifications.

Biography • Isaac Asimov immigrated to the United States with his Russian Jewish parents when he was three years old; they settled in Brooklyn, New York. Encountering early science-fiction magazines at his father's candy store, where he began working when his mother was pregnant with his brother, led him to follow dual careers as a scientist and author. Asimov was the oldest of three children; he had a sister, Marcia, and a brother, Stanley. He considered himself an American and never learned to speak Russian, although in later life he studied Hebrew and Yiddish. He started at Columbia University at the age of fifteen. By age eighteen, he sold his first story to the magazine *Amazing Stories.* He had been writing a regular column for his high school newspaper prior to that.

After graduating from Columbia with a bachelor's degree in chemistry in 1939, Asimov applied to all five New York City medical schools and was turned down. He was also rejected for the master's program at Columbia but persuaded the department to accept him on probation. He earned his master's degree in chemistry in 1941. His doctoral program was interrupted by his service in World War II as a junior chemist at the Philadelphia Naval Yard from 1942 through 1945. He worked there with fellow science-fiction writer Robert Heinlein. Asimov earned his doctorate in biochemistry in 1948.

After earning his doctorate, Asimov worked for a year as a researcher at Columbia, then became an instructor at Boston University School of Medicine. He was granted tenure there in 1955, but he gave up his duties to write full-time, while retaining his academic title. The university promoted him to the rank of full professor in 1979. Asimov married Gertrude Blugerman in July of 1942. They had two children, a son named David and a daughter named Robyn Joan. They were divorced on November 16, 1973, and Asimov married Janet Opal Jeppson fifteen days later. They had no children, but they wrote the Norby robot children's books together.

Asimov was afraid of heights and flew in airplanes only twice in his life. On the other hand, he enjoyed enclosed places. He enjoyed working in windowless rooms and thought that the city he describes in his book *The Caves of Steel* would be a very appealing place to live. Asimov was not religious but was proud of his Jewish ethnic heritage. He enjoyed public speaking almost as much as he enjoyed writing and had an exuberant personality.

Analysis • Asimov was especially known for his ability to explain complicated scientific concepts clearly. Although his writing reputation was based on his science fiction, his nonfiction writings are useful reference works on the many subjects he covered. His goal was not only to entertain but also to inform.

Asimov's novels are primarily science fiction, and of these almost half, fourteen novels, are tied together at some point with part of the Foundation series. Early in his writing career Asimov established four series of stories: the Empire series, consisting of three novels and collections of short stories; the Foundation series, consisting of seven novels, with more that Asimov outlined to be finished by other authors; the Robot series, consisting of four novels and collections of short stories; and the Lucky Starr series, a collection of six juvenile novels not related to the Foundation series. Asimov borrowed heavily from history, specifically the history of the Roman Empire, to create his plot lines for the Foundation books. Of all his novels, *The Gods Themselves,* a Hugo and Nebula Award winner, was Asimov's favorite.

The Empire series • The Empire series consists of three novels, *Pebble in the Sky, The Stars Like Dust,* and *The Currents of Space.* Later Foundation series books attempt to tie these three into that series. Asimov's first published novel, *Pebble in the Sky,* is the best of these. The writing is not Asimov's most polished, but the hero, Joseph Schwartz,

Library of Congress

provides an interesting middle-aged counterpoint to Bel Arvardan, a younger man of action coping with a postapocalyptic, radioactive Earth.

The Foundation series • The Foundation series began as a trilogy. The first three Foundation books, known for some time as the Foundation trilogy, were written during the 1950's and took much of their plot line from the history of the Roman Empire. Because of the length of the trilogy, it is rarely taught in schools, but the first two of the three books, *Foundation* and *Foundation and Empire*, are examples of Asimov's fiction at its best.

The hero of these novels is Hari Seldon, a mathematician who invents the discipline of psychohistory. Using psychohistory, Seldon is able to predict the coming fall of the empire and to help set up the Foundation in order to help humankind move more quickly through the coming "dark ages" that will be caused by the collapse of the empire. Psychohistory is unable to predict individual mutations and events in human history, however, so Seldon's Foundation is unable to predict the rise to power of the Mule, a mutant of superior intelligence. Asimov's introduction of the concept of psychohistory, a science that could predict the future course of humankind, has inspired many history, psychology, sociology, and economics majors, and was significant in the creation of an actual psychohistory major at some colleges and universities.

By the third book, *Second Foundation*, Asimov was tired of the Foundation story and came up with two alternate endings that he hoped would let him be free of it. In the first, the Mule discovers the secret second Foundation and destroys it, thereby ending Seldon's plan. Asimov's editor talked him out of this ending, so he wrote another, in which the Second Foundation triumphs. Seldon's plan is restored to course and nothing of interest happens again to the human species—thus freeing Asimov from the need to write further Foundation novels. Time and financial incentives eventually overcame Asimov's boredom with the Foundation trilogy, and thirty years later, during the 1980's and 1990's, he began filling in the gaps around the original stories with four other novels. He went on to produce *Foundation's Edge*, *Foundation and Earth*, *Prelude to Foundation*, and *Forward the Foundation*. None has quite the same magic as the first two Foundation novels.

The Robot series • The ideas introduced by Asimov in the Robot series are perhaps his most famous. Asimov's robots are human in form and have "positronic" brains. During the late 1980's and 1990's, the television program and films of *Star Trek: The Next Generation* contributed to public awareness of this concept through the character of the android Data, who, like Asimov's robots, has a positronic brain. Asimov also invented the three Laws of Robotics, which he tended not to let other people use. His invention of mechanical creatures with built-in ethical systems is used freely, however, and from that standpoint Data is an Asimovian robot. The concept of a tool designed for safety in the form of a robot was new to science-fiction writing when Asimov introduced it, and it stood in sharp contrast to the usual mechanical men of science-fiction pulp magazines, which tended to be dangerous and run amok.

There are exciting ideas and parts in each of the four Robot novels, *The Caves of Steel, The Naked Sun, The Robots of Dawn,* and *Robots and Empire. The Caves of Steel* is a good place to start. The character R. Daneel Olivaw is introduced in this novel and appears in six additional novels. The "R." stands for robot. This particular novel is also notable for its blending of two genres, science fiction and mystery. Additionally, the title describes Asimov's solution to an overcrowded Earth, an incredible complex of multilayered mega-cities covering the entire planet.

The Lucky Starr series • Because he was intentionally writing juvenile novels of the Lucky Starr series for a hoped-for television series and was afraid that they would affect his reputation as a serious science-fiction writer, Asimov originally published them under the pseudonym Paul French. In these novels, David Starr and his friend Bigman Jones travel around the solar system in a spaceship. Asimov adapted Western stereotypes to create these plots, but he used his amazing ability to explain science to create plot devices and solutions based on science.

***The Gods Themselves* •** *The Gods Themselves* is one of Asimov's best novels and one of the few unrelated to any others. However, to single it out as a "stand-alone" novel would imply that the books of his series are dependent upon one another, which is not true. *The Gods Themselves* is one of the few Asimov novels dealing with aliens.

The Gods Themselves (the title is taken from a quote by German dramatist Friedrich Schiller, "Against stupidity the gods themselves contend in vain") is actually a series of three interrelated stories treating stupidity and responses to it. Humans exchange energy with aliens in a parallel universe with the Inter-Universe Electron Pump. When one human realizes the pump will eventually cause the sun to explode, he works to warn others, but nobody listens. Meanwhile, in the parallel universe, one of the "para-men" also attempts to shut down the pump. Although neither succeeds due to stupidity on the part of their peers, the problem eventually is solved by others, and the human universe is saved.

***Fantastic Voyage* and *Fantastic Voyage II* •** *Fantastic Voyage* was contracted as a novelization of the 1966 film of the same name. However, because of the rapidity of Asimov's writing and the slow pace of filmmaking, the book actually appeared before the film. In the novel Asimov attempted to explain and justify some of the scientific impossibilities and inaccuracies of the film but never succeeded to his own satisfaction. *Fantastic Voyage II: Destination Brain* was in many ways a second attempt at rectifying the science of the first.

Novelettes into Novels • As a publishing ploy, it was arranged that Robert Silverberg would expand three of Asimov's best and most famous novelettes, "Nightfall," "The Bicentennial Man" (which became *The Positronic Man*), and "The Ugly Little Boy," into full novels. Although Silverberg is an excellent and literary writer, his style and Asimov's do not blend particularly well. Given the opportunity, readers should begin by reading the original award-winning work. "Nightfall" in particular has won worldwide acclaim and is the most mentioned and remembered of Asimov's stories. Its premise concerns what happens to the psyches of a people who live in a world that only experiences total darkness once every two thousand years.

B. Diane Blackwood

Other major works

SHORT FICTION: *I, Robot*, 1950; *The Martian Way*, 1955; *Earth Is Room Enough*, 1957; *Nine Tomorrows*, 1959; *The Rest of the Robots*, 1964; *Asimov's Mysteries*, 1968; *Nightfall, and Other Stories*, 1969; *The Early Asimov*, 1972; *Tales of the Black Widowers*, 1974; *Buy Jupiter, and Other Stories*, 1975; *More Tales of the Black Widowers*, 1976; *The Bicentennial Man, and Other Stories*, 1976; *Good Taste*, 1977; *The Key Word, and Other Mysteries*, 1977; *Casebook of the Black Widowers*, 1980; *Computer Crimes and Capers*, 1983; *The Union Club Mysteries*, 1983; *The Winds of Change, and Other Stories*, 1983; *Banquets of the Black Widowers*, 1984; *The Disappearing Man, and Other Mysteries*, 1985; *Alternative Asimovs*, 1986; *Isaac Asimov: The Complete Stories*, 1990-1992 (2 volumes).

NONFICTION: *The Chemicals of Life: Enzymes, Vitamins, Hormones*, 1954; *Inside the Atom*, 1956; *The World of Carbon*, 1958; *The World of Nitrogen*, 1958; *Realm of Numbers*, 1959; *Words of Science and the History Behind Them*, 1959; *The Intelligent Man's Guide to Science*, 1960; *The Wellsprings of Life*, 1960; *Life and Energy*, 1962; *The Search for the Elements*, 1962; *The Genetic Code*, 1963; *A Short History of Biology*, 1964; *Asimov's Biographical Encyclopedia of Science and Technology*, 1964; *Planets for Man*, 1964 (with Stephen H. Dole); *The Human Body: Its Structures and Operation*, 1964; *The Human Brain: Its Capacities and Functions*, 1964; *A Short History of Chemistry*, 1965; *The Greeks: A Great Adventure*, 1965; *The New Intelligent Man's Guide to Science*, 1965; *The Genetic Effects of Radiation*, 1966; *The Neutrino: Ghost Particle of the Atom*, 1966; *The Roman Republic*, 1966; *The Universe: From Flat Earth to Quasar*, 1966; *Understanding Physics*, 1966; *The Egyptians*, 1967; *The Roman Empire*, 1967; *Asimov's Guide to the Bible*, 1968-1969 (2 volumes); *Science, Numbers, and I*, 1968; *The Dark Ages*, 1968; *The Shaping of England*, 1969; *Asimov's Guide to Shakespeare*, 1970 (2 volumes); *Constantinople: The Forgotten Empire*, 1970; *Electricity and Man*, 1972; *The Shaping of France*, 1972; *Worlds Within Worlds: The Story of Nuclear Energy*, 1972; *The Shaping of North America from Earliest Times to 1763*, 1973; *Today, Tomorrow, and . . .*, 1973; *Before the Golden Age*, 1974 (autobiography); *Earth: Our Crowded Spaceship*, 1974; *Our World in Space*, 1974; *The Birth of the United States, 1763-1816*, 1974; *Our Federal Union: The United States from 1816 to 1865*, 1975; *Science Past—Science Future*, 1975; *The Collapsing Universe*, 1977; *The Golden Door: The United States from 1865 to 1918*, 1977; *A Choice of Catastrophes: The Disasters That Threaten Our World*, 1979; *Extraterrestrial Civilizations*, 1979; *In Memory Yet Green: The Autobiography of Isaac Asimov, 1920-1954*, 1979; *Asimov on Science Fiction*, 1980; *In Joy Still Felt: The Autobiography of Isaac Asimov, 1954-1978*, 1980; *The Annotated "Gulliver's Travels,"* 1980; *Visions of the Universe*, 1981; *Exploring the Earth and the Cosmos: The Growth and Future of Human Knowledge*, 1982; *The Roving Mind*, 1983; *The History of Physics*, 1984; *Asimov's Guide to Halley's Comet*, 1985; *Exploding Suns*, 1985; *Robots: Machines in Man's Image*, 1985 (with Karen A. Frenkel); *The Edge of Tomorrow*, 1985; *The Dangers of Intelligence, and Other Science Essays*, 1986; *Beginnings: The Story of Origins—of Mankind, Life, the Earth, the Universe*, 1987; *Past, Present, and Future*, 1987; *Asimov's Annotated Gilbert and Sullivan*, 1988; *The Relativity of Wrong*, 1988; *Asimov on Science*, 1989; *Asimov's Chronology of Science and Discovery*, 1989; *Asimov's Galaxy*, 1989; *Frontiers*, 1990; *Asimov's Chronology of the World: The History of the World from the Big Bang to Modern Times*, 1991; *Atom: Journey Across the Subatomic Cosmos*, 1991; *I, Asimov: A Memoir*, 1994; *Yours, Isaac Asimov: A Lifetime of Letters*, 1995 (Stanley Asimov, editor); *It's Been a Good Life*, 2002 (Janet Jeppson Asimov, editor; condensed version of his 3 volumes of autobiography); *Conversations with Isaac Asimov*, 2005 (Carl Freedman, editor).

CHILDREN'S LITERATURE: *David Starr: Space Ranger*, 1952; *Lucky Starr and the Pirates of the Asteroids*, 1953; *Lucky Starr and the Oceans of Venus*, 1954; *Lucky Starr and the Big Sun of Mercury*, 1956; *Lucky Starr and the Moons of Jupiter*, 1957; *Lucky Starr and the Rings of Saturn*, 1958.

Bibliography

Asimov, Isaac. *Asimov's Galaxy: Reflections on Science Fiction*. Garden City, N.Y.: Doubleday, 1989. This compilation of sixty-six essays presents readers with Asimov's unique perspective on a genre to which he made many important contributions for fifty years. The topics deal with religion and science fiction, women and science fiction, time travel, science-fiction editors, and magazine covers. Particularly interesting are the items in the final section, "Science Fiction and I," in which Asimov writes frankly about his life and work. No index.

____________. *I, Asimov: A Memoir*. New York: Doubleday, 1994. Spans his entire life in more introspective and anecdotal form.

____________. *In Memory Yet Green: The Autobiography of Isaac Asimov, 1920-1954*. New York: Doubleday, 1979. Asimov's autobiographies are the three best sources about the life and times of this author. Covers Asimov's life through 1954.

____________. *In Joy Still Felt: The Autobiography of Isaac Asimov, 1954-1978*. Garden City, N.Y.: Doubleday, 1980. Continues from 1954 to 1978 and provides vignettes of the publishing world and other science-fiction authors.

"A Celebration of Isaac Asimov: A Man for the Universe." *Skeptical Inquirer* 17 (Fall, 1992): 30-47. Asimov is praised as a master science educator, perhaps of all time; he was responsible for teaching science to millions of people. Tributes are made by Arthur C. Clarke, Frederik Pohl, Harlan Ellison, L. Sprague de Camp, Carl Sagan, Stephen Jay Gould, Martin Gardner, Paul Kurtz, Donald Goldsmith, James Randi, and E. C. Krupp.

Goble, Neil. *Asimov Analyzed*. Baltimore: Mirage, 1972. This unusual study of Asimov's work concentrates on his style in his science fiction and nonfiction. The analyses are detailed, with the author going so far as to perform word-frequency counts to make some of his points.

Gunn, James. *Isaac Asimov: The Foundations of Science Fiction*. New York: Oxford University Press, 1982. Rev. ed. Lanham, Md.: Scarecrow Press, 2005. A professor of English at the University of Kansas, Gunn was a prominent science-fiction writer in his own right and a historian and critic of the genre. He used his long personal friendship with Asimov to show how science fiction shaped Asimov's life and how Asimov in turn shaped the field. The bulk of Gunn's book is devoted to painstaking analyses of Asimov's entire science-fiction corpus. The book concludes with a chronology, a checklist of works by Asimov, a select list of works about him, and an index.

Hutcheon, Pat Duffy. "The Legacy of Isaac Asimov." *The Humanist* 53 (March/April, 1993): 3-5. A biographical account, noting Asimov's efforts to bring scientific understanding to people and to make people realize that to study humanity is to study the universe, and vice versa; claims that Asimov saw the possibility of an eventual organization of a world government, warned against the abandonment of technology in our search for solutions, and predicted the end of sexism, racism, and war.

Palumbo, Donald. *Chaos Theory, Asimov's Foundations and Robots, and Herbert's Dune: The Fractal Aesthetic of Epic Science Fiction.* Westport, Conn.: Greenwood Press, 2002. Looks at the history of epic science fiction through its two most outstanding examples. Includes bibliographical references and index.

Patrouch, Joseph F., Jr. *The Science Fiction of Isaac Asimov.* Garden City, N.Y.: Doubleday, 1974. Patrouch, a teacher of English literature at the University of Dayton, published science-fiction stories, and many reviewers found his critical survey of Asimov's writings in science fiction the best book-length study yet to appear. Patrouch discusses Asimov's style, his narrative skills, and his themes; he also provides detailed analyses of the principal short stories and novels.

Touponce, William F. *Isaac Asimov.* Boston: Twayne, 1991. Part of Twayne's United States Authors series, this volume is a good introduction to the life and works of the author. Includes bibliographical references and an index.

White, Michael. *Asimov: The Unauthorised Life.* London: Millennium, 1994. An unauthorized biography published after Asimov's death. Includes bibliographic references.

Margaret Atwood

Born: Ottawa, Ontario, Canada; November 18, 1939

Principal long fiction • *The Edible Woman*, 1969; *Surfacing*, 1972; *Lady Oracle*, 1976; *Life Before Man*, 1979; *Bodily Harm*, 1981; *The Handmaid's Tale*, 1985; *Cat's Eye*, 1988; *The Robber Bride*, 1993; *Alias Grace*, 1996; *The Blind Assassin*, 2000; *Oryx and Crake*, 2003; *The Penelopiad: The Myth of Penelope and Odysseus*, 2005.

Other literary forms • A skillful and prolific writer, Margaret Atwood has published many volumes of poetry. *Double Persephone* (1961), *The Animals in That Country* (1968), *The Journals of Susanna Moodie* (1970), *Procedures for Underground* (1970), *Power Politics* (1971), *You Are Happy* (1974), *Selected Poems* (1976), *Two-Headed Poems* (1978), *True Stories* (1981), *Interlunar* (1984), and *Selected Poems II* (1987) have enjoyed a wide and enthusiastic readership, especially in Canada. During the 1960's, Atwood published in limited editions poems and broadsides illustrated by Charles Pachter: *The Circle Game* (1964), *Kaleidoscopes Baroque: A Poem* (1965), *Speeches for Dr. Frankenstein* (1966), *Expeditions* (1966), and *What Was in the Garden* (1969). Atwood has also written and illustrated books for children, including *Up in the Tree* (1978) and *Anna's Pet* (1980). Her volumes of short stories, a collection of short fiction and prose poems (*Murder in the Dark*, 1983), a volume of criticism (*Survival: A Thematic Guide to Canadian Literature*, 1972), and a collection of literary essays (*Second Words*, 1982) further demonstrate Atwood's wide-ranging talent. In 1982, Atwood coedited the revised *New Oxford Book of Canadian Verse . She has also written articles and critical reviews too numerous to list. She has contributed prose and poetry to literary journals such as Acta Victoriana* and *Canadian Forum*, and her teleplays have been aired by the Canadian Broadcasting Corporation.

Achievements • Early in her career, Atwood's work was recognized for its distinction. This is particularly true of her poetry, which has earned her numerous awards, including the E. J. Pratt Medal in 1961; the President's Medal from the University of Western Ontario in 1965; and the Governor-General's Award, Canada's highest literary honor, for *The Circle Game* in 1966. Twenty years later, Atwood again won this prize for *The Handmaid's Tale.* Atwood won first prize from the Canadian Centennial Commission Poetry Competition in 1967, and won a prize for poetry from the Union League Civic and Arts Foundation in 1969. Honorary doctorates were conferred by Trent University and Queen's University. Additional prizes included the Bess Hoskins Prize for poetry (1974), the City of Toronto Award (1977), the Canadian Bookseller's Association Award (1977), the St. Lawrence Award for Fiction (1978), the Canada Council Molson Prize (1980), and the Radcliffe Medal (1980).

Two of Atwood's novels have been selected for CBC Radio's *Canada Reads* competition: *The Handmaid's Tale*, supported by former prime minister Kim Campbell in 2002, and *Oryx and Crake*, supported by Toronto city councillor Olivia Chow in 2005.

Biography • Margaret Atwood was born in Ottawa, Ontario, Canada, on November 18, 1939, the second of Carl Edmund and Margaret Killam Atwood's three children.

At the age of six months, she was backpacked into the Quebec wilderness, where her father, an entomologist, pursued his special interests in bees, spruce budworms, and forest tent caterpillars. Throughout her childhood, Atwood's family spent several months of the year in the bush of Quebec and northern Ontario. She did not attend school full-time until she was twelve.

Though often interrupted, Atwood's education seems to have been more than adequate. She was encouraged by her parents to read and write at an early age, and her creative efforts started at the age of five, when she wrote stories, poems, and plays. Her serious composition, however, did not begin until she was sixteen.

In 1961, Atwood earned her bachelor's degree in the English honors program from the University of Toronto, where she studied with poets Jay Macpherson and Margaret Avison. Her master's degree from Radcliffe followed in 1962. Continuing graduate work at Harvard in 1963, Atwood interrupted her studies before reentering the program for two more years in 1965. Although she found graduate studies interesting, Atwood's energies were largely directed toward her creative efforts. To her, the doctoral program was chiefly a means of support while she wrote. Before writing her doctoral thesis, Atwood left Harvard.

Returning to Canada in 1967, Atwood accepted a position at Sir George Williams University in Montreal. By this time, her poetry was gaining recognition. With the publication of *The Edible Woman* and the sale of its film rights, Atwood was able to concentrate more fully on writing, though she taught at York University and was writer-in-residence at the University of Toronto. In 1973, Atwood divorced her American husband of five years, James Polk. After the publication of *Surfacing*, she was able to support herself through her creative efforts. Atwood moved to a farm near Alliston, Ontario, with Canadian novelist Graeme Gibson. A daughter, Eleanor Jess Atwood Gibson, was born in 1979. In 1980, Atwood's family returned to Toronto, where Atwood and Gibson became active in the Canadian Writers' Union, Amnesty International, and the International Association of Poets, Playwrights, Editors, Essayists, and Novelists (PEN).

Analysis • For Atwood, an unabashed Canadian, literature became a means to cultural and personal self-awareness. "To know ourselves," she writes in *Survival*, "we must know our own literature; to know ourselves accurately, we need to know it as part of literature as a whole." Thus, when she defines Canadian literary concerns, she relates her own as well, for Atwood's fiction grows out of this tradition. In her opinion, Canada's central reality is the act of survival: Canadian life and culture are decisively shaped by the demands of a harsh environment. Closely related to this defining act of survival, in Atwood's view, is the Canadian search for territorial identity—or, as literary theorist Northrop Frye put it, "Where is here?"

Atwood's heroines invariably discover themselves to be emotional refugees, strangers in a territory they can accurately label but one in which they are unable to feel at home. Not only are they alienated from their environment, but also they are alienated from language itself; for them, communication becomes a decoding process. To a great degree, their feelings of estrangement extend from a culture that, having reduced everything to products, threatens to consume them. Women are particularly singled out as products, items to be decorated and sold as commodities, though men are threatened as well. Indeed, Canadian identity as a whole is in danger of being engulfed by an acquisitive American culture, though Atwood's "Americans" symbolize exploitation and often turn out to be Canadian nationals.

Courtesy, Vancouver International Writers Festival

Reflective of their time and place, Atwood's characters are appropriately ambivalent. Dead or dying traditions prevent their return to a past, a past most have rejected. Their present is ephemeral at best, and their future inconceivable. Emotionally maimed, her heroines plumb their conscious and unconscious impressions, searching for a return to feeling, a means of identification with the present.

Atwood often couches their struggle in terms of a journey, which serves as a controlling metaphor for inner explorations: The unnamed heroine of *Surfacing* returns to the wilderness of Quebec, Lesje Green of *Life Before Man* wanders through imagined Mesozoic jungles, Rennie Wilford of *Bodily Harm* flies to the insurgent islands of Ste. Agathe and St. Antoine. By setting contemporary culture in relief, these primitive sites define the difference between nature and culture and allow Atwood's heroines to gain new perspectives on their own realities. They can see people and places in relation to each other, not as isolated entities. Ultimately, however, this resolves little, for Atwood's novels end on a tenuous note. Although her heroines come to terms with themselves, they remain estranged.

Supporting her characters' ambivalence is Atwood's versatile narrative technique. Her astringent prose reflects their emotional numbness; its ironic restraint reveals their wariness. Frequent contradictions suggest not only the complexity of her characters but also the antagonistic times they must survive. By skillful juxtaposition of past and present through the use of flashbacks, Atwood evokes compelling fictional landscapes that ironically comment on the untenable state of modern men and women. There remains some hope, as her characters survive with increased understanding of their world. Despite everything, life does go on.

Surfacing • The first of Atwood's novels to arouse critical praise and commentary, *Surfacing* explores new facets of the *Bildungsroman.* What might have been a conventional novel of self-discovery develops into a resonant search for self-recovery imbued with mythic overtones and made accessible through Atwood's skillful use of symbol and ritual. At the same time, Atwood undercuts the romantic literary conventions of ultimate self-realization as a plausible conclusion. To accept the heroine's final emergence as an end in itself is to misread this suggestively ironic novel.

The unnamed heroine of *Surfacing*, accompanied by her lover Joe and a married couple named David and Anna, returns to the Canadian wilderness where she was reared in hopes of locating her missing father. His sudden disappearance has recalled her from a city life marked by personal and professional failures that have left her emotionally anesthetized. While her external search goes forward, the heroine conducts a more important internal investigation to locate missing "gifts" from both parents. Through these, she hopes to rediscover her lost ability to feel. In order to succeed, however, she will need to expose the fiction of her life.

At the outset of her narrative, the heroine warns her readers that she has led a double life when she recalls Anna's question, "Do you have a twin?" She denies having one, for she apparently believes the elaborate fiction she has created, a story involving a spurious marriage, divorce, and abandonment of her child. As additional protection, the heroine has distanced herself from everyone. She refers to her family as "they," "as if they were somebody else's family." Her relationship with Joe is notable for its coolness, and she has only known Anna, described as her best friend, for two months.

By surrounding herself with friends whose occupation of making a film significantly titled *Random Samples* reveals their rootlessness, the heroine seeks to escape the consequences of her actions. Indeed, she describes herself both as a commercial artist, indicating her sense of having sold out, and as an escape artist. Reluctantly approaching the past she sought to escape, the heroine feels as if she is in foreign territory.

The fact that she feels alienated by the location of her past is not surprising, for she is an outsider in a number of telling ways: of English descent in French territory; a non-Roman Catholic, indeed a nonreligious person among the devout; a woman in a man's world. Her French is so halting that she could be mistaken for an American, representing yet another form of alienation, displacement by foreigners. Most of all, she is a stranger to herself. Rather than focusing on her self-alienation, she is consumed by the American usurpation of Canada, its wanton rape of virgin wilderness, in order to avoid a more personal loss of innocence.

Canada's victimization by Americans reflects the heroine's victimization by men. Having been subjected to the concept that "with a paper bag over their head they're all the same," the protagonist is perceived as either contemptible or threatening. Her artistic skills are denigrated by a culture in which no "important" artists have been women. Even her modest commercial success is treated as a personal assault by Joe, who has an "unvoiced claim to superior artistic skills." By telling herself that the wilderness can never recover from abuse, the protagonist denies her own recovery. Although she feels helpless at the beginning of the novel, she soon rediscovers her own capabilities, and as these are increasingly tested, she proves to be a powerful survivor. Thus, the wilderness, a self-reflection, provides the key to self-discovery.

Perhaps the most important lesson the heroine learns is that the wilderness is not innocent. Her encounter with and response to a senselessly slaughtered heron evoke a sense of complicity, leading her to reflect on similar collusion in her brother's animal experiments when they were children. Finding her refuge in childhood innocence blocked, the heroine goes forward with her search. Once again, nature provides information, for in discovering her father's body trapped under water, she finally recognizes her aborted child, her complicity in its death by yielding to her lover's demands. On a broader scale, she acknowledges death as a part of life and reclaims her participation in the life-process by conceiving a child by Joe.

In a ceremony evocative of primitive fertility rites, she seduces her lover. Then, assured of her pregnancy, she undergoes a systematic purgation in order to penetrate to the very core of reality. During this process, the protagonist discovers her parents' gifts—her father's sense of sight and her mother's gift of life. With body and mind reunited, she takes an oath in which she refuses to be a victim. Whole, she feels free to reenter her own time, no longer either victim or stranger.

Atwood's procedure for bringing her heroine to this state of consciousness is remarkable for its intricacy. Though she distrusts language, the protagonist proceeds to tell her story by describing what she sees. Because she has lost her ability to feel, much of this description seems to be objective—until the reader realizes just how unreliable her impressions can be. Contradictions abound, creating enormous uncertainty as intentional and unintentional irony collide, lies converge, and opinion stated as fact proves to be false. Given this burden of complexity, any simple conclusion to *Surfacing* is out of the question. Clearly, Atwood hints at a temporary union with Joe, but this is far from resolving the heroine's dilemma. Outer reality, after all, has not altered. Thus, Atwood's open-ended conclusion is both appropriate and plausible, for to resolve all difficulties would be to give in to the very romantic conventions that her fiction subverts.

Life Before Man • Coming after the gothic comedy of *Lady Oracle, Life Before Man* seems especially stark. Nevertheless, its similarity with all of Atwood's novels is apparent. A penetrating examination of contemporary relationships, it peels away protective layers of deceptions, stripping the main characters until their fallible selves are presented with relentless accuracy. Lesje Green and Elizabeth and Nate Schoenhof are adrift in a collapsing culture in which they struggle to survive. As she focuses on each character, Atwood reveals unrecognized facets of the others.

In this novel, wilderness and culture converge in the Royal Ontario Museum, where Lesje works as a paleontologist and Elizabeth works in public relations. There is little need for the bush country of Quebec, since culture is something of a jungle itself. Unlike the Mesozoic, however, the present anticipates its own extinction because of abundant evidence: pollution, separatist movements, political upheaval, lost traditions, disintegrating families. Humanity is in danger of drowning in its own waste. Whatever predictability life held in the past seems completely absent; even holidays are meaningless. Nevertheless, the novel is fascinated with the past, with the behavior of animals, both human and prehistoric, and with the perpetuation of memory, particularly as it records the history of families.

As in *Surfacing*, a violent death precipitates emotional withdrawal. Most affected is Elizabeth Schoenhof, whose lover Chris has blown off his head as a final gesture of defiance, the ultimate form of escape. His act destroys Elizabeth's sense of security, which resides both in her home and in her ability to manipulate or predict the actions of others. A supreme manipulator, Elizabeth attempts to make everyone act as reasonably as she. Not surprisingly, Elizabeth has at least two selves speaking different languages, genteel chic and street argot, and what passes for "civilized" behavior is merely an escape from honest confrontation with such basic human emotions as love, grief, rejection, and anger. In fact, all of the novel's characters prefer escape to self-realization, and while they pay lip service to social decorum, they quietly rebel.

The characters' rebellious emotions are reflected in the larger world, a political world aflame with separatist zeal. René Lévesque, with whom Nate identifies, is gaining momentum for the separation of Quebec and the reestablishment of French as the major language, threatening to displace the English. Indeed, the world seems to be coming apart as international, national, and personal moves toward separation define this novel's movement. As a solution, however, separation fails to satisfy the characters' need to escape, for no matter how far they run, all carry the baggage of their past.

Elizabeth in particular has survived a loveless past, including abandonment by both parents, the painful death of her alcoholic mother, her sister's mental breakdown and drowning, and her Auntie Muriel's puritanical upbringing. All of this has turned Elizabeth into a determined survivor. Beneath her polished exterior is a street fighter from the slums, a primitive. Indeed, Elizabeth recognizes an important part of herself in Chris. Nate and Lesje share a different kind of past, where love created as much tension as affection. Lesje's Jewish and Ukrainian grandmothers treated her as disputed territory, speaking to her in languages she could not understand and driving her to seek refuge in her fantasy world of Lesjeland.

Feeling like a refugee in treacherous territory, each character attempts to build a new, stable world, notwithstanding the continual impingement of the old, messy one. Nate, having forsaken his mother's futile idealistic causes to save the world, falls in love with Lesje, whom he envisions as an exotic subtropical island free from rules. For a time, Elizabeth inhabits a clean expanse of space somewhere between her bed and the ceiling, and Lesje explores prehistoric terrain, wishing for a return to innocence. When these fantasies diminish in power, the characters find substitutes, challenging the reader to reexamine the novel's possibilities.

Despite its bleak tone, its grimy picture of a deteriorating culture, its feeling of estrangement and futility, its rejection of simplistic resolutions, *Life Before Man* is not without hope. Each character emerges at the end of this novel with something he or she has desired. Nate has Lesje, now pregnant with his child—a child who, in turn, confirms Lesje's commitment to life by displacing her preoccupation with death. Having exorcised the evil spirits of her past, Elizabeth experiences a return of direct emotion.

There is, however, a distinct possibility that the apparent resolution is as ambivalent as that of *Surfacing*. What appears to be a completely objective third-person point of view, presiding over chapters neatly cataloged by name and date, sometimes shifts to first-person, an unreliable first-person at that. Through her revolving characters, their identification with one another, and their multiple role-reversals, Atwood creates contradictory, problematic, and deceptive human characters who defy neat categorization. Taken separately, Nate, Elizabeth, and Lesje can easily be misinterpreted; taken as a whole, they assume an even more complex meaning, reflecting not only their own biased viewpoints but also the reader's. Atwood's ability to capture such shifting realities of character and place is one of her chief artistic distinctions.

Bodily Harm • Rather like the narrator of *Surfacing*, Rennie Wilford in *Bodily Harm* has abandoned her past, the stifling world of Griswold, Ontario, to achieve modest success as a freelance journalist. To Rennie, Griswold represents values of duty, self-sacrifice, and decency found comic by contemporary standards. It is a place where women are narrowly confined to assigned roles that make them little better than servants. Rennie much prefers city life, with its emphasis on mobility and trends such as slave-girl bracelets and pornographic art. In fact, Rennie has become an expert on just such trends, so adept that she can either describe or fabricate one with equal facility. Having learned to look only at surfaces, Rennie has difficulty accepting the reality of her cancerous breast, which *looks* so healthy.

Her cancer serves as the controlling metaphor in the novel, spreading from diseased personal relationships to a political eruption on St. Antoine. Indeed, the world seems shot through with moral cancer. The symptoms are manifest: Honesty is a liability, friends are "contacts," lovers are rapists, pharmacists are drug pushers, and no one wants to hear about issues. What should be healthy forms of human commerce have gone out of control, mirroring the rioting cells in Rennie's breast. When confronted by yet another manifestation of this malaise, a would-be murderer who leaves a coil of rope on her bed, Rennie finds a fast escape route by landing a magazine assignment on St. Antoine.

Her hopes of being a tourist, exempt from participation and responsibility, are short-lived as she is drawn into a political intrigue more life-threatening than her cancer. Before reaching St. Antoine, she learns of its coming election, ignoring Dr. Minnow's allusions to political corruption and makeshift operations. What puzzles her most about their conversation is his reference to the "sweet Canadians." Is he being ironic or not, she wonders. Her superficial observations of island life reveal little, though plenty of evidence points to a violent eruption. Rennie seems more concerned about avoiding sunburn and arrest for drug possession than she is about the abundant poverty and casual violence. Her blindness allows her to become a gunrunner, duped by Lora Lucas, a resilient survivor of many injurious experiences, and Paul, the local connection for drugs and guns, who initiates Rennie into genuine, albeit unwilling, massive involvement.

As a physical link to life, Paul's sexual attention is important to Rennie, who appreciates the value of his touch. His hands call forth the "missing" hands of her grandmother, her doctor's hands, and Lora's bitten hands, hands that deny or offer help. Paul's "aid" to the warring political factions, like Canada's donation of canned hams and Rennie's assistance, is highly questionable, and the results are the reverse of what was planned. Trying to escape from his botched plan, Rennie is brought to confront her own guilt.

Again, Atwood uses flight as a route to self-discovery and deprivation as a source of spiritual nourishment. In Rennie's case, however, these are externally imposed. In her underground cell, with only Lora as company, Rennie ultimately sees and understands the violent disease consuming the world, a disease growing out of a human need to express superiority in a variety of ways and at great spiritual expense. Rennie becomes "afraid of men because men are frightening." Equally important, she understands that there is no difference between *here* and *there*. Finally, she knows that she is not exempt: "Nobody is exempt from anything."

If she survives this ordeal, Rennie plans to change her life, becoming a reporter who will tell what truly happened. Once again, though, Atwood leaves this resolution open to questions. Rennie is often mistaken about what she sees and frequently misinterprets events. Her entire story may well be a prison journal, an account of how she arrived there. When projecting her emergence from prison, she uses the future tense. For Atwood's purposes, this is of relative unimportance, since Rennie has been restored in a way she never anticipated. In the end, stroking Lora's battered hand, Rennie finally embodies the best of Griswold with a clear vision of what lies beneath the surface of human reality.

The Handmaid's Tale • In *The Handmaid's Tale*, Atwood's fiction turns from the realistic to the speculative, though she merely takes the political bent of the 1980's to its logical—and chilling—conclusion. Awash in a swill of pollution, promiscuity, pornography, and venereal disease, late twentieth century America erupts into political and religious battles. Rising from the ashes is the Republic of Gilead, a theocracy so conservative in its reactionary bent that women are channeled into roles as Daughters, Wives, Marthas (maids), Econowives, and Handmaids (mistresses).

The narrator, Offred (referring to her status as a possession *of* her master), is among the first group of Handmaids, fertile women assigned to high-ranking government officials. Weaving between her past and present in flat, almost emotionless prose, Offred draws a terrifyingly real picture of a culture retreating to fundamentalist values in the name of stability. At first, her prose seems to be accurate, a report from an observer. Deeper in the story, readers come to understand that Offred is numb from all that has changed in her life. Besides, she does not trust anyone, least of all herself. As a survivor, she determines to stay alive, even if that means taking risks.

Her loss of freedom and identity create new hungers in Offred: curiosity about the world, a subversive desire for power, a longing for feeling, a need to take risks. In many ways, *The Handmaid's Tale* is a novel about what loss creates. Gilead, in fact, is created partially in response to men's loss of feeling, according to Fred, Offred's Commander. However, Offred takes little comfort in his assurance that feeling has returned.

As she knows, feeling is ephemeral, often unstable, impossible to gauge. Perhaps this is why her characterization of others in the novel seems remote. Although Offred observes gestures, facial movements, and voice tone, she can only guess at intent. Implicit in the simplest statement may be an important message. Thus, Offred decodes all kinds of communication, beginning with the Latin inscription she finds scratched in her wardrobe: "Nolite te bastardes carborundorum." Even this injunction, however, which becomes her motto, is a corruption. Though desperate for communication, Offred cautiously obscures her own message. Her struggle to understand reflects Atwood's familiar theme of the inability to truly understand another person, another situation.

By having Offred acknowledge the impossibility of accurately decoding messages, Atwood calls attention to the narrative itself. Another interesting fictional element is the narrative's remove in time. Offred tells her story in the present, except when she refers to her life before becoming a Handmaid. Ironically, readers learn that not only is she telling her story after events, but her narrative has been reconstructed and presented to an audience at a still greater temporal remove. All of this increases the equivocal quality of the novel and its rich ambiguity.

Although Atwood demands attention, she provides direction in prefatory quotations. Most revealing is her quotation from Jonathan Swift's "A Modest Proposal." Like Swift's satire, Atwood's skates on the surface of reality, often snagging on familiar actions and only slightly exaggerating some attitudes, especially those commonly held about women. Perennial issues of a woman's place, the value of her work, and her true role in society, are at the center of this novel.

Cat's Eye • These concerns appear again in *Cat's Eye*, but in a more subdued form. In subject and theme, *Cat's Eye* is an artistic retrospective. Elaine Risley, a middle-aged painter, is called to Toronto to prepare for her first artistic retrospective. Risley takes the occasion to come to terms with the dimensions of self in time, which she perceives as a "series of transparencies, one laid on top of another." Her return to Toronto, where she grew up, gives her an opportunity to look through the layers of people and events from her present position on the curve of time. This perspective, often ironic and tenuous, allows Risley to accept herself, including her foibles.

Cat's Eye takes full advantage of Atwood's visual style as it reiterates the importance of perspective in relation to change. The novel's art theme emphasizes interpretation while simultaneously satirizing the kind of inflated yet highly subjective criticism published for public consumption. Atwood's most personal novel to date, *Cat's Eye* tackles the physics of life and art and arrives at Atwood's least ambiguous conclusion. Returning to her family in Vancouver, Risley notes that the starlight she sees is only a reflection. Still, she concludes, "it's enough to see by."

The Robber Bride • In *The Robber Bride* communication as a decoding process occurs both figuratively and literally, as one of the four protagonists, the historian Antonia (Tony) Fremont, seeks to discover the underlying meaning of the past. In her own storytelling she sometimes uses a reverse code, transforming herself into her imagined heroine Ynot Tnomerf. In fact, each of the women in the novel has renamed herself to gain distance from past traumas: Karen becomes Charis to cast out the memory of sexual abuse; Tony hopes to escape the "raw sexes war" that characterized her family; Roz Grunwald becomes Rosalind Greenwood as her family climbed the social ladder. Although cast in comic form, the novel explores issues of identity, reality versus fiction, and women's friendship. The three friends meet for lunch and reminisce about their betrayal at the hands of Zenia, a mysterious femme fatale who seduced Tony's and Roz's husbands and Charis's lover. Zenia has multiple stories about her origins, all dramatic but plausible. By preying on their fears and hopes, she ensnares her victims. Speaking about the novel, Atwood has remarked that Zenia is the equivalent of the fiction writer, a liar, a trickster who creates stories to captivate her audience.

Alias Grace • *Alias Grace* is a historical novel based on the character of Grace Marks, a nineteenth century Irish immigrant to Canada accused of being an accomplice in the murder of her employer and his housekeeper-mistress. The novel combines gothic elements, social commentary, and conventions of nineteenth century fiction to tell its story. Spinning out several parallel courtship plots, the novel elucidates the implications of class and gender: Servant women were often the victims of wealthy employers or their bachelor sons. Grace's friend Mary Whitney dies of a botched abortion when she becomes pregnant.

The story is told through letters and narration by Grace and Dr. Simon Jordan, a young physician who has been employed by Grace's supporters to discover the truth of the murder. Dr. Jordan is a foil to Grace: As her fortunes rise, his fall. Hoping to win a pardon from her prison sentence, the shrewd Grace narrates her life story in great detail but claims she cannot clearly remember the events surrounding the murder. Dr. Jordan hopes to restore her faulty memory and to learn the facts of the case. However, in an ironic twist of plot he becomes embroiled in a shabby romantic liaison and, to avoid the consequences, flees Canada in haste. He is injured while serving as a physician in the American Civil War and loses his recent memory. Grace is released from prison, given a job as a housekeeper, and marries her employer. Dr. Jordan remains in the care of his mother and the woman she has chosen to be her son's wife. At the end of the novel all the plot threads are conveniently tied together as in the conventional nineteenth century novel, but at the heart of the story Grace herself remains a mystery.

Atwood's own vision is as informed and humane as that of any contemporary novelist. Challenging her readers to form their own judgments, she combines the complexity of the best modern fiction into the moral rigor of the great nineteenth century novelists. Atwood's resonant symbols, her ironic reversals, and her example challenge readers and writers alike to confront the most difficult and important issues of the contemporary world.

Oryx and Crake • In this 2003 novel, as in *The Handmaid's Tale*, Atwood creates a futuristic dystopia in which she places her protagonist, Snowman. Although Snowman has managed to survive some kind of catastrophe, the specifics surrounding the event are not revealed until the end of the work. The only other forms of life that Snowman meets on the barren seaside landscape are humanoids and animals that have resulted from bioengineering. The humanoids are called Crakers, innocent beings that are tractable and resistant to diseases. These green-eyed mutants manifest selected traits; they are uninterested in sex and violence, and their skin is impervious to ultraviolet light.

Along with the narrative of Snowman's daily existence, the reader learns of his youth via flashbacks. As a child he was called Jimmy (he has renamed himself Snowman), and his best friend was named Glenn, who later adopts the name Crake. Both lived in a compound built by a bioengineering firm for its employees. The compound was isolated from other cities. Crake, a scientific whiz, and Jimmy were raised in dysfunctional families. Jimmy's mother left the family because of her moral resistance to her husband's work; he was responsible for creating genetic hybrids.

Crake's father appears to have been murdered in the wake of a scandal with the firm. Crake grows from a youth who spends his time surfing the Web to a scientific mastermind in charge of a secret project. First he studies at the Watson-Crick Institute, which has a reputation like that of Harvard University—before Harvard ceased to exist. Jimmy attends Martha Graham Academy, a more liberal setting with a focus on the humanities. Even though Crake is fundamental to the story, his character is never fully developed, and he proves to be more of an instrument for the plot.

As the gap between the friends grows, and time passes, Jimmy does little more than hold menial employment and seduce women. The naïve Jimmy finally reconnects with Crake, who employs him. Crake reveals that he is altering human embryos to eliminate their faulty features; in a sense, Crake is playing a godlike role. Jimmy also comes into contact with Oryx, a captivating woman whom Jimmy recognizes from pornography. Oryx imparts snippets of her life to Jimmy, although she remains a hazy figure throughout.

Finally, it is revealed that the apocalyptic event was not a nuclear war; the cause was a potent and fatal plague. When the deadly virus took hold, it spanned the earth from Hong Kong to Toronto. Snowman perpetuates the myth of Oryx and Crake to keep the green-eyed mutants alive. At the end of the novel, there is a suggestion that a new humanity has evolved; the Crakers may be exhibiting some of the traits that Crake had attempted to eliminate in them, such as the desire to lead or to organize religion.

In this cautionary tale, Atwood manages to keep the reader riveted with her careful use of dark humor and asides. The author is known for her ability to create authentic female voices in her novels; in *Oryx and Crake*, she manages to construct a realistic male voice and to convey both the twisted emotional environment in which he matured and a society propelled by commercialism, pornography, and technology.

Karen Carmean
Updated by Karen F. Stein and Jamie Sondra Sindell

Other major works

SHORT FICTION: *Dancing Girls, and Other Stories*, 1977; *Bluebeard's Egg*, 1983; *Murder in the Dark: Short Fictions and Prose Poems*, 1983; *Wilderness Tips*, 1991; *Good Bones*, 1992 (pb. in U.S. as *Good Bones and Simple Murders*, 1994); *Moral Disorder: Stories*, 2006.

POETRY: *Double Persephone*, 1961; *The Circle Game*, 1964 (single poem), 1966 (collection); *Kaleidoscopes Baroque: A Poem*, 1965; *Talismans for Children*, 1965; *Expeditions*, 1966; *Speeches for Dr. Frankenstein*, 1966; *The Animals in That Country*, 1968; *What Was in the Garden*, 1969; *Procedures for Underground*, 1970; *The Journals of Susanna Moodie*, 1970; *Power Politics*, 1971; *You Are Happy*, 1974; *Selected Poems*, 1976; *Two-Headed Poems*, 1978; *True Stories*, 1981; *Snake Poems*, 1983; *Interlunar*, 1984; *Selected Poems II: Poems Selected and New, 1976-1986*, 1987; *Selected Poems, 1966-1984*, 1990; *Poems, 1965-1975*, 1991; *Poems, 1976-1989*, 1992; *Morning in the Burned House*, 1995; *Eating Fire: Selected Poems, 1965-1995*, 1998.

NONFICTION: *Survival: A Thematic Guide to Canadian Literature*, 1972; *Second Words: Selected Critical Prose*, 1982; *The CanLit Foodbook: From Pen to Palate, a Collection of Tasty Literary Fare*, 1987; *Margaret Atwood: Conversations*, 1990; *Deux sollicitudes: Entretiens*, 1996 (with Victor-Lévy Beaulieu; *Two Solicitudes: Conversations*, 1998); *Negotiating with the Dead: A Writer on Writing*, 2002; *Moving Targets: Writing with Intent, 1982-2004*, 2004 (pb. in U.S. as *Writing with Intent: Essays,Reviews, Personal Prose, 1983-2005*, 2005); *Waltzing Again: New and Selected Conversations with Margaret Atwood*, 2006 (with others; Earl G. Ingersoll, editor).

EDITED TEXTS: *The New Oxford Book of Canadian Verse in English*, 1982.

MISCELLANEOUS: *The Tent*, 2006.

Bibliography

Bloom, Harold, ed. *Margaret Atwood*. Philadelphia: Chelsea House, 2000. Collection of critical essays about Atwood that have been assembled for student use, from the series Modern Critical Views. Includes an introduction by Bloom.

Brown, Jane W. "Constructing the Narrative of Women's Friendship: Margaret Atwood's Reflexive Fiction." *Literature, Interpretation, Theory* 6 (1995): 197-212. In this special issue on Atwood, Brown argues that Atwood's narrative reflects the struggle of women to attain friendship. Maintains Atwood achieves this with such reflexive devices as embedded discourse, narrative fragmentation, and doubling. Discusses the difficulty women have in creating friendships because few women think such friendships are important.

Cooke, Nathalie. *Margaret Atwood: A Critical Companion*. Westport, Conn.: Greenwood Press, 2004. Part of the publisher's series of reference books on popular contemporary writers for students, this volume provides detailed plot summaries and analyses of Atwood's major works, along with character portraits, a biography of Atwood and an extensive bibliography. Nathalie Cooke is also the author of *Margaret Atwood: A Biography* (1998).

Deery, June. "Science for Feminists: Margaret Atwood's Body of Knowledge." *Twentieth Century Literature* 43 (Winter, 1997): 470-486. Shows how the themes of feminine identity, personal and cultural history, body image, and colonization in Atwood's fiction are described in terms of basic laws of physics. Comments on Atwood's application of scientific concepts of time, space, energy, and matter to the experience of women under patriarchy in an adaptation of male discourse.

Howells, Coral Ann. *Margaret Atwood*. New York: St. Martin's Press, 1996. In this lively critical and biographical study, Howells elucidates issues that have energized all of Atwood's work: feminist issues, literary genres, and her own identity as a Canadian, a woman, and a writer. Focuses on the fiction.

Ingersoll, Earl G., ed. *Margaret Atwood: Conversations.* Princeton, N.J.: Ontario Review Press, 1990. Contains many interviews with Atwood.

McCombs, Judith, ed. *Critical Essays on Margaret Atwood.* Boston: G. K. Hall, 1988. This indispensable volume contains thirty-two articles and essays, including assessments of patterns and themes in her poetry and prose. The entries are arranged in the chronological order of Atwood's primary works, beginning with *The Circle Game* and ending with *The Handmaid's Tale.* It includes a primary bibliography to 1986 and a thorough index. McCombs's introduction provides an illuminating overview of Atwood's writing career and is a satisfying rationale for her choices of the critical pieces included in the book.

Nischik, Reingard M., ed. *Margaret Atwood: Works and Impact.* Rochester, N.Y.: Camden House, 2000. This sturdy gathering of original (not reprinted) criticism covers a wide variety of aspects of Atwood's writing, including her long fiction.

Stein, Karen F. *Margaret Atwood Revisited.* New York: Twayne, 1999. A lucid and thorough overview of Atwood's writing in all genres. Includes references and a selected bibliography. This volume supersedes an equally fine volume in the same series, Jerome Rosenberg's *Margaret Atwood* (above).

Sullivan, Rosemary. *The Red Shoes: Margaret Atwood, Starting Out.* Toronto: HarperFlamingo Canada, 1998. A biography focusing on Atwood's early life until the end of the 1970's. Attempts to answer the question of how Atwood became a writer and to describe the unfolding of her career.

York, Lorraine M., ed. *Various Atwoods.* Concord, Ont.: Anansi, 1995. Critical essays chiefly on the later poetry and fiction.

Louis Auchincloss

Born: Lawrence, New York; September 27, 1917

Principal long fiction • *The Indifferent Children*, 1947 (as Andrew Lee); *Sybil*, 1951; *A Law for the Lion*, 1953; *The Great World and Timothy Colt*, 1956; *Venus in Sparta*, 1958; *Pursuit of the Prodigal*, 1959; *The House of Five Talents*, 1960; *Portrait in Brownstone*, 1962; *The Rector of Justin*, 1964; *The Embezzler*, 1966; *A World of Profit*, 1968; *I Come as a Thief*, 1972; *The Partners*, 1974; *The Dark Lady*, 1977; *The Country Cousin*, 1978; *The House of the Prophet*, 1980; *The Cat and the King*, 1981; *Watchfires*, 1982; *Exit Lady Masham*, 1983; *The Book Class*, 1984; *Honorable Men*, 1985; *Diary of a Yuppie*, 1986; *The Golden Calves*, 1988; *Fellow Passengers*, 1989; *The Lady of Situations*, 1990; *Three Lives*, 1993 (novellas); *The Education of Oscar Fairfax*, 1995; *Her Infinite Variety*, 2001; *The Scarlet Letters*, 2003; *East Side Story*, 2004.

Other literary forms • Although best known as a novelist, Louis Auchincloss became a prolific and successful writer in a variety of other literary forms. Among his strongest collections of short fiction are *The Romantic Egoists* (1954), *Powers of Attorney* (1963), and *Tales of Manhattan* (1967), each of which presents stories linked by narration, characters, or theme in such a way as to resemble a novel. An accomplished critic, Auchincloss published studies of a wide range of writers, from William Shakespeare to Edith Wharton; among his best-known critical works are *Reflections of a Jacobite* (1961) and *Reading Henry James* (1975). *Life, Law, and Letters: Essays and Sketches* (1978) consists chiefly of essays on literary subjects, while the autobiographical memoir *A Writer's Capital* (1974) provides valuable insight into the formation of Auchincloss's outlook. Finally, Auchincloss published several heavily illustrated biographies and works of nonfiction intended for a general readership; among these works are *Richelieu* (1972), *Persons of Consequence: Queen Victoria and Her Circle* (1979), *False Dawn: Women in the Age of the Sun King* (1984), *The Vanderbilt Era: Profiles of a Gilded Age* (1989), and *La Gloire: The Roman Empire of Corneille and Racine* (1996).

Achievements • During the 1950's, Auchincloss emerged as a strong social satirist and novelist of manners, rivaling in his best work the accomplishments of John Phillips Marquand and John O'Hara. Unlike those writers, however, Auchincloss was clearly an "insider" by birth and breeding, belonging without reservation to the social class and power structure that he so convincingly portrayed. With the waning of the tradition represented by figures such as Marquand and O'Hara, Auchincloss stands nearly alone as an American novelist of manners, unrivaled in his analysis of social and political power.

Freely acknowledging his debt to Henry James and Edith Wharton as well as to Marcel Proust and the Duc de Saint-Simon, Auchincloss transforms the stuff of success into high art, providing his readers with convincing glimpses behind the scenes of society and politics where top-level decisions are often made for the most personal and trivial of reasons. As a rule, his featured characters are credible and well developed, if often unsympathetic; Auchincloss's apparent aim is to describe what he has seen, even at the risk of alienating readers who care so little about his charac-

Inge Morath

ters as not to wonder what will become of them. At the same time, Auchincloss's characteristic mode of expression leaves him open to accusations that he is an "elitist" writer, featuring characters who are almost without exception white, Anglo-Saxon, and Protestant. Such accusations, however, do little to undermine the basic premise that emerges from the body of Auchincloss's work: For good or for ill, the people of whom he writes are those whose decisions and behavior have determined the shape of the American body politic.

Biography • Louis Stanton Auchincloss was born September 27, 1917, in Lawrence, New York, a village on Long Island where his parents owned a vacation house. Their permanent residence was New York City's upper East Side, where Auchincloss spent his entire life except for his years of education and military service. His parents, Joseph and Priscilla Auchincloss, were related to many prominent families in New York City society. Auchincloss attended the Bovee School for Boys and graduated from the prestigious Groton School, where his English teacher, Malcolm Strachan, fostered his literary interests. He entered Yale University in 1935 with plans to become a writer, only to withdraw several months short of graduation in 1939 after his initial efforts at publication had been rejected. Deciding instead to pursue a career in law, he received his degree from the University of Virginia in 1941 and worked briefly for the firm of Sullivan and Cromwell in New York before joining the Navy.

During World War II, Auchincloss served in Naval Intelligence in the Panama Canal Zone and as a gunnery officer on landing ship tanks off the coast of France. Later he was commanding officer on similar craft in the Pacific Ocean. Returning to Sullivan and Cromwell after World War II, Auchincloss again tried his hand at creative writing, this time with demonstrable success. His first novel, *The Indifferent Children,* incorporated some of his experiences in the Navy and used an upper-class military officer as its protagonist, but it was published under the pseudonym Andrew Lee. Auchincloss's parents disapproved of the novel because they thought it might diminish his social standing and harm his legal career.

In 1951, Auchincloss withdrew from the practice of law and devoted himself to writing full-time, only to decide after some three years that law and literature were indeed compatible, even symbiotic, and that the writer's life excluding all other pursuits was a bore. During this period he also had intensive psychotherapy. In 1954, he returned to the practice of law with the Manhattan firm of Hawkins, Delafield, and Wood, of which he became a partner in 1958. The previous year, he had married the former Adele Lawrence, to whom he dedicated several of his publications. Three children were born to them: John Winthrop Auchincloss in 1958, Blake Leay Auchincloss in 1960, and Andrew Sloane Auchincloss in 1963. Auchincloss retired from Hawkins, Delafield, and Wood in 1986.

During the 1960's, Auchincloss achieved critical acclaim, but during the next decade he experienced persistent doubts about his creative ability and his reputation as a writer. After several years in which he wrote mainly nonfiction, he became more productive and began to explore new forms. After 1980 he wrote historical fantasies such as *Exit Lady Masham* and stories that are more decidedly comic, such as those in *Narcissa, and Other Fables* (1983).

After retiring from the law firm in 1986, Auchincloss remained in New York City, living on Park Avenue and spending summers at a second home in Bedford, New York. He continued to write and produced such new novels as *The Scarlet Letters* (2003) and *East Side Story* (2004). He also published important nonfiction works, including three impressive biographies: *J. P. Morgan: The Financier as Collector* (1990), *Woodrow Wilson* (2000), and *Theodore Roosevelt* (2001). Publication of *The Collected Stories of Louis Auchincloss* in 1994 moved critics to reassess his short fiction, which they found as finely crafted as his longer works. Although Auchincloss has long been considered the best novelist of manners of his time.

In addition to his work as writer and lawyer, Auchincloss has been active in civic and cultural affairs. He served as president of the Museum of the City of New York and was a member of the advisory board of *Dictionary of Literary Biography*. He also became a life fellow of the Pierpont Morgan Library.

Analysis • For a writer with a full-time professional career, Louis Auchincloss proved astoundingly prolific, producing nearly one book of fiction or nonfiction each year from the 1950's into the early twenty-first century. Like that of many highly prolific writers, the quality of his work is decidedly uneven. At his best, however, Auchincloss meets and surpasses the standard set by John P. Marquand and John O'Hara for twentieth century American social satire, displaying a resonant erudition that somehow eluded the two older writers even in their brightest moments. Even in the best of his novels, the results of Auchincloss's erudition are sometimes too conspicuous for the reader's comfort, but they can easily be overlooked in favor of the authenticity displayed by characters portrayed in convincing situations.

Auchincloss's reputation as a major writer rests primarily on novels written during the 1960's, a time somewhat past the vogue of social satire in the United States but coinciding neatly with the author's full maturity: The worst of his mistakes were behind him, and he had not yet experienced the temptation to repeat himself. *Pursuit of the Prodigal*, published in 1959, shows Auchincloss approaching the height of his powers, yet not quite free of his earlier mode as he portrays the tribulations of a "maverick" lawyer who is uncomfortable with the conventions into which he was born. Set in the immediate postwar years, *Pursuit of a Prodigal*, despite the distinct insider's voice, shows a clear indebtedness to Marquand's *Point of No Return*, published a decade earlier. The following year, however, Auchincloss broke new and enviable ground with *The House of Five Talents*, ostensibly the memoirs, composed in 1948, of the septuagenarian Miss Gussie Millinder, heir to and survivor of an impressive nineteenth century New York fortune. The author's demonstrated skill at characterization and narration served clear notice of his new, mature promise, soon to be fulfilled with *Portrait in Brownstone*, *The Rector of Justin*, and *The Embezzler*, any one of which would suffice to confirm Auchincloss's reputation as the successor to O'Hara and Marquand as a master observer of American society and a superior stylist.

It is hardly surprising that Auchincloss achieved his greatest success with books narrated by the characters themselves, frequently by two or more characters in successive sections of one novel. Although his early novels and certain of his short stories bear witness to his control of third-person narration, Auchincloss is doubtless at his best when assuming the voice and persona of a featured character, striking a thoroughly convincing tone of vocabulary, style, and reflection. At times, his narrators are authentically unreliable without, however, approaching the virtuoso performances sought and achieved by Marquand in such works as *The Late George Apley* (1937) or *H. M. Pulham, Esq.* (1941). Unlike Marquand, Auchincloss seeks less to ridicule his characters than to represent them true to life, allowing readers to draw their own conclusions. It is to Auchincloss's credit that he can credibly assume such diverse personae as those of Miss Gussie Millinder and the three main characters of *The Embezzler*, as well as the slightly fussy schoolmaster who narrates *The Rector of Justin.*

Given the fact that Auchincloss has chosen to serve as a chronicler of his generation and those immediately preceding, it stands to reason that a number of his featured characters are drawn rather closely upon recognizable models—perhaps too closely in *The House of the Prophet*, rather less so in *The Embezzler* and *The Rector of Justin.* Such a practice has both its benefits and its pitfalls. At his best, Auchincloss meets and surpasses the aims of the finest historical fiction, showing rounded characters where the record presents only flatness. On other occasions, however, his presentation is so sparse as to require the readers' knowledge of the facts behind the fiction. This is not to say, however, that any of Auchincloss's novels are simple romans à clef; in each case, Auchincloss is careful to discover and point a message that goes far deeper than a simple recitation of documented facts.

Together with the highest minded of his characters, Auchincloss exhibits and values a strong sense of moral and ethical responsibility; unlike certain of his predecessors and erstwhile competitors in the genre, he never indulges in sensationalism or exposé for its own sake. Even when scandal invades the lives of his characters, as often it must, there is no perceptible intent to scandalize or titillate readers. Indeed, given the Proustian atmosphere that reigns in many of Auchincloss's novels, readers often wait in vain for the comic catharsis, however slow to build, with which Marcel Proust frequently rewards his readers' patience. It must be noted that Auchincloss presents all but the meanest of his characters with considerable indulgence, providing a human warmth that is totally lacking in the work of such satirists as Sinclair Lewis and often absent in the more bitter works of O'Hara and Marquand.

A New Yorker by proclivity as well as by birth, Auchincloss remains, above all, a New York novelist; his characters spend most of their time in the metropolis, leaving it only for such traditional watering places as Newport and Bar Harbor or for higher civic duty in Washington, D.C. The author's sense of place serves to illustrate and to explain the dominant role traditionally played by New Yorkers in the shaping of American society.

The House of Five Talents • In the first work of his "mature" period, *The House of Five Talents*, Auchincloss undertakes a personal record of upper-level Manhattan society through the still-perceptive eyes of one Augusta Millinder, age seventy-five, whose immigrant grandfather, Julius Millinder, founded one of the less conspicuous but more durable of the major New York fortunes. The Millinders had, by the time of Augusta's birth in 1873, established a position of quiet dominance, based upon diversified investments. The world in which Augusta and her more attractive elder sister Cora grew to maturity was thus one of easy movement and understated privilege, pursued frequently aboard yachts and in private railroad cars. As a memoirist, Augusta remains securely inside the closed world that she describes, yet she is privileged to have a gift for shrewd observation.

As the second and less attractive of two daughters, "Gussie" Millinder learned at an early age to view male admiration with a jaundiced eye. Indeed, the only man to whom she ever became engaged had proposed several years earlier to her vacuous sister Cora, who subsequently married a French prince. Although it seems likely that Lancey Bell, a rising young architect, has proposed to Gussie in good faith, she remains so skeptical that she breaks the engagement, having developed such inner resources that she no longer believes marriage to be necessary or desirable. In fact, the marriages in and around Gussie's family do little to encourage her faith in that institution. Soon after ending her engagement, Gussie becomes a reluctant participant in the dismantling of her own parents' marriage and household. Her father, aged sixty, has become enamored of a former actor half his age and wishes to marry her, supported in his folly by Gussie's older brother Willie and sister-in-law Julia.

Although the divorce and remarriage eventually take place as planned, Gussie has discovered in the meantime her own increasingly formidable talent for high-minded meddling. She has also begun to explore the extent of a freedom uniquely available to rich and well-read spinsters. Although dissuaded from attending college in her youth, she has taken enough courses at Columbia during her early adulthood to qualify her for part-time teaching in a private school. Later, around the age of forty, she becomes deeply involved in volunteer work. By 1948, when she at last addresses herself to her memoirs, she has led a life both independent and fulfilling, but not without its disappointments.

Appropriately, Gussie's greatest disappointments have less to do with spinsterhood than with her various relatives, many of whom seem to have a singular talent for ruining their lives, at least when measured by Gussie's demanding but forgiving standards. Gussie's personal favorite appears to have been her nephew Lydig, a versatile and talented former army flight instructor who tries his hand at various pursuits successfully but without commitment, only to seek fulfillment in a life of adventure. Having taken up mountain-climbing, he dies in an avalanche around the age of thirty, a year before the stock market crash of 1929.

The changes wrought by the Great Depression and its consequences upon the Millinders are recorded with a sympathetic but dispassionate eye by Gussie, whose own personal fortune is sufficiently great to sustain major loss without requiring more than minimal changes in her privileged lifestyle. Among the few things she is obliged to forfeit is her private railroad car, while the chauffeured limousine remains. To the others, Gussie remains a rock of stability in a river of change, able to avert disaster with a well-placed loan (or gift) and a bit of timely meddling. At the age of seventy-five, however, she admits that her interventions have not always been the right ones, much as they may have seemed so at the time. Several marriages remain broken beyond all possible repair and certain of her cousins face congressional investigation for their leftist sympathies.

Self-aware, yet not too much so for credibility, Gussie Millinder remains one of Auchincloss's most engaging narrators and one of his most satisfying creations, combining in her large and slightly outrageous person the best qualities of observer and participant in the action that she records.

Portrait in Brownstone • Auchincloss's next novel, *Portrait in Brownstone*, attempts a broader picture of New York society. Although fulfilling much of the promise held forth by *The House of Five Talents*, it falls short of its predecessor in tightness of construction, in part because of a multiplicity of narrative voices and viewpoints. Each chapter is presented from the viewpoint of a particular character, and while certain characters speak for themselves, others do not, presumably because their self-awareness is so limited as to require the author's third-person intervention.

The principal character of *Portrait in Brownstone*, although never a viewpoint character, is one Derrick Hartley, a minister's son from New England whose Harvard education and contacts facilitate his rapid rise within the presumably closed world of New York high finance. In the hands of O'Hara or Marquand, such a character as Derrick would emerge as a perceptive outsider with just a hint of the romantic hero; Auchincloss, however, presents Derrick as a thoroughgoing professional and opportunist, quick to impose his own stamp upon the closed world that almost did not allow him within its confines. He is also quick to enjoy and exploit the attentions of two female cousins, nieces of the employer whom he will eventually replace.

Set principally in the period during and surrounding World War I, *Portrait in Brownstone* underlines the contrast between "old money" and well-bred industry. Derrick, although polished and considerably less of an arriviste than certain of Auchincloss's later protagonists, has a talent for making money that renders him conspicuous among the Denison descendants, for whom the presence of money has obviated the need for making it.

After a brief and disastrous infatuation with the treacherous and ultimately unhappy Geraldine, Derrick returns his attentions to the younger, somewhat plainer cousin, Ida Trask, who had been his first love. Although disabused of her earlier illusions, Ida agrees to marry Derrick and soon bears him two children, a daughter and then a son. Ida, as a main viewpoint character, narrates much of the novel's action, developing considerably as a character in proportion to a growing awareness of her own innate strengths; Ida is a survivor, a resourceful, intelligent woman who, born in a later time, might well have rivaled her own husband's success. In any case, she is the only woman in the novel who could possibly handle the strains of marriage to a hard-driving businessman such as Derrick, whose strongest attentions and affections are reserved for his work. Like Gussie Millinder, Ida has developed character and intelligence in the absence of great beauty. Unlike Gussie, however, she is willing and able to function competently within the demands of marriage and parenthood. Because of her intelligence and understanding, her marriage to Derrick survives a number of shocks, including their daughter's marital problems and a late-blooming affair between Derrick and Geraldine.

Minor character that she may be, it is Ida's cousin Geraldine whose life and eventual suicide polarize the action of the novel. Although it is Ida who should resent Geraldine and not the other way around, Geraldine continues to envy Ida's relatively stable marriage and often genuine happiness. As Ida observes,

> She remained to the end the little girl who had come down with a bright face and bright flowing hair to find in her Christmas stocking a switch and a book of sermons while mine was crammed with packages that I dared not open.

Childless despite several marriages, resentful of Derrick's mechanical approach to lovemaking during their brief affair, Geraldine begins drinking heavily to dull the pain of bright promise unfulfilled.

Among the other characters portrayed in some detail are the Hartleys' two children, born shortly before World War I. Dorcas, who has inherited her father's temperament but little of his discipline, seeks a career of her own in publishing that is cut short by her marriage to a rebellious young editor who accepts the Hartley's largesse while professing to scorn its source. Eventually, Dorcas enters into a second marriage with one Mark Jesmond, an associate of Derrick who, during an earlier career as a lawyer, had handled the details of her divorce from the editor. Dorcas at last finds fulfillment of sorts in assisting Mark in efforts to "depose" her father from headship of his firm, much as Derrick himself had done years earlier to Ida's uncle Linnaeus Tremain. Dorcas's brother Hugo, meanwhile, is beginning to enter adulthood at the age of thirty-five, thanks mainly to his mother's direct intervention in the choice of his wife and career: Ida, it seems, has begun to assert herself as a matriarch.

Although marred by loose construction and a multiplicity of viewpoints, *Portrait in Brownstone* is notable for the keenness of its observation and the presentation of several memorable scenes. In any case, Auchincloss's readers did not have long to wait before the publication of *The Rector of Justin*, considered by several critics to be the finest of his novels.

The Rector of Justin • Despite the fact that it shares with *Portrait in Brownstone* the potential pitfalls of loose construction and multiple viewpoints, *The Rector of Justin* is considerably more successful both as novel and as document. Auchincloss manages to broaden the appeal of the novel through his choice of subject matter, focusing upon the concept and execution of the American preparatory school. In analyzing the life and career of one Francis Prescott, founder of "Justin Martyr, an Episcopal boys' boarding school thirty miles west of Boston," Auchincloss provides through various viewpoint characters a thoughtful examination of a powerful American institution.

The main narrator of *The Rector of Justin* is Brian Aspinwall, whose arrival at Justin coincides with the outbreak of World War II in Europe. Brian has recently returned to the United States after several years of study at Oxford, where doctors have diagnosed a heart murmur that renders him unfit for service in the British Army. Unsure as yet of his vocation to become an Episcopal priest, Brian welcomes the prospect of teaching at Justin as an opportunity to test his suitability for the priesthood as well as for teaching, another possibility. Drawn gradually deeper into the affairs of the school and its founder-headmaster, Brian records his observations and experiences in a journal that forms the backbone of the book. Later, as the idea of recording the school's history begins to take form in his mind, he includes the testimony—both oral and written—of Dr. Prescott's family, friends, and former students. The result is thus more unified and better organized than *Portrait in Brownstone*, despite the old-maidish Brian's obvious limitations both as narrator and as observer.

By the time of Brian's arrival, Francis Prescott is nearly eighty years of age and long overdue for retirement; as both founder and headmaster, however, he is such an institution that no one has given serious thought to replacing him. Brian vacillates between admiration and harsh criticism for the old man and his "muscular Christianity." To Brian's incredulity, the aging Prescott remains unfailingly democratic in pronouncements both public and private, seemingly unaware of the fact that he and his school have helped to perpetuate an American class system that Prescott personally deplores. This basic irony continues to animate the novel, providing as it does the subject matter for Brian's continuing research.

Early in the novel, Brian learns that Prescott, as a young man, took pains to examine at close range the British public-school system preparatory to founding a boarding school of his own; at no point does Prescott or anyone near him appear to have considered the difference between British aristocracy and American democracy. In fact, many of the questions raised in Brian's mind are left hanging, at least for readers, calling attention to the anomalous role of private education in America. Prescott, for his part, continues to deny the existence of an American ruling class even when faced with evidence to the contrary from his own alumni rolls.

Brian's continuing research gradually uncovers a wealth of conflicting evidence concerning Prescott's accomplishment. It is clear in any case that the realization of Prescott's lifelong dream has been achieved only at great personal cost. Brian finds the darker side of Justin's history in both a document penned by the long-dead son of the school's charter trustee, on whose behalf Prescott's efforts failed miserably, and in the spoken recollections of Prescott's youngest daughter, ironically named Cordelia. When Brian meets her, Cordelia is in her middle forties, an unreconstructed Greenwich Village bohemian with nymphomaniacal tendencies that, on one occasion, send Brian fleeing for his life. Prescott, it seems, did much to ruin not only her early first marriage but also a later liaison with a mortally wounded veteran of World War I. Cordelia ascribes much of her unhappiness to the fact that both men, as "old boys" of Justin Martyr, perceived a higher obligation to her father than to herself.

Ending with Prescott's death in retirement at the age of eighty-six, *The Rector of Justin* concludes much as it began, undecided as to the ultimate value of Prescott's achievement. Brian, however, has made a decision; now a fully ordained priest, he continues as a member of the faculty at Justin Martyr.

Together with *The House of Five Talents, The Rector of Justin* stands as one of Auchincloss's more impressive accomplishments; in few of his other novels are the interdependent questions of privilege and responsibility discussed with such thoughtfulness or candor. If the book has a major weakness it is that the characters, especially Prescott himself, are often stretched so flat as to strain the readers' belief; even then, it is possible to accept flatness in the case of a character who adamantly refuses to admit life's ambiguities.

The Embezzler • Published two years after *The Rector of Justin, The Embezzler* builds on the author's known strengths to provide a strong social satire in the tradition of O'Hara and Marquand, yet it transcends the accomplishments of both authors with its spareness and authority. Recalling in its essentials one of the subplots in *The House of Five Talents*, wherein Gussie Millinder reluctantly covers the defalcations of a distant relative threatened with exposure, *The Embezzler* credibly re-creates the heyday of high finance in America before, during, and after the crash of 1929.

The title character and initial narrator of *The Embezzler* is Guy Prime, writing in 1960 to set straight the record of his notoriety some twenty-five years earlier. His antagonist and eventual successor as narrator is Reginald (Rex) Geer, an erstwhile friend and associate since college days. The gathering tension between the two men, reflected in the conflict between their recollections of the same events, provides the novel with its major human interest. Throughout the novel, it is up to readers to weigh conflicting testimony and to form their own considered judgments.

Grandson of a former Episcopal bishop of New York, Guy Prime has grown up less rich than other of Auchincloss's main characters. His breeding and Harvard education, however, qualify him to function competently at the upper reaches of Manhattan's financial establishment. His classmate Rex Geer, like Derrick Hartley the son of a rural New England parson, is perhaps even better suited than Guy to the "art" of making money. Rex is not, however, a social climber; to interpret him as such, as a number of the characters do, is to oversimplify a personality of multiple and often conflicting motivations. Guy, for his part, is hardly less complex, an essentially humane man whose interactions with his fellow mortals are almost inevitably compounded by a flair for the dramatic and a tendency toward hero-worship.

From the start, the friendship of Guy Prime and Rex Geer is complicated by their interlocking relationships with women whom neither man quite understands. The first of these is Guy's wealthy cousin Alix Prime, a doll-like heir with whom Rex falls suddenly and disastrously in love, quite to his own consternation. Although ambitious and industrious, Rex is immune to the blandishments of inherited wealth and quite undone by the common opinion that he covets Alix for her money. The second woman is Guy's wife Angelica, reared mainly in Europe by her expatriate mother. An affair in middle life between Rex and Angelica permanently alters the lives of all three characters, serving at least in part as Guy's justification for his ventures into thievery. To Guy's way of thinking, the affair between his wife and his best friend suffices to suspend his belief in permanent values; the fact remains, however, that Guy has already begun to borrow large sums of money from Rex to cover high-risk stock market activities. With the increase of risk, Guy "simply" begins to pledge the value of securities that have been left in trust with his firm.

Later testimony supplied by Rex (and by Angelica herself in a short concluding chapter) casts serious doubt upon some of the assertions made by Guy in the brief memoir that has been discovered following his death in 1962. Even so, there are few hard-and-fast answers to the questions that remain in the readers' mind. Auchincloss does not make any serious attempt to justify the plainly unethical conduct of his principal character; what he seeks, rather, is a credible re-creation of a significant moment in recent American history, leading immediately to the extensive financial reforms implemented by the administration of Franklin D. Roosevelt. To a far greater degree than in his earlier novels, Auchincloss presents characters caught and portrayed in all their understandably human ambiguity. Despite its limited scope and relative brevity, *The Embezzler* may well be the tightest and finest of Auchincloss's novels.

The House of the Prophet • A prophet, according to Scripture, is not without honor save in his own house. In *The House of the Prophet*, Auchincloss, drawing from that proverb, has fashioned a novel based loosely on the life of the prominent political journalist Walter Lippmann. The novel's protagonist, Felix Leitner, a respected attorney, widely read pundit, and adviser to presidents, emerges diminished from the examination of his life undertaken by Roger Cutter, an erstwhile assistant and aspiring biographer. A variety of lesser narrative voices, including those of Leitner's two former wives, do their best to show the private truth behind the public image.

As in many of his later efforts, Auchincloss in *The House of the Prophet* returns with diminished success to a number of conventions and devices that have served him well in the past: The basic format of the novel, including the fussy, would-be "historian," owes much to *The Rector of Justin*, while Leitner, speaking occasionally in his own voice, recalls both Rex Geer and Guy Prime of *The Embezzler*. Although the action and characters are both credible and engrossing, *The House of the Prophet* gives the disturbing impression of a novel that one has already read, in which only the names and certain of the circumstances have been changed.

In its weakest moments, *The House of the Prophet* borders upon self-parody. Roger Cutter, the "main" narrator whose memories and intentions form the backbone of the novel, often comes across as Brian Aspinwall in caricature: Rendered impotent for life by a diabetic crisis sustained in early adulthood, Roger is (even more obviously than the old-maidish Brian) cast in the role of house eunuch, free to observe and record the master's movements while remaining immune to any possible entanglement with the numerous female characters. Only in its documentary interest and its plausible interpretations of recent American history does *The House of the Prophet* bear serious comparison with the strongest of the author's earlier novels.

Viewed purely as a "political" novel, *The House of the Prophet* is a creditable example of the genre, showing that Auchincloss, when he chooses, can examine politics with the same shrewd powers of observation that he customarily applies to business and the law. As Leitner the pundit grows increasingly conservative with the onset of old age, his changing opinions are attributed less to the ossification of his mind than to the necessary tension between the "prophet" and his changing times. Toward the end of his life, for example, Leitner prepares a brilliant but outrageous column suggesting that America, through the forced resignation of Richard Nixon, "is engaging in one of the most ancient of tribal rituals: the burial of the fisher king." Roger Cutter, appalled by the likely consequences should such opinions be allowed to appear in print under Leitner's respected byline, acts quickly and effectively to have the column suppressed. Leitner's intelligence, however touched by senility, remains as keen and sensitive as ever; he has simply outlived his own time.

The Lady of Situations • By entitling his 1990 book *The Lady of Situations*, Auchincloss points to the fact that his heroine, Natica Chauncey, attains success by treating every difficult situation not as an obstacle but as an opportunity. Her independent spirit and her clear-sightedness qualify Natica for her role as a heroine. However, her life story suggests that a woman such as Natica will often sacrifice others in order to fulfill her own potential.

The Lady of Situations is for the most part narrated by an omniscient author. However, the novel is framed by first-person narratives titled "Ruth's Memoir," in which Natica's aunt, Ruth Felton, reports her observations, thus functioning much like a Greek chorus. A similar passage appears at three other points in the book. The story begins during the 1960's, with Ruth, now in her seventies, recalling the time three decades before when Natica's difficulties began. Natica's bankrupt father spends his time perfecting his fly-fishing technique; her mother refuses to admit that the Chauncey name no longer means anything. She is too obtuse to let Ruth pay Natica's way through a prestigious private school, where she could make the friendships that would serve her in later life.

The primary narrator now takes up Natica's story. After graduating from Barnard College, Natica meets and marries Thomas Barnes, an assistant rector at Averhill School. Unlike her naïve husband, Natica sees Averhill as it is, a hotbed of hypocrisy and malice. However, after autocratic headmaster Reverend Rufus Lockwood makes Natica his secretary, she enjoys feeling powerful and is almost happy. Unfortunately, when Lockwood's wife realizes that Natica has some influence over him, he is forced to fire her.

By now, Natica is so bored with her husband and the school that she embarks upon an affair with a new teacher, the wealthy, charming Stephen Hill. After she becomes pregnant, Hill insists on her divorcing Barnes and marrying him. Ever the pragmatist, Natica agrees. Though he is the innocent party, Barnes is dismissed from Averhill, becomes a military chaplain, and is later killed in wartime.

Meanwhile, Natica has miscarried. She is somewhat relieved, however, because she feared that the child would resemble Barnes, who was probably his father. Back in the United States, Hill's mother, who adores Natica, arranges for her to be accepted by society. However, Hill proves to be lazy and moody. Realizing that he resents her success in business, Natica quits her job and persuades Hill's mother to buy them a bookstore. When he learns from Barnes that he was not the father of the child Natica lost, Hill shoots himself.

Again, Natica makes the best of things. She persuades Hill's mother to pay her way through law school and then joins a law firm, where she finally meets a man she can both love and respect. When she appears in the final "Memoir," set in 1966, Natica is happily married and has three children, as well as a flourishing law practice.

Ruth points out, however, that Natica has made her way to success by manipulating some people and destroying others, notably two husbands. Natica just laughs, but Ruth muses that she would rather be an old maid than have Natica's memories. Ruth fulfills the role of the Greek chorus, raising the moral questions that Natica does not choose to ask.

Honorable Men • Political controversy provoked by the Vietnam War is an important issue in *Honorable Men*, but this novel remains primarily a treatment of personal and family crises. Spanning four decades (the 1930's through the 1960's), the book displays the troubled lives of Chip Benedict and his wife Alida. Sections of the novel focusing on Chip use third-person narration, but Alida's sections use first-person and thereby elicit more sympathy.

As a young woman, Alida Struthers dabbles in adolescent rebellion but eventually re-creates herself as the most famous debutante in America. By this means she escapes the genteel poverty into which her family has fallen and marries the rich and handsome Chip.

Chip is the only male descendant in a New England family who has become wealthy from manufacturing glass, a commodity as fragile as many relationships in the novel. Born with great privileges but also burdened by family expectations, Chip displays both self-righteous hypocrisy and guilt at his own inadequacies. He continually searches for Puritanical moral certainty as a buttress against his own less honorable impulses. As his name implies, he can scarcely define himself except as a chip off the family block. In a key episode that echoes the novel's title, Chip forces his best friend to resign from law school for presumably violating the honor code. Chip's action shows that he can adhere rigidly to the rules but has no larger faith that might give real meaning to the code of honor.

Chip's actions always appear good, but eventually his active support of the Vietnam War shatters his family. Alida leaves him, his daughter becomes an antiwar activist, and his son goes to Sweden to escape the draft. In an ending that some readers may find too facile, Chip finally receives assurance of his mother's unqualified love and apparently finds happiness by marrying his adoring secretary.

The Education of Oscar Fairfax • In *The Education of Oscar Fairfax* Auchincloss revisits much of the territory explored in *Honorable Men* and other novels. Spanning seventy years, the narrative takes Oscar through a New England boys' school, on to Yale University, and eventually to a partnership in the Wall Street law firm founded by his grandfather. The chapters are loosely linked, but each episode provides an opportunity for Oscar's further enlightenment.

At St. Augustine's School, for example, he learns the possible dangers of close male relationships and saves a senior master from damaging accusations. At Yale he regretfully acknowledges the limits of his own literary talents but heartily condemns the ruthless tactics of a more brilliant classmate. As a wealthy and successful lawyer, Oscar repeatedly ponders the appropriate use of his power—in influencing the opinion of a Supreme Court justice regarding New Deal legislation, in introducing an idealistic young man from Maine into his own jaded social and professional realm, in meddling with his son's rigorous ethics. Early in the novel Oscar's future wife accuses him of caring more for art than for people. Throughout the book, however, Oscar is a keen observer of all those around him. In keeping his eyes open and exercising subtle power, he also manages to change the lives of many for the better.

David B. Parsell
Updated by Albert Wilhelm
and Rosemary M. Canfield Reisman

Other major works

SHORT FICTION: *The Injustice Collectors*, 1950; *The Romantic Egoists*, 1954; *Powers of Attorney*, 1963; *Tales of Manhattan*, 1967; *Second Chance: Tales of Two Generations*, 1970; *The Winthrop Covenant*, 1976; *Narcissa, and Other Fables*, 1983; *Skinny Island: More Tales of Manhattan*, 1987; *Fellow Passengers: A Novel in Portraits*, 1989; *False Gods*, 1992 (fables); *Tales of Yesteryear*, 1994; *The Collected Stories of Louis Auchincloss*, 1994; *The Atonement, and Other Stories*, 1997; *The Anniversary, and Other Stories*, 1999; *Manhattan Monologues*, 2002; *The Young Apollo, and Other Stories*, 2006.

NONFICTION: *Reflections of a Jacobite*, 1961; *Pioneers and Caretakers: A Study of Nine American Women Novelists*, 1965; *Motiveless Malignity*, 1969; *Edith Wharton: A Woman in Her Time*, 1971; *Richelieu*, 1972; *A Writer's Capital*, 1974; *Reading Henry James*, 1975; *Life, Law and Letters: Essays and Sketches*, 1979; *Persons of Consequence: Queen Victoria and Her Circle*, 1979; *False Dawn: Women in the Age of the Sun King*, 1984; *The Vanderbilt Era: Profiles of a Gilded Age*, 1989; *J. P. Morgan: The Financier as Collector*, 1990; *Love Without Wings: Some Friendships in Literature and Politics*, 1991; *The Style's the Man: Reflections on Proust, Fitzgerald, Wharton, Vidal, and Others*, 1994; *La Gloire: The Roman Empire of Corneille and Racine*, 1996; *The Man Behind the Book: Literary Profiles*, 1996; *Woodrow Wilson*, 2000; *Theodore Roosevelt*, 2001; *Writers and Personality*, 2005.

Bibliography

Bryer, Jackson R. *Louis Auchincloss and His Critics*. Boston: G. K. Hall, 1977. A comprehensive, annotated bibliography of works by and about Auchincloss from 1931 to 1976. The first secondary sourcebook dealing exclusively with Auchincloss and his work, it remains authoritative in its record of his developing reputation as a writer.

Dahl, Christopher C. *Louis Auchincloss*. New York: Frederick Ungar, 1986. The first book-length study of Auchincloss's work, examining his novels and stories in chronological order and offering a balanced view of his accomplishments. Of special interest is the investigation of the boundaries between fiction and fact, which explores possible historical antecedents for characters and plot in *The Embezzler, The House of the Prophet,* and *The Rector of Justin.*

Gelderman, Carol W. *Louis Auchincloss: A Writer's Life.* New York: Crown, 1993. A good, updated biography of the writer. Includes bibliographical references and an index.

Milne, Gordon. *The Sense of Society.* Madison, N.J.: Fairleigh Dickinson University Press, 1977. This overview of the American novel of manners devotes a chapter to Auchincloss, stressing his characterizations and prose style.

Parsell, David B. *Louis Auchincloss.* Boston: Twayne, 1988. Parsell's sixth chapter, titled "The Novel as Omnibus: Auchincloss's Collected Short Fiction," is recommended for those seeking to explore Auchincloss's singular approach to short and long fiction.

Piket, Vincent. *Louis Auchincloss: The Growth of a Novelist.* Basingstoke, England: Macmillan, 1991. Part of the New Directions in American Studies series, this critical look at Auchincloss's career includes bibliographical references and an index.

Plimpton, George. "The Art of Fiction CXXXVIII: Louis Auchincloss." *Paris Review* 36 (Fall, 1994): 72-94. In this interview, Auchincloss discusses his fiction and nonfiction, commenting on his relationship with editors, how important plot and character are in his fiction, and his notion of literary style as a reflection of the personality of the writer.

Tuttleton, James W. "Louis Auchincloss at 80." *New Criterion* 16, no. 2 (October 1, 1997): 32-36. Brief appreciation of Auchincloss at the end of his eighth decade of life.

Vidal, Gore. "The Great World and Louis Auchincloss." In *United States.* New York: Random House, 1993. An assessment of Auchincloss by one of the leading figures in American letters.

James Baldwin

Born: New York, New York; August 2, 1924
Died: St. Paul de Vence, France; December 1, 1987

Principal long fiction • *Go Tell It on the Mountain,* 1953; *Giovanni's Room,* 1956; *Another Country,* 1962; *Tell Me How Long the Train's Been Gone,* 1968; *If Beale Street Could Talk,* 1974; *Just Above My Head,* 1979.

Other literary forms • Before he published his first novel, James Baldwin had established a reputation as a talented essayist and reviewer. Many of his early pieces, later collected in *Notes of a Native Son* (1955) and *Nobody Knows My Name: More Notes of a Native Son* (1961), have become classics; his essays on Richard Wright, especially "Everybody's Protest Novel" (1949) and "Many Thousands Gone" (1951), occupy a central position in the development of "universalist" African American thought during the 1950's. Culminating in *The Fire Next Time* (1963), an extended meditation on the relationship of race, religion, and the individual experience in America, Baldwin's early prose demands a reexamination and redefinition of received social and cultural premises. His collections of essays *No Name in the Street* (1971) and *The Devil Finds Work* (1976) reflected a more militant stance and were received less favorably than Baldwin's universalist statements. *The Evidence of Things Not Seen* (1985) is a book-length essay on the Atlanta child-murders, while *The Price of the Ticket: Collected Nonfiction 1948-1985* (1985) includes all of Baldwin's essay collections as well as a number of previously uncollected pieces. Less formal and intricate, though in some cases more explicit, reflections of Baldwin's beliefs can be found in *A Rap on Race* (1971), an extended discussion with anthropologist Margaret Mead, and *A Dialogue* (1975), a conversation with poet Nikki Giovanni.

Baldwin also wrote children's fiction (*Little Man, Little Man,* 1975), the text for a photographic essay (*Nothing Personal,* 1964, with Richard Avedon), an unfilmed scenario (*One Day, When I Was Lost: A Scenario Based on "The Autobiography of Malcolm X,"* 1972), drama, and short stories. Most critics prefer Baldwin's first play, *The Amen Corner* (produced 1954), to *Blues for Mister Charlie* (1964) despite the latter's four-month Broadway run. Although he published little short fiction after the collection *Going to Meet the Man* (1965), Baldwin was an acknowledged master of the novella form. "Sonny's Blues" (1957), the story of the relationship of a jazz musician to his "respectable" narrator-brother, anticipates many of the themes of Baldwin's later novels and is widely recognized as one of the great American novellas.

Achievements • Baldwin's public role as a major African American racial spokesman of the 1950's and 1960's guarantees his place in American cultural history. Though not undeserved, this reputation more frequently obscures than clarifies the nature of his literary achievement, which involves his relationship to African American culture, existential philosophy, and the moral tradition of the world novel. To be sure, Baldwin's progression from an individualistic, universalist stance through active involvement with the integrationist Civil Rights movement to an increasing sympathy with militant Pan-Africanist thought parallels the general development of African

©John Hoppy Hopkins

American thought between the early 1950's and the mid-1970's. Indeed, his novels frequently mirror both Baldwin's personal philosophy and its social context. Some, most notably *Another Country*, attained a high degree of public visibility when published, leading to a widely accepted vision of Baldwin as a topical writer. To consider Baldwin primarily as a racial spokesman, however, imposes a stereotype that distorts many of his most penetrating insights and underestimates his status as a literary craftsman.

More accurate, though ultimately as limited, is the view of Baldwin primarily as an exemplar of the African American presence in the "mainstream" of the American tradition. Grouped with Ralph Ellison as a major "post-Wright" black novelist, Baldwin represents, in this view, the generation that rejected "protest literature" in favor of "universal" themes. Strangely at odds with the view of Baldwin as racial spokesman, this view emphasizes the craftsmanship of Baldwin's early novels and his treatment of "mainstream" themes such as religious hypocrisy, father-son tensions, and sexual identity. Ironically, many younger African American novelists accept this general view of Baldwin's accomplishment, viewing his mastery of Jamesian techniques and his involvement with continental literary culture as an indication of alienation from his racial identity. Recasting political activist Eldridge Cleaver's political attack on Baldwin in aesthetic terms, the African American writer Ishmael Reed dismisses Baldwin as a great "white" novelist. A grain of truth lies in Reed's assertion; Baldwin rarely created new forms. Rather, he infused a variety of Euro-American forms, derived from Wright and William Faulkner as well as from Henry James, with the rhythms and imagery of the African American oral tradition.

Like the folk preacher whose voice he frequently assumed in secular contexts, Baldwin combined moral insight with an uncompromising sense of the concrete realities of his community, whether defined in terms of family, lovers, race, or nation. This indicates the deepest level of Baldwin's literary achievement; whatever his immediate political focus or fictional form, he possessed an insight into moral psychology shared by only a handful of novelists. Inasmuch as the specific circumstances of this psychology involve American racial relations, this insight aligns Baldwin with Wright, Faulkner, Mark Twain, and Harriet Beecher Stowe. His insight involves the symbolic alienation of the individual and places him with American romantics such as Nathaniel Hawthorne and European existentialists such as Albert Camus.

Because Baldwin's insight recognizes the complex pressure exerted by social mechanisms on individual consciousness, it reveals affinities with James Joyce,

George Eliot, and Ellison. As a writer who combined elements of all of these traditions with the voice of the anonymous African American preacher, Baldwin cannot be reduced to accommodate the terms of any one of them. Refusing to lie about the reality of pain, he provided realistic images of the moral life possible in the inhospitable world that encompasses the streets of Harlem and the submerged recesses of the mind.

Biography • James Baldwin once dismissed his childhood as "the usual bleak fantasy." Nevertheless, the major concerns of his fiction consistently reflect the social context of his family life in Harlem during the Great Depression. The dominant figure of Baldwin's childhood was clearly that of his stepfather, David Baldwin, who worked as a manual laborer and preached in a storefront church. Clearly the model for Gabriel Grimes in *Go Tell It on the Mountain,* David Baldwin had moved from New Orleans to New York City, where he married Baldwin's mother, Emma Berdis. The oldest of what was to be a group of nine children in the household, James assumed a great deal of the responsibility for the care of his half brothers and sisters. Insulated somewhat from the brutality of Harlem street life by his domestic duties, Baldwin, as he describes in *The Fire Next Time,* sought refuge in the church. Undergoing a conversion experience, similar to that of John in *Go Tell It on the Mountain,* at the age of fourteen in 1938, Baldwin preached as a youth minister for the next several years. At the same time, he began to read, immersing himself in works such as *Uncle Tom's Cabin* (1852) and the novels of Charles Dickens. Both at his Harlem junior high school, where the African American poet Countée Cullen was one of his teachers, and at his predominantly white Bronx high school, Baldwin contributed to student literary publications. The combination of family tension, economic hardship, and religious vocation provides the focus of much of Baldwin's greatest writing, most notably *Go Tell It on the Mountain, The Fire Next Time,* and *Just Above My Head.*

If Baldwin's experience during the 1930's provided his material, his life from 1942 to 1948 shaped his characteristic approach to that material. After he graduated from high school in 1942, Baldwin worked for a year as a manual laborer in New Jersey, an experience that increased both his understanding of his stepfather and his insight into America's economic and racial systems. Moving to Greenwich Village in 1943, Baldwin worked during the day and wrote at night for the next five years; his first national reviews and essays appeared in 1946. The major event of the Village years, however, was Baldwin's meeting with Richard Wright in the winter of 1944-1945. Wright's interest helped Baldwin secure first a Eugene F. Saxton Memorial Award and then a Rosenwald Fellowship, enabling him to move to Paris in 1948.

After his arrival in France, Baldwin experienced more of the poverty that had shaped his childhood. Simultaneously, he developed a larger perspective on the psychocultural context conditioning his experience, feeling at once a greater sense of freedom and a larger sense of the global structure of racism, particularly as reflected in the French treatment of North Africans. In addition, he formed many of the personal and literary friendships that contributed to his later public prominence. Baldwin's well-publicized literary feud with Wright, who viewed the younger writer's criticism of *Native Son* (1940) as a form of personal betrayal, helped establish Baldwin as a major presence in African American letters. Although Baldwin's first novel, *Go Tell It on the Mountain,* was well received critically, it was not so financially successful that he could devote his full time to creative writing. As a result, Baldwin continued to travel widely, frequently on journalistic assignments, while writing *Giovanni's*

Room, which is set in France and involves no black characters.

Returning to the United States as a journalist covering the Civil Rights movement, Baldwin made his first trip to the American South in 1957. The essays and reports describing that physical and psychological journey propelled Baldwin to the position of public prominence that he maintained for more than a decade. During the height of the movement, Baldwin lectured widely and was present at major events such as the March on Washington and the voter registration drive in Selma, Alabama. In addition, he met with most of the major African American activists of the period, including Martin Luther King, Jr., Elijah Muhammad, James Meredith, and Medgar Evers. Attorney General Robert Kennedy requested that Baldwin bring together the most influential voices in the black community, and, even though the resulting meeting accomplished little, the request testifies to Baldwin's image as a focal point of African American opinion. In addition to this political activity, Baldwin formed personal and literary relationships—frequently tempestuous ones—with numerous white writers, including William Styron and Norman Mailer. A surge in literary popularity, reflected in the presence of *Another Country* and *The Fire Next Time* on the best-seller lists throughout most of 1962 and 1963, accompanied Baldwin's political success and freed him from financial insecurity for the first time. He traveled extensively throughout the decade, and his visits to Puerto Rico and Africa were to have a major influence on his subsequent political thought.

Partly because of Baldwin's involvement with prominent whites and partly because of the sympathy for homosexuals evinced in his writing, several black militants, most notably Eldridge Cleaver, attacked Baldwin's position as "black spokesman" beginning during the late 1960's. As a result, nationalist spokesmen such as Amiri Baraka and Bobby Seale gradually eclipsed Baldwin in the public literary and political spotlights. Nevertheless, Baldwin, himself sympathetic to many of the militant positions, continued his involvement with public issues, such as the fate of the Wilmington, North Carolina, prisoners, which he addressed in an open letter to Jimmy Carter shortly after Carter's election to the presidency. In his later years, though he returned periodically to the South, Baldwin lived for much of the time in France and Turkey. It was in St. Paul de Vence, France, that he died, in late 1987.

Analysis • Uncompromising in his demand for personal and social integrity, James Baldwin from the beginning of his career charged the individual with full responsibility for his or her moral identity. Both in his early individualistic novels and in his later political fiction, he insisted on the inadequacy of received definitions as the basis for self-knowledge or social action. Echoing the existentialist principle "existence precedes essence," he intimated the underlying consistency of his vision in the introductory essay in *Notes of a Native Son*:

> I think all theories are suspect, that the finest principles may have to be modified, or may even be pulverized by the demands of life, and that one must find, therefore, one's own moral center and move through the world hoping that this center will guide one aright.

Baldwin's insistence on the moral center and movement in the world cautions against associating him with the atheistic or solipsistic currents of existential thought. Never denying the possibility of transcendent moral power—which he frequently imaged as the power of love—he simply insisted that human conceptions must remain flexible enough to allow for the honest perception of experience. Fully recognizing the reality of existential pain and despair, Baldwin invoked honesty and self-acceptance as the necessary supports for the love capable of generating individual communication and at least the groundwork for political action.

Baldwin's social vision, reflecting his experience in a racist culture, acknowledges the forces militating against self-knowledge and moral responsibility. Each of his novels portrays a series of evasive and simplifying definitions built into religious, economic, and educational institutions. These definitions, which emphasize the separation of self and other, control the immediate contexts of individual experience. As a result, they frequently seem to constitute "human nature," to embody the inevitable limits of experience. Although sympathizing with the difficulty of separating the self from context without simultaneously denying experience, Baldwin insists that acquiescing to the definitions inevitably results in self-hatred and social immorality. The individual incapable of accepting his or her existential complexity flees to the illusion of certainty provided by the institutions that assume responsibility for directing moral decisions.

This cycle of institutional pressure encouraging existential evasion ensuring further institutional corruption recurs in each of Baldwin's novels. On both personal and social levels, the drive to deny the reality of the other—racial, sexual, or economic—generates nothing save destruction. Derived from the streets of Harlem rather than from Scripture, Baldwin's response echoes Christ's admonition to "love thy neighbor as thyself." The derivation is vital; in Baldwin's novels, those who extract the message from the Bible rather than from their lives frequently aggravate the pain that makes evading reality seem attractive.

The immediate focus of Baldwin's attention gradually shifted from consciousness to context, creating the illusion of a change in his basic concerns. Although he always worked in the realistic tradition of the novel, his choice of specific forms paralleled this shift in thematic focus, though again his later work indicates an underlying unity in his fiction. His first novel, *Go Tell It on the Mountain*, employs a tightly focused Jamesian form to explore the developing awareness of the adolescent protagonist John Grimes, who is not yet aware of the evasive definitions conditioning his experience. After a second Jamesian novel, *Giovanni's Room*, Baldwin adapted the relatively unstructured Dreiserian mode in *Another Country* and *Tell Me How Long the Train's Been Gone*. Characters such as Rufus Scott and Vivaldo Moore in *Another Country* continue to struggle for individual awareness, but Baldwin's new narrative stance emphasizes the impact of the limiting definitions on a wide range of particular social circumstances. Attempting to balance the presentation of consciousness and context, Baldwin's last two novels, *If Beale Street Could Talk* and *Just Above My Head*, synthesize the earlier technical approaches. Returning to the immediate focus on the individual consciousness in these first-person narratives, Baldwin creates protagonists capable of articulating their own social perceptions. Consciousness and context merge as Baldwin's narrators share their insights and, more important, their processes with their fellow sufferers.

These insights implicitly endorse William Blake's vision of morality as a movement from innocence through experience to a higher innocence. Beginning with an unaware innocence, individuals inevitably enter the deadening and murderous world of experience, the world of the limiting definitions. Those who attempt to deny the world and remain children perish alongside those who cynically submit to the cruelty of the context for imagined personal benefit. Only those who plunge into experience, recognize its cruelty, and resolve to forge an aware innocence can hope to survive morally. Specifically, Baldwin urges families to pass on a sense of the higher innocence to their children by refusing to simplify the truth of experience. This painful honesty makes possible the commitment to love despite the inevitability of pain and isolation. It provides the only hope, however desperate, for individual or social rejuvenation. To a large extent, Baldwin's career developed in accord with the Blakean pattern. John Grimes begins his passage from innocence to experience in *Go Tell It on the Mountain*; Rufus Scott and Vivaldo Moore, among others, struggle to survive experience in *Another Country*, which intimates the need for the higher innocence. Baldwin's last two novels portray the entire process, focusing on the attempt first to find and then to pass on the higher innocence. *Just Above My Head*, with its middle-aged narrator and his teenage children, clearly represents a more highly developed and realistic stage of the vision than *If Beale Street Could Talk*, with its teenage mother-narrator and her newborn infant.

Go Tell It on the Mountain • *Go Tell It on the Mountain* centers on the religious conversion and family relationships of John Grimes, whose experience parallels that of Baldwin during his youth. Although he believes himself to be the natural son of Gabriel Grimes, a preacher who, like Baldwin's stepfather, moved to New York after growing up in the South, John is actually the son of Gabriel's wife, Elizabeth, and her lover, Richard, who committed suicide prior to John's birth. Growing up under the influence of his hypocritical and tyrannical stepfather, John alternately attempts to please and transcend him. Gabriel expends most of his emotional energy on his openly rebellious son Roy, whose immersion in the violent life of the Harlem streets contrasts sharply with John's involvement with the "Temple of the Fire Baptized," the storefront church where his conversion takes place. To the extent that Baldwin organizes *Go Tell It on the Mountain* around John's attempt to come to terms with these pressures, the novel appears to have a highly individualistic focus.

The overall structure of the novel, however, dictates that John's experience be viewed in a larger context. Of the three major sections of *Go Tell It on the Mountain*, the first, "The Seventh Day," and the third, "The Threshing Floor," focus directly on John. The long middle section, "The Prayers of the Saints," a Faulknerian exploration of history, traces the origins of John's struggle to the experience of his elders, devoting individual chapters to Elizabeth, Gabriel, and Gabriel's sister Florence. Together the prayers portray the Great Northern Migration of African Americans from the South, from rural to urban settings. Far from bringing true freedom, the movement results in a new indirect type of oppression. As Elizabeth recognizes:

> There was not, after all, a great difference between the world of the North and that of the South which she had fled; there was only this difference: the North promised more. And this similarity: what it promised it did not give, and what it gave, at length and grudgingly with one hand, it took back with the other.

Even in his most individualistic phase, Baldwin is aware of the power of institutional pressures. The origins of John's particular struggle against the limiting definitions go back to their impact on both Elizabeth and Gabriel.

Elizabeth's relationship with John's true father, at least in its early stages, appears to offer hope for at least a limited freedom from external definition. Highly intelligent and self-aware, Richard struggles to transcend the limitations imposed on black aspiration through a rigorous program of self-education, which he shares with Elizabeth. Despite his intelligence and determination, however, Richard maintains a naive innocence concerning the possibility of self-definition in a society based on racist assumptions. Only when arrested on suspicion of a robbery he had nothing to do with does he recognize that his context defines him simply as another "nigger." Unable to reconcile this imposed definition with his drive for social transcendence, he despairs and commits suicide. This act, in turn, destroys Elizabeth's chance for obtaining a greater degree of freedom. She is not, however, simply a victim. Fearing that Richard will be unable to cope with the responsibility of a family, she fails to tell him of her pregnancy. Far from protecting him, this evasion contributes to his destruction by allowing Richard to view his situation as purely personal. Elizabeth's own choice, conditioned by the social refusal to confront reality, combines with the racist legal system to circumscribe her possibilities. Forced to care for her infant son, she marries Gabriel, thus establishing the basic terms for John's subsequent struggle.

Seen in relation to John in "The Seventh Day," Gabriel appears to be one of the most despicable hypocrites in American literature. In relation to his own history in "The Prayers of the Saints," however, he appears victimized by the institutional context of his youth. In turn, he victimizes his family by attempting to force them into narrowly defined roles. The roots of Gabriel's character lie in the "temple-street" dichotomy of his southern childhood. Encouraged by his religious mother to deny his sensuality, Gabriel undergoes a conversion experience and immerses himself in the role of preacher. As a result, he enters into a loveless asexual marriage with his mother's friend Deborah, herself a victim of the racist psychology—enforced by black and white people—which condemns *her* after she has been brutally raped by a group of whites. Eventually, Gabriel's repressed street self breaks out and he fathers a son by the sensual Esther. Again attempting to deny his sensuality, Gabriel refuses to acknowledge this son, Royal. Like John's half-brother Roy, the first Royal immerses himself in the street life that Gabriel denies; he dies in a Chicago barroom brawl. Gabriel fears that Roy will share Royal's fate, but his attempt to crush his second son's street self merely strengthens the resulting rebellion. Faced with the guilt of Royal's death and the sense of impending doom concerning Roy, Gabriel retreats into a solipsism that makes a mockery of his Christian vocation. Far from providing a context for moral responsibility, the church—both in the South and in the North—simply replaces the original innocence of religious fervor with a cynical vision of religion as a source of the power needed to destroy the innocence of others.

Against this backdrop, John's conversion raises a basic question that will recur in slightly different circumstances in each of Baldwin's novels: Can an individual hope to break the cycle of evasion that has shaped his personal and social context? In John's case, the problem takes on added dimensions, since he remains ignorant of many of the events shaping his life, including those involving his own birth. By framing the prayers with John's conversion, Baldwin stresses the connection between past and present, but the connection can be perceived as either oppressive or liberating. The complex irony of "The Threshing Floor" section allows informed readings of John's conversion as either a surrender to evasion or as a movement toward existential responsibility. Focusing primarily on John's internal experience as he lies transfixed on the church floor, "The Threshing Floor" revolves around a dialogue between an "ironic voice" that challenges John to return to the street and the part of John that seeks traditional salvation. Throughout John's vision, the narrative voice shifts point of view in accord with John's developing perception. As John accepts the perceptions implied by his vision, the ironic voice shifts its attention to yet deeper levels of ambiguity. To the extent that John resolves these ambiguities by embracing the

Temple, his experience seems to increase the risk that he will follow Gabriel's destructive example.

Several image patterns, however, indicate that John may be moving nearer to a recognition of his actual complexity. Chief among these are those involving the curse of Ham, the rejection of the father, and the acceptance of apparent opposites. From the beginning of the vision, the ironic voice ridicules John for accepting the curse of Ham, which condemns him both as son and as "nigger." Manipulating John's sense of guilt for having indulged his street self by masturbating, the ironic voice insists that John's very existence "proves" Gabriel's own sexual weakness. If Gabriel condemns John, he condemns himself in the process. As a result, John comes to view himself as the "devil's son" and repudiates his subservience before his "father." Without this essentially negative, and ultimately socially derived, definition of himself, John finds himself in an existential void where "there was no speech or language, and there was no love."

Forced to reconstruct his identity, John progresses from this sense of isolation to a vision of the dispossessed with whom he shares his agony and his humanity. John's vision of the multitude whose collective voice merges with his own suggests suffering as the essential human experience, one obliterating both the safety and the isolation of imposed definitions. Significantly, this vision leads John to Jesus the Son rather than God the Father, marking an implicit rejection of Gabriel's Old Testament vengeance in favor of the New Testament commitment to an all-encompassing love. The son metamorphoses from symbol of limitation to symbol of liberation. Near the end of his vision, John explicitly rejects the separation of opposites—street and temple, white and black—encouraged by his social context: "The light and the darkness had kissed each other, and were married now, forever, in the life and the vision of John's soul." Returning to his immediate environment from the depths of his mind, John responds not to the call of Gabriel but to that of Elisha, a slightly older member of the congregation with whom he has previously engaged in a sexually suggestive wrestling match reminiscent of that in D. H. Lawrence's *Women in Love* (1920). John's salvation, then, may bring him closer to an acceptance of his own sensuality, to a definition of himself encompassing both temple and street. Baldwin ends the novel with the emergence of the newly "saved" John onto the streets of Harlem. His fate hinges on his ability to move ahead to the higher innocence suggested by his vision of the dispossessed rather than submitting to the experiences that have destroyed and deformed the majority of the saints.

Another Country • *Another Country*, Baldwin's greatest popular success, analyzes the effects of deforming pressure and experience on a wide range of characters, black and white, male and female, homosexual and heterosexual. To accommodate these diverse consciousnesses, Baldwin employs the sprawling form usually associated with political rather than psychological fiction, emphasizing the diverse forms of innocence and experience in American society. The three major sections of *Another Country*, "Easy Rider," "Any Day Now," and "Toward Bethlehem," progress generally from despair to renewed hope, but no single consciousness or plot line provides a frame similar to that of *Go Tell It on the Mountain*. Rather, the novel's structural coherence derives from the moral concerns present in each of the various plots.

Casting a Melvillean shadow over the novel is the black jazz musician Rufus Scott, who is destroyed by an agonizing affair with Leona, a white southerner recently arrived in New York at the time she meets him. Unable to forge the innocence necessary for love in a context that repudiates the relationship at every turn, Rufus destroys Leona psychologically. After a period of physical and psychological destitution, he kills himself by jumping off a bridge. His sister Ida, an aspiring singer, and his friend Vivaldo Moore, an aspiring white writer, meet during the last days of Rufus's life and fall in love as they console each other over his death. Struggling to overcome the racial and sexual definitions that destroyed Rufus, they seek a higher innocence capable of countering Ida's sense of the world as a "whorehouse." In contrast to Ida and Vivaldo's struggle, the relationship of white actor Eric Jones and his French lover Yves seems Edenic. Although Baldwin portrays Eric's internal struggle for a firm sense of his sexual identity, their shared innocence at times seems to exist almost entirely outside the context of the pressures that destroyed Rufus. The final major characters, Richard and Cass Silenski, represent the cost of the American Dream. After Richard "makes it" as a popular novelist, their personal relationship decays, precipitating Cass's affair with Eric. Their tentative reunion after Richard discovers the affair makes it clear that material success provides no shortcut to moral responsibility.

Baldwin examines each character and relationship in the context of the institutional pressures discouraging individual responsibility. His portrait of Rufus, the major accomplishment of *Another Country*, testifies to a moral insight and a raw artistic power resembling that of Wright and Émile Zola. Forgoing the formal control and emotional restraint of his earlier novels, Baldwin opens *Another Country* with the image of Rufus who "had fallen so low, that he scarcely had the energy to be angry." Both an exceptional case and a representative figure, Rufus embodies the seething anger and hopeless isolation rendering Baldwin's United States a landscape of nightmare. Seeing his own situation as unbearable, Rufus meditates on the fate of a city tormented by an agony like his own: "He remembered to what excesses, into what traps and nightmares, his loneliness had driven him; and he wondered where such a violent emptiness might drive an entire city." Forcing readers to recognize the social implications of Rufus's situation, Baldwin emphasizes that his specific situation originates in his own moral failure with Leona. Where Gabriel Grimes remained insulated from his immorality by arrogance and pride, Rufus feels the full extent of his self-enforced damnation. Ironically and belatedly, his destitution clarifies his sense of the extent of his past acceptance of the social definitions that destroy him.

Wandering the streets of Manhattan, Rufus feels himself beyond human contact. Desperately in need of love, he believes his past actions render him unfit for even minimal compassion. His abuse of Leona, who as a white woman represents both the "other" and the source of the most obvious social definitions circumscribing his life as a black male, accounts for his original estrangement from family and friends, who find his viciousness uncharacteristic. All, including Rufus, fail to understand soon enough that his abuse of Leona represents both a rebellion against and an acceptance of the role dictated by racial and sexual definitions. Separated from the psychological source of his art—jazz inevitably rejects the substructure of Euro-American definitions of reality—Rufus falls ever further into a paranoia that receives ample reinforcement from the racist context. Largely by his own choice, he withdraws almost entirely from both his black and white acquaintances. When he is on the street following Leona's breakdown, he begins to recognize not only his immediate but also his long-term acceptance of destructive definitions. Thinking back on a brief homosexual affair with Eric to which he submitted out of pity rather than love, Rufus regrets having treated his friend with contempt. Having rejected the "other" in

Eric and Leona, Rufus realizes he has rejected a part of himself. He consigns himself to the ranks of the damned, casting himself beyond human love with his plunge off the bridge.

Although not absolving Rufus of responsibility for his actions, Baldwin treats him with profound sympathy, in part because of his honesty and in part because of the enormous power of the social institutions that define him as the "other." Throughout *Another Country*, Baldwin emphasizes that white heterosexual men possess the power of definition, although their power destroys them as surely as it does their victims. Television producer Steve Ellis, a moral cripple embodying the worst values of the American economic system, nearly destroys Ida and Vivaldo's relationship by encouraging Ida to accept a cynical definition of herself as a sexual commodity. Vivaldo, too, participates in the cynicism when he visits the Harlem prostitutes, indirectly perpetuating the definitions that reduce black people to sexual objects, and thus implicating himself in Rufus's death. In fact, every major character with the exception of Eric bears partial responsibility for Rufus's destruction, since each at times accepts the definitions generating the cycle of rejection and denial. The constituting irony, however, stems from the fact that only those most actively struggling for moral integrity recognize their culpability. Vivaldo, who attempts to reach out to Rufus earlier on the night of his suicide, feels more guilt than Richard, who simply dismisses Rufus as a common "nigger" after his mistreatment of Leona.

This unflinching portrayal of moral failure, especially on the part of well-meaning liberals, provides the thematic center of *Another Country*. Baldwin concludes the novel with the image of Yves's reunion with Eric, who is apparently on the verge of professional success with a starring role in a film of a Fyodor Dostoevski novel. This combination of personal and financial success seems more an assertion of naïve hope than a compelling part of the surrounding fictional world. The majority of the narrative lines imply the impossibility of simple dissociation from institutional pressure. Ultimately, the intensity of Rufus's pain and the intricacy of Ida and Vivaldo's struggle overshadow Eric and Yves's questionable innocence. As Ida tells Vivaldo, "Our being together doesn't change the world." The attempt to overcome the cynicism of this perception leads to a recognition that meaningful love demands total acceptance. Ida's later question, "How can you say you loved Rufus when there was so much about him you didn't want to know?" could easily provide the epitaph for the entire society in *Another Country*.

Just Above My Head • In *Just Above My Head*, Baldwin creates a narrator, Hall Montana, capable of articulating the psychological subtleties of *Go Tell It on the Mountain*, the social insights of *Another Country*, and the political anger of *Tell Me How Long the Train's Been Gone*. Like other observer-participants in American literature, such as Nick Carraway in *The Great Gatsby* (1925) and Jack Burden in *All the King's Men* (1946), Hall tells both his own story and that of a more publicly prominent figure, in this case his brother Arthur, a gospel singer who dies two years prior to the start of the novel. Significantly, *Just Above My Head* also reconsiders Baldwin's own artistic history, echoing countless motifs from his earlier writings. Though not precisely a self-reflexive text, *Just Above My Head* takes on added richness when juxtaposed with Baldwin's treatment of religious concerns in *Go Tell It on the Mountain*; the homosexuality theme in *Giovanni's Room*; the relationship between brothers and the musical setting in "Sonny's Blues"; racial politics in *Blues for Mister Charlie* and *Tell Me How Long the Train's Been Gone*; the Nation of Islam in *The Fire Next Time* and *No Name in the*

Street; and, most important, the intermingled family love and world politics in *If Beale Street Could Talk*. Baldwin's reconsideration of his own history, which is at once private like Hall's and public like Arthur's, emphasizes the necessity of a continual reexamination of the nature of both self and context in order to reach the higher innocence.

Similarly, Hall's resolve to understand the social and existential meaning of Arthur's experience originates in his desire to answer honestly his children's questions concerning their uncle. Refusing to protect their original innocence—an attempt he knows would fail—Hall seeks both to free himself from the despair of experience and to discover a mature innocence he can pass on to the younger generation. Tracing the roots of Arthur's despair to pressures originating in numerous limiting definitions and failures of courage, Hall summarizes his, and Baldwin's, social insight:

> [T]he attempt, more the necessity, to excavate a history, to find out the truth about oneself! is motivated by the need to have the power to force others to recognize your presence, your right to be here. The disputed passage will remain disputed so long as you do not have the authority of the right-of-way. . . . Power clears the passage, swiftly: but the paradox, here, is that power, rooted in history, is also, the mockery and the repudiation of history. The power to define the other seals one's definition of oneself.

Recognizing that the only hope for meaningful moral freedom lies in repudiating the power of definition, Hall concludes: "Our history is each other. That is our only guide. One thing is absolutely certain: one can repudiate, or despise, no one's history without repudiating and despising one's own."

Although Baldwin recognizes the extent to which the definitions and repudiations remain entrenched in institutional structures, his portrayal of Hall's courage and honesty offers at least some hope for moral integrity as a base for social action. If an individual such as Hall can counteract the pressures militating against personal responsibility, he or she may be able to exert a positive influence on relatively small social groups such as families and churches, which in turn may affect the larger social context. Nevertheless, Baldwin refuses to encourage simplistic optimism. Rather than focusing narrowly on Hall's individual process, he emphasizes the aspects of the context that render that success atypical. Although Hall begins with his immediate context, his excavation involves the Korean War, the Civil Rights movement, the rise of Malcolm X, and the role of advertising in American culture.

Hall's relation with his family and close friends provides a Jamesian frame for the Dreiserian events of the novel, somewhat as John's conversion frames the historical "The Prayers of the Saints" in *Go Tell It on the Mountain*. *Just Above My Head*, however, leaves no ambiguity concerning the individual's ability to free himself or herself from history. Only a conscious decision to accept the pain and guilt of the past promises any real hope for love, for the higher innocence. Similarly, Baldwin reiterates that, while the desire for safety is understandable, all safety is illusion. Pain inevitably returns, and, while the support of friends and lovers may help, only a self-image based on existential acceptance rather than repudiation makes survival possible.

Arthur's death, occupying a thematic and emotional position similar to Rufus's in *Another Country*, provides the point of departure for Hall's excavation. A gifted gospel singer as a teenager, Arthur rises to stardom as the "emperor of soul." Despite his success, however, he never frees himself from doubts concerning his own identity or feels secure with the experience of love. Even though his parents offer him a firm base of love and acceptance, Arthur feels a deep sense of emotional isolation even as a child, a sense reinforced by his observations of life in Harlem and, later, in the South. Though he accepts his own homosexuality with relatively little anxiety, his society refuses the freedom necessary for the development of a truly satisfying emotional life. The Edenic innocence of Eric and Yves clearly fails to provide a sufficient response to the institutional context of *Just Above My Head.*

Arthur's childhood experiences provide clear warnings against the attempt to maintain innocence through simplistic self-definition. Julia Miller, like John in *Go Tell It on the Mountain,* undergoes a salvation experience and embarks on a career as a child evangelist. Encouraged by her parents, friends of the Montanas who rely on their daughter for economic support, she assumes a sanctimonious attitude that she uses to manipulate her elders. Arthur's parents deplore the indulgence of Julia, unambiguously rejecting the idea that her religious vocation lifts her beyond the "naughty" street side of her personality. Ultimately, and in great pain, Julia confronts this truth. After her mother's death, she discovers that her father, Joel, views her primarily as an economic and sexual object. His desire to exploit her earning potential even when she says she has lost her vocation reflects his underlying contempt for the spirit. This contempt leads to an incestuous rape that destroys Julia's remaining innocence and drives her to a life as a prostitute in New Orleans. Eventually, Julia recovers from this brutalization, but her example provides a clear warning to Arthur against confusing his vocation as a gospel singer with a transcendence of human fallibility.

The experiences of the members of Arthur's first gospel group, the Trumpets of Zion, reveal how institutions infringe even on those not actively committed to simplifying definitions. At one extreme, the social definitions establish a context that accepts and encourages murder—symbolic and real—of the other. Peanut, a member of the Trumpets and later Arthur's companion on the road, vanishes into the Alabama night following a civil rights rally, presumably murdered by whites seeking to enforce the definition of African Americans as "niggers."

Equally devastating though less direct is the operation of the context on Red, another member of the Trumpets, who turns to drugs in an attempt to relieve the pain of the Harlem streets. Even Hall finds himself an unwilling accomplice to the imposition of social definitions when he is drafted and sent to Korea. Powerless to alter the institutional structure, Hall recognizes, and tells Arthur, that the American military spreads not freedom but repudiation in the Third World. Hall's subsequent employment by an advertising agency involves him in another aspect of the same oppressive system. Viewed as an anomaly by his employers, as an atypical high-class "nigger," Hall nevertheless participates in the creation of images designed to simplify reality for economic gain, which will be used to strengthen the oppressive system. The juxtaposition of Julia's false innocence with the destructive experiences of Peanut, Red, and Hall protects Arthur against the urge to dismiss any aspect of his awareness. A large part of his power as a singer derives from his recognition of the reality of both street and temple, expressed in his ability to communicate sexual pain in gospel songs and spiritual aspiration in the blues.

Arthur, then, appears ideally prepared for the responsible exercise of existential freedom. His failure even to survive underscores the destructive power of the corrupt institutional context. The roots of Arthur's doom lie in his homosexual relationship with Crunch, the final member of the Trumpets. Highly desirable physically, Crunch feels locked into a definition of himself as a sexual object prior to his involvement with Arthur. In its early stages, Arthur and Crunch's love, like that of Yves and Eric in *Another Country*, seems an idyllic retreat, a spot of innocence in the chaos of experience. The retreat, however, proves temporary, in part because Crunch cannot free himself from the urge for self-simplification and in part because of the continuing presence of the outside world. Uneasy with his sexual identity, Crunch becomes involved with Julia when he discovers the extent of her father's abuse. Arthur recognizes that Crunch is not abandoning him by reacting to Julia's pain and accepts the relationship. Granted sufficient time for adjustment, Arthur and Crunch seem capable of confronting their experience and forging a higher innocence as the basis for a lasting love. The time does not exist. Crunch is drafted and sent to Korea. Separated from Arthur's reassurance and tormented by self-doubt, Crunch never fully accepts his sexuality. After his return to Harlem, he and Arthur gradually lose contact.

The repeated losses—of Peanut, Red, and Crunch—create a sense of isolation that Arthur never overcomes. The expectation of loss periodically overpowers his determination to communicate, the determination that makes him a great singer. Even during periods of real joy, with his French lover Guy in Paris or with Julia's brother Jimmy, who is both his pianist and his lover, Arthur suffers acute emotional pain. Attempting to survive by rededicating himself to communication, to his artistic excavation of history, Arthur drives himself past the limits of physical and psychological endurance. He dies in the basement bathroom of a London pub after a lover's quarrel, clearly only temporary, with Jimmy. By concluding Arthur's life with an image of isolation, Baldwin emphasizes the power of the limiting definitions to destroy even the most existentially courageous individual.

Arthur's death, however, marks not only a conclusion but also the beginning of Hall's quest for the higher innocence, which he, along with his wife Ruth, Julia, and Jimmy, can pass on to the younger generation. This higher innocence involves both individual and social elements, ultimately demanding the mutual support of individuals willing to pursue excavation of their own histories. This support expresses itself in the call and response dynamic, a basic element of African American oral culture that Arthur employs in his interaction with audiences while singing. As Baldwin recreates the traditional form, the interaction begins with the call of a leader who expresses his own emotional experience through the vehicle of a traditional song that provides a communal context for the emotion. If the community recognizes and shares the experience evoked by the call, it responds with another traditional phrase that provides the sense of understanding and acceptance that enables the leader to go on. Implicitly the process enables both individual and community to define themselves in opposition to dominant social forces. If the experience of isolation is shared, it is no longer the same type of isolation that brought Rufus to his death. In *Just Above My Head*, the call and response rests on a rigorous excavation requiring individual silence, courage, and honesty expressed through social presence, acceptance, and love. Expressed in the interactions between Arthur and his audiences, between Hall and his children, between Baldwin and his readers, this call and response provides a realistic image of the higher innocence possible in opposition to the murderous social definitions.

As in John's vision in *Go Tell It on the Mountain* and Rufus's self-examination in *Another Country*, the process begins in silence, which throughout Baldwin's novels offers the potential for either alienation or communication. The alienating silence coincides thematically with institutional noise—mechanical, social, political. The majority of Americans, Baldwin insists, prefer distracting and ultimately meaningless sounds to the silence that allows self-recognition. Only individuals sharing Arthur's willingness to remove himself from the noise can hope to hear their own voices and transform the silence into music. Every moment of true communication in *Just Above My Head* begins in a moment of silence that effectively rejects the clamor of imposed definitions. The courage needed for the acceptance of silence prepares the way for the honest excavation of history that must precede any meaningful social interaction. The excavation remains a burden, however, without that interaction. No purely individual effort can alter the overwhelming sense of isolation imposed by social definitions. The individual stage of the process merely heightens the need for acceptance, presence, and love. Arthur sounds the call amid the noise; he cannot provide the response. Perhaps, Baldwin indicates, no one, not even Jimmy, can provide a response capable of soothing the feeling of isolation emanating from early experiences. Nevertheless, the attempt is vital. Julia recognizes both the necessity and the limitation of presence when she tells Hall of her relationship with Jimmy: "I don't know enough to change him, or to save him. But I know enough to be there. I *must* be there."

If presence—being there—is to provide even momentary relief, it must be accompanied by the honest acceptance underlying love. Refusing to limit his acceptance, Hall answers his son Tony's questions concerning Arthur's sexuality with complete honesty. Understanding fully that his acceptance of Arthur entails an acceptance of the similar complexity in himself and in Tony, Hall surrenders his voice to Jimmy's, imaginatively participating in a love that repudiates social definition, which rises up out of the silence beyond the noise. Implicitly, Hall offers both Tony and his daughter Odessa the assurance of presence, of acceptance, of love. They need not fear rejection if they have the courage to accept their full humanity. The assurance cannot guarantee freedom, or even survival. It can, and does, intimate the form of mature innocence in the world described by the composite voice of Baldwin, Jimmy, and Hall, a world that

> doesn't have any morality. Look at the world. What the world calls morality is nothing but the dream of safety. That's how the world gets to be so f—ing moral. The only way to know that you are safe is to see somebody else in danger—otherwise you can't be sure you're safe.

Against this vicious safety, a safety that necessitates limiting definitions imposed on others, Baldwin proposes a responsibility based on risk. Only by responding to the call sounding from Arthur, from Jimmy and Hall, from Baldwin, can people find freedom. The call, ultimately, emanates not only from the individual but also from the community to which he or she calls. It provides a focus for repudiation of the crushing definitions. Hall, using Jimmy's voice, describes the call: "The man who tells the story isn't *making up* a story. He's listening to us, and can only give back, to us, what he hears: from us." The responsibility lies with everyone.

Craig Werner

Other major works

SHORT FICTION: *Going to Meet the Man*, 1965.

PLAYS: *The Amen Corner*, pr. 1954, pb. 1968; *Blues for Mister Charlie*, pr., pb. 1964; *A Deed from the King of Spain*, pr. 1974.

SCREENPLAYS: *One Day, When I Was Lost: A Scenario Based on "The Autobiography of Malcolm X,"* 1972.

POETRY: *Jimmy's Blues: Selected Poems,* 1983.

NONFICTION: *Notes of a Native Son,* 1955; *Nobody Knows My Name: More Notes of a Native Son,* 1961; *The Fire Next Time,* 1963; *Nothing Personal,* 1964 (with Richard Avedon); *A Rap on Race,* 1971 (with Margaret Mead); *No Name in the Street,* 1971; *A Dialogue,* 1975 (with Nikki Giovanni); *The Devil Finds Work,* 1976; *The Evidence of Things Not Seen,* 1985; *The Price of the Ticket,* 1985; *Conversations with James Baldwin,* 1989; *Collected Essays,* 1998.

CHILDREN'S LITERATURE: *Little Man, Little Man,* 1975.

Bibliography

Balfour, Lawrie, and Katherine Lawrence Balfour. *The Evidence of Things Not Said: James Baldwin and the Promise of American Democracy.* Ithaca, N.Y.: Cornell University Press, 2001. Explores the political dimension of Baldwin's essays, stressing the politics of race in American democracy.

Campbell, James. *Talking at the Gates: A Life of James Baldwin.* New York: Viking, 1991. Full biography of Baldwin completed shortly after his death.

Hardy, Clarence E. *James Baldwin's God: Sex, Hope, and Crisis in Black Holiness Culture.* Knoxville: University of Tennessee Press, 2003. Brief exploration of some the most troubling themes in Baldwin's writing.

Harris, Trudier, ed. *New Essays on "Go Tell It on the Mountain."* American Novel series. Cambridge, England: Cambridge University Press, 1996. These essays examine the composition, themes, publication history, public reception, and contemporary interpretations of Baldwin's first novel.

Kinnamon, Keneth, ed. *James Baldwin: A Collection of Critical Essays.* Englewood Cliffs, N.J.: Prentice-Hall, 1974. A good introduction to Baldwin's early work featuring a collection of diverse essays by such well-known figures as Irving Howe, Langston Hughes, Sherley Anne Williams, and Eldridge Cleaver. Includes a chronology of important dates, notes on the contributors, and a select bibliography.

Leeming, David. *James Baldwin: A Biography.* New York: Alfred A. Knopf, 1994. A biography of Baldwin written by one who knew him and worked with him for the last quarter century of his life. Provides extensive literary analysis of Baldwin's work and relates his work to his life.

McBride, Dwight A. *James Baldwin Now.* New York: New York University Press, 1999. Stresses the usefulness of recent interdisciplinary approaches in understanding Baldwin's appeal, political thought and work, and legacy.

Miller, D. Quentin, ed. *Re-Viewing James Baldwin: Things Not Seen.* Philadelphia: Temple University Press, 2000. Explores the way in which Baldwin's writing touched on issues that confront all people, including race, identity, sexuality, and religious ideology.

Scott, Lynn Orilla. *James Baldwin's Later Fiction: Witness to the Journey.* East Lansing: Michigan State University Press, 2002. Analyzes the decline of Baldwin's reputation after the 1960's, the ways in which critics have often undervalued his work, and the interconnected themes in his body of work.

Standley, Fred L., and Nancy V. Burt, eds. *Critical Essays on James Baldwin.* Boston: G. K. Hall, 1988. An attempt to anthologize the important criticism on Baldwin in one definitive volume. More than thirty-five articles focus on Baldwin's essays, fiction, nonfiction, and drama.

Tomlinson, Robert. "'Payin' One's Dues': Expatriation as Personal Experience and Paradigm in the Works of James Baldwin." *African American Review* 33 (Spring, 1999): 135-148. A discussion of the effect of life as an exile in Paris had on Baldwin. Argues that the experience internalized the conflicts he experienced in America. Suggests that Baldwin used his homosexuality and exile as a metaphor for the experience of the African American.

Troupe, Quincy, ed. *James Baldwin: The Legacy.* New York: Simon & Schuster, 1989. Contains eighteen essays by and about Baldwin, five of which were written for this collection, and homage and celebration from many who were profoundly influenced by him, including Pat Mikell's account of Baldwin's last days in St. Paul de Vence. With a foreword by Wole Soyinka.

Weatherby, W. J. *James Baldwin: Artist on Fire.* New York: Donald I. Fine, 1989. A lengthy personal reminiscence of Baldwin by a close friend who calls his biography a portrait. Rich in intimate detail and based on conversations with more than one hundred people who knew Baldwin. Reveals the man behind the words.

Toni Cade Bambara

Born: New York, New York; March 25, 1939
Died: Philadelphia, Pennsylvania; December 9, 1995

Principal long fiction • *The Salt Eaters,* 1980; *Those Bones Are Not My Child,* 1999.

Other literary forms • Toni Cade Bambara is best known for her short stories, which appear frequently in anthologies. She has also received recognition as a novelist, essayist, journalist, editor, and screenwriter, as well as a social activist and community leader. Her stories depict the daily lives of ordinary people who live in the black neighborhoods of Brooklyn, Harlem, and sections of New York City and the rural South. Although she wrote in other genres, her short stories established her reputation. In *Gorilla, My Love* (1972), a collection of fifteen stories, Bambara focuses on the love of friends and neighborhood as she portrays the positive side of black family life and stresses the strengths of the African American community. These fast-paced stories, characterized by her use of the black dialect of the street, are full of humorous exchanges and verbal banter. *The Sea Birds Are Still Alive* (1977) is a collection of short stories that reflect Bambara's concern with people from other cultures; the title story focuses on the plight of Vietnamese refugees at the end of the Vietnam War. *Deep Sightings and Rescue Missions,* a collection of Bambara's writings, most of which never appeared before in print, was published posthumously in 1996.

Achievements • Bambara received the Peter Pauper Press Award in Journalism from the *Long Island Star* in 1958, the John Golden Award for Fiction from Queens College in 1959, and the Theater of Black Experience Award in 1969. She was also the recipient of the George Washington Carver Distinguished African American Lecturer Award from Simpson College, Ebony's Achievement in the Arts Award, and the American Book Award, for *The Salt Eaters,* in 1981. *The Bombing of Osage Avenue* won the Best Documentary of 1986 Award from the Pennsylvania Association of Broadcasters and the Documentary Award from the National Black Programming Consortium in 1986.

As an editor of anthologies of the writings of African Americans, Bambara introduced thousands of college students to the works of these writers. She was a founder of the Southern Collective of African American Writers and played a major role in the 1984 Conference on Black Literature and the Arts at Emory University.

During the last fourteen years of her life, Bambara devoted much of her energies to the film industry, writing screenplays. She also completed what some critics regard as her most important work, *Those Bones Are Not My Child,* a fictional reconsideration of the Atlanta child murder case.

Biography • Miltona Mirkin Cade was born in New York on March 25, 1939, to Helen Brent Henderson Cade. She grew up in Harlem, Bedford-Stuyvesant, and Queens, where she lived with her mother and brother, Walter. She credited her mother with "cultivating her creative spirit and instilling in her a sense of independence and self-sufficiency." In 1970, after finding the name Bambara written in a sketchbook in her grandmother's trunk, she legally changed her surname to Bambara. She received a bachelor's degree in theater arts and English literature from Queens College in 1959, and that same year her first short story, "Sweet Town," was published in *Vendome* magazine. After studying in Italy and Paris, she earned a master's degree in American literature at City College of New York and completed additional studies in linguistics at New York University and the New School for Social Research. She was a social worker for the Harlem Welfare Center and director of recreation in the psychiatric division of Metro Hospital in New York City. She taught in the Search for Education, Elevation, Knowledge (SEEK) program at City College.

In 1970, under the name of Toni Cade, she published *The Black Woman: An Anthology*, a collection of essays, short fiction, poetry, and letters exploring the experiences of black women, with emphasis on their involvement with the Civil Rights movement and the women's movement. In 1971 she edited *Tales and Stories for Black Folks*, a collection of writings from students in her composition class, along with the work of well-known authors.

As an assistant professor at Livingston College at Rutgers University from 1969 to 1974, Bambara was active in black student organizations and arts groups. She was a visiting professor in Afro-American Studies at Emory University and an instructor in the School of Social Work at Atlanta University. In 1973 on a visit to Cuba, Bambara met with the Federation of Cuban Women, and in 1975 she traveled to Vietnam. These experiences served to broaden Bambara's view of the importance of community involvement and political action and provided subject matter for stories in *The Sea Birds Are Still Alive.*

Bambara and her daughter, Karma, lived in Atlanta from 1974 to 1986, during which time Bambara continued to be active in community political and artistic organizations, hosting potluck dinners in her home and organizing writers and artists in the community. In 1986 Bambara moved to Philadelphia, where she continued her active participation in the community and worked on *The Bombing of Osage Avenue*, a 1986 documentary on the bombing of a house where a group of black nationalists lived. She also worked on a film about African American writer Zora Neale Hurston. Bambara was known as a writer, civil rights activist, teacher, and supporter of the arts. Her work represents her dedication to the African American community and her desire to portray the ordinary lives of the people who live in those communities. As a lecturer and teacher she worked to raise the consciousness of other African Americans and to encourage a sense of pride in their heritage. Bambara died in a suburb of Philadelphia on December 9, 1995, of cancer.

Analysis • Toni Cade Bambara's work reflects her experiences with political action committees and her belief in the necessity for social responsibility. The political activism of the 1960's and 1970's provides the subject matter for her work, as she explores the consequences of the Civil Rights movement and the divisions in the African American community. In describing this community, Bambara portrays the individual characters with affection and humor.

The Salt Eaters • Set during the 1970's, Bambara's novel *The Salt Eaters* focuses on the effects of the Civil Rights movement on the inhabitants of the small town of Claybourne, Georgia. The plot centers on the attempted suicide of its main character, Velma Henry, a community activist who has tried to kill herself by slitting her wrists and sticking her head in an oven. The other major character is Minnie Ransom, a conjure woman who uses her healing powers to restore Velma to health.

Joyce Middler

Minor characters include Fred Holt, the bus driver; Obie, Velma's husband; and Dr. Julius Meadows. These members of the African American community are suffering from the fragmentation and alienation that have occurred in the wake of the Civil Rights movement. Velma was so filled with rage that she sought death as an answer to her pain. The novel traces Velma's journey from despair to mental and spiritual health. Bambara's own experiences with political activism provide her with the background for the events of the novel.

Throughout the novel, Bambara stresses the importance of choice. In the opening line of the novel, Minnie Ransom asks Velma, "Are you sure, sweetheart, that you want to be well?" Freedom of choice requires acceptance of responsibility. If Velma is to heal herself, she must make a conscious choice of health over despair. Characters in the novel are seen in relationship to the larger community. Godmother Sophie M'Dear reminds Velma that her life is not solely her own, but that she has a connection and obligation to her family and community. Other characters are reminded of their responsibility to others. When Buster gets Nadeen pregnant, her uncle Thurston arrives with a gun, ordering Buster to attend parenting classes. Doc Serge tells Buster that abortion is not a private choice but a choice that involves the whole community. The characters echo Bambara's belief that membership in a community entails responsibilities to that community.

For most of the novel Velma sits on a stool in a hospital, suffering from depression, overwhelming fatigue, and a mental collapse. She remains immobile and seemingly frozen as scenes from the past and present play in her mind in no particular order. Other characters seem to whirl past Velma and blend into one another, reflecting the problems that have brought Velma to this hospital room. Bambara shows that these problems are a result of alienation from the community. Because of his light skin, education, and profession, Dr. Julius Meadows has lost touch with his roots. Through a chance encounter with two young black men, Julius begins his journey back to the black community. Reflecting on the encounter, Julius feels that "whatever happened, he wasn't stumbling aimlessly around the streets anymore, at loose ends, alone." Meadows's journey back into the black community parallels Velma's journey to health. Alienation from the community had brought Velma to the brink of destruction, and realignment with the community heals her. Velma's journey is similar to the spiritual journey of Tayo, the Native American protagonist in Leslie Marmon Silko's *Ceremony* (1977). The horrors Tayo experienced as a prisoner of the Japanese during World War II and the sense of alienation he experiences when he returns to his Laguna reservation have nearly destroyed his will to survive. Through immersion in the Native American culture, traditions, beliefs, and stories, Tayo finds his way back to health. As Tayo and Velma embrace their cultural heritages, they begin to heal.

The predominant image in the novel is the vision of the mud mothers painting the walls of their cave. This recurring vision haunts Velma until she sees the cave as a symbol of cultural history and identity. Other characters reflect on the responsibility of the older generation to educate and nurture the children of the community. If the children are forgetting the values of the community, it is because the elders have failed in their responsibility to instill community values in the young.

Bambara believes that to keep traditions alive, every generation has to be nurtured and educated, has to be taught the old stories. At times the novel seems to be a catalog of African American cultural history, which includes African tribal customs and rituals, slave ships, and names of famous leaders. In the early part of the novel, Ruby, one of the most politically active characters, laments the loss of leaders and causes: "Malcolm gone, King gone, Fanni Lou gone, Angela quiet, the movement splintered, enclaves unconnected." Near the end of the novel, Velma realizes how much she has learned from the leaders and influences that are part of her background, "Douglass, Tubman, the slave narratives, the songs, the fables, Delaney, Ida Wells, Blyden, DuBois, Garvey, the singers, her parents, Malcolm, Coltrane."

Bambara enriches the novel with background from folk legends and literary works. At times she merely mentions a name, such as Shine, the famous African American trickster, or the legendary Stagolee, who killed a man for his hat. Fred's friend Porter, borrowing a term from Ralph Ellison's novel *Invisible Man* (1952), explains his feelings about being black: "They call the Black man the Invisible Man. . . . Our natures are unknowable, unseeable to them." The following lines show how Bambara packs cultural, historical, and political history into one sentence: "Several hotheads, angry they had been asleep in the Sixties or too young to participate, had been galvanized by the arrival in their midst of the legless vet who used to careen around Claybourne fast and loose on a hot garage dolly."

In contrast to the positive images, Bambara shows the negative side of society in describing the "boymen" who hang around women in grocery stores begging for money in a ritual she calls "market theater." In another scene, Ruby complains about the way women have had to carry the burden of improving society, "taking on . . . drugs, prisons, alcohol, the schools, rape, battered women, abused children," while the men make no contribution to the organization.

One of the most distinctive aspects of Bambara's style is her use of black dialect with its colorful vocabulary, playful banter, and unique phrasing and speech patterns. At times the rhythm and rhyme of phrases give a musical quality to the prose: "Cause the stars said and the energy belts led and the cards read and the cowries spread." At other times Bambara describes the atmosphere in musical terms: "the raga reggae bumpidity bing zing was pouring out all over Fred Holt" and "the music drifted out over the trees . . . maqaam now blending with the bebop of Minnie Ransom's tapes."

The major theme of the novel is that identification with one's cultural history can be liberating and empowering. In *The Salt Eaters*, loss of cultural identity has brought despair. Bambara provides flashbacks to the civil rights struggles of the 1960's and the legacy of slavery. As they struggle for political power, African Americans must remember the past and maintain their best traditions. As Velma begins to heal she thinks that she knows "how to build resistance, make the journey to the center of the circle . . . stay centered in the best of her people's traditions."

Those Bones Are Not My Child • Considered by some critics to be Bambara's most important work, this posthumously published novel offers a chilling reimagination of the child murder case that rocked Atlanta, Georgia, in 1979 and 1980. During those two years, more than forty African American children living in the Atlanta area were brutally abused and murdered. As most serial killers are typically white men, the murders were believed to be racially motivated hate crimes until a black man, Wayne Williams, was arrested and was convicted of the crimes in 1981. In *Those Bones Are Not My Child,* Bambara revisits Atlanta during the summer of 1980 and offers an alternative vision of events.

Bambara's African American protagonist is Marzala Rawls Spencer, the single mother of three children who is struggling to get by when her twelve-year-old son, Sundiata, disappears. Terrified that Sundiata is the latest victim of the serial killer, Marzala joins with her estranged husband, Spence, to learn what has become of her son. Their first discovery is that Atlanta's police and political leaders have a shocking lack of interest in finding their missing son. The novel then conveys Marzala and Spence on a nightmarish journey through the complex web of Atlanta politics and racial divisions that get in the way of the search for the truth.

During the dozen years leading up to her death in 1995, Bambara worked on *Those Bones Are Not My Child* but was not able to polish it before she died. Nevertheless, the novel is notable for the strength of its well-drawn characters, its dissection of the harsh realities of African American family life, and the powerful emotions that it evokes.

Judith Barton Williamson
Updated by the Editors

Other major works

SHORT FICTION: *Gorilla, My Love,* 1972; *The Sea Birds Are Still Alive: Collected Stories,* 1977; *Raymond's Run: Stories for Young Adults,* 1989.

SCREENPLAYS: *The Bombing of Osage Avenue,* 1986 (documentary); *W. E. B. Du Bois—A Biography in Four Voices,* 1995 (with Amiri Baraka, Wesley Brown, and Thulani Davis).

EDITED TEXTS: *The Black Woman: An Anthology,* 1970; *Tales and Stories for Black Folks,* 1971; *Southern Exposure,* 1976 (periodical; Bambara edited volume 3).

MISCELLANEOUS: "What It Is I Think I'm Doing Anyhow," *The Writer on Her Work,* 1981 (Janet Sternburg, editor); *Deep Sightings and Rescue Missions: Fiction, Essays, and Conversations,* 1996.

Bibliography

Alwes, Derek. "The Burden of Liberty: Choice in Toni Morrison's *Jazz* and Toni Cade Bambara's *The Salt Eaters.*" *African American Review* 30, no. 3 (Fall, 1996): 353-365. In comparing the works of Morrison and Bambara, Alwes argues that while Morrison wants readers to participate in a choice, Bambara wants them to choose to participate. Bambara's message is that happiness is possible if people refuse to forget the past and continue to participate in the struggle.

Bone, Martyn. "Capitalist Abstraction and the Body Politics of Place in Toni Cade Bambara's *Those Bones Are Not My Child.*" *Journal of American Studies* 37, no. 2 (August, 2003): 229-246. Analysis of the racial and political dynamics depicted in Bambara's last novel.

Butler-Evans, Elliott. *Race, Gender, and Desire: Narrative Strategies in the Fiction of Toni Cade Bambara, Toni Morrison, Alice Walker.* Philadelphia: Temple University Press, 1989. The first book-length study to treat Bambara's fiction to any extent, this study uses narratology and feminism to explore Bambara's works.

Collins, Janelle. "Generating Power: Fission, Fusion, and Post-modern Politics in Bambara's *The Salt Eaters.*" *MELUS* 21, no. 2 (Summer, 1996): 35-47. Collins argues that Bambara's nationalist and feminist positions inform the text of the novel as she advocates political and social change.

Evans, Mari, ed. *Black Women Writers (1950-1980): A Critical Evaluation.* Garden City, N.Y.: Anchor Press/Doubleday, 1984. In the essay "Salvation Is the Issue," Bambara says that the elements of her own work that she deems most important are laughter, use of language, sense of community, and celebration.

Vertreace, Martha M. *Toni Cade Bambara.* New York: Macmillan Library Reference, 1998. The first full-length work devoted to the entirety of Bambara's career. A part of the successful Twayne series of criticism, this will be quite helpful for students interested in Bambara's career.

Willis, Susan. "Problematizing the Individual: Toni Cade Bambara's Stories for the Revolution." In *Specifying: Black Women Writing the American Experience.* Madison: University of Wisconsin Press, 1987. Though largely centered on an analysis of *The Salt Eaters,* this essay also has clear and informative analysis of Bambara's most important short fiction.

John Barth

Born: Cambridge, Maryland; May 27, 1930

Principal long fiction • *The Floating Opera,* 1956; *The End of the Road,* 1958; *The Sot-Weed Factor,* 1960; *Giles Goat-Boy: Or, The Rev. New Syllabus,* 1966; *Chimera,* 1972 (three novellas); *Letters,* 1979; *Sabbatical: A Romance,* 1982; *The Tidewater Tales: A Novel,* 1987; *The Last Voyage of Somebody the Sailor,* 1991; *Once upon a Time: A Floating Opera,* 1994; *Coming Soon!!!,* 2001.

Other literary forms • Although John Barth's novels have ensured his eminence among contemporary American writers, his short fictions have been no less influential or controversial. In addition to his novels, he published a collection of shorter works, *Lost in the Funhouse* (1968), the technical involutions of which plumb the nature of narrative itself and disrupt conventional relationships between teller and tale. Barth also wrote two essays of particular significance. In "The Literature of Exhaustion," he discusses those writers whose suspicion that certain forms of literature have become obsolete is incorporated both thematically and technically in the fictions they produce. He highlights the successes of Jorge Luis Borges, Vladimir Nabokov, and Samuel Beckett in the face of apparent artistic impasse; they acknowledge and push beyond the boundaries staked out by their literary predecessors and employ a potentially stifling sense of "ultimacy" in the creation of new work, so that their forms become metaphors for their aesthetic concerns. "The Literature of Replenishment" seeks to correct any misreading of the former essay as a complaint that contemporary writers have little left to accomplish save the parody of conventions that they arrived upon too late to benefit from themselves.

Barth's method is to define and legitimize postmodernism by placing its most interesting practitioners—he singles out Italo Calvino and Gabriel García Márquez for praise—in a direct line of succession that may be traced through the great modernists of the first half of the twentieth century back to eighteenth century novelist Laurence Sterne and sixteenth century writer Miguel de Cervantes. "The Literature of Replenishment" makes clear that Barth is not averse to admitting realistic elements into his fictional worlds, provided they do not constrain the imagination. Both of these essays are collected in *The Friday Book: Essays, and Other Nonfiction* (1984). *The Friday Book* and its companion volume, *Further Fridays* (1995), also contain many essays dealing with Barth's affection for and interest in his native state of Maryland.

Achievements • Perhaps Barth's method is a mark of a growing receptivity among readers and critics to formally venturesome fiction; perhaps it is merely a result of the writer's almost inevitable passage from unexpected new voice to mature artist. Whatever the case, Barth infiltrated the literary establishment with relative ease, with no perceptible compromise. He became America's foremost existential novelist, but his approach to the rather somber question of the arbitrariness of moral values and the absence of intrinsic meaning has always been richly overlaid with humor that is at times intricate and esoteric and often expansive and full of delight in its own verbal virtuosity. He has shown a career-long obsession with mythology, with how classical tales may be reconstituted in and provide resonance for contemporary fiction, and with how the novel may continue to respond to the age-old and seemingly insatiable need for the coherent pleasures of narrative.

Barth still has his detractors, whose accusations typically focus on his tendency to overwork his jokes (a condemnation that often attends *Giles Goat-Boy*) or to surrender to vulgar effects (as in his revisionist history of John Smith's encounter with Pocahontas in *The Sot-Weed Factor*). Nevertheless, few would dispute Barth's stature as the most widely appreciated postmodernist, a designation that he embraces despite its connotation of self-absorption and unreadability. He won the National Book Award in 1973 for *Chimera*. His other awards include the F. Scott Fitzgerald Award (1997), the PEN/Malamud Award (1998), and the Lannan Literary Awards lifetime achievement award (1998).

Biography • John Barth was born John Simmons Barth on May 27, 1930, in Cambridge, Maryland, the contemporary and historical environs of which have provided the setting for much of his writing. He attended Cambridge High School, after which he accommodated his passion for jazz and the drums with a brief stay at the Juilliard School of Music. His unspectacular showing there led him to enroll at Johns Hopkins University, a move made possible when he won a scholarship he forgot he had applied for. He achieved the highest grade point average in the College of Arts and Sciences upon receiving a bachelor's degree in 1951.

To pay off tuition debts and support his wife (Harriet Anne Strickland, whom he had married in 1950), Barth took a job in the Classics Library, where he first became absorbed in the Asian tale-cycles that would later inform the style and content of his own fiction. During this period came his first publications in student literary magazines, including one story, "Lilith and the Lion," whose appearance in *The Hopkins Review* when Barth was twenty may rightly be considered his first professional work. His master's project was *The Shirt of Nessus*, a novel based on a love triangle including a father and son and populated by rapists, murderers, bootleggers, and lunatics; Barth confesses it a miscarriage, and he says it now rests in the Dorchester marshes on Chesapeake Bay.

After receiving his master's degree in the spring of 1952, Barth began studying for a doctorate in the aesthetics of literature while tutoring and teaching freshman composition courses, until the cost of supporting both his family (his third child was born in January, 1954) and his education compelled him to teach full-time. He took a position at Pennsylvania State University in 1953; his experience with freshman composition there would eventually find its way into *The End of the Road*. (He did not earn his doctorate until 1969, from the University of Maryland.) While at Penn State, Barth began a series of one hundred stories, in the bawdy manner of Giovanni Boccaccio's *The Decameron* (1348-1353), detailing the history of Dorchester County. He abandoned the project within a year, but fifty of the proposed hundred stories were completed; a handful were published separately and others later were incorporated into *The Sot-Weed Factor.*

Barth advanced from instructor to associate professor at Penn State, where he taught until 1965, and it was during this twelve-year period that he established his reputation. In the fall of 1954, he found a photograph of an old showboat; borrowing something of the conversational style of Sterne's *Tristram Shandy* (1759-1767) and some plot devices from *Don Casmurro* (1900), by the Brazilian novelist Joaquim Maria Machado de Assis, he began *The Floating Opera* in January, 1955. It was completed in three months, but several publishers rejected it, and Appleton-Century-Crofts demanded many revisions before publishing it in 1956. By the fall of 1955, however, Barth was already at work on *The End of the Road*. Like *The Floating Opera*, with which it is often associated as a philosophical companion-piece, it was finished in three months. It was ultimately published by Doubleday in 1958.

The Floating Opera was nominated for a National Book Award, which it failed to win; neither the book nor its successor sold well. Barth was denied a Guggenheim grant in 1958, but his school's research fund did manage $250 to send him to Maryland to gather information for his next project. He had expected *The Sot-Weed Factor* to be another three-month venture, but that mammoth refurbishing of the eighteenth century picaresque turned out to be nearly three years in the writing. That novel, too, met with relative public indifference, but it later became his first major critical success when it was released in paperback in 1964.

Giles Goat-Boy was begun in 1960, and it would be six years from inception to publication. In 1965, Barth left Penn State for a full professorship at the State University of New York in Buffalo. *Giles Goat-Boy* introduced Barth to the best-seller lists in 1966, but he was already at work on *Lost in the Funhouse*, a brain-teasing, technically probing collection of multimedia pieces that came out in 1968, for which Barth received his second unsuccessful nomination for a National Book Award.

Barth's next book did earn that elusive honor, however; *Chimera*, Barth's most direct confrontation of ancient narrative in the form of three metafictions, won the National Book Award in 1973. In that same year, Barth changed locale once more, accepting a post at his alma mater, Johns Hopkins. It was not until 1979 that his next book, *Letters*, was published. Instead of creating a new form, Barth decided, as he had done in *The Sot-Weed Factor*, to resuscitate a traditional one: in this case, the epistolary novel. *Letters* plumbs the author's personal literary history as well, for its principal correspondents are characters from Barth's earlier novels.

Whether the familiar hybrid of writer-teacher nourishes or diminishes creativity will not be decided on the basis of one man's example, but Barth has found the academic atmosphere to be not only hospitable to his talents but also generous as an occasion and setting for his fiction: Two of his novels are set specifically in college communities, and the theme of education—be it in a school, under the auspices of a spiritual adviser, or in the shifting, multifarious outside world of affairs—has been repeatedly highlighted in Barth's work. In 1970, Barth married Shelley Rosenberg, a former student of his at Penn State whom he reencountered after some years. Shelley Barth, a high school literature teacher, is often alluded to in the various heroines in Barth's later works, many of which feature an enriching second marriage that helps frame the novel's story. From the 1970's onward, Barth taught writing at Johns Hopkins University. In August, 1979, he bought a weekend and summer residence on Langford Creek in Dorchester County, Maryland, where he did most of his writing. As with his fictional protagonists, traveling, especially sailing, became one of his favorite avocations. In 1992, he formally retired from teaching at Johns Hopkins. Barth was, however, named professor emeritus there and would occasionally teach writing seminars. He continued to write and published the novel *Coming Soon!!!* in 2001 and *The Book of Ten Nights and a Night: Eleven Stories* in 2004, and the collection *Where Three Roads Meet* in 2005.

Analysis • The literary historian and the literary technician meet in the novels and attitudes of John Barth. His eagerness to affirm the artificiality of the art he creates enables him to strip-mine the whole range of narrative that precedes his career for usable personalities and devices; similarly, by beginning with the premise of literature as a self-evident sham, he greatly enlarges the field of possibility within his own fictions, so that outrageous plot contrivances, protean characters (or characters who are essentially banners emblazoned with ruling philosophies), and verbal acrobatics all become acceptable. Barth's general solution for handling the fracture between art and reality is not to heal it, but rather to heighten his readers' awareness of it. This is why, despite his penchant for intellectual confrontation and long interludes of debate in his novels, Barth most often looks to humor—jokes and pranks, parody, and stylistic trickery—to make the philosophy palatable.

Barth meticulously reconstructs the fabric and feel of allegory (*Giles Goat-Boy*) or of the *Künstlerroman* (*The Sot-Weed Factor*), then minimizes the appropriateness of such patterns in the contemporary world by vigorously mocking them. He takes on formidable intellectual questions—the impossibility of knowing external reality, the unavailability of intrinsic values, the fragility of the self in an incurably relativistic universe—but chooses to do so in, to borrow one of his own most durable metaphors, a funhouse atmosphere. In fact, in Barth's fiction, abstract discussion is consistently revealed as a dubious alternative to passionate participation in life. Given the ambiguous state of the self, exposure to the world could be fatal if not for the strategy of fashioning and choosing from among a variety of masks that afford the beleaguered self a sense of definition and a schedule of valid responses to whatever situations the world presents. The willful choosing of masks is Barth's main theme; it suggests that the alternative to despair in the face of universal chaos and indifference is the responsibility to exercise one's freedom, much as an artist exercises his creative faculties in writing and editing tales that satisfy him. In this sense, Barth's heroes are artists of the self, who view the elasticity of character as a challenge to their mythmaking abilities, and who treat their private lives as fictions that are amenable to infinite revision.

Teturo Maruyama

The Floating Opera • "Good heavens," complains Todd Andrews in *The Floating Opera*, "how does one write a novel! I mean, how can anybody stick to the story, if he's at all sensitive to the significance of things?" The doubts and false starts that frustrate the progress of this protagonist's Inquiry—a hodgepodge of papers contained in peach baskets in his hotel room, for which, life being on so tenuous a lease from eternity, he pays rent on a daily basis—reflect those that would potentially stymie Barth himself, were he not to make them part of his subject. Like his narrator/alter ego in *The Floating Opera*, Barth contends with the problem of making art out of nihilism. In Andrews's hands, that problem takes the shape of a book-long (and, he confesses, lifelong) obsession with how, and whether, to live. There is little of traditional suspense to propel the narrative; after all, this is an examination of a decision *not* to commit suicide, so that Andrews's private undertaking of Hamlet's well-known question has led him to accept life, at least provisionally and despite its absence of intrinsic values.

The quality of life is described by the title of the novel and symbolized by the barge show—part vaudeville, part minstrel show—which flashes in and out of view as it moves along the river. No other image in literature so effectively captures the idea of Heraclitean flux: The "performance" is never the same for any two spectators, nor can one resume watching it at the same place in the show as when it last passed by. Furthermore, the nature of this floating phenomenon is operatic: sentimental, bizarre, wildly melodramatic, and often simply laughable. The players are amateurish, and they are best appreciated by an unrefined audience who are not bothered by the gaps in their understanding or by the unevenness of the performance. Andrews entertains the notion of building a showboat that has a perpetual play going on, and the novel itself is the alternative result; like the floating extravaganza, it is "chock-full of curiosities" and considers every possible taste: games, violence, flights of fancy and philosophy, legal and sexual intrigue, war and death, artwork and excrement. The implication here, as emphasized by T. Wallace Whittaker's rendition of William Shakespeare (one of the more delicate turns on the bill, to please the ladies), is that not only are all people players on a stage, but also they are apparently purposeless, scriptless players at that.

There is something of the floating opera in the stylistic range of the novel as well. Todd Andrews is a monologist in the comic, voluble tradition of Tristram Shandy. In fact, both men write autobiographical inquiries into the strangeness of the human condition that digress and associate so frequently that they are destined to become life works; both are artists racing to create against death, although Andrews is as likely to be felled by rational suicide as by his heart murmur; and both combine intellectual pursuits with technical "entertainments" (which include, in Barth's novel, repeated paragraphs, a double column of narrative "options," and a reproduction of the handbill announcing the schedule of events in "Adam's Original and Unparalleled Ocean-Going Floating Opera").

Motivation sets these two narrators apart, however, for if Tristram is compelled by life's delights, Andrews is alienated by its absurdity. Andrews is engaged in a search for purpose; his life hangs in the balance. His Inquiry began as an attempt to come to terms with his father's suicide in 1930, an event too complex to chalk up to an escape from debts incurred after the stock-market crash. It then absorbed a letter to his father that, with the obsessive diligence of Franz Kafka in a similar enterprise, Andrews had begun in 1920 and continued to redraft even after his father's death. The Inquiry continued to blossom until, by the time the novel opens in 1954, it is autobiography, journal, and religious/philosophical treatise all in one, and it floats by at the moment of focus on the decision (made on one of two days in June, 1937), after a failed effort, not to commit suicide. (Todd Andrews admonishes readers not to confuse his name with its meaning of "death" in German; his name, which misspells the German word, is more aptly read as "almost death.")

Given the kinds of experience he relates, his final acceptance of life is rather surprising. His father's suicide is but one of a series of incidents that suggest that life may not be worth the salvaging effort. Sexuality, for example, is represented by his wonder at the ridiculousness of the act when, at the age of seventeen, he spies himself in a mirror in the midst of intercourse, and later, when his five-year affair with Jane Mack is revealed to have been directed by her husband, Harrison. Andrews's most profound confrontation with his own self, during World War I, reveals him to be "a shocked, drooling animal in a mudhole." When an enemy soldier stumbles upon him, they share their terror, then silent communion and friendship . . . and then Andrews stabs him to death. All actions are equally pointless; all commitments are arbitrary; all attempts to solve human incomprehension are laughable.

From rake to saint to cynic, Andrews endures without much joy as an expert lawyer, although he does admit to a certain detached interest in the law's arbitrary intricacies, epitomized in the search for the legitimate will among the seventeen left to posterity by Harrison Mack, Sr., which, when found, decides the fate of more than one hundred pickle jars brimming with his excrement. Andrews is actually comfortable enough living in the Dorset Hotel among a collection of society's aged castoffs, until a casual reference by his mistress to his clubbed hands initiates a kind of Sartrean nausea at the utter physical fact of himself; his growing detestation of that mortal coil, coupled with an absolute conviction that all value is artificially imposed, leads him to the brink of suicide, in the form of a scheme to blow up the opera boat (which, in the restored 1967 edition of the novel, would include hundreds of spectators, with the Macks and Jeannine, their—or possibly Andrews's—daughter among them).

What stays him is the revelation that, if all values are arbitrary, suicide is not less arbitrary; furthermore, even arbitrary values may offer a way to live. This uneasy treaty with a relativistic universe is Andrews's provisional conclusion to the Inquiry, for the suicide does not come off. Some accident—a psychological shudder, an instinct beyond the intellect's dominion, or a spasm of sentimental concern for the little girl who had suffered a sudden convulsion—disrupts the plan, so the novel's philosophical journey concludes in the anticlimax promised by the narrator at the outset. If Barth frustrates some readers by forsaking the questions he has so fastidiously prepared them for, they must understand that the willingness to handle the sublime and the ridiculous alike with a shrug of good humor is part of the point: In the end, even nihilism is shown to be yet one more posture, one more mask.

The End of the Road • In his next novel, *The End of the Road*, Barth's speculations on the nature and necessity of masks becomes more formulaic, although with somewhat bleaker results for his hero. Jake Horner—the name is borrowed from William Wycherley's sly seducer in *The Country Wife* (1673)—suffers from "cosmopsis," a disease of hyperconsciousness: the awareness that one choice is no more inherently valid or attractive than another. When a nameless black doctor materializes near a bench at Pennsylvania Station, he discovers Jake as hopelessly rooted to the spot as the statuette Jake keeps of the tortured Laocoön. The doctor recognizes his paralysis and initiates a program of therapy that forces his patient into action. He explains that no matter how arbitrary the system of "choosing" that he advocates may appear, "Choosing is existence: to the extent that you don't choose, you don't exist." All of Jake's subsequent activities—the plot of the novel—represent his execution of the doctor's precepts.

At the outset, Jake's quest is meticulously prescribed *for* him. He is advised to begin with simple, disciplined choices between well-defined alternatives; should he happen to get "stuck" again beyond his mentor's reach, he is to choose artificially according to Sinistrality, Antecedence, and Alphabetical Priority. He is made to worship the hard facts of an almanac and to travel in straight lines to scheduled locations; because it is a monument to fixity, he is to devote himself to teaching of prescriptive grammar at Wicomico State Teachers College. In short, Jake is to undergo Mythotherapy: the regular assignment of roles to the befuddled ego in order to facilitate participation in the world.

After Jake's quest is complicated by relationships that overextend the narrative "masks" behind which he operates, that neatly contrived therapy proves insufficient. Joe and Rennie Morgan, characters analogous to Harrison and Jane Mack in *The Floating Opera*, confuse his roles: Joe is a strident god whose rational self-control and mechanical theorizing make him his wife's mentor and Jake's intimidator; Rennie's sexuality and mixture of admiration and helplessness toward her husband are provocative, but she involves Jake in a script he cannot handle. His "road" grows tortuous and overwhelming, as his strictly plotted career is diverted into adulterous liaisons and philosophical tournaments, deceit and death. The profundity of his relapse into irresponsibility is much greater this time, however, for he is not the only one victimized by it. By failing to control his roles at critical times, he becomes the instrument of Rennie's death: Rennie will not lie to ensure a safe operation, and Jake's frantic role-playing in order to secure an abortion ends in a grisly death at the hands of Jake's doctor. The reality of Rennie's bleeding on the table is one that, unlike his callous affair with the lonely Peggy Rankin, Jake cannot manipulate or evade; it is the end of the road for him as a free agent in the world. Because he apparently requires further training in order to function successfully, he escapes with the doctor to a new site of the Remobilization Farm.

Jake's intellectual adversary fares little better under the pressure of real events. Joe Morgan personifies Todd Andrews's supposition that an arbitrary value could be transformed into the "subjective equivalent of an absolute" that might then provide the coherent way of life so crucial to a man who deifies the intellect. Both Jake and Joe begin from the premise of relativism, which explains their mutual attraction, but while Jake tends to succumb to "weatherlessness" (a numbness incurred by the randomness of events and the loss of an essential I), Joe is smug about the rational system he and his wife abide by. That self-assurance sanctions Rennie's being exposed to Jake's influence and provokes Jake to undermine him. When Joe is revealed as something less than pure mind and standards (Jake and Rennie spy him through a window masturbating, grunting, picking his nose), the god loses his authenticity, and the affair merely emphasizes Joe's fall from eminence. Rennie does bring her guilt to Joe, but he returns her to Jake to reenact the betrayal until she can account for it rationally. In the same way, Joe refuses to face up to the fact of Rennie's death, which was indirectly engineered by his experimental obsession, and proves himself to be far more comfortable in handling abstract ideas than in facing up to the welter of uncertainties beyond his field of expertise.

The road's end serves as a final blessing to Jake; the conclusion of the novel is not the completion of a quest but a relief from it. Because the turbulence of the world of affairs has proved unmanageable, he capitulates and numbly offers his "weatherless" self up to the auspices of the doctor, the price for performing Rennie's abortion. Jake retreats into submission after a disastrous initiation into the world.

The Sot-Weed Factor • In his next two novels, Barth grants his philosophical preoccupations the panoramic expansiveness and formal openness of a Henry Fielding or François Rabelais, as if seeking epic dimension for what might well be considered in his first novels to be merely the idiosyncrasies of constipated personalities. *The Sot-Weed Factor* features a riotously inventive plot and a cast of characters including poets and prostitutes, lords and brigands, landowners and Indians, merchants and thieves, but the triumph of the novel is in its authentic language and texture: For some eight hundred pages, Barth's novel impersonates one of those sprawling eighteenth century picaresque English novels, complete with protracted authorial intrusions, outrageous coincidences, dizzying turns of plot, and a relish for lewd humor.

Barth borrows a satirical poem on colonial America by Ebenezer Cooke (1708) for the foundation of his novel and resuscitates Cooke himself to be his hero. Barth's Eben Cooke is a timid, awkward fellow, who, unlike Andrews and Horner, maintains a steadfast virginity—sexual, social, and political—in a world teeming with sin and subterfuge. His steadfast adherence to a chosen mask—that of poet laureate of Maryland—with its requisite responsibilities keeps him on course. Until he happens upon that identity, Eben is overwhelmed by "the beauty of the possible," so much so that he cannot choose among careers; a broad education shared with his twin sister, Anna, at the hands of the ubiquitous Henry Burlingame, serves to increase his wonder rather than to specify a direction, so that readers discover him as a young man who haunts the London taverns, somewhat ill at ease among more raucous peers. He cannot muster an identity reliable enough to survive the pressure of alternatives.

What could have become a lifelong "cosmopsic" stagnation is interrupted by an encounter with a whore, Joan Toast; instead of having sex, Eben chooses to defend his innocence, for he sees in it a symbolic manifestation of his ultimate role. He exalts the deliciously earthy Joan into a bodiless goddess of verse; it is this indifference to reality that will enable him to survive, if not to transcend, the subversive and often grotesque facts of the New World, and the astounding contrasts between the poet's rhapsodizing and the world's stubborn brutishness provide much of the novel's ironic humor.

That confrontation with the New World is set into motion by Eben's father, who, when advised of his son's failure to lead a useful life in London, commands him to set off for his tobacco (sot-weed) estate in Maryland. Armed with a sense of his true calling, Eben wins from Lord Baltimore an agreement to write the "Marylandiad," a verse epic glorifying the province he knows nothing about, and is granted the laureateship in writing. The balance of *The Sot-Weed Factor* is a prolonged trial of Eben's confidence: His initiation into political intrigue and worldly corruption lays siege to his high-flown illusions about humankind. The people he meets are rapacious victimizers, ravaged victims, or crass simpletons, and Eben's promised land, his Malden estate, turns out to be an opium den and brothel. One illusion after another is stripped away, until the poet's tribute to Maryland is metamorphosed into the bitter satire on the deformities of America and Americans found in the poem by the historical Cooke.

Eben would not survive the conspiracies and uglinesses of reality were it not for the tutelage and example of Henry Burlingame. Whereas Eben labors to maintain one role—his "true" self—after years of aimlessness, Burlingame accepts and celebrates a series of roles, for he argues that, in a world of "plots, cabals, murthers, and machinations," an elastic personality will prove most useful. Therefore, he ducks in and out of the novel unpredictably, assuming a variety of guises (including that of

John Coode, Baltimore's devilish enemy, Lord Baltimore himself, and even Eben Cooke) as the situation demands. Eben's discussions with his mentor, although they do not cause him to forsake his belief in the essential truth of humankind's perfectibility and of his own career, do instruct him in how to dissemble when necessary, as exemplified during the voyage to America, when an exchange of roles with his servant, Bertram, proves expedient. In a sense, *The Sot-Weed Factor* boils down to the contrast and the tentative accommodations made between the ideal and the real, or between innocence and experience, as represented by the virgin-poet, who is linked to a past (his father) and to a future (his commission), and by the orphaned jack-of-all-trades, who embraces adventures and lovers with equal vivacity.

The Sot-Weed Factor insists on no conclusive resolution between these attitudes; as is Barth's custom throughout his fiction, the struggles between theoretical absolutes must end in compromise. If Eben's first problem is to rouse himself out of languor, his second is to realize the inadequacy of a single, unalterable role. Accordingly, Eben repudiates his sexual abstinence in order to wed the diseased, opium-addicted Joan Toast—his ruined Beatrice, who has followed him secretly to America—and so accepts a contract between the ideal and the actual. Similarly, Burlingame can only win and impregnate his beloved Anna after he completes his search for his family roots, which is to say, after he locates a stable identity. The novel ends in good comic fashion: Lovers are finally united; plot confusions are sorted out. Significantly, however, Barth adds twists to these conventions, thereby tempering the comic resolution: Joan dies in childbirth, and Burlingame disappears without a trace. Barth replicates the eighteenth century picaresque novel only to parody it; he seduces readers into traditional expectations only to undermine them.

For many readers, the most satisfying passages in *The Sot-Weed Factor* are not the philosophical or the literary exercises but rather the bawdy set pieces, the comic inventories and the imaginative diaries; nor should any discussion of this novel neglect to mention the war of name-calling between whores, or the "revisionist" rendition of Captain Smith's sexual assault on the otherwise impregnable Pocahontas. Barth has written of his enjoyment of Tobias Smollett's *Roderick Random* (1748) for its "nonsignificant surfaces," and in such glittering surfaces lie the charm of *The Sot-Weed Factor* as well. Fiction invades history and finds in its incongruities and intricacies of plot, character, and motivation a compatible form. Of all the deceptions perpetrated in the novel, perhaps none is so insidious as that of American history itself—the ultimate ruse of civilization, an imperfect concealment of savagery and selfishness. To remain innocent of the nature of history is irresponsible; Eben Cooke's practiced detachment, as implied by his virginity, is morally unacceptable. This lesson enables him to mature both artistically and ethically, and to dedicate himself to the world of which he claims to be poet laureate.

Giles Goat-Boy • Following immediately upon his satire of the historical past is Barth's satire of the future—a computer narrative. The novel-long analogy ruling *Giles Goat-Boy* transforms the universe into a university; this Newest Testament portrays a world divided (between East and West Campus) and waiting for the Grand Tutor, the Savior of the academic system, to protect Studentdom from the satanic Dean o' Flunks.

Barth provides Giles, an amalgam of worldwide messiah-heroes, as the updated instrument of human destiny. Giles (Grand-Tutorial Ideal, Laboratory Eugenical Specimen) is the child of the prodigious WESCAC computer and a virgin, who later appears as Lady Creamhair. Raised as a goat (Billy Bocksfuss) by an apostate scientist-mentor, Max Spielman, he eventually leaves the herd to join humanity as a preacher of the Revised New Syllabus on the West Campus of New Tammany College. The novel traces his attempts to verify and institute his claim to be Grand Tutor. Such a task entails a loss of innocence comparable in kind (although far more extensive in its implications for humanity) to those undertaken by his predecessors in Barth's canon. In *Giles Goat-Boy*, the initiation into complexity assumes a mythical overlay, as the hero passes from his exotic birth to his revelation of purpose in the womb of WESCAC (in whose mechanical interior he and Anastasia, a student who serves as Female Principle, come together) to a series of "assignments" through which he must prove his worth to his role as lawgiver and deposer of the false prophet, Harold Bray, and finally, to his sacrificial death for the sake of humankind.

Giles's career invokes Lord Raglan's systematic program for the stages of the hero's life, yet readers are irresistibly drawn to make correlations between the novel's allegorical personalities and events, and counterparts in journalistic reality. East and West Campus are barely fictional versions of Russia and the United States, with the H-bomb, in the form of WESCAC, the source of their power struggle. John F. Kennedy, Nikita Khrushchev, Joseph McCarthy, Albert Einstein, and other contemporary world figures populate the novel, as do such ancient luminaries as Moses, Socrates, and Christ Himself (Enos Enoch, accompanied by Twelve Trustees). These textures give *Giles Goat-Boy* the authority of sociopolitical history, but as is the case in *The Sot-Weed Factor*, Barth's penchant for discovering his own artifice casts a thick shadow of unreliability over the proceedings. For example, readers must share in the doubts over Giles's legitimacy, both filial and messianic: Not only do many people fail to accept his Grand Tutorhood (he predicts betrayal by the masses, who will drive him out on a rusty bicycle to his death on Founder's Hill), but also he himself is never completely certain that his words have not been programmed into him by WESCAC. The document itself—the pages before the readers—brought to "J. B." by Giles's son, is framed by disclaimers, editorial commentaries, footnotes, and postscripts, so that, finally, the "true text" is indistinguishable from the apocrypha. Moreover, Barth's liberal infusion of verse, puns, allusions, and stylistic entertainments strains the heroic conventions, which he has assembled from a great variety of literary and mythic sources. In short, the quality of revelation as espoused by Gilesianism is consistently affected by the doubt and self-effacement implied in the structure of the narrative.

Despite Barth's typical supply of structural equivocations, *Giles Goat-Boy* is his most ambitious attempt to recognize correspondences between factual and fictional accounts, between politics and mythology, between public and personal history. If the hero's quest leads him into a world of complexity, there is at least, by virtue of these correspondences, the promise of insight. Under Burlingame's direction in *The Sot-Weed Factor*, readers learn that the human personality, correctly apprehended, is a compendium of various, even contradictory, selves; in *Giles Goat-Boy*, this lesson is applied to the whole history of human learning and progress. Only when Giles accepts the all-encompassing nature of truth—PASS ALL and FAIL ALL are inextricably connected, not separable opposites but parts of a mystical oneness—does he mature into effectiveness. His passage through experience will include failure, but failure will guarantee growth, itself evidence of passage. Giles is a condenser in whom worldly paradoxes and dichotomies—knowledge and instinct, asceticism and responsibility, Spielman and Eirkopf, West and East Campus, and all other mutually resistive characters and systems of thought—manage a kind of synthesis. Keeping in mind that

Giles's story originates from a fundamental willingness to accept his humanity over his "goathood," one comes to appreciate that, although the novel is a satirical fantasy, it is inspired by the same receptivity to experience and the same optimistic energy in the face of desperate circumstances that are exalted by the tradition of quest literature.

The image of Giles and Anastasia united in WESCAC is the philosophical center of the novel; at this climactic moment, flesh is integrated with spirit, animal with human, and scientific hardware with "meaty tubes," all in the service of the improvement of the race. The gospel of *Giles Goat-Boy* is that the very impulse to enter the labyrinth is an affirmation, however unlikely the hero's chances against the beasts and devils (such as Stoker, the gloomy custodian of the power station) who reside within. Giles's victory is a transcendence of categories, a faith in the unity of the universe, and that revelation is enough to overcome the lack of appreciation by the undergraduates. No obstacle or imposture of the dozens that antagonize the hero obscures the meeting of goat-boy with computer; the circuitry of myth remains intact, even in this age of broken atoms.

Letters • "When my mythoplastic razors were sharply honed, it was unparalleled sport to lay about with them, to have at reality." So proclaimed Jake Horner in *The End of the Road* while praising articulation as his nearest equivalent to a personal absolute. The narrative impulse is the principal source of faith for Barth's array of protagonists, insofar as faith is possible in an undeniably relativistic environment. In *Letters,* he allows those characters a fuller opportunity to engage in an authorial perspective. *Letters* solidifies Barth's associations with modernists such as James Joyce and Samuel Beckett; here Barth takes license not only with established literary forms—specifically, the epistolary novel—but also with his private literary past, as he nonchalantly pays visits and respects to old fictional personalities. Because *Letters,* by its very form, intensifies one's awareness of the novel as a fabricated document (and, for that matter, of characters as collections of sentences), it is Barth's most transparently metafictional work; as the novel's subtitle unabashedly declares, this is "an old time epistolary novel by seven fictitious drolls and dreamers each of which imagines himself actual." *Letters* breaks down into seven parts, one for each letter of the title, and covers seven months of letter-writing. Place the first letter of each of the eighty-eight epistles in *Letters* on a calendar so that it corresponds with its date of composition, and the title of the novel will appear; like *Ulysses* (1922), *Letters* testifies to the diligence, if not to the overindulgence, of the craftsman.

Among these letter-writers are a group recycled from previous works as well as two figures, Germaine Pitt (Lady Amherst) and the Author, newly created for this book. In spite of Barth's assertions to the contrary, an appreciation of these characters is rather heavily dependent on a familiarity with their pre-*Letters* biographies: Todd Andrews emerges from *The Floating Opera* as an elderly lawyer who writes to his dead father and is drawn to incest while enjoying one last cruise on Chesapeake Bay; Jake Horner remains at the Remobilization Farm to which he had resigned himself at the conclusion of *The End of the Road,* and where his latest Information Therapy demands that he write to himself in an elaborate reconstitution of the past; Ambrose Mensch, the now-mature artist out of "Lost in the Funhouse," directs his correspondences to the anonymous "Yours Truly" whose message he found in a bottle years earlier, and constructs his life, including an affair with Germaine Pitt, in accordance with Lord Raglan's prescription for the hero. Readers also meet descendants of previous creations: Andrew Burlingame Cook VI busily attempts to shape the nation's destiny in a Second American Revolution, and Jerome Bonaparte Bray, a mad rival to Barth himself who may be a gigantic insect, seeks to program a computer-assisted novel, *Numbers,* to compete with the authority of the one that treated him so shabbily.

The third level of writers in *Letters* includes the two who have no prior existence in Barth's works: Germaine Pitt, a colorful widow who had been the friend of James Joyce, H. G. Wells, Aldous Huxley, and other literary notables, anxiously campaigns as Acting Provost to ensure the prestige of her college against the administrative dilutions and hucksterism of one John Schott; the Author enters the novel as Pitt's own alternative candidate for an honorary doctorate (which Schott proposes to give to the dubious activist, State Laureate A. B. Cook VI), and he writes to everyone else in the vicinity of *Letters.*

The most consistent theme tying the letters and authors together is the conflict between restriction and freedom. The setting is the volatile America of the 1960's, when sexual, moral, political, and even academic norms underwent the most serious reevaluation in American history. Obviously, Barth's creative history is the most evident aspect of this theme, and the repetitions and echoes among his novels and within *Letters* seduce readers into joining his search for pattern in the flux of human affairs. The ambiguous nature of history itself has also been one of his most durable themes—one recalls a chapter in *The Sot-Weed Factor* that examined the question of whether history is "a Progress, a Drama, a Retrogression, a Cycle, an Undulation, a Vortex, a Right-or Left-Handed Spiral, a Mere Continuum, or What Have You"—and the suggestion here is that any sort of orthodoxy can be revealed, especially in times of social crisis, as fictional. Student protests against the establishment are replicated in the antagonism between characters and an established text; the societal disruptions in the novel disrupt and contaminate the narrative.

A. B. Cook VI, one of the novel's seven correspondents, is the descendant of Ebenezer Cooke in *The Sot-Weed Factor.* Taking his cue from his ancestor, he is involved in the political intrigues of his own time, but he also attempts to rewrite history, providing alternative versions of storied events in the American past. The history of the Cook family is an antiestablishment one, filled with various attempts to launch "The Second American Revolution." This involves both rolling back the original American Revolution (for instance, during the War of 1812 the Cooks are on the British side) and extending it by making America more democratic. The Cooks, for instance, frequently ally with Native American peoples.

In contrast to Cook's historical vision stands the aesthetic one of Ambrose Mensch. Mensch is the prototypical modern artist, as presented in modern novels by writers such as James Joyce and Thomas Mann. His goal in life is to mold his own experience into a finished object, remote from the contingencies of time and place. Barth recognizes that both Cook's and Mensch's visions are partial. To bring together the two polarities, his instrument is Germaine Pitt, Lady Amherst, who serves in many ways as the muse of the book. Germaine reconciles art and history and shows the way for the novel, and life itself, to have a productive future.

In contrast to Samuel Richardson's definitive use of the epistolary form, *Letters* is populated by characters who are more than vaguely aware of their unreality, and therefore of the need to bargain with Barth for personal status and support. When the Author intrudes as a character, no convention is above suspicion; although he describes himself as turning away from the "fabulous irreal" toward "a détente with the realistic tradition," if this novel is the result, it is a severely qualified détente, indeed.

Perhaps the structural "confusion" of the novel explains the smugness of Reg Prinz, an avant-garde filmmaker who wants to create a version of all of Barth's books in a medium that he feels to be superior and more up-to-date. What had been a playful interest in the relationships between creative media in *Lost in the Funhouse* has escalated in *Letters* into a battle for aesthetic dominance between the word-hating Prinz and the word-mongering Barth. (The fact that Prinz is a prisoner of the novel enables Barth to sway the outcome of this battle, at least temporarily.)

Letters, like history itself, concludes in blood and ambiguity; one suspects that Barth means to undergo a catharsis of the books and characters that have obsessed him and that continue to infiltrate his creative consciousness. It is testimony to Barth's ability to elicit admiration for his craft that readers do not leave *Letters*—or, for that matter, most of his fictions—with a sense of defeat. The keynote of his literary career is exuberance; if nihilism and existential gloom have been his thematic preoccupations, their potentially numbing effects are undercut by Barth's cleverness, his stylistic ingenuity, and his campaign for the rewards of narrative.

Sabbatical • Barth's *Sabbatical* continues to bend philosophy into escapade. Subtitled "A Romance," *Sabbatical* is rather a postmodernization of romance: All the well-established Barthian formal intrigues, ruminative digressions, plot coincidences (the married pair of main characters, in the same vein as *The Sot-Weed Factor*, are both twins), and other examples of literary self-consciousness complicate the vacation cruise of Fenwick Scott Key Turner, a former CIA agent and a contemporary novelist, and his wife, Susan, herself an established academic and critic. The nine-month sea journey—a frequent theme for Barth—leads to the birth of the novel itself, in whose plot the narrating "parents" seek clues to some conspiratorial Agency "plot" against them. (Fenwick has written an exposé that makes his "life as voyage" a perilous journey indeed—even when on sabbatical.) So the creative couple prepare, nurture, take pride in, and exhaustively analyze their verbal offspring, while the real world blows into their story from the shore in another dizzying mixture of fact and fiction.

As readers have come to expect from Barth, the imagination is exalted above and beyond its moorings in the "real world," all the while calling attention to its own altitude. As Fenwick declares to his loving coauthor: "I won't have our story be unadulterated realism. Reality is wonderful; reality is dreadful; reality is what it is." The intensity, the scope, and the truth of reality are more appropriately the province of experimental technique.

The Tidewater Tales • *The Tidewater Tales: A Novel* is closely related to *Sabbatical*. Fenwick Scott Key Turner reappears in the guise of Franklin Key Talbott, and Carmen B. Seckler has become the main character Peter Sagamore's mother-in-law, Carla B. Silver. Following the theme of twins in *Sabbatical*, Peter's wife, Katherine, is eight and a half months pregnant with twins. In fact, much of the plot consists of Peter and Katherine sailing around in their sloop *Story* while waiting for Katherine to come to term.

The sloop's name is an obvious reference to both Peter's and Katherine's (and Barth's) profession. Peter is a writer, and Katherine is an oral history expert—a storyteller. The intricate narratives become a line of stories within stories, as Barth concentrates on capturing all of reality within his fictive form.

The Last Voyage of Somebody the Sailor • *The Last Voyage of Somebody the Sailor* is a retelling of the Arabic short-story cycle *The Arabian Nights' Entertainments* (c. fifteenth century), with an interesting difference. Whereas traditionally the Arabian Nights stories have been valued as exotic fantasies wholly divergent from conventional modern realism, Barth demonstrates that what is usually considered realism can often also be considered fantastic. When Somebody (also known as Simon Behler), a modern-day sailor whose biography parallels Barth's own to some degree, arrives in medieval Baghdad, his stories of American boyhood, sexual awakening, and marital trouble are seen as amazing and weird by his Arabian audience, for whom the "marvelous" is all too familiar. Though this novel may lack the psychological depth of some of Barth's earlier works, such as *The End of the Road*, it does attempt a serious moral critique. Somebody's Arabian equivalent is the renowned sailor Sindbad, who initially appears to be a hero but whose avarice and cruelty are soon found out and duly punished. Somebody marries the beautiful princess Yasmin, with whom he has a happy relationship (though readers are perpetually reminded that it is a fictional one). Somebody's better adjusted, more humane kind of heroism is eventually celebrated by the Arabian Nights society, and thus the novel becomes an even happier version of Mark Twain's time-travel novel *A Connecticut Yankee in King Arthur's Court* (1889).

Once upon a Time: A Floating Opera • *Once upon a Time* is a hybrid of fiction and autobiography. Barth gives readers a bare-bones account of his life and career, sometimes fleshed out with extended anecdotes. Interspersed with this, however, are scenes of voyages to the Caribbean and back, as well as meditations on the nature of storytelling itself. The strongest fictional element of the book is a totally invented character, Jay Scribner. Scribner serves as Barth's alter ego in the book. He is a more outwardly vigorous and outspoken figure who bounces off the character of the author. Scribner at once comments upon and frames Barth's own sensibility. As the book proceeds on its jaunty course, Barth appends footnotes of what is going on, politically and otherwise, in the "real" world. The gently made point of the narrative is that autobiography is as much a fiction as fiction itself. What is real and what is imaginary (especially in the life and mind of a novelist) are always intertwining and cannot definitively be separated from each other. Readers in search of truly enlightening entertainment would not want such a thing to occur.

Arthur M. Saltzman
Updated by Nicholas Birns

Other major works

SHORT FICTION: *Lost in the Funhouse*, 1968; *On With the Story*, 1996; *The Book of Ten Nights and a Night: Eleven Stories*, 2004; *Where Three Roads Meet*, 2005.

NONFICTION: *The Friday Book: Essays, and Other Nonfiction*, 1984; *Further Fridays: Essays, Lectures, and Other Nonfiction*, 1995.

Bibliography

Barth, John. "Interview." *Short Story*, n.s. 1 (Spring, 1993): 110-118. Discusses Barth's love for the short story and why he does not write more of them. Talks about minimalism and self-reflexivity; examines the nature of the story in *The Arabian Nights' Entertainments* and Edgar Allan Poe; explains why he tries to stay as non-ideological as possible; surveys the changes in short fiction from the mid-1970's to the early 1990's.

Bowen, Zack. "Barth and Joyce." *Critique* 37 (Summer, 1996): 261-269. Discusses how

Barth followed James Joyce in the grandness of his narrative scheme, his ironic focus on a region, and his personal overtones in his fiction. Explores Barth's anxiety about this influence.

____________. *A Reader's Guide to John Barth.* Westport, Conn.: Greenwood Press, 1994. A concise overview of Barth's first ten books of fiction (through *The Last Voyage of Somebody the Sailor*), with a short but thoughtful chapter on *Lost in the Funhouse.* Contains good bibliographies (including one of articles and book chapters on *Lost in the Funhouse*), a brief biographical sketch, and an interesting appendix: "Selected List of Recurrent Themes, Patterns, and Techniques."

Fogel, Stan, and Gordon Slethaug. *Understanding John Barth.* Columbia: University of South Carolina Press, 1990. In this text, the authors present a comprehensive interpretation of Barth's works, from *The Floating Opera* to *The Tidewater Tales.* Chapter 6 is devoted entirely to *Lost in the Funhouse,* with discussion of how Barth's short fiction fits into his oeuvre. Each chapter includes notes at its end. Fogel and Slethaug have included both a primary and a secondary bibliography. The primary bibliography is especially useful for its list of uncollected short stories, and it includes the stories' date and place of publication. An index divided by work and a general index conclude the book.

Harris, Charles B. *Passionate Virtuosity: The Fiction of John Barth.* Urbana: University of Illinois Press, 1983. This work has a chapter titled "'A Continuing, Strange Love Letter': Sex and Language in *Lost in the Funhouse,*" which concentrates on Barth's stories from the aspect of the reader and writer relationship. Exhaustive notes at the end of the chapter direct the reader to further sources, as does the secondary bibliography at the end of the book. Includes an index.

Schulz, Max F. *The Muses of John Barth: Tradition and Metafiction from "Lost in the Funhouse" to "The Tidewater Tales."* Baltimore: Johns Hopkins University Press, 1990. Schulz concentrates on the themes of "romantic passion and commonsense love" in Barth's work, with an emphasis on "the textual domestication of classical myths." In the chapter titled "Old Muses and New: Epic Reprises, Self-Reflexive Bedtime Stories, and Intertextual Pillow Talk," Schulz discusses what he calls the "Thalian design" of *Lost in the Funhouse.* Notes to the chapters are included at the end of the text, as is an index.

Scott, Steven D. *The Gamefulness of American Postmodernism: John Barth and Louise Erdrich.* New York: Peter Lang, 2000. Comparative study of Barth and the Native American writer Louise Erdrich as postmodernist writers.

Walkiewicz, E. P. *John Barth.* Boston: Twayne, 1986. This book is very useful for biographical details: It includes a chronology of Barth's life and work. Contains also considerable discussion of *Lost in the Funhouse,* which makes this book a good all-around reference. Supplemented by primary and secondary bibliographies as well as notes and an index.

Ann Beattie

Born: Washington, D.C.; September 8, 1947

Principal long fiction • *Chilly Scenes of Winter,* 1976; *Falling in Place,* 1980; *Love Always,* 1985; *Picturing Will,* 1989; *Another You,* 1995; *My Life, Starring Dara Falcon,* 1997; *The Doctor's House,* 2002.

Other literary forms • Ann Beattie has published numerous short stories, including those anthologized in *Distortions* (1976) and a children's book titled *Goblin Tales* (1975).

Achievements • Hailed by many as the spokesperson for her generation, Beattie won numerous awards for her novels and short stories focusing on vapid, upper-middle-class characters. Along with several scholastic honors, Beattie also received a literary award from the American Academy and Institute of Arts and Letters and a Distinguished Alumnae award from American University, both in 1980. A member of the International Association of Poets, Playwrights, Editors, Essayists, and Novelists (PEN) and of the Authors Guild, in 1992 she was elected to the American Academy and Institute of Arts and Letters.

Biography • The daughter of an administrator in the U.S. Department of Health, Education, and Welfare, James A. Beattie, and Charlotte (née Crosby) Beattie, Ann Beattie was born in Washington, D.C., in 1947 and grew up in its suburbs. As a child, she was encouraged to paint, read, and write. An avid scholar, she enrolled at American University in Washington, D.C., in 1966 and received her bachelor's degree only three years later, in 1969. During this short tenure, she edited the university literary journal and was chosen by *Mademoiselle* magazine to be a guest editor in 1968. After her graduation, Beattie entered the master's degree program at the University of Connecticut as a graduate assistant to study eighteenth century literature. She received her degree in 1970 and began to work toward a doctorate; however, she quickly became frustrated and turned to writing short stories. It was then that—encouraged by her mentor, John O'Hara—she submitted several stories to small-press literary journals. After initial, moderate success with these publications, she finally had "A Platonic Relationship" published by *The New Yorker* in 1974. Later that same year, *The New Yorker* printed two more Beattie short stories, a signal of her arrival in the literary world.

At this, Beattie quit the university to concentrate on her writing. After that, she served on the faculties of several universities as a writing instructor. In 1972 she married David Gates, a fellow University of Connecticut student; they were divorced in 1980. In 1985, a mutual friend introduced Beattie to the painter Lincoln Perry, a visiting professor at the University of Virginia, where Beattie had taught several years before. They were married in 1988. After several years in Charlottesville, they moved to Maine. Meanwhile, with her fourth novel, *Picturing Will* (1989), Beattie extended her literary domain dramatically; the novel was well received, gaining a front-page review in the book review section of *The New York Times*. Beattie has homes in Charlottesville, Virginia, and Key West, Florida, with Perry.

Analysis • Although Beattie's work has often been criticized as pointless and depressing, there is a method to her seeming madness. The stories and novels are not a mix of ennui and untapped angst but rather detailed examinations of the lives of several apparently different—but uniquely similar—people. Not one specific character is repeated in any story, but some, like the Vietnam veteran, appear in different versions and perform different functions, as plot catalysts, for example. At the same time, all Beattie's characters share the same vague feelings of discontent and lack of fulfillment, the knowledge that something is missing in their lives.

Chilly Scenes of Winter • Initially, a Beattie character may seem feisty and self-assured, even defensive about his or her lack of enthusiasm. In Beattie's first novel, *Chilly Scenes of Winter*, one player remarks, "[Y]ou could be happy, too, Sam, if you hadn't had your eyes opened in the 60's." The promise of a better life that was given to these characters has been transmogrified into unhappiness and loneliness without relief. Beattie's novels are, accordingly, laced with irony.

It is the acknowledgment of this transgression through the use of irony that provides a saving grace for the stories and novels. The main character of *Chilly Scenes of Winter* is granted all that he wishes; in the end, however, all that he wants is to escape his gratification. Charles, the protagonist, is in love with Laura, a married woman. His desire for her eventually dominates his life, so that he is unable to function without that desire or—as he would believe—without her.

Charles's obsession with Laura colors his relationship with his own family: his mother, Clara; her second husband, Pete; and Charles's sister, Susan. Even though his sister has accepted Pete, Charles refuses to acknowledge him as a replacement for their father, a man whose good qualities are magnified by the virtue of his death. Charles regards Pete as both a loser and a catalyst for Clara's chronic hypochondria. He claims that Pete refuses to accept life as it is and, instead, continues to make excuses for Clara's instability. The irony is that what Charles so clearly perceives as Pete's faults are really his own. Charles cannot—or will not—admit that he, too, fantasizes about the woman he loves and constructs absurd ideas about her that are founded on nothing but his own imagination. Charles will never be able to have a normal life with Laura, just as Pete will never be able to have one with Clara.

There is also the thought, which runs throughout the novel, that marriage itself is not a desirable norm. Sam, Clara's friend, comments, "It's nuts to get married," and indeed none of the relationships in *Chilly Scenes of Winter* seems to bode well for the participants. Pete and Clara's marriage is tainted by her mental illness, Jim and Laura's seems emptied by their lack of interest, and Charles and Laura's relationship is adulterous (and thus unable to be acknowledged).

The lack of sanction for Charles's love is typical of his whole existence. Nothing in his life lives up to his expectations, so he wanders pathetically, searching for both the ideal and the unreal. He is terrified of discovering a truth in his miserable existence, and this fear prevents him from completing his quest for love and a meaningful life. Charles is consumed by the thought that he will develop an "inoperable melanoma," even though there is no indication that he will; it is merely a phrase he has overheard in a hospital room. After Laura leaves Jim, Charles refuses to contact her; he will only drive past her house, hoping for a signal that will never be given.

Sigrid Estrada

Falling in Place • In contrast to this world where the characters are forced to wander endlessly, searching for a direction, the players in *Falling in Place* are given a very clear signal when a significant event occurs. The story opens with John Knapp, his estranged wife Louise, their children Mary and John Joel, and John's mistress Nina. During the week, John lives with his mother, ostensibly to be close to his job in New York City but really to be far away from Louise and the children and closer to Nina. Naturally, this situation affects his children, and they become bitter and distanced not only from their father but also from their mother. Instead of swimming in a maelstrom of their own emotions, however, the characters in *Falling in Place* actually reach out to others and are influenced by them. John Joel's deviant friend Parker brings the action of the novel to a head: He provides John Joel with a handgun, and the latter proceeds to shoot his sister Mary in the side. When asked why he shot her, John Joel explains to his father, "She was a bitch."

Perhaps this phrase succinctly sums up Beattie's child characters in the story. Instead of behaving like real children, their circumstances force them to become miniature adults, faced with adult problems and desires. John Joel has an eating disorder, his friend Parker smokes a pack of cigarettes a day, and cold Mary dreams of sacrificing her virginity to singer Peter Frampton. They are a sad band of children, imitating the worst habits of their adult counterparts in the worst possible way. John Joel mouths adult words and defines his teenage sister in adult terms.

Finally, John and Louise divorce, freeing themselves and their children to pursue meaningful existences. None however, really believes that he or she will be able to attain this. At one point, John complains to Mary, "Don't you think I might already realize that my existence is a little silly?" Mary replies, "[T]hat's what *Vanity Fair* is like. Things just fall into place." John wonders if his daughter's advocacy of predestination seals her fate or if she simply cannot, or will not, try to imagine a future over which she has any control. Mary is not, however, the only member of her family who refuses to admit to a future. After Nina and John finally unite, Nina begs him to consider her wants: "Acres of land. Children. A big house. Try to *realize* what you love." John only replies, "You're what I want."

John, then, refuses to realize, to make real, his existence with Nina and any sort of happiness they might have. He and his fellow characters are moderately pleased with their ties to the past and present; one boasts of a once-removed acquaintance with singer Linda Ronstadt. No one, however, will consider the effect of his or her present actions on the future. No one wants to be responsible for shaping a future; all merely accept whatever happens as a logical consequence of an illogical life.

Love Always • In contrast, the characters in *Love Always* begin by rejoicing that they are "beating the system." Hildon and his ex-student friends run a slick journal named *Country Daze*, the success of which, Hildon maintains, is "proof positive that the whole country is coked-out." Because America, or at least the readership of *Country Daze*, has gone to rack and ruin, Hildon and associates decide that their behavior does not have to measure up to any modern-day standards. Hildon continues his long-standing affair with coworker and advice columnist Lucy, despite his marriage. Lucy's fourteen-year-old niece, Nicole, is taking a brief vacation with her aunt from her role as a teenage junkie on a popular soap opera.

Nicole is yet another of Beattie's adult children, as are John Joel and Mary in *Falling in Place*. She serves as a foil for the adults in her world who are childishly hiding from the responsibilities and terrors of the outside world in a world of their own devising. Nicole's aunt, Lucy, writes under the name Cindi Coeur. Ironically, she does not wear her heart on her sleeve but rather flees from mature relationships. Lucy is equally unhappy about Nicole's adult behavior, but she does not know what to do about it.

Picturing Will • During the mid-1980's, the direction of Beattie's fiction began to change. While there were still passive, directionless characters in her novels, there were also instances of redemption, primarily through a commitment to other human beings that no one in the earlier works seemed willing or able to make. There are still a great many characters in these novels who fail both themselves and others, however. In *Picturing Will*, for example, the needs of the five-year-old protagonist are ignored by both of his divorced parents. His mother Jody is more interested in becoming a famous photographer than in taking care of her son, and his shiftless father Wayne would rather drink and womanize than pay attention to Will. The real hero of the story is Jody's lover, and later her second husband, Mel Anthis. It is Mel who sacrifices his own literary ambitions in order to dedicate his life to child-rearing, thus ensuring that Will becomes the secure man and the loving husband and father we meet at the end of the novel.

Another You • In *Picturing Will*, Mel is introduced as a caring person, capable of loving a woman as difficult as Jody, and his affection for Will is believable. In the protagonist of *Another You*, however, a striking change in personality occurs, one that promises redemption. At the beginning of the book, Marshall Lockard seems much like the passive characters in Beattie's earlier novels, except that he is quite content with his purposeless life; in fact, Marshall has deliberately arranged his way of life. As an English professor at a small New Hampshire college, he can live vicariously through literary characters, and he has so well mastered the art of sarcasm that he can repel his students at will. Because his wife Sonja believes him too vulnerable to be subjected to any emotional stress, it is she, not Marshall, who goes to the nursing home to visit Marshall's stepmother, who reared him and loves him dearly. Although Sonja has become bored enough with this well-ordered existence to indulge in a little adultery with her employer, she does not mean for her husband to find out about it.

Despite all his precautions, however, Marshall is drawn into the untidy world. It all begins with a simple request from one of his students: She wants him to speak to someone on campus about her friend, who is claiming that she was assaulted by Marshall's colleague Jack MacCallum. Soon Marshall finds himself kissing the student and worrying about repercussions, explaining to the police why MacCallum was stabbed by his pregnant wife in the Lockard home, and dealing with his stepmother's death and his wife's infidelity, not to mention the two students' having fabricated their story and the supposed victim's turning out to be a narcotics agent. Marshall is so shaken by these heavy blows of reality that he decides to go to Key West, visit his older brother Gordon, and ask about some events in their childhood that have always haunted him. Although only Beattie's readers find out the truth, not Marshall, by simply confronting the issue Marshall gains new strength. Instead of becoming another drifter in Key West, he heads back to New Hampshire, cold weather, and real life, hopefully with Sonja.

My Life, Starring Dara Falcon • In Beattie's early works, the characters are often far more interested in the lives of celebrities, such as Janis Joplin and Lucille Ball, than in their own lives. After all, it is much less risky to invest in a tabloid than in another person. A similar kind of vicarious existence is the subject of *My Life, Starring Dara Falcon*. Here, however, the protagonist, Jean Warner, is so young and so malleable that this is obviously a coming-of-age novel. Beattie even reassures her readers of a happy ending by beginning her book two decades after most of its events and by showing the narrator as a happily married, mature woman who understands herself and others. Thus readers know from the outset that Jean did escape from her husband's large extended family, which smothered her rather than giving her the security she sought, from a rather dull husband who is ruled by his family, and, most important, from the manipulations of the Machiavellian Dara Falcon.

In both *My Life, Starring Dara Falcon* and *Another You*, the protagonists begin as passive creatures who live vicariously through others, but they can and do choose to change, first by coming to terms with their own identities, then by daring to care about others. If in her early works Beattie showed what was wrong with the members of her generation, in her later works she offers hope to them and, indeed, to all of us.

Jennifer L. Wyatt
Updated by Rosemary M. Canfield Reisman

Other major works

SHORT FICTION: *Distortions*, 1976; *Secrets and Surprises*, 1978; *Jacklighting*, 1981; *The Burning House*, 1982; *Where You'll Find Me, and Other Stories*, 1986; *What Was Mine, and Other Stories*, 1991; *Park City: New and Selected Stories*, 1998; *Perfect Recall: New Stories*, 2001; *Follies and New Stories*, 2005.

NONFICTION: *Alex Katz*, 1987.

CHILDREN'S LITERATURE: *Goblin Tales*, 1975; *Spectacle*, 1985.

Bibliography

Aldridge, John. "Less Is a Lot Less (Raymond Carver, Ann Beattie, Amy Hempel, Frederick Barthelme)." In *Talents and Technicians*. New York: Charles Scribner's Sons, 1992. Comparative study of the economical writing style of Beattie and three other contemporary authors.

Barth, John. "A Few Words About Minimalism." *The New York Times Book Review*, December 28, 1986, 1, 2, 25. Explores Beattie's spare style and considers her fiction as it represents a current stylistic trend in the American short story. Spends a considerable amount of space describing the origins of the contemporary minimalist movement in American short fiction. Sees this form as a nonverbal statement about theme: the spareness of life in America. Places Beattie's work among that of other minimalists, including Raymond Carver, Bobbie Ann Mason, James Robison, Mary Robison, and Tobias Wolff. Discusses Edgar Allan Poe as an early proponent of minimalism. Says that Beattie's fiction is clearly shaped by the events surrounding the Vietnam War. A helpful essay for gaining an understanding of Beattie as a minimalist.

Beattie, Ann. "An Interview with Ann Beattie." Interview by Steven R. Centola. *Contemporary Literature* 31 (Winter, 1990): 405-422. Contains a photograph of Beattie. This article is useful to the general reader, providing information about Beattie's biography. Beattie discusses herself as a feminist writer and talks about how she goes about creating credible male protagonists. Asserts that most of her fiction centers on exploring human relationships. Discusses *Falling in Place, Love Always, Chilly Scenes of Winter,* and *Picturing Will.* Talks about F. Scott Fitzgerald and his novel, *The Great Gatsby* (1925). Says that she is not interested in capturing American society but in capturing human nature.

Lee, Don. "About Ann Beattie." *Ploughshares* 21, no. 2-3 (1995): 231-235. A good biographical and critical essay, based on an interview and including extensive quotations. Beattie points out that as she has matured, her novels have become more complex and therefore more time-consuming to produce. She describes her difficulties with *Another You,* which left her even more partial than before to short fiction.

Montresor, Jaye Berman, ed. *The Critical Response to Ann Beattie.* Westport, Conn.: Greenwood Press, 1993. Includes contemporary reaction to Beattie's novels and collections of short stories, as well as scholarly and academic analyses of her work by various critics.

Murphy, Christina. *Ann Beattie.* Boston: Twayne, 1986. Good general introduction to Beattie's work. Discusses her major stories, illustrating her central themes and basic techniques. Discusses the relationship of her stories to her novels and her place in the development of the contemporary American short story.

Opperman, Harry, and Christina Murphy. "Ann Beattie (1947-): A Checklist." *Bulletin of Bibliography* 44 (June, 1987): 111-118. A useful guide to Beattie's work. Contains a helpful brief introductory essay that identifies Beattie as an important authorial voice that came of age during the 1960's. Views her as a descendant of Ernest Hemingway. Her characters are refugees from the Woodstock generation, idealistic dreamers caught by ennui, drifters and people who are emotional burnouts. Says that her characters resemble F. Scott Fitzgerald's: Both have outlived their youthful romanticism and are now materialistic rather than idealistic. Also compares her to John Cheever and John Updike. Provides both primary and secondary bibliographies through 1986.

Porter, Carolyn. "The Art of the Missing." In *Contemporary American Women Writers: Narrative Strategies,* edited by Catherine Rainwater and William J. Scheick. Lexington: University Press of Kentucky, 1985. Argues that Beattie economizes not by developing a symbolic context, as James Joyce and Sherwood Anderson did, but rather by using the present tense and thus removing any temptation to lapse into exposition, forcing the background to emerge from dialogue of character consciousness.

Stein, Lorin. "Fiction in Review." *Yale Review* 85, no. 4 (1997): 156-165. After an excellent summary of Beattie's early fiction, the writer proceeds to analyze *My Life, Starring Dara Falcon*, which he thinks has been underrated by critics.

Wyatt, David. "Ann Beattie." *The Southern Review* 28, no. 1 (1992): 145-159. Presents evidence that during the mid-1980's there was a marked alteration in Beattie's fiction. Instead of withdrawing from life and its dangers, her characters chose to care about other people and to commit themselves to creativity. A perceptive and convincing analysis.

Saul Bellow

Born: Lachine, Quebec, Canada; June 10, 1915
Died: Brookline, Massachusetts; April 5, 2005

Principal long fiction • *Dangling Man*, 1944; *The Victim*, 1947; *The Adventures of Augie March*, 1953; *Seize the Day*, 1956; *Henderson the Rain King*, 1959; *Herzog*, 1964; *Mr. Sammler's Planet*, 1970; *Humboldt's Gift*, 1975; *The Dean's December*, 1982; *More Die of Heartbreak*, 1987; *A Theft*, 1989; *The Bellarosa Connection*, 1989; *The Actual*, 1997 (novella); *Ravelstein*, 2000; *Novels, 1944-1953*, 2003 (includes *Dangling Man, The Victim,* and *The Adventures of Augie March*).

Other literary forms • In addition to his many novels, Saul Bellow published short stories, plays, and a variety of nonfiction. His stories have appeared in *The New Yorker, Commentary, Partisan Review, Hudson Review, Esquire,* and other periodicals, and he published two collections of short stories, *Mosby's Memoirs, and Other Stories* (1968) and *Him with His Foot in His Mouth, and Other Stories* (1984; includes short novels). His full-length play *The Last Analysis* was produced for a short run on Broadway in 1964, while three one-act plays, *Orange Soufflé, A Wen,* and *Out from Under,* were staged in 1966 in America and Europe. Another one-act play, *The Wrecker,* was published, though not staged, in 1954. Throughout his career, Bellow wrote numerous articles on a variety of topics. In 1976, for example, he published an account of his trip to Israel, *To Jerusalem and Back: A Personal Account.*

Achievements • Often described as America's best contemporary novelist, Bellow earned enormous critical praise and a wide readership as well. He was awarded the Nobel Prize in Literature in 1976. His popularity is somewhat surprising, however, as his novels do not contain the usual ingredients one expects to find in best-selling fiction—suspense, heroic figures, and graphic sex and violence. In fact, his novels are difficult works that wrestle with perplexing questions, sometimes drawing from esoteric sources such as the anthroposophy of Rudolf Steiner and the psychology of Wilhelm Reich. One of America's most erudite novelists, Bellow often alluded to the work of philosophers, psychologists, poets, anthropologists, and other writers in his fiction. He once stated that the modern movelist should not be afraid to introduce complex ideas into his work. He found nothing admirable about the anti-intellectualism of many modern writers and believed that most of them failed to confront the important moral and philosophical problems of the modern age. Opposed to the glib pessimism and the "complaint" of the dominant tradition of modern literature, Bellow struggled for affirmation at a time when such a possibility was seen by many writers as merely an object of ridicule.

In contrast to many American writers, who produced their best work when they were young and then wrote mediocre or poor fiction as they grew older, Bellow is known for the consistent high quality of his work. Moreover, his fiction reveals an immense versatility. In his work, one finds highly structured Flaubertian form as well as picaresque narrative, naturalistic realism as well as romance.

Bellow earned a reputation as a master of narrative voice and perspective, a great comic writer (perhaps the best in America since Mark Twain), and a fine craftsman whose remarkable control of the language allowed him to move easily from the highly formal to the colloquial. Most important, his novels illuminate the dark areas of the psyche and possess immense emotional power. Bellow once complained that many contemporary authors and critics are obsessed with symbolism and hidden meanings. A literary work becomes an abstraction for them, and they contrive to evade the emotional power inherent in literature. Bellow's novels do not suffer from abstraction; they deal concretely with passion, death, love, and other fundamental concerns, evoking the whole range of human emotions for his readers.

Biography • Saul Bellow was born in Lachine, Quebec, Canada, on June 10, 1915, the youngest of four children. Two years before, his parents, Abraham and Liza (Gordon) Bellow, had immigrated to Canada from St. Petersburg, Russia. The family lived in a very poor section of Montreal, where Bellow learned Yiddish, Hebrew, French, and English. In 1923, Bellow was diagnosed with tuberculosis and spent half a year in Montreal's Royal Victoria Hospital. When he was nine, his family moved to Chicago, where they lived in the tenements of Humboldt Park.

In 1933, after graduating from Tuley High School on the Northwest Side, Bellow entered the University of Chicago. Two years later he transferred to Northwestern University, where he received a bachelor's degree with honors in sociology and anthropology. In 1937, he entered the University of Wisconsin at Madison to study anthropology but left school in December to marry Anita Goshkin and to become a writer. He was employed briefly with the Works Progress Administration Writers' Project and then led a bohemian life, supporting himself with teaching and odd jobs. During World War II, he served in the merchant marine and published his first novel, *Dangling Man*.

After publishing his second novel, *The Victim*, Bellow was awarded a Guggenheim Fellowship in 1948, which enabled him to travel to Europe and work on *The Adventures of Augie March*, parts of which he published in various periodicals before publishing the novel in 1953. This third novel won the National Book Award for Fiction in 1953 and established Bellow as one of America's most promising novelists.

After his return from Europe in 1950, Bellow spent a large part of the next decade in New York City and Dutchess County, New York, teaching and writing before moving back to Chicago to publish *Herzog*. Although *Seize the Day* and *Henderson the Rain King* did not receive the critical attention they deserved, *Herzog* was an enormous critical and financial success, even becoming a best-seller for forty-two weeks and selling 142,000 copies, making Bellow wealthy for the first time in his life. *Herzog*, which prompted several thousand readers to send letters to Bellow pouring out their souls, is not only Bellow's masterpiece but also the most autobiographical of his novels. The impetus for the novel was the breakup of his second marriage, to Sondra Tschacbasov, because of her affair with his best friend, the writer Jack Ludwig. Although the novel reveals all of the important episodes of Bellow's life up to the time of the writing of *Herzog*, the primary focus of the novel is on the triangle of Herzog (Bellow), an academic suffering from writer's block, his beautiful and strong-willed wife Madeleine (Sondra), and the flamboyant charlatan Valentine Gersbach (Jack Ludwig). The shameless Gersbach pretends to be Herzog's best friend and even provides marital counseling for the despondent husband while cuckolding him.

Bellow's next two novels, *Mr. Sammler's Planet* and *Humboldt's Gift*, helped increase

© The Nobel Foundation

his reputation but also created some controversy. *Mr. Sammler's Planet* was critical of the excesses of the late 1960's, and some complained that Bellow had become a reactionary. Although Bellow opposed the Vietnam War, he found it difficult to identify with the "counterculture." *Humboldt's Gift* disturbed some critics, who complained that his interest in the ideas of Austrian social philosopher Rudolf Steiner indicated that he was becoming an escapist; it was a mistaken assumption. An ardent supporter of Israel, Bellow traveled to that country in 1975 and published an account of his journey, *To Jerusalem and Back.* Winning the Nobel Prize in Literature in 1976 did not result in a loss of Bellow's creativity, and he published important books during the 1980's and 1990's that challenge conventional thinking on political, aesthetic, and philosophical matters.

Bellow married five times and had three sons by his first three wives. At the age of 84, he had a daughter by his fifth wife. After living in Chicago for many years, he moved to Massachusetts in 1994, where he became a professor of literature at Boston University. He published his last novel, *Ravelstein,* in 2000. It might be seen as his literary farewell, as it voices his concern about the survival of the human spirit amid the luxurious entanglements of contemporary life. Bellow died in Brookline, Massachusetts in April, 2005, at the age of eighty-nine.

Analysis • Saul Bellow's mature fiction can be considered as a conscious challenge to modernism, the dominant literary tradition of the age. For Bellow, modernism is a "victim literature" because it depicts an alienated individual who is conquered by his environment. According to him, this "wasteland" tradition originated in the middle of the nineteenth century with the birth of French realism and culminates in the work of Samuel Beckett and other nihilistic contemporary writers. This victim literature reveals a horror of life and considers humanist values useless in a bleak, irrational world. Modernism assumes that the notion of the individual self that underlies the great tradition of the novel is an outmoded concept, and that modern civilization is doomed.

Dangling Man • Bellow's first two novels owe a large debt to the wasteland modernism that he would explicitly reject during the late 1940's. *Dangling Man* is an existentialist diary that owes much to Fyodor Dostoevski's *Notes from the Underground* (1864). The demoralized protagonist Joseph is left "dangling" as he waits to be drafted during World War II. A moral casualty of war, he has no sense of purpose and feels weary of a life that seems boring, trivial, and cruel. Excessively self-conscious and critical of those around him, he spends most of his time alone, writing in his journal. He can no longer continue his past work, writing biographical essays on philosophers of the Enlightenment. Although he is alienated, he does realize that he should not make a doctrine out of this feeling. The conclusion of the novel reveals Joseph's ultimate failure to transcend his "victimization"; he is drafted and greets his imminent regimentation enthusiastically.

The Victim • Bellow's next novel, *The Victim*, also depicts a passive protagonist who is unable to overcome his victimization. As Bellow admitted, the novel is partially modeled on Dostoevski's *The Eternal Husband* (1870) and uses the technique of the doppelgänger as Dostoevski did in *The Double* (1846). Bellow's novel presents the psychological struggle between Asa Leventhal, a Jew, and Kirby Allbee, his Gentile "double." A derelict without a job, Allbee suggests that Leventhal is responsible for his grim fate. Leventhal ponders the problem of his guilt and responsibility and tries to rid himself of his persecuting double. Despite his efforts to assert himself, he is still "dangling" at the end of the book—still a victim of forces that, he believes, are beyond his control.

The Adventures of Augie March • After his second novel, Bellow became disenchanted with the depressive temperament and the excessive emphasis on form of modernist literature. His first two novels had been written according to "repressive" Flaubertian formal standards; they were melancholy, rigidly structured, restrained in language, and detached and objective in tone. Rebelling against these constricting standards, Bellow threw off the yoke of modernism when he began to write his third novel. The theme, style, and tone of *The Adventures of Augie March* are very different from his earlier novels, for here one finds an open-ended picaresque narrative with flamboyant language and an exuberant hero who seeks to affirm life and the possibility of freedom. Although the environment has a profound influence upon Joseph and Asa Leventhal, Augie refuses to allow it to determine his fate. During the course of many adventures, a multitude of Machiavellians seek to impose their versions of reality upon the good-natured Augie, but he escapes from them, refusing to commit himself.

With his third novel, then, Bellow deliberately rejected the modernist outlook and aesthetic. The problem was to find an alternative to modernism without resorting to glib optimism. It seems that he found an alternative in two older literary traditions—in nineteenth century English Romantic humanism and in a comedy that he considers typically Jewish. Unlike the modernists, who denigrate the concept of the individual, Bellow believes in the potential of the self and its powerful imagination that can redeem ordinary existence and affirm the value of freedom, love, joy, and hope.

Although comedy in Bellow is a complex matter, its primary function seems to be to undercut the dejection that threatens his heroes. The comic allows Bellow's protagonists to cope with the grim facts of existence; it enables them to avoid despair and gain a balanced view of their problematical situation. Comedy, the spirit of reason, allows them to laugh away their irrational anxieties. Often Bellow seemed to encourage his worst anxieties in order to bring them out into the open so that he could dispose of them by comic ridicule.

Seize the Day • If *The Adventures of Augie March* presents Bellow's alternative to a "literature of victimization," his subsequent novels can be regarded as probing, exploratory studies in spiritual survival in a hostile environment.

Seize the Day is a much more somber novel than *The Adventures of Augie March.* Bellow believed that his liberation from Flaubertian formalism had gone too far, and that he must use more restraint in his fourth novel. He realized that Augie was too effusive and too naïve. The protagonist of *Seize the Day* is similar to the protagonists of the first two novels, but while Tommy Wilhelm is a "victim," Bellow's attitude toward him is different from his attitude toward Joseph and Asa Leventhal. In his fourth novel, Bellow sought to show the spiritual rebirth of such a "victim."

The short novel, divided into seven parts, presents the day of reckoning in the life of a forty-four-year-old ex-salesman of children's furniture whose past consists of a series of blunders. Living in the Hotel Gloriana (which is also the residence of his wealthy father, Dr. Adler), Wilhelm feels that he is in a desperate situation. He is unemployed and unable to obtain money from his unsympathetic father. He gives his last seven hundred dollars to be invested for him by the mysterious psychologist Dr. Tamkin, a man who has become not only his surrogate father and financial adviser but also his instructor in spiritual and philosophical matters. Furthermore, Wilhelm's wife, Margaret, from whom he is separated, is harassing him for money. Depressed and confused by the memories of his failures in the past and absorbed by his problems in the present, Wilhelm needs love and compassion. Dr. Adler, Dr. Tamkin, and Margaret all fail him.

Seize the Day is a harsh indictment of a money-obsessed society, where a father is unable to love a son who is unsuccessful. Tamkin's speech on the two souls, no doubt the most important passage in the novel, helps clarify Bellow's social criticism. The psychologist argues that there is a war between man's "pretender soul," his social self, and his "real soul." When the pretender soul parasitically dominates its host, as is common in modern society, one becomes murderous. If one is true to the real soul, however, and casts off the false pretender soul, one can learn to love and "seize the day."

Bellow shows that all of the characters in the novel are products of an exploitative, materialistic society—all are dominated by their pretender souls. Dr. Adler has fought his way up the economic ladder to success. Revered by the residents of the Hotel Gloriana, he is full of self-love. He desires to spend his remaining years in peace and refuses to acknowledge his paternal obligation to his desperate son. Wilhelm's appeals for money are actually pleas for some sign of paternal concern. He provokes his father, trying to disturb the polite barrier of aloofness that the old man has constructed to prevent any kind of real communication between father and son. Although Wilhelm is a difficult son for a father to cherish, Dr. Adler is a cold-hearted man who has no real affection for his son, or for anyone else except for himself. When, at the end of the novel, Wilhelm begs him for some kind of sympathy, the hard-boiled Adler brutally rejects him, revealing his hatred for his "soft" son.

Dr. Adler's failure as a father results in Wilhelm's turning to the strange psychologist Dr. Tamkin. Down on his luck, Tamkin is a confidence man hoping to make easy money. He is another one of Bellow's eccentric fast talkers, full of fantastic stories and philosophical and psychological insights. Wilhelm is attracted to him not only because he is a father figure who promises to save him from his dire financial crisis but also because he is one man in a cynical society who speaks of spiritual matters. The direct result of Tamkin's advice is the loss of Wilhelm's money, but while the doctor is a phony whose flamboyant personality enables him to dupe the naïve ex-salesman, he does indirectly allow Wilhelm to obtain a kind of salvation.

Wilhelm is the only character in the novel who is able to forsake his pretender soul. He is a product of society as the other characters are, but he is different from them in his instinctive distaste for the inveterate cynicism at the heart of society. Accepting society's definition of success, he considers himself a failure. He suffers immensely and constantly ponders his life and his errors in the past. However, while he can at times degenerate into a buffoon indulging in self-pity and hostility, he is also attracted to the idealism that Tamkin occasionally expounds.

A significant moment occurs near the end of the novel when Wilhelm suddenly feels a sense of brotherhood with his fellow travelers in the New York subway. For once he has transcended his self-absorption, though he is immediately skeptical of this intuitive moment. At the very end of the novel, there is another heightened moment in which he does make the breakthrough foreshadowed in the subway scene. Having lost all of his money, he pursues into a funeral home a man who resembles Tamkin. Suddenly he finds himself confronting a corpse, and he begins to weep uncontrollably. His weeping is not merely out of self-pity, as some have suggested, but for humankind. Understanding that death and suffering are an inextricable part of the human condition, he feels humility and is able to overcome his excessive self-absorption. He is finally able to cast off his pretender soul. The work concludes with a powerful affirmation and suggests an alternative to the spiritual death of a materialistic, predatory society.

Henderson the Rain King • Bellow's next novel, *Henderson the Rain King*, is the first fully realized work of his maturity. It is Bellow's first novel of which one can say that no other writer could have conceived it, much less written it. Although it has some characteristics of the picaresque, the fable, and the realistic novel, *Henderson the Rain King* assumes the most widely used form for longer works during the English romantic era—the quest-romance. The tone of the novel is somewhat different from that typically heard in the quest-romance, however; it is exuberant and comic, and the book is full of wit, parody, farce, and ironic juxtapositions.

The novel might be seen as Bellow's version of Joseph Conrad's *Heart of Darkness* (1902). Like Conrad's Marlow, Eugene Henderson recalls his journey into the heart of Africa and his bizarre adventures there, which culminate in his meeting with a Kurtz-like instructor who has a profound influence upon him. Although Kurtz reveals to Marlow man's potential for degradation, Dahfu conveys to Henderson man's promise of nobility. With its allusions to William Wordsworth, Samuel Taylor Coleridge, Percy Bysshe Shelley, and William Blake, the novel affirms the possibility of the individual's regeneration by the power of the human imagination; it is a trenchant rejection of Conrad's pessimism.

The novel can be divided into three basic parts: Chapters 1-4 depict Henderson's alienation; chapters 5-9 present his journey to the African tribe of the Arnewi; and chapters 10-22 portray his journey to the African tribe of the Wariri and his spiritual regeneration.

The first section presents Henderson's discursive recollections of his life before he set out for Africa, in which he attempts to reveal the reasons for the journey. Although these chapters provide a plethora of information about him, he is never able to articulate the reasons for his "quest," as he calls it. Bellow is suggesting in this section that there are no clear-cut reasons for the African journey. Henderson leaves his wife and family for the African wilderness because of his dissatisfaction with his meaningless existence. A millionaire with tremendous energy but no scope for it, Henderson has spent most of his life suffering or making others suffer. Middle-aged, anxious about his mortality, and unable to satisfy the strident inner voice of "I want, I want," he leaves for Africa, hoping to burst "the spirit's sleep," as he phrases it, echoing Shelley's *The Revolt of Islam* (1818).

With his loyal guide Romilayu, he first visits the Arnewi tribe. These people are "children of light" who represent a healthy existence; they are gentle, peaceful, and innocent. Queen Willatale, who rules the tribe, informs Henderson that man wants to live—"grun-tu-molani." It is an important message for Henderson, but he soon demonstrates that he is unable to follow Willatale's wisdom. Desiring to help the tribe, whose water supply has been infested by frogs, he decides to kill the creatures. His bomb is too powerful and destroys the cistern as well as the frogs. Henderson has violated the code of the Arnewi, who abhor violence and have love for all living creatures.

After Henderson leaves the Arnewi, he visits the Wariri, "the children of darkness," who are violent and hostile, reminiscent of the predatory society of Bellow's earlier novels. He does meet one extraordinary individual, however, and establishes a friendship with him. King Dahfu is a noble man who completes Henderson's education begun with the Arnewi. He perceptively observes that Henderson's basic problem is his avoidance of death: He is an "avoider." Dahfu helps him by persuading him to go down into a lion's den to overcome his anxiety over mortality. Dahfu believes, too, that Henderson can absorb qualities of the lion and slough off his porcine characteristics.

Dahfu is another one of Bellow's eccentric teachers who speaks both wisdom and nonsense. His greatest importance for Henderson is that he embodies the nobility of man, who can by the power of his imagination achieve spiritual regeneration. At the end of the novel, Henderson finally bursts the spirit's sleep and leaves Africa for America. He has a sense of purpose and can love others. He plans to become a physician and will return home to his wife.

Herzog • *Herzog* is by most accounts Bellow's best and most difficult novel. It is a retrospective meditation by a middle-aged professor who seeks to understand the reasons for his disastrous past. A complex discursive work, pervaded by sardonic humor, it defies traditional labeling but owes a debt to the novel of ideas, the psychological novel, the epistolary novel, and the romantic meditative lyric. *Herzog* is a meditative work in which the protagonist compulsively remembers and evaluates his past, striving to avoid complete mental breakdown. There are reminiscences within reminiscences, and the story of Moses Herzog's life is related in fragments. Bellow's method enables the reader to see how Herzog's imagination recollects and assembles the fragments of the past into a meaningful pattern.

Distraught over his recent divorce from his second wife, Madeleine, Herzog has become obsessed with writing letters to everyone connected with that event as well as to important thinkers, living and dead, who concern him. He associates his domestic crisis with the cultural crisis of Western civilization, and therefore he ponders the ethics of Friedrich Nietzsche as well as those of his psychiatrist, Dr. Edvig. His letter-writing is both a symptom of his psychological disintegration and an attempt to meditate upon and make sense of suffering and death.

At his home in the Berkshires, Herzog recalls and meditates upon the events of his recent past; the five-day period of time that he recalls reveals the severity of his psychological deterioration. His mistress Ramona believes that a cure for his nervous state can be found in her Lawrentian sexual passion, but he considers her "ideology" to be mere hedonism; impulsively, he decides to flee from her to Martha's Vineyard, where he has friends. After arriving there, the unstable professor leaves almost immediately and returns to New York. The next evening he has dinner with Ramona and spends the night with her, waking in the middle of the night to write another letter. The following morning he visits a courtroom while waiting for a meeting with his lawyer to discuss a lawsuit against Madeleine. Hearing a brutal child-abuse and murder case causes the distraught professor to associate Madeleine and her lover with the brutal child-murderers; he flies to Chicago to murder them. As he spies upon them, he realizes his assumption is absurd and abandons his plan. The next morning he takes his young daughter Junie for an outing but has a car accident and is arrested by the police for carrying a gun. He confronts an angry Madeleine at the police station and manages to control his own temper. Later, he is released and returns to his run-down home in the Berkshires, and the novel ends where it began.

Interspersed within these recollections of the immediate past are memories of the more distant past. By piecing these together, one learns the sad story of Herzog's domestic life. Feeling a vague dissatisfaction, the successful professor divorced his first wife Daisy, a sensible midwestern woman, and began affairs with a good-natured Japanese woman, Sono, and the beautiful, bad-tempered Madeleine. After marrying Madeleine, Herzog purchased a house in the Berkshires, where he intended to complete his important book on the Romantics. Soon they returned to Chicago, however, where both saw a psychiatrist, and Madeleine suddenly announced that she wanted a divorce. The shocked Herzog traveled to Europe to recuperate, only to return to Chicago to learn that Madeleine had been having an affair with his best friend and confidant the whole time their marriage had been deteriorating.

Herzog's grim past—his disastrous marriages and the other sad events of his life that he also recalls—becomes emblematic of the pernicious influence of cultural nihilism. Herzog is devoted to basic humanist values but wonders if he must, as the ubiquitous "reality-instructors" insist, become another mass man devoted to a brutal "realism" in the Hobbesian jungle of modern society. His antipathy for the wastelanders' cynicism is strong, but he knows his past idealism has been too naïve. Repeatedly, the "reality instructors" strive to teach ("punish") Herzog with lessons of the "real"—and the "real" is always brutal and cruel. Sandor Himmelstein, Herzog's lawyer and friend, proudly announces that all people are "whores." It is an accurate description not only of Himmelstein but also of his fellow reality instructors. Their cynical view is pervasive in modern society, in which people play roles, sell themselves, and seduce and exploit others for their own selfish ends.

The turning point of the novel is Herzog's revelation in the courtroom episode. Intellectually, he has always known about evil and suffering, but emotionally he has remained innocent. His hearing of the case in which a mother mistreats and murders her son while her lover apathetically watches is too much for him to bear; here is a monstrous evil that cannot be subsumed by any intellectual scheme. In a devastating moment the professor is forced to realize that his idealism is foolish.

At the end of the novel, Herzog has achieved a new consciousness. He recognizes that he has been selfish and excessively absorbed in intellectual abstractions. A prisoner of his private intellectual life, he has cut himself off from ordinary humanity and everyday existence. He sees that his naïve idealism and the wastelanders' cruel "realism" are both escapist and therefore unacceptable attitudes; they allow the individual to evade reality by wearing masks of naïve idealism or self-serving cynicism. The exhausted Herzog decides to abandon his compulsive letter-writing and to stop pondering his past. The threat of madness has passed, and he is on the road to recovery.

Mr. Sammler's Planet • *Mr. Sammler's Planet* is a meditative novel of sardonic humor and caustic wit. The "action" of the novel centers upon the protagonist's recollection of a brief period of time in the recent past, though there are recollections of a more distant past, too. Once again, the mental state of the protagonist is Bellow's main concern. Like Herzog, Artur Sammler has abandoned a scholarly project because he finds rational explanations dissatisfying; they are unable to justify suffering and death. The septuagenarian Sammler is yet another of Bellow's survivors, a lonely humanist in a society populated by brutal "realists."

This seventh novel, however, is not merely a repetition of Bellow's previous works. Sammler is detached and basically unemotional, yet he reveals a mystical bent largely absent in Bellow's other protaganists. He is drawn to the works of Meister Eckhart and other thirteenth century German mystics. Although he does not literally believe in their ideas, he finds reading their works soothing. His religious inclination is a recent phenomenon.

Sammler had been reared in a wealthy, secular Jewish family in Krakow. As an adult, he became a haughty, cosmopolitan intellectual, useless to everyone, as he readily admits. On a visit to Poland in 1939, when the Germans suddenly attacked, he, his wife, and others were captured and ordered to dig their own graves as the Nazis waited to murder them. Although his wife was killed in the mass execution, miraculously he escaped by crawling out of his own grave. After the war ended, Sammler and his daughter Shula were rescued from a displaced persons camp by a kind nephew, Dr. Elya Gruner, who became their patron.

The experience of the Holocaust destroyed what little religious inclination Sammler possessed, but in his old age he has become concerned with his spiritual state. However, it is difficult to pursue spiritual interests in a materialistic society hostile to them. The basic conflict in the novel is between Sammler's need to ponder the basic questions of existence—a need accentuated by the dying of the noble Gruner—and the distractions of contemporary society. In the primary action of the novel, Sammler's main intention is to visit the dying Gruner, who finds Sammler a source of great comfort. Several "accidents" distract Sammler from his goal, and on the day of his nephew's death, he arrives too late.

The "accidents" that encumber Sammler reveal clearly the "degraded clowning" of contemporary society. Sammler is threatened by a black pickpocket who corners the old man and then exposes himself. In the middle of a lecture he is shouted down by a radical student who says that Sammler is sexually defective. His daughter Shula steals a manuscript from an Indian scholar, and Sammler must waste precious time to recover it. Even Gruner's self-centered children, who have little compassion for their dying father, distract Sammler by their thoughtless actions.

Opposed to Gruner, who is part of the "old system" that esteems the family, the expression of emotion, and the traditional humanist values, is the contemporary generation, a kind of "circus" characterized by role-playing, hedonism, amorality, self-centeredness, and atrophy of feeling. Despite its flaws, Bellow sympathizes with the "old system." The novel concludes after Sammler, despite the objections of the hospital staff, goes into the postmortem room and says a prayer for Gruner's soul.

Humboldt's Gift • As in Bellow's previous novels, the tension and the humor of *Humboldt's Gift* have their origin in the protagonist's attempt to free himself from the distractions of contemporary society and pursue the needs of his soul. The protagonist Charlie Citrine strives to define for himself the function of the artist in contemporary America. He tries to come to terms with the failure and premature death of his one-time mentor, Von Humboldt Fleisher, who had the potential to be America's greatest modern poet but achieved very little. Charlie wonders if the romantic poet can survive in a materialistic society; he wonders, too, if he can overcome his fear of the grave and exercise his imagination. A writer who has squandered his talent, Charlie has intimations of terror of the grave and intimations of immortality. He spends much time reading the anthroposophical works of Rudolf Steiner; although he is skeptical of some of Steiner's more esoteric teachings, he is sympathetic to the spiritual world view of anthroposophy, even finding the notion of reincarnation quite persuasive.

The primary nemesis of Charlie's spiritual life is Ronald Cantabile, a small-time criminal. Renata, Charlie's voluptuous mistress, Denise, his ex-wife, and Pierre Thaxter, a confidence man, are also major distractions. When Charlie, on the advice of a friend, refuses to pay Cantabile the money he owes him from a poker game, the criminal harasses him. In fact, the proud, psychopathic Cantabile refuses to leave Charlie alone even after he agrees to pay him the money. He continually humiliates Charlie and even tries to involve him in a plot to murder the troublesome Denise.

Denise, Renata, and Thaxter also distract Charlie from pondering the fate of Humboldt and meditating upon fundamental metaphysical questions. Hoping Charlie will return to her, Denise refuses to settle her support suit and continues to demand more money. When Charlie is forced to put up a $200,000 bond, he is financially ruined, and the loss of his money results in the loss of the voluptuous Renata, who decides to marry a wealthy undertaker. A third disillusioning experience involves Thaxter, who has apparently conned Charlie. Charlie had invested a small fortune in a new journal, *The Ark*, which was supposed to restore the authority of art and culture in the United States. Thaxter, the editor of *The Ark*, never puts out the first issue and has, it appears, stolen the money. His confidence game symbolizes America's lack of respect for art and culture, impractical subjects in a practical, technological society.

Charlie does, however, overcome these "distractions." Humboldt's posthumously delivered letter, accompanied by an original film sketch (his "gift") and a scenario that the two had written at Princeton years before, provides the genesis for Charlie's salvation. The original film idea and the scenario of their Princeton years enable Charlie to attain financial security, but more important, Humboldt's letter provides the impetus for Charlie's decision at the end of the novel to repudiate his past empty life and to pursue the life of the imagination. Humboldt's ideas, bolstered by the poetry of Blake, Wordsworth, and John Keats, enable Charlie to avoid the fate of the self-destructive artist. He decides to live in Europe and meditate upon the fundamental questions—in short, to take up a different kind of life.

When, at the end of the novel, Charlie gives Humboldt and the poet's mother a proper burial, Bellow suggests that Charlie's imagination is ready to exert itself and wake him from his self-centered boredom and death-in-life. The final scene of the novel promises Charlie's spiritual regeneration.

The Dean's December • Bellow's 1982 novel, *The Dean's December*, is "a tale of two cities," Chicago and Bucharest, in which the protagonist, a dean at an unnamed college in Chicago, ponders private and public problems. Albert Corde experiences at first hand the rigid penitentiary society of the communist East as well as the anarchic society of the noncommunist West, which seems on the verge of disintegration. The novel is a protest against the dehumanization of the individual. The East has enslaved its population, while the West has "written off" its doomed "Underclass." Like *Humboldt's Gift*, this novel can be seen as a kind of retrospective crisis meditation in which the protagonist attempts to come to terms with an immensely complex and threatening "multiverse," as Augie March calls it.

The complicated plot defies a succinct summary, but one can outline the basic situation. The dean and his wife, Minna, arrive in Rumania to visit her dying mother. Corde tries to help his despairing wife, who is unable to reconcile herself to the grim reality of her mother's death. He also ponders the controversy that he has provoked in Chicago. The dean has published two articles in *Harper's* in which he comments upon the political and social problems of the city. The articles outrage the powerful members of Chicago society, and the administration of his college disapproves of the controversy that the dean has provoked. Moreover, Corde creates another controversy when he pressures the police to solve the murder of a white graduate student, Rickie Lester. A sensational trial, a media "circus," is the result of the dean's search for justice.

Although more than any other novel by Bellow, *The Dean's December* is concerned with contemporary public issues, especially the vile conditions of the inner city, it is also concerned with the spiritual state of the individual. In fact, Bellow suggests that there is a connection between the spiritual malady of the individual and the spiritual anarchy of society. The novel is a protest against not only people's lack of political freedom but also the spiritual enslavement that is the result of their inability to see clearly and to experience reality. Corde implies that this inability to experience reality is largely a product of "seeing" the world with a kind of reductive journalism completely lacking in imagination. Disgusted with contemporary journalism that provides only substitutes for reality, Corde intends to incorporate "poetry" into writing. The novel suggests that in Corde's kind of poetic vision there is hope for the spiritual rebirth of the individual and society.

More Die of Heartbreak • Three years after the publication of his collection *Him with His Foot in His Mouth, and Other Stories*, Bellow published *More Die of Heartbreak*. This comic novel does not have a highly structured plot but might be best described as an elaborate monologue from the overstimulated mind of the bachelor narrator, Kenneth Trachtenberg. Kenneth, an expert in Russian history and culture, is preoccupied with his uncle, Benn Crader, a renowned botanist. The only important "action" in the novel revolves around the attempt of Dr. Layamon, his daughter Matilda, and her fiancé Benn Crader to "extort" money from Benn's relative, Harold Vilitzer, a political racketeer in bad health. Years before, Vilitzer had cheated the Crader family in a real estate deal. The greedy Dr. Layamon sees his daughter's marriage to Benn as a marvelous opportunity to acquire a fortune if Benn will agree to pressure Vilitzer for the money the corrupt politician stole from the Crader family. Although he wants to please his beautiful fiancé and her father, Benn is not enthusiastic about the plan. As the narrator suggests, Benn is a man who should be in search of "higher meanings."

At the end of the novel, Benn flees from the Layamons to the North Pole to carry out his research. The implication is that now he will be able to pursue his neglected aesthetic and metaphysical goals.

A Theft • After being rejected by two periodicals because it was "too long," the short novel *A Theft* was published in 1989 as a paperback original. Like so many of Bellow's works, the plot of this 109-page novel is subordinate to Bellow's interest in character. Just as *Seize the Day* might be considered an intimate psychological exploration of Wilhelm, *A Theft* is a detailed exploration of the soul of the heroine. Clara Velde was brought up on old-time religion but has led a disorganized life, including disappointing love affairs, suicide attempts, and four marriages. Her fourth marriage is not successful, and she is actually in love with "an old flame," Ithiel Regler, a Henry Kissinger-like high-powered adviser to statesmen. For Clara, transcendent love between her and Ithiel is symbolized by an emerald ring that he gave her years ago. When this ring is stolen, Clara finds herself in a troubling search for it and experiences a kind of spiritual quest as well. She feels a special sense of kinship with her self-possessed au pair girl, Gina. In its epiphany-like quality, the conclusion of the novel is reminiscent of *Seize the Day.*

The Bellarosa Connection • Another paperback original, the short novel *The Bellarosa Connection* is narrated by the wealthy founder of the Mnemosyne Institute in Philadelphia. The institute instructs businesspersons and others in the use of memory. The narrator, a retired widower, focuses his immense powers of recollection on two relatives who haunt him—Harry and Sorella Fonstein. Harry narrowly escaped the Nazi death camps, thanks to the Broadway producer Billy Rose, who made use of his gangster connections in Italy to help Fonstein and others escape to freedom. Billy Rose's generosity is particularly noteworthy, the narrator implies, because the Broadway producer has a sleazy reputation.

In the United States, Harry marries the intelligent, capable Sorella and becomes successful but is frustrated by Rose's repulsing Harry's repeated attempts to meet him and express his gratitude. The central scene of the novel is the dramatic encounter between Sorella and Billy Rose, in which the determined woman attempts to coerce the stubborn producer into meeting her husband by threatening to reveal sordid details of Rose's private life. Despite Sorella's "blackmail," Rose refuses to meet Harry.

As in "The Old System," Bellow in this short novel is pondering how the assimilation of Jews into American life can corrupt not only their values but also their souls. Sorella reflects: "The Jews could survive everything that Europe threw at them. I mean the lucky remnant. But now comes the next test—America." Apparently the United States proves "too much" for at least some of them.

The Actual • The novella *The Actual* is narrated by Harry Trellman, an introspective man in his sixties who grew up in a lower-middle-class Jewish neighborhood in Chicago. His father was a simple carpenter; his mother's family was wealthy. Harry was put in an orphanage despite the fact that both his parents were alive because his hypochondriacal mother did not have the time to care for him; she spent much time abroad and in the United States at various sanitariums looking for a cure for her disease of the joints. The bills for sojourns abroad and at home were paid by the mother's family; her brothers were successful sausage manufacturers who could pay for the cures she took at Bad Nauheim or Hot Springs, Arkansas.

After the Korean War, the government sent Harry to study Chinese at a "special school." He spent a number of years in the Far East, the final two in Burma, where he made business connections, and then returned to Chicago, where he had "unfinished emotional business." Although the precise source of Harry's income is not clear, apparently he is well off. Semiretired and without financial concerns, Harry is nevertheless far from being content. For more than four decades he has loved Amy Wustrin, whom he first knew in high school. When Harry returned to Chicago after his Far East sojourn, he and Amy met again. Despite for Harry a momentous sexual encounter in which he kissed Amy "under the breast and inside the thigh," the relationship did not progress. After divorcing her first husband, she married Jay Wustrin, Harry's best friend in high school. Both Jay and Amy did not pay much heed to their marriage vows, and the result was a bitter divorce that culminated in Jay's playing tapes in divorce court of Amy's adulterous lovemaking in which one could hear her orgasmic cries. None of this disheartening history dampened Harry's ardent love for Amy.

Harry and Amy are brought together by the ninety-two-year-old billionaire Sigmund Adletsky, for whom Amy is working as an interior decorator and Harry as adviser in his "brain trust." Harry accompanies Amy in her emotionally arduous task of exhuming Jay's body from his cemetery plot next to the grave of Amy's mother so that Amy can bury her father there. (A practical joker with nihilistic proclivities, Jay had purchased the plot from Amy's father.) In the grave scene that concludes the novel, the withdrawn intellectual Harry takes decisive action by confessing his love for Amy and asking her to marry him. This scene is reminiscent of the conclusion to *Humboldt's Gift*, when the protagonist in the cemetery achieves an epiphany and the work ends with the implication that the protagonist, keenly aware of mortality and the death-in-life of his past existence, will be spiritually reborn.

Ravelstein • Like its title character, *Ravelstein*, is a puzzling work. At once a mass of fact and observations on history, philosophy, and the world-at-large, the book appears to be composed of a series of discontinuous scenes and repetitious pronouncements affirming the genius of Abe Ravelstein, professor, best-selling author, and would-be celebrity. Yet when the narrator, Chick, reveals that as Ravelstein's friend and admirer he has been selected by the professor to write his memoirs, the scheme of the novel's structure becomes clear, the apparent disjointedness a mark of the narrator's admiration and puzzlement. *Ravelstein* is thus a tribute to a great man and a cautionary tale illustrating his weaknesses.

Though Ravelstein is a worldly success, a big man with big appetites, almost a kind of cult leader among young intellectuals, he is, as his name implies, a "complicated" fellow whose real sympathies lie "knotted" and "tangled" amid the blandishments of the physical world. Seduced by success and fame into pursuing an extravagant lifestyle, Ravelstein enjoys all the pleasures of the modern world while pontificating to Chick in a tone of hardened cynicism.

Chick is amused, even impressed by the breadth and seeming wisdom of Ravelstein's knowledge, from the political origins of twentieth century Germany to the courtship rituals of native South American headhunters. Ravelstein's opinions permeate Chick's life, and Abe Ravelstein himself is the last of a long line of fast-talking hustlers and con men who fill Bellow's books, characters such as Einhorn in *The Adventures of Augie March* and Tamkin in *Seize the Day*.

Though there is a bit of the charlatan in Abe Ravelstein, he is not spiritually bankrupt. While he gently mocks what he considers Chick's conventional idealism and his capacity for hope, he insists that Chick write his biography, thus revealing his own yearning for immortality, for the human need to be remembered. Throughout this final novel, Abe Ravelstein, this "raveled" human being who is both "complicated" and at "loose ends," admits to Chick that he is a confirmed nihilist. Ravelstein dies of acquired immunodeficiency syndrome (AIDS), and Chick himself survives a near-fatal illness near the end of the book. Chick realizes that his friend's hard-core reliance on pleasure and materialism actually disguised his basic human empathy. When he tells Chick, for instance, that the Jewish people are living witnesses to the absence of redemption, Ravelstein is confronting the great question that all of Bellow's heroes face: How does a human being come to terms with the allurements of the physical world and still preserve a spiritual integrity?

Allan Chavkin
Updated by Edward Fiorelli

Other major works

SHORT FICTION: *Mosby's Memoirs, and Other Stories*, 1968; *Him with His Foot in His Mouth, and Other Stories*, 1984; *Something to Remember Me By: Three Tales*, 1991; *Collected Stories*, 2001.

PLAYS: *The Wrecker*, pb. 1954; *The Last Analysis*, pr. 1964; *Under the Weather*, pr. 1966 (also known as *The Bellow Plays*; includes *Out from Under*, *A Wen*, and *Orange Soufflé*).

NONFICTION: *To Jerusalem and Back: A Personal Account*, 1976; *Conversations with Saul Bellow*, 1994 (Gloria L. Cronin and Ben Siegel, editors); *It All Adds Up: From the Dim Past to the Uncertain Future*, 1994.

EDITED TEXTS: *Great Jewish Short Stories*, 1963.

Bibliography

American Studies International 35 (February, 1997). A special issue on Bellow, in which a number of distinguished contributors discuss the importance of Bellow's work as a symbol of the civilization of the United States. The issue contains tributes, critiques, and analyses of Bellow's thought and art.

Atlas, James. *Bellow.* New York: Random House, 2000. A full and accessible biography, written with the cooperation of its subject. Bibliography.

Bellow, Saul. "Moving Quickly: An Interview with Saul Bellow." *Salmagundi* (Spring/Summer, 1995): 32-53. In this special section, Bellow discusses the relationship between authors and characters, John Updike, intellectuals, gender differences, Sigmund Freud, and kitsch versus avant-garde art.

Bigler, Walter. *Figures of Madness in Saul Bellow's Longer Fiction.* Bern, Switzerland: Peter Lang, 1998. This study examines the psychological makeup of Bellow's characters. Includes bibliographical references.

Bloom, Harold, ed. *Saul Bellow.* New York: Chelsea House, 1986. This volume, with an introduction by Bloom, is an omnibus of reviews and essays on Bellow. Collected here are comments on Bellow by writers such as Robert Penn Warren, Malcolm Bradbury, Tony Tanner, Richard Chase, and Cynthia Ozick. Gives the reader a good sense of early critical responses to Bellow.

Cronin, Gloria L., and L. H. Goldman, eds. *Saul Bellow in the 1980's: A Collection of Critical Essays.* East Lansing: Michigan State University Press, 1989. This anthology brings together a sampling of a wave of criticism that focuses variously on Bellow's women, his debts to Judaism, connections to theories of history, and modernism.

Freedman, William. "Hanging for Pleasure and Profit: Truth as Necessary Illusion in Bellow's Fiction." *Papers on Language and Literature* 35 (Winter, 1999): 3-27. Argues that Bellow's realism is a search for truth, not the discovery of it. Discusses how Bellow deals with the question of whether a man is isolated or a member of a human community. Contends that for Bellow the value of literature is the ceaseless search for truth in a world that promises truth but seldom provides it.

The Georgia Review 49 (Spring, 1995). A special issue on Bellow in which a number of contributors discuss his life and art, his contribution to American thought and culture, and the wide range of his works.

Hollahan, Eugene, ed. *Saul Bellow and the Struggle at the Center.* New York: AMS Press, 1996. Part of the Georgia State Literary Studies series, this volume includes bibliographical references and an index.

Kiernan, Robert. *Saul Bellow.* New York: Continuum, 1989. Provides a useful chronology of Bellow's life and production. Traces the writer's development from *Dangling Man* to *More Die of Heartbreak.* The best book on Bellow for the general reader.

Miller, Ruth. *Saul Bellow: A Biography of the Imagination.* New York: St. Martin's Press, 1991. Traces Bellow's travels, linking the author's life to his work. Contains useful appendixes, a bibliography, a listing of interviews, and a table of contents from *The Noble Savage,* a journal edited by Bellow.

Pifer, Ellen. *Saul Bellow Against the Grain.* Philadelphia: University of Pennsylvania Press, 1990. In a study that deals comprehensively with the writer's oeuvre, Pifer's central observation is that Bellow's heroes are divided against themselves and conduct an inner strife that dooms and paralyzes them. Their struggle, like Bellow's, is a search for language to articulate the modern condition.

Arna Bontemps

Born: Alexandria, Louisiana; October 13, 1902
Died: Nashville, Tennessee; June 4, 1973

Principal long fiction • *God Sends Sunday*, 1931; *Black Thunder*, 1936; *Drums at Dusk*, 1939.

Other literary forms • Arna Bontemps was a prolific author and editor. He wrote or cowrote many children's books, biographies, and histories. He edited or coedited more than a dozen works, including African American poetry anthologies, histories, slave narratives, and a folklore collection. His short stories were collected in *The Old South* (1973), and his poetry collection, *Personals*, appeared in 1963. He and Countée Cullen adapted Bontemps's novel *God Sends Sunday* for the New York stage in 1946 as *St. Louis Woman*. Bontemps's forty-two-year correspondence with writer Langston Hughes was published in 1980.

Achievements • Bontemps's finely honed poems quietly reflect his lifelong Christian beliefs. After winning several prizes for his poems and short stories during the 1920's and 1930's, Bontemps was granted the first of two Rosenwald Fellowships in Creative Writing in 1939 (the other came in 1943). In 1949 and 1954 he received Guggenheim Fellowships for creative writing. He was given the Jane Addams Children's Book Award in 1956 for *The Story of the Negro* and was also runner-up for the Newbery Award. In 1969 he was appointed writer-in-residence at Fisk University, and in 1972 he was named honorary consultant to the Library of Congress in American cultural history. Beginning during the 1960's he was a popular national speaker, and he always offered encouragement to struggling black writers. He was loved and respected by his students, wherever he served as a teacher.

Biography • Arna Wendell Bontemps's parentage was Louisiana Creole. He was born in the front bedroom of his maternal grandfather's comfortable home at the corner of Ninth and Winn Streets in Alexandria, Louisiana. The house is still standing, though it has been moved, and is today the Arna Bontemps African American Museum. Bontemps's father, a skilled stonemason, bricklayer, and former trombonist with a New Orleans marching band, moved with his wife, children, and in-laws to California following a racial incident in Louisiana. The elder Bontemps also served as a Seventh-day Adventist preacher after he abandoned Roman Catholicism.

Bontemps's earliest childhood was spent happily in his grandparents' house in Alexandria. Later, in California, he recalled being greatly influenced by a great-uncle, Uncle Buddy, who came from Alexandria to stay with his relatives in California. Though Uncle Buddy was a down-at-the-heels alcoholic, he nevertheless represented, for young Bontemps, the essence of Louisiana culture, folklore, and history with his colorful stories and speech. Self-educated, intelligent, and articulate, Uncle Buddy was a good reader and storyteller and awakened in his grandnephew a love of hearing and telling stories and of reading and reciting poetry. Most important, Uncle Buddy reminded young Bontemps of his Louisiana and southern roots, which

Library of Congress

were later to be a great literary storehouse for the budding author.

Bontemps's mother died when he was ten, and he and his sister went to live on his grandmother's farm near Los Angeles. Bontemps completed his secondary schooling at a private boarding school and his bachelor's degree at Pacific Union College in California. In New York he joined the Harlem Renaissance, which was in full swing, and began a close, lifelong friendship with writer Langston Hughes.

Bontemps taught school in New York, married Alberta Jones when he was twenty-four, and subsequently fathered six children. In 1931 Bontemps and his family moved to Alabama, where he taught in a junior college and observed southern behavior and customs. In 1934 Bontemps and his family left Alabama because of a hostile racial climate following the trial of the Scottsboro Nine, black men who were unjustly convicted of raping two white women, and moved into his father's small house in California. There the author worked on his second novel, frequently writing outdoors with his small portable typewriter on a makeshift desk.

By 1943 he had moved to Chicago, where he earned a master's degree in library science. Accepting an appointment as full professor and head librarian at Fisk University in Nashville, he served there until the mid-1960's, when he accepted a professorship in history and literature at the University of Illinois at Chicago Circle. He also served as curator of the James Weldon Johnson Collection.

In 1969 he retired to work on his autobiography, which was unfinished at his death. In 1972 he published *The Harlem Renaissance Remembered* and returned to visit his birthplace in Louisiana. He died on June 4, 1973, and was honored at both Protestant and Roman Catholic memorial services.

Analysis • Though he lived and taught in many parts of America, Bontemps always identified with the South and set most of his fictional works there. Bontemps greatly valued his African American inheritance and tried to increase both racial pride and understanding through his many books about African American figures, life, and culture.

God Sends Sunday • *In God Sends Sunday*, set during the 1890's, Bontemps depicts a diminutive black jockey, Little Augie, who lives on a Red River plantation in Louisiana with his older sister. Because he was born with a caul over his face, he is thought to be lucky. He discovers a talent for riding horses, which serves him well when he escapes to New Orleans on a steamboat and becomes a jockey. Augie grows rich, arrogant, and ostentatious. He falls in love with a beautiful young mulatto, Florence Desseau, but learns, to his sorrow, that she is the mistress of his rich white patron. Going to St. Louis to find a woman like Florence, Augie falls in with a crowd of prostitutes, gamblers, and "sugar daddies," one of whom he murders when the man bothers Augie's woman. Returning to New Orleans, Augie at last has Florence as his lover. However, she deserts him, taking his money and possessions. Augie's luck fades, and he declines rapidly into penury and alcoholism. In California, Augie commits another "passion murder" and escapes to Mexico.

The novel exhibits a remarkable joie de vivre among its black characters, but they are primarily caricatures within a melodramatic plot. Bontemps uses black dialect and folklore effectively, however, especially the blues, for which Augie has a great affection.

Black Thunder • Bontemps's second novel, first published in 1936, was reissued in 1968 with a valuable introduction by Bontemps. In this essay, he describes finding a treasured store of slave narratives in the Fisk Library; he read the stories of slave insurrectionists Nat Turner, Denmark Vesey, and Gabriel Prosser. Bontemps identified Prosser as the slave-rebel-hero whose yearning for freedom most greatly resembled his own.

Black Thunder is generally acknowledged by readers and critics alike to be Bontemps's best novel; it has even been called the best African American historical novel. The French Revolution and the slave rebellion in Santo Domingo are a significant background; the story dramatizes an enslaved people's long-restrained desire for freedom. Bundy, an old black peasant, longs for the freedom that the legend of Haitian liberator Toussaint-Louverture has inspired in many slaves. When Bundy is viciously flogged to death, Gabriel Prosser, a strong young coachman, feels driven to seek freedom for himself and his people. This feeling is even held by already-freed slaves, such as Mingo, a leather worker, who plays a major role in the rebellion effort. The white Virginians, both patricians and common folk, hold Creuzot, a French painter, and Biddenhurst, a British lawyer, responsible for the slaves' disquiet. Moreover, the white population does not believe the slaves to be human; thus, they cannot understand why they would want freedom. The whites' interpretation of the Bible supports their racial beliefs.

Gabriel too is deeply religious, though not fanatical, and often echoes scripture, believing that God will free his people because Armageddon is at hand. He plans, with the assistance of free blacks, slaves, and a few sympathetic whites, to capture the arsenal at Richmond in order to seize the weapons and overpower the city. However, a monsoonlike rainstorm on the night of the rebellion causes a delay in the insurrection. Bontemps's powers as a prose artist are especially strong as he describes, in haunting cadences, the revolt's defeat by nature's wrath. The slaves believe that it was ill luck and fateful weather that led to the revolt's collapse, though in actuality two elderly, spoiled house servants betrayed the cause. The collapse of the rebellion marks the climax of the story; what follows tells of the insurrectionists' capture and execution. Bontemps makes astute use of court records as he dramatizes Gabriel's trial.

Bontemps is in firmer control of his literary material in *Black Thunder* than in his other novels. All his characters—white planter-aristocrats, free blacks, and French zealots—are drawn with objectivity and restraint. Profreedom views are not praised at the expense of antifreedom beliefs. Furthermore, Bontemps's characters, even minor ones, are richly complex. For example, Ben and Pharoah, the betrayers of the rebellion, evidence conflicting loyalties both to their aristocratic masters and to their African American brothers. In a memorable interior monologue, Ben condemns himself for the narcissism that made his own survival more important to him than that of his fellow slaves. His ironic curse is that he must live under the threat of a horrible revenge at the hands of his own people.

Bontemps's special achievement in *Black Thunder* is the skill with which he integrates Gabriel's revolt into the fabric of Virginian, and American, life by using a documentary style of exposition. While Virginia legislators debate further segregation of African Americans as a way of dealing with race issues, quoted reports from Federalist newspapers oppose the liberal ideas of former president Thomas Jefferson and attribute Gabriel's revolt to his evil influence. These same newspapers support John Quincy Adams's presidential campaign.

Even more impressive is Bontemps's use of interior monologues and passages that present the point of view of several individual characters, Caucasian and African American. First-and third-person perspectives are blended in order to present both objective and subjective forces. Bontemps's careful synthesis of history and imagination helps him demonstrate the universal, age-old struggles of humankind to surmount barriers of race, class, and caste and gain equality, liberty, respect, and security. Because Bontemps allows Gabriel to maintain and even increase his integrity, he becomes a truly tragic figure for whom, at the end of the novel, "excellent is strength, the first for freedom of the blacks . . . [he is] perplexed but unafraid, waiting for the dignity of death."

Drums at Dusk • *Drums at Dusk,* like *Black Thunder,* is a historical novel in which Bontemps makes use of slave narratives and legal records to establish background for the black rebellion leading to Haiti's independence and Toussaint-Louverture's ascendancy. Bontemps centers the story around a young girl of French ancestry, Celeste Juvet, and Diron de Sautels, an aristocratic young Frenchman who claims membership in Les Amis des Noirs, embraces enthusiastically the ideas of writers of the French Revolution, and works as an abolitionist. Celeste and her grandmother reside on a large plantation where the owner's cousin, Count Armand de Sacy, abuses ailing slaves and mistreats his mistresses, abandoning them at his uncle's. De Sacy is deeply disliked, and when several slaves foment an insurrection, the aristocrats are overturned and rebel leaders successfully seize power.

Diron de Sautels's radical opinions influence young black people, and they fight with three other groups for political control of Santo Domingo: rich aristocrats, poor whites, and free mulattos. *Drums at Dusk* describes with melodramatic sensationalism the sybaritic lives of the wealthy and their sexual exploitation of light-skinned black women. Moreover, the novel describes graphically the heinous conditions on the slave ships and on many of the plantations. The patricians' cruelty and abuse lead to a rapid spread of liberal ideology and the rise of such leaders as Toussaint-Louverture.

In spite of its faults, Bontemps's last novel, like his second one, emphasizes the universal need and desire for freedom, which he intimates is as necessary for the survival of human beings as water, air, food, and shelter.

Philip A. Tapley

Other major works

SHORT FICTION: *The Old South,* 1973.

PLAY: *St. Louis Woman,* pr. 1946 (with Countée Cullen).

POETRY: *Personals,* 1963.

NONFICTION: *Father of the Blues,* 1941 (with W. C. Handy; biography); *They Seek a City,* 1945 (with Jack Conroy; revised as *Anyplace but Here,* 1966); *One Hundred Years of Negro Freedom,* 1961 (history); *Free at Last: The Life of Frederick Douglass,* 1971; *Arna Bontemps-Langston Hughes Letters: 1925-1967,* 1980.

CHILDREN'S LITERATURE: *Popo and Fifina: Children of Haiti,* 1932 (with Langston Hughes); *You Can't Pet a Possum,* 1934; *Sad-Faced Boy,* 1937; *The Fast Sooner Hound,* 1942 (with Jack Conroy); *We Have Tomorrow,* 1945; *Slappy Hooper: The Wonderful Sign Painter,* 1946 (with Conroy); *The Story of the Negro,* 1948; *Chariot in the Sky: A Story of the Jubilee Singers,* 1951; *Sam Patch,* 1951 (with Conroy); *The Story of George Washington Carver,* 1954; *Lonesome Boy,* 1955; *Frederick Douglass: Slave, Fighter, Freeman,* 1959; *Famous Negro Athletes,* 1964; *Mr. Kelso's Lion,* 1970; *Young Booker: Booker T. Washington's Early Days,* 1972; *The Pasteboard Bandit,* 1997 (with Hughes); *Bubber Goes to Heaven,* 1998.

EDITED TEXTS: *The Poetry of the Negro,* 1949 (revised, 1971; with Langston Hughes); *The Book of Negro Folklore,* 1958 (with Hughes); *American Negro Poetry,* 1963; *Great Slave Narratives,* 1969; *Hold Fast to Dreams,* 1969; *The Harlem Renaissance Remembered,* 1972.

Bibliography

Bone, Robert. "Arna Bontemps." *Down Home: A History of Afro-American Short Fiction From Its Beginnings to the End of the Harlem Renaissance.* New York: G. P. Putnam's Sons, 1975. Brief but incisive analyses of four of the stories from *The Old South:* "Boy Blue," "A Summer Tragedy," "The Cure," and "Three Pennies for Luck." Notes the use of nature symbolism and folklore in Bontemps's short stories.

Canaday, Nicholas. "Arna Bontemps: The Louisiana Heritage." *Callaloo* 4 (October-February, 1981): 163-169. Traces the significant influence of Bontemps's Louisiana great-uncle, Buddy (Joe Ward), on the author's novel *God Sends Sunday* and on "The Cure" in *The Old South.*

Fleming, Robert E. *James Weldon Johnson and Arna Wendell Bontemps: A Reference Guide.* Boston: G. K. Hall, 1978. Contains a biography of Bontemps, as well as indexes and extensive bibliographical information.

Jones, Kirkland C. "Bontemps and the Old South." *African American Review* 27, no. 2 (1993): 179-185. Argues that the Old South is employed more greatly in Bontemps's fiction than in that of any other Harlem Renaissance writer. Brief but perceptive critiques of five of *The Old South* selections: "Summer Tragedy," "The Cure," "Talk to the Music," "Boy Blue," and "Why I Returned."

____________. *Renaissance Man from Louisiana, A Biography of Arna Wendell Bontemps.* Westport, Conn.: Greenwood Press, 1992. The first full-scale biography of Bontemps. Treats the author's life and career in detail but only cursorily analyzes or evaluates the writings.

Reagan, Daniel. "Voices of Silence: The Representation of Orality in Arna Bontemps's *Black Thunder.*" *Studies in American Fiction* 19 (Spring, 1991): 71-83. Examines the use of African American vernacular traditions in *Black Thunder* and concludes that the novel's significant statements of black cultural identity occur in the oral discourse that Bontemps portrays through figurative language.

Stone, Albert. "The Thirties and the Sixties: Arna Bontemps's *Black Thunder.*" In *The Return of Nat Turner: History, Literature, and Cultural Politics in Sixties America.* Athens: University of Georgia Press, 1992. Examines Bontemps's successful synthesis of history and his own imagination in *Black Thunder.*

Yardley, Jonathan. Review of *The Old South. The New York Times Book Review* (December, 1973): 11. Comments on the impression of informality and chattiness the reader gets on a first reading of Bontemps's stories, but a second reading reveals the author's concern about race relations while avoiding bitterness.

Paul Bowles

Born: New York, New York; December 30, 1910
Died: Tangier, Morocco; November 18, 1999

Principal long fiction • *The Sheltering Sky,* 1949; *Let It Come Down,* 1952; *The Spider's House,* 1955; *Up Above the World,* 1966.

Other literary forms • Paul Bowles is probably critically appreciated best for his short fiction, even though he is also known for his novels. Also famous as a translator especially of Moroccan fiction, he translated from Arabic, French, and Spanish and wrote poetry, travel literature, and even music, to which he devoted himself during the 1930's. His autobiography, *Without Stopping,* was well received when it was published in 1972.

Achievements • Bowles holds a unique place in American literature. As an exile, he shared with 1920's expatriate novelist Gertrude Stein, among others, a distanced perspective on his native culture. Through his translations, he earned an international reputation as an author with a North African sensibility. His fiction reflects a world akin to that written about by existentialists Jean-Paul Sartre or Albert Camus, and indeed he has been described as America's foremost existentialist writer, a label more likely to restrict him to a time period than to characterize his fiction accurately. Although his nihilism does strike one as a bit pretentious, it also has a modern application, reflecting as it does a dark vision of the world as contemporary as the times demand.

Bowles became a guru of sorts to the Beat generation, although Bowles's attraction for them was as much for his writings about drugs as for his generally pessimistic philosophy. Never an author of wide appeal, he has nevertheless had a loyal following among those interested in experimental and avant-garde writing, and his work has reflected a steady maturation, his 1982 experimental work *Points in Time* receiving praise from, among others, Tobias Wolfe, who wrote that the book was a completely original performance. Perhaps in the last analysis, Bowles will be best remembered for his originality, his willingness to challenge definitions and the status quo in his fiction. With every work, he tried to forge new ground.

Biography • Paul Frederic Bowles spent most of his adult life living abroad, in permanent exile, mostly in Morocco, although for brief periods he also lived in France, Mexico, and South America. Admonished as a young man by his disapproving father that he could not expect merely to sit around and loaf as a writer when at home, Bowles found places where he could sit and invite his soul.

Bowles was born in the Jamaica section of New York City, the only child of a dentist and a mother who was a former schoolteacher. He was a precocious child and began writing at an early age. By the time he was in grade school, he had also begun composing music, a passion that occupied him more than did writing until after World War I. Immediately after high school, he attended very briefly the School of Design and Liberal Arts before enrolling in the fall of 1928 as a freshman at the University of

Cherie Nutting

Virginia, a choice made primarily because it was the school attended by Edgar Allan Poe. In March, he left the university and ran off to Paris, where he was already known as the writer whose poem "Spire Song" had been published in Eugène Jolas's little magazine *transition.* Bowles returned home the next fall and went to work for Dutton's bookstore while trying to write a novel in his spare time. In the spring, he returned to Virginia to complete his freshman year, at that point he ended forever his college career.

By 1929, Bowles had met and been encouraged by American composer Aaron Copland to pursue a career as a composer by returning to Paris to study with Nadia Boulanger, which he did in the spring of 1931. His second Paris sojourn began his literary life when he met and became friends with Gertrude Stein, who took him under her ample wing and tutored him in writing. It was Stein's companion Alice Toklas who suggested that Bowles and Copland, who had joined him abroad, live someplace warm, and she suggested Morocco, to which the two composers moved in the late summer of 1931. It was the beginning of Bowles's love affair with North Africa and his life as a writer: From Tangier Bowles sent Stein his first prose efforts and received back from her the encouragement to continue writing, although, as he admitted later, it was not until the 1940's, while watching his wife, Jane, compose her first novel, that he began to work seriously at the writer's trade.

From 1931 to 1933, Bowles traveled between Europe and North Africa, gathering the impressions that would later shape his first novel, *The Sheltering Sky.* In 1933 he moved to New York City, where he made a living writing music reviews for the *Herald Tribune* and composing theater music for works by Orson Welles, Lillian Hellman, Tennessee Williams, and others.

In 1938, Bowles married Jane Auer. The couple moved to Mexico in 1940, where Jane Bowles wrote *Two Serious Ladies* (1943), the novel that inspired Bowles to take his own literary craft seriously. While he was in Mexico, Bowles composed his opera *The Wind Remains,* which premiered in New York in 1943. The opera's failure deepened Bowles's interest in pursuing fiction writing.

During that same year the Bowleses moved back to New York. There, in 1947, Paul Bowles had an overpowering dream of Tangier. The dream inspired him to begin *The*

Sheltering Sky and prompted his return to North Africa, where he traveled for a year seeking material for the novel in progress. Jane joined him in 1948, and the two settled in Tangier, where they would become the center of a lively artistic community that included writers William S. Burroughs and Brion Gysin and visitors Tennessee Williams and Truman Capote.

The Sheltering Sky was published in October of 1949, and by December it was on *The New York Times* best-seller list. During that same month, Bowles plunged into his second novel, *Let It Come Down*. Appearing in 1952, it did not receive the popular success or critical acclaim of his first novel.

While working on novels, short stories, and poems, Bowles became interested in the tales of Moroccan oral storytellers, which he began to translate. By the 1960's, he was translating Moroccan writers as well.

Jane Bowles's declining literary career came to a close with her stroke in 1957. Although she survived the illness, its debilitating effects stopped her writing and increased her problems with depression. By 1967, she had been committed to a psychiatric hospital in Spain; she died in 1973. Reacting to Jane's death, Bowles did little writing for nearly a decade, although he still actively translated. The critically acclaimed appearance of *Points in Time* (1982), an avant-garde approach to history, marked Bowles's return to writing.

Public interest in Bowles increased dramatically with the 1990 release of Bernardo Bertolucci's film version of *The Sheltering Sky*, in which Bowles had a minor part, and with the 1995 Lincoln Center Paul Bowles celebration and symposium, which Bowles attended despite failing health. On November 18, 1999, Bowles died in Tangier.

Analysis • Because of Bowles's small output of novels and because of his problematic relationship with American writing, his reputation has yet to be firmly established. A writer who always attracted attention, and serious attention at that, he has not been accorded sufficient critical notice to measure his significance as a writer. To paraphrase Johannes Willem Bertens, one of his most perceptive critics, who has written on the critical response to Bowles's work, Bowles as a novelist can be classified in three categories: romantic, existentialist, and nihilist. As a romantic, Bowles saw the modern world in a disjunctive relationship with nature, and that vision pushed him to depict the march of Western progress in very pessimistic terms, which accounts for one of his most frequently recurring themes, namely, that of a sophisticated Westerner confronting a less civilized and more primitive society in a quest of self-discovery. Such Romantic attitudes suggest the reasons for labeling Bowles as an existentialist. The search for an authentic life amid the self-doubts and the fragile, provisional nature of the civilized instincts, as Theodore Solotaroff describes it, places Bowles squarely within the existentialist tradition made more formal and philosophical by such writers as Camus and Sartre. The search for values in a world without God, a world with an ethical vacuum, suggests the third possible interpretation of Bowles's fiction, that of nihilism.

There are those critics, especially Chester E. Eisinger, who understand the novelist's universe as totally without hope, a region devoid of meaning and purpose and thereby representing a nihilistic philosophical position. This position is worked out through the clash between civilizations, or rather through the tension between civilization and the savage. Even Bowles himself remarked that life is absurd and the whole business of living hopeless, a conviction he would share with most of his central characters, thereby giving credence to any nihilistic interpretation of his fiction.

Whichever position one takes, the central details of Bowles's novels remain the same: A Westerner, often an intellectual, searches through an Eastern, less civilized culture for meaning and direction, usually finding neither by the end of the book.

The Sheltering Sky • *The Sheltering Sky* is both Bowles's first novel and his best-known novel. It was the book in which the author set forth those topics or themes that he would pursue throughout the rest of his fiction with almost obsessive tenacity. The story follows an American couple, Port and Kit Moresby, who have traveled to Morocco in search of themselves and to reinvigorate their marriage after years of indifference. The couple appear in Oran shortly after World War II and there experience a series of devastating events that eventually kill Port and destroy the mental stability of his wife, Kit.

Soon after their arrival, Port insists that they travel inland into the desert. Kit is opposed, so Port, accompanied by an Australian photographer and her son, depart, leaving Kit with Tunner, their American friend, who is to escort her on the night train later that day. Bored by the ride, Kit wanders into the fourth-class, or "native," section of the train and passes a frightening night among the Arabs, later sleeping with Tunner. Meanwhile, Port has come to the realization that he desires a reconciliation with his wife. The novel follows this hapless pair as they progress farther and farther into the heart of the country, leaving civilization more distantly behind them. Port contracts typhoid and dies, leaving his wife alone to face the rigors of the desert. She is picked up by a passing caravan and made the sexual slave of the leaders of the group. She is both entranced and repulsed by the experience and is soon completely disoriented by her subjugation. Finally, she is rescued by a member of the American embassy only to disappear once again, this time for good, into the Casbah, or "native" quarter, in Oran.

The Sheltering Sky is considered Bowles's most uncompromisingly existential work and has been read by the critics along this line, with the fragile and provisional nature of civilized instincts being put to the test against the brutality and savagery of the primitive desert. Not only does Port test his febrile psyche against overwhelming powers of the North African terrain, but also he must face the fact that he harbors in himself no reserves, no hope—for it is all too late—of anything better. Unable to commit himself to his wife, or to anything else for that matter, Port is left with a void that, in the end, exacts a heavy price, leaving him utterly alone and unequipped to face the hostile environment. So, too, Kit is stripped of her defenses and forced back on herself, only to discover that she has no inner resolve either. In the end, these two civilized Americans lack the inner strength to combat the primitive forces, both within and without, which they encounter in their North African adventures.

The novel offers a convincing portrait of the disintegration of a couple of innocents thrust into a cruel environment for which they are totally unprepared. The writing in places is luminescent, the locale wonderfully realized—so much so that the novel's shortcomings pale by comparison, leaving a work, if flawed, at least magnificently so, and convincing in its portrait of nihilism in the modern world.

Let It Come Down • Bowles's second novel, *Let It Come Down*, continues an existentialist quest by following Nelson Dyer, an American bank clerk, who throws over his job to join an old acquaintance who lives in Tangier and who offers Dyer a position in the travel agency he runs there. When he arrives, Dyer finds that his friend Jack Wilcox does not operate a successful agency and in fact seems to possess a mysterious source of income. As the story advances, Dyer's relationship with Wilcox takes on a Kafkaesque tone, as he is obviously not needed at the agency.

Out of money and in desperate need of a job, Dyer accepts an offer to help in a money scheme by transporting cash between a local bank and a shop. Realizing that he is being used for illegal purposes, Dyer takes the money he has been given and flees Tangier, only to discover that he is utterly helpless in a country where he neither speaks the language nor understands the customs. After he has killed his native guide, the novel concludes with Dyer alone and hunted in a foreign country but curiously pleased with his state of affairs as an isolated individual.

Once again, Bowles has thrust an upper-middle-class American into a North African environment and allowed him to become submerged in the native and alien culture. With his loss of identity, Dyer discovers something far more authentic about himself as he is systematically stripped of his civilized supports and is forced to fall back on what little reserves he possesses as an individual human being. This peeling away of the veneer of civilization reveals underneath an emptiness and void that leaves the protagonist, like Port Moresby, totally unprepared for the unfamiliar culture into which he is thrust. Under such pressure, he collapses and must seek refuge in internal strength, of which he possesses precious little. His plunge into an exotic culture, instead of rejuvenating him, debilitates his vigor, leaving him in a weakened if also enlightened condition.

As with other American writers, such as Edgar Allan Poe and Herman Melville, Bowles wrote of the exhaustion exacted by primitive cultures on the more civilized. It is a reversal of the romantic notion that cultured man, tired of his culture, can find rejuvenation through immersion in a more savage environment. Instead, like Joseph Conrad's heroes, Dyer finds only confusion and despair. At least, it may be argued, he discovers the truth, however unpalatable it might be, and the conclusion of the novel leaves him possessed of a dark actuality, if robbed of a comforting illusion.

The Spider's House • Bowles's next novel, *The Spider's House*, was set in 1954 against the political upheaval caused by the deposition of Morocco's hereditary ruler, Sultan Mohammed, by the colonial regime of the French. The fiction traces the tension caused by the collapse of the traditional way of life of the native inhabitants of the city of Fez through a fifteen-year-old boy, Amar, who, halfway through the novel, is befriended by John Stenham, an expatriate American writer, who has fallen in love with an American woman tourist named Lee Burroughs. By the conclusion of the novel, John leaves Fez with Lee, abandoning Amar to deal with the destruction of his way of life any way he can.

Although it is not a political novel, *The Spider's House* uses the tensions of the French colonial rule not only to highlight the theme of the disintegration of Muslim culture under the French but also to provide a backdrop against which to play out the drama of the on-again, off-again love affair between Lee and John. Amar is from a devout family but one that is not caught up in the political conflicts between the Istiqlal, the Nationalist party, with their use of terror, and the colonials. Both the French and the Nationalists are bent on stopping the ritual religious festival of *Aid el Kabir*, and Amar, who has been forbidden to leave the Medina where his family resides, gets caught outside the city's walls and is rescued by Lee and John, who have been observing the unfolding cycle of violence that is developing between the French and the Moroccans. John helps Amar return to his family through the city's walls, and Amar offers to take the couple to see the religious celebration in a village outside Fez. The

Americans are fascinated by the exotic quality of the Arab life around them and agree to accompany Amar. The festival turns out badly for them, however, when Lee is shocked and repulsed by the rituals of the feast. After a quarrel, Lee and John decide that they are beginning a love affair.

Meanwhile, Amar has received a large sum of money from Lee so that he can join the Nationalists in their fight against the French. Still apolitical, Amar again gets caught up in the action of the revolution and is manipulated by the Istiqlal, barely avoiding capture by the French. At the end of the novel, he wants to rejoin John and Lee but is rebuffed by the novelist, who is set on going off with his new lover. The fiction concludes when Amar is abandoned by his newly won friend into the political turmoil of a struggle he barely understands.

As the critics have pointed out, *The Spider's House* contains a nostalgia for a past that does not belong to either John Stenham or to Bowles, but it is a longing that is nevertheless keenly felt. It has also been described as a deeply religious book, one in which Bowles mourns for a lost religious belief no longer possible in Western civilization, with its emphasis on the rational and the scientific. Certainly, the book focuses on the consequences of destroying a traditional way of life and on a myopic colonialism that blunders along in an attempt to apply Western methods to a totally unsuitable situation. It is the story of all colonial experiences in which a foreign power tries to forge a new life for a people it only partially understands, which accentuates one of the main achievements of the book, the faithful rendering of the North African landscape with its traditions and cultures.

Up Above the World • For his fourth novel, Bowles shifted his location to South America and his plot to that of the detective novel. Yet, although seen by many critics as a genre fiction of the whodunit variety, *Up Above the World* is a far cry from a run-of-the-mill thriller. It is, in fact, a deeply psychological study of the disintegration of another couple, Taylor and Day Slade, who, much in the same vein as the Moresbys, undergo a tragic transformation that ultimately destroys them.

The Slades arrive by ship in an unidentified South American country at the port town of Puerto Farol. A woman whom they had befriended on the ship is found dead in her hotel room—murdered, it is discovered later, at the behest of her son by a thug named Thorny. The son, Grover Soto, afraid that the Slades have been a witness to the killing, hunts down the couple, who have by now taken a train to the interior of the country. The Slades are finally subjected to the use of drugs and a variety of brainwashing techniques in order to erase the memory of Mrs. Rainmantle, the murdered woman, from their minds. While recuperating at the ranch of Grover Soto, Day sees some written instructions that were to have been destroyed, and in a moment of panic, Soto drugs and then kills Taylor. As the novel concludes, he is about to do the same with Day.

The novel is a psychological thriller much in the vein of Graham Greene's "entertainments," a lesser work not demanding the exertion either to read or to write that a more serious novel requires. However, there are certain themes and characters that immediately label the book as one of Bowles's. The wandering Americans confronting themselves amid the exotic background of a less civilized and unknown world, their eventual disintegration as they experience an alien culture, and the search for meaning in what appears to be meaningless lives echo his earlier novels. Even the appearance of chance events, encounters onto which the critics have latched to tie the volume to the thriller genre, are also present in his earlier work. The big difference in *Up Above the World* is the novel's compactness. It is streamlined, and in that sense it provides a faster, perhaps more accessible read, but it is a novel no less interesting for all that.

The critics, especially Bertens, have been particularly hard on this book, largely because of its thriller status, which is unfair, since the novel goes beyond the requirements of mere genre fiction and into a netherworld of the truly black. In many ways, this book is Bowles's most pessimistic and most nihilistic, and, writing in the thriller vein, Bowles has made a contribution to the American fictional form most foreboding and dark, a form, in short, closest to his own hopeless vision.

Bowles's fiction will remain attractive both to the few who truly admire advanced writing and thinking and to a general reading audience. It is unfortunate that Bowles's reputation as a writer's writer has limited the enjoyment of his work by the public, since he not only deserves a wider readership but also has much to offer the general reader. Too easily dismissed as the product of an expatriate writer and therefore of little interest to students of American literature, Bowles's work is nevertheless central to the American literary experience, dealing as it does with the protagonist facing the frontier on the edge of civilization, a position that recalls that of Melville's Ishmael, James Fenimore Cooper's Natty Bumppo, and even Mark Twain's Huck Finn. Finally, critics and the public alike need to read Bowles's fiction for its relevant encounters between modern humankind and an increasingly mechanistic and depersonalized world, a place truly of nihilism and despair.

Charles L. P. Silet
Updated by John Nizalowski

Other major works

SHORT FICTION: *A Little Stone: Stories*, 1950; *The Delicate Prey, and Other Stories*, 1950; *The Hours After Noon*, 1959; *A Hundred Camels in the Courtyard*, 1962; *The Time of Friendship*, 1967; *Pages from Cold Point, and Other Stories*, 1968; *Three Tales*, 1975; *Things Gone and Things Still Here*, 1977; *Collected Stories of Paul Bowles, 1939-1976*, 1979; *Midnight Mass*, 1981; *In the Red Moon*, 1982; *A Distant Episode: The Selected Stories*, 1988; *Call at Corazón, and Other Stories*, 1988; *Unwelcome Words*, 1988; *A Thousand Days for Mokhtar, and Other Stories*, 1989; *The Stories of Paul Bowles*, 2001.

POETRY: *Scenes*, 1968; *The Thicket of Spring: Poems, 1926-1969*, 1972; *Next to Nothing*, 1976; *Next to Nothing: Collected Poems, 1926-1977*, 1981.

NONFICTION: *Yallah*, 1957; *Their Heads Are Green and Their Hands Are Blue*, 1963; *Without Stopping*, 1972; *Points in Time*, 1982; *Days: Tangier Journal, 1987-1989*, 1991; *Conversations with Paul Bowles*, 1993 (Gena Dagel Caponi, editor); *In Touch: The Letters of Paul Bowles*, 1994 (Jeffrey Miller, editor).

TRANSLATIONS: *The Lost Trail of the Sahara*, 1952 (of R. Frison-Roche's novel); *No Exit*, 1958 (of Jean-Paul Sartre's play); *A Life Full of Holes*, 1964 (of Driss ben Hamed Charhadi's autobiography); *Love with a Few Hairs*, 1967 (of Mohammed Mrabet's fiction); *M'Hashish*, 1969 (of Mrabet's fiction); *The Lemon*, 1969 (of Mrabet's fiction); *The Boy Who Set the Fire*, 1974 (of Mrabet's fiction); *The Oblivion Seekers*, 1975 (of Isabelle Eberhardt's fiction); *Harmless Poisons, Blameless Sins*, 1976 (of Mrabet's fiction); *Look and Move On*, 1976 (of Mrabet's fiction); *The Big Mirror*, 1977 (of Mrabet's fiction); *The Beggar's Knife*, 1985 (of Rodrigo Rey Rosa's fiction); *Dust on Her Tongue*, 1989 (of Rey Rosa's fiction); *Chocolate Creams and Dollars*, 1992 (of Mrabet's fiction).

EDITED TEXTS: *Claudio Bravo: Drawings and Paintings*, 1997 (revised, 2005).

MISCELLANEOUS: *Too Far from Home: The Selected Writings of Paul Bowles*, 1993; *The Paul Bowles Reader*, 2000.

Bibliography

Caponi, Gena Dagel. *Paul Bowles*. New York: Twayne, 1998. An excellent introduction to Bowles and his writings. After a brief chronology and biography, Caponi explores the breadth of Bowles's canon through various critical lenses: existentialism, postcolonial literature, detective fiction, surrealism, extraordinary consciousness, travel writing, historical fiction, and late work.

____________. *Paul Bowles: Romantic Savage*. Carbondale: Southern Illinois University Press, 1994. A biographical/critical study of Bowles's life and art that examines the sources of his fiction, his major themes and techniques, and his methods of story composition.

____________, ed. *Conversations with Paul Bowles*. Jackson: University Press of Mississippi, 1993. In this collection of reprinted and unpublished interviews, Bowles talks about his life and art, even though he claims that the man who wrote his books does not exist except in the books. Bowles has a penchant for perverse responses to interview questions but still communicates a great deal about the relationship between himself and his work.

Carr, Virginia Spencer. *Paul Bowles: A Life*. New York: Charles Scribner's Sons, 2004. First major biography of Bowles to appear after his death.

Dillon, Millicent. "Tracing Paul Bowles." *Raritan* 17 (Winter, 1998): 47-63. In these excerpts from her biography of Bowles, *You Are Not I*, Dillon traces the relationship between Bowles and his wife Jane Auer Bowles, revaluates earlier views in her biography of Jane Bowles, and recounts her own speculations on his life and work.

Green, Michelle. *The Dream at the End of the World: Paul Bowles and the Literary Renegades in Tangier*. New York: HarperCollins, 1991. A lively account of the artistic and socialite sets that congregated in Tangier during the 1940's and 1950's. Investigates the lives of Bowles and those who came to stay with him in Morocco. Green gives some interesting background details for readers of Bowles's fiction. Includes an index and photographs.

Hibbard, Allen. *Paul Bowles: A Study of the Short Fiction*. New York: Twayne, 1993. This introduction to Bowles's short fiction discusses his debt to Edgar Allan Poe's theories of formal unity and analyzes his short-story collections as carefully organized wholes. Also includes material from Bowles's notebooks and previously published critical essays by other critics.

Lacey, R. Kevin, and Francis Poole, eds. *Mirrors on the Maghrib: Critical Reflections on Paul and Jane Bowles and Other American Writers in Morocco*. Delmar, N.Y.: Caravan Books, 1996. This collection of critical essays on the Bowleses and the Beats explores the relationship between the concept of otherness and Morocco. The book includes a number of essays by Moroccan critics, who provide a North African viewpoint on the strengths and weaknesses of Bowles's depiction of their homeland.

Miller, Jeffrey. *Paul Bowles: A Descriptive Bibliography*. Santa Barbara, Calif.: Black Sparrow Press, 1986. Full and very useful guide to published works on Bowles.

Patterson, Richard. *A World Outside: The Fiction of Paul Bowles*. Austin: University of Texas Press, 1987. This scholarly examination of Bowles's work is comprehensive in its analysis. *The Sheltering Sky* is given much attention. Patterson's notes and index are quite good.

Pounds, Wayne. *Paul Bowles: The Inner Geography.* New York: Peter Lang, 1985. A good introduction to Bowles and his use of landscape. Demonstrates the connection between setting and the spiritual states of Bowles's characters.

Sawyer-Laucanno, Christopher. *An Invisible Spectator: A Biography of Paul Bowles.* New York: Weidenfeld & Nicolson, 1989. Sawyer-Laucanno presents a very readable account of the writer's life and offers some intriguing speculation on the connection between the events of Bowles's life and the plots of his stories. The index and notes are useful, and a select bibliography lists Bowles's major works in literature and music.

T. Coraghessan Boyle

Born: Peekskill, New York; December 2, 1948

Principal long fiction • *Water Music*, 1981; *Budding Prospects: A Pastoral*, 1984; *World's End*, 1987; *East Is East*, 1990; *The Road to Wellville*, 1993; *The Tortilla Curtain*, 1995; *Riven Rock*, 1998; *A Friend of the Earth*, 2000; *Drop City*, 2003; *The Inner Circle*, 2004; *Talk Talke*, 2006.

Other literary forms • T. Coraghessan Boyle published several collections of mostly satirical short stories that generally address the same themes seen in his longer fiction.

Achievements • Boyle's novels have been praised for their originality, style, and comic energy. At a time when his contemporaries seem obsessed with the mundane details of everyday life—presented in a minimalist style—Boyle approaches fiction as an iconoclastic storyteller who embraces and borrows from the entire history of narrative literature, celebrating the profane, often-absurd complexities of human endeavors. His first collection of stories won the St. Lawrence Award for Short Fiction, *Water Music* received the Aga Khan Award, and the PEN/Faulkner Award for Fiction was given to *World's End*. Boyle also has been a recipient of the PEN short-story award. Film director Alan Parker adapted *The Road to Wellville* for the screen in 1994, and several of Boyle's stories have been adapted for broadcast on cable television. Boyle also won a Creative Writing Fellowship from the National Endowment for the Arts in 1977. *Descent of Man*, based on his dissertation, was published in 1979. Its stories won the Coordinating Council of Literary Magazines Award for Fiction and the St. Lawrence Award for Fiction. He also received O. Henry Awards for "Sinking House" (1988), "The Ape Lady in Retirement" (1989), "The Underground Gardens" (1999), "The Love of My Life" (2001), and "Swept Away" (2003). *T. C. Boyle Stories: The Collected Stories of T. Coraghessan Boyle* (1998) won the Bernard Malamud Prize in Short Fiction from the PEN/Faulkner Foundation. In 2003, he was a National Book Award finalist for *Drop City*. In 2004, "Tooth and Claw" was a Best American Stories selection.

Biography • Born into a lower-middle-class family in Peekskill, New York, in 1948, Thomas John Boyle was a rebellious youth who played drums, sang in a rock-and-roll band, and drove fast cars. He did not get along with his father, a school-bus driver who died of alcoholism at the age of fifty-four in 1972. Boyle's mother, a secretary, was also an alcoholic and died of liver failure. Assuming the name T. Coraghessan Boyle at the State University of New York at Potsdam, Boyle studied saxophone and clarinet until he realized that he lacked the necessary discipline for music and drifted into creative writing. After college, to avoid military service during the Vietnam War, he taught English for two years at Lakeland High School in Shrub Oak, New York, while increasing his use of drugs, including heroin.

In 1972, Boyle entered the creative writing program at the University of Iowa, where he studied under Vance Bourjaily, John Cheever, and John Irving. He also studied nineteenth century English literature and received a doctoral degree in

1977, with a short-story collection, later published as *Descent of Man* (1979), serving as his dissertation. He became head of the writing program at the University of Southern California and settled in Woodland Hills, a suburb of Los Angeles, with his wife, Karen Kvashay (whom he met when they were undergraduates), and their children, Kerrie, Milo, and Spencer.

Boyle's first novel, *Water Music* (1981), a picaresque work based on the adventures of Mungo Park, an eighteenth century Scottish explorer, was received by critics as a virtuoso performance. Boyle's delight in playing with the language was infectious, and the book was admired more for its exuberant style than for its thematic depth. Turning to a more realistic approach and a contemporary setting in his second novel, Boyle published *Budding Prospects: A Pastoral* (1984), a satiric treatment of the American Dream in which hippies growing marijuana in the Northern California backwoods are presented as modern models of Benjamin Franklin and Henry David Thoreau.

Boyle continued to write short stories during this period, publishing his collection *Greasy Lake, and Other Stories* in 1985, which was widely praised for its satire and humor. A particularly ambitious work is *World's End* (1987), a sprawling picaresque novel covering several generations of Hudson Valley families was called Boyle's "peak achievement" in *The New York Times Book Review.* Boyle's third collection of short stories, *If the River Was Whiskey* (1989), was less enthusiastically received, with critics complaining that it did not contain any stories equal to some of the masterpieces in Boyle's first two collections. *East Is East* (1990), about a young half-Japanese man who jumps ship and lands on a small island near Georgia, similarly received only lukewarm response.

Analysis • T. Coraghessan Boyle's novels concern the misconceptions people of different sexes, races, nationalities, and backgrounds have about one another and the misunderstandings—some violent—that result. The clashes between Britons and Africans in *Water Music,* drug entrepreneurs and Northern California rednecks in *Budding Prospects,* Indians and Dutch settlers in New York in *World's End,* Americans and a half-American Japanese in *East Is East,* and privileged white Southern Californians and destitute illegal Mexican immigrants in *The Tortilla Curtain* all allow Boyle to satirize the prejudices, eccentricities, and excesses of several cultures.

Boyle's ironic fiction is populated by a multitude of diverse characters, all convinced that theirs is the only possible way of perceiving and dealing with a complex, changing, often-hostile world. Boyle alternates the viewpoints of these protagonists to present events and issues from all possible sides and increase the irony of the situations. He writes both in a straightforward, economical style and in more ornate prose resembling that of such popular writers as John Barth and Thomas Pynchon. Far from being didactic, Boyle's serious fiction entertains through his masterful storytelling ability and through his control of his vivid style.

Water Music • *Water Music* alternates between the stories of Scottish explorer Mungo Park and London criminal Ned Rise until their destinies converge in Africa. Park (1771-1806), the first European to see West Africa's upper Niger River, wrote a best-selling account of his adventures, *Travels in the Interior Districts of Africa* (1797), led a larger expedition into the interior of Africa, and drowned in the rapids of the Niger during an attack by Africans. Boyle's fictionalized Park and the low-born Rise are used to contrast the levels of English society and attitudes toward the British Empire.

A public hero, Park is less than heroic as imagined by Boyle. He thinks that he has had unique experiences because he is unable to recognize the humanity of the Africans he encounters. He selfishly ignores Ailie, his long-suffering fiancé and later devoted wife, thinking nothing of leaving her behind for years while he strives for glory. Park is less concerned with any benefits to humankind resulting from his expeditions than with mere adventure and fame. This need leads him to distort and romanticize his experiences in his writings. The irony of these exploits is that Park would be totally lost without the assistance of such nonwhites as Johnson, born Katunga Oyo. Sold into slavery in America, Johnson learns to read, wins his freedom, becomes a highly respected valet in London, and translates Henry Fielding's *Amelia* (1751) into Mandingo before returning to Africa. His earthy yet sophisticated realism strongly contrasts with Park's muddled idealism. Park's moral blindness suggests some of the causes of the collapse of the empire.

Ned Rise, on the other hand, is a victim in the tradition of the picaros created by Fielding, Daniel Defoe, and Charles Dickens. (Dickens's mixture of colorful characterizations, humor, and moral outrage, as well as his use of odd names, seems to be a major influence on Boyle.) Rise is stolen from his mother at birth and forced to become a beggar when old enough. He has his right hand mutilated by a cleaver, is nearly drowned, is robbed, is wrongfully imprisoned and hanged—coming to life as he is about to be dissected—loses his true love, Fanny Brunch, is imprisoned again, and is shipped to Africa to become part of Park's fatal expedition. Park's Great Britain represents culture and privilege; Ned's stands for the poverty and depravity at the extreme other end of the social scale. However, the ironically named Rise learns to survive.

In the tradition of such classics of the American picaresque novel as John Barth's *The Sot-Weed Factor* (1960) and Thomas Berger's *Little Big Man* (1964), *Water Music* is an entertaining black comedy, a deliberately anachronistic, self-conscious narrative that frequently calls attention to its form and style. Boyle's delight in being a literary show-off, a tendency he has subdued as his career has progressed, led some of the novel's reviewers to dismiss it as a stunt, but *Water Music* quickly developed a cult following and has come to be seen as a clear announcement of the debut of an original, irreverent talent.

Budding Prospects • Boyle presents another ill-conceived adventure, though on a much smaller scale, in *Budding Prospects: A Pastoral.* Its thirty-one-year-old protagonist, Felix Nasmyth, is a chronic failure given another shot at success by the mysterious Vogelsang, a Vietnam War veteran and sociopath. With the assistance of Boyd Dowst, holder of a master's degree in botany from Yale University, Felix is to grow marijuana in rural Northern California. Vogelsang promises the desperate Felix that he will earn a half-million dollars from the enterprise.

Felix and his inept friends Phil and Gesh experience culture shock in isolated Willits, whose aggressively antagonistic citizens consider themselves morally superior to the rest of the decadent world. Obstacles to raising a productive marijuana crop include rain, fire, a hungry bear, a 320-pound alumnus of the state mental hospital's violent ward, and John Jerpbak, a menacing policeman who, like everyone in Willits, knows what Felix is doing. The comedy of *Budding Prospects* results from the dogged perseverance of Felix and friends in this doomed endeavor.

Beside his usual theme of individuals out of their element in a strange environment, Boyle offers a satire of the American free-enterprise system. As he interprets it, the system is motivated primarily by greed, with success coming less through intelligence or hard work than through luck. The dubious morality of Felix's project only adds to the irony. He and his friends want to get rich quickly and are honest only in admitting that they care about nothing but money. The fact that they work harder to fail in an illegal business than they would to earn money honestly is yet another irony in a highly ironic tale. Felix's unreliable narration as he constantly compares himself to the pioneers who settled America adds comic hyperbole. Such humor keeps Boyle's examination of the materialistic side of the American Dream from being preachy.

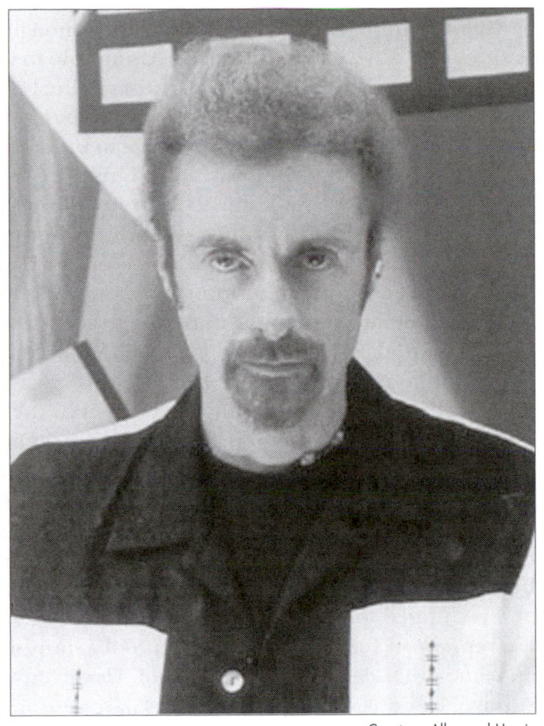

Courtesy, Allen and Unwin

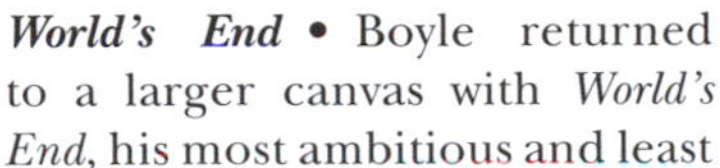

World's End • Boyle returned to a larger canvas with *World's End*, his most ambitious and least comic novel, a consideration of America's self-destructive impulse. The Van Brunts, Dutch settlers in what is now northern Westchester County, New York, in the late seventeenth century, experience conflicts with a hostile nature and the voracious Van Warts, the patroons who own the land they farm. The lives of the Van Brunts become intertwined with those of the Kitchawanks, their Indian neighbors. The greedy machinations of the Van Warts lead to misery for the settlers and Indians and death for several of them.

Boyle alternates chapters about these characters with ones dealing with their twentieth century descendants, including Jeremy Mohonk, the last of the Kitchawanks, whose efforts to regain his birthright (stolen by the Van Warts) earn for him seventeen years in prison. Truman Van Brunt betrays his friends and relatives to save himself, just as one of the original Van Brunts had done. The protagonist of the twentieth century chapters is Walter Van Brunt, reared by communists after Truman runs away and his mother dies. During the late 1960's, Walter is torn between the countercultural life led by his friends and the wealth and social position of the Van Warts. After losing his wife when she finds him in bed with Mardi Van Wart and losing both his feet in separate motorcycle accidents, Walter tracks down his lost father in Barrow, Alaska, to discover that Truman has spent years researching his family's history to justify his actions. Walter returns home thoroughly disillusioned, and Jeremy Mohonk gains revenge against his enemies by impregnating the wife of the current Van Wart, ironically allowing the despised line to continue.

In *World's End*, Boyle shows how people of different races, sexes, and social and economic backgrounds exploit, betray, and fail one another. The characters either are desperate to control their destinies or consider themselves the victims of fates they are incapable of overcoming. Almost everyone is self-deluding, from the right-wing fanatic Dipe Van Wart in his pathetic attempts to resist change, to Walter, who sees himself as an alienated, existential antihero in the tradition of Meursault in Albert Camus's *L'Étranger* (1942; *The Stranger*, 1946). Walter thinks that his life will fall into place if he can understand his father, yet finding Truman leads only to confusion.

As Boyle rifles English literary traditions as part of his satire in *Water Music*, in *World's End* he draws upon the mythical views of America espoused by such writers as Washington Irving, James Fenimore Cooper, Nathaniel Hawthorne, Herman Melville, and William Faulkner. From the destruction of the virgin wilderness to the exploitation of the Indian to the curses inflicted upon several generations of characters to fatal obsession with the inexplicable, the novel is virtually a catalog of traditional American literary themes.

World's End represents a new maturity in Boyle as an artist. In it he eschews the too-easy irony and too-obvious satire that occasionally weaken his earlier fiction, while he confirms his skill at storytelling. Though *World's End* is a sprawling novel with more than one hundred characters, Boyle exerts masterful control over his complicated, overlapping plots, expecting his readers to share his joy in the manipulation of so many coincidences, parallels, and ironies.

East Is East • The inability of people of different backgrounds to understand one another is even more at the center of *East Is East* than of Boyle's other novels. Hiro Tanaka, a twenty-year-old cook on a Japanese ship, jumps overboard off the coast of Georgia. Hiro, another Boyle orphan, has never known his father, an American rock musician who loved and left Hiro's mother, an eventual suicide. Ostracized by Japanese society for being half American, Hiro longs to lose himself in the great melting pot but unfortunately washes ashore on isolated Tupelo Island, site of Thanatopsis House, an artists' colony.

After a series of confused encounters with the local people, Hiro finds refuge in the cottage of Ruth Dershowitz. A mediocre writer from California, Ruth is at Thanatopsis thanks to being the lover of Saxby Lights, son of Septima Lights, the colony's founder. Ruth pities the hungry, frightened fugitive from immigration authorities but also longs to incorporate Hiro into a short story with which she is having difficulty. Saxby finds out about Hiro, who is imprisoned, escapes to the Okefenokee Swamp, and is arrested again when near death.

Both the white and the black residents of Tupelo Island are frightened by their Japanese visitor, who is equally bewildered by them. Detlef Abercorn, the immigration official sent to find Hiro, is from Los Angeles and feels totally alienated in the South. An albino, he, like Hiro, has never truly fit in anywhere. Abercorn is assisted by Lewis Turco, a veteran of covert operations in Southeast Asia, who prides himself on being in control in any environment, but he is so paranoid that he creates nothing but chaos. No one in *East Is East* understands or trusts anyone else. The writers, painters, sculptors, and composers at Thanatopsis, who should be able to transcend the cultural differences that handicap the others, are instead so self-absorbed and crippled by petty jealousies that they are totally ineffective as human beings.

Hiro is another Boyle innocent destroyed by his inability to deal with the world's complexities and hostilities and by his own foolishness. Hiro has a system of beliefs—based on Japanese writer Yukio Mishima's theory of the samurai—to help guide him, but Mishima proves tragicomically ineffective in the Georgia swamps. Hiro trusts Ruth, to a degree, because he has no one else, and while she genuinely wants to help, her needs must come first. Ruth, the most fully developed female character in Boyle's novels, ironically finds success through being caught harboring an illegal immigrant, for she then lands a book contract to tell her story. The unscrupulousness of supposedly sensitive artists is as much the target of Boyle's satirical ire as are cultural differences.

The Road to Wellville • Similar to each other in scheme and scope, *The Road to Wellville* and *Riven Rock* elaborate the wry appraisal of human nature and American values found in *Budding Prospects* and *East Is East* in period tales whose vivid historical tableaux call to mind Boyle's achievement in *Water Music* and *World's End.*

The Road to Wellville is a farcical examination of the career of Dr. John Harvey Kellogg, inventor of the corn flake and other "gastrically correct" natural foods. A devout vegetarian and zealous promoter of physical culture, Kellogg opens his Battle Creek Sanitarium to men and women at the beginning of the twentieth century, hoping to win them over to his vision of a healthier lifestyle through carefully restricted diets, vigorous exercise regimens, and crackpot medical interventions that include yogurt enemas and sinusoidal baths. Kellogg's "Temple of Health," as some deem it, is a magnet for celebrities, socialites, eccentrics, and connivers who represent a cross section of Boyle's America.

Among them is Eleanor Lightbody, an independent woman and self-proclaimed "Battle Freak" whose sense of liberation is tied to her willing embrace of Kellogg's instruction. Intelligent and principled, Eleanor is blind to the absurdity of Kellogg's methods and to the misery they cause her sickly husband, Will, who suffers the increasingly dangerous indignities of rehabilitation at the sanitarium out of love for his wife. Boyle interweaves the adventures of the Lightbodys with those of Charlie Ossining, a likable scalawag who has squandered the money given him by a patron to establish a competing health food company in Battle Creek. Ossining's inept efforts to duplicate Kellogg's products through cheap and eventually devious means offer a comic reflection on the underside of entrepreneurism and the free-enterprise system.

The book's most interesting character is George Kellogg, one of Dr. Kellogg's numerous adopted children and a symbol of the Kellogg method's failure. George spends most of the novel dissipated and disorderly, deliberately embarrassing his father to extort money from him. He embodies the tendency toward entropy that undermines the best-laid plans in all of Boyle's novels and the irrepressible primitive appetites that get the better of even the most sophisticated characters.

Riven Rock • Boyle develops these character types and traits further in *Riven Rock.* Set at approximately the same time as *The Road to Wellville,* Riven Rock portrays another American captain of industry whose personal shortcomings reflect an inherent flaw in the human condition. Stanley McCormick, heir to the McCormick Reaper fortune, is afflicted with an apparently hereditary schizophrenia that manifests as sexual psychopathy. He spends most of the novel locked away at Riven Rock, a family retreat in Santa Barbara, deprived of the company of women—his wife included—because a mere glimpse of them provokes him to profane and lewd attacks. In flashbacks, Boyle portrays Stanley as a naïve and sensitive young man who has perhaps been driven mad by the pressure of family responsibilities, and almost certainly by the insensitivity of women in his life, including his domineering mother and his crusading wife.

As in his other panoramic novels, Boyle refracts the central conflicts and issues through the experiences of a number of characters. Chief among these is Stanley's wife, Katherine, a caring but ambitious woman who bears a striking resemblance in her attitudes to Eleanor Lightbody of *The Road to Wellville.* Educated and fiercely independent, Katherine is dedicated to Stanley's rehabilitation partly out of affection, but also as part of her selfish quest to have a child and know the fulfilled expression of her privilege and will. Edward O'Kane, Stanley's nurse and caretaker, complements Katherine. Sexually profligate and perpetually hostage to his lusts, he impregnates several women over the course of the novel, which leads to repeated comic complications with their families and his employer. In their own ways, Katherine and O'Kane embody the same appetites that govern Stanley. Boyle emphasizes this point through the efforts of Stanley's doctors to cure him by studying the insatiable sex drives of monkeys brought to the secluded estate. *Riven Rock* is possibly Boyle's most direct attempt to present the competing interests and compelling drives behind a culture and citizens as an expression of Darwinian biological imperatives.

The anger in Boyle's novels is tempered by the comedy. Even a relatively somber work such as *World's End* has moments of sublime silliness, as Dipe Van Wart fights middle-age depression by eating dirt from beneath his ancestral home—a fitting comic metaphor for his family's neuroticism and mindless consumption of the land. Boyle's fiction is also notable for the diversity of his style, which changes not only from novel to novel but also from chapter to chapter. He understands well how to play upon the natural rhythms of convoluted sentences and when to resort to the subtler joys of simpler ones, has a vocabulary rivaling Vladimir Nabokov's, and delights in parody. *East Is East* offers the mock Faulkner appropriate to a comic novel set in the South, but it avoids the overkill occasionally seen in Boyle's short stories and earlier novels. *The Road to Wellville* and *Riven Rock* are kaleidoscopic narratives in the style of Charles Dickens and William Makepeace Thackeray; their broad historical context accommodates their sweeping social satire. Most important is Boyle's ability to create believable, usually sympathetic, characters caught in absurd quests for truths they are incapable of understanding.

The Inner Circle • During the late 1940's and early 1950's, the Kinsey Report, compiled by Dr. Alfred Kinsey, documented the results of a scientific study of male and female sexuality. Boyle's 2004 novel, *The Inner Circle,* explores Kinsey's influence on American sexual and social mores through the voice of John Milk, Kinsey's assistant and first disciple, who assists Kinsey both in the office and in bed and with both Kinsey's wife and his own in group sex.

The fictionalization of Kinsey's story provides a lens through which the book examines the sexual revolution in sharp, provocative detail, especially as Kinsey's research grows increasingly voyeuristic and exhibitionistic. As Milk becomes part of the "inner circle" of researchers, he and his wife are drawn into experiments that become increasingly uninhibited and increasingly problematic for his marriage. The shyness regarding sexuality that permeates the era in which the book is set makes the research both alluring and alarming to Milk, whose sensibility reflects that of the readers of the Kinsey Report and chronicles the transformation of public attitudes and private behavior.

The book's primary theme is sex, marriage, and jealousy and the difficulties of attempting to quantify or classify personal interactions. Boyle explores the division between human pride and human animal natures and whether the act of sex can be separated from its emotional and spiritual context. In Kinsey's crusade to separate sex and morality, his attempt is doomed by his own uncompromising idealism. The novel also serves as a case study of what it means to become another person's apostle as it explores the impact of Kinsey's methods on Milk and his marriage.

Michael Adams
Updated by Stefan Dziemianowicz and Catherine Rambo

Other major works

SHORT FICTION: *Descent of Man*, 1979; *Greasy Lake, and Other Stories*, 1985; *If the River Was Whiskey*, 1989; *Without a Hero*, 1994; *T. C. Boyle Stories: The Collected Stories of T. Coraghessan Boyle*, 1998; *After the Plague: Stories*, 2001; *Tooth and Claw*, 2005; *The Human Fly and Other Stories*, 2005.

EDITED TEXTS: *Doubletakes: Pairs of Contemporary Short Stories*, 2003.

Bibliography

Boyle, T. Coraghessan. Interview by David Stanton. *Poets and Writers* 18 (January/February, 1990): 29-34. Boyle explains his need to promote himself through readings and interviews, his strong self-confidence in his abilities, his doubts about creative-writing programs, and the positive effect that writing novels has had on his short fiction. He believes that his earlier stories call attention to themselves too much.

____________. "The Maximalist Novelist." Interview by Helen Dudar. *The Wall Street Journal*, November 5, 1990, p. A13. This interview discusses Boyle's work habits; his attitudes toward his art, teaching, and success; and his fear of running out of material.

____________. "A Punk's Past Recaptured." Interview by Anthony DeCurtis. *Rolling Stone*, January 14, 1988, 54-57. In his most revealing interview, Boyle talks about his drug use, the importance of understanding history, and the autobiographical element in his fiction. He expresses the desire to be like Kurt Vonnegut, in showing that literature can be both serious and entertaining, and like John Updike, in constantly changing his approach to fiction and improving as an artist.

____________. "Rolling Boyle." Interview by Tad Friend. *The New York Times Magazine*, December 9, 1990, 50, 64, 66, 68. Boyle portrays himself as a missionary for literature who promotes himself to ensure that he is read. He comments on the new maturity and reality in some of his fiction but admits that the absurd and bizarre are more natural for him. Boyle also expresses pessimism about the future of the human race.

Burke, Matthew. "Fortress Dystopia: Representations of Gated Communities in Contemporary Fiction." *Journal of American and Comparative Cultures* 24 (Spring, 2001): 115-122. Discusses the social dynamics of *The Tortilla Curtain*.

Carnes, Mark C., ed. *Novel History: Historians and Novelists Confront American's Past (and Each Other)*. New York: Simon & Schuster, 2001. The essay by Michael Kamen discusses Boyle's fictional use of history and historical characters.

Chase, Brennan. "Like, Chill!" *Los Angeles* 38 (April, 1993): 80-82. A biographical sketch, focusing on Boyle's successful literary career and celebrity status in Hollywood. Boyle maintains that he is an academic whose purpose is to write.

Hume, Kathryn. *American Dream, American Nightmare: Fiction Since 1960.* Urbana: University of Illinois Press, 2000. Boyle's work is discussed in an extensive study of the tension between utopian and dystopian tendencies in late twentieth century American fiction.

Pope, Dan. "A Different Kind of Post-Modernism." *Gettysburg Review* 3 (Autumn, 1990): 658-669. A discussion of Boyle's collection *If the River Was Whiskey*, along with a collection of short fiction by Rick DeMarinis and Paul West, as typifying the work of a new generation of writers who look beyond "the age of innocent realism."

Schenker, Daniel. "A Samurai in the South: Cross-Cultural Disaster in T. Coraghessan Boyle's *East Is East.*" *The Southern Quarterly* 34 (Fall, 1995): 70-80. Penetrating analysis of the cultural clashes and intransigence that inform the tragicomic vision of Boyle's novel.

Shelden, Michael. "T. Coraghessan Boyle: The Art of Fiction CLXI." *Paris Review* 155 (Summer, 2000): 100-126. General appreciation of Boyle's writings.

Spencer, Russ. "The Jester Who Hath No King." *The Book Magazine*, December, 1998-January, 1999, 38-43. Day-in-the-life type feature based on a visit to Boyle's home, with Boyle—described as "the Bacchus of American letters"—assessing his career and personal philosophies following the publication of *Riven Rock* and *T. C. Boyle Stories.*

Ray Bradbury

Born: Waukegan, Illinois; August 22, 1920

Principal long fiction • *Fahrenheit 451*, 1953; *Dandelion Wine*, 1957; *Something Wicked This Way Comes*, 1962; *Death Is a Lonely Business*, 1985; *A Graveyard for Lunatics: Another Tale of Two Cities*, 1990; *Green Shadows, White Whale*, 1992; *From the Dust Returned: A Family Remembrance*, 2001; *Let's All Kill Constance*, 2003; *Farewell Summer*, 2006.

Other literary forms • Ray Bradbury's principal literary form is the short story, and he published several important collections, including *Dark Carnival* (1947), *The Golden Apples of the Sun* (1953), and *I Sing the Body Electric!* (1969). A one-hundred-story collection, *The Stories of Ray Bradbury* (1980), seemed to sum up his life's work, but it was later followed by anthologies of new stories, *Quicker than the Eye* (1996) and *Driving Blind* (1997). In addition to his short stories and novels, he published in a wide variety of literary forms, from light verse and poetry to screenplays and dramas. A notable screenplay, which he wrote in collaboration with film director John Huston, is a 1956 adaptation of Herman Melville's *Moby Dick* (1851). A representative example of his poetry is *When Elephants Last in the Dooryard Bloomed: Celebrations for Almost Any Day in the Year* (1973) and of his plays is *The Pedestrian* (1966).

Achievements • Although Bradbury became arguably the best-known American science-fiction writer, the majority of his work, which ranges from gothic horror to social criticism, centers on humanistic themes. His best works are powerful indictments of the dangers of unrestrained scientific and technological progress. However, his works also foster the hope that humanity will deal creatively with the new worlds it seems driven to construct. Aficionados of the science-fiction genre have criticized his science-fiction stories for their scientific and technological inaccuracies, a criticism that Bradbury shrugs off, stating that his dominating concerns are social, cultural, and intellectual issues, not scientific verisimilitude. His stories, which often explore the dehumanizing pressures of technocracies and the mesmerizing power of the imagination, are widely anthologized and translated into many foreign languages. His ascent from pulp magazines to literary respectability was intermittently recognized with several awards, including appearances in Martha Foley's annual best American short-story collections, two O. Henry prizes, the *Benjamin Franklin Magazine* Award, the National Institute of Arts and Letters Award, an Academy Award nomination, and a Golden Eagle Award for his screenplay *Icarus Montgolfier Wright* (1961). He was named a Nebula Grand Master and received the Bram Stoker Life Achievement Award as well as the Body of Work Award from the International Association of Poets, Playwrights, Editors, Essayists, and Novelists (PEN). His other awards have included the World Fantasy Convention's life achievement award (1977), a Gandalf "Grand Master" award at the Hugo Award Ceremonies of 1980, the Jules Verne Award (1984), the PEN Body of Work Award (1985), a star on the Hollywood Walk of Fame (2002), and the National Medal of the Arts (2004).

Biography • Ray Bradbury was born on August 22, 1920, in Waukegan, Illinois. His father, Leonard Spaulding Bradbury, whose distant ancestor Mary Bradbury was among those tried for witchcraft in Salem, was a lineman with the Waukegan Bureau of Power and Light; his mother, Esther Marie (née Moberg) Bradbury, emigrated as a child from Sweden. When he was three years old, his mother took him to his first film, *The Hunchback of Notre Dame* (1923), and he was frightened and entranced by Lon Chaney in this film and, later, in *The Phantom of the Opera* (1925). As a child, Bradbury passed through a series of enthusiasms, from monsters to circuses to dinosaurs and eventually to the planet Mars. His development through childhood was aided by an older brother and by an aunt, Neva Bradbury, a costume designer, who introduced him to the theater and to the stories of Edgar Allan Poe.

In 1932, Bradbury's family moved to Arizona, where they had previously spent some time in the mid-1920's, largely because of his father's need to find work. In 1934 the family left behind both Arizona and Waukegan, settling in Los Angeles, which became Bradbury's permanent home. He attended Los Angeles High School and joined the Science Fiction Society (he had earlier begun reading Hugo Gernsback's *Amazing Stories*, which, he said, made him fall in love with the future). After graduation, Bradbury worked for several months in a theater group sponsored by the actor Laraine Day, and for several years he was a newsboy in downtown Los Angeles. He took these jobs to support his writing, an avocation that he hoped would soon become a vocation.

Bradbury's poor eyesight prevented him from serving in the U.S. Army during World War II, which left him free to launch his writing career. During the early 1940's he began to publish his stories in such pulp magazines as *Weird Tales* and *Amazing Stories*, but by the late 1940's his work was appearing in such mass-market magazines as *Collier's, The Saturday Evening Post, The New Yorker, Harper's Magazine,* and *Mademoiselle.* Because these magazines paid well, he was able, on September 27, 1947, to marry Marguerite Susan McClure, a former English teacher at the University of California in Los Angeles. He remained married to her for fifty-six years and had four daughters with her. Marguerite died in 2003.

During the 1950's, Bradbury continued to write for the pulp and mass-market magazines, and he routinely collected his stories for publication in books. During the mid-1950's, he traveled to Ireland in connection with a screenplay of *Moby Dick* that he wrote with John Huston. Upon his return to the United States, Bradbury composed a large number of television scripts for such shows as *Alfred Hitchcock Presents, Suspense,* and *The Twilight Zone.* During the late 1950's and early 1960's, Bradbury's stories and novels focused mostly on his midwestern childhood—for example, *Dandelion Wine* and *Something Wicked This Way Comes,* the latter his favorite book.

During the 1960's and 1970's, Bradbury's output of fiction decreased, and his ideas found outlets in such forms as plays, poems, and essays. He also became involved in a number of projects, such as "A Journey Through United States History," the exhibit that occupied the upper floor of the United States Pavilion for the New York World's Fair in the mid-1960's. Because of this display's success, the Walt Disney organization hired him to help develop the themes for Spaceship Earth, an important part of Epcot Center at Disney World in Florida. Bradbury also helped design a twenty-first century city near Tokyo. He continued to diversify his activities during the 1980's and 1990's by collaborative and consultative work, and he also found time to return to his first love, the short story, and to write four novels. He collaborated with Jimmy Webb by composing lyrics for a musical version of *Dandelion Wine,* which was not successful, though critics praised the Bradbury novel that provided the inspiration for this production. These excursions into other fields were part of his expressed plan to work in "every writing medium," but his successes continued to be in the traditional forms of the novel and short story. He published two detective novels, *Death Is a Lonely Business* and *A Graveyard for Lunatics*, and a roman à clef, *Green Shadows, White Whale.* He also wrote a large number of short stories, some of them in his customary fields of science fiction, fantasy, and horror, but many dealing with extraordinary characters in ordinary life. These were collected in anthologies: *The Toynbee Convector* (1988), *Quicker than the Eye*, and *Driving Blind.*

Thomas Victor

Analysis • Paradoxically, Bradbury's stories look both backward and forward. For him, each story is a way of discovering a self, and the self found in one story is different from the self found in another. Bradbury, like all human beings, is made of time, and human beings, like rivers, flow and change. Adapting the ancient Greek philosopher Heraclitus's famous statement that one cannot step into the same river twice, one could say that no person ever steps twice into the same self. Sometimes Bradbury discovered a self in the past, and sometimes, particularly in his science fiction, he discovered a self in the future. Several critics have pictured him as a frontiersman, ambivalently astride two worlds, who has alternately been attracted to an idealized past, timeless and nostalgic, and to a graphic future, chameleonic and threatening. This creative tension is present both in his own life and in the generation of Americans he liked to depict. It is also intimately connected with the genre—science fiction—with which he became so closely identified.

Bradbury has been called a Romantic, and his Romanticism often surfaces in the themes he investigates: the conflict between human vitality and spiritless mechanism, between the creative individual and the conforming group, between imagination and reason, between intuition and logic, between the innocence of childhood and the corruptions of adulthood, and between the shadow and light in every human soul. His stories make clear that, in all these conflicts, human beings, not machines, are at the center of his vision. An ambivalence about technology characterizes his life and work. For example, he never learned to drive, even while spending most of his life in Los Angeles, a city that has made the automobile not only an apparent necessity but also an object of worship. He also refused to use a computer, and he successfully avoided flying in an airplane for the first six decades of his life.

Each of these attitudes is rooted in some profoundly emotional experience; for example, he never learned to drive because, as a youth, he witnessed the horrible deaths of five people in an automobile accident. Because of his emphasis on basic human values against an uncritical embracing of technical progress, because of his affirmation of the human spirit against modern materialism, and because of his trust in the basic goodness of small-town life against the debilitating indifference of the cities, several critics have accused him of sentimentality and naïveté. Bradbury responded by saying that critics write from the head, whereas he writes from the heart.

The poetic style that Bradbury developed was admirably suited to the heartfelt themes that he explored in a cornucopia of highly imaginative stories. He cultivated this style through eclectic imitation and dogged determination. As an adolescent, he vowed to write several hundred words every day, for he believed that quantity would eventually lead to quality. Experience and the example of other writers would teach him what to leave out. According to Bradbury, his style was influenced by such writers as Charles Dickens, Mark Twain, Thomas Wolfe, and Ernest Hemingway. On another occasion, however, he stated that his style came as much from silent-film actor Charles Chaplin as from Aldous Huxley, as much from Tom Swift as from George Orwell, as much from cowboy actor Tom Mix as from Bertrand Russell, and as much from Edgar Rice Burroughs as from C. S. Lewis. Bradbury was also influenced by such poets as Alexander Pope, Gerard Manley Hopkins, and Dylan Thomas, and such dramatists as William Shakespeare and George Bernard Shaw. Furthermore and surprisingly, such painters as El Greco and Tintoretto and such composers as Wolfgang Amadeus Mozart and Franz Joseph Haydn showed him how to add color and rhythm to his writing.

According to Bradbury, all these influences—writers, poets, painters, and musicians—gloried in the joy of creating, and their works overflow with animal vigor and intellectual vitality. Their ardor and delight are contagious, and their honest response to the materials at hand calls forth a similar response in their readers, viewers, and listeners. This enchanting of the audience, similar to casting a magic spell, is what Bradbury attempted to do with his kaleidoscopic style: to transform colorful pieces of reality into a glittering picture that will emotionally intensify the lives of his readers.

Bradbury's writing is profoundly autobiographical, and childhood, adolescent, and adult experiences generated many of his stories. Graham Greene once said that there is always one moment in childhood when the door opens and lets the future in. Actually, for Bradbury, there were many such moments. He once said that everything he had ever done—all his activities, loves, and fears—were created by the primitive experiences of monsters and angels he had when he was five years old. He also said, however, that the most important event in his childhood occurred when he was twelve years old, at a carnival, when the performance of a magician, Mr. Electrico, so energized his imagination that he began to write stories to communicate his fervid visions to others.

Numerous Bradbury stories, including several in his first collection, *Dark Carnival*, have as their provenance specific childhood events. For example, "The Small Assassin," which metamorphoses some of his childhood experiences and fears, tells of a newborn infant, terrified at finding himself thrust into a hostile world, taking revenge on his parents by first terrorizing, then murdering them. This story also reveals that Bradbury's view of childhood innocence is more complex than many critics realize, for, in Bradbury's view, beneath the façade of innocence lies a cauldron of sin—a dark vision of the human condition that some critics have called Calvinistic.

Another tale, "The Lake," is based on Bradbury's experience as a seven-year-old, when his cousin nearly drowned in Lake Michigan. These and other early stories, which he published in such pulp magazines as *Weird Tales*, *Amazing Stories*, and *Astounding Science Fiction*, served as his apprenticeship, an opportunity to perfect his style, deepen his vision, and develop the themes on which he would play variations in his later, more accomplished short stories, novels, poems, and dramas.

One of these early themes that also haunted his later fiction is alienation. Bradbury himself experienced cultural alienation when he traveled to Mexico in 1945. Americans were then mostly Protestant, individualistic, and preoccupied with getting ahead. Mexicans, on the other hand, were mostly Roman Catholic, communalistic, and preoccupied with death. On his trip to Guanajuato, northwest of Mexico City, Bradbury was both horrified and fascinated by the catacombs with their rows of propped-up mummified bodies. A story collected in *Dark Carnival*, "The Next in Line," grew out of this experience. In this story, a young American wife finds herself, after her traumatic ordeal in the Guanajuato crypts, alienated both from the strange Mexican society and from her own body, which she obsessively realizes is a potential mummy. Bradbury uses the metaphor of death to help the reader comprehend one reality, life, in terms of another, death. Metaphor thus becomes a medicine, a way of healing ourselves by envisioning ourselves into new modes of experiencing, learning, and surviving.

Despite his forays into long fiction, Bradbury's forte is the short story, and three major collections of his tales appeared during the 1980's and 1990's: *The Toynbee Convector*, *Quicker than the Eye*, and *Driving Blind*. Many of the later stories are either slightly camouflaged, grossly exaggerated, or an "absolutely accurate" detailing of events in the author's own life. Whatever the source of these stories, they are part of what Bradbury calls "the history of ideas." In the afterword to *Quicker than the Eye*, he confesses that he is not a writer of science fiction, fantasy, or Magical Realism; rather, he sees himself as a word magician who does not really "write these stories, *they* write *me*." He calculated that he had written close to five hundred stories, but he believed that "there must be at least 1,000 more . . . waiting to be discovered."

Several critics during the late 1980's and the 1990's detected a decline in the quality of Bradbury's later work, but the standard he set during the 1950's was very high. Because his work took so many different literary forms, and because, within each of these forms, his treatment of a potpourri of subjects was equally variegated, it is difficult to make neat generalizations about his oeuvre. The public has recognized him as a science-fiction writer, but only a third of his work has been in this genre. Certainly, his science-fiction stories have revealed that cultivated and craftsmanlike writing is possible in what was seen, before him, as a vulgar genre. Within the science-fiction community, however, a sharp difference of opinion exists about Bradbury's contributions. A sizable segment sees his work as reactionary, antitechnological, and antiutopian. As one of these critics put it, Bradbury is a science-fiction writer for people who do not really like science fiction. On the other hand, a large group, which includes a significant segment of the literary community (viewing him as one of their own), sees him as a humanist and a regional writer. This group draws some good arguments from Bradbury's stories: For example, even when he writes about Mars, the planet symbolizes for him the geography—emotional and intellectual—of the American Midwest. In this sense, his regionalism is one of the mind and heart.

Actually, both sides of this debate can find evidence for their views in Bradbury's motley work. He can be both enthusiastic about a future transformed by technology and critical of the dangers posed by technocracies. Ultimately, for him, technology is a *human* creation, and it is therefore subject to the labyrinthine goods and evils of the human heart. Although his best work is deeply humanistic and includes a strong critique of unrestrained technology, he is no Luddite. It is true that the technological society has produced many problems—pollution, for example—but human beings love to solve problems; it is a defining characteristic of the species.

Those who see only Bradbury's critique of technology view him as a pessimistic writer. In the proper light, however, his work is really profoundly optimistic. His fiction may rest upon the gloomy foundation of the Fall, but, in traditional theology, the counterpart of the Fall is Redemption, and Bradbury believes that human beings will renew themselves, particularly in space, which he sees as modern humanity's religious quest. Space, then, is Bradbury's new wilderness, with an infinity of new challenges. In that inexhaustible wilderness, human beings will find themselves and be saved.

The Martian Chronicles • Although, at first glance, many of Bradbury's early stories seem notable for their great variety, he did deal, especially in his stories about Mars, with a set of conflicts that had a common theme, and so, when an editor suggested in 1949 that he compose a continuous narrative, he took advantage of the opportunity, since several of his stories about the colonization of Mars by Earthlings lent themselves to just such a treatment. Using the chronological frame of 1999 to 2026, Bradbury stitched these stories together with bridge passages that gave the book a semblance of unity (it also presented categorizers of his works with a problem: Some have listed the book as a novel, others as a short-story collection). Many critics have called *The Martian Chronicles* Bradbury's masterpiece, a magical and insightful account of the exploitation of a new frontier, Mars, by Earthlings whose personalities appear to have been nurtured in small midwestern American towns.

By placing normal human beings in an extraordinary setting, Bradbury was able to use the strange light of an alien world to illuminate the dark regions of human nature. The apparatus of conventional science fiction makes an appearance, including monsters and supermachines, but Bradbury's basic intent is to explore the conflicts that were troubling postwar America: imperialism, alienation, pollution, racism, and nuclear war. He therefore depicts not a comforting human progress but a disquieting cycle of rises and falls. He also sees the Martian environment, itself transformed by human ingenuity, transforming the settlers. Thus, his ultimate view seems optimistic: Humanity will, through creative adaptation, not only survive but thrive. In *The Martian Chronicles* Earthlings metamorphose into Martians, an action that serves as a Bradburian metaphor for the human condition, which is to be always in the process of becoming something else.

Even though scientists criticized *The Martian Chronicles* for its portrayal of Mars as a planet with a breathable atmosphere, water, and canals (known by astronomers in 1950 to be untrue), and even though science-fiction devotees found Bradbury's portrayal of Martian colonies implausible, the book was a triumphant success, largely, some have suggested, because of these "weaknesses." Bradbury's Mars mirrored the present and served as the stage upon which his eccentric characters—the misfits, opportunists, and romantics—could remake Mars in their own images (only to find themselves remade by Mars in the process). *The Martian Chronicles* has proved to be enduringly popular. It has passed through several editions, sold millions of copies, and been translated into more than thirty foreign languages.

The Illustrated Man • Another book of interlinked stories, *The Illustrated Man*, followed soon after the publication of *The Martian Chronicles*. In *The Illustrated Man* the device linking the stories together is the tattoos on the skin of one of the characters. Bradbury sets some of his stories on Mars, and a few bear some relation to the cycle of stories in *The Martian Chronicles*. By the early 1950's, Bradbury was a well-established writer, able to place his stories in both pulp and popular magazines and able to profit again when his collections of these stories were published as books. His fourth collection, *The Golden Apples of the Sun*, abandoned the frame narrative that he had been using and instead simply juxtaposed stories from a wide variety of genres—science fiction, fantasy, crime, and comedy.

Fahrenheit 451 • During this most prolific period in Bradbury's literary life, he also published the book that would generate, along with *The Martian Chronicles*, his greatest success and influence. The story that came to be called *Fahrenheit 451* went through several transformations. In 1947 he had written a short story, "Bright Phoenix," in which the residents of a small town counter government book-burning edicts by memorizing the banned books. In 1951 he expanded this idea into a long story, "The Fireman," which appeared in *Galaxy Science Fiction*. A fire chief informed him that book paper first bursts into flame at 451 degrees Fahrenheit, which gave him the title for his novel-length story set in a future totalitarian state. Some critics interpreted this dystopian novel as an attack against McCarthyism, then at the height of its power, but the book also attacks the tyrannical domination of mass culture, especially in this culture's tendency to eschew complexity of thought and to embrace the simple sentiments of pressure groups. The central irony of the novel concerns firemen whose job is to set fires (burn books) rather than to put them out. Bradbury, a lifelong book lover, used his novel to show how important books are to freedom, morality, and the search for truth. His novel concludes with Montag, a fireman who has rejected his role as book burner, joining a community that strives to preserve books by memorizing them. Some critics have pointed out that this new society, where individuals abandon their identities to "become" the books they have memorized, inculcates a mass behavior as conformist as the one from which they and Montag have escaped, but Bradbury would respond that this new culture allows for a multiplicity of ideas and attitudes and thus provides the opportunity for human creativity to shape a hopeful legacy for the next generation.

Dandelion Wine • From the mid-1950's to the mid-1960's, Bradbury's writings tended to center on his midwestern childhood, without being camouflaged by a science-fiction or fantasy setting. His novel *Dandelion Wine* is a nostalgic account of a small Illinois town in the summer of 1928. Again, as in so much of his earlier work, his novel was composed of previously published stories, and the superficial unity he imposed on this material was not sufficiently coherent to satisfy several critics. Another similarity to his previous work was his theme of the twin attractions of the past and the future. The twelve-year-old hero finds himself between the secure, uncomplicated world of childhood and the frightening, complex world of adulthood. Despite the loneliness, disease, and death that seem to plague adults, the young man, like the colonists in *The Martian Chronicles*, must transform his past to create his future. Critics accused Bradbury of sentimentality in *Dandelion Wine*, pointing out how depressed and ugly Waukegan, Illinois (the model for Green Town), was at this time. Bradbury answered that he was telling his story from the viewpoint of the child, and factories, trains, pollution, and poverty are not ugly to children. Adults teach children what is ugly, and their judgments about ugliness are not always sound. For a child, as for Bradbury, Green Town was like William Butler Yeats's Byzantium, a vision of creativity and a dream for action.

Something Wicked This Way Comes • Bradbury returned to some of these themes in another novel, *Something Wicked This Way Comes*, in which a father tries to save his son and his son's friend from the evil embodied in a mysterious traveling carnival. The friend, Jim Nightshade (a name indicative of the symbolic burden the characters in this novel must bear), is particularly susceptible to the carnival's temptations, since his shadow side is so powerful. The father ultimately achieves victory by using the power of laughter as his weapon; however, the father also points out that human victories are never final and that each individual must constantly struggle never to permit the good that is in him or her to become a passive rather than an activating force. The potential for evil exists in every human being (a Christian idea, original sin, that surfaces in many of Bradbury's stories), and unless humans keep their goodness fit through creativity, evil will take over. For Bradbury, love is the best humanizing force that human beings possess.

Something Wicked This Way Comes marked a turning point in Bradbury's career. After this work failed to enhance his status as a significant American novelist, he turned increasingly to plays, poems, and essays. His turn to drama was essentially a return, since he had acted, as a boy, on the stage and on radio, and because he had written several plays when he was young (they were so bad that he vowed never to write plays again until he learned to write competently in other forms). Many of his plays are adaptations of his stories, and most of them have been staged in California, though a few have had productions Off-Broadway in New York. The majority of his plays have been published. His first collection, *The Anthem Sprinters and Other Antics*, appeared in 1963 (the "anthem sprinters" are Irishmen who flee from motion-picture theaters before the national anthem is played). Although his short-story writing diminished during the 1960's, it did not vanish, and in 1969 he published another collection, *I Sing the Body Electric!*, which was a miscellany of science-fiction and fantasy stories. Throughout his life, Bradbury has also been an avid reader of poetry. He often made use of poetic diction in his stories, but, as in the case of his playwriting, he refrained from publishing his poetry until late in his career, because he wanted it to be accomplished and stylistically refined. Heavily indebted to Gerard Manley Hopkins, Dylan Thomas, Walt Whitman, and others, his poetry has not had the success of his stories. Much of the poetry, whimsical in tone, can be categorized as light verse.

Death Is a Lonely Business • During the 1980's and 1990's, Bradbury's audacious approach to writing continued with new twists on such old forms as short and long fiction, poetry, and plays, but he also found himself in such new roles as librettist for a musical and an opera. Though his poetry was collected as *The Complete Poems of Ray Bradbury* in 1982, this did not prevent him from publishing new volumes of poetry during the late 1980's and into the 1990's. In 1985 he published his first novel in twenty-three years, *Death Is a Lonely Business*, which also marked his entry into a new genre, the detective story, though its offbeat characters and elements of fantasy give it a distinctly Bradburian slant. Some reviewers considered the clash between the hard-boiled and the fantastic disconcerting and frustrating, but others found his re-creation of a bygone era in Southern California history appealing.

A Graveyard for Lunatics • Bradbury's next novel, *A Graveyard for Lunatics: Another Tale of Two Cities*, used the same unnamed narrator and several other characters as *Death Is a Lonely Business.* The two cities of the subtitle are Venice and Hollywood, and the narrator, who is a young writer of stories for fantasy and detective magazines, has many adventures in the "graveyard" of Maximus Films, "the most successful studio in history," which also serves as a burial ground for the fantastic schemes of several eccentrics the narrator meets.

Green Shadows, White Whale • *Green Shadows, White Whale* represented Bradbury's fictionalization of the experiences he had more than forty years before, when he traveled to Ireland to write the screenplay for *Moby Dick* for director John Huston. He recounts entertaining incidents with a customs inspector, a priest, and the habitual denizens of an Irish pub, but Bradbury's exaggerated and barbed depiction of director Huston is what actually holds the book together.

Robert J. Paradowski

Other major works

SHORT FICTION: *Dark Carnival*, 1947; *The Martian Chronicles*, 1950; *The Illustrated Man*, 1951; *The Golden Apples of the Sun*, 1953; *The October Country*, 1955; *A Medicine for Melancholy*, 1959; *Twice Twenty-two*, 1959; *The Machineries of Joy*, 1964; *Autumn People*, 1965; *Vintage Bradbury*, 1965; *Tomorrow Midnight*, 1966; *I Sing the Body Electric!*, 1969; *Long After Midnight*, 1976; *"The Last Circus," and "The Electrocution,"* 1980; *The Stories of Ray Bradbury*, 1980; *Dinosaur Tales*, 1983; *A Memory of Murder*, 1984; *The Toynbee Convector*, 1988; *Quicker than the Eye*, 1996; *Driving Blind*, 1997; *One More for the Road: A New Short Story Collection*, 2002; *Bradbury Stories: One Hundred of His Most Celebrated Tales*, 2003; *The Best of Ray Bradbury: The Graphic Novel*, 2003; *The Cat's Pajamas*, 2004.

PLAYS: *The Anthem Sprinters and Other Antics*, pb. 1963; *The World of Ray Bradbury: Three Fables of the Future*, pr. 1964; *The Day It Rained Forever*, pb. 1966; *The Pedestrian*, pb. 1966; *Dandelion Wine*, pr. 1967 (adaptation of his novel); *Madrigals for the Space Age*, pb. 1972; *The Wonderful Ice Cream Suit, and Other Plays*, pb. 1972; *Pillar of Fire, and Other Plays for Today, Tomorrow, and Beyond Tomorrow*, pb. 1975; *That Ghost, That Bride of Time: Excerpts from a Play-in-Progress*, pb. 1976; *The Martian Chronicles*, pr. 1977; *Fahrenheit 451*, pr. 1979 (musical); *A Device Out of Time*, pb. 1986; *On Stage: A Chrestomathy of His Plays*, pb. 1991.

SCREENPLAYS: *It Came from Outer Space*, 1952 (with David Schwartz); *Moby Dick*, 1956 (with John Huston); *Icarus Montgolfier Wright*, 1961 (with George C. Johnson); *The Picasso Summer*, 1969 (with Ed Weinberger).

POETRY: *Old Ahab's Friend, and Friend to Noah, Speaks His Piece: A Celebration*, 1971; *When Elephants Last in the Dooryard Bloomed: Celebrations for Almost Any Day in the Year*, 1973; *Where Robot Mice and Robot Men Run Round in Robot Towns: New Poems, Both Light and Dark*, 1977; *The Bike Repairman*, 1978; *Twin Hieroglyphs That Swim the River Dust*, 1978; *The Aqueduct*, 1979; *The Haunted Computer and the Android Pope*, 1981; *The Complete Poems of Ray Bradbury*, 1982; *Forever and the Earth*, 1984; *Death Has Lost Its Charm for Me*, 1987; *Dogs Think That Every Day Is Christmas*, 1997; *With Cat for Comforter*, 1997 (with Loise Max); *I Live by the Invisible: New and Selected Poems*, 2002.

NONFICTION: *Teacher's Guide to Science Fiction*, 1968 (with Lewy Olfson); *"Zen and the Art of Writing" and "The Joy of Writing": Two Essays*, 1973; *Mars and the Mind of Man*, 1973; *The Mummies of Guanajuato*, 1978; *The Art of the Playboy*, 1985; *Zen in the Art of*

Writing: Essays on Creativity, 1989; *Yestermorrow: Obvious Answers to Impossible Futures*, 1991; *Bradbury Speaks: Too Soon from the Cave, Too Far from the Stars*, 2005.

CHILDREN'S LITERATURE: *Switch on the Night*, 1955; *R Is for Rocket*, 1962; *S Is for Space*, 1966; *The Halloween Tree*, 1972; *Fever Dream*, 1987; *Ahmed and the Oblivion Machines: A Fable*, 1998.

EDITED TEXTS: *Timeless Stories for Today and Tomorrow*, 1952; *The Circus of Dr. Lao, and Other Improbable Stories*, 1956.

Bibliography

Bloom, Harold, ed. *Ray Bradbury*. New York: Chelsea House, 2001. Critical essays cover the major themes in Bradbury's works, looking at, among other topics, his Martian stories, his participation in the gothic tradition, the role of children in his work, and his use of myth.

____________. *Ray Bradbury's "Fahrenheit 451."* New York: Chelsea House, 2001. Eight essays on one of Bradbury's most important novels. Includes a chronology, a bibliography, and an introduction by Bloom.

Bolhafner, J. Stephen. "The Ray Bradbury Chronicles." *St. Louis Post-Dispatch*, December 1, 1996. An interview with Bradbury on the occasion of the publication of his collection of short stories *Quicker than the Eye*. Bradbury reminisces about the beginnings of his career, talks about getting over his fear of flying, and discusses *The Martian Chronicles* as fantasy, mythology, and Magical Realism.

Bradbury, Ray. "Sci-fi for Your D: Drive." *Newsweek* 126 (November 13, 1995): 89. In this interview-story, Bradbury discusses why he is putting his most widely acclaimed short-story collection, *The Martian Chronicles*, on CD-ROM. Bradbury also discusses the role of imagination in technology, the space program, and his favorite literary figures.

Eller, Jonathan R., and William F. Touponce. *Ray Bradbury: The Life of Fiction*. Kent, Ohio: Kent State University Press, 2004. First full biography of Bradbury.

Greenberg, Martin Henry, and Joseph D. Olander, eds. *Ray Bradbury*. New York: Taplinger, 1980. This anthology of Bradbury criticism is part of the Writers of the Twenty-first Century series. Some of the articles defend Bradbury against the charge that he is not really a science-fiction writer but an opponent of science and technology; other articles defend him against the charge that he is mawkish. Includes an extensive Bradbury bibliography compiled by Marshall B. Tymn and an index.

Johnson, Wayne L. *Ray Bradbury*. New York: Frederick Ungar, 1980. Although this volume is the work of a fan rather than a critic, it provides a good general introduction to Bradbury's stories of fantasy and science fiction. Johnson's approach is thematic rather than chronological (he uses the categories of magic, monsters, and machines to facilitate his discussion of Bradbury's principal approaches, ideas, and themes). Index.

Reid, Robin Ann. *Ray Bradbury: A Critical Companion*. Westport, Conn.: Greenwood Press, 2000. Part of the publisher's series of reference books on popular contemporary writers for students, this volume provides detailed plot summaries and analyses of Bradbury's novels, along with character portraits, a biography of Bradbury and an extensive bibliography.

Touponce, William F. *Naming the Unnameable: Ray Bradbury and the Fantastic After Freud*. Mercer Island, Wash.: Starmont House, 1997. Touponce finds the psychoanalytic ideas of Sigmund Freud and Carl Jung helpful in plumbing the effectiveness of much of Bradbury's work (though in a letter to the author, Bradbury himself denies any direct influence, since he has "read little Freud or Jung"). Nevertheless, Touponce believes that Bradbury has given us stories of a modern consciousness that often forgets its debt to the unconscious.

Weist, Jerry, and Donn Albright. *Bradbury, an Illustrated Life: A Journey to Far Metaphor.* New York: William Morrow, 2002. A "visual biography" of Bradbury, consisting largely of images from pulps, films, television, and other mass media that both influenced Bradbury and have been influenced by him. An innovative approach to understanding a writer who transcends the printed page.

Weller, Sam. *The Bradbury Chronicles.* New York: William Morrow, 2005. This authorized biography was written with access to Bradbury and his personal papers and correspondence. Not a critical work, but rather an admiring portrait of the writer.

Marion Zimmer Bradley

Born: Albany, New York; June 3, 1930
Died: Berkeley, California; September 25, 1999

Principal long fiction • *The Door Through Space*, 1961; *"The Planet Savers" and "The Sword of Aldones,"* 1962; *The Bloody Sun*, 1964; *Star of Danger*, 1965; *The Winds of Darkover*, 1970; *The World Wreckers*, 1971; *Darkover Landfall*, 1972; *Hunters of the Red Moon*, 1973 (with Paul Edwin Zimmer); *The Spell Sword*, 1974; *The Heritage of Hastur*, 1975; *The Shattered Chain*, 1976; *The Forbidden Tower*, 1977; *The House Between the Worlds*, 1980; *Two to Conquer*, 1980; *Sharra's Exile*, 1981; *The Mists of Avalon*, 1983; *Thendara House*, 1983; *Web of Light*, 1983; *The Firebrand*, 1987; *Witch Hill*, 1990; *Renunciates of Darkover*, 1991; *Rediscovery: A Novel of Darkover*, 1993; *The Forest House*, 1993; *The Forest of Darkover*, 1993; *Towers of Darkover*, 1993; *Glenraven*, 1996 (with Holly Lisle); *Witchlight*, 1996; *Gravelight*, 1997; *Lady of Avalon*, 1997; *The Shadow Matrix: A Novel of Darkover*, 1997; *Heartlight*, 1998; *In the Rift*, 1998 (with Holly Lisle); *Traitor's Sun: A Novel of Darkover*, 1998; *Priestess of Avalon*, 2000; *The Fall of Neskaya*, 2001 (with Deborah J. Ross).

Other literary forms • Marion Zimmer Bradley wrote short fiction but is mostly known as a novelist. She published several collections of short stories and a few essays. In addition to her writing, Bradley made a name for herself as an editor. She founded *Marion Zimmer Bradley's Fantasy Magazine* in 1988. She also edited numerous anthologies, notably the Darkover anthologies and the Sword and Sorceress series.

Achievements • Bradley is one of the most prolific authors to write science fiction, with more than sixty novels to her name and others written under pseudonyms. Though she was nominated for both the Hugo and Nebula Awards, she never won either of science fiction's highest honors. Nevertheless, her novels contributed to the growth of science fiction in numerous ways. Bradley pushed the boundaries of sexual taboos, especially on homosexuality, with her sympathetic homosexual characters. It could also be argued that she, like fellow fantasy writer Andre Norton, served as a role model for many women who wanted to write science fiction and fantasy. As an editor, Bradley published many authors' debut stories and helped other women writers become established in what had been traditionally a male-oriented field. She will always be known for creating one of the most enduring worlds and series in science fiction.

Biography • Marion Zimmer was born in Albany, New York, in 1930. As a teenager, she was a science-fiction and fantasy fan. She made her first amateur sale to a fiction contest in *Fantastic/Amazing Stories* in 1949. During that same year, she married Robert Alden Bradley. Her oldest son, David, was born in 1950. Bradley wrote during these early years, but only for amateur fanzines and school magazines. Her first professional sale came in 1953 when she sold a short story to *Vortex Science Fiction*.

Bradley published her first novel in 1961. In 1962, she published two novels together, including the first novel set on the planet Darkover. The Darkover novels eventually became her best-known works. She published several more novels during the 1960's, while going to college. Some of her work at this time was done under

various pseudonyms, since she was earning her living by writing. She graduated from Hardin-Simmons University in Texas in 1964 with a bachelor's degree. From 1966 to 1967, she did graduate work at the University of California at Berkeley. During that time she and Robert Bradley divorced. Marion then married Walter Breen, with whom she later had two children, Patrick and Moira.

During the 1970's, Bradley published an average of two books per year, usually one Darkover novel and another novel. The Darkover series generated fan groups specifically dedicated to that series. Also during the 1970's, Bradley became a pastoral counselor in California and began to study religion and counseling. Her writing career continued to flourish during the 1980's. In 1983, she published *The Mists of Avalon*, a best-seller. In 1980, she became an ordained priest of the Pre-Nicene Roman Catholic Church and established the Centre for Nontraditional Religion. Religious themes also are demonstrated in her novels.

During the late 1980's, Bradley began editing her own magazine and anthologies. She helped nurture up-and-coming writers, particularly female authors. In her magazine and the Sword and Sorceress anthologies, she made an effort to publish first-time authors. In 1990, Bradley divorced Breen. Her writing career continued, even though she suffered health problems. She was still editing her magazine and the anthologies until shortly before her death in September, 1999.

Analysis • Bradley's early years fit the conventional mold of the science-fiction and fantasy genres in which she was publishing. However, as she matured as a writer, she explored nonconventional themes, particularly in the areas of religion and sexuality. She also moved away from hard science fiction into more traditional fantasy. Many of her characters possess psychic abilities or some sort of power that sets them apart from others. Most of the critical work on Bradley has been done on her as a woman writer and a writer of women characters and issues. She created memorable female characters, such as Morgaine from *The Mists of Avalon*, and female sisterhoods, such as the Free Amazons of Darkover. Though Bradley did not call herself a feminist, she was both criticized and applauded by those who have.

Darkover Landfall • *Darkover Landfall* is not the first book published about Darkover; however, it is the first book in the chronological order of that series. *Darkover Landfall* details the origin of humans on the planet Darkover. A colonization ship, heading for another planet, crashes on the inhospitable planet. While trying to repair their ship, the crew and colonists are exposed to the Ghost Wind, a natural occurrence that spreads a psychoactive pollen over the crash party. The pollen activates latent psychic abilities and lowers sexual inhibitions. Various sexual unions occur among the survivors. Eventually, they realize that they will have to make their home on the world.

The plot is a fairly conventional one for a science-fiction novel. This book shows Bradley's interest in and use of psychic abilities in her novels. On a nonconventional level, the book, without giving details, explores alternate sexualities and alternate standards of marriage and partnerships. To ensure a broad gene pool, everyone must have children with different partners. What caused the biggest controversy for the novel, though, was the fact that Camilla Del Rey, the first officer, is forbidden to have an abortion when she wishes one. If it had not been for the crash, there would have been no problem with her choice, but since the colony knows fertility and infant survival rates will be low for the first several years, she is forced to have the child. This position, though defended in the world of the book, sparked controversy and ire among fans, feminists, and other writers. It was not until later books that Bradley changed their minds.

The Shattered Chain • *The Shattered Chain* is another Darkover novel, but it differs from earlier works because it focuses on the Free Amazons, or Renunciates, of Darkover. Centuries after the crash of the starship, Darkover has become a planet with a harsh caste system and a mostly feudal political and economic system. Women have few or no rights in most of this society. The exception is the Free Amazons. The Free Amazons have renounced their allegiance and reliance on their former families and men. They renounce marriage. They swear an oath that they will give themselves to men and will have children only when they want to. They are often ridiculed by Darkoveran society. This novel in many ways answers the criticisms leveled at Bradley after the publication of *Darkover Landfall*. In this novel, the women are the protagonists and the capable characters.

The story is told in three sections, with twelve years separating part 1 from part 2. Parts 1 and 2 focus on rescues. In the first part, Rohanna Ardais, a telepathic noblewoman, hires the Free Amazons to rescue her abducted kinswoman because the men in her family have given up on her. Melora, Rohanna's cousin, is trapped in a Dry Town. In the Dry Towns, all women are chained, wearing the outward sign that they belong to the men. The Free Amazons rescue Melora and her daughter Jaelle so that Jaelle will not be chained. In part 2, Magda Lorne, a Terran sociologist, impersonates a Free Amazon to ransom her male friend, Peter Haldane, from a thief. She meets the grown Jaelle and her band and is forced to pledge the oath of the Amazons. She then realizes that she believes the oath. Part 3 focuses on the ramifications of Magda and Jaelle's oath.

Although the first two parts carry most of the action for the story, it is the last section that reveals Bradley's themes. Throughout the section, the three female protagonists confront the choices they have made and the prices they have paid or will pay. Rohanna renounced her freedom of choice for security in marriage. Jaelle gained her freedom but renounced the ability to ever marry. Magda has to renounce her Terran allegiance to live as a Free Amazon. Bradley's point is that what is important is the choice—women should always have a choice in what they do. Rohanna did not have that choice and learns to live with it. Jaelle did have that choice but realizes it requires a price. She eventually chooses to live as a freemate with Peter Haldane. The fact that she wants to give herself to a man is her choice as well.

There is a brief mention of the theme of fate in this novel, a theme Bradley explores in greater depth in later works. It seems to be pure chance that Magda meets Jaelle on her way to free Haldane. However, Lady Rohanna does not think it mere coincidence that Haldane looks exactly like Rohanna's son or that Magda meets Jaelle, the one person who could uncover her masquerade as a Free Amazon. Bradley suggests that there is a higher power at work. Although feminists hated *Darkover Landfall*, many hailed *The Shattered Chain* as a feminist novel. Reviewer Joanna Russ, critical of the earlier work, later included *The Shattered Chain* in a listing of feminist utopias. The exploration of woman's choice continued in later Bradley works.

The Mists of Avalon • Although she will be known forever among the science-fiction community for creating Darkover, Bradley is known to a wider literary audience for *The Mists of Avalon*. It could be considered her magnum opus. An impressive length, it stayed on *The New York Times* best-seller list for months after it was published in 1983. It was her first and most successful crossover mainstream novel.

The themes Bradley explored in *The Shattered Chain* reappear in *The Mists of Avalon*. This is the story of the women of the Arthurian legend and their struggles with fate, religion, and the social strictures of that time. It deals with the matters of choice, or lack thereof. Though principally the story of Morgaine and Gwenhwyfar, attention is also given to Ingraine, the mother of Morgaine and Arthur; Viviane, the Lady of the Lake; Morguase, Morgaine's aunt and the mother of Gawaine; and Nimue, daughter of Lancelot and the nemesis of the Merlin, Kevin Harper. Through these women, Bradley reimagines the Arthurian legends into a woman's history and story.

Bradley reimagines the thematic conflict of the legend. In the book, the old ways of the Goddess religion are dying out to the encroachments of Christianity. The Lady of the Lake is the high priestess of the Goddess faith, with Avalon as her seat of power. The Merlin is the chosen messenger of the gods. Viviane, the Lady of the Lake, and Taliesin, the Merlin, plan to put Uther on the throne of Great Britain so that he can protect the people from both the Saxons and the Christians. They further arrange that Uther's son Arthur should be king of both Britain and Avalon. Their plans go awry when Gwenhwyfar turns out to be overly pious and converts Arthur into a Christian king.

Morgaine is raised on Avalon as priestess of the Goddess and vows to do Her will. However, when Viviane arranges for Arthur and Morgaine to participate in the ancient rites and have sexual intercourse, Morgaine feels betrayed and leaves Avalon. She joins Arthur's court, though she never gives up her ways. She continually tries to make Arthur be true to his oath to Avalon. In Bradley's version of the legend, this is the source of the conflict between Arthur and Morgaine—the struggle of one religion over another. Mordred, the son of Arthur and Morgaine, is also incorporated into this struggle, as he has been raised in Avalon and sees himself as the one to return Britain to its old ways. To do so, he must remove his father. Morgaine never hates Arthur in this version; in fact, the siblings love each other. Morgaine has always been Arthur's first love.

The conflict between the religions spurs social conflict as well. Under the old ways, women had the choice of whom they would mate with or love. The priests bring patriarchy and the concept of adultery. Bradley makes it clear that few of these women have choices. Ingraine, at the age of fifteen, is given in marriage to the old duke of Cornwall. Morgaine is given to Arthur in the rites. Gwenhwyfar is given to Arthur as part of a deal for horses. Arthur later arranges a marriage for Morgaine with the aged Uriens, king of North Wales. The women do what is expected of them, however much they internally question those rules. Besides having no social choices, Bradley suggests that the women have no choices at all. Viviane and Morgaine both have the Sight, a gift from the Goddess that gives them knowledge of the future. The implication is that everyone has a destiny to be carried out, and there is little that can be done to change that destiny.

The success of this novel may be attributed to many things. First, the Arthurian legend holds a certain mystique of its own, and Bradley captures that sense of awe in her own way. Second, Bradley manages to portray the conflict that many women feel regarding traditional Judeo-Christian religions. Bradley, through Gwenhwyfar, often mentions how priests teach that sin came into the world through a woman, and therefore all women are evil. Morgaine's character dismisses that notion with contempt, and even Gwenhwyfar seems to finally reject it, entering the embrace of the Goddess in the aspect of the Virgin Mary.

P. Andrew Miller

Other major works

SHORT FICTION: *The Dark Intruder, and Other Stories,* 1964; "A Sword of Chaos," 1981; "The Lesson of the Inn," 1981; *The Best of Marion Zimmer Bradley,* 1985; *Lythande,* 1986.

NONFICTION: "Responsibilities and Temptations of Women Science Fiction Writers," 1985.

CHILDREN'S LITERATURE: *The Brass Dragon,* 1970.

EDITED TEXTS: *Sword and Sorceress: An Anthology of Heroic Fantasy,* 1985-(series; 19 volumes as of 2002); *Snows of Darkover,* 1994.

Bibliography

Arbur, Rosemarie. *Leigh Brackett, Marion Zimmer Bradley, Anne McCaffrey: A Primary and Secondary Bibliography.* Boston: G. K. Hall, 1982. A comprehensive bibliography through the early 1980's in the Masters of Science Fiction and Fantasy series. Includes indexes.

____________. *Marion Zimmer Bradley.* Mercer Island, Wash.: Starmont House, 1985. A great overall look at Bradley's work. Gives biographical and chronological overview of Bradley's writing as well as analysis of her books by type, such as Darkover, non-Darkover science fiction, and fantasy.

Browne, Pat, ed. *Heroines of Popular Culture.* Bowling Green, Ohio: Bowling Green State University Press, 1987. Contains an essay discussing Bradley's debt to the Beguinal societies in the use of sisterhood in her Darkover novels.

Hildebrand, Kristina. *The Female Reader at the Round Table: Religion and Women in Three Contemporary Arthurian Texts.* Uppsala, Sweden: Uppsala University Library, 2001. Places Bradley in the context of the history of the Arthurian legends and women's literature.

King, Betty. *Women of the Future: The Female Main Character in Science Fiction.* Metuchen, N.J.: Scarecrow Press, 1984. Places Bradley's work in historical perspective.

Roberson, Jennifer, ed. *Return to Avalon: A Celebration of Marion Zimmer Bradley.* New York: DAW Books, 1996. A collection of appreciative essays, written primarily by other female luminaries writing in the science-fiction and fantasy genres.

Russ, Joanna. "Recent Feminist Utopias." In *Future Females: A Critical Anthology*, edited by Marleen S. Barr. Bowling Green, Ohio: Bowling Green State University Press, 1981. Critical article that draws comparisons among many feminist utopias, including *The Shattered Chain.*

Schwartz, Susan M. "Marion Zimmer Bradley's Ethic of Freedom." In *The Feminine Eye*, edited by Tom Staicar. New York: Frederick Ungar, 1982. Critical chapter on women in the Darkover novels, particularly *The Shattered Chain.* Schwartz examines Bradley's themes of choice and the price of choice. Also emphasizes the importance of risk taking and tests of will in the Darkover novels.

Tober, Lee Ann. "Why Change the Arthur Story? Marion Zimmer Bradley's *The Mists of Avalon.*" *Extrapolation* 34, no. 2 (Summer, 1993): 147-157. Academic article that argues the feminist significance of Bradley's novel as an inversion of the male-centered Arthurian legend.

Richard Brautigan

Born: Tacoma, Washington; January 30, 1935
Died: Bolinas, California; September, 1984

Principal long fiction • *A Confederate General from Big Sur*, 1964; *Trout Fishing in America*, 1967; *In Watermelon Sugar*, 1968; *The Abortion: An Historical Romance*, 1971; *The Hawkline Monster: A Gothic Western*, 1974; *Willard and His Bowling Trophies: A Perverse Mystery*, 1975; *Sombrero Fallout: A Japanese Novel*, 1976; *Dreaming of Babylon: A Private Eye Novel 1942*, 1977; *The Tokyo-Montana Express*, 1980; *So the Wind Won't Blow It All Away*, 1982; *An Unfortunate Woman*, 2000.

Other literary forms • Richard Brautigan began his literary career as a poet. "I wrote poetry for seven years," he noted, "to learn how to write a sentence." Though a poet for many years, Brautigan maintained that his ambition was to write novels: "I figured I couldn't write a novel until I could write a sentence." Although most of Brautigan's later work was in novel form, he continued to publish poetry and also produced a collection of short stories (*Revenge of the Lawn: Stories 1962-1970*, 1971).

Achievements • Short-story writer, novelist, and poet, Brautigan created a stream of works that resist simple categories—in fact, defy categorization altogether. Much of his popularity can be attributed to his peculiar style, his unconventional plots, simple language, and marvelous humor, which together provide a melancholy vision of American life and the elusive American Dream.

Much of Brautigan's work involves the search for simplicity—an expansion of the Emersonian search for pastoral America. Yet, the complacent rural life is no longer available in Brautigan's world: All the trout streams have been sold to the highest bidder, all the campgrounds are already filled, in fact overflowing; yet, the search must go on for new places where the imagination can still roam free—to a pastoral America where the individual can escape the suffocating din of technocracy.

Brautigan's work evolved into a new, unorthodox version of the American novel. His experimentation with language, structure, characterization, plot, and motif broke new ground. Because of this, many critics have been unable to characterize his work with ease. Unable to pinpoint his exact standing, they have dismissed him as a counterculture phenomenon, a faddish nonentity. Although Brautigan's oeuvre is indeed very uneven, his best work is genuinely original and ensures him a lasting place in American literature.

Biography • Richard Brautigan was born and reared in the Pacific Northwest. The son of Bernard F. Brautigan and Lula Mary Keho Brautigan, he spent his early years in Washington and Oregon. His literary career took hold when, in 1958, he moved to San Francisco and began writing poetry in the company of Lawrence Ferlinghetti, Robert Duncan, Philip Whalen, and Michael McClure. The company he kept led to his initial identification as a Beat poet, but Brautigan's unique and now well-known style defied the classification.

Resisting crass commercialism and the profits linked with corporate America,

Brautigan's first books were published primarily for the benefit of his friends and acquaintances. Success finally forced him to allow a New York publication of his work during the 1960's, however, and Grove Press published his *A Confederate General from Big Sur.* Shortly after his change of allegiance from Four Seasons Foundation in San Francisco to Grove Press in New York, Brautigan was invited to become poet-in-residence at Pasadena's California Institute of Technology. Although he had never attended college, he accepted the invitation and spent the 1967 academic year at the prestigious school.

In 1957, Brautigan married Virginia Diorine Adler. They had one daughter, Ianthe, and later were divorced. In his later years, Brautigan divided his time among three places: Tokyo, San Francisco, and, when in retreat or fishing, a small town in Montana. He died in 1984, an apparent suicide.

Analysis • Richard Brautigan's novels are generally characterized by the appearance of a first-person narrator (sometimes identified in the third person as Brautigan himself) who presents an autobiographical, often whimsical story. Brautigan's work employs simple, direct, short, and usually repetitive sentences. In his best work, he has an uncanny ability to create vibrant and compelling scenes from apparently banal subject matter. It is the voice of the "I," however, that carries the Brautigan novel, a voice that often unifies virtually plotless and quite heterogeneous materials.

A Confederate General from Big Sur • Brautigan's first published novel, *A Confederate General from Big Sur,* is perhaps his funniest. A burlesque of American society long after the Civil War, the story is told by Jesse, a gentle, shy, withdrawn narrator (not unlike Brautigan himself) who meets Lee Mellon, a rebel, dropout, and activist living in San Francisco. Lee soon moves to Oakland, California, where he lives, rent-free, at the home of a committed mental patient. The story then moves to Big Sur, where Lee and Jesse live in a cabin, again owned by a mental patient. As Jesse and Lee figure out how to cope with life and no money, they find a fortune of six dollars and some loose change, get rip-roaring drunk in Monterey, and discover Elaine and a great deal of money. Johnston Wade, a crazed insurance man, arrives on the scene, informing everyone that he is fleeing from his wife and daughter (they want to commit him to a mental institution). He leaves as abruptly as he arrived, remembering an important business appointment he must keep. The book ends, as it must, without ending.

In *A Confederate General from Big Sur,* Brautigan is facing the question of how to cope with civilization. The flight from technology toward wilderness holds risks of its own. Brautigan offers no answers. Human life is not unlike that of the bugs sitting on the log Jesse has thrown into the fire. They sit there on the log, staring out at Jesse as the flames leap around them.

The theme of the novel is the ambition to control one's life and destiny. The ownership of the Big Sur log cabin by a mental patient and Johnston Wade's mental aberrations only serve to illustrate the fleeting control all people have over their lives. Brautigan introduces Wade to burlesque the myth of American destiny. He is a parody, a ridiculous image of American business and technocracy: the self-made man running away from his wife and child who suddenly remembers an important business engagement.

In Watermelon Sugar • Although not published until 1968, *In Watermelon Sugar* was written in 1964, during Brautigan's evolution from poet to novelist. The book reflects

Library of Congress

this evolutionary change, for in many ways it is more poetic than novelistic in its form. The story is that of a young man who lives in a small community after an unspecified cataclysm. In the first of the three parts of the book, the shy and gentle narrator tells the reader about himself and his friends. Their peaceful life was not always so, he explains, and he tells about iDEATH, a central gathering place that is more a state of mind than an actual physical location. In the second part of the novel, the narrator has a terrible dream of carnage and self-mutilation. The third part of the book begins with the narrator's awakening, strangely refreshed after the terrible dream. The gentle, leisurely pace of the first part then restores itself.

In Watermelon Sugar is like Aldous Huxley's *Brave New World* (1932): a utopian novel of the Garden of Eden, springing forth out of the chaos of today's world. It is his vision of the rustic good life in postindustrial society. From watermelons comes the juice that is made into sugar, the stuff of the lives and dreams of the people of iDEATH. By controlling their own lives, by creating their own order, the people of iDEATH recover society from chaos. The sense of order and recurrence is set in the very first line of the book, which both begins and ends "in watermelon sugar." That phrase is also used as the title of the first part of the book, as well as the title of the first chapter. Like a refrain, it sets a pattern and order in a world in which people live in harmony with nature.

The Abortion • Like several of Brautigan's books, *The Abortion: An Historical Romance* spent some time in the library of unpublished books that it describes, where dreams go (and can be found). The world of *The Abortion* is that of a public library in California: not an ordinary library, but one where losers bring their unpublishable books. Again Brautigan's narrator is a shy, introverted recluse—the librarian, unnamed because he is ordinary, like the people who bring their books to the library to have them shelved. Brautigan himself visits the library at one point in the novel to bring in *Moose*; he is tall and blond, with an anachronistic appearance, looking as if he would be more comfortable in another era. That circumstance is certainly the case with the narrator as well.

There is less action in *The Abortion* than in most of Brautigan's novels; the book plods along slowly, mimicking its central theme, which is that a series of short, tentative steps can lead one out of a personal and social labyrinth and toward the promise of a new life. Before the reader knows it, however, the librarian is out in the rain with a young woman; she gets pregnant; and they journey to Tijuana so she can have an abortion. The woman is called Vida, and she represents life in the twentieth century. The librarian struggles with his inner self, afraid to move from the old ways, afraid to let go of his innocence. Brautigan contrasts him with his partner, Foster, a wild caveman who takes care of the books that have been moved from the library to dead storage in a cave. Foster is loud and outgoing—the opposite of the timid librarian—and he thinks of the library as an asylum.

With Vida, the librarian becomes embroiled in a quest for survival. Vida brings him out of the library into the world of change and conflict. He is frightened by it, but, step by tentative step, he confronts it.

The Abortion is a commentary on American culture. Brautigan draws a loose parallel between the library and American history: The librarian-narrator is the thirty-sixth caretaker of the library; at the time the book was written, there had been thirty-six presidents of the United States. The origins of the mysterious library go back into the American past as well, just as Brautigan himself appears as an anachronism from an earlier, easier time.

Although Brautigan laments the times gone by and yearns for the "good old days" and the leisurely pace of the library, he also holds out hope for a fresh alternative. American culture has nearly been destroyed—the playboy beauty queen named Vida hates herself, and bombs and industrial technocracy threaten lives and deaden spirits. Strangely enough, by destroying life—by the abortion—one can begin anew, start a new life. The narrator and Vida share this hopefulness, which was widespread in the counterculture when *The Abortion* was published.

The Hawkline Monster • With *The Hawkline Monster: A Gothic Western*, Brautigan began a series of novels that adapt the conventions of genre fiction in a quirky, unpredictable manner. Not strictly parodies, these hybrids sometimes achieve wonderful effects—odd, unsettling, comical—and sometimes fall flat. Combining the gothic novel, the Western, and a dash of romance, *The Hawkline Monster* is set in eastern Oregon during 1902 and centers on a magical Victorian house occupied by two equally baffling Victorian maidens with curious habits. The unreality of the situation does not affect the two unruffled Western heroes of the book, however, who methodically go about their task of killing the Hawkline Monster. The problem is not only to find the monster but also to discover what it is; the ice caves under the house complete the unreality of the situation. Brautigan moves lyrically from the mundane to the magical in this fusion of the real and the surreal.

Trout Fishing in America • *Trout Fishing in America*, Brautigan's most famous novel and his best, is a short, visionary inscape of the American nightmare. Brautigan has created a tragic symbol of what has happened to America: The trout streams are all gone, the campgrounds are full; escape to the American pastoral is no longer possible. However, Brautigan assures his readers that all is not lost—there is still a place where they can find freedom. If all the land is being used and one cannot physically escape the city, then one must escape to the pastoral realm of one's imagination. Trout fishing, Brautigan insists, is thus a way of recapturing the simple while remaining aware of the complex.

Trout Fishing in America, like much of Brautigan's work (including his last novel, *So the Wind Won't Blow It All Away*), is autobiographical. The gentle, withdrawn narrator uses trout fishing as a central metaphor. A victim of the technological world, the narrator creates his own watery realm, complete with its own boundaries—a place where he can find solace from the technological stranglehold. His vision implies that all people have a fundamental right to the abundant richness and good life that America can provide but that are denied to many because the bankrupt ideas of the past still hold sway. Aware of the complexities of American life, Brautigan seems to be exhorting his readers to recapture the simple life, to escape the confinement of the city for the freedom of the wilderness. If that wilderness in the actual sense is cut off and no longer accessible; if all the trout streams have been developed, disassembled, and sold; if the horizon is now not new but old and despoiled; if the parks are already overcrowded; if there is no other way, then one must escape through the imagination.

So the Wind Won't Blow It All Away • In *So the Wind Won't Blow It All Away*, Brautigan gives readers a glimpse of what post-*Trout Fishing in America* life has become. Billed as an "American tragedy," *So the Wind Won't Blow It All Away* focuses on the tragedy that America and American life have become: "dust . . . American . . . dust."

Written, as are most of his novels, in the first person, Brautigan's novel is the memoir of an anonymous boy reared in welfare-state poverty somewhere in the Pacific Northwest. Unloved but tolerated by his mother, the boy and his family go from town to town, meeting an odd assortment of minor characters. Although undeveloped, these characters serve to carry the novel's theme and serve as victims of the technocracy America has become. There is an old pensioner who lives in a packing-crate shack; adept at carpentry, the old man built a beautiful dock and boat and knows all the best fishing spots on the pond near his home, but he does not use his knowledge or equipment. A gas-station attendant who cares nothing about selling gas but likes to sell worms to fishermen also appears on the scene. There is a thirty-five-year-old alcoholic who traded ambition for beer; charged with the safety of the sawmill, the man dresses in finery (although readers are told that his appearances are not true-to-life), cares nothing about his job, and is continually encircled by boys who swoop like vultures to take his empty bottles back to the store for credit. Like America itself, the guard has brittle bones resembling dried-out weeds. Finally, Brautigan introduces a husband and wife who, each night, carry their living-room furniture to the pond, set it up, and fish all night.

Brautigan presents America as having come to the end of its greatness, like the end of a summer afternoon. The technological success that spurred the country to greatness has resulted in its downfall. The husband and wife have changed all their electrical lamps to kerosene and await the cool evening with its refreshing possibilities, but as they patiently fish in the wrong spot, America goes on, killing its imagination with the technology of mindless television.

So the Wind Won't Blow It All Away ends with the horrible climax of the death of a boy, shot by mistake in an orchard that has been left to die. With that end, however, is the beginning of a new life, for, though the orchard has been left alone to die, new fruit will grow. The novel recalls the message of *The Abortion*: The substitutions of the confinement of the city for the freedom of the wilderness, and of television for imagination, are choices people have. With this novel, Brautigan returned to the successful themes of his earliest novels, warning that to go on will result only in dust.

David Mike Hamilton

Other major works

SHORT FICTION: *Revenge of the Lawn: Stories 1962-1970*, 1971.

POETRY: *The Return of the Rivers*, 1957; *The Galilee Hitch-Hiker*, 1958; *Lay the Marble Tea: Twenty-four Poems*, 1959; *The Octopus Frontier*, 1960; *All Watched over by Machines of Loving Grace*, 1967; *Please Plant This Book*, 1968; *The Pill Versus the Springhill Mine Disaster*, 1968; *Rommel Drives on Deep into Egypt*, 1970; *Loading Mercury with a Pitchfork*, 1976; *June 30th, June 30th*, 1978.

MISCELLANEOUS: *The Edna Webster Collection of Undiscovered Writings*, 1995.

Bibliography

Abbott, Keith. *Downstream from "Trout Fishing in America."* Santa Barbara, Calif.: Capra Press, 1989. Abbott recounts his memories of Brautigan from their first meeting in San Francisco in 1966, through the Montana years, and back to 1982 in San Francisco. Abbott's last chapter, "Shadows and Marble," is a critical essay devoted to Brautigan's language and strategy of fiction.

Barber, John F. *Richard Brautigan: An Annotated Bibliography*. Jefferson, N.C.: McFarland, 1990. A good source for students of Brautigan.

Boyer, Jay. *Richard Brautigan*. Boise, Idaho: Boise State University Press, 1987. Offers criticism and interpretation. Includes a bibliography.

Bradbury, Malcolm. *The Modern American Novel*. Oxford, England: Oxford University Press, 1983. Chapter 7, "Postmoderns and Others: The 1960s and 1970s," cites Brautigan, placing him in the genre of writers who "celebrated the hippie youth spirit." Bradbury gives succinct but insightful critical commentary on Brautigan's novels. He sees Brautigan as much more than a hippie writer, whose spirit of "imaginative discovery" has spawned a number of literary successors.

Brautigan, Ianthe. *You Can't Catch Death: A Daughter's Memoir*. New York: St. Martin's Press, 2000. Brautigan's daughter offers her recollections of a childhood spent bouncing between her two bohemian parents' homes.

Chénetier, Marc. *Richard Brautigan*. New York: Methuen, 1983. A semiotic examination of Brautigan's approach to structure and elements of style that generate meaning. This slender volume touches on several works, with particular attention to *Trout Fishing in America*.

Foster, Edward Halsey. *Richard Brautigan*. Boston: Twayne, 1983. This blend of biography and criticism deals primarily with Brautigan's work within his own cultural ambience, referring to other contemporary fiction, the Beat movement, and Zen Buddhism as an overall influence. Not always flattering, Foster discusses most of Brautigan's short fiction and novels.

Horvath, Brooke. "Richard Brautigan's Search for Control Over Death." *American Literature* 57 (October, 1985): 435-455. Horvath explores possible limits to Brautigan's response of imagination as a strategy for countering the basic issue of death in his four early novels and one of the stories in *The Tokyo-Montana Express*.

Keeler, Greg. *Waltzing with the Captain: Remembering Richard Brautigan*. Boise, Idaho: Limberlost Press, 2004. Appreciative study of Brautigan's life and writings.

Mills, Joseph. *Reading Richard Brautigan's "Trout Fishing in America."* Boise, Idaho: Boise State University Press, 1998. A brief volume in the Boise State University Western Writers series.

Seymore, James. "Author Richard Brautigan Apparently Takes His Own Life, but He Leaves a Rich Legacy." *People Weekly* 22 (November 12, 1984): 40-41. Provides a biographical background leading up to Brautigan's suicide, including his heavy drinking and depression at the loss of his readers.

Stull, William L. "Richard Brautigan's *Trout Fishing in America:* Notes of a Native Son." *American Literature* 56 (March, 1984): 69-80. Stull approaches general themes in *Trout Fishing in America* by examining some of the book's many allusions to other literature and Americana. A good get-acquainted piece.

Wright, Lawrence. "The Life and Death of Richard Brautigan." *Rolling Stone,* April 11, 1985, 29. A biographical sketch, noting Brautigan's early fame and cult following and the fading of his reputation and his suicide. Notes that when friends describe him, he seems two different people; at one point he was diagnosed as a paranoid schizophrenic.

Pearl S. Buck

Born: Hillsboro, West Virginia; June 26, 1892
Died: Danby, Vermont; March 6, 1973

Principal long fiction • *East Wind: West Wind,* 1930; *The Good Earth,* 1931; *Sons,* 1932; *The Mother,* 1934; *A House Divided,* 1935; *House of Earth,* 1935; *This Proud Heart,* 1938; *The Patriot,* 1939; *Other Gods: An American Legend,* 1940; *China Sky,* 1942; *Dragon Seed,* 1942; *The Promise,* 1943; *China Flight,* 1945; *Portrait of a Marriage,* 1945; *The Townsman,* 1945 (as John Sedges); *Pavilion of Women,* 1946; *The Angry Wife,* 1947 (as Sedges); *Peony,* 1948; *Kinfolk,* 1949; *The Long Love,* 1949 (as Sedges); *God's Men,* 1951; *Bright Procession,* 1952 (as Sedges); *The Hidden Flower,* 1952; *Come, My Beloved,* 1953; *Voices in the House,* 1953 (as Sedges); *Imperial Woman,* 1956; *Letter from Peking,* 1957; *Command the Morning,* 1959; *Satan Never Sleeps,* 1962; *The Living Reed,* 1963; *Death in the Castle,* 1965; *The Time Is Noon,* 1967; *The New Year,* 1968; *The Three Daughters of Madame Liang,* 1969; *Mandala,* 1970; *The Goddess Abides,* 1972; *All Under Heaven,* 1973; *The Rainbow,* 1974.

Other literary forms • An overwhelmingly prolific writer, Pearl S. Buck wrote short stories, juvenile fiction and nonfiction, pamphlets, magazine articles, literary history, biographies, plays (including a musical), educational works, an Asian cookbook, and a variety of books on America, democracy, Adolf Hitler and Germany, Japan, China, Russia, the mentally disabled, the sexes, and the Kennedy women. In addition, she translated *Shui Hu Chuan* (1933, *All Men Are Brothers*) and edited a book of Asian fairy tales, several Christmas books, and a book of Chinese woodcuts.

Besides *The Good Earth,* her finest works are her biographies of her parents, *The Exile* (1936) and *Fighting Angel: Portrait of a Soul* (1936). *The Exile* portrays the unhappy and frustrating life of her mother, a missionary wife. *Fighting Angel,* a better biography because of its greater objectivity, shows the ruthless missionary zeal of Buck's father. Of her early articles, "Is There a Case for Foreign Missions?," printed in *Christian Century* in 1933, created a furor in its charges that missionaries, and churches themselves, lacked sympathy for the people, worrying more about the numbers of converts than the needs of the flock.

Buck also delivered several important addresses that reveal much about her own literary philosophy, including her 1938 Nobel Prize lecture on the Chinese novel. *Of Men and Women* (first issued in 1941; reissued in 1971 with a new epilogue) is one of Buck's most important nonfiction works because it gives her views of Chinese and American family life and her warnings about "gunpowder" American women who are educated for work yet lead idle and meaningless lives at home.

During World War II, Buck delivered many speeches and published articles, letters, and pamphlets on the Asian view of the war, particularly on colonial rule and imperialism. Her most famous war essay is probably "Tinder for Tomorrow." Buck's canon further includes personal works, such as the autobiographical *My Several Worlds: A Personal Record* (1954) and *A Bridge for Passing* (1962). Several of her plays were produced Off-Broadway or in summer stock.

Achievements • Buck has been enormously successful with popular audiences, more so than with the literati. She is the most widely translated author in all of American literary history. In Denmark, for example, her popularity exceeded that of Ernest Hemingway and John Steinbeck during the 1930's, and in Sweden, ten of her books were translated between 1932 and 1940, more than those of any other American author. *The Good Earth*, her most famous work, has been translated into more than thirty languages (seven different translations into Chinese alone) and made into a play and a motion picture.

Buck's early novels received much acclaim. *The Good Earth* was awarded the Pulitzer Prize; in 1935, she was awarded the William Dean Howells Medal by the American Academy of Arts and Letters for the finest work in American fiction from 1930 to 1935, and in 1936, she was elected to membership in the National Institute of Arts and Letters. In 1938, she was awarded the Nobel Prize in Literature, the third American and the fourth woman to receive it, for her "rich and generous epic description of Chinese peasant life and masterpieces of biography." *The Good Earth*, a staple of high school and undergraduate reading, is undoubtedly a masterpiece, and her missionary biographies, *The Exile* and *Fighting Angel*, though currently neglected, have merit in the depth of their analysis. Three other books of the 1930's—*Sons*, *The Mother*, and *The Patriot*—have effective passages. In all her works, Buck evinces a deep humanity, and she did much to further American understanding of Asian culture.

Buck has not fared so well with the literary establishment. Critics of the 1930's disdained her work because she was a woman, because her subjects were not "American," and because they thought she did not deserve the Nobel Prize. Her success in writing best-seller after best-seller and her optimistic faith in progress and humanity have irked later critics. She did, however, achieve success by her own standards. Her books have reached and touched middle-class American women, an enormous body of readers largely ignored by serious writers. Her innate storytelling ability does "please," "amuse," and "entertain" (her three criteria for good writing), but even the kindest of her admirers wish that she had written less, spending more time exploring the minds of her characters and polishing her work.

Biography • Pearl S. Buck was born Pearl Comfort Sydenstricker on June 26, 1892, in the family home at Hillsboro, West Virginia, to Absalom and Caroline (Stulting) Sydenstricker. Her parents were missionaries in China, home on a furlough. After five months she was taken to China. Her parents' marriage was not a particularly happy one because of their disparate natures. Her mother, fun-loving and witty, was torn by her devotion to God; her father, single-minded and zealous, had success with his mission but not with his family. Buck grew up in Chinkiang, an inland city on the Yangtze River. In 1900, during the Boxer Rebellion, her family was forced to flee, and she experienced the horrors of racism. Her education included one year at boarding school in Shanghai and four years at Randolph-Macon Women's College in Virginia.

In 1917, she married John Lossing Buck, an agricultural specialist. They lived in Nanhsuchon in Anhwei Province (the setting of *The Good Earth*). Buck learned much about farming from her husband and from her own observations. After five years, they moved southward to Nanking, where her husband taught agriculture and she taught English at the university. She published her first article in *The Atlantic Monthly* (January, 1923); "In China, Too" described the growing Western influence in China.

Tragedy struck Buck's life with the birth of Carol, her only biological child, who was mentally disabled (she later adopted eight children). She took Carol to the United States for medical treatment in 1925. When her husband took a year's leave of absence, Buck studied English at Cornell University and received her master's degree. Her first published novel, *East Wind: West Wind*, combined two short stories, one of which was originally published in 1925 in *Asia* magazine. She had written a novel before *East Wind: West Wind*, but the novel was destroyed by soldiers entering her home in the 1926-1927 Nationalist Communist uprising. (During the takeover of Nanking, Buck and her family barely escaped, hiding in a mud hut until relief came.) On March 2, 1931, *The Good Earth* appeared, creating a literary sensation.

Edward Steichen/Courtesy, George Bush Presidential Library and Museum

Buck's early literary influences included her parents and her old Chinese nurse. Her parents encouraged her to read the Bible and told her tales of their American homeland, while her nurse told her fantastic Buddhist and Daoist legends of warriors, devils, fairies, and dragons. She learned to speak Chinese before English, but she learned to read and write in English sooner than in Chinese. She read incessantly, Charles Dickens as a child and later Theodore Dreiser. Émile Zola and Sinclair Lewis were also important in her adult life. She paid particular tribute to Dickens: "He opened my eyes to people, he taught me to love all sorts of people." Even as a child, she decided to write: "One longs to make what one loves, and above all I loved to hear stories about people. I was a nuisance of a child, I fear, always curious to know about people and why they were as I found them." Her first writing appeared in the children's section of the *Shanghai Mercury*; in college, she contributed stories to the campus monthly and helped write the class play.

The Bucks were divorced in 1932, and that same year Pearl married her publisher, Richard J. Walsh, president of John Day and editor of *Asia* magazine. Their marriage lasted until his death in 1960. Buck loved both the United States and China throughout her life, serving as an intermediary between the two. In her last years, she was bitterly disappointed when the Chinese communists would not grant her a visa despite the rapprochement between the United States and China.

Buck's parents instilled in their daughter principles of charity and tolerance. Her love for the needy was also awakened by Miss Jewell, the mistress of her boarding school. Jewell took Buck along as an interpreter on errands of mercy—to visit institutions for slave girls who had fled from their masters and institutions where prostitutes went for help. Buck's own humanitarian efforts began in 1941 with the founding of the East and West Association, which endeavored to increase understanding between diverse cultures. During World War II, Buck actively spoke against racism, against the internment of Japanese Americans, and against the yielding of democratic privileges during wartime.

Her sympathy extended to all, but especially to children and the helpless. In 1949, she and her husband founded Welcome House, an adoption agency for Asian American children. In 1954, her letter of protest to *The New York Times* led to the changing of a policy that put immigrants in federal prisons with criminals. In 1964, she founded the Pearl S. Buck Foundation to care for Asian American children who remained overseas. She also worked for the Training School, a school for the mentally disabled in Vineland, New Jersey. For her many humanitarian efforts, she received the Brotherhood Award of the National Conference of Christians and Jews, the Wesley Award for Distinguished Service to Humanity, and more than a dozen honorary degrees from American colleges and universities.

Along with her extensive humanitarian activities, Buck continued to write. Because her American novels *This Proud Heart* and *Other Gods* were not well received, Buck assumed the pen name "John Sedges" to write with freedom on American subjects. Between 1945 and 1953, five novels were published under this name, while she wrote Asian stories under her own name. However, as Buck's humanitarian efforts increased, the quality of her fiction declined. Its strident and moralistic tone reflected her growing concern with social issues rather than artistic technique. She continued writing, however, and by the time of her death in 1973 had written more than eighty novels and novellas.

Analysis • Pearl S. Buck's reputation for excellence as a writer of fiction rests primarily on *The Good Earth* and segments of a few of her other novels of the 1930's. The appeal of *The Good Earth* is undeniable and easy to explain: Its universal themes are cloaked in the garments of an unfamiliar and fascinating Chinese culture.

***The Good Earth* •** Echoing many elements of life, *The Good Earth* speaks of animosity between town and country, love of land, decadent rich and honest poor, marital conflicts, interfering relatives, misunderstandings between generations, the joys of birth and sorrows of old age and death, and the strong bonds of friendship. Added to these universal themes is the cyclical movement of the growth and decay of the crops, the decline of the House of Hwang and the ascent of the House of Wang, the changes of the years, and the birth and death of the people.

Buck fittingly chose to tell her story in language reminiscent of the Bible, with its families and peoples who rise and fall. Her style also owes something to that of the Chinese storytellers, to whom she paid tribute in her Nobel Prize lecture, a style that flows along in short words "with no other technique than occasional bits of description, only enough to give vividness to place or person, and never enough to delay the story." Most of Buck's sentences are long and serpentine, relying on balance, parallelism, and repetition for strength. Although the sentences are long, the diction is simple and concrete. She chooses her details carefully: Her descriptions grow out of close observation and are always concise. The simplicity of the diction and the steady, determined flow of the prose fit the sagalike plot. In Chinese folk literature, the self-effacing author, like a clear vessel, transmits but does not color with his or her personality the life that "flows through him." So, also, Buck presents her story objectively. Her authorial presence never intrudes, though her warm feeling for the characters and her own ethical beliefs are always evident.

The strength of the novel also lies in its characterization, particularly that of the two main characters, O-lan and her husband Wang Lung. Whereas characters in Buck's later novels too easily divide into good and bad, the characters of *The Good*

Earth, like real people, mix elements of both. Ching, Wang Lung's faithful, doglike friend and later overseer, early in the novel joins a starving mob that ransacks Wang Lung's home for food; Ching takes Wang Lung's last handful of beans. The eldest son is a pompous wastrel, but he does make the House of Hwang beautiful with flowering trees and fish ponds, and he does settle into the traditional married life his father has planned for him. Even O-lan, the almost saintly earth mother, seethes with jealousy when Wang Lung takes a second wife, and she feels contempt and bitterness for the House of Hwang in which she was a slave. Her major flaw is her ugliness. Wang Lung delights the reader with his simple wonder at the world and with his perseverance to care for his family and his land, but he, too, has failings. In middle age, he lusts for Lotus, neglecting the much-deserving O-lan, and in old age, he steals Pear Blossom from his youngest son. Rather than confusing the morality of the novel, the intermingling of good and bad increases its reality. Buck acknowledged literary indebtedness to Émile Zola, and the influence of naturalism is evident in *The Good Earth* in its objective, documentary presentation and its emphasis on the influence of environment and heredity. Unlike the naturalists, however, Buck also credits the force of free will.

The Good Earth aroused much fury in some Chinese scholars, who insisted that the novel portrays a China that never was. Younghill Kang criticized the character of Wang Lung. Professor Kiang Kang-Hu said that Buck's details and her knowledge of Chinese history were inaccurate. Buck defended herself by granting that customs differed in the many regions of China. In later novels, she retaliated by harshly portraying Chinese scholars such as Kang and Kiang, who, she believed, distorted the picture of the real China either because of their ignorance of peasant life or because of their desire to aid propagandistic efforts of the Chinese government. Other native Chinese, including Phio Lin Yutang, sprang to Buck's defense, insisting on the accuracy of her portrayal.

The Mother • Like *The Good Earth, The Mother* follows the cyclical flow of time: The protagonist, who begins the novel in vigorous work, caring for an elderly parent, ends the novel as an elderly parent himself, cared for by the new generation. *The Mother* is also written in the simple, concrete, and sometimes poetic style of *The Good Earth.* The old mother-in-law, for example, in her early morning hunger, "belched up the evil winds from her inner emptiness." *The Mother,* however, portrays a different side of Chinese peasant life from that seen in *The Good Earth*—a more brutal one. The main character, named only "the mother," is carefully drawn; the other characters are flat and undeveloped, serving only as objects for her attention.

Deserted by her irresponsible, gambling husband, the mother lies about her spouse's absence to protect her family and cover her shame. She proves easy prey for her landlord's agent, by whom she becomes pregnant, later aborting the baby by taking medicine. Her eldest son eventually supports her, but his unfeeling wife will not tolerate having his blind sister underfoot. A husband is found for the blind girl, but when the mother travels to visit her daughter after a year, she discovers that the husband is witless and her daughter, after much mistreatment, has died. Even more sorrow darkens the mother's life. Her younger and most beloved son joins the Communists, is used as their dupe, and finally is arrested and beheaded.

This is not the honest-work-brings-rewards world of Wang Lung, but a world of victims, deformity, hatred, and cruelty. It is a portrait of the life of a woman in China, where girl babies routinely were killed and young girls of poor families were sold as slaves. Only new life—the excitement of birth and spring—balances the misery of the mother's life.

In *The Good Earth* and *The Mother*, Buck provides compelling visions of old age. Her children are mostly silent and inconsequential, her adolescents merely lusty and willful, but her elderly are individuals. The old father in *The Good Earth* cackles with life, drawing strength from his grandchildren-bedfellows. Wang Lung drowses off into a peaceful dream with his Pear Blossom. The mother-in-law basks in the sun and prides herself on wearing out her burial shrouds. The elderly mother in *The Mother* is frustrated because she no longer has the strength to work the land but remains as active as possible, trying to save her blind daughter and her Communist son, finally turning her affections to a new grandchild.

The main flaw in *The Mother* is that the mother seems too distant, too self-contained, for the reader to identify with her, to accept her as the universal mother that Buck intends her to be. The mother's story is interesting, but one does not feel her shame or her misery as one does O-lan's, nor does one feel her delight or her pride as one does Wang Lung's. Also, Buck's feelings about Communism are blatantly evident in the simplistic and oft-repeated phrase that the Communists are a "new kind of robber."

As Buck became more interested in social and political issues and in the media—magazines, film, and radio—her fiction began to deteriorate. She claimed, "The truth is I never write with a sense of mission or to accomplish any purpose whatever except the revelation of human character through a life situation." Her fiction, however, did not demonstrate this belief: More and more it became a forum for her own social and political ideas rather than an exploration of human character and life. Further, Hollywood and women's magazines began to influence her stories: They became drippingly romantic.

Dragon Seed • *Dragon Seed* is one of Buck's most popular post-1930's works, with the first half of the novel containing many of the strengths of her earlier work. Her characters are not as fully realized as the mother or Wang Lung, but the story is intriguing. A peasant farming family works the land, much as their ancestors have done for centuries, until the coming of war—flying airships and enemy troops—thrusts them into a world of violence and deprivation. As long as Buck keeps her eye sharp for details, describing the atrocities the people must endure and their struggles to understand what is happening to them, the novel remains interesting.

In the second half of the novel, however, Buck's purposes split. Rather than concentrating on the war story—the people and their experiences—she uses the novel to argue that the Western world is blind and uncaring about the troubles of the Chinese in World War II. In contrast to this didacticism are the Hollywood-style love stories of Lao-Er and Jade and Lao San and Mayli. The dialogue between the happily married Lao-Er and Jade seems straight from a B-film, and the overly coincidental coming together of Lao San and Mayli is a women's magazine romance of the self-made man and the rich, beautiful woman. Buck tries to portray the strong new woman of China (and the Western world) in Jade and Mayli, but they are *too* strong, *too* clever, almost always posturing with a defiant chin against the sunset. At one point in the novel, Buck even writes that Jade is so skillful in disguising herself that she should have been a film actor. O-lan, in her stoic silence—grudging, jealous, yet loving—is a believable woman; Jade and Mayli are creatures of fantasy.

Buck's power as a novelist derived from her intelligence, her humanity, her interesting stories, and her ability to make Chinese culture real to readers from all over the world. Her weaknesses as a novelist include didacticism, sentimentalism, and an inability to control her energy long enough to explore deeply, revise, and improve. In her later novels, she lost control of her point of view, her language, and her characterization. Her legacy is an enduring masterpiece, *The Good Earth*, and an inestimable contribution to cultural exchange between China and the West.

Ann Willardson Engar

Other major works

SHORT FICTION: *The First Wife, and Other Stories*, 1933; *Today and Forever*, 1941; *Twenty-seven Stories*, 1943; *Far and Near, Stories of Japan, China, and America*, 1947; *American Triptych*, 1958; *Hearts Come Home, and Other Stories*, 1962; *The Good Deed, and Other Stories*, 1969; *Once Upon a Christmas*, 1972; *East and West*, 1975; *Secrets of the Heart*, 1976; *The Lovers, and Other Stories*, 1977; *The Woman Who Was Changed, and Other Stories*, 1979.

NONFICTION: *East and West and the Novel*, 1932; *Fighting Angel: Portrait of a Soul*, 1936; *The Exile*, 1936; *The Chinese Novel*, 1939; *Of Men and Women*, 1941 (expanded, 1971); *American Unity and Asia*, 1942; *What America Means to Me*, 1943; *China in Black and White*, 1945; *Talk About Russia: With Masha Scott*, 1945; *Tell the People: Talks with James Yen About the Mass Education Movement*, 1945; *How It Happens: Talk About the German People, 1914-1933, with Erna von Pustau*, 1947; *American Argument: With Eslanda Goods*, 1949; *The Child Who Never Grew*, 1950; *My Several Worlds: A Personal Record*, 1954; *Friend to Friend: A Candid Exchange Between Pearl Buck and Carlos F. Romulo*, 1958; *A Bridge for Passing*, 1962; *The Joy of Children*, 1964; *Children for Adoption*, 1965; *The Gifts They Bring: Our Debt to the Mentally Retarded*, 1965; *The People of Japan*, 1966; *To My Daughters with Love*, 1967; *China as I See It*, 1970; *The Kennedy Women: A Personal Appraisal*, 1970; *Pearl S. Buck's America*, 1971; *The Story Bible*, 1971; *China Past and Present*, 1972.

CHILDREN'S LITERATURE: *The Young Revolutionist*, 1932; *Stories for Little Children*, 1940; *The Chinese Children Next Door*, 1942; *The Water-Buffalo Children*, 1943; *The Dragon Fish*, 1944; *Yu Lan: Flying Boy of China*, 1945; *The Big Wave*, 1948; *One Bright Day, and Other Stories for Children*, 1952; *The Man Who Changed China: The Story of Sun Yat-Sen*, 1953; *Johnny Jack and His Beginnings*, 1954; *The Beech Tree*, 1954; *Fourteen Stories*, 1961; *The Little Fox in the Middle*, 1966; *The Chinese Story Teller*, 1971.

TRANSLATIONS: *All Men Are Brothers*, 1933 (of Shih Nai-an's novel).

Bibliography

Bentley, Phyllis. "The Art of Pearl S. Buck." *English Journal* 24 (December, 1935): 791-800. Analyzes Buck's early works from a technical perspective, focusing on setting, style, characterization, plot, and theme. Concludes that the great strength of Buck's fiction is its emphasis on the "continuity of life" from generation to generation.

Cevasco, George A. "Pearl Buck and the Chinese Novel." *Asian Studies* 5 (December, 1967): 437-450. Provides important insights into Buck's understanding of the novel as a form for the general public, not the scholar, and shows her debt to Chinese beliefs about the function of plot and characterization in fiction.

Conn, Peter. *Pearl S. Buck: A Cultural Biography*. New York: Cambridge University Press, 1996. Attempts to revise the "smug literary consensus" that has relegated Pearl Buck to a "footnote" in literary history. Conn does not rehabilitate Buck as a great author but shows how her best work broke new ground in subject matter and is still vital to an understanding of American culture.

Dickstein, Lore. "Posthumous Stories." *The New York Times Book Review,* March 11, 1979, 20-21. Praises Buck's best work as having subject matter with a universal appeal and an easy, graceful style. Finds the late stories, however, to be excessively didactic and sentimental.

Doyle, Paul A. *Pearl S. Buck.* Boston: Twayne, 1980. A valuable survey of Buck's literary achievements, strengths, and weaknesses. Contains a biographical chapter and excellent bibliographies of both primary and secondary materials.

__________. "Pearl S. Buck's Short Stories: A Survey." *English Journal* 55 (January, 1966): 62-68. One of the few critical works devoted exclusively to Buck's short fiction. Her best stories, Doyle believes, contain realistic description, clearly delineated characters, and narrative interest. Too often, however, she wrote slick magazine fiction, excessively sentimental or filled with improbable incidents.

Gao, Xiongya. *Pearl S. Buck's Chinese Women Characters.* Selinsgrove, Pa.: Susquehanna University Press, 2000. A brief volume examining the Chinese women portrayed by Buck, presented by a Chinese woman.

Liao, Kang. *Pearl S. Buck: A Cultural Bridge Across the Pacific.* Westport, Conn.: Greenwood Press, 1997. Examines Buck's political and social views and her means of expressing them. Studies the East-West cultural divide in the fiction.

Lipscomb, Elizabeth J., Frances E. Webb, and Peter Conn, eds. *The Several Worlds of Pearl S. Buck: Essays Presented at a Centennial Symposium, Randolph-Macon Woman's College, March 26-28, 1992.* Westport, Conn.: Greenwood Press, 1994. Includes bibliographical references and an index.

Stirling, Nora. *Pearl Buck: A Woman in Conflict.* Piscataway, N.J.: New Century, 1983. A balanced, well-researched biography that provides important insights into Buck's personality and the experiences that shaped her writings.

William S. Burroughs

Born: St. Louis, Missouri; February 5, 1914
Died: Lawrence, Kansas; August 2, 1997

Principal long fiction • *Junkie*, 1953; *The Naked Lunch*, 1959 (republished as *Naked Lunch*, 1962); *The Soft Machine*, 1961; *The Ticket That Exploded*, 1962; *Dead Fingers Talk*, 1963; *Nova Express*, 1964; *The Wild Boys: A Book of the Dead*, 1971; *Port of Saints*, 1973; *Cities of the Red Night*, 1981; *The Place of Dead Roads*, 1983; *The Burroughs File*, 1984; *Queer*, 1985; *The Western Lands*, 1987; *Ghost of Chance*, 1995; *My Education: A Book of Dreams*, 1995.

Other literary forms • Because of their experimental techniques, William S. Burroughs's works are especially difficult to classify within established literary forms. *Exterminator!* (1973), for example, although published as a "novel," is actually a collection of previously published poems, short stories, and essays. Other unclassifiable works are book-length experiments, often written in collaboration and in the "cut-up, fold-in" technique pioneered by Burroughs, which might be considered novels by some. Examples of such works are *Minutes to Go* (1960), written in collaboration with Sinclair Beiles, Gregory Corso, and Brion Gysin; *The Exterminator* (1960), written with Gysin; *Time* (1965), which contains drawings by Gysin; and *Œuvre Croisée* (1976), written in collaboration with Gysin and reissued as *The Third Mind* in 1978. *White Subway* (1965), *Apomorphine* (1969), and *The Job: Interviews with William S. Burroughs* (1970), written in collaboration with Daniel Odier, are additional short-story and essay collections.

The Dead Star (1969) is a journalistic essay that contains photocollage inserts; *APO-33 Bulletin: A Metabolic Regulator* (1966) is a pamphlet; and *Electronic Revolution 1970-71* (1971) is an essay that fantasizes bizarre political and business uses for the cut-up, fold-in technique. Burroughs has also published scores of essays, stories, and articles in numerous journals, periodicals, and short-lived magazines. One of Burroughs's most revealing publications, *The Yage Letters* (1963), collects his correspondence with Allen Ginsberg concerning Burroughs's 1952 expedition to South America in search of yage, a legendary hallucinogen. In these letters, Burroughs is Govinda, the master, to Ginsberg's Siddhartha, the disciple.

Achievements • Although his novel *Naked Lunch* was made notorious by American censorship attempts and consequently became a best-seller, Burroughs wrote primarily for a cult audience. He is essentially a fantasist and satirist, is often misread, and in these respects has accurately been compared to Jonathan Swift. Both writers focus on the faults and evils of humankind and society, employ fantastic satire to ridicule these shortcomings, and hope through this vehicle to effect some positive change in the human condition. Burroughs's works are exceptionally vicious satires, however, "necessarily brutal, obscene and disgusting"—his own description of them—because they must mime the situations from which their recurring images and metaphors (of drug addiction, aberrant sexual practices, and senseless violence) are drawn.

Archive Photos

Superficially, Burroughs's satiric attacks are aimed at humanity's "addictions" to pleasure or power in any of the many forms either craving might take. Those who, obeying the dictates of "the algebra of need," will stop at nothing to fulfill their desires have, in the terms of the moral allegory Burroughs creates, "lost their human citizenship" and become nonhuman parasites feeding on the life essences of others. They shamelessly lie, cheat, and manipulate to attain what Burroughs's associative imagery repeatedly equates with perversion, excrement, and death. Burroughs's satire, however, cuts deeper than this. It attacks not only humankind and its addictions but also the structures of the cultures that enable these addictions to flourish and proliferate. It attacks the myths and linguistic formulas that imprison the human race, the stone walls of patriotism and religion. It demands that people first free themselves from these "word and image addictions" before they kick their more obvious habits and regain their humanity, and thus calls for nothing less than a revolution of consciousness.

The Grove Press edition of *Naked Lunch* became a national best-seller and was cleared of obscenity charges in Los Angeles in 1965 and in Massachusetts in 1966. Ginsberg and Norman Mailer, who asserted that Burroughs is "the only American novelist living today who may conceivably be possessed by genius," were among those who testified in the book's defense. Although it does detail with exceptional brutality the ugly, revolting, and perverse, *Naked Lunch* is at bottom a strikingly moral but darkly comic work that employs irony and allegory, as well as more unconventional techniques, to satirize much that is false and defective in modern American life in particular and human nature in general. Especially effective as a subliminal argument against heroin abuse, the book's successful publication in America elevated its heretofore practically unknown author to membership in the literary elite.

Many reviewers—some seemingly oblivious to the irony of Burroughs's works—have not been responsive or sympathetic to his themes and techniques, and none of his novels after *Naked Lunch*, with the exception of *The Wild Boys: A Book of the Dead*, received comparable critical acclaim. Although *Naked Lunch* was lauded by Terry Southern, Mary McCarthy, Karl Shapiro, and Marshall McLuhan, as well as by Ginsberg and Mailer, the less successfully realized subsequent novels were considered by some critics, not totally inaccurately, as "language without content" and "the world's greatest put-on." Burroughs himself admitted that "*Naked Lunch* demands silence from the reader. Otherwise he is taking his own pulse." He warned that his novels do not present their "content" in the manner the reader ordinarily anticipates. One of the triumphs of Burroughs's unique style is that he has created a low-content form, a narrative near vacuum, upon which the unwary reader is tempted to project his own psyche, personal myths, or forgotten dreams. Although they do have their own message to convey, his works also encourage the reader to develop or invent his or her private fictions and to append them to the skeletal narrative structure provided by the author. Readers are thus invited to create the work as they read it. In place of relying on the easily perceived, clearly coherent story the reader might have expected, Burroughs's best work keeps one reading through the hypnotic fascination of the author's flow of images and incantatory prose.

Biography • William Seward Burroughs was born on February 5, 1914, in St. Louis, Missouri, to Perry Mortimer Burroughs, son of the industrialist who invented the cylinder that made the modern adding machine possible, and Laura Lee, a direct descendant of Robert E. Lee, the commander of the Confederacy's Army of Northern Virginia during the Civil War. Dominated by his mother's obsessive Victorian prudery and haunted by vivid nightmares and hallucinations, Burroughs led a restless childhood. He was educated in private schools in St. Louis and Los Alamos, New Mexico, where he developed seemingly disparate fascinations with literature and crime, and later studied ethnology and archaeology at Harvard University, where he encountered a set of wealthy homosexuals. He graduated with a bachelor's degree in 1936.

After finishing college, Burroughs traveled to Europe, briefly studied medicine at the University of Vienna, and returned to the United States and Harvard to resume his anthropological studies, which he soon abandoned because of his conviction that academic life is little more than a series of intrigues broken by teas. Although he attempted to use family connections to obtain a position with the Office of Strategic Services, Burroughs was rejected after he deliberately cut off the first joint of one finger in a Vincent van Gogh-like attempt to impress a friend. Moving to New York City, he worked as a bartender and in an advertising agency for a year and underwent psychoanalysis. Burroughs entered the U.S. Army in 1942 as a glider pilot trainee, engineered his discharge for psychological reasons six months later, and then moved to Chicago, where he found work as an exterminator and a private detective, among other odd jobs.

In 1943, Burroughs returned to New York City and met Joan Vollmer, a student at Columbia University, whom he married on January 17, 1945. His wife introduced him to Jack Kerouac, who in turn introduced him to Ginsberg. The Beat generation was born in Burroughs's 115th Street apartment after Burroughs acquainted Kerouac and Ginsberg with the writings of William Blake, Arthur Rimbaud, and others; the three friends soon emerged as leaders of the movement. Late in 1944, Herbert Huncke, a Times Square hustler involved in criminal activity to support his drug habit, introduced Burroughs to the use of morphine and its derivatives. Burroughs was for most of the next thirteen years a heroin addict who frequently altered his place of residence to evade the police.

Burroughs moved to Waverly, Texas, where he tried farming, in 1946; had a son, William, Jr., in 1947; and voluntarily entered a drug rehabilitation center at Lexington, Kentucky, in 1948. Returning to Waverly and already back on drugs, Burroughs was hounded by the police until he moved to Algiers, Louisiana, later that same year. To avoid prosecution for illegal possession of drugs and firearms after a 1949 raid on his Algiers farm, Burroughs relocated to Mexico City in 1950, where he began writing *Junkie.* He continued his archaeological studies at Mexico City University, pursuing an interest in the Mayan codices. On September 7, 1951, Burroughs accidentally killed his wife while allegedly attempting to shoot a champagne glass off her head while playing "William Tell." Although Mexican authorities let the matter drop, Burroughs soon left Mexico for the jungles of Colombia.

Burroughs returned again to New York City in 1953, the year *Junkie* was published, lived for a while with Ginsberg, and then settled in Tangier, Morocco, where from 1955 to 1958 he was frequently visited by other Beat writers and worked on the manuscript that would develop into his quartet of science-fiction-like novels: *Naked Lunch, The Soft Machine, Nova Express,* and *The Ticket That Exploded.* In 1957, Burroughs again sought treatment for his heroin addiction. This time he placed himself in the care of John Yerby Dent, an English physician who treated drug addicts with apomorphine—a crystalline alkaloid derivative of morphine—a drug Burroughs praises and mythologizes in his writings. The following year, cured of his addiction, Burroughs moved to Paris, where *The Naked Lunch* was published in 1959.

In 1960, Gysin, who had helped Burroughs select the Paris edition of *The Naked Lunch* from a suitcase full of manuscript pages, introduced his experimental "cut-up" technique to Burroughs and collaborated with him on *The Exterminator* and *Minutes to Go.* Burroughs's literary reputation was firmly established with the American publication of *Naked Lunch* in 1962, and by the mid-1960's Burroughs had settled in London. He returned to St. Louis for a visit in 1965, covered the Democratic National Convention for *Esquire* in 1968, and moved again to New York to teach writing at City College of New York in 1974. In 1975, he embarked on a reading tour of the United States and conducted a writers' workshop in Denver, Colorado. After returning to London briefly, Burroughs settled in New York. In 1983, he was inducted into the American Academy and Institute of Arts and Letters.

Burroughs published a number of novels and collections throughout the 1980's and 1990's, including 1987's *The Western Lands,* the last novel in the trilogy that included *Cities of the Red Night* and *The Place of Dead Roads.* He moved to rural Kansas shortly after the publication of this novel and died there in August, 1997.

Analysis • William S. Burroughs did not begin writing seriously until 1950, although he had unsuccessfully submitted a story titled "Twilight's Last Gleaming" to *Esquire* in 1938. His first novelistic effort, *Queer,* which deals with homosexuality, was not published until 1985. Allen Ginsberg finally persuaded Ace Books to publish Burroughs's first novel, *Junkie,* which originally appeared with the pseudonym William Lee, as half of an Ace double paperback. It was bound with Maurice Helbront's *Narcotic Agent.* Although strictly conventional in style, *Junkie* is a luridly hyperbolic, quasi-autobiographical first-person account of the horrors of drug addiction. Of little literary merit in itself, this first novel is interesting in that it introduces not only the main character, Lee, but also several of the major motifs that appear in Burroughs's subsequent works: the central metaphor of drug addiction, the related image of man reduced to a subhuman (usually an insectlike creature) by his drug and other lusts, and the suggestion of concomitant and pervasive sexual aberration.

In *Naked Lunch* and its three less celebrated sequels, *The Soft Machine, Nova Express,* and *The Ticket That Exploded,* Burroughs weaves an intricate and horrible allegory of human greed, corruption, and debasement. Like Aldous Huxley's *Brave New World* (1932) and George Orwell's *Nineteen Eighty-Four* (1949), these four works seize on the evils or tendencies toward a certain type of evil—which the author sees as particularly malignant in the contemporary world—and project them into a dystopian future, where, magnified, they grow monstrous and take on an exaggerated and fantastic shape. Although progressively clarifying and developing Burroughs's thought, these novels share themes, metaphorical images, characters, and stylistic mannerisms. In them, Burroughs utilizes the "cut-up, fold-in" technique that has its closest analog in the cinematic technique of montage. He juxtaposes one scene with another without regard to plot, character, or, in the short view, theme, to promote an association of the reader's negative emotional reaction to the content of certain scenes (sexual perversion, drug abuse, senseless violence) with the implied allegorical content of others (examples of "addictions" to drugs, money, sex, power). The theory is that if such juxtapositions recur often enough, the feeling of revulsion strategically created by the first set of images will form the reader's negative attitude toward the second set of examples.

In these novels, Burroughs develops a science-fiction-like, paranoid fantasy wherein, on a literal level, Earth and its human inhabitants have been taken over by the Nova Mob, an assortment of extraterrestrial, non-three-dimensional entities who live parasitically on the reality of other organisms. Exploitation of Earth has reached such proportions that the intergalactic Nova Police have been alerted. The Nova Police are attempting to thwart the Nova Mob without so alarming them that they will detonate the planet in an attempt to destroy the evidence (and thus escape prosecution in the biologic courts) while trying to make what escape they can. The most direct form of Nova control, control that enables the Nova Mob to carry on its viruslike metaphysical vampirism with impunity, is thought control of the human population through control of the mass communication media. Nova Mob concepts and perspectives attach themselves to and are replicated by the terrestrial host media much as a virus invades and reproduces through a host organism, a thought-control process analogous to the "cut-up, fold-in" technique itself. By the middle of *Nova Express*, the reader is caught up in a war of images in which the weapons are cameras and tape recorders. The Nova Police and the inhabitants of Earth have discovered how to combat the Nova Mob with their own techniques (of which these novels are examples) and are engaged in a guerrilla war with the Nova Criminals, who are desperately trying to cut and run. The ending of *The Ticket That Exploded* is optimistic for Earth but inconclusive, leaving the reader to wonder if Earth will be rid of the Nova Mob or destroyed by it.

Naked Lunch • A vividly and relentlessly tasteless fantasy-satire that portrays humankind's innate greed and lack of compassion in general and contemporary American institutions and values in particular, *Naked Lunch* immerses the reader in the impressions and sensations of William Lee (Burroughs's pseudonym in *Junkie*). Lee is an agent of the Nova Police who has assumed the cover of a homosexual heroin addict because with such a cover he is most likely to encounter Nova Criminals, who are all addicts of one sort or another and thus prefer to operate through human addict collaborators. Nothing of importance seems to occur in the novel, and little of what does happen is explained. Only toward the conclusion does the reader even suspect that Lee is some sort of agent "clawing at a not-yet of Telepathic Bureaucracies, Time Monopolies, Control Drugs, Heavy Fluid Addicts." The "naked lunch" of the title is that reality seen by Lee, that "frozen moment when everyone sees what is on the end of every fork." The random scenes of mutilation and depravity, bleak homosexual encounters, and desperate scrambles for drug connections into which the book plunges yield its two key concepts: the idea of addiction, the central conceit that men become hooked on power, pleasure, illusions, and so on much as a junkie does on heroin, and that of "the algebra of need," which states simply that when an addict is faced with absolute need (as a junkie is) he will do anything to satisfy it.

The Nova Criminals are nonhuman personifications of various addictions. The Uranians, addicted to Heavy Metal Fluid, are types of drug addicts. Dr. Benway, Mr. Bradley Mr. Martin (a single character), and the insect people of Minraud—all control addicts—are types of the human addiction to power. The green boy-girls of Venus, addicted to Venusian sexual practices, are types of the human addiction to sensual pleasure. The Death Dwarf, addicted to concentrated words and images, is the analog of the human addiction to various cultural myths and beliefs; he is perhaps the most pathetic of these depraved creatures. Burroughs explains that "Junk yields a basic formula of 'evil' virus: the face of evil is always the face of total need. A dope fiend is a man in total need of dope. Beyond a certain frequency need knows absolutely no limit or control." As poet and literary critic John Ciardi noted,

> Only after the first shock does one realize that what Burroughs is writing about is not only the destruction of depraved men by their drug lust, but the destruction of all men by their consuming addictions, whether the addiction be drugs or over-righteous propriety or sixteen-year-old girls.

The Soft Machine • Burroughs sees *The Soft Machine* as "a sequel to *Naked Lunch,* a mathematical extension of the Algebra of Need beyond the Junk virus." Here, the consuming addiction, displayed again in juxtaposition with scenes of drug abuse and sexual perversion, and through a number of shifting narrators, is the addiction to power over others. The central episode is the destruction by a time-traveling agent of the control apparatus of the ancient Mayan theocracy (Burroughs's primary archaeological interest), which exercises its control through the manipulation of myths; this is a clear analog of the present-day struggle between the Nova Police and the Nova Mob that breaks into the open in the subsequent two novels.

The time traveler uses the same technique to prepare himself for time travel as Burroughs does in writing his novels, a type of "cut-up, fold-in" montage: "I started my trip in the morgue with old newspapers, folding in today with yesterday and typing out composites." Because words tie men to time, the time traveler character is given apomorphine (used to cure Burroughs of his heroin addiction) to break this connection.

The "soft machine" is both the "wounded galaxy," the Milky Way seen as a biological organism diseased by the viruslike Nova Mob, and the human body, riddled with parasites and addictions and programmed with the "ticket," obsolete myths and dreams, written on the "soft typewriter" of culture and civilization. Burroughs contends that any addiction dehumanizes its victims. The Mayan priests, for example, tend to become half-men, half-crab creatures who eventually metamorphosize into giant centipedes and exude an erogenous green slime. Such hideous transformations also strike Lee, a heroin addict, and other homosexuals. Bradley the Buyer, who reappears as Mr. Bradley Mr. Martin, Mr. and Mrs. D., and the Ugly Spirit, has a farcical habit of turning into a bloblike creature who is addicted to and absorbs drug addicts.

Nova Express* and *The Ticket That Exploded • Instances of metamorphosis are almost innumerable in *Nova Express* and *The Ticket That Exploded.* These novels most clearly reveal the quartet's plot and explore the Nova Mob's exploitation of media. Here addiction to language is investigated. As Stephen Koch argues,

> Burroughs's ideology . . . is based on an image of consciousness in bondage to the organism: better, of consciousness as an organism, gripped by the tropisms of need. Consciousness is addicted—it is here the drug metaphor enters—to what sustains it and gives it definition: in particular, it is addicted to the word, the structures of language that define meaning and thus reality itself.

Thus, while in *The Soft Machine* the time traveler is sent to Trak News Agency (whose motto is "We don't report the news—we write it") to learn how to defeat the Mayan theocracy by first learning "how this writing the news before it happens is done," in *The Ticket That Exploded* it is axiomatic that "you can run a government without police if your conditioning program is tight enough but you can't run a government without [nonsense and deception]."

Contemporary existence is seen ultimately as a film that is rerun again and again, trapping the human soul like an insect imprisoned in amber, negating any possibility of choice or freedom. In these last two novels, Burroughs issues a call for revolt against humanity's imprisoning addiction to language. In *Nova Express,* he notes that "their garden of delights is a terminal sewer" and demands that everyone heed the last words of Hassan I Sabbah (cribbed out of context from Fyodor Dostoevski's Ivan Karamazov): "Nothing is True—Everything is Permitted." In *The Ticket That Exploded,* he rages, "Better than the 'real thing'?—There is no real thing—Maya—Maya—It's all show business."

The Wild Boys • Burroughs's other notably science-fiction-like novel, *The Wild Boys,* is also composed of scenes linked more by associated images than by any clearly linear narrative framework. Here, the author posits a bizarre alternative to the problematical apocalypse-in-progress depicted in his earlier quartet. In a world wrecked by famine and controlled by police, the wild boys, a homosexual tribe of hashish smokers, have withdrawn themselves from space and time through indifference and have developed into a counterculture complete with its own language, rituals, and economy. The existence of this counterculture poses a threat to those who create the false images upon which the larger, repressive, external society is based; but the wild boys cannot be tamed because their cold indifference to the mass culture entails a savagery that refuses to submit to control. Although Burroughs's thinking clearly becomes more political in *The Wild Boys* and in the book that followed it, *Exterminator!,* a collection of short stories and poems that revolve around the common theme of death through sinister forces, his primary concern for freedom from the controllers and manipulators—chemical, political, sexual, or cultural—has remained constant from the beginning of his literary career.

Cities of the Red Night • Continuing the utopian vision of *The Wild Boys,* but encompassing it into a larger, more anthropological context, Burroughs's next three works form a trilogy to expand his vision of society and its place in the natural order. The first book in the series, *Cities of the Red Night,* continues the twin themes of freedom from control and the power of mythmaking, but does so on a much larger scale. One of Burroughs's longest works, *Cities of the Red Night* is unique in that in it he sustains a rather conventional narrative voice, utilizing conventional popular genre, to achieve a re-creation of history through fantasy and myth.

The novel begins with three distinct plots, which seem at first to be only tenuously related. One plot concerns a retroactive utopia founded by eighteenth century pirates, which Burroughs uses as a foundation for social criticism. A second plot, from which the title comes, depicts mythical "cities of the red night," which existed in prehistoric time and function as a dystopia through which the reader views present culture. A third plot involves a present-day investigator who traces the mystery of a deadly virus known as B-23 to its historical origins in the "cities of the red night." Each plot employs conventions from one popular genre or another: The story of the utopian pirates' colony reads very much like a boys' adventure story, the story of the advanced prehistoric cities takes its structure from science fiction, and the story of the investigation of the virus lends itself to the conventions of the hard-boiled detective story.

The Place of Dead Roads • In the second book of the trilogy, *The Place of Dead Roads,* Burroughs continues the process of mythmaking. His protagonist is Kim Carsons, a late nineteenth century gunslinger who utilizes a sort of "hole in time," a phenomenon introduced in *Cities of the Red Night.* Through this hole, Carsons becomes a time-traveler, moving precariously across time and space, encountering different cultures and time periods in an effort to forge some sense of the whole, some sense of control over his own destiny. He seeks fulfillment in disparate, almost lonely, homosexual encounters, in drugs, and in the sense of power he feels by manipulating others.

The story begins with a clipping from a Boulder, Colorado, newspaper that tells the reader that William Seward Hall, who writes Western novels under the pen name Kim Carsons, was shot in a gunfight during the year 1899. The story then introduces the character Carsons and, after a disjointed series of adventures and misadventures, returns the reader to that same date when Carsons loses his life, as if to say that destiny will not be averted in the end. The similarity of Carsons's true name to Burroughs's is striking here because, like Hall, Burroughs tends to fictionalize himself as author, as though an author can reach his true potential only through the life of his character—perhaps another way of understanding Burroughs's fascination with somehow circumventing destiny through manipulation.

The Western Lands • In the third book of the trilogy, *The Western Lands,* the reader learns that Carsons was not shot by his opponent, Mike Chase, but by a killer from the Land of the Dead named Joe, described as a NO (Natural Outlaw), whose job it is to break natural laws. The Western land itself is a mythical place, a utopian vision of a place beyond one's images of earth and heaven—a land where natural law, religious law, and human law have no meaning. It is a paradise, but a paradise difficult to reach.

The intent of Burroughs's trilogy is first to create a science-fiction myth that explains all of human history; then to reveal the power of fantasy and myth to offer alternative histories; and finally, by realizing these alternative histories, to explore alternative anthropological patterns by which to organize society. The three separate plots interrelate and merge at various points throughout the trilogy, but eventually each is abandoned before completion—a technique that, Burroughs claims, allows the reader to create his or her own stories, to engage his or her own sense of mythmaking. The reader is encouraged to play a kind of "what if" game along with Burroughs: What if the Spanish had not defeated the New World into submission? What if the true foundations of liberty and individual freedom had taken hold in the Third World? What if all of our assumptions, whether religious, historical, or psychological, are wrong? This process of mythmaking in Burroughs is not a means to an end but rather the object of the struggle—the great creative process of defining and redefining ourselves, which is our ultimate defense against those who would manipulate us.

Although Burroughs's innovative, highly unconventional fictive style and often abrasive thematic preoccupations were not without their detractors, by the end of his career Burroughs had firmly established his place as one of late twentieth century fiction's most significant innovators. In fact, his "cut-up" technique has reached beyond the bounds of obscure cult fiction to influence both mainstream cinema and popular music. Burroughs played a semiautobiographical role as Tom the Priest in Gus Van Sant's 1989 film about drug addiction, *Drugstore Cowboy*; in 1991, acclaimed director David Cronenberg adapted *Naked Lunch* to the screen. In her introduction to his unprecedented reading on the popular American television show *Saturday Night Live* in 1981, actor Lauren Hutton lauded Burroughs as "America's greatest living writer," while rock music icons Lou Reed and David Bowie have both recognized Burroughs's disjointed and surreal but surprisingly moralistic approach to writing as enormously influential on their own work. "Heavy metal," a genre of rock-and-roll music prominent during the 1980's, borrows its name from a phrase in Burroughs's *Naked Lunch*.

Upon his death in 1997 at the age of eighty-three, Burroughs was eulogized as everything from the "most dangerous" of Beat writers to the undisputed patriarch of this important movement in twentieth century American writing. Although Burroughs's lifelong penchant for the cutting edge of fiction continues to intimidate some scholars and critics, none can dispute his role as a significant innovator and catalyst for change in twentieth century fiction and popular culture.

Donald Palumbo
Updated by Gregory D. Horn

Other major works

NONFICTION: *The Yage Letters*, 1963 (with Allen Ginsberg); *APO-33 Bulletin: A Metabolic Regulator*, 1966; *The Job: Interviews with William S. Burroughs*, 1970 (with Daniel Odier); *Electronic Revolution, 1970-71*, 1971; *Letters to Allen Ginsberg, 1953-1957*, 1983; *The Adding Machine: Collected Essays*, 1985; *The Cat Inside*, 1992; *The Letters of William S. Burroughs, 1945-1959*, 1993 (Oliver Harris, editor); *Word Virus: The William S. Burroughs Reader*, 1998 (James Grauerholz and Ira Silverberg, editors); *Conversations with William S. Burroughs*, 1999 (Allen Hibbard, editor); *Last Words: The Final Journals of William S. Burroughs*, 2000.

MISCELLANEOUS: *Minutes to Go*, 1960 (with Sinclair Beiles, Gregory Corso, and Brion Gysin); *The Exterminator*, 1960 (with Brion Gysin); *Time*, 1965 (drawings by Gysin); *White Subway*, 1965; *Apomorphine*, 1969; *The Dead Star*, 1969; *The Last Words of Dutch Schultz*, 1970; *Exterminator!*, 1973; *The Book of Breeething*, 1974; *Œeuvre Croisée*, 1976 (with Brion Gysin; also known as *The Third Man*, 1978); *Blade Runner: A Movie*, 1979; *Interzone*, 1989; *Word Virus: the William S. Burroughs Reader*, 1998 (James Grauerholz, and Ira Silverberg, editors).

Bibliography

Burroughs, William S. *Conversations with William S. Burroughs.* Jackson: University Press of Mississippi, 1999. Edited by Allen Hibbard. Collection of interviews with Burroughs over a number of years, in which Burroughs reveals much about himself and his writings.

____________. *Burroughs Live: The collected Interviews of William S. Burroughs.* Edited by Sylvère Lotringer. Cambridge, Mass.: MIT Publisher, 2001. This collection of interviews, along with the title above, are recommended for the reader hoping for a personal glimpse of the novelist. Burroughs, however, was notorious with interviewers for being a difficult subject to draw out.

Caveney, Graham. *Gentleman Junkie: The Life and Legacy of William S. Burroughs.* Boston: Little, Brown, 1998. An unconventional biography of Burroughs with an imaginative visual presentation that superimposes the text on reproductions of photographs, newspaper clippings, and other visual features, all printed on multicolored pages. Caveney considers the myths and legends surrounding Burroughs as well as his life and influence on later generations of musicians, writers, and artists.

Cook, Bruce. *The Beat Generation.* New York: Charles Scribner's Sons, 1971. Cook's survey of the Beat generation emphasizes their social impact rather than their literary importance. He devotes a chapter to Burroughs's work, notably *Naked Lunch,* describing it as primarily self-revelation. He includes a biography of Burroughs and an interview that takes place in London.

Goodman, Michael Barry. *Contemporary Literary Censorship: The Case History of Burroughs's "Naked Lunch."* Metuchen, N.J.: Scarecrow Press, 1981. Goodman offers a narrative history of the writing, publication, critical reception, and subsequent censorship of *Naked Lunch* in the United States, a work he describes as one of the last to receive such treatment in such a universal way. Provides much previously unpublished Burroughs material.

Lardas, John. *The Bop Apocalypse: The Religious Visions of Kerouac, Ginsberg, and Burroughs.* Urbana: University of Illinois Press, 2001. A study of the spiritualism of the Beats.

Lee, Robert A. "William Burroughs and the Sexuality of Power." *Twentieth Century Studies* 2 (November, 1969): 74-88. Lee analyzes the structure and imagery in several of Burroughs's novels, including *Junkie, The Soft Machine, The Ticket That Exploded,* and *Nova Express.* Lee argues that Burroughs's theme of the sexuality of power forms a basis for his mythology. He praises Burroughs as a moralist and serious social critic.

Lydenberg, Robin. *World Cultures: Radical Theory and Practice in William S. Burroughs' Fiction.* Urbana: University of Illinois Press, 1987. Analyzes the work of Burroughs from the stance of literary theory.

Morgan, Ted. *Literary Outlaw: The Life and Times of William S. Burroughs.* New York: Holt, 1988. Still useful study that was considered the definitive source on Burroughs at the time of its publication.

Mottram, Eric. *William Burroughs: The Algebra of Need.* London: Marion Boyars, 1977. Mottram sees Burroughs's works as a radical critique of Western power structures and the myths that support them, classifying the writer as an anarchic individualist. Mottram's comparisons of Burroughs with other radical thinkers is insightful and unique.

Skerl, Jennie. *William S. Burroughs.* Boston: Twayne, 1985. Skerl attempts to provide an overview of contemporary thought on Burroughs's art and life for the general reader and literary historian. She also argues, in a rather concise analysis section, that Burroughs's art comes from a worldview that revolves around the "hipsterism" ideas of Norman Mailer.

Tanner, Tony. *City of Words: American Fiction, 1950-1970.* New York: Harper and Row, 1971. Tanner's influential survey of the contemporary American novel includes a lengthy chapter on Burroughs. His discussion centers on *Junkie, The Yage Letters, Naked Lunch, The Ticket That Exploded,* and *Nova Express.* Tanner sees Burroughs as giving major emphasis to a central theme in contemporary American literature—namely, the conflict between the dream of freedom and the dread of control.

Octavia E. Butler

Born: Pasadena, California; June 22, 1947
Died: Seattle, Washington; February 25, 2006

Principal long fiction • *Patternmaster,* 1976; *Mind of My Mind,* 1977; *Survivor,* 1978; *Kindred,* 1979; *Wild Seed,* 1980; *Clay's Ark,* 1984; *Dawn,* 1987; *Adulthood Rites,* 1988; *Imago,* 1989; *Parable of the Sower,* 1993; *Parable of the Talents,* 1998; *Fledgling,* 2005.

Other literary forms • Octavia E. Butler contributed short stories to various science-fiction collections and periodicals, including *Isaac Asimov's Science Fiction Magazine, Future Life,* and *Clarion.* Her story "Speech Sounds" won the Hugo Award in 1984; a short work of fiction, "Bloodchild," was honored with the Hugo and various other prizes in 1985.

Achievements • Broad and growing popularity among readers of science fiction greeted first Butler's Patternist series of novels and then her Xenogenesis series. She won multiple prizes for her short fiction as well as critical acceptance for her longer work. Her portrayal of the "loner" of science and adventure fiction is given depth and complexity by the implied treatment of sexual and racial prejudices and the direct treatment of social power structures. Entertaining stories with alien settings, sometimes narrated by alien characters, provide a platform for her contemplative approach to human dynamics. Love and miscegenation, male-female roles, the responsibilities of power, and the urge to survive are among the recurring themes that insistently invite the reader to reexamine long-standing attitudes.

Biography • Octavia E. Butler grew up in a family that reflected some of the hard realities of life in the United States for African Americans. Her father, who died when she was very young, shined shoes; her mother, who had been taken from school at the age of ten, supported herself by working as a maid. Reared by her mother, grandmother, and other relatives, Butler felt most comfortable in the company of her adult relatives, even while she was uncomfortable with a social system that routinely denied their humanity. She was tall for her age, shy, bookish, and further set off from her peer group by strict Baptist prohibitions against dancing and the use of makeup. Her escape from a less-than-satisfactory everyday life was provided by her ability to write. She began writing when she was about ten years old and began to experiment with science fiction one day at the age of twelve, when she decided that she could write a better story than the poor science-fiction film she happened to see on television.

Butler's family did not support her decision to write, and her teachers did not support her choice of science fiction as a medium. She attended Pasadena City College and what was then California State College at Los Angeles, where she was unable to major in creative writing but took a potpourri of other subjects. After attending evening writing classes at the University of California at Los Angeles (UCLA), she found a long-sought entrée into science-fiction writing when she met writer Harlan Ellison through the Writers Guild of America. Ellison brought her to the six-week Clarion Science Fiction Writers Workshop in 1970. She continued her study of science-fiction writing in classes occasionally taught by Ellison at UCLA. Although she had sold some of her science fiction as early as 1970, her breakthrough publication came in 1976 with *Patternmaster,* with which she began the Patternist series. Except for *Kindred,* a novel about a modern black woman transported to the antebellum South to experience slavery, all Butler's novels through 1984 were Patternist tales.

Analysis • Octavia E. Butler presented a version of humanity as a congenitally flawed species, possibly doomed to destroy itself because it is both intelligent and hierarchical. In this sense, her work does not follow the lead of Isaac Asimov's Foundation series (1951-1993), Arthur C. Clarke's *2001: A Space Odyssey* (1968), and similar science fiction in offering an optimistic, rational, and agreeable view of humanity. As Butler herself said, she does not believe that imperfect human beings can create a perfect world.

Butler's diverse societies are controlled by Darwinian realities: competition to survive, struggle for power, domination of the weak by the strong, parasitism, and the like. Within this framework, there is room for both pain and hope, for idealism, love, bravery, and compassion, for an outsider to challenge the system, defeat the tyrant, and win power. There is, however, no happy ending but a conclusion in which the lead characters have done their best and the world (wherever it is) remains ethically and morally unchanged.

In contemplative but vividly descriptive prose, Butler tells her story from the first-or third-person perspective of someone who is passive or disfranchised and is forced by events or other characters to take significant action. In order to fulfill her destiny, often the protagonist—most often a black woman—must do or experience something not only unprecedented but also alien and even grotesque. What begins as an act of courage usually ends as an act of love, or at least understanding. Through an alien, alienated, or excluded person, a crucial compromise is struck, civilization is preserved in some form, and life goes on.

Beth Gwinn

Butler's fiction reflects and refracts the attempts—and failures—of the twentieth century to deal with ethnic and sexual prejudice. She frequently uses standard images of horror, such as snakelike or insectlike beings, to provoke an aversion that the reader is unable to sustain as the humanity of the alien becomes clear. Being human does not mean being faultless—merely familiar. Therefore, each of her human, nonhuman, and quasi-human societies displays its own form of selfishness and, usually, a very clear power structure. The maturity and independence achieved by the protagonists imply not the advent of universal equality and harmony but merely a pragmatic personal obligation to wield power responsibly. Characters unable to alter or escape the order of things are expected to show a sort of noblesse oblige.

Kindred • Butler's most atypical work in terms of genre is *Kindred*, published in 1979. While the protagonist is shuttled helplessly back and forth between 1824 and 1976 in a kind of time travel, this device is of no intrinsic importance to the message of the story. At one point, the heroine, Edana, asks herself how it can be that she—the as-yet unborn black descendant of a nineteenth century slaveholder—can be the instrument of keeping that slaveholder alive until he fulfills his destiny and fathers her ancestor. By asking, she preempts the reader's own curiosity, and when there is no answer, the story simply moves forward.

Kindred uses a black woman of the 1970's and her white husband to probe beneath the surface stereotypes of "happy slave" on the one hand and "Uncle Tom" on the other. When Edana and Kevin are separated by the South of 1824 into slave and master, they each begin unwillingly to imbibe the feelings and attitudes of the time from that perspective. The impact of the novel results from Butler's ability to evoke the antebellum South from two points of view: the stubborn, desperate attempts of African Americans to lead meaningful lives in a society that disregards family ties and disposes of individuals as marketable animals; and the uncomprehending, sometimes oppressively benevolent ruthlessness of a ruling class that defines slaves in terms of what trouble or pleasure they can give.

The Patternist series • Butler began her science-fiction novels with the Patternist series, and in this series the reader can observe the beginning of her development from a writer of well-crafted science/adventure fiction to a writer who recalls in her own way the reflectiveness of Ray Bradbury.

Survivor • First written but third published was *Survivor*, the tale of an orphaned Afro-Asian girl who becomes a "wild human" in order to survive in a harsh environment. She is found and adopted, in an atypical act of reaching out, by two members of the Missionaries—a nouveau-Fundamentalist Christian sect. The Missionaries' escape from a hostile Earth takes them to a planet inhabited by furred bipeds, whom they regard as less than human. These beings are, in fact, a science-fiction version of the noble savage, but the protagonist is alone in recognizing their nobility. Internally untouched by Missionary dogma, she is truly socialized as a captive of the Tehkohn and, in the end, chooses them as her own people. Her survival and success require an understanding of the color classes of fur among the Tehkohn, where blue is the highest color, suggesting a tongue-in-cheek reference to "blue blood." She makes her own way by dint of qualities often found in protagonists of adventure novels: physical agility, courage, and adaptability.

Patternmaster • *Patternmaster* features an appealing duo, with the younger son of the Patternmaster—the psychic control-central of a society of advanced human beings—confronting and defeating his brutal older brother in an unwanted competition to succeed their father. His helper, mentor, and lover is a bisexual Healer; he trusts her enough to "link" with her in order to pool their psionic power. She teaches him that Healing is, paradoxically, also a deadly knowledge of the body with which he can defeat his brother. Thus, trust and cooperation overcome ambition and brutality. The "mutes" of this novel are nontelepathic human beings whose vulnerability to cruelty or kindness and inability to control their own destinies reflect the earlier status of slaves in America.

Mind of My Mind • Mary, in *Mind of My Mind,* is a "latent" who must undergo a painful transition in order to become a full-fledged telepath. The pain and danger of this passage from adolescence to adulthood are emblematic of the turmoil of coming of age everywhere and of the physical or psychological pain that is required as the price of initiation in many, if not all, societies. The deadened, sometimes crazed, helplessness of latents who cannot become telepaths but must continue to live with the intrusive offal of other people's thoughts is a powerful metaphor for people trapped in poverty, and some of the horrors Butler paints are familiar.

Mary has no choice at first. The founder of her "people," a nontelepathic immortal named Doro, prescribes her actions until she acquires her power. He senses danger only when she reaches out reflexively to control other, powerful telepaths, thus forming the first Pattern. Mary's destruction of the pitiless Doro, like the death of the older brother in *Patternmaster* and of the rival alien chief in *Survivor,* is foreordained and accomplished with a ruthlessness appropriate to the society and to the character of the victim. The incipient change in Butler's style is evident here in the comparative lack of adventure-action sequences and in the greater concentration on psychological adaptation to and responsible use of social power.

Wild Seed • The technique of historical reconstruction is seen again in *Wild Seed,* whose evocation of Ibo West Africa owes something to the work of writers such as Chinua Achebe. *Wild Seed* traces Doro and Anyanwu from their seventeenth century meeting in West Africa to the establishment of Doro's settlements in America. Doro is a centuries-old being who lives by "taking" another man's or woman's body and leaving his previous body behind. Anyanwu, the Emma of *Mind of My Mind,* is a descendant of Doro. She is a "wild seed" because she has unexpectedly developed the power to shape-shift, becoming young or old, an animal, fish, or bird, at will. Their relationship is completely one-sided, since Doro could "take" her any time he chose, although he would not acquire her special abilities. His long life and unremitting efforts to create a special people of his own have left him completely insensitive to the needs and desires of others. Anyanwu finally achieves some balance of power simply by being willing to die and leave Doro without the only companion who could last beyond a mortal lifetime.

Clay's Ark • The last Patternist novel, *Clay's Ark,* introduces the reader to those brutish enemies of both Patternist and "mute" humanity, the Clayarks, so named because the disease that created them was brought back to Earth on a spaceship called "Clay's Ark." The disease culls its victims, killing some and imbuing others with a will to live that overcomes the horror of their new existence. They become faster and stronger, and their children evolve even further, taking on animal shapes and attributes of speed, power, and heightened senses, but retaining human thought and use of their hands. In the guise of a horror story, *Clay's Ark* follows the first Clayarks' attempt to come to terms with their condition and live responsibly, shut off from civilization. Their failed attempt demonstrates that it is not possible to contain cataclysmic natural change, but the story enlists the reader's sympathy for human beings who suffer even as they afflict others.

The Xenogenesis series • With the exception of *Clay's Ark*, where there is much action, the pace of Butler's novels slows progressively; action is increasingly internalized and psychological. Moral judgmentalism and the contest of right versus wrong dwindle to insignificance. The next, and quite logical, development is the Xenogenesis series: *Dawn*, *Adulthood Rites*, *Imago*. This series confirmed Butler as a science-fiction writer of sufficient depth to be of significance beyond the genre.

The change from her originally projected title for the series is informative. "Exogenesis" would have implied merely genesis effected from outside humanity. "Xenogenesis" has both text and subtext. Its meaning is the production of an organism altogether and permanently unlike the parent. The subtext is a function of the best-known English word built on the same root: xenophobia, fear and dislike of that which is foreign or alien. Butler makes the series title a statement of the thesis she will address.

Many of the techniques and themes of her earlier, developing style come to fruition here: the alternating use of first-and third-person narrative, the slow pace of a plot laden with psychological development and sensory perceptions, the meticulous foreclosure of value judgments, the concern with hierarchy and responsibility, the objective observation of feelings of revulsion for that which is alien, and those feelings' gradual dissipation as the alien becomes familiar and therefore less threatening. Action in the series is sparse, normally kept to the minimum necessary to maintain the pace of psychological and social observation. In some ways, it is a chilling series of seductions of human beings by an alien, benevolent oppressor not entirely unlike Rufus of *Kindred* in his better moments. In some ways, it is a demonstration of the infinite capacity of humanity to seek satisfaction in the destruction of itself and others.

Words used to describe two of Butler's shorter works in the 1984 and 1987 issues of *The Year's Best Science Fiction* may serve here as a characterization of the Xenogenesis series: "strange, grotesque, disturbing . . . and ultimately moving," a "tale of despair, resignation, and, most painfully, hope." It is apparently to examine the capacity of human beings to adapt, to survive, and perhaps stubbornly to pursue a self-destructive course of action that Butler has created the nightmarish situation that the reader encounters in *Dawn*.

Dawn • In a world devastated by nuclear exchange between East and West, the dying remnants of humanity survive largely in the Southern Hemisphere. The heroine of *Dawn* is an African, Lilith, whose name suggests the demonic goddess of Hebrew tradition, the famous medieval witch who appears in Johann Wolfgang von Goethe's *Faust* (1808, 1833), and the medieval, alternate "first mother" who was put aside in favor of Eve.

Enter the Oankali, a nonviolent race of benevolent parasites and genetic engineers, who exist for the opportunity of combining with other species to acquire new cellular "knowledge" and capabilities. They live for miscegenation. They are trisexual: male, female, and ooloi. The ooloi is the indispensable link between male and female, channeling, altering, or amplifying all genetic material and sexual contact, including transfer of sperm and pleasurable sensations. The ooloi is capable of internal healing; for example, one cures Lilith of a cancer and finds the cancer to be an exciting new biological material with which to work.

The Oankali blend with another species by linking a male and female of that species and a male and female Oankali through an ooloi. Thereafter, independent conception is not possible for those members of that species. The progeny are "constructs," who, at least at first, resemble their direct parents but carry genetic change within them. Lilith's first husband is killed in *Dawn*, but she bears his child posthumously because Nikanj, the ooloi that has chosen her, has preserved his seed. The resultant humanoid male child is the protagonist of *Adulthood Rites*, while a much later child of Lilith with another husband and the same Oankali parents is the protagonist of *Imago*.

Lilith is at first appalled by even the more humanoid Oankali, with their Medusan tentacles and sensory arms. She is gradually acclimated to them, cooperates with them to save humanity, bears children with them, is overwhelmed by the sensory pleasure they can give, and becomes sympathetic to their need to unite with other species, but she is never fully resigned. In *Imago*, Lilith compares the Oankali's description of the "flavors" of human beings to physical cannibalism and implies that the spiritual equivalent is no less predatory.

Lilith's conversion from complete repugnance in *Dawn*, a stylistic tour de force, shapes the following novels, as human beings are ultimately allowed a choice of living with the Oankali, staying behind on a doomed and barren Earth, or living in an experimental, all-human world on Mars. The Oankali, who seem to make decisions as a kind of committee-of-the-whole, foresee that the same old combination of intelligence and hierarchical tendencies (in a rather Darwinian sense) will lead this last outpost of humanity to destroy itself. No one convincingly denies it.

Adulthood Rites* and *Imago • Butler's stylistic virtuosity also extends to narrative person. *Dawn* is a third-person account of Lilith's absorption into the Oankali social structure; *Adulthood Rites* is the third-person narrative of Akin, a male-human construct, who persuades the more rational human beings left on Earth to trust the Oankali, and persuades the Oankali to offer the humans the choice of planetary residences; *Imago* is a first-person account of Jodahs, a child whose transformation to adulthood reveals it to be an ooloi. Use of the first-person narrative to tell the story of an apparent human who becomes wholly alien in both psychology and physiology is risky but rewarding. Through the eyes of a being routinely referred to as "it" in its own society, the reader observes its benevolent stalking and drug-induced brainwashing of human mates and the final planting of a seed that will grow into an organic town and then an organic spaceship, which will carry Jodahs and his people to new worlds for new genetic blendings.

Imago's conclusion serves as a reminder that Butler's imaginary worlds are primarily arenas for hard, necessary decisions in the business of survival. There is compassion as well as bitterness, and love as well as prejudice, but there is no triumph or glory. There is only doing what must be done as responsibly as possible.

Parable of the Sower • *Parable of the Sower* was published in 1993. It is set in California in 2024. The narrator is a fifteen-year-old African American girl who lives with her family in the fictitious town of Robledo, some twenty miles from Los Angeles. At the time of the story, the social order has nearly disintegrated. Society consists of "haves" and "have-nots." The haves live in walled and fortified neighborhoods; the have-nots roam outside the walls along with packs of wild dogs and drug addicts called "Paints," whose addiction imbues them with an orgasmic desire to burn things. Apparently due to the follies of humankind, the climate has been altered, and the entire world is in a state of near-collapse. Disease is rampant, natural disasters are frequent, and though there are stores, some jobs, and even television programming, the social order, at least in California, is almost gone.

Against this backdrop, the heroine, Lauren Olamina, founds a new religion named Earthseed. The novel takes the form of a journal Lauren keeps. Entries are dated, and each chapter is prefaced with a passage from the new religion, the essence of which is that everything changes, even God. In fact, God is change.

Butler said that humankind is not likely to change itself, but that humans will go elsewhere and be forced to change. When the Paints destroy Lauren's neighborhood and most of her family, she treks north toward Canada, and new members join her group, one by one. Most survive and reach their destination, a burned farm in Oregon. The ending is a classic Butler resolution: There is no promised land; people who have not changed generally perish. Lauren has changed nothing in society; she has merely adapted and learned to survive. The structure, style, and plot of *Parable of the Sower* are all deceptively simple. Beneath the surface of the story, the novel deals directly with social power, its use and abuse, and its possible consequences.

James L. Hodge
Updated by John T. West III

Other major works

SHORT FICTION: "Crossover," 1971; "Near of Kin," 1979; "Speech Sounds," 1983; "Bloodchild," 1984; "The Evening and the Morning and the Night," 1987.

NONFICTION: "Birth of a Writer," 1989 (later renamed "Positive Obsession"); "Furor Scribendi," 1993.

MISCELLANEOUS: *Bloodchild, and Other Stories*, 1995 (collected short stories and essays).

Bibliography

Barr, Marleen S. *Lost in Space: Probing Feminist Science Fiction and Beyond.* Chapel Hill: University of North Carolina Press, 1993. Places Butler's themes within feminist fiction.

Butler, Octavia. "Interview with Octavia Butler." Interviewed by Joan Fry. *Poets and Writers Magazine* 25, no. 2 (March/April, 1997): 58-69. Interview with Butler after she had published all but two of her novels.

____________. "Interview with Octavia E. Butler." Interviewed by Larry McCaffery. *Across the Wounded Galaxies.* Urbana: University of Illinois Press, 1990. Among the best of numerous Butler interviews.

Dubey, Madhu. "Folk and Urban Communities in African American Women's Fiction: Octavia Butler's *Parable of the Sower.*" *Studies in American Fiction* 27, no. 1 (1999): 103-128. Explores Butler's representation of the dilemmas and crises of urban life in her fiction.

Foster, Frances Smith. "Octavia Butler's Black Female Future Fiction." *Extrapolation* 23 (Spring, 1982): 37-49. A very early article, published before Butler had completed the Patternmaster series. The article outlines the way "Butler consciously explores the impact of race and sex on future society." Unfettered by the pretentious writing common to much later Butler criticism, Foster illuminates the early texts and remains among the best Butler criticism.

Govan, Sandra Y. "Connections, Links, and Extended Networks: Patterns in Octavia Butler's Science Fiction." *Black American Literature Forum* 18 (1984): 82-87. Demonstrates how Butler uses elements of slave narratives and historical novels to produce a new kind of science fiction, one that features black characters, especially black women, as major heroic figures. Govan's clear and convincing demonstration is enlightening and thought-provoking.

Jesser, Nancy. "Blood, Genes, and Gender in Octavia Butler's *Kindred* and *Dawn*." *Extrapolation* 43, no. 1 (2002): 36-61. Analyzes Butler's heroines Lilith and Dana in terms of Butler's "biological essentialism as it relates to the human body" and its influence on her feminism.

Mitchell, Angelyn. "Not Enough of the Past: Feminist Revisions of Slavery in Octavia Butler's *Kindred*." *MELUS* 26, no. 3 (2001): 51-75. Explores the way in which Butler uses the device of time travel to bridge nineteenth and twentieth century attitudes about slavery.

Roberts, Robin. *A New Species: Gender and Science in Science Fiction*. Urbana: University of Illinois Press, 1993. Explores Butler's role in the maturation of feminist science fiction.

Shinn, Thelma. "The Wise Witches: Black Woman Mentors in the Fiction of Octavia E. Butler." In *Conjuring: Black Women, Fiction, and Literary Tradition*, edited by Marjorie Pryse and Hortense Spillers. Bloomington: Indiana University Press, 1985. An interesting discussion of some of Butler's early heroines. Shinn draws on Annis Pratt's work, which defines archetypal patterns in women's fiction. She then demonstrates convincingly how Butler employs wise witches in her fiction.

George Washington Cable

Born: New Orleans, Louisiana; October 12, 1844
Died: St. Petersburg, Florida; January 31, 1925

Principal long fiction • *The Grandissimes,* 1880; *Madame Delphine,* 1881; *Dr. Sevier,* 1884; *Bonaventure,* 1888; *John March, Southerner,* 1894; *The Cavalier,* 1901; *Bylow Hill,* 1902; *Kincaid's Battery,* 1908; *Gideon's Band,* 1914; *Lovers of Louisiana,* 1918.

Other literary forms • In addition to nine novels, George Washington Cable published a novella, *Madame Delphine* (1881), and four collections of short stories: *Old Creole Days* (1879); *Strong Hearts* (1899); *Posson Jone' and Père Raphaël* (1909); and *The Flower of the Chapdelaines* (1918). He also wrote a dramatized version of one of his novels, *The Cavalier.* His eight books of nonfiction cover miscellaneous subjects. *The Creoles of Louisiana* (1884) is a collection of history articles, and *Strange True Stories of Louisiana* (1889) is a collection of factual stories; both collections are set in Cable's native state. *The Silent South* (1885) and *The Negro Question* (1890) are collections of essays on southern problems. *The Busy Man's Bible* (1891) and *The Amateur Garden* (1914) grew out of Cable's hobbies of Bible-teaching and gardening. *A Memory of Roswell Smith* (1892) is a memorial tribute to a friend. *The Cable Story Book: Selections for School Reading* (1899) is a book of factual and fictional material for children. Cable also wrote magazine articles and a newspaper column.

Achievements • In his study *George W. Cable* (1962), Philip Butcher shows the high position that Cable held in American literature in the last years of the nineteenth century. In 1884, the *Critic* ranked him ahead of fourteenth-place Mark Twain on its list of "Forty Immortals." A cartoon in *Life* (May 27, 1897) depicted Cable among the ten most popular authors of the day. In the American edition of *Literature* in 1899, he was tenth on the list of greatest living American writers.

Popular both with critics and with the reading public in his own time, Cable is little known today. His reputation as a writer of fiction rests on three works: the novel *The Grandissimes,* the novella *Madame Delphine,* and the collection of short stories *Old Creole Days,* later editions of which include *Madame Delphine* as the lead story. Although *Dr. Sevier* and *John March, Southerner* contain serious commentary, the three novels that followed in the first decade of the twentieth century are trivial romances. His last two novels, *Gideon's Band* and *Lovers of Louisiana,* signal only an incomplete return to the artistic level and social worth of his first three books. Because much of his energy went into provocative social essays on southern racial problems, into humanitarian reforms in such areas as prisons and insane asylums, into cultural projects, and, as a major source of income, into platform tours, Cable found insufficient time for the fiction he might otherwise have created. Nevertheless, as late as 1918 he published a collection of short stories and a novel, and up to his death in 1925 he was working on still another novel.

Cable was much admired by his contemporaries. William Dean Howells praised him privately and in print. Twain took him as a partner on a reading tour, and for four months (1884-1885) the two shared the stage as they read from their respective works. Cable also read on programs that included Hamlin Garland, James Whitcomb Riley, Eugene Field, and other popular writers of the day.

Popular in Great Britain as well, he was invited to England by Sir James Barrie for the first of two trips abroad (1898, 1905). For nearly three months in 1898, he traveled and visited in the homes of Barrie, Arthur Conan Doyle, Rudyard Kipling, Henry James, and other well-known figures. He was an interesting conversationalist, an effective speaker, and an entertaining performer. His British friends arranged for him to read his fiction, play a guitar, and sing Creole-black songs in their homes and in public halls. Andrew Carnegie, his host at Skibo Castle, was so impressed with Cable's personality and writing that he later bestowed a lifetime pension on him. Among his honorary degrees was the Doctorate of Letters given by Yale University in 1901 to Cable, Twain, Howells, Theodore Roosevelt, Woodrow Wilson, and other contemporary notables.

Cable's reputation began to decline before his death and has never recovered. During the 1980's, he was considered too important a writer to be omitted from southern literature anthologies and American literature textbooks, but at the end of the twentieth century he had yet to be deemed worthy of widespread revival.

Biography • George Washington Cable was born in New Orleans, Louisiana, on October 12, 1844. Ancestors of his mother, Rebecca Boardman Cable, had lived in New England since the seventeenth century and had moved to Indiana in 1807. The background of his father, the elder George Washington Cable, dates back to pre-Revolutionary times in Virginia. The elder Cable lived in Virginia and Pennsylvania with his parents before moving to Indiana, where he married Rebecca in 1834. The Cable family migrated to New Orleans in 1837, where George, their fifth child, was born.

During the 1840's, the Cables lived a comfortable existence, owning several household slaves until the father's business failed. Through the 1850's, the elder Cable worked at a series of jobs until, weakened in health, he died on February 28, 1859. Because young George's older brother, along with an older sister, had died of scarlet fever, his father's death required him, not yet fourteen, to leave school to support the family. Until the third year of the Civil War, he held his father's former position as a clerk at the customhouse.

Slight in size—only five feet five inches and weighing one hundred pounds—and deceptively youthful in features, Cable enlisted in the Confederate Army on October 9, 1863, three days before his nineteenth birthday. Incurring two slight wounds during his service, he was discharged in 1865.

After the war, Cable worked as errand boy, store clerk, and, until malaria stopped him, as a rodsman with a surveying party on the Red River. In 1868, he became a bookkeeper for two cotton firms in New Orleans. He married Louise Stewart Bartlett on December 7, 1869, and soon fathered the first of a large family of children. At one time, he worked simultaneously for the cotton house of William C. Black and Company, the New Orleans Cotton Exchange, and the National Cotton Exchange.

Newspaper work provided Cable's first opportunity to see his writing in print. While continuing as an accountant, he worked for newspapers as a freelance contributor and then as a full-time reporter. For eighteen months, beginning February 27, 1870, he wrote the column "Drop Shot" weekly, and then daily, for the New Orleans *Picayune*. While working for the *Picayune*, his research into Louisiana history at city hall, the cathedral, and the Cabildo, former seat of colonial government, led him to

Library of Congress

factual stories later to be shaped into fiction. In addition, his newspaper reports on contemporary local affairs interested him in reform on civic, regional, and national levels.

Appearing in *Scribner's Monthly*, Cable's stories were based on his knowledge of the people and activities of New Orleans and of events in Louisiana history. Six of the stories appearing in *Scribner's Monthly* and a seventh story, "Posson Jone'," which was published in *Appleton's Journal*, were later collected as *Old Creole Days*, published by Scribner's. His first novel, *The Grandissimes*, also based on the people and history of Louisiana, was serialized in *Scribner's Monthly* over a twelve-month period and then published in book form in 1880. Next came the novella *Madame Delphine*, first printed in *Scribner's Monthly* as a three-part serial, and then published in book form in 1881.

In 1881, Cable gave up his position as an accountant, depending for the rest of his life on lectures and public readings of his fiction to supplement his income as a writer. One of his successes was a series of six lectures at Johns Hopkins University in 1883, and he continued to find himself in demand on platforms in many cities. In 1884, his regional history *The Creoles of Louisiana* appeared, and in the same year his second novel, *Dr. Sevier*, was published. In 1884-1885 he went on a successful reading tour with Mark Twain, but afterward, the two writers had a permanent falling out.

The son of a slaveholding family, Cable was a loyal Confederate soldier during the Civil War and apparently remained unchanged in political stance for some time thereafter. Later, however, he began to express feeling against racial injustice. Although criticism of discrimination is present in his fiction, it was only through the direct statements of his magazine articles and public lectures that fellow southerners became fully aware of his radical stance. The publication of a volume of his essays, *The Silent South* (1885), made his stand clear. Newspaper editorialists who had acclaimed his fiction now began to attack his social and political views.

Cable had two households to support—one including his wife and children, and the other his mother, his sisters, and the children of his widowed sister. His wife, who traced her ancestry back to the *Mayflower*, was born and reared in New England. Cable believed that a return to the climate of New England would be beneficial for his wife's frail health. In addition, the attraction that a location near his publishers in New York held for him, and a sensitivity to the criticism aimed at him in the South, influenced his decision to leave New Orleans after forty years of residence there. Having previously visited Northampton, Massachusetts, he moved his wife and children to a home there in 1885, and his mother, sisters, and cousins followed soon thereafter.

Despite his desire to write fiction, Cable allowed other interests to take much of his time. In 1885, he championed black rights in an essay read nationwide, "The Freedman's Case in Equity." In 1886, he founded the first of the Home Culture Clubs, in which he would be involved for the next thirty-five years. Through his Open Letter Club (1888-1890), in whose name he lectured, wrote, and published, Cable completed the period identified as his greatest effort for reform in the South. From 1887 to 1889, he undertook an extensive program of religious writing and teaching; he conducted a large Bible class in Northampton each Sunday, traveling to Boston on Saturdays to hold a similar class.

For five years, Cable published a book annually; *Bonaventure, Strange True Stories of Louisiana, The Negro Question, The Busy Man's Bible,* and *A Memory of Roswell Smith* were all published during this period. At the same time, he was giving readings and lectures from coast to coast. A popular speaker, he was frequently invited to deliver commencement addresses and to give talks on literary subjects, southern problems, and Creole history. Despite his endeavors, however, he remained constantly in debt—receiving advances on royalties from his publishers, obtaining loans, repaying old debts, and incurring new ones.

By this time, Cable had ceased actively campaigning for civil rights, and his writing developed a noncontroversial tone. His third novel, *John March, Southerner,* although concerned with Reconstruction problems, avoided racial issues, as did his collection of short stories *Strong Hearts. The Cable Story Book,* needless to say, offended no one. The following novels, *The Cavalier* and *Bylow Hill,* veered even more sharply from controversy to entertainment, their artistic value diminishing proportionately.

Meanwhile, in 1898, Cable had made a triumphal reading tour in Britain. Philanthropist Andrew Carnegie, with whom Cable became friends while in Scotland, donated money to one of Cable's long-enduring projects. In 1903, Carnegie agreed to give fifty thousand dollars for a building for the Home Culture Clubs on the condition that five thousand dollars a year be guaranteed locally for five years.

Dimming Cable's good fortune, his beloved wife died on February 27, 1904, ending a devoted marriage of nearly thirty-five years. Cable continued to write, although without immediately readying a book for publication. Two years and nine months after Louise's death, he married Eva C. Stevenson. In 1908, he published the novel *Kincaid's Battery,* and in 1909 he put two of his short stories (one of them selected from the *Old Creole Days* collection) into book form, *Posson Jone' and Père Raphaël.* In 1911, Carnegie began sending Cable one thousand dollars a year to support his writing. Three years later, *Gideon's Band* and *The Amateur Garden* were published.

Despite his debts, Cable managed to travel outside the United States even before Carnegie began to subsidize him. When traveling, he often carried with him an unfinished manuscript, working on it when he had time. In later years, no longer dependent on the platform circuit, he began staying in Northampton in the summer, spending the winter in New Orleans, Florida, and Bermuda. In 1918, at the age of seventy-four, he published two books—*The Flower of the Chapdelaines,* a collection of short stories, and *Lovers of Louisiana.*

When Carnegie died in 1919, his will provided Cable with five thousand dollars a year for life, the annuity to be transferred to Eva if she survived her husband. Eva, however, died on June 7, 1923. Six months after her death, Cable married his third wife, Hanna Cowing. A little more than a year later, on January 31, 1925, he died. Among his literary papers was an unfinished novel on which he had been working.

Analysis • Although George Washington Cable's reputation rests primarily on one collection of short stories and two pieces of longer fiction, his total output includes twenty-two books. For an understanding of Cable as a writer of fiction, one should first consider his nonfiction and his reasons for writing it. Cable's interest in history is shown in two books centered on Creole culture, *The Creoles of Louisiana,* a collection of history articles, and *Strange True Stories of Louisiana,* a collection of factual stories about the Creoles. On a juvenile level, *The Cable Story Book* is a combination of factual and fictional material that emphasizes the same Creole subjects as his fiction. *The Silent South* and *The Negro Question,* his best-known works of nonfiction, are collections of essays on controversial southern problems, notably the problem of racial discrimination. Characteristic of Cable's prose is a moral posture and a humanitarian zeal, openly stated in his nonfiction and imaginatively expressed in the most important of his fiction. He worked for the reform of people and institutions and for a reversal in racial attitudes.

The Grandissimes • Cable's first novel, *The Grandissimes,* is his unqualified masterpiece. Louis D. Rubin, Jr., has called it the first "modern" southern novel, dealing realistically as it does with the role of the black in American society. Added to the rich portrayal of aristocratic Creole settings and family problems, a panoramic array of characters of Native American, black, and mixed bloods vivify problems of social castes and racial discrimination in Louisiana in 1803, the year of the Louisiana Purchase. Using the historical actuality of racially tangled bloodlines as the theme for dramatic episodes, Cable emphasizes the ramifications of black-white relationships. The free quadroon caste, for example, had its special role in southern society, as shown historically in the New Orleans "quadroon balls." Beautiful young women of one-quarter black blood (quadroons) or, perhaps, one-eighth (octoroons) danced at these balls with white men, were chosen by them as mistresses, and were set up in separate households in the city.

Two principal quadroons interact in *The Grandissimes.* A male quadroon is the identically named half-brother of the aristocratic Creole Honoré Grandissime. The darker Honoré Grandissime flouts the law by refusing to inscribe the letters "f.m.c." (free man of color) after his name. Educated in Paris along with his half-brother and heir to most of their deceased father's wealth, the quadroon nevertheless remains unrecognized as a legitimate member of the Grandissime family. The Creoles' acceptance of an American Indian chieftain as ancestor is introduced to point up their unwonted prejudice against the taint of black blood. The main female quadroon is Palmyre Philosophe, a freed slave who bears a hopeless love for the all-white Honoré Grandissime and, in turn, is loved by his quadroon half-brother. To illustrate the injustices perpetrated against blacks, Cable inserts the episode of the black Bras-Coupé, a historical figure used earlier in Cable's unpublished short story "Bibi." Palmyre hates Agricola Fuselier, her former owner and uncle to Honoré Grandissime, who forced her unconsummated marriage to Bras-Coupé.

The character who serves throughout the novel as spokesman for Cable is Joseph Frowenfeld, a German American newcomer to New Orleans, who observes, participates in, and comments critically on the action. Honoré Grandissime, the leading male character, is a Creole who recognizes the faults of his society and works with moderation to correct them. He provides a liberal Creole viewpoint, supplementary to the rigid moral judgment of Frowenfeld. Agricola Fuselier, in direct contrast to Frowenfeld, represents the proud old Creoles who insist on purity of race.

Action antecedent to the yearlong events of the novel goes back to 1673, the year of the birth of the American Indian girl whose choice of a De Grapion suitor began a feud between two Creole families, the De Grapions and the Grandissimes. Preceding the main plot by eight years comes the tale of Bras-Coupé. Otherwise, the action takes place between September, 1803, and September, 1804.

The leading female character, Aurora Nancanou, daughter of a De Grapion, is the young widow of a man killed by Agricola Fuselier in a duel over a card game. Agricola took Nancanou's estate in payment for the gambling debt, passing the estate on to his nephew, the white Honoré, and leaving Aurora and her daughter Clotilde without land or money. The novel opens at a masked ball in New Orleans where Aurora and Honoré meet, unaware of each other's identity, thus beginning a romantic complication. Paralleling the love triangle of Palmyre and the Grandissime half-brothers, Joseph Frowenfeld falls in love with Clotilde, who, at the same time, is desired by Frowenfeld's friend Dr. Charlie Keene.

Honoré Grandissime, as leader of the Grandissime family and as Cable's symbol of right-thinking Creoles, upsets his relatives on several occasions: Endangering the Grandissime finances, he returns Aurora Nancanou's property to her; in an act socially degrading to the family, he becomes a partner with the quadroon Honoré, under the business title "The Grandissime Brothers"; on an uneasy political level, he cooperates with Claiborne, the newly appointed territorial governor.

Romance, realism, and melodrama are mingled in *The Grandissimes.* In a romantic resolution, the De Grapion-Grandissime feud is ended, and marriage is imminent for two sets of lovers—Aurora and the white Honoré Grandissime, Clotilde and Frowenfeld. On the realistic side—with an admixture of melodramatic incidents—the two leading quadroons of the story are defeated. After Palmyre's several attempts to get revenge on the object of her hate, Agricola Fuselier, and after he is stabbed by the quadroon Honoré, she is forced to flee for safety to Paris. She is accompanied by her fellow refugee, Honoré Grandissime (f.m.c.), who commits suicide by drowning because of her final rejection of him.

Intentional obscurity is a characteristic of Cable's style in *The Grandissimes.* Lack of direct statement and slow revelation of relationships mark the progress of the plot. Facts are given through hints and implication; full information is withheld in a dense accumulation of incidents. This technique, typical of his early and best works, has been praised for its artistry and criticized for its lack of clarity.

Cable's portrayal of slaveholders, slaves, and the stubbornly held traditions of French Louisiana added a new dimension to southern literature. Succeeding in his aim as a novelist, Cable found that fame brought a painful backlash. His radical views caused this native son to be identified as a traitor to New Orleans and the South.

Madame Delphine • In 1881, Cable published the novella *Madame Delphine,* the third in the three-year sequence of Cable's finest literary works (after the short-story collection *Old Creole Days* and the novel *The Grandissimes*). First published as a three-part novelette in *Scribner's Monthly* from May to July, 1881, *Madame Delphine* was published by Scribner's in book form later that year. In editions of *Old Creole Days* succeeding its initial publication, *Madame Delphine* is included and given lead position in the book.

The story begins with beautiful Olive Delphine returning from France on a ship that is boarded by the Creole pirate Ursin Lemaitre. Confronted by Olive's piety and charm, Lemaitre is struck with repentance for his sinful life and with love for the unidentified stranger. Settling in New Orleans, the reformed Lemaitre changes his name to Vignevielle and turns from piracy to banking. When not in his banker's office, he wanders through the streets, searching for the mysterious young woman.

Eventually, the lovelorn banker and Olive develop a friendship, and marriage becomes their intention. Olive, however, is not legally able to become Lemaitre's wife, for she has black ancestry. Her mother, Madame Delphine, is a quadroon, the mistress to a white man, Olive's father. Madame Delphine, despite the laws against miscegenation, approves of the marriage. Indeed, she has made it clear that she is seeking a white husband for her daughter.

Vignevielle's relatives and friends, knowing that Madame Delphine is a quadroon, attempt to stop the illegal marriage, going so far as to threaten to turn him over to government agents who are searching for him. Madame Delphine meanwhile puts forth the ultimate effort to make the union possible. Producing fabricated evidence, she perjures herself by swearing that she is not the girl's blood mother. After Vignevielle and Olive are married, Madame Delphine goes for confession to the priest Père Jerome, admits her lie, and dies. Père Jerome speaks the closing line: "Lord, lay not this sin to her charge!"

The style of *Madame Delphine* is leisurely. Little mysteries cling to characters and actions, with revelation coming in glimpses, suggestions, and half-expressed statements. Early reviewers compared Cable to Nathaniel Hawthorne in achievement of mood, atmosphere, and ambiguity. Adverse criticism of *Madame Delphine*, however, finds the work excessively obscure; most troubling to critics is the needlessly complicated unfolding of the plot.

Furthermore, the characterization of the lovers is weak. Vignevielle's switch from dashing pirate to banker is inadequately motivated. Olive is a shadowy figure without distinguishable traits. Madame Delphine, despite her maneuvers, approaches the stereotype of the helpless mother. The only strong character is Père Jerome, a compassionate observer and spokesman for Cable. Père Jerome sees that society deserves blame, both for its actions and for its failure to act. Society acquiesces in evil—from its unprotesting profit in Lemaitre's smuggled goods to its deliberate manipulation of the lives of mulattoes.

More significant than the style of *Madame Delphine* is its portrayal of the southern attitude toward miscegenation. Although romanticism embellishes the outwardly happy ending of the story, Cable's recognition of the female mulatto's untenable position is clear. Looking beyond the temporary bliss of the wedding day, the reader realizes that prospects for Olive in New Orleans are not favorable. Madame Delphine's perjury has made the marriage legally permissible, but in the eyes of Lemaitre's friends, Olive is not and will never be an acceptable member of their aristocratic society.

The developing social consciousness revealed by Cable in *Madame Delphine* gives the work a lasting value. After this novella, though, he confined the most telling of his indictments to essays, disappointing readers who waited for his familiar critical tone in future novels. He was never able to duplicate the blend of artistic craftsmanship, authentic local color, and social commentary that distinguishes *Madame Delphine*, *The Grandissimes*, and *Old Creole Days*.

Bernice Larson Webb

Other major works

SHORT FICTION: *Old Creole Days*, 1879; *Strong Hearts*, 1899; *Posson Jone' and Père Raphaël*, 1909; *The Flower of the Chapdelaines*, 1918.

NONFICTION: *The Creoles of Louisiana*, 1884; *The Silent South*, 1885; *Strange True Stories of Louisiana*, 1889; *The Negro Question*, 1890; *The Busy Man's Bible*, 1891; *A Memory of Roswell Smith*, 1892; *The Amateur Garden*, 1914.

MISCELLANEOUS: *The Cable Story Book: Selections for School Reading*, 1899.

Bibliography

Benfey, Christopher E. G., *Degas in New Orleans: Encounters in the Creole World of Kate Chopin and George Washington Cable.* Berkeley: University of California Press, 1999. Exploration of the culture of late nineteenth century New Orleans that touches on how George Washington Cable and Kate Chopin used New Orleans themes in their writings.

Biklé, Lucy Leffingwell Cable. *George W. Cable: His Life and Letters.* New York: Charles Scribner's Sons, 1928. This biography, written by Cable's daughter, has the advantage of immediacy to, and intimacy with, the subject. Biklé covers the life of Cable primarily through the many letters that he wrote.

Butcher, Philip. *George W. Cable.* New York: Twayne, 1962. This literary biography studies the life of Cable in the context of his work and vice versa. Like other biographies in the Twayne authors series, it provides a useful general introduction. Butcher covers the major phases of Cable's life—from New Orleans and *Old Creole Days* to the friendship with Mark Twain to his social and political involvement—in an honest, engaging fashion.

Cleman, John. *George Washington Cable Revisited.* New York: Twayne, 1996. Revision of an earlier critical introduction to Cable's life and work; discusses Cable's major work and the social context that frames it. Cleman also includes chapters devoted to Cable's advocacy of civil rights for African Americans, his political writing, and his later works of "pure fiction."

Ekstrom, Kjell. *George Washington Cable: A Study of His Early Life and Work.* New York: Haskell House, 1966. Ekstrom focuses on Cable's Creole fiction, giving much historical, literary, and cultural background to Cable's early work. In addition to the biographical information on Cable's early years, Ekstrom also discusses literary and nonliterary sources for the Creole short stories and novels.

Elfenbein, Anna Shannon. *Women on the Color Lines: Evolving Stereotypes and the Writings of George Washington Cable, Grace King, Kate Chopin.* Charlottesville: University Press of Virginia, 1989. Argues that Cable identified racism with sexism and classism and subverted the traditional literary categories that have segmented white women and women of color. Discusses how in the story "Tite Poulete" Cable moves beyond racism to a consideration of the shared oppression of all women.

Jones, Gavin. "Signifying Songs: The Double Meaning of Black Dialect in the Work of George Washington Cable." *American Literary History* 9 (Summer, 1997): 244-267. Discusses interaction of African American and French-Creole culture in Cable's works; argues that African American dialect, song, and satire were transmitted to the white community subversively.

Ladd, Barbara. *Nationalism and the Color Line in George W. Cable, Mark Twain, and William Faulkner.* Baton Rouge: Louisiana State University Press, 1996. Argues that racial thinking of the lower Mississippi River area, on which Cable focused, is colonialist and assimilationist.

Petry, Alice Hall. *A Genius in His Way.* Cranbury, N.J.: Associated University Presses, 1988. A literary study focusing on the short stories from *Old Creole Days,* but opening with a chapter on *Madame Delphine,* this book is rather scholarly, but accessible to an advanced high school student. The bibliography includes only items cited in the text.

Roberson, William H. *George Washington Cable: An Annotated Bibliography.* Metuchen, N.J.: Scarecrow Press, 1982. An important resource, this volume has the most extensive bibliographical listings on Cable yet published

Rubin, Louis D., Jr. *George W. Cable: The Life and Times of a Southern Heretic.* New York: Pegasus, 1979. By Rubin's own admission, the biography in this book is dependent on the work of Arlin Turner, but Rubin's comments on the individual stories are insightful and helpful. Has complete chapters on *Old Creole Days, The Grandissimes, Dr. Sevier,* and *John March, Southerner.*

Turner, Arlin. *George W. Cable: A Biography.* Durham, N.C.: Duke University Press, 1957. Turner's thoroughly researched biography in many ways set the standard for further Cable studies. Turner discusses in great detail not only Cable's life but also his literary work, political involvement, geographical contexts, and the important historical events that affected Cable's life and work. As with the rest of this biography, the index and bibliography are extensive.

Morley Callaghan

Born: Toronto, Ontario, Canada; February 22, 1903
Died: Toronto, Ontario, Canada; August 25, 1990

Principal long fiction • *Strange Fugitive*, 1928; *It's Never Over*, 1930; *No Man's Meat*, 1931 (novella); *A Broken Journey*, 1932; *Such Is My Beloved*, 1934; *They Shall Inherit the Earth*, 1935; *More Joy in Heaven*, 1937; *The Varsity Story*, 1948; *The Loved and the Lost*, 1951; *The Many Coloured Coat*, 1960; *A Passion in Rome*, 1961; *A Fine and Private Place*, 1975; *Season of the Witch*, 1976; *Close to the Sun Again*, 1977; *"No Man's Meat," and "The Enchanted Pimp,"* 1978; *A Time for Judas*, 1983; *Our Lady of the Snows*, 1985; *A Wild Old Man on the Road*, 1988.

Other literary forms • Morley Callaghan's early reputation was based primarily on his short stories, many of which appeared in European and American magazines such as *The Transatlantic Review*, *The Exile*, *Transition*, *The New Yorker*, *Esquire*, *The Atlantic Monthly*, and *Scribner's Magazine*. Several significant collections of these stories have been published, including *A Native Argosy* (1929), *Now That April's Here, and Other Stories* (1936), *Morley Callaghan's Stories* (1959), and *The Lost and Found Stories of Morley Callaghan* (1985). In addition to the novels and stories, Callaghan wrote a few plays and published many articles in *The Toronto Star*, *New World*, *Maclean's*, and *Saturday Night*. In 1963, he published *That Summer in Paris: Memories of Tangled Friendships with Hemingway, Fitzgerald, and Some Others*, a memoir of his early years as a writer in the company of Ernest Hemingway, F. Scott Fitzgerald, Robert McAlmon, James Joyce, and Ford Madox Ford.

Achievements • It seems almost typical of the Canadian literary scene that Callaghan has been more widely praised outside his home country than within it. Many American and European critics have compared Callaghan's work, especially the short stories, to that of the great Russians: Leo Tolstoy, Anton Chekhov, and Ivan Turgenev. Edmund Wilson claimed that Callaghan was probably the most neglected novelist in the English-speaking world. From the beginning of his career during the 1920's, Callaghan attracted the attention of some of the foremost figures in the literary world: Fitzgerald, Hemingway, Sinclair Lewis, James T. Farrell, Ezra Pound, Erskine Caldwell, and Ford, to name but a few. These writers praised his direct, laconic style, which was unencumbered by many of the excesses in language and description prevalent in the fiction of the 1920's and 1930's. American and European editors also found a special quality in Callaghan's work and promoted it in the leading magazines of the day: *The Exile*, *Transition*, and *The New Yorker*.

In Canada, on the other hand, Callaghan's early critical reception was often less than positive, as if there were some acute embarrassment in having a local author achieve international success. Callaghan himself was particularly sensitive to the vicissitudes of his reputation, and in *A Fine and Private Place*, using the persona of neglected author Eugene Shore, he placed himself at the forefront of Canadian letters. Certainly, much of the international praise of Callaghan has been extravagant, and much Canadian criticism has been parochial, but in the late twentieth century a more incisive and serious approach to this work created a well-deserved and long overdue balance. Callaghan was awarded the Lorne Pierce Medal for Literature by the Royal Society of Canada and Canada's most prestigious literary prize, the Governor-General's Award (1951), for his novel *The Loved and the Lost.*

Biography • Edward Morley Callaghan was born in Toronto, Ontario, on February 22, 1903. His parents, both of whom encouraged his literary bent, were Roman Catholics of Irish descent. Callaghan was educated at Riverdale Collegiate and St. Michael's College, University of Toronto, where he excelled in academics and in sports. His college interests are often illustrated in his writing, most prominently in *The Varsity Story,* a novel of university life written on the occasion of a fund-raising campaign, and *That Summer in Paris,* which includes his account of his famous boxing match with Ernest Hemingway. During his university days, Callaghan worked as a reporter on the *Toronto Daily Star*; in 1923, he met Ernest Hemingway, who was the European correspondent for the paper. The two became good friends, and Hemingway not only provided stimulating conversation concerning Callaghan's favorite authors, Sherwood Anderson (Callaghan's "literary father"), Joyce, Pound, and Fitzgerald, but also encouraged him to continue writing fiction.

Callaghan graduated with a bachelor's degree from St. Michael's in 1925 and enrolled in Osgoode Law School, from which he graduated in 1928. From 1926 to 1928, he made numerous trips to New York, where he met many friends of Hemingway who were to help him in his career. Among them were Katherine Anne Porter, William Carlos Williams, Nathan Asch, and Maxwell Perkins of Charles Scribner's Sons. Perkins, after reading Callaghan's material, decided to publish his first novel, *Strange Fugitive,* and a collection of stories, *A Native Argosy.* Following his marriage to Loretto Dee in 1929, Callaghan traveled to Paris, where in a few months he completed a novel, *It's Never Over,* a novella, *No Man's Meat,* and a number of stories.

In 1930, Callaghan returned to Toronto permanently and began to produce his mature work, including *Such Is My Beloved, The Loved and the Lost,* and *Close to the Sun Again.* Although his work has a universal appeal that distinguishes it from much Canadian fiction, it is rooted in his observations of ordinary Canadian life and the particular attitudes of people as they respond to social and institutional forces. Into his eighties, Callaghan continued to write effectively, challenging the moral and social complacency that threatens the individual consciousness. He died in Toronto on August 25, 1990.

Analysis • Much has been made of Morley Callaghan's streamlined style—in his own words, the art of getting the writing down "so directly that it wouldn't feel or look like literature." Callaghan wished to get an effect that was "transparent as glass." Life should be delineated without embellishment and to a large extent without metaphor. The language should be stripped of all artistic and symbolic associations, and objects should be seen as they are, like Paul Cezanne's apples, which are merely apples and yet capture the essence of apples. The central idea of Callaghan's style is that reality must be accepted for what it is and that it can be conveyed directly and simply. Leon Edel suggests that this method has its origins in Callaghan's journalism, that Callaghan, like Hemingway, transfers the clipped, almost perfunctory prose of the newsroom into the realm of the novel, evading the images and symbols so often used in fiction. In its formative stages, Callaghan's style was perhaps also affected by the naturalism that was popular during the 1920's and 1930's, especially with American writers who wanted a mode of expression to capture the grim realities of the Great Depression.

Whatever its antecedents, Callaghan's style, especially in the early novels such as *Strange Fugitive* and *It's Never Over*, is handicapped by its programmatic simplicity; the prose is ill equipped to handle complexities of character. Callaghan's novels, even the later ones, are also marked by a structural simplicity, with a limited number of characters, few subplots, and, usually, a single controlling consciousness. They seem to plod on to an almost inevitably tragic but morally ambiguous conclusion, giving an illusion of time that is almost static, reduced to its elemental character.

Callaghan did not, however, adhere slavishly to the avowed principles of his early fiction. Beginning with *Such Is My Beloved*, the sentences are more complex; the dialogue is richer, less stylized in the Hemingway manner; the prose is more rhythmic; and the structure of the novels is more intricate. All of Callaghan's work is characterized by an unremarkable surface, which at first glance has little aesthetic appeal. A more discriminating appraisal must therefore be made that accounts for the enduring quality of his work. Some critics have noted the parabolic nature of Callaghan's fiction, which limits the need for rounded characterization and necessitates simplicity of structure. Others argue that Christian humanism, especially in *Such Is My Beloved, More Joy in Heaven*, and *A Passion in Rome*, with their obvious biblical titles, informs Callaghan's work, giving it veracity and insight. Finally, some conclude that Callaghan's power derives from the influence of Charles Darwin, Karl Marx, and Sigmund Freud and a particular setting in history.

To a certain extent, all these theories are true, but all are equally unsatisfying as comprehensive theories. Underlying each of the novels is an ironic point of view that defeats easy answers and leaves the reader with both an unsatisfying vision of life with few moral or aesthetic certainties, and a sense of mystery, an awareness of the infinite complexities of human action and thought that make life worthwhile. This deliberate ambiguity is a narrative strategy designed to force the reader into reevaluating his own observations of life and his own moral stance. Callaghan's novels, then, demand an involved sensibility and a questioning attitude; perhaps what is needed is the passionate intensity that Callaghan so frequently hints is the key to self-realization and independence.

John Martin

Many of Callaghan's novels are animated by the tension between an individual and the institutions that circumscribe his behavior.

The Church, the government, and the business community insist on a patterned, prudent existence that gives society stability and order. As such, they serve a useful function in most people's lives, but they are no substitute for a personal, compassionate, and intuitive vision which, in everyday relationships, often subverts the legalistic intentions of the institutions. An individual can be caught betraying society because he refuses to betray his own conscience. Thus, Father Dowling in *Such Is My Beloved* befriends two prostitutes to rescue them, and himself, with the power of love. His seemingly inordinate concern for them strikes a local parishioner and Dowling's bishop as unorthodox, and Dowling is relieved of his position and finally is admitted to a sanatorium. In *The Loved and the Lost,* Jim McAlpine is torn between his ambition to be a respectable columnist on a Montreal newspaper and the love of a mysterious woman who inhabits the seamier region of the city. By losing faith in Peggy at a crucial moment, Jim allows the circumstances that bring about her death and a loss of faith in himself.

In *Close to the Sun Again,* a more complex relationship between private and public values is explored. Ira Groome, former "lord" of the Brazilian Power Company and now chairman of Toronto's police commission, reflects to no avail on why he has become impersonal and detached from the stream of life. After suffering severe injuries in a car accident, he relives his career as a naval commander and realizes that he had tried to escape the pain of human involvement by representing an institutional view of life. In a final epiphany, he accepts the voices in his own heart and dies with the profound self-knowledge that had been lacking in the earlier part of his life. In all of these works, the ultimate irony is that the individual can rarely reconcile the public demands of the world with a passionate, often barbaric, private vision.

Such Is My Beloved • The dedication to Callaghan's finest early novel, *Such Is My Beloved,* reads, "To Those Times With M. In The Winter Of 1933"; "M." was Jacques Maritain, the world-renowned philosopher, who came to St. Michael's College Institute for Medieval Studies as a visiting lecturer. Perhaps from his discussions with Maritain, especially concerning the nature of Christian humanism and the role of the saint in the world, Callaghan chose to concentrate on an explicitly religious theme, probing the relationship between the Roman Catholic Church, an agency of worldly prudence, and its priests, who must minister to individuals' needs through the love of Christ. The title suggests the focus of the novel; as Brandon Conron has noted, it is an echo of God's expression of love for his son on the occasion of Christ's baptism. The epigraph confirms the theme of the nature of love and the consequences of the spiritual attitude of the novel. Taken from the Song of Songs, it reads: "Many waters cannot quench love, neither can the floods drown it: if a man give all the substance of his house for love, it would utterly be contemned."

The story is simple. Father Dowling, the central figure of the novel, befriends two prostitutes, Veronica (Ronnie) Olsen and Catherine (Midge) Bourassa, in order to save them from their degrading way of life. He soon realizes that they need not only love but also material necessities to sustain them through the Great Depression. Aware that the money he earns from his parish will not be enough, Dowling enlists the help of a wealthy parishioner, James Robison, to provide jobs for them. Robison, however, is not willing to risk the possibility of scandal and reports Dowling to his bishop. The two women are forced to leave the city (ostensibly Toronto), and Dowling, driven by these betrayals to madness, has only momentary periods of lucidity in the sanatorium.

Brandon Conron and Malcolm Ross both have argued that the novel presents at least a superficial allegory, with Dowling as Christ, Robison as Judas, and the bishop as Pontius Pilate, with certain minor characters also serving symbolic roles. The success of the novel, however, resides in Callaghan's ability to draw these characters as vulnerable human beings and not merely as types. Dowling conveys a disturbing naïveté that, despite his powerful love, causes his downfall. He brings Ronnie and Midge presents and money in an effort to keep them off the streets, but the gifts are ineffective. Dowling exhibits many other traits that seduce the reader into a kind of Conradian belief in him as "one of us." In the confessional, he is so consumed by his thoughts for the women that he is harsh with others. He is jealous of Father Jolly's room, which Dowling himself covets; he admits to the natural sexual feelings of a young man his age; he hates the owner of the bawdy house, Henry Baer; and he lies about his involvement with the two prostitutes. Ironically, these human weaknesses make his love seem more potent.

The other characters, although not as well portrayed as Dowling, are effective in that the reader's responses to them are never wholly one-sided. Robison, much of the time, is a kind, helpful Christian who is confused by Dowling's love. The bishop, representing the position of the worldly Church, doubts himself and does not seem secure in his opinion of Dowling. Ronnie's pimp, Joe Wilenski, is a brutish man who often takes advantage of her, yet respects her as a person. Ronnie, coming from a broken home in Detroit, and Midge, abandoned by her lover, react with affecting girlishness, especially when Dowling gives them pretty clothes. The ambivalent, realistic natures of these people condition the reader's response to the novel as a whole. One sees human beings with limited control over their circumstances; the Church and society seem to conspire to destroy the idealistic impulse in the individual consciousness.

Professor David Dooley identifies the central moral problem of the novel as the conflict between quixotic idealism and worldly prudence, with no satisfactory conclusion being evinced. Father Dowling tries to love the prostitutes as Christ loved sinners; all people are worthy of love without distinction, despite their failures. Love, he thinks, will overcome worldly considerations, but his faith cannot change the economic conditions that have driven the women into sin. Dowling also tries to console the Canzanos, a family with twelve children living in abject poverty. Mr. Canzano says that they need money, not faith, and there is nothing left for him but despair. Even Dowling's great love is unconvincing here; he spends so much time with the prostitutes that he can give little to his other parishioners. Although the bishop is satirized by Callaghan for his concern that the scandal will hurt his charity campaign, he is perhaps correct in thinking that the Church should play a more material part in helping people such as the Canzanos.

Dowling's best friend, Charlie Stewart, a medical student who is an avowed Marxist, also views the world in terms of economics. Because he is a secular idealist, he believes that the ideal state could transform society and put an end to poverty. For him, there is no religious problem, only an economic one. The Church, the business community (represented by Robison and his uncharitable wife), Stewart, and Dowling are all caught up in the same dilemma. The personal qualities of spiritual love and secular compassion are defeated by institutions that must force their representatives to make rational, pragmatic choices. Even though these choices are often hypocritical, they are necessary to sustain order in society.

Such Is My Beloved ends with the two prostitutes forced out of the city by the police, and Dowling, in the sanatorium, is left to think of them as two of the many restless souls who cannot find peace. Dowling has occasional moments of clarity in which he offers his sanity as a sacrifice to God so that he might spare their souls. The priest is content in this offering and, at peace with himself, plans to write a commentary on the Song of Songs. The only positive note in the book is that this powerful love of Dowling's is somehow good, and although it cannot change society, it can transcend it, making even the tragic elements of life worthwhile.

In his next two novels, *They Shall Inherit the Earth* and *More Joy in Heaven*, Callaghan continued to examine the theme of love and its relation to society in explicitly religious terms. Neither novel is as well wrought as *Such Is My Beloved*, but they are nevertheless effective renderings of complex human motives. In the period between 1937 and 1948, his "dark period," Callaghan published no major novels. In 1948, however, his period of "spiritual dryness" over, Callaghan published *Luke Baldwin's Vow* and *The Varsity Story* and began work on *The Loved and the Lost*, which appeared in 1951.

The Loved and the Lost • Although the religious dimension is understated in *The Loved and the Lost*, the inner opposition between the individual and the dictates of society is again explored. For the most part, the narrative consciousness is that of Jim McAlpine, through whose eyes the reader receives impressions of Montreal's clearly divided social strata. Formerly an associate professor of history at the University of Toronto, Jim is brought to the city by a publisher, Joseph Carver, to write a political column for the Montreal *Sun*. Carver, a professed "liberal," admired Jim's article, "The Independent Man," in *The Atlantic Monthly*. Living on "the mountain," an affluent district in Montreal, Carver and his divorced daughter, Catherine, represent the social status to which Jim has aspired all his life. Through a friend, Jim meets Peggy Sanderson, a seemingly generous and warm-hearted woman. Jim falls in love with her innocence and her compassion, knowing that their relationship, as elusive as it may be, could destroy his ambitions. After a brawl involving Peggy at Café St. Antoine, a black jazz club on the river, Jim feels compelled to protect her and to profess his love for her. When Peggy's need for him is greatest, however, Jim loses faith in her, inadvertently leaving her to be raped and murdered. Unable to choose between the stable values of "the mountain" and the uncertain values of the river, Jim betrays not only Peggy but also himself.

The novel works in parallels of discrete oppositions between the mountain and the river, with Jim at the center, torn by the attractiveness of each and unable to reconcile the contradictions inherent in both. Carver has wealth and power, which he uses to operate a newspaper dedicated, like *The New York Times* or *Manchester Guardian*, to the principles of independent thinking. His editorial stance, however, is compromised by his personal objection to giving his own writers freedom of thought; he wants supreme loyalty from his staff, and he is disturbed by the possibility that Jim may be an embarrassment to him. His daughter, Catherine, embodies the beauty and social grace of her class, but she is unsure of herself and hides her ardent character. She sees a hockey game with Jim, remarking on the artistic patterns of play. For her, life is a pattern, like her orderly room, which should not be disturbed. When Jim seems to side with the hockey player breaking the pattern by receiving a penalty, she asks why he is not "with us." In the end, however, discovering Jim's complicity in the murder, she empathizes with Peggy, violently slapping Jim for what she thinks is his betrayal.

Evoking similarly complex responses in all those who know her, Peggy Sanderson is an extremely ambiguous character. She has an air of innocence that enchants Jim and makes him want to protect her, but there is also a suggestion of carnality; as a young girl she admired the body of a naked black boy, and there are many comments made on her promiscuity with the blacks at the Café St. Antoine, although they are not verified. In her indiscriminate, but platonic, love for all souls "without distinction" (here she echoes Father Dowling), she is seen as Saint Joan and Christ. This spiritual gift, however, invites fear and resentment, not peace and understanding. Symbolically, she is associated with a carved leopard and a small antique church, both of which she takes Jim to see. The fierce, uncertain jungle violence of the leopard contrasts with the stable religious feeling of the church, but Callaghan never lets the reader know if these are indeed Peggy's responses to these objects. Jim thinks that her innocence is attracted to violence, that in fact her actions are self-destructive. By refusing to compromise her personal vision to social prudence, she is destroyed; the reader is never really sure of the extent to which she is culpable for her own fate.

Much of the novel is controlled by Jim's subjective, ambivalent feelings. He is estranged from the world of status as a child, a boy outside the hedge of the wealthy Havelocks, so his ambition is understandable even if excessively rationalized. Although he is drawn to Catherine and her tidy universe, he feels more comfortable in the "middle world" of the Chalet restaurant. Peggy shatters his balance by showing him a different side of life, where society's rules are broken and ambition becomes mere illusion. At the hockey game, he dismisses the patterns and sees the ice surface as a pit with writhing sacrificial figures. His vision, however, is only refracted, not significantly altered, and rather than accept Peggy for what she is, he tries to mold her into his possession. Like Peter denying Christ, Jim denies knowing Peggy at Angela Murdoch's party on the mountain, hoping at some later date to bring the two worlds into harmony.

Wolfgast, the owner of the Chalet restaurant, tells Jim the story of a white horse he believed belonged to him although it was owned by his father's landlord. The circumstances of losing the horse impressed upon him the need for some definitive personal possession. In buying the Chalet, he achieved his dream. Peggy becomes Jim's "white horse," and he tries to own her by using her apartment to write his articles. Every day he tidies it up and makes a change that reflects his own personality. Only after her death does he recognize that his sin resided in not accepting Peggy for herself. Ironically, by not abandoning himself completely, by losing faith in Peggy as Orpheus lost faith in Euridice, he loses his own sense of identity as well. Confused about the values of high and low society and the mysterious values embodied by Peggy, Jim is left only with a dream of Peggy being trampled by white horses from the mountain as he draws back. In desperation, he attempts to find Peggy's antique church, hoping that in this symbol of belief Peggy will be with him always. The gesture is futile: Jim does not find the church.

The reader, too, is left without a clear moral resolution. Is Peggy really a virgin, a pure innocent? Is she a saint like Saint Joan, destroyed by an insensitive society? Is there really something primitive in her character that attracts violence? Could Jim cope with Peggy as a human being and not as the ideal he made her out to be? How do the symbols clarify and support meaning? After all, Wolfgast's "white horse," the possession of his restaurant, is something quite different from the possession of a human being. Does the church symbolize religious values or innocence, or is there a more ephemeral quality to it? Does the leopard represent the passionate nature of humankind or perhaps only independence? Beneath the surface of a straightforward, well-told story, then, there are ambiguities admitting no easy resolutions.

Through the 1950's, 1960's, and early 1970's, Callaghan continued to write many interesting stories; his novels, however, met with mixed reviews. His style became more ambitious, and his ideas remained adventurous, but his plots were clumsy, his dialogue often unrealistic, and his characterizations more stereotyped than ever before. In *A Fine and Private Place,* an entertaining roman à clef for Callaghan followers, there is even a strident attack on critics unwilling to accept him as a major novelist. With *Close to the Sun Again,* however, Callaghan returned to some earlier themes with great success. The values of the novel are less ambiguous, and the story is simply but powerfully told in his characteristic clipped style, which suits the material admirably.

Close to the Sun Again • The story relates the psychic journey of former naval commander Ira Groome, who quits his job as head of the Brazilian Power Corporation to become chairman of the police commission in a large, metropolitan city, probably Toronto. After the death of his alcoholic wife, Julia, he feels a sense of astonishment that shocks him into the realization that imperceptibly he has lost the passion that makes life real. He has, in fact, become so detached that his wife only felt comfortable calling him "Commander," and his son has rejected him as a father. Voices from within challenge him to break the pattern of impersonality that has characterized his life, but they do not completely penetrate his conscious mind.

As introspective as he was in Brazil, Groome still projects the image of stable authority in Toronto, demanding and getting loyalty from the members of the police commission and starting a casual, uninvolved affair with Mrs. Oscar Finley (Carol) of the prestigious Hunt Club set. Still seeking some "enchantment," however, he begins to drink gin, which softens his disciplined view of life but forces him into the Maplewood rest home every few weeks for a temporary "cure." One night, shocked by some harsh but vaguely familiar words from Carol, he leaves Maplewood for home in an excited state, only to be involved in a serious car accident. In the hospital, holding the hand of his former ship's boatswain, Horler, Groome experiences the enchantment he so badly desires and drifts into a dream world of memory and heightened perception.

Groome relives an important part of his life in which he is again Lieutenant Groome on a ship in the North Atlantic during the war. Upon realizing that he is alive after being severely wounded in action, he sees people as unique individuals, each inhabiting a wonderful private world, and is then able to respond to his men with a sensitivity rarely shown by officers. Groome's life is changed radically, however, when two survivors of a torpedo raid board his ship. Gina Bixby, trying to reach England to see her father, a boxing promoter, is accompanied by huge, silent Jethroe Chone, her father's bodyguard. They are escaping Marty Rosso, a mobster involved in fixing fights, who wants to use Gina to prevent her father from testifying to the boxing commission. Rosso has already caused the death of Robert Riopelle, a naïve boxer duped into believing in himself: With his hands smashed by Rosso, Riopelle perceived that his whole being was corrupted and committed suicide. During their escape from Rosso, the mysterious Chone raped Gina but feels no remorse for an act that "kills" part of her. Although there still seems to be a perverse bond between them, Gina confesses to Groome that, when they reach London, she will kill Chone for this brutal betrayal.

Groome is disturbed by this world so unlike the well-ordered naval existence; it is a world of violent passions beyond his experience. In her questioning of Groome, however, Gina brings to the surface his fascination for the Mayan religious rituals he had encountered as a young archaeology student on the Yucatán peninsula. This society with its sacrificial violence seems to parallel Gina's world in a strange way. Groome recalls a Mayan girl, Marina, an image of light suffusing his memory, who gave him the ancient piece of wisdom that in a cruel, senseless world, all one can do is create something beautiful from the nightmare.

Before they can reach the safety of London, the ship is torpedoed, leaving Groome, Horler, Gina, a wounded Chone, and a few sailors on a life raft. Defiantly, Chone tells Groome that no one knew or loved Gina more than he did; soon after, Chone rolls himself into the water to die at sea. Yelling for him to come back, in the same words that Carol later spoke to Groome, Gina swims after Chone, her passion overcoming any sense of safety. She is also lost in the water. Groome is horrified at the emotions he feels—the jungle terrors of involvements with people living in intense personal worlds. He rationalizes that getting too close to people, being intoxicated by violent passions, only causes pain and suffering. Groome closes his heart to these sufferings and resists the voices in his own heart. He changes into secure Ira Groome, the Commander, dedicated to a high purpose in life, a world of order unencumbered by the depth of personal relationships.

Remembering all this from his hospital bed, Groome realizes that he has committed treason to his own nature. He finally understands the significance of Chone's life. He sees the brightness from a sunlit jungle clearing into which a white leopard emerges, and finally, Groome understands himself. Recognizing the necessity of leading a life of passion in all respects, bearing the suffering and sacrifice that enrich the individual sensibility, Groome dies, "close to the sun again."

In this novel, Callaghan reiterates the themes of his other works but makes it clear that passion should not be compromised to suit the values of society. In earlier novels, the conflict between private passions and the imposed, prudent views of society is unresolved, but *Close to the Sun Again* concludes with an epiphany that clearly emphasizes that the individual's responsibility is above all to himself. Throughout his career, Callaghan offered his readers a vision which is thought-provoking, humane, and replete with the passions that touch everyone's life. There is little doubt that in the future his reputation as a significant twentieth century novelist will remain secure.

James C. MacDonald

Other major works

SHORT FICTION: *A Native Argosy*, 1929; *Now That April's Here, and Other Stories*, 1936; *Morley Callaghan's Stories*, 1959; *The Lost and Found Stories of Morley Callaghan*, 1985.

PLAYS: *Turn Home Again*, pr. 1940 (also known as *Going Home*); *To Tell the Truth*, pr. 1949; *Season of the Witch*, pb. 1976.

NONFICTION: *That Summer in Paris: Memories of Tangled Friendships with Hemingway, Fitzgerald, and Some Others*, 1963; *Winter*, 1974.

CHILDREN'S LITERATURE: *Luke Baldwin's Vow*, 1948.

Bibliography

Boire, Gary A. *Morley Callaghan: Literary Anarchist.* Toronto: ECW Press, 1994. A very good biography of Callaghan. Includes bibliographical references.

Callaghan, Barry. *Barrelhouse Kings*. Toronto: McArthur, 1998. A memoir by Morley Callaghan's son.

Conron, Brandon. *Morley Callaghan*. New York: Twayne, 1966. A comprehensive, carefully organized analysis of Callaghan's short fiction and novels up to *A Passion in Rome*. Its straightforward style and format make this book accessible to students. Also includes a useful biographical chronology and a selected bibliography.

Cude, Wilfred. "Morley Callaghan's Practical Monsters: Downhill from Where and When?" In *Modern Times*. Vol. 3 in *The Canadian Novel*, edited by John Moss. Toronto: NC Press, 1982. This florid essay treats the darker side of Callaghan's vision through a discussion of characterization in several of his short stories and in some of his novels such as *Luke Baldwin's Vow* and *A Passion in Rome*.

Gooch, Bryan N. S. "Callaghan." *Canadian Literature* 126 (Autumn, 1990): 148-149. Discusses *A Wild Old Man on the Road*, comparing it to *Such Is My Beloved* and *They Shall Inherit the Earth*. Praises the novel's compelling quality and suggests that this "short tense" fiction ranks with the best of Callaghan's work.

Hoar, Victor. *Morley Callaghan*. Toronto: Copp Clark, 1969. The style and thematic concerns in Callaghan's fiction to 1963 are treated in this book's two sections, "The Technique" and "The Themes." Hoar supports his commentary with plentiful quotations from Callaghan's works. A useful bibliography is included.

Kendle, Judith. "Morley Callaghan: An Annotated Bibliography." In *The Annotated Bibliography of Canada's Major Authors*, edited by Robert Lecker and Jack David. Vol. 5. Toronto: ECW Press, 1984. Contains the most exhaustive listing of primary sources and secondary sources for Callaghan's work up to 1984 that a student is likely to need. The categories cover the spectrum from books and articles to interviews to audiovisual material. A helpful "Index to Critics Listed in the Bibliography" is also included.

Marin, Rick. "Morley Callaghan." *The American Spectator* 24 (February, 1991): 36-37. A biographical sketch, noting that Callaghan was a famous literary figure during the 1920's when he was part of the Parisian expatriate set of Ernest Hemingway, James Joyce, and F. Scott Fitzgerald; asserts that Callaghan's decision to remain in his native Toronto affected his status in the literary world, but he accepted his relative obscurity with resignation rather than bitterness.

Morley, Patricia. *Morley Callaghan*. Toronto: McClelland and Stewart, 1978. This study considers Callaghan's fiction to the mid-1970's, including thorough, useful analysis of his short fiction.

Stuewe, Paul. "The Case of Morley Callaghan." In *Clearing the Ground: English-Canadian Fiction After "Survival."* Toronto: Proper Tales Press, 1984. In this chapter, Stuewe takes Callaghan to task for sloppy writing and his critics to task for concentrating on Callaghan's thematic concerns to the exclusion of his technical flaws. Stuewe's own writing and tone are lively and incisive.

Woodcock, George. "Possessing the Land: Notes on Canadian Fiction." In *The Canadian Imagination: Dimensions of a Literary Culture*, edited by David Staines. Cambridge, Mass.: Harvard University Press, 1977. Callaghan's fiction is discussed in the context of Canadian fiction and its development and direction since the nineteenth century. The student is provided with a valuable overview that underscores the significance of Callaghan's contribution to Canadian literature.

Truman Capote

Born: New Orleans, Louisiana; September 30, 1924
Died: Los Angeles, California; August 25, 1984

Principal long fiction • *Other Voices, Other Rooms,* 1948; *The Grass Harp,* 1951; *A Christmas Memory,* 1956 (serial); *In Cold Blood,* 1966; *The Thanksgiving Visitor,* 1967 (serial); *Answered Prayers: The Unfinished Novel,* 1986; *Summer Crossing,* 2005 (found manuscript).

Other literary forms • In addition to writing fiction, Truman Capote worked principally in two other forms: the drama (stage, film, and television) and reportage. Capote's first work for the stage was his adaptation of his novel *The Grass Harp,* which was produced in New York in the spring of 1952. In 1954, he collaborated with Harold Arlen on the Broadway musical *House of Flowers,* based on his short story. He also wrote the film scenario for *Beat the Devil* (1954) and dialogue for *Indiscretion of an American Wife* (1954). He adapted Henry James's 1898 short story *The Turn of the Screw* for film as The Innocents (1961). Two Hollywood films, *Breakfast at Tiffany's* (1961) and *In Cold Blood* (1967), were based on his work, but Capote himself did not contribute to the screenplays. He did, however, with Eleanor Perry, adapt three of his stories—"Miriam," "Among the Paths to Eden," and *A Christmas Memory*—for television. *A Christmas Memory* won the Peabody Award in 1967, and the three-story dramatizations were later released as a film, *Trilogy: An Experiment in Multimedia* (1969).

Capote's first venture in reportage was *Local Color* (1950), a series of impressionistic sketches of New Orleans, New York, and other places where he had lived or visited in America and Europe. *Local Color* was followed by *The Muses Are Heard* (1956), an urbane account of his trip to Leningrad and the opening-night performance of the American cast of *Porgy and Bess.* Other sketches of the 1950's appeared in *Observations* (1959), with photographs by Richard Avedon. His masterpiece in this form is *In Cold Blood,* although Capote preferred to regard this work as a "nonfiction novel." *The Dogs Bark: Public People and Private Places* (1973) collects his earlier nonfiction writing and includes some additional sketches, while *Music for Chameleons* (1980) includes new reportage and a short "nonfiction novel," *Handcarved Coffins,* an account of multiple murders in the American Southwest.

Achievements • With the publication of his first novel, *Other Voices, Other Rooms,* Capote achieved fame at the young age of twenty-four. His precocity, the bizarre nature and brilliant quality of the novel, and the astonishing photograph of the author on the book's dust jacket (a figure, childlike in stature, who reclines on a period sofa and looks out with an expression of unsettling maturity and aloofness) made him widely discussed in both America and Europe. This debut set the tone of Capote's later career, in which he consistently attained remarkable popularity while yet appealing to an elite audience of serious readers.

The publication one year later of *A Tree of Night, and Other Stories* (1949) consolidated Capote's reputation as an author of baroque fiction, fiction concerned with the strange, often dreamlike inner states of estranged characters. A peculiarity of

Library of Congress

this volume, however, is that several of the stories it contains are lightly whimsical. *The Grass Harp,* which shares this more "sunlit" vision, shows Capote emerging, tentatively, from his "private," subjective fiction; in this work, whimsy predominates as the individual gropes for his relationship to others. *Breakfast at Tiffany's: A Short Novel and Three Stories* (1958) moves further out into the world, and this tendency becomes more pronounced still in his nonfiction novel *In Cold Blood.*

Capote's unfinished novel, *Answered Prayers,* with its large gallery of precisely observed characters, was Capote's fullest effort to engage the many-sided world of actual social experience. In whatever form he wrote, however, whether sequestered fantasy or fiction with a social orientation, Capote's preoccupations remained constant—loneliness and isolation, the dichotomy between the world and the self, the deprivations of the innocent or unconventional and their moments of grace.

Capote's strength was mainly in the briefer modes—in the vignette, short story, and short novel. Of his longer works, the best is *In Cold Blood,* the most accomplished "nonfiction novel" of its time. Called by Norman Mailer "the most perfect writer of my generation . . . word for word, rhythm upon rhythm," Capote is known for being a great stylist. There is no question that he belongs in the first rank of modern American writers.

In 2005, Truman Capote began receiving new attention with the release of the feature film *Capote,* directed by Bennett Miller. The film chronicles the five years of Capote's life when he was writing *In Cold Blood* and earned Philip Seymour Hoffman a best-actor Academy Award for his portrayal of Capote. Director Douglas McGrath's 2006 film *Infamous* covers the same period in Capote's life and stars Toby Jones as Capote.

Biography • Truman Capote, whose name at birth was Truman Streckfus Persons, was born in New Orleans on September 30, 1924. His mother, Nina (Faulk) Persons, only sixteen when he was born, had married a traveling salesman, Joseph Persons, to escape the drabness of her hometown, Monroeville, Alabama. The marriage soon proved unhappy, and by the time Capote was four years old his parents had become divorced. When his mother moved to New York, she sent her son (an only child) to live with a variety of relatives in the South. From the time Capote was four until he was ten, he lived outside Monroeville, where one of his neighbors was Nelle Harper Lee, who later put him into her novel *To Kill a Mockingbird* (1960) as Dill, the strange, brilliant little boy who is "passed from relative to relative." The relatives with whom he stayed were four elderly, unmarried cousins—three women and their brother. One of the women was Sook Faulk, a childlike, simple woman, wise in ways that mattered to a small boy who otherwise lived much to himself and within his own imagination. Sook Faulk inspired the character of Dolly Talbo in *The Grass Harp*, and Capote later commemorated his childhood friendship with her in his autobiographical stories *A Christmas Memory* and *The Thanksgiving Visitor*. In his secluded life in rural Alabama, he read the works of Charles Dickens and other novelists at an early age and made his first attempts at fiction at the age of ten. Feeling himself different from others, without the love of a mother or father, uncertain even of a home, Capote developed the sense of isolation that informs all of his fiction.

Capote's childhood wanderings continued after he left Monroeville in 1934. At different times, he stayed with cousins in New Orleans, and at one point he lived with a family in Pass Christian, Mississippi, which provided the setting for *Other Voices, Other Rooms*. In 1939, when he was sixteen, he went to New York to join his mother and her second husband, Joseph Garcia Capote, a Cuban textile manufacturer who legally adopted him and whose surname he took. At this time, he was sent to a series of boarding schools in New York and then to Greenwich High School in Millbrook, Connecticut, where his parents had moved. At the age of seventeen, he dropped out of school and found work with *The New Yorker* magazine. After two years, he left his job to live with relatives in Alabama and begin a first novel, *Summer Crossing*, later discarded when he began work on *Other Voices, Other Rooms*.

Capote had been sending out stories for publication since he was fifteen; by the time he was seventeen he had his first acceptances, and in Alabama he wrote his first important stories—"Miriam" and "A Tree of Night." With a fifteen-hundred-dollar advance from Random House for his novel-in-progress, he traveled to New Orleans, then to New York and Nantucket, where the novel, the result of two years' work, was completed. The novel drew upon his own childhood experiences—his exposure to rural localities in the South, his crisis of identity as a nomadic child, and his early preoccupation with homosexuality.

Reviews of *Other Voices, Other Rooms* were mixed, yet many praised Capote enthusiastically for his evocation of the dream states of the subconscious, his "uncanny ability to make a weird world come alive" with a kind of magical radiance. One reviewer called Capote's talent "the most startling American fiction has known since the debut of Faulkner." For a time, Capote was regarded as a writer of southern gothic fiction; during the 1950's, however, he moved away from this school. *The Grass Harp*, although set in the rural South, was more lyrical than gothic; *Breakfast at Tiffany's*, which followed it, was set in New York and was urban in its idiom, its manner, and its implication. *The Muses Are Heard*, with its detached, worldly intelligence, shows how fully Capote had adopted a cosmopolitan stance.

During much of the 1950's, Capote lived abroad, but by autumn of 1959 he was living in New York, and while exploring the possibilities of "nonfiction fiction," he read in the newspapers of the macabre and seemingly inexplicable murder of the Herbert Clutter family in the Midwest. Acting on the intuition that he had found his "subject," he went immediately to Holcomb, Kansas, and began to familiarize himself with the town and with the circumstances of the Clutters. This project soon developed into a major undertaking, to which he devoted himself almost exclusively from November,

1959, to April, 1965. After their apprehension, the murderers, Richard Hickok and Perry Smith, were tried and sentenced to be executed in 1960, but the executions were stayed for five years, during which Capote held more than two hundred interviews with them. He also personally retraced the route they had taken in the course of their wandering after the murders and compiled extensive notes from his conversations with all the parties concerned with the case.

The psychological strain Capote experienced at this time was particularly great because of his empathetic involvement with one of the murderers, Perry Smith. Like Capote, Smith had come from a shattered home and had been a nomadic dreamer; the two were physically similar, both being five feet, four inches tall. The intensity of Capote's imaginative involvement can be felt on every page of *In Cold Blood*, a work that, almost paradoxically, combines objective reporting with deep feeling.

On its publication, *In Cold Blood* became a phenomenal best-seller while winning great critical acclaim. The literary year of 1966 belonged to Capote. It was at this time that he gave his black and white masked ball for five hundred friends at the Plaza Hotel in New York, sometimes called "the Party of the Decade." After the publication of *In Cold Blood*, Capote became a media celebrity and a member of wealthy and fashionable society. After that, however, he produced relatively no new work—chiefly, two volumes of reportage: *The Dogs Bark* and *Music for Chameleons*. During the late 1960's, he announced that he was at work on a new book, *Answered Prayers*, a lengthy, Proustian novel that would be a "major work."

By the mid-1970's, four chapters of the work-in-progress had been published in *Esquire* magazine, which perhaps was done to prove that Capote was actually working on the novel. By this time, Capote had developed drug and alcohol problems, and his lack of professional output reflected his personal disintegration.

Answered Prayers has a stronger sexual frankness than any of Capote's other works; its complicated, darkly intriguing narrative is sometimes scabrous in its revelation of envied lives. In its suggestive handling of reality and illusion, *Answered Prayers* also reveals Capote's familiar sense of loneliness—loneliness among the members of the haut monde. Capote died in California at the home of his close friend Joanne Carson on August 25, 1984, of heart and liver failure caused by multiple drug ingestion. As biographer Gerald Clarke observed, it is unknown whether Capote committed suicide or his health had failed due to the effects that his chemical addictions had on his body.

Analysis • The pattern of Truman Capote's career suggests a divided allegiance to two different, even opposing literary forms—objective realism and romance. Capote's earliest fiction belongs primarily to the imagination of romance. It is intense, wondrously evocative, subjective; in place of a closely detailed outlining of a real social world, it concentrates on the inner states of its characters, usually with the full resources of romance, including archetypal journeys or a descent into the subconscious. His characters' inner life is fixed through the use of telling imagery and controlling symbols. In "The Headless Hawk," for example, the real world exists hardly at all; what little there is of it seems subaqueous, has the liquid flow of things seen underwater. In "A Tree of Night," the heroine is subjected to real terror, complete with gothic phantoms in the form of two strangers on a train. The journey of the train itself is complementary to Kay's journey into the dark places of her soul, where the "wizard man" and irrational fear prevail. In "Miriam," an elderly woman's sense of reality and personal identity give way before the presence of an implike child.

It is not surprising that these early stories have been compared to those of Edgar Allan Poe, for, like Poe, Capote was fascinated by the psyche at the point of disintegration. Similarly, in *Other Voices, Other Rooms*, the boy Joel Knox inhabits a vaguely outlined social world; what is ultimately most real is the terror that surrounds and threatens him. The scenes that pinpoint his experience are all charged with moral, symbolic implication; rather than unfolding through a study of social relationships, the narrative moves episodically through assaults on Joel's mind, imagistic storm points keeping him in agitation and crisis; the identities of the characters surrounding Joel are fixed from the beginning and have only to be revealed through psychic drama. The shape of the work is, finally, that of a romantic moral parable.

How strange it is, then, that as Capote's career progressed he revealed a pronounced interest in the literature of realism, even a kind of superrealism, implied by "nonfiction fiction." He began working in this genre with *Local Color*, a poetic literature of pure "surface." The texture of surface is the real subject of *The Muses Are Heard*. With a sleepless vigilance, Capote observes his fellow travelers and in the finest, most precise detail captures their idiosyncrasies, the gestures and unguarded remarks that reveal them, as it were, to the quick. Tart, witty, detached, *The Muses Are Heard* assumes no depths of meaning in the Cold War world it portrays; eye, ear, and social intelligence are what are important. Capote's career also shows a desire to bring together the opposing parts of his nature and his equipment as a writer, however, and in *In Cold Blood* he actually achieved such a fusion. Capote himself never intrudes on the narration, makes no commentary, stands back reporting "impartially" on what occurs. This effacement of self is so complete that the reader believes he is witnessing the events as they occur. However, at the same time the work contains many, not always obvious, romantic urgings, forcing the reader to put himself in the place of Perry Smith on death row. Strict categories of good and evil break down before the sense of the inextricable mixture of both in life, and the helplessness of humankind before an obscure and ominously felt cosmic drama. The lyric note of baffled yearning at the end is romantic, in spite of the work's judicious, almost judicial, realism.

Other Voices, Other Rooms • The plot of *Other Voices, Other Rooms*, Capote's first novel, is not extremely complicated. Joel Knox, a thirteen-year-old, motherless boy, is sent from the home of his Aunt Ellen in New Orleans to Skully's Landing to be united with his father, Mr. Edward Sansom. Arriving eventually at the Landing, a plantation house partly in ruins, Joel is cared for by a woman named Amy, her languid, artistic cousin Randolph, and two family retainers, Jesus Fever, an ancient black man, and his granddaughter Missouri Fever, known as Zoo. The boy's inquiries about his father are mysteriously unanswered by the adults, and it is only later in the novel that the boy confronts his father—a paralytic invalid who neither speaks nor understands, his eyes fixed in a wide, crazed stare. The crisis experienced by the boy in the decaying house is largely inward; he attempts to free himself of his situation, but in a series of strange episodes his failure to do so becomes evident, and at the end he embraces his fate, which is complementary to that of Randolph, the dream-bound homosexual. He accepts whatever love and solace Randolph (evoked as mother-father, male-female, and "ideal lover" in one) can give him.

In its atmosphere of sinister enchantment, of the bizarre and weird, *Other Voices, Other Rooms* exploits many of the resources of the gothic mode. William Faulkner stands distantly in the background; Carson McCullers is more immediately evident.

Capote's theme of a quest for love and understanding in a world apparently incapable of providing either, and his use of freakish characters, suggest the generic influence of McCullers's *The Heart Is a Lonely Hunter* (1940). Even the "normal" world of Noon City is filled with oddity—a one-armed barber, a female restaurant proprietor who has an apelike appearance. Such oddity is minor, however, compared to the characters who inhabit the Landing—Jesus Fever, a brokeback dwarf; Zoo, whose long, giraffelike neck reveals the scars from Keg Brown's razor assault upon her; Randolph, who, in an upper-floor room, dressed in a gown and wig, becomes a "beautiful lady." At the same time, and often with the most powerful effect, the novel draws on the imagery of surrealism. The late scene at the carnival, for example, is spectacular in its evocation of an irrational world struck by lightning, a sequence followed by the nocturnal pursuit of Joel through an abandoned house by the midget Miss Wisteria, and the coma Joel experiences in which his life is relived while a pianola composes its own jazz and the plantation lurches into the earth.

Essentially, *Other Voices, Other Rooms* is a romance. It has been compared with Nathaniel Hawthorne's 1831 story "My Kinsman, Major Molineux," which also deals with a youth who, in a dark and dreamlike world, searches for his identity and is initiated into life. Joel's journey, in its various stages, has a symbolic shading. At the opening, he leaves the morning world of Paradise to travel to Noon City, where he continues his journey through the backcountry in a mule-drawn wagon, with Jesus Fever asleep at the reins; arriving at the Landing in darkness, Joel is himself asleep and cannot remember entering the house when he awakens the next morning in an upstairs bedroom. With the effect of a wizard's spell, the house comes to claim him. Complicated patterns of imagery—of fire and fever, knifing and mutilation, death and drowning—evoke the extremity of the boy's fear and loneliness as avenues of escape from the Landing are closed to him, one by one. Mythic patterns also emerge—the search for the "father," the Grail quest, Christian crucifixion, Jungian descent into the unconscious—to reinforce the romantic contour of his experience. Although in some ways Joel's guide ("I daresay I know some things I daresay you don't"), Randolph is himself held under an enchantment, dating back to the inception of his homosexual life. At the end, Joel and Randolph become one. As the ancient "slave bell" in the ruined garden seems to ring in Joel's head, he goes forward to join Randolph, leaving his childhood behind him.

Other Voices, Other Rooms is less perfectly achieved than *The Heart Is a Lonely Hunter.* Randolph, for example, a major character, is more a pastiche of English decadence than a real person. Moreover, the ending becomes snarled in obscurity. In accepting Randolph, Joel accepts his own nature, an act that brings liberation and even some limited hope of love. However, Randolph is so sterile, so negative, and so enclosed within his own narcissism that the reader cannot share the upsurge of joy that Joel is supposed to feel. Capote's strength in the novel lies elsewhere—in his ability to create a sustained poetry of mood, to capture psychic states of rare intensity and beauty. His experimentalism in this respect is far more adventurous than that of McCullers. The image-making power of Capote's language is so impressive in this precocious novel as to leave one fearful that he may have exhausted the resources of the southern gothic mode in a single flight.

The Grass Harp • Capote's next novel, *The Grass Harp,* derives from the rural southern fable of "Children on Their Birthdays." Like that tale, *The Grass Harp* has a narrative frame that begins and ends in the present, with the story placed in between.

Collin Fenwick looks back upon his rearing as an orphan in the home of two maiden women, Dolly Talbo, a gentle, childlike woman, and her sister Verena, who has property and investments in town. He is spared the intense ordeal of Joel Knox but is like him in his sense of personal isolation and in his search for love and identity. When Verena takes it upon herself to exploit a home remedy that Dolly makes from herbs (her little scrap of identity), Dolly rebels, and with Collin and Catherine Creek, an eccentric half-breed factotum, she withdraws to a treehouse set amid a field of tall Indian grass. Eventually, they are joined by Riley Henderson, a rebellious youth, and Charlie Cool, a retired circuit court judge whose refinement makes him an anachronism to his married sons, at whose houses he stays in rotation. The adventure in the tree house does not have a long duration, but by the time it is over the characters all come to have an enlarged sense of who they are.

The narrative is flawed in various respects. It involves a number of plot contrivances (Morris Ritz's absconding with the money in Verena's safe); the "battle" scenes between the tree house occupants and the law-and-order characters from town rely too much on slapstick; and Riley Henderson's reformation and marriage to Maude Riordan is a trite conception. However, there are many fine touches in this fragile, not wholly successful tale—the portrait of Judge Cool and his late-in-life courtship of Dolly; Verena's recognition that it is she who is more alone than Dolly, whose "heart" has been the pillar of the house; the controlling symbols of freedom and imagination versus rigidity and dry rationality (the Indian grass "harp" and the cemetery) that enclose the work and give it life beyond its conclusion. A meditation on freedom and restriction, *The Grass Harp* reveals Capote moving away from his earlier studies in isolation toward a concern with a discovery of identity through relation to others.

Breakfast at Tiffany's • The novella *Breakfast at Tiffany's* marks a new stage of Capote's career, since it brings him fully into the world outside his native South. In this short novel, Capote captures New York and its denizens—Joe Bell, the sentimental bartender with a sour stomach; Madame Sapphia Spanella, a husky coloratura who rollerskates in Central Park; O. J. Berman, the Hollywood agent; and Sally Tomato, the surprisingly unsinister mobster with a Sing Sing address. José Ybarra-Jaegar, the Argentine diplomat, is perceived acutely and never more so than when he writes a mendacious letter to the novella's protagonist, Holly Golightly, breaking off a relationship with her when her dreamlife becomes "unsafe."

Capote's novel employs a retrospective narrative frame like the one in F. Scott Fitzgerald's *The Great Gatsby* (1925), in which the pale, conventional Nick Carraway observes the strange career of his larger-than-life neighbor. In both cases, the narration is dominated by nostalgia and the sense of loss, accentuated by the use of a reiterated autumnal motif. Holly's origins go far back in Capote's writing. In *Other Voices, Other Rooms*, Randolph's dream initiator Dolores dries her washed hair in the sun and strums a guitar, as does Holly. Miss Bobbit models her too, her "precious papa" having told her to "live in the sky." Holly is a Miss Bobbit in her late teens, a child-adult whose ideal of happiness lies "beyond." An "innocent" immoralist, Holly is, however, a somewhat sentimental conception (a "good" sensitive character misprized by a nasty and unfeeling world), and a rather underdeveloped character. As Alfred Kazin has observed, she is partly New York chic and partly Tulip, Texas, naïve, but in neither case does she become a real person. The fusion of realism and romantic fable attempted in *Breakfast at Tiffany's* is not achieved fully until Capote's next work, *In Cold Blood.*

In Cold Blood • *In Cold Blood*, which remained on the best-seller lists for more than one year and has since been translated into twenty-five languages, is Capote's most popular and widely read book. It is also one of his most notable works artistically. F. W. Dupee has called it "the best documentary account of an American crime ever written," and Capote himself claimed that it creates a new literary genre, the "nonfiction novel." Although nothing exactly like *In Cold Blood* had appeared previously, there are clearly precedents for it—Theodore Dreiser's *An American Tragedy* (1925), for example, a documentary novel of crime and punishment, and Ernest Hemingway's *Green Hills of Africa* (1935), as well as the reportage of Rebecca West and Lillian Ross. Moreover, *In Cold Blood*'s objectivity is more apparent than real, since the material Capote draws from has been heightened, muted, and selected in many ways, subjected to his aesthetic intelligence. *The New Yorker* style of objective reportage clearly was an influence on the book; another may have been Capote's experience as a scenarist. His use of "intense close-ups, flashbacks, traveling shots, [and] background detail," as Stanley Kauffmann has observed, all belong to the "structural" method of the cinema.

A cinematic method is particularly noticeable in the earlier part of the work, where Capote cuts back and forth between the murderers and the victims as the knot tightens and their paths converge. It is the convergence of a mythic as well as a literal kind of two Americas—one firmly placed in the wheat belt of the Midwest, decent in its habits, secure in its bounty, if a little stiff in its consciousness of being near to God; the other aimless and adrift, powered by garish and fantastic dreams, dangerous in its potential for violence. The horrible irony of Capote's description of "Bonnie" Clutter suggests the ominousness of this section. "Trust in God sustained her," he writes, "and from time to time secular sources supplemented her faith in His forthcoming mercy." The account of the actual murders, suspensefully postponed until later in the work, is chilling in its gratuitous nature while at the same time, through a steady building of telling details, it has the force of a vast inevitability.

The slaughter of the Clutters is "gratuitous" insofar as it might well not have occurred, has nothing to do with them personally, and gains for the young men responsible nothing except a few dollars, a fugitive life, arrest, and execution. As "haves" and "have-nots" come together, as Smith's long pent-up rage against his father becomes projected onto Mr. Clutter, a lighted match explodes a powder keg. Contributing to this act of unreason is the stand-off between Hickok and Smith, each having told lies about himself to the other; rather than surrender this "fiction" of himself, which would involve confronting the truth of his maimed and powerless life, Smith is driven to a senseless murder. The irrationality of the crime is complemented later by the irrationality implicit in the trial and execution, so that ultimately *In Cold Blood* deals with the pervasive power of irrationality.

The psychological interest of the book is heightened by Capote's drifting narrative and use of multiple "perceptors"—the Clutters themselves, Alvin Dewey, the Kansas Bureau of Investigation agent, and many of Holcomb's townspeople. Of overshadowing interest, however, is Perry Smith, who could, as Capote said, "step right out of one of my stories." A young dreamer and "incessant conceiver of voyages," he is at the same time a dwarfish child-man with short, crippled legs. A series of Capote's earlier characters stand behind him. Holly Golightly, dreamer-misfit and child-woman, is a not-so-distant cousin. However, in this work, Capote's sentimental temptation has been chastened by a rigorous actuality, and what results is an extraordinary portrait. Sensitive and sympathetic, Smith is yet guilty of heinous murders. His romantic escapism (he dreams of diving for treasure but cannot swim, imagines himself a famous tap dancer but has hopelessly maimed legs) becomes comprehensible in the light of his homeless, brutalized background, more bizarre than any fiction; his undoing is elaborately plausible.

In the book's final scene, reminiscent of the ending of *The Grass Harp*, Capote brings the memory of Nancy Clutter together with the memory of Smith—entangled in an innocence blighted by life; in this way, *In Cold Blood* becomes a somber meditation on the mysterious nature of the world and the ways of Providence. This questioning quality and lyric resonance were undoubtedly what Rebecca West had in mind in referring to *In Cold Blood* as "a grave and reverend book." It is a work in which realism and romance become one.

Answered Prayers • After the publication of *In Cold Blood*, Capote produced no new major work. During this period, which included bouts of suicidal depression as well as serious physical illnesses, he continued to write for films and to write shorter pieces, while also supposedly at work on *Answered Prayers*. Of the four chapters originally published, Capote later decided that "Mojave" did not belong in the novel, being a self-contained short story written by the character P. B. Jones. With its drifting narrative, including flashbacks and a story within the story, it is extremely suggestive. Its theme is never directly stated, but its cumulative effect makes it clear that its concern is with illusion, particularly of those who love others and find their love betrayed. "La Côte Basque: 1965" is set at a fashionable restaurant on New York's East Side, where all the diners indulge in or are the subject of gossip. P. B. Jones lunches with Lady Ina Coolbirth, who, herself on the eve of divorce, tells stories of broken marriages, while at the next table Gloria Vanderbilt Cooper and Mrs. Walter Matthau tell similar tales. This mood piece closes at the end of the afternoon in an "atmosphere of luxurious exhaustion."

Jones himself is the focal figure in "Unspoiled Monsters," which details his career as an opportunistic writer and exploiter of others, exploitation and disillusion being the observed norm among the members of the international set. However, even these few chapters reveal the depth to which Capote's writing had sunk. His "gossip column" approach simply reveals that Capote had lost the capability of producing anything original—he was merely telling thinly disguised tales out of school. Indeed, the publication of "La Côte Basque" alienated many of Capote's society friends. Its topicality also ensured that *Answered Prayers* would not have stood the test of time—or of the critics, for that matter—and probably that, more than any other reason, is why Capote never finished it.

Capote excelled in a number of literary forms—as a memoirist, journalist, travel writer, dramatist, short-story writer, and novelist. The body of his work is comparatively small, and it has neither the social range nor the concern with ideas of the work of certain of his contemporaries, but it is inimitable writing of great distinction. He is a brilliant and iridescent stylist, and his concern with craft belongs to that line of American writers that includes Henry James, Edith Wharton, Willa Cather, and Fitzgerald. Like Fitzgerald particularly, whose romantic themes and classical form he shares, Capote has the abiding interest of sensibility.

Robert Emmet Long

Other major works

SHORT FICTION: *A Tree of Night, and Other Stories*, 1949; *Breakfast at Tiffany's: A Short Novel and Three Stories*, 1958; *One Christmas*, 1983; *I Remember Grandpa: A Story*, 1986; *The Complete Collected Stories of Truman Capote*, 2004.

PLAYS: *The Grass Harp: A Play*, pr., pb. 1952 (adaptation of his novel); *House of Flowers*, pr. 1954 (with Harold Arlen).

SCREENPLAYS: *Beat the Devil*, 1954 (with John Huston); *The Innocents*, 1961.

NONFICTION: *Local Color*, 1950; *The Muses Are Heard*, 1956; *Observations*, 1959 (with Richard Avedon); *The Dogs Bark: Public People and Private Places*, 1973.

MISCELLANEOUS: *Selected Writings*, 1963; *Trilogy: An Experiment in Multimedia*, 1969 (with Eleanor Perry and Frank Perry); *Music for Chameleons*, 1980; *A Capote Reader*, 1987; *Too Brief a Treat: The Letters of Truman Capote*, 2004 (edited by Gerald Clarke).

Bibliography

Bloom, Harold, ed. *Truman Capote*. Philadelphia: Chelsea House, 2003. Collection of critical essays about Capote assembled for student use.

Brinnin, John Malcolm. *Truman Capote: Dear Heart, Old Buddy*. Rev. ed. New York: Delacorte Press, 1986. Chronicles Capote's life from before the success of *In Cold Blood* to his ruin from alcoholism and drugs. Most useful is the insight into the literary circles in which Capote moved. Includes an index.

Clarke, Gerald. *Capote: A Biography*. New York: Simon & Schuster, 1988. Arguably the definitive biographical work on Capote, this lengthy text covers all the ups and downs of his career. Contains copious references and an index.

Dunphy, Jack. *"Dear Genius": A Memoir of My Life with Truman Capote*. New York: McGraw-Hill, 1989. Written by Capote's friend and close companion of more than thirty years and a novelist in his own right. Details the disintegration of Capote's life as a result of drugs and alcohol. Includes an index.

Garson, Helen S. *Truman Capote: A Study of the Short Fiction*. New York: Twayne, 1992. Divided into three sections: a critical analysis of the short fiction, an exploration of Capote's biography and his "inventing a self," and a selection of essays by Capote's most important critics. Also includes a chronology and bibliography.

Grobel, Lawrence. *Conversations with Capote*. New York: New American Library, 1985. This biography uses interview material to flesh out its information. Grobel covers Capote's life from childhood to his fall from society's grace and his subsequent death. In chapter 4, titled "Writing," Capote discusses his writing career and the authors who he believed had the greatest influence on him. Includes a brief primary bibliography that lists films that Capote scripted and an index.

Hardwick, Elizabeth. "Tru Confessions." *The New York Review of Books* 45 (January 15, 1998): 4-5. Discusses George Plimpton's recording the remarks of those who came into contact with Capote's journey to literary fame; notes that Plimpton arranges these voices to produce the effect of the unrehearsed, companionable exchange at a cocktail party; argues that the method and result suit their subject, given that Capote, when not writing, was partying, forever receiving and producing banter.

Inge, M. Thomas, ed. *Truman Capote: Conversations*. Jackson: University Press of Mississippi, 1987. This book is a collection of interviews with Capote done by interviewers who range from Gloria Steinem to George Plimpton to Capote himself, in a section called "Self-Portrait." The index allows the reader to find specific references to individual short stories.

Plimpton, George. *Truman Capote: In Which Various Friends, Enemies, Acquaintances, and Detractors Recall His Turbulent Career.* New York: Doubleday, 1997. This oral biography based on interviews provides dramatic, primary information, but it also must be checked against the more reliable biography by Gerald Clarke. Includes biographies of contributors and a chronology.

Rudisill, Marie. *The Southern Haunting of Truman Capote.* Nashville, Tenn.: Cumberland House, 2000. Study of the impact of the South on Capote's worldview and writing.

Windham, Donald. *Lost Friendships: A Memoir of Truman Capote, Tennessee Williams, and Others.* New York: William Morrow, 1987. A friend of the major literary lights of the 1950's and 1960's, as well as a novelist himself, Windham dedicates the first half of *Lost Friendships* to his relationship with Capote and its subsequent decline. No reference material is included.

Willa Cather

Born: Back Creek Valley, near Gore, Virginia; December 7, 1873
Died: New York, New York; April 24, 1947

Principal long fiction • *Alexander's Bridge*, 1912; *O Pioneers!*, 1913; *The Song of the Lark*, 1915; *My Ántonia*, 1918; *One of Ours*, 1922; *A Lost Lady*, 1923; *The Professor's House*, 1925; *My Mortal Enemy*, 1926; *Death Comes for the Archbishop*, 1927; *Shadows on the Rock*, 1931; *Lucy Gayheart*, 1935; *Sapphira and the Slave Girl*, 1940.

Other literary forms • Willa Cather was a prolific writer, especially as a young woman. By the time her first novel was published when she was thirty-eight, she had written more than forty short stories, at least five hundred columns and reviews, numerous magazine articles and essays, and a volume of poetry. She collected three volumes of her short stores: *The Troll Garden* (1905), *Youth and the Bright Medusa* (1920), and *Obscure Destinies* (1932). Those volumes contain the few short stories she allowed to be anthologized, most frequently "Paul's Case," "The Sculptor's Funeral" (*The Troll Garden*), and "Neighbour Rosicky" (*Obscure Destinies*). Since her death, additional volumes have been published that contain other stories: *The Old Beauty and Others* (1948), *Willa Cather's Collected Short Fiction: 1892-1912* (1965), and *Uncle Valentine and Other Stories: Willa Cather's Collected Short Fiction, 1915-1929* (1973).

Many of Cather's early newspaper columns and reviews have been collected in *The Kingdom of Art: Willa Cather's First Principles and Critical Statements, 1893-1896* (1966) and in *The World and the Parish: Willa Cather's Articles and Reviews, 1893-1902* (1970, 2 volumes). Three volumes of essays, which include prefaces to the works of writers she admired, have been published. Cather herself prepared the earliest volume, *Not Under Forty* (1936), for publication. The other two, *Willa Cather on Writing* (1949) and *Willa Cather in Europe* (1956), have appeared since her death. Her single volume of poetry, *April Twilights*, appeared in 1903, but Cather later spoke apologetically of that effort, even jokingly telling a friend that she had tried to buy up and destroy all extant copies so that no one would see them. Cather's novel *A Lost Lady* has been adapted for the screen. A second screen version of that novel was so distasteful to her that in her will she prohibited any such attempts in the future. One story, "Paul's Case," was presented on public television. Cather's will also forbids the publication of her letters. Cather continued to write short stories after she began writing novels, but she wrote them less frequently.

Achievements • Cather actually had at least two careers in her lifetime. Prior to becoming a novelist, she was a highly successful journalist and writer of short fiction, as well as a high school English teacher. She began her career as a writer while still in college, where she published several short stories and wrote a regular newspaper column for the *Nebraska State Journal*. Later she also wrote for the Lincoln *Courier*. Her columns were on a variety of subjects, but many of them were related to the arts. She discussed books and authors and reviewed the many plays, operas, and concerts that came through Lincoln on tour. She gained an early reputation as an astute (and opinionated) critic. Even after she moved to Pittsburgh, the Lincoln papers continued to print her columns.

Over the years, Cather published stories in such national magazines as Century, *Collier's, Harper's, Ladies' Home Journal, Woman's Home Companion, The Saturday Evening Post,* and *McClure's,* the popular journal for which she served as an editor for several years.

Edward Steichen/Courtesy, George Bush Presidential Library and Museum

During her affiliation with *McClure's,* Cather traveled widely gathering materials for stories and making contacts with contributors to the magazine. She helped many a struggling young writer to find a market, and she worked regularly with already prominent writers. Cather had been a student of the classics since childhood, and she was unusually well read. She was also a devoted and knowledgeable student of art and music, a truly educated woman with highly developed, intelligent tastes. She was friendly with several celebrated musicians, including Metropolitan Opera soprano Olive Fremstad, after whom she patterned Thea Kronborg in *The Song of the Lark*; songwriter Ethelbert Nevin; and the famous child prodigies the Menuhins. She also knew Sarah Orne Jewett briefly.

Typically, Cather did not move in writers' circles but preferred to work by her own light and without the regular association of other writers of her time. She never sought the public eye, and as the years went on she chose to work in relative solitude, preferring the company of only close friends and family. Known primarily as a novelist, in the second half of the twentieth century she enjoyed a growing reputation as a writer of short fiction. She was awarded the Pulitzer Prize for *One of Ours,* and an ardent admirer, Sinclair Lewis, was heard to remark that she was more deserving than he of the Nobel Prize he won. Cather is particularly appealing to readers who like wholesome, value-centered art. She is held in increasingly high regard among critics and scholars of twentieth century literature and is recognized as one of the finest stylists in American letters.

Biography • Willa Cather was born in Back Creek Valley, Virginia, on December 7, 1873, the first of seven children. Her father's side of the family came to Virginia during colonial times. Her grandfather, William Cather, did not believe in slavery and favored the Union cause during the Civil War, creating a rift in a family of Confederate sympathizers. Her grandfather on her mother's side, William Boak, served three terms in the Virginia House of Delegates. He died before Cather was born, while serving in Washington in the Department of the Interior. Cather's grandmother, Rachel Boak, returned with her children to Back Creek Valley and eventually moved to Nebraska with her son-in-law Charles, Willa Cather's father, and his wife, Mary Virginia. Rachel Boak is an important figure in Cather's life and fiction. A courageous and enduring woman, she appears as Sapphira's daughter Rachel in Cather's last completed novel and as the grandmother in a late story, "Old Mrs. Harris." Rachel's maiden name was Seibert, a name that Cather adopted (spelling it "Sibert" after her uncle William Sibert Boak) as a young woman and then later dropped.

In 1883, when Cather—named Wilella, nicknamed Willie, and later renamed Willa by her own decree—was nine years old, her family sold their holdings at Back Creek and moved to Webster County, Nebraska. In that move from a lush Virginia countryside to a virtually untamed prairie, Cather experienced what Eudora Welty has called a "wrench to the spirit" from which she never recovered. It proved to be the most significant single event in her young life, bringing her as it did face to face with a new landscape and an immigrant people who were to make a lasting impression on her imagination. The move was a shock, but a shock that was the beginning of love both for the land and the people, and for the rest of her life, Cather was to draw from this experience in creating her fiction.

Cather always had a special affection for her father; he was a gentle, quiet-mannered man who, after eighteen months on his parents' prairie homestead, moved his family into Red Cloud, sixteen miles away. There he engaged in various business enterprises with no great success and reared his family. Unlike her husband, Mary Cather was energetic and driving, a hard disciplinarian, but generous and life-loving. A good many scenes and people from Cather's years on the farm and in Red Cloud appear in her fiction. Her third novel, *The Song of the Lark*, though its central character is a musician, recounts some of Cather's own struggles to develop her talent amid the strictures and jealousies of small-town life.

Cather's years at the university in Lincoln were extremely busy ones. Not a metropolis by any means, Lincoln was still many times larger than Red Cloud, and Cather gratefully discovered the joys of the theater and of meeting people with broad interests and capabilities. Her experience is much like that of Jim Burden as she describes it in *My Ántonia*. At first she planned to study science but switched to the humanities, she later confessed, when she saw an essay of hers printed in the newspaper. As she tells it, she was hooked for life. While at the university, she was active in literary circles, serving as an editor for the *Lasso* and the *Hesperian*, two student literary magazines. Several of her stories appeared in those magazines and in others. She spent the year after her graduation, in 1895, in and around Red Cloud, where she began writing for the weekly Lincoln *Courier* as well as for the *Nebraska State Journal* and published her first story in a magazine of national circulation, the *Overland Monthly*. Then in June, 1896, she left Nebraska to take a position with the *Home Monthly*, a small, rather weak family magazine in Pittsburgh.

Cather knew she had to leave Red Cloud to forward her career, and even the drudgery of the *Home Monthly* was an important opportunity. Later, she secured a position with the Pittsburgh *Daily Leader*, and then taught high school English and Latin for five years. While in Pittsburgh, Cather continued to write short fiction while pursuing an active social life. It was there that she met Isabelle McClung, who was to become her dearest friend. For a time, Cather lived with Isabelle and her parents, and in their home she enjoyed the quiet seclusion she needed for her writing. Cather's big break in her journalistic career came in 1903 when S. S. McClure, the dynamic publisher of *McClure's* magazine, became aware of her work and summoned her to his office. That interview began an association that led to an important position with

McClure's and eventually made it possible for Cather to leave the world of journalism and devote her full energies to the writing of fiction. The publication of *The Troll Garden* in 1905 announced that a major new talent had arrived on the literary scene. McClure knew ability when he saw it.

Cather's first novel, *Alexander's Bridge*, was written while she was still with *McClure's*, and it was first conceived as a serial for the magazine. It appeared as a novel in 1912, the year she left *McClure's* to try writing on her own. Not until *O Pioneers!* came to fruition the next year did Cather believe she had hit what she called "the home pasture" and discovered herself as a novelist. In this book, she turned to her memories of the Nebraska prairie and wrote powerfully of immigrant efforts to come to terms with the land. From then on, Cather was on her way. In 1920, she began a long and satisfying professional relationship with Alfred A. Knopf, who became her publisher and remained so for the rest of her life.

Cather lived most of her professional life in New York City with a friend and literary associate, Edith Lewis. Her many trips to Europe confirmed her great admiration for France and the French people, an appreciation that receives repeated expression in her novels. She also visited the American West a number of times and drew upon her experiences there for some of her work. She developed a special affection for the area around Jaffrey, New Hampshire, where she liked to go for uninterrupted work. She even chose to be buried there.

Cather's classmates in Lincoln remembered her as strong-willed, bright, gifted, and somewhat eccentric. Certainly, she knew her own mind, and she had strong ideas about the difference between the cheap and the valuable. She was fiercely attached to her family and friends, but once her parents were dead, she never returned to Red Cloud. Prior to her death on April 24, 1947, Cather was working on a novel that was set in medieval France. After her death, the unfinished manuscript, as she had requested, was destroyed.

Analysis • Willa Cather once said in an interview that the Nebraska landscape was "the happiness and the curse" of her life. That statement reveals the ambivalence in Cather that produced in her a lifelong tug-of-war between the East and the western prairie. That ambivalence is the central tension in her novels. As long as her parents were alive, she made repeated trips back home to see them, and each time she crossed the Missouri River, she said, "the very smell of the soil tore [her] to pieces." As a young woman in Red Cloud and Lincoln, however, she was chafed by narrow attitudes and limited opportunities. She knew that she had to leave the prairie in order to fulfill her compelling desire for broader experiences and for art. Like Thea Kronborg in *The Song of the Lark*, Cather knew she would never find fulfillment unless she left her home. At the same time, however, she also discovered that her very being was rooted in the landscape of her childhood. Thus, going back to it, even if only in memory, was essential and inescapable.

Cather once remarked that the most important impressions one receives come before the age of fifteen, and it seems clear that she was referring particularly to her own experiences on the Nebraska prairie. She did use some Virginia memories in her work, but only sporadically, in a few early short stories, before turning to them in her last published novel, *Sapphira and the Slave Girl*. In her "Nebraska works," it is not only Nebraska that Cather evokes, but it is, also, what Nebraska symbolizes and means, for she is not simply a regional writer. The range of her work is as broad as the range of her experience, and Nebraska represents the westward necessity of her life. Wherever in her work the pull of the landscape is felt, there is Nebraska—whether the setting is Colorado, Kansas, New Mexico, or even rural Pennsylvania or frontier Quebec.

As has been suggested, her life had an eastward necessity too. The raw hardships of prairie life could sometimes mutilate the body and drain the spirit, and a human being often needed something else. A man of genuine sensitivity and culture, such as Ántonia Shimerda's father, for example, could not survive in a hard land. Cather's awareness of this fact made a great impression on her. One of the first stories she heard after arriving in Nebraska was the account of Francis Sadilek's suicide, an event that she reconstructed in *My Ántonia.* Not only could the beloved land be killingly cruel, but it also failed to provide the environment of training, discipline, and appreciation so necessary for the growth and development of an artist. Although the land provided the materials for memory to work with and the germinating soil for the seed of talent, it could not produce the final fruit.

Then, too, part of the Nebraska Cather experienced was small-town life and the limited opportunities it offered the artistically ambitious. Throughout her life, she felt misunderstood by some of the townspeople who had known her as a youngster. Letters to her lifelong friend in Red Cloud, Carrie Miner Sherwood (from whom she drew Frances Harling in *My Ántonia*), indicate how sharply Cather felt their disapproval of her. She rebelled against their codes and refused to remain among them but was stung by their criticism.

East and West • Thea Kronborg is not the only Cather character to be torn, like her creator, between East and West, civilization and the land. In *My Ántonia,* the young Jim Burden expresses Cather's own feelings of awe and fear upon his arrival in Nebraska. Later, when he goes to school in Lincoln and eventually leaves for a career in the East, the Nebraska landscape of his past stays with him, just as it stayed with Cather, even after long absences. Claude Wheeler, in *One of Ours,* also has a good deal of his maker in him. Much as he loves the beauty of the Nebraska landscape, he cannot find himself until he leaves it. Like Cather, the ultimate in civilization for him is France.

The opposing aspects of Cather's desire, the land and civilization—or, more specifically, art—were of equal value to her. She could never entirely give up one for the other or value one above the other. Thus, the land was "the happiness and the curse" of her life. She might well have said the same thing about her art. Ironically, however, at least according to her friend Elizabeth Sergeant, it was not until Cather made her feelings for the land a part of her art that she truly realized her potential as an artist. Though East and West, civilization (art) and the land—the very foundations of Cather's work—are sometimes at opposite poles in terms of the choices one must make, they are both valuable to her. The greatest threat to each is not the other; the greatest threat to each is an exploitative materialism that has no appreciation for the innate value of the land or of art.

In Cather's work, the same impulse that exploits the land is also destructive to art and the best qualities of civilization. The author's most despicable characters are those such as Ivy Peters in *A Lost Lady* and Bayliss Wheeler in *One of Ours,* who have no feeling for the land or for the past that it harbors. All that interests them is making money, as much as possible as quickly as possible. Cather had great admiration for the early railroad pioneers, wealthy men of immense courage, vision, and taste, as she pictures them in *A Lost Lady.* In too many people, however, the lust for wealth and the acquisition of it are destructive to character. They subvert what are for Cather some of life's most positive values, a relationship with the earth and an aesthetic sensibility.

Of Cather's twelve novels, only three, *Alexander's Bridge*, *My Mortal Enemy*, and *Sapphira and the Slave Girl*, do not deal centrally with the tension between East and West, with civilization and the land as values threatened by the spirit of acquisitiveness; yet even those touch the latter point. For example, Myra Henshawe's harshness of character comes partly as a result of her need to live in a style only money can provide; the desire to possess that style leads to the buying and selling of human beings, a central issue in *Sapphira and the Slave Girl*.

O Pioneers! • Cather's second novel, *O Pioneers!*, her first to use Nebraska materials, presents the conflict between the land and civilization and the threat of destructive materialism as its major concerns. The novel's principal character, Alexandra Bergson, is something of an earth mother, a being so closely linked with the soil and growing things that her very oneness with the earth seems to convert the harsh wild land into rich acreage that willingly yields its treasures. From the first, she believes in the land and loves it, even when her brothers and neighbors grow to despise and curse it. Two of Alexandra's brothers have such a fear of financial failure that they cannot see the land's potential.

Cather, however, does not simply present Alexandra's struggle and eventual triumph. There is another value, opposed to the land but equally important, with which Alexandra must contend. Her youngest brother, Emil, is sensitive in a way that does not lend itself to life on the Continental Divide, and she wants him to have opportunities that are available only in centers of civilization. His finely tuned spirit, though, leads him to disaster in a prairie environment where passions can run high, untempered by civilizing influences. Emil falls in love with Marie Shabata, a free, wild creature, and both of them are killed by her enraged husband. The book's final vision, however, returns to an affirmation of the enduring qualities of the land and the value of human union with it.

The Song of the Lark • The conflict between the landscape of home and art is played out dramatically in the central character of *The Song of the Lark*. Thea Kronborg is in many ways the young Willa Cather, fighting the narrowness of small-town life on the prairie, needing to leave Moonstone to develop her talent, but needing also to integrate the landscape of home with her artistic desire. Thea has to leave home, but she also has to have her sense of home with her in order to reach her potential as an opera singer. Much that she has set aside in her quest for art she must pick up again and use in new ways. In fact, Cather makes it clear that without the integration of home, Thea might never have become an artist. Moonstone, however, also has its materialists who obviously stand in opposition to the enduring, if sometimes conflicting, values of earth and art. The only villain of the piece is the wife of Thea's best friend and supporter, Doctor Archie. She is a mean, pinched woman, shriveled with stinginess.

After Thea leaves Moonstone and goes to Chicago to study music, the killing pace and the battle against mediocrity wear her to the breaking point. In an effort at self-renewal, she accepts an invitation to recuperate on a ranch near the Canyon de Chelly in Arizona. There, she spends many hours lying in the sun on the red rock, following the paths of ancient potters, examining the broken pieces of their pottery that still lie in the streambeds. It is there that Thea has the revelation that gives birth to her artist self. These ancient potters made their pottery into art by decorating it. The clay jars would not hold water any better for the artistic energy expended upon them, but their makers expended that energy nevertheless. This revelation comes to Thea out of the landscape itself, and it gives her the knowledge she needs in order to continue her studies: Artistic desire is universal, ageless, and she is a part of it.

Lucy Gayheart • The eponymous protagonist of *Lucy Gayheart* is not so hard and indomitable a character as Thea, nor is she destined to become a performing artist in her own right. Nevertheless, Lucy is much like Thea (and the young Willa Cather) in her need to leave the prairie landscape and pursue art in the only place where such pursuits are possible, the city. Lucy is, however, in many ways a child of the earth—she loves skating on the frozen river, and she begs for the preservation of an orchard that her sister Pauline, a plodding materialist, wants to cut down because it is no longer productive. Given her nature, it is no surprise that Lucy falls in love with the singer for whom she plays accompaniments at practice. He is the embodiment of the art for which her soul yearns. After his accidental drowning, Lucy returns home and she herself dies in a skating accident, her death a final union with the earth. There is also a "Doctor Archie's wife" in *Lucy Gayheart.* Ironically, she marries the one man in Haverford that Lucy might have married happily, the one man with the capacity to appreciate what a rare and lovely phenomenon Lucy was.

My Ántonia • Something of an earth mother like Alexandra Bergson, yet more malleable and human, Ántonia Shimerda of *My Ántonia* is for many readers Cather's most appealing character. She becomes a total embodiment of the strength and generosity associated with those who are one with the land and the forces of nature. Unlike Alexandra, her capacity for life finds expression not only in the trees and plants she tends but also in her many children, who seem to have sprung almost miraculously from the earth. It is in Jim Burden, who tells the story, and to some extent, in Ántonia's husband, Anton Cuzak, that the conflict between East and West occurs. Jim, like Cather, comes to Nebraska from Virginia as a youngster, and though he has to seek his professional life in eastern cities, he never gets Nebraska out of his soul. Even as a student at the University of Nebraska in Lincoln, he gazes out his window and imagines there the landscape and figures of his childhood. Ántonia represents for Jim, even after twenty years of city life, all the positive values of the earth for which no amount of civilization can compensate. At the end of the book, he determines to revitalize his past association with the land and yet still tramp a few lighted streets with Cuzak, a city man at heart.

The conflict between the harshness of life on the prairie and the cultural advantages of civilization is also presented in Ántonia's father, who had been a gifted musician in Europe, but who now, poverty-stricken and overworked, no longer plays the violin. Ántonia's deep appreciation for Cuzak's quality and for his gentle city ways and her pride in Jim's "city" accomplishments bridge the gap between prairie and civilization.

The materialists are also evident in *My Ántonia.* In fact, one of Cather's most memorable villains is the lecherous and greedy Wick Cutter, Black Hawk's nefarious moneylender. His last act is to devise a scheme whereby he can kill himself and his equally greedy wife and at the same time guarantee that her relatives will not get a cent of his money.

One of Ours • Claude Wheeler, the main character of *One of Ours*, is torn, like so many of Cather's young people, by the need to go and the need to stay. Claude is filled with yearnings he does not completely understand. All he knows is that he is burning to fulfill some inner desire, and everything he does seems to go wrong. Much as he loves the rivers and groves of his own landscape, he feels like a misfit there. His father's hearty, nonchalant materialism is only slightly less distressing to him than the hard, grasping greed of his older brother Bayliss, the bloodless, pious parsimony of his wife, Enid, and the cheerful selfishness of his younger brother Ralph. The world begins opening to him during the short period when he is allowed to attend the university at Lincoln, but Claude completely finds himself only when he enlists in the army and begins fighting in France. There, he meets Lieutenant David Gerhardt, a musician, and encounters a gracious cultural climate to which he responds with all his heart.

There is, however, a troubling aspect to this novel. Claude's real fulfillment comes in the midst of battle, surrounded by death and destruction. Only then does he feel at one with himself and his surroundings; only then is the old anguish gone, the tension released. In the end, he is killed, and his mother feels some sense of gratitude that at least he does not have to face the disillusionment of returning to a country that has given itself over to material pursuits. With the exception of *Alexander's Bridge*, this is probably Cather's least successful novel, perhaps partly because she was emotionally very close to her central character. Cather stated publicly that she modeled Claude after a young cousin of hers who died in World War I, but in a letter she indicated that Claude was, in fact, an embodiment of Cather herself. The novel is a poignant portrayal of the central tensions in her work between the land and civilization, and it also describes the ever-present threat of spiritually damaging materialism.

A Lost Lady • In *A Lost Lady*, Cather again shows a character's need for civilization's amenities, in spite of the appeal of the Western landscape. Here too, though the reader may fault Cather's main character for her sometimes expedient morality, Cather has publicly expressed her affection for the woman upon whom she based the character of Marian Forrester. Further, the ruthless, materialistic mind-set that nearly always characterizes "the enemy" in Cather's work is graphically portrayed in the coarse figure of Ivy Peters. As a boy, Ivy cruelly blinded a bird and then set it free, and as a man he drained what was once the Forresters' lovely marshlands in order to make them yield a profit. Unscrupulous and shrewd, he manages to compromise the beautiful Marian Forrester with as little conscience as he showed toward the helpless bird.

Until her husband's decline, Mrs. Forrester managed to have the best of both worlds, East and West, spending her summers in the beautiful countryside outside Sweet Water, on the Burlington line, and her winters in the lively social atmosphere of Denver and Colorado Springs. Captain Forrester, much her elder, had made his fortune pioneering Western railroad development. When the novel opens, the Captain's failing health has already begun to limit Mrs. Forrester's social and cultural opportunities, though she still enjoys visits to the city and entertains important guests at Sweet Water. It becomes apparent, however, much to the dismay of Marian Forrester's young admirer, Niel Herbert, that Marian's passion for life and high living has led her into an affair with the opportunistic, if handsome, Frank Ellinger even before the death of the captain. This affair foreshadows her later desperate sellout to Ivy Peters. It is significant, however, that Cather never judges Marian, though the prudish Niel does. It is not the life-loving Marian Forrester that Cather condemns but the grasping Ivy Peters and the unprincipled Frank Ellinger—and perhaps even the unforgiving Niel Herbert. The novel's hero is Captain Forrester, who willingly relinquishes his fortune to preserve his honor.

The Professor's House • There are two plot lines in *The Professor's House*, one of which centers around the growing life weariness of Professor Godfrey St. Peter, and the other around the experiences of his student, Tom Outland, on a faraway desert mesa. Both sets of experiences, however, illuminate the tension between civilization and the open landscape and focus upon the destructive nature of materialistic desire. St. Peter, a highly civilized man with refined tastes and a keen appreciation for true art, loses heart at his daughters' greed and selfishness and his wife's increasing interest in what he regards as ostentatious display. Near the end of the book, he focuses his imagination on the Kansas prairie, on his solitary, primitive boyhood self. He wants to recapture the self he was before he married and before his family and his colleagues began conjugating the verb "to buy" with every breath.

Tom Outland, the one remarkable student of St. Peter's teaching career, becomes equally disillusioned with society and its greed. Cather spares him from living out his life in such a society, however, by mercifully allowing him to die in the war in France, as she had allowed Claude Wheeler to die. Ironically, it is Tom's invention of a new engine, bequeathed in a romantic impulse to one of St. Peter's daughters, that makes her and her husband rich. While herding cattle on the great Western desert, Tom Outland and his partner Roddy Blake explore the great Blue Mesa across the river from their summer grazing range. On it, they find the remnants of ancient cliff dwellers, including many beautifully decorated jars. These jars provide for Tom, as they had for Thea Kronborg, a priceless link with the art and people and landscape of the past. In these jars, the tension between land and art is erased. While Tom is away on a fruitless trip to Washington, where he had hoped to interest someone in his find, Roddy Blake misguidedly sells the relics to a European art dealer. Recovering from two heartbreaking disappointments, the loss of the relics and the loss of Roddy, Tom makes his spiritual recovery through union with the mesa itself. He becomes one with the rock, the trees, the very desert air.

Death Comes for the Archbishop • Even though *Death Comes for the Archbishop* is not Cather's final novel, it is in a very real sense a culmination of her efforts at reconciling the central urges toward land and toward art, or civilization, that are the hallmark of her life and her work. Selfishness and greed are a threat in this book too, but their influence is muted by Cather's concentration on Father Jean Latour as the shaping force of her narrative. He is Cather's ideal human being, by the end of the book a perfect blend of the virtues of the untamed landscape and the finest aspects of civilization.

As a young priest, Latour is sent from a highly cultivated environment in his beloved France to revitalize Roman Catholicism in the rugged New Mexico Territory of the New World. Learned in the arts, genteel in manner, dedicated to his calling, this man of fine-textured intelligence is forced to work out his fate in a desolate, godforsaken land among, for the most part, simple people who have never known or have largely forgotten the sacraments of the civilized Church. His dearest friend, Father Joseph Vaillant, works with him—a wiry, lively man, Latour's complement in every way. Latour must bring a few greedy, unruly local priests into line, but his greatest struggle is internal as he works to convert himself, a product of European civilization, into the person needed to serve the Church in this vast desert land. In the end, his remarkable nature is imprinted indelibly on the barren landscape, and the landscape is imprinted indelibly on his nature. Instead of returning to France in his official retirement, he elects to remain in the New World. His total reconciliation with the land is symbolized in the fulfillment of his dream to build a European-style cathedral out of the golden rock of New Mexico. In that building, the art of civilization merges gracefully with the very soil of the Western landscape, just as Jean Latour's spirit had done.

Shadows on the Rock • *Shadows on the Rock*, a lesser book, takes for its landscape the rock of Quebec, but the tension is still between the old ways of civilized France and the new ways of the Canadians of the future, children of the uncharted, untamed land. It, too, focuses on the efforts of the Roman Catholic Church to bring spiritual civilization to the New World, but its central character is not a churchman. Rather, it is young Cécile Auclair who values the old ways, the civilities taught her by her mother and still priceless to her father, but who also responds to the wave of the future and marries a Canadian backwoodsman whose deepest ties are to the uncharted landscape.

Cather's work stands as something of an emotional autobiography, tracing the course of her deepest feelings about what is most valuable in human experience. For Cather, what endured best, and what helped one endure, were the values contained in the land, and in humanity's civilizing impulses, particularly the impulse to art. What is best in humanity responds to these things, and these things have the capacity to ennoble in return. Sometimes they seem mutually exclusive, the open landscape and civilization, and some characters never reconcile the apparent polarity. Cather says, however, that ultimately one can have both East and West. For her, the reconciliation seems to have occurred mainly in her art, where she was able to love and write about the land, if not live on it. A conflict such as this can be resolved, for it involves a tension between two things of potential value. Thus, in her life and her art it was not this conflict that caused Cather to despair; rather, it was the willingness of humanity in general to allow the greedy and unscrupulous to destroy both the land and civilization. At the same time, it was the bright promise of youth, in whom desire for the land and for art could be reborn with each new generation, that caused her to rejoice.

Marilyn Arnold

Other major works

SHORT FICTION: *The Troll Garden*, 1905; "Paul's Case," 1905; *Youth and the Bright Medusa*, 1920; *Obscure Destinies*, 1932; *The Old Beauty and Others*, 1948; *Willa Cather's Collected Short Fiction: 1892-1912*, 1965; *Uncle Valentine, and Other Stories: Willa Cather's Collected Short Fiction, 1915-1929*, 1973.

POETRY: *April Twilights*, 1903.

NONFICTION: *Not Under Forty*, 1936; *Willa Cather on Writing*, 1949; *Willa Cather in Europe*, 1956; *The Kingdom of Art: Willa Cather's First Principles and Critical Statements, 1893-1896*, 1966; *The World and the Parish: Willa Cather's Articles and Reviews, 1893-1902*, 1970 (2 volumes).

MISCELLANEOUS: *Writings from Willa Cather's Campus Years*, 1950.

Bibliography

Fryer, Judith. *Felicitous Space: The Imaginative Structures of Edith Wharton and Willa Cather.* Chapel Hill: University of North Carolina Press, 1986. Although there are many full-length studies on Cather's writing, this volume is particularly noteworthy for its examination of Cather using current feminist thinking. Fryer explores Cather's fiction in terms of the "interconnectedness between space and the female imagination" and cites her as a transformer of social and cultural structures. A thorough and interesting study, recommended for its contribution to women's studies in literature. Includes extensive notes.

Gerber, Philip L. *Willa Cather.* Rev. ed. New York: Twayne, 1995. In this revised edition, Gerber focuses more on Cather's short fiction than in the first edition, as well as on the resurgence of criticism of her work. Discusses the major themes of the experience of the artist and life in rural Nebraska in major Cather short stories.

Goldberg, Jonathan. *Willa Cather and Others.* Durham, N.C.: Duke University Press, 2001. A psychosexual study of Cather's novels.

Lathrop, JoAnna, ed. *Willa Cather: A Checklist of Her Published Writing.* Lincoln: University of Nebraska Press, 1975. An annotated list of all of Cather's works including the lesser known posthumously published essays on writing as well as her travel essays, reviews, and student works.

Lindermann, Marilee. *The Cambridge Companion to Willa Cather.* New York: Cambridge University Press, 2005. Thirteen essays examining Cather's most noted novels and short stories.

O'Connor, Margaret Anne, ed. *Willa Cather: The Contemporary Reviews.* New York: Cambridge University Press, 2001. A collection of reprinted reviews of Cather's works. Includes an introduction. Very useful for assessing contemporary critical opinions of Cather during her time.

Romines, Ann, ed. *Willa Cather's Southern Connections: New Essays on Cather and the South.* Charlottesville: University Press of Virginia, 2000. A collection of essays concentrating on Cather's *Saphira and the Slave Girl.*

Rosowski, Susan J. *The Voyage Perilous: Willa Cather's Romanticism.* Lincoln: University of Nebraska Press, 1986. This thematic study interprets Cather's writing within the literary tradition of Romanticism. Although the main focus is on her novels (with a chapter devoted to each), the volume also investigates the stories in *The Troll Garden* and includes a chapter on *Obscure Destinies.* See also *Cather Studies,* a forum for scholarship and criticism, which is edited by Rosowski and published biennially by the University of Nebraska Press.

Shanley, J. Lyndon. "Willa Cather's Fierce Necessity." *The Sewanee Review* 102 (Fall, 1994): 620-630. Notes that Cather's stories are about ordinary people and that one of her most important themes is youthful dreams; discusses Cather's clear prose and the apparent simplicity of her stories.

Shaw, Patrick W. *Willa Cather and the Art of Conflict: Re-visioning Her Creative Imagination.* Troy, N.Y.: Whitston, 1992. Separate chapters on all of Cather's major novels. Reexamines Cather's fiction in terms of her conflicts over her lesbian sexuality. The introduction provides a helpful overview of Cather criticism on the topic.

Skaggs, Merrill Maguire, ed. *Willa Cather's New York: New Essays on Cather in the City.* Madison, N.J.: Fairleigh Dickinson University Press, 2001. A collection of twenty essays focusing on Cather's urban fiction and her work for *McClure's.*

Stout, Janis P. *Willa Cather: The Writer and Her World.* Charlottesville: University Press of Virginia, 2000. A deconstructionist analysis of Cather's work, viewed in the context of crumbling modernism and the emerging "new woman."

____________, ed. *Willa Cather and Material Culture: Real-World Writing, Writing the Real World.* Tuscaloosa: University of Alabama Press, 2005. Collection of original essays on a variety of aspects of Cather's works.

Woodress, James. *Willa Cather: A Literary Life.* Lincoln: University of Nebraska Press, 1990. This definitive biography extends previous studies of Cather, including Woodress's own earlier work (*Willa Cather: Her Life and Art,* 1970), with fuller accounts of Cather's life and includes new and expanded critical responses to her work, taking feminist criticism into account. In preparing the volume, Woodress was able to use the papers of Cather scholar Bernice Slote. Scholars and students will appreciate the extensively documented sources. Includes photographs of Cather, as well as of people and places important to her.

Raymond Chandler

Born: Chicago, Illinois; July 23, 1888
Died: La Jolla, California; March 26, 1959

Principal long fiction • *The Big Sleep*, 1939; *Farewell, My Lovely*, 1940; *The High Window*, 1942; *The Lady in the Lake*, 1943; *The Little Sister*, 1949; *The Long Goodbye*, 1953; *Playback*, 1958; *The Raymond Chandler Omnibus: Four Famous Classics*, 1967; *The Second Chandler Omnibus*, 1973; *Poodle Springs*, 1989 (incomplete manuscript finished by Robert B. Parker); *Later Novels and Other Writings*, 1995.

Other literary forms • Raymond Chandler began his literary career with a false start in England in his early twenties, publishing an assortment of journalistic sketches, essays, poems, and a single story, most of which have been collected in *Chandler Before Marlowe* (1973). His real career as a writer began more than twenty years later, when he began to publish short stories in crime magazines. Chandler published twenty-three stories during his lifetime, most of which appeared in pulp magazines such as *Black Mask* or *Dime Detective Magazine*. Although the stories rarely approach the literary merit of his novels, they are representative of a popular type of American writing. They also show a versatility within the mystery formula that would later be developed by Chandler in his novels.

Chandler forbade the reissue during his lifetime of eight of his stories, but three of these were published, apparently without the author's consent. Chandler insisted that these stories be withheld because of a curious professional scruple. The materials had been incorporated in subsequent novels—in Chandler's word, "cannibalized"—and he believed that their republication would be unfair to readers of the novels. Some of the best of Chandler's stories are in this group and have, since his death, been published in the collection *Killer in the Rain* (1964).

Like William Faulkner and F. Scott Fitzgerald, Chandler was invited to Hollywood to write film scripts. He collaborated on several important screenplays and with Billy Wilder was nominated for an Academy Award for their adaptation of James M. Cain's novel *Double Indemnity* (1936). His original screenplay *The Blue Dahlia* also received a nomination, despite the fact that Chandler remained dissatisfied with the film. In 1948 he wrote, under contract with Universal, an original screenplay, *Playback*, which was not filmed but was rewritten, with new characters, as a novel during Chandler's final years.

Achievements • More than any of his contemporaries, Chandler attempted to use the devices of mystery fiction for serious literary purposes. The peculiarly American school of detective fiction came of age during the years of the 1930's Depression. The most influential outlet for this fiction was *Black Mask*, a pulp magazine founded by H. L. Mencken and George Jean Nathan and later edited by Captain Joseph T. Shaw.

Because the American detective had his origins in *Black Mask* and similar pulp magazines, he is often called the "hard-boiled detective." The character of the hard-boiled detective differs sharply from that of the traditional British sleuth. Chandler's heroes are not charming eccentrics in the tradition of Dorothy L. Sayers's Lord Peter

Wimsey, nor are they masters of unbelievable powers of deduction, such as Arthur Conan Doyle's Sherlock Holmes. When Chandler's Philip Marlowe tells his client (in *The Big Sleep*) that he is not Holmes or Philo Vance and humorously introduces himself as Philo Vance in *The Lady in the Lake*, Chandler is calling attention to the distance he intends to create between his character and the traditional heroes of detective literature. The American detective as created by Chandler, Dashiell Hammett, and a host of lesser contemporaries, is a loner, a man of ordinary intellect but of unusual perseverance and willingness to confront whatever adversary he encounters, whether that adversary be the criminal or the legal establishment. Kenneth Millar, who under the pen name Ross Macdonald would become the most worthy of Chandler's successors, said that from the *Black Mask* revolution came "a new kind of detective hero, the classless, restless men of American democracy, who spoke the language of the street."

Chandler found the formulaic plots of traditional detective fiction limiting and confining. He was less interested in challenging the deductive skills of the reader than in examining the milieu and sociocultural effects of criminal behavior. Chandler once told his publisher that he disliked those popular mystery titles that emphasized sheer deduction because such titles "put too much emphasis on the mystery itself, and I have not the ingenuity to devise the sort of intricate and recondite puzzles the purest aficionados go for." His mention of a lack of ingenuity is characteristic of the diffidence with which Chandler sometimes spoke of his own work; what is certain, both from his letters and from his essay "The Simple Art of Murder," is that such plots did not interest Chandler.

Although he should be credited, along with Hammett and other *Black Mask* writers, with the development of a peculiarly American form for detective fiction, Chandler himself always consciously sought to transcend the limitations of the genre. He regarded himself as a serious novelist who wrote detective fiction. His intent was to study the modern landscape of evil, and his work bears striking affinities with T. S. Eliot's *The Waste Land* (1922) and with Ernest Hemingway's novels. His evocation of a world dominated by malicious, sadistic, self-centered, ruthless, and psychopathic types led W. H. Hudson, in his essay "The Guilty Vicarage," to conclude that Chandler's interest was not in detective fiction at all but in "serious studies of the criminal milieu, the Great Wrong Place"; Auden argued that Chandler's "powerful but extremely depressing books should be read and judged, not as escape literature, but as works of art."

Auden states, admirably, only half the case. Chandler's books should be judged as works of art, but not merely as studies of the world of crime, or of the world gone bad. In his novels there is a constant quest, a search for heroic possibility in the ruined moral landscape of modern California. Chandler's fiction continually considers whether authentic heroism is possible in the modern world, and Marlowe's attempt to take heroic action places him at odds with the world he inhabits. By the time he was ready to write *The Long Goodbye*, Chandler had indeed transformed the detective story: In that book the elements of detection and mystery are clearly subordinate to psychological and cultural realism.

The achievement of Chandler thus discloses a paradox. Although he was instrumental in the discovery of an American style for detective fiction and has been widely and rightly respected for that accomplishment, his real achievement was to merge detective fiction with serious literature.

Library of Congress

Biography • Although his early ambition was to be a writer, Raymond Thornton Chandler did not begin the literary career that would win him fame until he was forty-five years old. This is only one of several incongruities in the life of one of America's original literary talents.

Chandler was born in Chicago in 1888, the only child of a railroad employee and an Irishwoman. The marriage was marred by his father's alcoholism and ended in divorce when the boy was seven years old. Chandler and his mother moved to London and became dependent on his maternal uncle, a successful solicitor. Chandler went to Dulwich College, where he received the solid classical education characteristic of English public schools. He was at the head of his classes in most of his subjects. After his graduation from Dulwich, Chandler claimed dual citizenship so that he could take the English civil service examinations, but he was unable to adapt to the bureaucratic environment and resigned his civil service appointment. He supported himself briefly by writing for magazines and newspapers and by publishing some undistinguished poems and a single story. He left England for America in 1912.

Upon his return to America, Chandler made his way to Southern California where he began a relationship that was to dominate his literary life. Chandler despised the superficiality and pretentiousness of the California culture, as well as its lack of tradition or continuity, but he intuited that this would be the culture of the future. One aim of his writing would be to record and comment on that culture. His immediate concern upon his return was to find work, and he was involved in a variety of minor jobs until he completed a three-year bookkeeping course in six weeks. Thereafter, he was involved in various business enterprises until 1917, when he joined the Canadian Army. He saw action in France; Chandler was the sole survivor of a raid on his outfit and was decorated for valor. When he returned to California, he briefly tried banking and eventually established himself as an extremely successful executive of the Dabney Oil Syndicate. He became vice president of the concern and was at one time director of eight subsidiary firms and president of three.

Shortly after he joined the Dabney firm, Chandler married Cissy Pascal, who filed for divorce in order to marry him. An accomplished pianist and a beauty, she was also eighteen years older than Chandler, a fact she deliberately concealed from him: He was thirty-five; she was fifty-three. Their marriage was a lasting but troublesome one.

Perhaps discoveries about his marriage, as well as problems and pressures in his business, led to the first appearance of Chandler's lifelong struggle with alcoholism.

In fact, several of Chandler's early stories, such as "Pearls Are a Nuisance," feature a hero who must contend with a drinking problem. In 1932, Dabney fired Chandler because of chronically poor job performance traced directly to excessive drinking.

Chandler took the shock of his firing as an indication that he had to take control of his life, and he turned again to the literary aspirations of his youth. Chandler was then reading and being influenced by Hemingway rather than by Henry James, whom he had read avidly in England, and he soon found the outlet his creative talent needed in the emerging American detective story. His first story appeared in *Black Mask* in 1933; he would be a successful novelist within the decade.

Fame and success came to Chandler during the 1940's. His sales were solid, studios sought the film rights to his novels, his books were being translated into several languages, and he was lured to Hollywood to write screenplays. There he enjoyed material success and stimulating camaraderie with other writers. Soon the pressures of studio deadlines, artistic compromise, and the pretentiousness around him—much of the satire of *The Little Sister* is directed at the phoniness of Hollywood—combined with personal ill health sent Chandler back to the bottle. His career in Hollywood ended in frustration, petty squabbles, and bitterness.

With material success and public acclaim, Chandler spent the final decade of his life alternating between despair and the hope for new beginnings. Always a lonely man, he became depressive after his wife died in 1954. He attempted suicide but after his recovery divided his time between life in London and La Jolla, between bouts with the bottle and the admiration of an appreciative public. He fell in love with his agent, Helga Greene, but the two were unable to marry. Chandler's death in 1959 ended the career of a shy, quiet man who was quite unlike his fictional hero Marlowe except for the essential loneliness and decency Chandler could not avoid projecting onto his most important creation.

Analysis • Many people who have never read a single word of Raymond Chandler's recognize the name of his fictional hero Philip Marlowe. This recognition results in part from the wide exposure and frequent dilution Chandler's work has received in media other than print. Several of his novels, and especially *Farewell, My Lovely* and *The Big Sleep*, have been filmed repeatedly; both were filmed again during the 1970's. Marlowe has been interpreted on film by such diverse actors as Humphrey Bogart, Dick Powell, Robert Montgomery, George Montgomery, Robert Mitchum, James Garner, and Elliot Gould. A series for radio and one for television were based somewhat loosely on Chandler's character.

This recognition amounts to more than exposure in multiple media; it is an indication of the legendary or even mythic proportions of Chandler's creation. Marlowe has become a central figure in the myth of the detective; the only comparable characters would be Arthur Conan Doyle's Sherlock Holmes and Agatha Christie's Hercule Poirot, even though they are quite different from Marlowe. Dashiell Hammett's Sam Spade, although well known, is developed in only one book and lacks the psychological depth of Marlowe. Marlowe has taken his place among characters of American myth, with Natty Bumppo, Captain Ahab, Huckleberry Finn, and Thomas Sutpen. There is something uniquely American about the self-reliance of this character, something that goes beyond Chandler's brilliant descriptions of the burned-out landscape of modern California.

Marlowe is in fact Chandler's great achievement, but that accomplishment in itself imposed a limitation of a sort. Because Marlowe had the dual role of central character and observer in all seven of Chandler's novels, the author was not consistently pressed to explore other characters except as they interacted with his hero. In his final novel, *Playback*, Chandler leads Marlowe through an ill-conceived plot at the expense of two neglected characters who had shown real literary promise. In this final project, the author had fallen victim to the temptation to rely on his primary character, and Marlowe's character suffers as a result.

Nevertheless, Marlowe remains an impressive artistic creation because of his remarkable combination of the detective with more traditional American heroic types, a combination discussed in Chandler's famous essay "The Simple Art of Murder." This essay attempts to define Chandler's intentions as a writer of detective fiction and has since become one of the classic texts concerning the scope and intention of mystery writing. Although a major point of "The Simple Art of Murder" is Chandler's rejection of the stylized mystery and his often-quoted tribute to Hammett—his claim that Hammett took murder "out of the Venetian vase and dropped it in the alley"—the essay makes its most important point in an argument for detective fiction as a heroic form in which modern readers can still believe. Claiming that all art must contain the quality of redemption, Chandler insists, perhaps too stridently, that the detective is "the hero; he is everything." In the character of Marlowe, Chandler tests the possibility of heroism in the modern cultural and spiritual wasteland of Southern California, to see whether traditional heroic values can survive the test of a realistic portrait of modern society.

In precisely this way, Chandler had to face a limitation that did not affect his American predecessors: the disappearance of the frontier. American heroes acted out the myth of Emersonian self-reliance against the background of a vast, unspoiled frontier. In the twentieth century, William Faulkner, attempting to study the ambivalent role of the hero, moved his fiery character Thomas Sutpen to the frontier in *Absalom, Absalom!* (1966).

Most twentieth century American novelists despaired of the possibility of reviving the heroic tradition and concentrated instead on victims, common people, and even criminals. Ernest Hemingway stood alone among the serious novelists looking for an affirmation by means of the code hero, and Chandler's intellectual debt to Hemingway is profound. He acknowledged that debt in two ways. In "The Simple Art of Murder," he points out that what is excellent in Hammett's (and by inference his own) work is implicit in Hemingway's fiction. In a more celebrated reference, a policeman in *Farewell, My Lovely* is called Hemingway by Marlowe. When Galbraith, the officer, asks who this Hemingway is, Marlowe explains, "A guy that keeps saying the same thing over and over until you begin to believe it must be good." This is a joke about the terse Hemingway style, and the character whom Marlowe calls Hemingway is indeed terse. The jest is not, however, a slap at Hemingway.

Galbraith is one of the few men with integrity whom Marlowe encounters in *Farewell, My Lovely*. He is a policeman who wants to be honest but who has to work in a corrupt system. By contrast, in the story from which this portion of *Farewell, My Lovely* was "cannibalized," "The Man Who Liked Dogs," Galbraith was as corrupt as any of the criminals Carmady (the detective) encountered. He was merely a sadistic cop who participated in cover-ups and even murder. The verbal association of this character with Hemingway corresponds nicely with Chandler's changing the personality of the officer so that he would represent the quality Chandler most admired in Hemingway's heroes, resignation to defeat while maintaining some measure of integrity.

The world Marlowe inhabits is, like that of Hemingway's characters, not conducive to heroism. Chandler coined a memorable phrase, "the mean streets," to describe the environment in which his hero would have to function. Marlowe was created to indicate that it is possible to maintain integrity in these surroundings, even if one cannot be uninfluenced by them. As Chandler put it, "down these mean streets a man must go who is not himself mean, who is neither tarnished nor afraid." Chandler emphasized that Marlowe is part of that environment—by necessity—but is not contaminated by it—by choice. He is not without fear. Marlowe often expresses the fear of a normal man in a dangerous situation, and in this way he differs from the heroes of the tough-guy school and from those of Chandler's apprentice stories. Like Hemingway's heroes, he must learn to control and to disguise his fear. Most important, he is not intimidated by his environment. As Chandler puts it in his essay, the detective "must be, to use a rather weathered phrase, a man of honor."

Although commonly used, the phrase "the mean streets" is somewhat misleading. Chandler's target is not merely, or even primarily, the cruelty and brutality of life at the bottom of the social and economic ladder. For him, the mean streets extend into the posh apartments and mansions of Hollywood and suburban Los Angeles, and he is more interested in exploring cruelty and viciousness among the very rich than among the people of the streets. Each of the novels treats the theme of the quest for and ownership of money and power as the source of evil; Chandler constantly emphasizes Marlowe's relative poverty as a symbol of his incorruptibility. *The High Window*, for example, is more a study in the corrupting influence of wealth than in the process of detection. Marlowe is shocked to discover that his client Mrs. Murdock not only murdered her husband to collect his life insurance, but also systematically conditioned her timid and neurotic secretary to believe that she was the murderess, dependent on Mrs. Murdock for forgiveness as well as for protection from the law. This instance is typical of Chandler's novels. The mean streets originate in the drawing rooms of those who may profit by exploiting others.

Marlowe's code of behavior differs from those of other fictional detectives, though his descendants, particularly Ross Macdonald's Lew Archer and Robert B. Parker's Spenser, resemble Chandler's hero. Marlowe is not, in the final analysis, a tough guy. He is a compassionate man who, as he half-ironically tells a policeman in *The Long Goodbye*, hears "voices crying in the night" and goes to "see what's the matter." Marlowe is instinctively the champion of the victims of the rich and powerful; in *The High Window* he insists that the secretary, Merle Davis, be set free of the psychological exploitation by the Murdock family and be allowed to return to her home in Kansas. To those who aspire to wealth and power, Marlowe is not so kind. In *The Little Sister*, he knowingly allows the amoral, ruthless murderess Dolores Gonzales to be killed by her husband.

This instinctive compassion for the weak accounts for much of Marlowe's fundamental decency, but it often gets him into trouble, for he is human enough to be occasionally deceived by appearances. The apparently innocent client in *The Little Sister*, Orfamay Quest from Kansas, deceives Marlowe with her piety and sincerity, and he is eventually depressed to learn that his compassion for her is wasted, that despite her apparent innocence she is compulsively materialistic and is willing to exploit even her brother's murder if she can profit by his scheme to blackmail a gangster.

Marlowe's compassion is what makes him interesting as a character, but it is also what makes him vulnerable in the mean streets. His defense against that vulnerability is to play the role of the tough guy. His wisecracks, which have since become obligatory in stories about private detectives, are nothing more than a shield. Chandler says in "The Simple Art of Murder" that the detective is a proud man who will take "no man's insolence without a due and dispassionate revenge." The mean streets have taught Marlowe that corrupt politicians, tired policemen, ambitious actors, rich people, and street toughs will insult and abuse him readily; his defense is the wisecrack. It is the attempt of an honorable man to stand up to a world that has gone sour.

The Big Sleep • *The Big Sleep,* Chandler's first full-length novel, makes explicit use of the associations with myth that had been implicit in the stories he had published over six years. It was in this book that the author settled on the name Marlowe for his detective, after he had experimented with such names as Carmady and Dalmas. In his first detective story, "Blackmailers Don't Shoot," he had called the detective Mallory, an obvious allusion to the chronicler of the Arthurian legends, Sir Thomas Malory. The association with the quest romance is worked out in several important ways in *The Big Sleep.* When the detective first arrives at the home of his client, he notices a stained-glass panel "showing a knight in dark armor rescuing a lady" and concludes that "if I lived in the house, I would sooner or later have to climb up and help him." Much later, upon returning to the house, the detective notes that the knight "wasn't getting anywhere" with the task of rescuing the lady.

These two references remind the reader of a heroic tradition into which Marlowe, a citizen of the twentieth century, is trying to fit his own experiences. Malory's knights lived in an age of faith, and the quest for the Holy Grail was a duty imposed by that faith as well as a test of the worthiness of the knight himself. Marlowe's adventures entangle him with a pornographer who is murdered, a small-time blackmailer whose effort to cut himself into the action leads to his death, a trigger-happy homosexual, a powerful criminal the law cannot touch, a district attorney eager to avoid scandal that might touch a wealthy family, and a psychopathic murderess. The environment is impossible to reconcile with the values suggested by the knight in the panel. At midpoint in the novel, Marlowe has a chess problem laid out (his playing chess against the problems defined in classical matches gives him an intellectual depth uncharacteristic of the tough-guy detective), and, trying to move a knight effectively on the board, he concludes that "knights had no meaning in this game. It wasn't a game for knights."

The implication of this set of images is that Marlowe aspires to the role of the traditional knight, but that such an aspiration is doomed to failure in the mean streets. His aspiration to the role of the knight is a hopeless attempt to restore order to the modern wasteland. At the same time, it is proof of his integrity that he tries to maintain that role in the face of certain and predictable frustration. In a subsequent novel, *The High Window,* a minor character invents a phrase that eloquently describes Marlowe's association with the romance tradition; he calls the detective a "shop-soiled Galahad," a reminder both of the knight who, in the romance, could not be corrupted, and of the pressures that wear down the modern hero.

Another important reference to the romance tradition in *The Big Sleep* is the client himself. General Sternwood is a dying man; he has to meet Marlowe in a greenhouse because the general needs the artificial warmth. He is lame, impotent, and distressed at the moral decay of his daughters. Chandler implicitly associates this character with the Fisher King of the archetypal romance, and *The Big Sleep* takes on revealing connections with T. S. Eliot's *The Waste Land* (1922), another modern version of this quest. Like Eliot's poem, Chandler's version of the quest is a record of failure. Marlowe's success in the work of detection points paradoxically to the failure of his quest. He is able to complete, even to go beyond, his assignment. His instinctive sympathy for the helpless general leads him to try to find out what happened to the general's son-in-law, Rusty Regan, whose charm and vigor had restored some vitality to the old man, much as the traditional knight might restore the Fisher King. Marlowe discovers that Regan has been murdered, hence, there is no hope that the general might be restored. He can only prepare to join Regan in "the big sleep."

"It was not a game for knights." This knight is able to sort through the many mysteries of *The Big Sleep*, to discover the killers of the various victims. He outsmarts a professional killer in a shoot-out and feels that in doing so he achieves some revenge for Harry Jones, a tough little victim whom Marlowe had respected. His actions do not, however, restore order to his surroundings. He is unable to reach, through law or intimidation, Eddie Mars, the operator of a gambling casino and several protection rackets, a parasite of society. His discovery that Regan was murdered leads him to the conclusion that all he can do is try to protect the general from "the nastiness," the inescapable and brutal facts of life. Even his discovery that Regan's killer was the general's daughter, Carmen, does not resolve anything: She is a psychopath, and her actions are gratuitous, not subject to reform. All Marlowe can do, ironically, is the same thing Eddie Mars and Regan's widow, Vivian, tried to do—protect the general from knowing that his own daughter was responsible for the death of the one person who brought happiness to his life. Marlowe's method differs from that of Mars. Rather than cover up the fact, he uses the leverage of his knowledge of the cover-up to force Vivian Regan, Carmen's sister as well as Rusty's widow, to have Carmen committed to a mental hospital. He makes this deal only after Vivian has tried to buy his silence.

What makes *The Big Sleep* such a rich novel, in addition to its mythic associations, is the question of what keeps Marlowe going. He knows that justice is not possible in a world controlled by Eddie Mars, and he learns that his efforts lead only to compound frustrations and personal danger. He continues to work, against the warnings of the criminal element, the official police, and the family of his client. Both Vivian and Carmen offer sexual bribes if Marlowe will get off the case. He is so personally affected by "the nastiness" around him that he has a nightmare after having encountered the perverse scene in which the pornographer Geiger was killed—a dream in which Marlowe implicates himself as an ineffective pornographer. He dreams about a "man in a bloody Chinese coat" (Geiger) who was chasing "a naked girl with long jade earrings" (Carmen) "while I ran after them and tried to take a photograph with an empty camera." This exposure to the corruption around him makes Marlowe doubt, in his nightmare, even his own ability to resist corruption.

Marlowe is able to continue in the face of these pressures because, like Joseph Conrad's Marlow in *Heart of Darkness* (1902), he believes in something greater than his personal interests. His idealism is of course shattered by the corruption around him, but like Conrad's character or Hemingway's heroes, he believes in a code: loyalty to his client. In the absence of a belief in an absolute good, Marlowe guides his behavior by weighing his options in the context of the principle of loyalty to the client. When the police and the district attorney threaten him, he explains that all he has to sell is "what little guts and intelligence the Lord gave me and a willingness to get pushed around in order to protect a client." He refuses an invitation to have sex with each of the attractive Sternwood daughters because of this principle. He tells Carmen, "It's a question of professional pride" after he has told Vivian that as a man he is tempted, but as a detective, "I work at it, lady. I don't play at it." Many bribes, monetary and sexual, are offered Marlowe in *The Big Sleep*. Even more threats, from criminals, police, and his client's family, are hurled at him. What gives him his sense of purpose in a world that seems to resonate to no moral standard is one self-imposed principle. This is the main theme of Chandler's fiction: If standards of behavior do not exist outside the individual, as they were believed to in the age of chivalry, then one must create them, however imperfect they may be, for oneself.

Writings During the 1940's • By the end of the 1940's, Chandler was well established as a master of detective fiction, but he was becoming increasingly impatient with the limitations of the form. Classically educated and somewhat aristocratic in his personal tastes, he found the conventions of the hard-boiled genre increasingly confining. However, he was not willing to dispose of Marlowe, partly because the detective had brought his creator success. More important, as biographer Frank MacShane has pointed out, Chandler's real interest was the variety of the life and the essential formlessness of Los Angeles, so his detective's ability to cut across class lines, to meet with criminals, police, the seedier citizens as well as the wealthy, gave the author a chance to explore in fiction the life of the entire community, much as two of his favorite novelists, Charles Dickens and Honoré de Balzac, had done for the cities in which they had lived.

Chandler had already pushed the mystery novel somewhat beyond its inherent limits, but he remained unsatisfied with what must be regarded as an impressive achievement. He had altered the formula to apply the quest myth in *The Big Sleep*; to study phony psychics and corrupt police in *Farewell, My Lovely*; to examine psychological and legal exploitation by the very wealthy in *The High Window*; to work with the devices of disguise and the anxieties of those who merely aspire to wealth and power in *The Lady in the Lake*; and to satirize the pretentiousness of Hollywood as well as to comment on the corrosive influence of materialism in *The Little Sister*.

***The Long Goodbye* •** *The Long Goodbye* abandons so many of the conventions of the detective formula that it simply uses what is left of the formula as a skeleton around which to build serious psychological and cultural themes. The actual detective work Marlowe is hired to perform is merely to search for the novelist Roger Wade, who has disappeared on a drunken spree, and eventually Marlowe discovers that the search itself was unnecessary. Wade's wife knew where Roger was but hired Marlowe to get him involved in Roger's life, so that he might possibly be persuaded to take a job as Wade's bodyguard. The search for Wade allows for some discussion of physicians who dispense drugs freely to the wealthy, but it depends more on persistent following of leads than on brilliant deduction. The real detective work in which he engages is entirely independent, work from which he is discouraged by the police, a gangster named Menendez, a wealthy businessman, and the Wades. It is a work of sentiment, not professionalism, and the book discloses that this task is worth neither the effort nor the integrity that Marlowe puts into it.

The Long Goodbye is finally a study in personal loyalties. The sustaining ethic of the earlier novels, loyalty to a client, does not really apply in this book, for most of the time Marlowe has no client or refuses to take up the assignments offered him. He is no longer satisfied with his work as a detective, and one of the book's best chapters details the monotony and triviality of a day in the life of a private investigator. His own ambivalence about his role is summed up after a series of absurd requests for his services: "What makes a man stay with it nobody knows. You don't get rich, and you don't often have much fun. Sometimes you get beaten up or shot at or tossed in the jailhouse." Each of these unpleasant things happens to Marlowe. He stays in business, but he has ceased to understand why.

At the heart of the book is Marlowe's relationship with Terry Lennox, who drifts into Marlowe's personal life. Lennox, a man with a mysterious past but at present married for the second time to the nymphomaniac daughter of a tycoon, impresses Marlowe with a jaded version of the Hemingway code. Lennox knows he is little more than a gigolo, but he has accepted himself with a kind of refined drunkenness. He and Marlowe become friends, but after his wife is brutally murdered, Lennox asks Marlowe to help him escape to Mexico. Marlowe, who agrees out of friendship rather than loyalty to Lennox as a client, is thus legally implicated as a possible accessory after the fact.

Lennox's action brings him into an almost inevitable conflict with the police, and he is roughly treated by a detective and his precinct captain. Marlowe's being at odds with the official police is far from a new occurrence in Chandler's work. His fiction always contains an innate distrust of the legal establishment, from the exposé of police corruption in *Farewell, My Lovely* through the abuse of police power by one of the killers in *The Lady in the Lake.* A lawyer in *The Long Goodbye* tells Marlowe, "The law isn't justice, it's a very imperfect mechanism. If you press exactly the right buttons and are also lucky, justice may show up in the answer." This distrust of the mechanism of law usually led Chandler to condemn separate kinds of justice for the wealthy and the powerless. Marlowe's reaction to his disillusionment includes verbal and physical conflict with the police as well as the routine concealment of evidence that might implicate a client.

What differentiates this conflict from previous ones in Chandler's work is that Marlowe is not really protecting the interests of a client. He acts out of a personal loyalty, based partly on his belief that Lennox could not have committed the sadistic murder of which he is accused. He keeps his silence during a week in jail, during which he is pressed to give evidence that would implicate both himself and Lennox.

Lennox's confession and suicide render Marlowe's actions futile. The arrival of a letter and a large sum of money rekindles a sentimental interest in the Lennox matter, and as it becomes clear that some connection exists between Lennox and the Wades, who have tried to hire him to help Roger stay sober long enough to finish his book, Marlowe continues to fit together evidence that points to Lennox's innocence. Proving Lennox innocent is another source of disillusionment: Marlowe learns that both the confession and the suicide were faked. In their final interview, Marlowe tells Lennox, "You had standards and you lived by them, but they were personal. They had no relation to any kind of ethics or scruples." Marlowe has himself come close to this moral relativism in his uncritical loyalty to Lennox, and has perhaps seen in his friend an example of the vague standard of ethical conduct to which such moral relativism can lead. The difference between Lennox and Marlowe is that the detective still recognizes the importance of having a code. He tells Lennox, "You're a moral defeatist." His work on behalf of Lennox has been a disappointment of the highest order, for he has seen the paralysis of will toward which the cynicism both men share leads. By returning Lennox's money, Marlowe implies that Lennox was not worth the risk and labor of proving his innocence.

The Long Goodbye is populated by "moral defeatists." Another character, Roger Wade, has given up on himself as a man and as a writer. Chandler creates in this character a representation of the writer who knowingly compromises his artistic talent for personal gain. Knowing that he is "a literary prostitute," Wade is driven to alcoholic sprees and personal despair. When he seeks Marlowe's sympathy for his predicament, Marlowe reminds him of Gustave Flaubert, an example of the genuine artist who was willing to sacrifice success for his art.

Marlowe's association with Wade develops the central theme of *The Long Goodbye*: personal responsibility. Wade's publisher and his wife want Marlowe to protect Wade from his depressive and suicidal tendencies. Realizing that Wade is trying to escape something inside himself, Marlowe knows that only Wade can stop his rush toward self-destruction. He refuses to take the lucrative job as Wade's bodyguard because he realizes he cannot prevent the author from being self-destructive. In fact, Marlowe is in the Wade house the day Roger Wade apparently commits suicide. Although he does try to remove Wade's gun from its customary desk drawer, he makes no effort to stop Wade from drinking. He knows that restraining Wade, whether by physical force or coercion, would be an artifical substitute for a real solution. If Wade's self-loathing makes him suicidal, Marlowe recognizes that nothing he can do will prevent the self-destructive act from taking place.

The theme of personal responsibility is even more directly apparent in Marlowe's relation with Eileen Wade. Initially, she impresses him as an ideal beauty, and the erotic implications of their relationship are always near the surface. In a scene after he has put the drunken Roger to bed, the detective comes close to his first sexual consummation in the novels. In this episode, it becomes clear that Eileen is mentally disturbed, and Marlowe's subsequent investigation reveals that she was once married to Lennox, who served in the war under another name. Her attempt to seduce Marlowe is in fact a clumsy attempt to establish a relationship with the Terry Lennox she knew before his cynicism turned to moral defeatism. From these premises, Marlowe deduces that Eileen murdered both Sylvia Lennox and Roger, who had been having an affair with Sylvia, a perverse revenge for her being twice defeated by a woman whose vulgarity she despised.

Marlowe has sufficient evidence to prove Lennox's innocence and to show that Wade's death was not suicide, but he does not go to the police. He confronts Eileen with the evidence and gives her time to commit suicide. He refers to himself as a "one-man death watch" and takes no action to prevent the self-destruction of this woman to whom he is so powerfully attracted. When he has to explain his conduct to the one policeman he trusts, Bernie Ohls, he says, "I wanted her to take a long look at herself. What she did about it was her business." This is a ruthless dismissal of a disturbed, though homicidal, person. What Chandler intends to emphasize is the idea that all humans must ultimately take full responsibility for their actions.

Even Marlowe's relationship with Bernie Ohls deteriorates. Ohls, the only policeman Marlowe likes or trusts, consents to leak a document so that Marlowe will use it unwittingly to flush out the racketeer Menendez, knowing that Marlowe will be abused psychologically and physically in the process. The ruse works, and Ohls ruthlessly sends Menendez off to possible execution by his fellow criminals. In the image used by another character, Marlowe has been the goat tied out by the police to catch the tiger Menendez. Marlowe understands why the police have used him this way, but the novel ends with a new note of mistrust between Marlowe and Ohls. Yet another human relationship has failed.

In *The Long Goodbye*, the business of detection is subordinate to the themes of personal responsibility, betrayal, and the mutability of all human relationships. The book is a powerful indictment of the shallowness of public values in mid-century America, and the emphasis is on characterization, theme, and atmosphere rather than on the matters typical of the mystery novel. It represents a remarkable transition from the detective novel to the realm of serious fiction, a transition that has subsequently been imitated but not equaled.

David C. Dougherty

Other major works

SHORT FICTION: *Five Murderers,* 1944; *Five Sinister Characters,* 1945; *Finger Man, and Other Stories,* 1946; *Red Wind,* 1946; *Spanish Blood,* 1946; *The Simple Art of Murder,* 1950; *Trouble Is My Business,* 1950; *Pick-up on Noon Street,* 1952; *Smart-Aleck Kill,* 1953; *Pearls Are a Nuisance,* 1958; *Killer in the Rain,* 1964 (Philip Durham, editor); *The Smell of Fear,* 1965; *The Midnight Raymond Chandler,* 1971; *The Best of Raymond Chandler,* 1977; *Stories and Early Novels,* 1995.

NONFICTION: *The Blue Dahlia,* 1946 (Matthew J. Bruccoli, editor); *Raymond Chandler Speaking,* 1962 (Dorothy Gardiner and Katherine Sorely Walker, editors); *Chandler Before Marlowe: Raymond Chandler's Early Prose and Poetry,* 1973 (Bruccoli, editor); *The Notebooks of Raymond Chandler and English Summer,* 1976 (Frank MacShane, editor); *Raymond Chandler and James M. Fox: Letters,* 1978; *Selected Letters of Raymond Chandler,* 1981 (MacShane, editor); *The Raymond Chandler Papers: Selected Letters and Nonfiction, 1909-1959,* 2000 (edited by Tom Hiney and MacShane).

Bibliography

Babener, Liahna K. "Raymond Chandler's City of Lies." In *Los Angeles in Fiction,* edited by David Fine. Albuquerque: University of New Mexico Press, 1984. The chapter on Chandler is a study of the image patterns in his novels. The volume as a whole is an interesting discussion of the importance of a sense of place, especially one as mythologically rich as Los Angeles. Includes notes.

Bruccoli, Matthew J., and Richard Layman. *Hardboiled Mystery Writers: Raymond Chandler, Dashiell Hammett, Ross Macdonald.* New York: Carroll and Graf, 2002. A handy supplemental reference that includes interviews, letters, and previously published studies. Illustrated.

Chandler, Raymond. *Raymond Chandler Speaking.* Edited by Dorothy Gardiner and Katherine Walker. Berkeley: University of California Press, 1997. Extracts from Chandler's letters, notebooks, and other sources that help to reveal how he wrote and what he thought of his characters.

"Chandler, Raymond." In *Mystery and Suspense Writers: The Literature of Crime, Detection, and Espionage,* edited by Robin W. Winks and Maureen Corrigan. New York: Charles Scribner's Sons, 1998. Appreciation of Chandler as a mystery wrier.

Hamilton, Cynthia S. "Raymond Chandler." In *Western and Hard-Boiled Detective Fiction: From High Noon to Midnight.* Iowa City: University of Iowa Press, 1987. This study provides an unusual insight into Chandler's detective fiction from the historical and generic perspective of the American Western novel. It includes three chapters on the study of formula literature. Complemented by a bibliography and an index.

Hiney, Tom. *Raymond Chandler: A Biography.* New York: Atlantic Monthly Press, 1997. A brief biography of Chandler that discusses his education in England, his relationship to Los Angeles, and the plots and characters of his most important detective novels and stories.

Jameson, F. R. "On Raymond Chandler." In *The Poetics of Murder: Detective Fiction and*

Literary Theory, edited by Glenn W. Most and William W. Stowe. San Diego: Harcourt Brace Jovanovich, 1983. This critic starts with the observation that Chandler's English upbringing in essence gave him an outsider's view of American life and language. A useful discussion of the portrait of American society that emerges from Chandler's works.

Knight, Stephen. "'A Hard Cheerfulness': An Introduction to Raymond Chandler." In *American Crime Fiction: Studies in the Genre*, edited by Brian Docherty. New York: St. Martin's Press, 1988. This is a discussion of the values and attitudes that define Philip Marlowe and that make him unusual in the genre of hard-boiled American crime fiction.

Lehman, David. "Hammett and Chandler." In *The Perfect Murder: A Study in Detection*. New York: Free Press, 1989. Chandler is represented in this comprehensive study of detective fiction as one of the authors who brought out the parable at the heart of mystery fiction. A useful volume in its breadth and its unusual appendices, one a list of further reading, the other, an annotated list of the critic's favorite mysteries. Includes two indexes, one of concepts, and one of names and titles.

Luhr, William. *Raymond Chandler and Film*. Rev. ed. New York: F. Ungar, 1991. Fascinating study of the translation of Chandler's stories to the screen.

MacShane, Frank. *The Life of Raymond Chandler*. New York: E. P. Dutton, 1976. Still the standard biography of Chandler.

Marling, William. *The American Roman Noir: Hammett, Cain, and Chandler*. Athens: University of Georgia Press, 1995. Comparative study of Dashiell Hammett, James Cain, and Raymond Chandler as noir writers

____________. *Raymond Chandler*. Boston: Twayne, 1986. Both a brief biographical summary and a literary analysis of Chandler's work.

Moss, Robert F., ed. *Raymond Chandler: A Literary Reference*. New York: Carroll & Graf, 2003. Lavishly illustrated collection of articles and extracts from writings by and about Chandler, his books, and film adaptations of his works.

Norrman, Ralf. *Wholeness Restored: Love of Symmetry as a Shaping Force in the Writings of Henry James, Kurt Vonnegut, Samuel Butler, and Raymond Chandler*. New York: Peter Lang, 1998. Discusses Chandler's *The Long Goodbye*.

Phillips, Gene D. *Creatures of Darkness: Raymond Chandler, Detective Fiction, and Film Noir*. Lexington: University Press of Kentucky, 2000. Though this work focuses largely on Chandler's Hollywood output, it contains some useful information.

Preiss, Byron, ed. *Raymond Chandler's Philip Marlowe: A Centennial Celebration*. New York: Alfred A. Knopf, 1988. Collection of appreciative essays on Chandler commemorating the one-hundredth anniversary of his birth.

Simpson, Hassell A. "'So Long, Beautiful Hunk': Ambiguous Gender and Songs of Parting in Raymond Chandler's Fictions." *Journal of Popular Culture* 28 (Fall, 1994): 37-48. Discusses the sexual ambiguity of Chandler's Philip Marlowe.

Skinner, Robert E. *The Hard-Boiled Explicator: A Guide to the Study of Dashiell Hammett, Raymond Chandler, and Ross Macdonald*. Metuchen, N.J.: Scarecrow Press, 1985. This volume is indispensable for the scholar interested in tracking down unpublished dissertations as well as mainstream criticism. Brief introductions of each author are followed by annotated bibliographies of books, articles, and reviews.

Steiner, T. R. "The Origin of Raymond Chandler's 'Mean Streets.'" *ANQ*, n.s. 7 (October, 1994): 225-227. Suggests that the origin of the expression "mean streets" is Arthur Morrison's *Tales of Mean Streets*, a classic of late Victorian slum literature. The phrase referred to the lack of purpose and joy in the East End of London.

Van Dover, J. K., ed. *The Critical Response to Raymond Chandler.* Westport, Conn.: Greenwood Press, 1995. A collection of essays examining Chandler's literary output. Includes bibliographical references and an index.

Widdicombe, Toby. *A Reader's Guide to Raymond Chandler.* Westport, Conn.: Greenwood Press, 2001. Comprehensive reference book on Chandler, his books, and dramatic adapations of his writings. Alphabetically arranged entries cover his major works, characters, and many other subjects. Includes a biographical overview, chronology, bibliography, and index.

John Cheever

Born: Quincy, Massachusetts; May 27, 1912
Died: Ossining, New York; June 18, 1982

Principal long fiction • *The Wapshot Chronicle*, 1957; *The Wapshot Scandal*, 1964; *Bullet Park*, 1969; *Falconer*, 1977; *Oh, What a Paradise It Seems*, 1982.

Other literary forms • Since the publication of his first fictional piece, "Expelled," in the October 10, 1930, issue of *The New Republic*, more than two hundred John Cheever stories have appeared in American magazines, chiefly *The New Yorker*. Fewer than half that number were reprinted in the seven collections Cheever published in his lifetime: *The Way Some People Live* (1943), *The Enormous Radio, and Other Stories* (1953), *The Housebreaker of Shady Hill, and Other Stories* (1958), *Some People, Places, and Things That Will Not Appear in My Next Novel* (1961), *The Brigadier and the Golf Widow* (1964), *The World of Apples* (1973), and *The Stories of John Cheever* (1978), which includes all but the earliest collected stories and adds four previously uncollected pieces. His one television play, *The Shady Hill Kidnapping*, aired on January 12, 1982, to inaugurate the Public Broadcasting Service's *American Playhouse* series. Cheever, however, made a clear distinction between fiction, which he considered humankind's most exalted and intimate means of communication, and literary works written for television, film, and theater. Consequently, he remained aloof from all attempts to adapt his literary work—the 1968 film version of "The Swimmer," for example, directed by Frank and Eleanor Perry and starring Burt Lancaster (which he found disappointing), or the adaptations of the three stories televised by the Public Broadcasting Service in 1979. In addition, he rarely turned his considerable energies to the writing of articles and reviews. One large and undoubtedly fascinating body of Cheever's writing is his journal, the keeping of which is part of a long family tradition.

Achievements • Until the publication of *Falconer* in 1977 and *The Stories of John Cheever* the following year, Cheever's position as a major American writer was not firmly established, even though as early as 1953 William Peden had noted that he was one of the country's most "undervalued" literary figures. Despite the fact that critics, especially academic ones, frequently invoked Cheever only to pillory his supposedly lightweight vision and preoccupation with upper-middle-class life, his reputation continued to grow steadily: four O. Henry Awards between 1941 and 1964; a Guggenheim Fellowship in 1951; the University of Illinois Benjamin Franklin Award in 1955; a grant from the National Institute of Arts and Letters in 1956 and election to that organization the following year; the National Book Award for his first novel, *The Wapshot Chronicle*, in 1958; the William Dean Howells Medal for its sequel, *The Wapshot Scandal*, seven years later; election to the American Academy of Arts and Letters in 1973; and cover stories in the nation's two most widely circulated weekly news magazines, *Time* (1964) and *Newsweek* (1977).

The overwhelmingly favorable reception of *Falconer* made possible the publication of *The Stories of John Cheever*, which in turn brought to its author additional honors: a second National Book Award; the National Book Critics Circle Award for best fiction; a Pulitzer Prize; the Edward MacDowell Medal; an honorary doctorate from Harvard University; and in April, 1982, the National Medal for Literature for his "distinguished and continuing contribution to American letters." The popular and critical success of those books and the televising of his work before a national audience brought Cheever the recognition he had long deserved and established his well-earned place in literature.

Biography • John Cheever was born in Quincy, Massachusetts, on May 27, 1912, and grew up during what he has called the "Athenian twilight" of New England culture. His father, Frederick, who was forty-nine when Cheever was born, lost his position in the shoe business in the 1929 Depression and much of his self-respect a short time later when his wife opened a gift shop in order to support the family. The parents' emotionally strained relationship eventually led to their separation and caused Cheever to become very close to his brother Fred, seven years his senior.

At the age of seventeen, Cheever was dismissed from Thayer Academy in South Braintree, Massachusetts, for smoking and poor grades; he promptly turned his experience into a story, "Expelled," which Malcolm Cowley published in *The New Republic* on October 10, 1930. John and Fred Cheever embarked on a walking tour of Europe. Upon their return, the brothers lived together briefly in Boston, where "Jon" (as he then identified himself) wrote while Fred worked in the textile business. The closeness of their relationship troubled Cheever, who then moved to a squalid rooming house on New York's Hudson Street. There, with the help of his Boston mentor, Hazel Hawthorne, he wrote synopses for Metro-Goldwyn-Mayer, subsisted on buttermilk and stale bread, associated with Cowley, E. E. Cummings, Sherwood Anderson, Edmund Wilson, Hart Crane, John Dos Passos, and Gaston Lachaise, and somehow managed to keep his art free of the political issues that dominated much of the literature of the period.

During that time Cheever began three of his most enduring relationships: with Yaddo, the writers' colony in Saratoga Springs, New York; with *The New Yorker*, which published his "Brooklyn Rooming House" in the May 25, 1935, issue; and with Mary Winternitz, the daughter of the dean of Yale Medical School, whom he married on March 22, 1941. They had three children: Susan, who would later become a best-selling writer herself; Benjamin, an editor at *Reader's Digest*; and Federico.

Midway through a tour of duty with the Army, Cheever published his first book to generally favorable reviews, and following his discharge, he was able to support himself and his family almost exclusively, if at times precariously, by his writing. Although he liked to give interviewers and others the impression that he was something of a country squire—the heavy Boston accent, the eighteenth century house with its extensive grounds in Ossining, New York—Cheever was in fact plagued throughout much of his life by financial as well as psychological insecurity.

The 1950's was an unsettling time for Cheever. As he explained to fellow writer Herbert Gold, the decade had begun full of promise, but halfway through it "something went terribly wrong"; confused by "the forceful absurdities of life" and, like another Quincy man, Henry Adams, unprepared to deal with them, he imagined himself "a man in a quagmire, looking into a tear in the sky." The absurdities of modern life are presented, often with a comic twist, in the three novels and six collections of short stories that Cheever published between 1953 and the early 1970's—at which time the author's life took an even darker turn: a massive heart attack in 1972, acute alcoholism that eventually forced Cheever to commit himself to the Smithers Rehabilitation Center in New York, financial difficulties, and the death of his brother in 1976. In the light of this background, it is clear that the writing of his triumphant novel *Falconer* freed Cheever from the same sense of confinement that plagues his characters.

Cheever was both deeply, though not narrowly, religious (a practicing Episcopalian) and physically active (biking, walking, skiing, and sawing were among his favorite pastimes). He was also active sexually and, often feeling rebuffed by his wife, pursued numerous love affairs both with men (including the composer Ned Rorem and a number of young writers) and with women (including the actor Hope Lange). As a writer, he incorporated into his fiction the same blend of the spiritual and the worldly that marked his own character. This blend shines most strongly in *Oh What a Paradise It Seems,* the novella Cheever published just three months before he died of cancer on June 18, 1982. In the novella, protagonist Lemuel Sears is introduced in a sentence that begins in the writing style of William Butler Yeats and ends in pure Cheever: "An aged man is but a paltry thing, a tattered coat upon a stick, unless he sees the bright plumage of the bird called courage—*Cardinalis virginius* in this case—and oh how his heart leapt." More than a literary work, *Oh What a Paradise It Seems* is the gift of an enormously generous writer whose loss is, to use one of John Cheever's favorite words, "inestimable."

Analysis • In a literary period that witnessed the exhaustion of literature, wholesale formal experimentation, a general distrust of language, the death of the novel, and the blurring of the lines separating fiction and play, mainstream art and the avant-garde, John Cheever consistently and eloquently held to the position that the writing of fiction is an intimate, useful, and indeed necessary way of making sense of human life and affirming its worth. Cheever's ambitious and overtly religious view of fiction not only is unfashionable today but also stands in marked opposition to those critics who pigeonhole, and in this way dismiss, his fiction as social criticism in the conventional realistic mode. Certainly, there is that element of realism in his work that one finds in the fiction of John O'Hara and Anton Chekhov, writers with whom he is often compared. Such a view, however, fails to account for the various nonrealistic components of his work: the mythic resonance of William Faulkner, the comic grotesquerie of Franz Kafka, and, most important, the lyric style that, while reminiscent of F. Scott Fitzgerald's finest prose, is nevertheless entirely Cheever's own, a cachet underscoring his essentially religious sensibility.

Humankind's inclination toward spiritual light, Cheever has said, "is very nearly botanical." His characters are modern pilgrims—not the Kierkegaardian "sovereign wayfarers" one finds in the novels of Walker Percy, another contemporary Christian writer, but instead the lonely residents of Cheever's various cities and suburbs whose search for love, security, and a measure of fulfillment is the secret undercurrent of their otherwise prosaic daily lives. Because the idea of Original Sin is a given in Cheever's fiction, his characters are men and women who have fallen from grace. At their worst, they are narcissists and chronic complainers. The best of them, however, persevere and, as a result, attain that redemptive vision which enables them "to celebrate a world that lies around them like a bewildering and stupendous dream."

This affirmation does not come easily to Cheever's characters, nor is it rendered sentimentally. Cheever well understands how social fragmentation and separation from the natural world have eroded the individual's sense of self-worth and debased contemporary life, making humanity's "perilous moral journey" still more arduous.

©Nancy Crampton

The outwardly comfortable world in which these characters exist can suddenly, and often for no clearly understandable reason, turn dangerously dark, bringing into sharper focus the emotional and spiritual impoverishment of their lives. What concerns Cheever is not so much the change in their fortunes as the way they respond to that change. Many respond in an extreme, sometimes bizarre manner—Melissa Wapshot, for one. Others attempt to escape into the past; in doing so, they deny the present by imprisoning themselves in what amounts to a regressive fantasy that Cheever carefully distinguishes from nostalgia, which, as he uses it, denotes a pleasurable remembrance of the past, one that is free of regret. Cheever's heroes are those who embrace "the thrust of life," taking from the past what is valuable and using it in their present situations. How a character responds to his world determines Cheever's tone, which ranges from open derision to compassionate irony. Although in his later work Cheever may have been, as Richard Schickel has claimed, less ironic and more forgiving, his finest stories and novels, including *Falconer*, derive their power from the balance or tension he creates between irony and compassion, comedy and tragedy, light and dark.

The social and moral vision that forms the subject of Cheever's fiction also affects the structure of his novels. The novel, Cheever said in 1953, is a form better suited to the parochial life of the nineteenth century than to the modern age with its highly mobile population and mass communications; but because critics and readers have continued to look upon the short story as inferior to the novel, the conscientious writer of short fiction has often been denied the recognition routinely awarded lesser writers who have worked in the longer form. One way out of this dilemma for Cheever was to publish a collection of stories having the unity of a novel: *The Housebreaker of Shady Hill*. Another was to write novels that had some of the fragmentary quality Cheever found at the heart of the modern age. His four novels are not, therefore, made up of short stories badly spliced together, as some reviewers have maintained; rather, they reflect—in various degrees according to the author's state of mind at the time of composition—Cheever's firm belief that wholeness of being is no longer readily apparent; instead, it is something that character, author, and reader must strive to attain. Moreover, Cheever develops his novels on the basis of "intuition, apprehensions, dreams, concepts," rather than plot, as is entirely consistent with the revelatory nature of his religious vision. Thus, although the story form is appropriate to the depiction of the discontinuity of modern life, only in the novel can that discontinuity be not only identified but also brought under some control, or, as happens in *Falconer*, transcended.

The Wapshot Chronicle • In *The Wapshot Chronicle*, Cheever's first novel, the discontinuity of modern life is apparent not only in the structure and the characterization but also in the complex relationship the author sets up between his fictional New England town and the modern world lying beyond its nineteenth century borders. The impulse to create St. Botolphs (loosely based on Quincy) came to Cheever while he stood at the window of a Hollywood hotel, gazing down on "the dangerously barbaric and nomadic world" beneath him. The strength of his novel, however, derives not from a rejection of the present or, as in the work of nineteenth century local colorists such as Sarah Orne Jewett, in a reverent re-creation of a vanished way of life, but in the way Cheever uses each to evaluate the other.

The novel traces the decline of once-prosperous St. Botolphs and the Wapshot clan and the picaresque adventures of the two Wapshot boys—the "ministerial" Coverly and his older and more worldly brother Moses—who go to seek their fortunes in New York, Washington, D.C., and elsewhere. By having the novel begin and end with an annual Fourth of July celebration, Cheever does not so much impose an arbitrary orderliness on his discursive narrative as affirm that ceremoniousness that, in his view, is necessary to spiritual and emotional well-being. The temporal frame is important for another reason: It implies that desire of human beings for independence equals their desire for tradition. Each must be accommodated if the individual is to prosper. If the modern world seems chaotic, even inhospitable to Leander Wapshot's sons, it nevertheless possesses a vitality and expansiveness that, for the most part, St. Botolphs lacks. While the town is to be treasured for its rich tradition and continuity, it is also to be considered a place of confinement. The burden of the novel, then, is to show that with "strength and perseverance" it is possible to "create or build some kind of bridge" between past and present.

Cheever intends this bridge to serve a larger, emblematic purpose in *The Wapshot Chronicle*, where, as in his other works, it is the distance between self and other, or, more specifically, between man and woman, that must be bridged. Although Cheever has repeatedly warned that fiction is not "cryptoautobiography," he obviously, if loosely, modeled the Wapshots on his own family and has even admitted that he wrote the novel to make peace with his father's ghost. Leander Wapshot is the book's moral center; he has the imaginative power to redeem his fallen world, to affirm what others can only whiningly negate. Lusty and romantic, a lover of nature as well as of women, he transmits to Coverly and Moses, by his example rather than by precept, his vision of wholeness. Fittingly, the novel concludes with his "Advice to my sons," which Coverly finds tucked into a volume of William Shakespeare's works: "Stand up straight. Admire the world. Relish the love of a gentle woman. Trust in the Lord."

Despite his affirmative stance, Leander is a diminished hero. Unlike earlier generations of Wapshot men who proved themselves by sailing around the world, Leander's sailing is limited to ferrying tourists across the bay in his barely seaworthy boat, the *Topaze*, which his wife, Sarah, later converts into a floating gift shop, thus further reducing Leander's self-esteem. At one point, a storm drives the boat upon some rocks, an image that captures perfectly what Leander and many other Cheever characters feel so acutely: "man's inestimable loneliness." One of Leander's friends, for example, is haunted by the knowledge that he will be buried naked and unceremoniously in a potter's field; another man sings of his "guest room blues," and a young girl who briefly stays with the Wapshots mistakenly believes that sexual intercourse will end her loneliness. Others, equally desperate, collect antiques or live in castles in a vain attempt to make themselves secure in a bewilderingly changeable world. Leander's vision and vitality keep him from the despair that afflicts these others; as a result, even his death by drowning seems less an end than an affirmation.

Leander, with his "taste for romance and nonsense," is quixotic and exuberant; his wife, Sarah, with her "air of wronged nobility," her "habitual reliance on sad conclusions," and his sister Honora, who substitutes philanthropy for love, are strong-willed and sexless. He affirms life; they deny it. Sarah, the town's civic leader, and Honora, the keeper of the Wapshot fortune, uncaringly strip Leander of his usefulness and self-worth (just as Cousin Justina, the reincarnation of Charles Dickens's Miss Havisham, aggressively plots to unman Moses). To some extent they are predatory, but even more they are incomplete because they are in need of someone to love. Similarly, Leander is portrayed as a man not without flaws. He is, like many of Cheever's male characters, impractical and, at times, inattentive to his family; he can also appear childishly petulant, even ridiculous, as in the scene in which he fakes suicide in order to attract attention. More important, he loves and is loved, as the large crowd of mourners at his funeral service attests—much to Honora's surprise.

Whether his sons will fare any better in their relationships with women is left uncertain in this novel. Both marry—Coverly his "sandwich shop Venus," called Betsey, and Moses the beautiful Melissa Scaddon, who plays Estella to Cousin Justina's Miss Havisham. Both, after briefly losing their wives, eventually father sons, thus fulfilling the terms of their inheritance as set by Honora. Melissa and Betsey are, however, tainted, or haunted, by their pasts (in Betsey's case this is only vaguely mentioned). Moreover, most marriages in Cheever's fiction, as in life, are difficult affairs. In sum, the Wapshot boys may yet be greatly disappointed in their expectations. What is more important is the fact that Moses and, more particularly, Coverly build the necessary bridge between past and present, holding firm to what is best in St. Botolphs (as evidenced in Leander's journal), while freeing themselves from that confinement that the town, in part, represents. This optimistic view is confirmed by the novel's lively style. Straight narrative sections alternate with large portions of two Wapshot journals, humorous parodies of biblical language, and frequent direct addresses to the reader. Tragic elements are present but always in muted tones and often undercut with humor. In *The Wapshot Chronicle*, the comic spirit prevails, as well it should in a novel that twice invokes Shakespeare's Prospero, the liberator of Ariel and tamer of Caliban.

The Wapshot Scandal • Outwardly, Cheever's first two novels are quite similar in theme, character, and structure. Like *The Wapshot Chronicle*, *The Wapshot Scandal* employs a framing device and interweaves three related stories: Honora's escape to Italy to avoid prosecution for income tax evasion and her return to St. Botolphs, where she promptly starves and drinks herself to death; Coverly and Betsey's life in yet another bland, middle-class housing development, Talifer; and Moses and Melissa's difficult existence in the affluent suburb of Proxmire Manor. Although reviewers generally responded less favorably to the second Wapshot book, finding it too discursive, Cheever has pointed out that both novels were carefully thought out in advance and has described the sequel as "an extraordinarily complex book built upon non sequiturs." Whether it is, as Samuel Coale has argued, Cheever's finest work, because it carefully balances comic and tragic elements, is open to question. More certain is that a considerably darker mood pervades *The Wapshot Scandal.*

At the time he began writing the book, Cheever told an audience that American life had become abrasive and debased, a kind of hell, and during its four-year composition he became severely depressed. In *The Wapshot Chronicle* the easy-to-answer refrain is "Why did the young want to go away?" but in *The Wapshot Scandal* the repeated question is Coverly's Hamlet-like "Oh, Father, Father, Father, why have you come back?"—a query that accurately gauges the extent of Coverly's and Cheever's disenchantment with a world that no longer seems either inviting or livable for men or ghosts. In the earlier book, Moses and Coverly had to escape the confinement of St. Botolphs; in the sequel, characters have too completely cut themselves off from the usable traditions, comforting stability, and vital, natural light that the town also represents. As a result, the communal center to which earlier Wapshot men had come back and, analogously, the narrative center to which *The Wapshot Chronicle* continually returned, are conspicuously absent from *The Wapshot Scandal*.

In the sequel, St. Botolphs, though by no means idealized, is rendered in less qualified terms, thus more firmly establishing Cheever's preference for its values and his impatience with the rootlessness and shallowness of the modern age. Honora, for example, is now a far more sympathetic figure endowed with two of Leander's most attractive qualities: a belief in ceremony and a love of nature. In the guise of an elderly senator, Cheever carefully distinguishes between the sentimentalizing of the past and the modern tendency to dispense with the past altogether. The modern Prometheus, the senator notes, is technologically powerful, but he lacks "the awe, the humility, that primitive man brought to the sacred fire."

Whereas earlier Wapshot men faced the terrors of the sea, Moses and Coverly face the greater terrors of daily life in the twentieth century: insecurity, boredom, loneliness, loss of usefulness and self-esteem, and the pervasiveness of death. As Cheever shows, the American Dream totters on the brink of nightmare. When one resident of Proxmire Manor suddenly finds her carefree days turn into a series of frozen water pipes, backed up toilets, exploding furnaces, blown fuses, broken appliances, unopenable packages of bacon, and vacationing repairmen, she turns first to alcohol and promiscuity, then to suicide. The few mourners her husband can persuade to attend the funeral are people they had briefly known on various sea cruises who, intuiting her disappointment and recognizing it as their own, burst into tears. Similarly, Melissa Wapshot becomes the Emma Bovary of Proxmire Manor, taking as her lover a delivery boy and eventually fleeing to Italy, where, perversely, she finds some "solace" for her disappointments in the Supra-Marketto Americano in Rome. Moses responds to his wife's infidelity by becoming a wandering alcoholic, and Betsey finds compensation for the wrongs she claims to have suffered by whittling away her husband's small store of self-esteem.

Coverly, now twelve years older than at the beginning of *The Wapshot Chronicle*, serves (as Leander did in the earlier work) as the novel's moral center. He survives, perhaps even prevails, partly because he chooses to follow the best of the past (Leander's advice to his sons) and partly because he adapts to his world without being overwhelmed by it. Trained as a computer programmer, he accepts the computer error that transforms him into a public relations man but resists the apocalyptic mood that infects nearly everyone else in the novel. Unlike Melissa, whose brief illness leads her to cultivate "a ruthless greed for pleasure," Coverly's narrow escape from a hunter's arrow prompts him to "make something illustrious of his life." His computer analysis of John Keats's poetry leads to the creation of new poetry and the realization of a universal harmony underlying not only the poems but also life itself. His brother Moses, whom he has saved for the moment from debauchery, claims to see through the pasteboard mask of Christmas morning to "the nothingness of things." Coverly, on the other hand, celebrates the "dazzling" day by romancing his wife and sharing Christmas dinner with his late aunt's blind guests, "the raw material of human kindness." Coverly's vision, as well as St. Botolphs's brand of decorum as "a guise or mode of hope," is certainly Cheever's own. Even so, that vision is tempered insofar as the author also shares Moses' pessimistic knowledge of decorum's other side: hypocrisy and despair.

Bullet Park • The contrasting visions of Coverly and Moses reappear as Eliot Nailles and Paul Hammer, the main characters of Cheever's third novel, *Bullet Park*. Nailles is the book's comic and decidedly qualified hero. Like Cheever, he has belonged to a volunteer fire department, loves to saw wood with a chainsaw, feels a kinship with the natural world, and has a realistically balanced view of suburban living as being neither morally perfect nor inherently depraved. However, while both character and author are optimistic, the quality of their optimism differentiates them, for Nailles's is naïve and ludicrously shallow: "Nailles thought of pain and suffering as a principality lying somewhere beyond the legitimate borders of western Europe." Just as Cheever's story "The Death of Justina" satirizes a community determined to defeat death by means of zoning regulations, so *Bullet Park* satirizes Nailles's myopic optimism, which, like Saint Paul's faith (Cheever quotes 2 Corinthians 11-12), is sorely tried during the course of the novel.

Beneath the appearance of respectability and comfort in *Bullet Park*, one finds the same unease that afflicts Talifer and Proxmire Manor. There is Mr. Heathcup, who interrupts his annual house painting to kill himself, claiming he could not stand "it" anymore. When Harry Shinglehouse is sucked under a passing express train and killed, only his shoe is found, an ironic memorial to a hollow life. Shaken by this and other reminders of mortality, Nailles turns to drugs. Drug addiciton is one of Nailles's escapes; another is the devising of soothing explanations. When asked about his work—he sells Spang mouthwash—Nailles claims to be a chemist. When his son Tony suddenly becomes melancholy and withdraws, Bartleby-fashion, from the outside world, his father, like the lawyer in Herman Melville's tale, rationalizes his son's illness as mononucleosis rather than confront the actual cause: He tried to murder his son when Tony echoed his misgivings about the quality of his life. Neither the father's drugged optimism nor the expensive services of a doctor, a psychiatrist, and a specialist in somnambulatory phenomena effect Tony's cure. That is accomplished by the Swami Rutuola, "a spiritual cheer-leader" whose vision is not altogether different from Nailles's.

The climax of Nailles's dark night of the soul occurs when he defeats his secret antagonist, Hammer, who, as John Leonard suggests, may represent a part of Nailles's own personality. Hammer is the illegitimate son of a wealthy socialist (such ironies abound in Cheever's fiction) and his name-changing secretary. Unloved and rootless, Hammer is haunted by a vaguely defined canard. To escape it he turns to various pursuits: aimless travel, alcohol, fantasizing, psychoanalysis, translating the pessimistic poetry of Eugenio Montale, and locating a room with yellow walls where, he believes, he will finally be able to lead "a useful and illustrious life." He finds the room, as well as a beautiful wife, but both prove disappointing, and his search for "a useful and illustrious life" continues to elude him. At this point, Hammer adopts the messianic plan formulated by his dissatisfied, expatriate mother: to live quietly in a place like Bullet Park, to single out one of its representative men, and to "crucify him on the door of Christ's Church. . . . Nothing less than a crucifixion will wake that world!"

Hammer fails in this, as in his other attempts, mainly for the same reasons he turned to it. One reason is his loneliness; feeling the need for a confidant, he explains his plan to the swami, who tells Nailles. The other is his having underestimated the depth of love, even in Bullet Park, where homes are associated not with the people who live in them but with real estate: number of bedrooms, number of baths, and market value.

This "simple" book about a father's love for his son greatly pleased its author. A number of reviewers, however, were troubled by the ending, which Guy Davenport called "shockingly inept." In a review that Cheever blames for turning the critical tide against the book, Benjamin DeMott charged that *Bullet Park* was broken-backed, its "parts tacked together." In retrospect, none of the charges appear merited. Cheever's narrative method and "arch"-like form (as he called it) are entirely consistent with his thematic purpose. In part 1, the third-person narration effectively establishes both the author's sympathy for and distance from his protagonist Nailles, whose confused state of mind is reflected in the confused chronology of this section. Part 2, Hammer's journal (the third-person narrator disappears after parenthetically remarking "Hammer wrote"), is the first-person monologue of a quietly desperate madman such as one finds in works by Edgar Allan Poe and Nikolai Gogol. The return to third-person narration in part 3 enables Cheever to use as centers of consciousness each of his two main characters. At the end of the novel, Tony is saved and returns to school, Hammer is sent to a hospital for the criminally insane, "and Nailles—drugged—went off to work and everything was as wonderful, wonderful, wonderful, wonderful as it had been." By undercutting Nailles's triumph without actually dismissing it, Cheever's ending resists those simplistic affirmations and negations that the rest of *Bullet Park* has explored.

Falconer • The prison setting is the most obvious difference between *Falconer* and Cheever's previous fiction. The more significant difference, however, is the absence of any qualifying irony in its concluding pages. Never has the author's and his protagonist's affirmation been so completely self-assured as in this, Cheever's finest achievement.

Falconer is a story of metaphoric confinement and escape. The realism here serves a larger purpose than verisimilitude; Cheever sketches the essentials of the religious experience and shows how that experience is reflected in a humankind's retreat from the natural world or in his acceptance of a responsible place in it. The relationship between two brothers (as in the Wapshot books) or two brotherlike figures (*Bullet Park*) is given a violent twist in *Falconer*, where the main character, a forty-eight-year-old college professor named Ezekiel Farragut, has been convicted of fratricide. Farragut's murderous act, as well as his addictions to heroin and methadone, imply his retreat into self, a retreat that is not without some justification—a narcissistic wife, a father who wanted his unborn child aborted, a mother who was hardly maternal, a jealous brother, and the violence of war—but self-pity is the sin Cheever has most frequently assailed. Farragut's task, then, is "to leach self-pity out of his emotional spectrum," and to do this he must learn inside Falconer prison what he failed to learn outside it: how to love.

Farragut's first, humble step away from self-love is the affection he has for his cat, Bandit, whose cunning he must adopt if he is to survive his time in prison and those blows that defeat Moses and Melissa Wapshot. More important is Farragut's relationship with a fellow prisoner, Jody. Neither narcissistic nor regressive, this homosexual affair is plainly shown to further Farragut's movement away from self and, in that from Jody's hideout Farragut is given an expansive view of the world he has lost, it also furthers his movement toward that world and "the invisible potency of nature." Jody teaches the professorial Farragut an important lesson concerning the usefulness of one's environment and the active role that must be assumed in order to effect one's own salvation, one's escape from the metaphoric prison. When Jody escapes from Falconer, the loss of his lover at first leads Farragut back to lonely self-love; directed by another prisoner, the Cuckold, to whose depths of self-pity Farragut could easily descend, Farragut goes to the Valley, a dimly lit lavatory where the prisoners masturbate. Here Farragut has a revelation; he suddenly understands that the target of human sexuality ought not to be an iron trough but "the mysteriousness of the bonded spirit and the flesh."

Farragut's continuing escape from useless fantasizing, from nostalgic re-creation of the past, and from passivity causes him to become more self-assured and more interested in the present moment and how to make use of it in realizing his future. The riot at nearby Amana prison (based on the September, 1971, Attica uprising, during which Cheever was teaching at Sing Sing) shows that Farragut is actually freer than his jailers, but it is at this point that Farragut overreaches himself. In his view, the Amana riot signals the salvation of all the dispossessed, and to aid himself in hearing the "word," that is, the news reports, Farragut begins to build a contraband radio. He hopes to get a crystal from Bumpo, who had earlier said he would gladly give up his diamond to save someone. Bumpo refuses to give up the crystal, his reason obviously being his own selfishness, yet there is something ridiculous in Farragut's vague plan for sweeping social reform when his own salvation is still in doubt. In the aftermath of his and the rioters' failures, Farragut briefly slips back into self-regarding passivity, from which he is saved by a dying prisoner. In place of the ineffectual and wholly impersonal charity of his plan to save humankind, Farragut takes upon himself the humbler and more truly charitable task of caring for his fellow man. For the first time, Farragut, prompted by the dying man's question, faces up to the enormity of his crime, making clear to the reader, and perhaps to himself, that in murdering his brother he was unconsciously trying to destroy the worst part of his own personality. The demon exorcised, Farragut becomes spiritually free, a creature of the light.

The visible sign of this freedom is his escape from Falconer in Chicken Number Two's burial box. Borrowing freely from Alexandre Dumas, fils's *The Count of Monte-Cristo* (1844-1845), Cheever treats the escape symbolically as a rebirth and a resurrection. The religious theme is effectively underscored by the novel's parablelike ending. Farragut meets a man who, although he has been evicted from his apartment because he is "alive and healthy," remains both cheerful and charitable, offering Farragut a coat, bus fare, and a place to stay. Miracles, it seems, do occur. The step from psychological retreat and spiritual darkness to freedom and light is not difficult to take, Cheever implies; it simply requires commitment and determination. As for the effect of this choice, which is as much Cheever's as Farragut's, that is summed up in the novel's final word: "rejoice."

Falconer recapitulates all of the major themes of Cheever's earlier fiction and, at the same time, evidences a number of significant changes in his art. One is the tendency toward greater narrative compression. Another, related to the first, is the inclusion of ancillary narratives, less as somewhat obtrusive sketches and more as integral parts of the main storyline. The third—a more overt treatment of the religious theme—appears to have influenced the characterization, style, and structure of *Fal-*

coner. Although Cheever always considered the novelist one who devotes himself to "enlarging" his peers rather than "diminishing" them, his two middle novels emphasize many of his characters' worst features. *Falconer* represents Cheever's return to the more certain affirmation of *The Wapshot Chronicle*; moreover, *Falconer* is Cheever's most lyrical and least bitingly humorous novel. The religious theme and the harmony it implies may also account for its being the most "novelistic" in structure of the four; this is not to say that Cheever had finally "out-grown" his earlier short-story style and mastered the more demanding form of the novel, for the structure of *The Wapshot Chronicle, The Wapshot Scandal,* and *Bullet Park* mirrors Cheever's vision of the 1950's and the 1960's. By the time he wrote *Falconer,* however, that sense of personal and cultural fragmentation no longer dominated his thinking, a change reflected in the relatively tight, more harmonious structure of his most affirmative work.

Oh What a Paradise It Seems • *Oh What a Paradise It Seems* is a slighter but in its own way no less triumphant work. The "bulky novel" that illness forced Cheever to cut short is, though brief, nevertheless remarkably generous in tone and spirit. It is also Cheever's most topical fiction yet strangely his least realistic—a self-regarding, even self-mocking fabulation, a *Walden* for the postmodern age, in which the irony falls as gently as the (acid) rain. Set in a future at once familiar (jogging, for example, has become popular) yet remote (highways with lanes in four digits)—a timeless present, as it were—the novel ends as it begins, by pretending to disclaim its own seriousness: "[T]his is just a story to be read at night in an old house on a rainy night."

Oh What a Paradise It Seems focuses on the "old but not yet infirm" Lemuel Sears. Twice a widower, Sears is financially well-off (he works for Computer Container Intrusion Systems, maker of "cerbical chips") and is as spiritually as he is sexually inclined. Sears's heart "leaps" in two not altogether different directions. One is toward Beasley's Pond, located near his daughter's home, where he ice-skates and in this way briefly satisfies his desire for fleetness, grace, pastoral innocence, and connectedness with the transcendental world of Emersonian Nature. When family connections (Mafia) and political corruption despoil the scene, however—transmogrifying pastoral pond into town dump—Beasley's Pond comes to symbolize for Sears not only imminent ecological disaster but, more important, the "spiritual vagrancy" of a "nomadic society" whose chief characteristics are "netherness" and "portability."

Sears's attraction to the pond parallels and in a way is offset by his physical attraction to the beautiful Renee Herndon, whose appetite for food and whose work as a real estate broker suggest that, despite the exoticism of her given name and the mysteriousness of her personal life, she represents everything that the prosaically named Beasley's, in its pristine state, does not. In his sexual pursuit of Renee, Sears is persistent to the point of clownishness. After numerous initial triumphs, Sears will eventually be rebuffed and come to see the waywardness of this attempt of his to attain what the pond, Sears's first wife, "the sainted Amelia," and even Renee in her own strange way symbolize, but not before a comical but nevertheless loving interlude with Eduardo, the elevator operator in Renee's apartment building, and a perfectly useless session with a psychiatrist named Palmer, "a homosexual spinster." The small but increasingly prominent part homosexuality plays in each of the novels reflects Cheever's ambivalence concerning his own bisexuality. Comically dismissed in the early works, it becomes in *Falconer* and *Oh What a Paradise It Seems* viable but, as Cheever would say in a letter to one of his many male lovers, not ultimate.

As in Cheever's other fictions, the narrative here progresses along parallel fronts.

Sears's dual lives, the sexual and the transcendental, become entwined in and simultaneously exist alongside those of Horace Chisholm, whose commitment to the environment evidences his longing for purity and human as well as spiritual attachment but also causes him to become estranged from his wife and family. Like Sears, he is also quixotic, which is to say both idealistic and absurd. Thanks to a number of those improbable plot complications that abound in Cheever's fiction, Chisholm, working for Sears to save Beasley's Pond, finds and returns a baby inadvertently left by the roadside after a family outing to the beach. The parents, the Logans, live next door to the Salazzos; Sammy Salazzo presides over the pond-turned-dump. Chisholm will be welcomed into the Logan family but eventually will be killed by the mob; an angry Betsey Logan will, however, complete his work, stopping the dumping by threatening to poison the teriyaki sauce in the local Buy Brite supermarkets. (A by-product of her action is that her hated neighbors, the Salazzos, will move away.) Sears, in turn, will utilize the latest technology to restore the pond to its original state, thus redeeming himself as well.

Cheever's ending is self-consciously "happy"—aware of its own improbability. It is, like the architecture of Hitching Post Lane, where the Logans and the Salazzos live, "all happy ending—all greeting card." However, Cheever's satire is more than offset by his compassion, his recognition of and sympathy for the waywardness of humankind's continuing search for both home and wholeness.

Robert A. Morace

Other major works

SHORT FICTION: *The Way Some People Live*, 1943; *The Enormous Radio, and Other Stories*, 1953; "The Country Husband," 1954; *The Housebreaker of Shady Hill, and Other Stories*, 1958; *Some People, Places, and Things That Will Not Appear in My Next Novel*, 1961; *The Brigadier and the Golf Widow*, 1964; *The World of Apples*, 1973; *The Stories of John Cheever*, 1978; *Thirteen Uncollected Stories*, 1994.

TELEPLAY: *The Shady Hill Kidnapping*, 1982.

NONFICTION: *The Letters of John Cheever*, 1988 (Benjamin Cheever, editor); *The Journals of John Cheever*, 1991; *Glad Tidings, a Friendship in Letters: The Correspondence of John Cheever and John D. Weaver, 1945-1982*, 1993.

Bibliography

Bloom, Harold, ed. *John Cheever.* Philadelphia: Chelsea House, 2004. Collection of critical essays about Cheever that have been assembled for student use.

Bosha, Francis J. *John Cheever: A Reference Guide.* Boston: G. K. Hall, 1981. Especially useful for its annotated listing of works about Cheever and for its brief overview of the critical response to Cheever's fiction. For a more complete listing of primary works, see Dennis Coale's checklist in *Bulletin of Bibliography* (volume 36, 1979) and the supplement in Robert G. Collins's book (below). Robert A. Morace's exhaustive assessment of all available biographical, bibliographical, and critical materials appears in *Contemporary Authors: Bibliographical Series: American Authors* (1986) and can be updated by reference to *American Literary Annual* (1985-).

____________, ed. *The Critical Response to John Cheever.* Westport, Conn.: Greenwood Press, 1994. A collection of reviews and critical essays on Cheever's novels and short-story collections by various commentators and critics.

Byrne, Michael D. *Dragons and Martinis: The Skewed Realism of John Cheever.* Edited by Dale Salwak and Paul David Seldis. San Bernardino, Calif.: Borgo Press, 1993. Focuses on Cheever's style in his fiction. Includes bibliographical references and an index.

Cheever, John. *Conversations with John Cheever.* Edited by Scott Donaldson. Jackson: University Press of Mississippi, 1987. Until his final years a rather reticent man, Cheever granted relatively few interviews. The most important ones are reprinted here, along with the editor's thorough chronology and brief but useful introduction.

Cheever, Susan. *Home Before Dark.* Boston: Houghton Mifflin, 1984. This memoir by Cheever's daughter is especially important for fleshing out his troubled early years and providing an insider's look at his marital and other personal difficulties (alcoholism, illnesses, sexual desires). Suffers from lack of documentation and indexing. More valuable as a synthesis of previously published material than as a daughter's intimate revelations.

Coale, Samuel. *John Cheever.* New York: Frederick Ungar, 1977. This volume in Ungar's Literature and Life series includes a brief biography, two chapters on selected short stories, individual chapters on Cheever's first four novels, and a brief conclusion. Coale focuses on the development of Cheever's style (from realism to fantasy) and concern for moral issues.

Collins, Robert G., ed. *Critical Essays on John Cheever.* Boston: G. K. Hall, 1982. Reprints an excellent sampling of reviews, interviews, and early criticism (including many dubbed "new" that are in fact only slightly reworked older pieces). Of the truly new items, three deserve special mention: Collins's biocritical introduction, Dennis Coale's bibliographical supplement, and particularly Samuel Coale's "Cheever and Hawthorne: The American Romancer's Art," arguably one of the most important critical essays on Cheever.

Donaldson, Scott. *John Cheever: A Biography.* New York: Random House, 1988. Scrupulously researched, interestingly written, and judiciously argued, Donaldson's biography presents Cheever as both author and private man. Donaldson fleshes out most of the previously unknown areas in Cheever's biography and dispels many of the biographical myths that Cheever himself encouraged. The account is sympathetic yet objective.

Meanor, Patrick. *John Cheever Revisited.* New York: Twayne, 1995. The first book-length study of Cheever to make use of his journals and letters published during the late 1980's and early 1990's. Focuses on how Cheever created a mythopoeic world in his novels and stories. Includes two chapters on his short stories, with detailed analyses of stories in *The Enormous Radio* and *The Brigadier and the Golf Widow.*

Salwak, Dale, and Paul David Seldis, eds. *Dragons and Martinis: The Skewed Realism of John Cheever,* by Michael D. Byrne. San Bernardino, Calif.: Borgo Press, 1993. Focuses on Cheever's style in his fiction. Includes bibliographical references and an index.

Waldeland, Lynne. *John Cheever.* Boston: Twayne, 1979. This volume in Twayne's United States Authors series is introductory in nature. Although it lacks the thematic coherence of Samuel Coale's work, it has greater breadth and evidences a greater awareness of previous critical commentary.

Kate Chopin

Born: St. Louis, Missouri; February 8, 1851
Died: St. Louis, Missouri; August 22, 1904

Principal long fiction • *At Fault*, 1890; *The Awakening*, 1899.

Other literary forms • In addition to her novels, Kate Chopin wrote nearly fifty poems, approximately one hundred stories and vignettes, and a small amount of literary criticism. Her poems are slight, and no serious claims can be made for them. Her criticism also tends to be modest, but it is often revealing. In one piece written in 1896, for example, she discloses that she discovered Guy de Maupassant eight years earlier, that is, when she first began to write. There is every indication that Maupassant remained one of her most important models in the short-story form. In another essay, she pays tribute to Mary Wilkins Freeman, the New England local colorist whose depiction of repressed passion in women was probably an influence on Chopin's own work. Elsewhere, she seems to distinguish between her own writing and that of the "local-color" school. She is critical of Hamlin Garland for his concern with social problems, "which alone does not insure the survival of a work of art," and she finds the horizons of the Indiana local-color writers too narrow. The subject of genuine fiction is not regional quaintness, she remarks, but "human existence in its subtle, complex . . . meaning, stripped of the veil with which ethical and conventional standards have draped it." Like Thomas Huxley, much read in her circle, she finds no moral purpose in nature, and in her fiction she frequently implies the relativity of morals and received standards.

Chopin's most important work, apart from her novels, lies in the short story. It was for her short stories that she was chiefly known in her time. Her earliest stories are unexceptional, but within only a few years she was producing impressive work, including a fine series of stories set in Nachitoches Parish, her fictional region. Many of these mature stories are included in the two volumes published during her lifetime—*Bayou Folk* (1894) and *A Night in Acadie* (1897). All of the stories and sketches were made available in *The Complete Works of Kate Chopin* (1969). Had she never written *The Awakening*, these stories alone, the best of which are inimitable and gemlike, would ensure Chopin a place among the notable writers of the 1890's.

Achievements • Chopin's reputation today rests on three books—her two short-story collections, *Bayou Folk* and *A Night in Acadie*, and her mature novel, *The Awakening*. *Bayou Folk* collects most of her fiction of the early 1890's set in Nachitoches (pronounced Nack-i-tosh) Parish. The characters it generally portrays, although belonging to different social levels, are Creole, Acadian (Cajun), or African American. In many cases they are poor. Not all of the stories in *Bayou Folk* are perfectly achieved, for when Chopin departs from realism into more fanciful writing she loses her power, but three of the stories in this volume—"Beyond the Bayou," "Désirée's Baby," and "Madame Célestin's Divorce"—are among her most famous and most frequently anthologized.

A Night in Acadie collects Chopin's stories from the mid-and late 1890's. In many of the stories, the protagonists come to sudden recognitions that alter their sense of the

Missouri Historical Society

world; Chopin's recurring theme is the awakening of a spirit that, through a certain set of circumstances, is liberated into conscious life. Passion is often the agent of liberation; while in the fiction of William Dean Howells, for example, characters frequently meet and fall putatively in love; in Chopin's fiction, they do so from the inmost springs of their being. There is nothing putative or factitious about Chopin's characters who are brought to the point of love or desire. *A Night in Acadie* differs from *Bayou Folk* somewhat in the greater emphasis it gives to the erotic drives of its characters.

Chopin's authority in this aspect of experience, and her concern with the interaction of the deeply inward upon the outward life, set her work apart from other local-color writing of the time. In her early novel *At Fault*, she had not as yet begun to probe deeply into the psychology of her characters. David Hosmer and Thérèse Lafirme are drawn too much at the surface level to sustain the kind of writing that Chopin does best. After she had developed her art in her stories, however, she was able to bring her psychological concerns to perfection in *The Awakening*, her greatest work. Chopin's achievement was somewhat narrowly bounded, without the scope of the fiction of manners that occupied Howells and Henry James, but in *Bayou Folk*, *A Night in Acadie*, and *The Awakening*, Chopin gave to American letters works of enduring interest—the interest not so much of local color as of a strikingly sensuous psychological realism.

Biography • Kate Chopin was born Katherine O'Flaherty on February 8, 1851, in St. Louis, Missouri, into a socially prominent family with roots in the French past of both St. Louis and New Orleans. Her father, Thomas O'Flaherty, an immigrant to America from Ireland, had lived in New York and Illinois before settling in St. Louis, where he prospered as the owner of a commission house. In 1839, he married into a well-known Creole family, members of the city's social elite, but his wife died in childbirth only a year later. In 1844, he married Eliza Faris, merely fifteen years old but according to French custom eligible for marriage. Faris was the daughter of a Huguenot man who had migrated from Virginia and a woman who descended from the Charlevilles, among the earliest French settlers in America.

Kate was one of three children and the only one to live to mature years. In 1855, tragedy struck the O'Flaherty family when her father, now a director of the Pacific Railroad, was killed in a train wreck; thereafter, Kate lived in a house of many widows—her mother, grandmother, and great-grandmother Charleville. In 1860, she entered the St. Louis Academy of the Sacred Heart, a Roman Catholic institution where French history, language, and culture were stressed—as they were, also, in her own household. Such an early absorption in French culture would eventually influence Chopin's own writing, an adaptation in some ways of French forms to American themes.

Chopin graduated from the Academy of the Sacred Heart in 1868, and two years later she was introduced to St. Louis society, becoming one of its ornaments, a vivacious and attractive girl known for her cleverness and talents as a storyteller. The following year, she made a trip to New Orleans, and it was there that she met Oscar Chopin, whom she married in 1871. After a three-month honeymoon in Germany, Switzerland, and France, the couple moved to New Orleans, where Chopin's husband was a cotton factor (a businessman who financed the raising of cotton and transacted its sale). Oscar Chopin prospered at first, but in 1878 and 1879, the period of the great "Yellow Jack" epidemic and of disastrously poor harvests, he suffered reverses. The Chopin family then went to live in rural Louisiana, where, at Cloutierville, Oscar Chopin managed some small plantations he owned. By all accounts, the Chopin marriage was an unusually happy one, and in time Kate became the mother of six children. This period in Kate's life ended, however, in 1883 with the sudden death, from swamp fever, of her husband. A widow at the age of thirty, Chopin remained at Cloutierville for a year, overseeing her husband's property, and then moved to St. Louis, where she remained for the rest of her life. She began to write in 1888, while still rearing her children, and in the following year she made her first appearance in print. As her writing shows, her marriage to Oscar Chopin proved to be much more than an "episode" in her life, for it is from this period in New Orleans and Natchitoches Parish that she drew her best literary material and her strongest inspiration. She knew this area personally, and yet as an "outsider" was also able to observe it with the freshness of detachment.

Considering the fact that she had only begun to have her stories published in 1889, it is remarkable that Chopin should already have written and published her first novel, *At Fault*, by 1890. The novel is apprenticeship work and was published by a St. Louis company at her own expense, but it does show a sense of form. She then wrote a second novel, *Young Dr. Gosse*, which in 1891 she sent out to a number of publishers, all of whom refused it, and that she later destroyed. After finishing this second novel, she concentrated on the shorter forms of fiction, writing forty stories, sketches, and vignettes during the next three years. By 1894, her stories began to find a reception in eastern magazines, notably in *Vogue*, *The Atlantic Monthly*, and *Century*. In the same year, her first short-story collection, *Bayou Folk*, was published by Houghton Mifflin to favorable reviews. Even so, because short-story collections were not commercially profitable, she had difficulty placing her second collection, *A Night in Acadie*, which was brought out by a relatively little-known publisher in Chicago in 1897.

Although having achieved some reputation as an author of what were generally perceived to be local-color stories set in northern Louisiana, Chopin was still far from having established herself as a writer whose work was commercially profitable. Under the advice of editors that a longer work would have a broader appeal, she turned again to the novel form, publishing *The Awakening* in 1899. *The Awakening*, however, received uniformly unfavorable reviews, and in some cities it was banned from library shelves. In St. Louis, Chopin was cut by friends and refused membership in a local fine arts club. Chopin had never expected such a storm of condemnation and, although she withstood it calmly, she was, according to those who knew her best, deeply hurt by the experience. She wrote little thereafter and never published another book. In 1904, after attending the St. Louis World's Fair, she was stricken with a cerebral hemorrhage and died two days later.

With her death, Chopin's reputation went into almost total eclipse. In literary histories written early in the century, her work was mentioned only in passing, with brief mention of her local-color stories but none at all of *The Awakening*. Even in the first biography of Chopin, Daniel S. Rankin's *Kate Chopin and Her Creole Stories* (1932), *The Awakening* was passed over quickly as a "morbid" book. The modern discovery of Chopin did not begin until the early 1950's, when the French critic Cyrille Arnavon translated *The Awakening* into French, with an introduction in which he discussed Chopin's writing as early realism comparable in some respects to that of Frank Norris and Theodore Dreiser.

In essays written in the mid-1950's, Robert Cantwell and Kenneth Eble called attention to *The Awakening* as a neglected work of classic stature. The belated recognition of *The Awakening* gained momentum during the 1960's when Edmund Wilson included a discussion of Chopin in *Patriotic Gore: Studies in the Literature of the American Civil War* (1963), in which he described *The Awakening* as a "quite uninhibited and beautifully written [novel] which anticipates D. H. Lawrence in its treatment of infidelity." By the mid-1960's, *The Awakening* was reprinted for the first time in half a century, and critics such as Werner Berthoff, Larzer Ziff, and George Arms all praised it warmly; Ziff called the novel "the most important piece of fiction about the sexual life of a woman written to date in America." With the publication of Per Seyersted's *Kate Chopin: A Critical Biography* (1969) and his edition of her writing, *The Complete Works of Kate Chopin* (1969), Chopin's work at long last became fully available. She has been of particular interest to feminist scholars, but interest in her has not been limited to a single group. It is now generally conceded that Chopin was one of the significant writers of the 1890's, and *The Awakening* is commonly viewed as a small masterpiece.

Analysis • When Kate Chopin began to publish, local-color writing, which came into being after the Civil War and crested during the 1880's, had already been established. Bret Harte and Mark Twain had created a special ambience for their fiction in the American West; Sarah Orne Jewett and Mary Wilkins Freeman had drawn their characters in the context of a New England world in decline; and the Creole culture of New Orleans and the plantation region beyond it had been depicted by George Washington Cable, Grace King, and Ruth McEnery Stuart.

At Fault • A late arriver to the scene, Chopin was at first, as her stories show, uncertain even of her locale. *At Fault*, her first novel, was a breakthrough for her in the sense that she found her rural Louisiana "region." The novel is set in the present, a setting that is important to its sphere of action. Place-du-Bois, the plantation, represents conservative, traditional values that are challenged by new, emergent ones. David Hosmer, from St. Louis, obtains lumber rights on Place-du-Bois, and with him comes conflict. *At Fault* deals with divorce, but beyond that, it addresses the contradictions of nature and convention. Place-du-Bois seems at times idyllic, but it is shadowed by the cruelties of its slaveholding past, abuses created by too rigidly held assumptions. St. Louis is almost the opposite, a world as much without form as Hosmer's pretty young wife, who goes to pieces there and again at Place-du-Bois.

A problem novel, *At Fault* looks skeptically at nature but also at received convention. Intelligent and thought out, it raises a question that will appear again in *The Awakening*: Are individuals responsible to others or to themselves? The characters in *At Fault* tend to be merely vehicles for ideas, while in the short stories that follow it,

Chopin's ability to create characters with an emotional richness becomes apparent. If *At Fault* suggests the symmetrical social novels of William Dean Howells, *Bayou Folk* gives the impression of southern folk writing brought to a high degree of perfection. The dominant theme in this collection is the universality of illusion, while the stories in *A Night in Acadie* prepare for *The Awakening*, in which a married woman, her self-assertion stifled in a conventional marriage, is awakened to the sensuous and erotic life.

Comparable in kind to Gustave Flaubert's *Madame Bovary* (1857), *The Awakening* is Chopin's most elaborate orchestration of the theme of bondage and illusion. Dramatic in form, intensely focused, it makes use of imagery and symbolism to an extent never before evident in Chopin's work. The boldness of her possession of theme in *The Awakening* is wholly remarkable. Her earliest effort in the novel, *At Fault*, asked if individuals were responsible to others or to themselves, a question that is raised again in *The Awakening*. *At Fault*, however, deals with its characters conventionally, on the surface only, while in *The Awakening* Chopin captures the deep, inner life of Edna Pontellier and projects it powerfully upon a world of convention.

In *At Fault*, Chopin drew upon her familiarity with two regions, St. Louis and the plantation country north of New Orleans. The hero, David Hosmer, comes to Louisiana from St. Louis, like Chopin herself, and at least one segment of the novel is set in St. Louis. The heroine, Thérèse Lafirme, proprietress of Place-du-Bois, is similar to Chopin—a widow at the age of thirty who carries on the management of her late husband's property. Moreover, her plantation of four thousand acres is of the same size as and seems suggested by that of Chopin's father-in-law, who had purchased it from the notorious Robert McAlpine, the model for Harriet Beecher Stowe's Simon Legree in *Uncle Tom's Cabin* (1852). In Chopin's novel, attention is called specifically to McAlpine, the former owner of the property, whose ghost is said to walk abroad at night in expiation of his cruel deeds.

Apart from its two settings, *At Fault* does not seem autobiographical. It has the form of a problem novel, reminiscent of the novels of Howells, to whom Chopin sent a copy of the work when it was published. As in certain of Howells's novels, a discussion takes place at one point that frames the conflict that the characters' lives illustrate. In this case it is the conflict between nature and convention, religious and social precept versus the data of actual experience. Thérèse Lafirme, although a warm and attractive woman, is accustomed to thinking about human affairs abstractly. When she learns that David Hosmer, who owns a sawmill on her property, is divorced from his young wife, a weak and susceptible woman who drinks, she admonishes him to return to her and fulfill his marriage pledge to stand by and redeem her. Hosmer admires Thérèse to such an extent that, against his own judgment, and most reluctantly, he returns to St. Louis and remarries Fanny Larimore. They then return to the plantation to live, and in due course history repeats itself. Despite Hosmer's dutiful attentions and her acceptance into the small social world of Place-du-Bois, Fanny begins to drink and to behave unreasonably. Near the end of the novel, having become jealous of Thérèse, Fanny ventures out in a storm and, despite Hosmer's attempt to rescue her, dies in a river flood.

Running parallel to this main plot is a subplot in which Hosmer's sister Melicent feels a romantic attraction to Thérèse's impetuous young nephew Grégoire, but decides on the most theoretical grounds that he would not be suitable for a husband. When he becomes involved in a marginal homicide, she condemns him utterly, literally abandoning him. He then returns to Texas, where he goes from bad to worse and is eventually killed in a lawless town. At the end, a year after these events, Hosmer and Thérèse marry and find the happiness they had very nearly lost through Thérèse's preconceptions. It is clear to her that Fanny never *could* have been redeemed, and that her plan to "save" her had brought suffering to all parties concerned—to Hosmer, herself, and to Fanny as well. Left open, however, is the question of Melicent's responsiblity to Grégoire, whom she had been too quick to "judge." *At Fault* appears to end happily, but in some ways it is pessimistic in its view of nature and convention.

At Fault shows a questioning intelligence and has an architectural competence, but it is still apprenticeship work. The St. Louis setting, especially in comparison to her southern one, is pallid, and the characters encountered there are lifeless. Fanny's associates in St. Louis include Mrs. Lorenzo (Belle) Worthington, who has dyed blond hair, and Mrs. Jack (Lou) Dawson, who has an expressionless face and "meaningless blue eyes set to a good humored readiness for laughter." These lady idlers, Belle and Lou, are stick figures. Although given a stronger individuality, the more important characters also tend to be typed. Grégoire is typed by his vulnerability and impetuousness, just as Melicent is drawn to type as an immature girl who does not know her mind.

The plot of *At Fault* is perhaps too symmetrical, too predictable in its outcome, with the irredeemability of Fanny Larimore a foregone conclusion. Moreover, in attempting to add emotional richness to the work, Chopin has sometimes resorted to melodramatic occurrences, such as Joçint's setting fire to the mill, his death at the hands of Grégoire, the death of Joçint's father, Morico, the death of Grégoire, and the scene in which Fanny perishes in the storm. *At Fault* is essentially a realistic novel but resorts at times to romantic or melodramatic conventions. If Chopin fails to bring her novel to life, she does at times create suggestive characters such as Aunt Belindy, Thérèse's cook, who asks pointedly, "Whar you gwine live if you don' live in de worl'?" One also notes a tonal richness in the drawing of Thérèse Lafirme. Thérèse is not allowed in this work to be fully "herself," but she points the way to Chopin's later successes in fiction, the women Chopin creates from the soul.

The Awakening • In *The Awakening*, Chopin achieved her largest exploration of feminine consciousness. Edna Pontellier, its heroine, is always at the center of the novel, and nothing occurs that does not in some way bear upon her thoughts or developing sense of her situation. As a character who rejects her socially prescribed role as a wife and mother, Edna has a certain affinity with the "New Woman," much discussed during the 1890's, but her special modeling and the type of her experience suggest a French influence. Before beginning the novel, Chopin translated eight of Guy de Maupassant's stories. Two of these tales, "Solitude" and "Suicide," share with *The Awakening* the theme of illusion in erotic desire and the inescapability of the solitary self. Another, "Reveil," anticipates Chopin's novel in some incidents of its plot. At the same time, *The Awakening* seems to have been influenced by *Madame Bovary*. Certain parallels can be noticed in the experience of the two heroines—their repudiation of their husbands, estrangement, and eventual suicides. More important, Flaubert's craftsmanship informs the whole manner of Chopin's novel—its directness, lucidity, and economy of means; its steady use of incident and detail as leitmotif. The novel also draws upon a large fin de siècle background concerned with a hunger for the exotic and the voluptuous, a yearning for the absolute. From these diverse influences, Chopin has shaped a work that is strikingly, even startlingly, her own.

The opening of the third section of *The Awakening*, the chapter set at Grand Isle, is particularly impressive. Here one meets Edna Pontellier, the young wife of a well-to-do Creole *negociant* and mother of two small boys. Mrs. Pontellier, an "American" woman originally from Kentucky, is still not quite accustomed to the sensuous openness of this Creole summer colony. She walks on the beach under a white parasol with handsome young Robert Lebrun, who befriends married Creole women in a way that is harmless, since his attentions are regarded as a social pleasantry, nothing more. In the background are two young lovers, and not far behind them, keeping pace, a mysterious woman dressed in black who tells her beads. Edna Pontellier and Robert Lebrun have just returned from a midday swim in the ocean, an act undertaken on impulse and perhaps not entirely prudent, in view of the extreme heat of that hour and the scorching glare of the sun. When Edna rejoins her husband, he finds her "burnt beyond recognition." Léonce Pontellier is a responsible husband who gives his wife no cause for complaint, but his mind runs frequently on business and he is dull. He is inclined to regard his wife as "property," but by this summer on Grand Isle she has begun to come to self-awareness, suppressed by her role as a "mother-woman." Emboldened by her unconventional midday swim, she goes out swimming alone that night, and with reckless exhilaration longs to go "further out than any woman had ever swum before." She quickly tires, however, and is fortunate to have the strength to return to the safety of the shore. When she returns to their house, she does not go inside to join her husband but drowses alone in a porch hammock, lost in a long moonlit reverie that has the voluptuous effulgence of the sea.

As the novel proceeds, it becomes clear that Edna has begun to fall in love with Lebrun, who decides suddenly to go to Mexico, following which the Pontelliers themselves return to their well-appointed home in New Orleans. There Edna begins to behave erratically, defying her husband and leading as much as possible an independent existence. After moving to a small house nearby by herself, she has an affair with a young roué, Alcée Arobin; Lebrun returns from Mexico about the same time, and, although in love with her, does not dare to overstep convention with a married woman and the mother of children. Trapped once again within her socially prescribed role, Edna returns to the seashore and goes swimming alone, surrendering her life to the sea.

In its own time, *The Awakening* was criticized both for its subject matter and for its point of view. Reviewers repeatedly remarked that the erotic content of the novel was disturbing and distasteful and that Chopin had not only failed to censure Edna's "morbid" awakening but also had treated it sympathetically. What the reviewers failed to take into account was the subtlety and ambiguity of the novel's vision. For if Chopin enters deeply into Edna's consciousness, she also stands outside it with a severe objectivity. A close examination of *The Awakening* reveals that the heroine has been involved in illusion from the beginning. Edna sometimes meditates, for example, on the self-realization that has been blunted by her role as wife and mother; but in her rejection of her responsibilities she constantly tends toward vagueness rather than clarity.

The imagery of the sea expresses Edna's longing to reach a state in which she feels her own identity and where she feels passionately alive. The "voice" of the sea, beckoning Edna, is constantly in the background of the work. "The voice of the sea," Chopin writes, "speaks to the soul. The touch of the sea is sensuous, enfolding the body in its soft, close embrace." In this "enfolding," however, Edna discovers her own solitude and loses herself in "mazes of inward contemplation." In *Moby Dick* (1851), Herman Melville contrasts the land and the sea, the one convention bound, the other "open" and boldly, defiantly speculative, but Edna is no thinker; she is a dreamer who, in standing apart from conditioned circumstance, can only embrace the rhapsodic death lullaby of the sea.

At the end of her life, Edna returns to her childhood, when, in protest against the aridness of her Presbyterian father's Sunday devotions, she had wandered aimlessly in a field of tall meadow grass that made her think of the sea. She had married her Roman Catholic husband despite her father's objection, or rather, one thinks, *because* of his objection. Later, discovering the limitations that her life with her husband imposes upon her, she rebels once again, grasping at the illusion of an idealized Robert Lebrun. Edna's habit of idealization goes far back in her past. As a girl, she had fallen in love with a Confederate officer whom she had glimpsed, a noble figure belonging to a doomed cause, and also with a picture of a "tragedian."

The last lines of the novel, as Edna's consciousness ends, are: "The spurs of the cavalry officer clanged as he walked across the porch. There were the hum of bees, and the musky odor of pinks filled the air." Her consciousness at the end thus reverts back to its beginning, forming a circle from which she cannot escape. The final irony of *The Awakening*, however, is that even though Edna is drawn as an illusionist, her protest is not quite meaningless. Never before in a novel published in America was the issue of a woman's suppressed erotic nature and need for self-definition, apart from the single received role of wife and mother, raised so forcefully. *The Awakening* is a work in which the feminist protest of the present had already been memorably imagined.

During the mid-1950's, Van Wyck Brooks described *The Awakening* as a "small perfect book that mattered more than the whole life work of many a prolific writer." In truth, *The Awakening* is not quite "perfect." Chopin loses some of her power when she moves from Grand Isle to New Orleans. The guests at her dinner party, characters with names such as Mrs. Highcamp and Miss Mayblunt, are two-dimensional and wooden, and at times the symbolic connotation of incidents seems too unvaried. *The Awakening*, certainly, would be embarrassed by comparison with a large, panoramic novel of marital infidelity such as Leo Tolstoy's *Anna Karenina* (1875-1877). Yet, within its limits, it reveals work of the finest craftsmanship and is a novel that, well after having been read, continues to linger in the reader's consciousness. Chopin was not prolific; all but a few of her best stories are contained in *Bayou Folk* and *A Night in Acadie*, and she produced only one mature novel, but these volumes have the mark of genuine quality. Lyric and objective at once, deeply humane and yet constantly attentive to illusion in her characters' perception of reality, these volumes reveal Chopin as a psychological realist of magical empathy, a writer having the greatness of delicacy.

Robert Emmet Long

Other major works

SHORT FICTION: *Bayou Folk*, 1894; *A Night in Acadie*, 1897.

NONFICTION: *Kate Chopin's Private Papers*, 1998.

MISCELLANEOUS: *The Complete Works of Kate Chopin*, 1969 (2 volumes; Per Seyersted, editor).

Bibliography

Beer, Janet, and Elizabeth Nolan, eds. *Kate Chopin's "The Awakening": A Sourcebook.* New York: Routledge, 2004. Handy guide for students studying Chopin's best-known novel.

Benfey, Christopher E. G., *Degas in New Orleans: Encounters in the Creole World of Kate Chopin and George Washington Cable.* Berkeley: University of California Press, 1999. Exploration of the culture of late nineteenth century New Orleans that touches on how George Washington Cable and Kate Chopin used New Orleans themes in their writings.

Bonner, Thomas, Jr. *The Kate Chopin Companion.* New York: Greenwood Press, 1988. A guide, arranged alphabetically, to the more than nine hundred characters and over two hundred places that affected the course of Chopin's stories. Also includes a selection of her translations of pieces by Guy de Maupassant and one by Adrien Vely. Contains interesting period maps and a useful bibliographic essay.

Boren, Lynda S., and Sara de Saussure Davis, eds. *Kate Chopin Reconsidered: Beyond the Bayou.* Baton Rouge: Louisiana State University Press, 1992. Although most of these essays focus on *The Awakening*, several discuss such stories as "Charlie," "After the Winter," and "At Cheniere Caminada." Other essays compare Chopin with playwright Henrik Ibsen in terms of domestic confinement and discuss her work from a Marxist point of view.

Brown, Pearl L. "Awakened Men in Kate Chopin's Creole Stories." *ATQ*, n.s. 13, no. 1 (March, 1999). Argues that in Chopin's Creole stories, in intimate moments women discover inner selves buried beneath socially imposed ones, and men discover subjective selves buried beneath public personas.

Erickson, Jon. "Fairytale Features in Kate Chopin's 'Désirée's Baby': A Case Study in Genre Cross-Reference." In *Modes of Narrative*, edited by Reingard M. Nischik and Barbara Korte. Würzburg: Königshausen and Neumann, 1990. Shows how Chopin's story conflicts with the expectations set up by the fairy-tale genre on which it is based; for example, the prince turns out to be the villain. Argues that the ending of the story is justified, for in the fairy tale the mystery of origin must be solved and the villain must be punished.

Petry, Alice Hall, ed. *Critical Essays on Kate Chopin.* New York: G. K. Hall, 1996. A comprehensive collection of essays on Chopin. This volume reprints early evaluations of the author's life and works as well as more modern scholarly analyses. In addition to a substantial introduction by the editor, it also includes seven original essays by such notable scholars as Linda Wagner-Martin and Heather Kirk Thomas.

Seyersted, Per. *Kate Chopin: A Critical Biography.* Baton Rouge: Louisiana State University Press, 1980. Seyersted's biography, besides providing invaluable information about the New Orleans of the 1870's, examines Chopin's life, views, and work. Provides lengthy discussions not only of *The Awakening* but also of her many short stories. Seyersted sees her as a transitional literary figure, a link between George Sand and Simone de Beauvoir.

Skaggs, Peggy. *Kate Chopin.* Boston: Twayne, 1985. Skaggs reads Chopin's work in terms of the theme of the search for identity, which pervades the two chapters devoted to Chopin's short fiction. Also included in this helpful overview of Chopin's life and work are a biographical chapter, a chronology, and a select bibliography. The book is indispensable for readers of Chopin's short fiction.

Toth, Emily. *Kate Chopin.* New York: William Morrow, 1990. Toth's thoroughly documented, exhaustive work is the definitive Chopin biography. She covers not only Chopin's life but also her literary works and discusses many of the short stories in considerable detail. Toth updates Per Seyersted's bibliography of Chopin's work, supplies a helpful chronology of her life, and discusses the alleged banning of *The Awakening.* The starting point for Chopin research.

———. *Unveiling Kate Chopin.* Jackson: University Press of Mississippi, 1999. Using newly discovered manuscripts, letters, and diaries of Chopin, Toth examines the source of Chopin's ambition and passion for her art, arguing that she worked much harder at her craft than previously thought.

James Fenimore Cooper

Born: Burlington, New Jersey; September 15, 1789
Died: Cooperstown, New York; September 14, 1851

Principal long fiction • *Precaution: A Novel,* 1820; *The Spy: A Tale of the Neutral Ground,* 1821; *The Pilot: A Tale of the Sea,* 1823; *The Pioneers: Or, The Sources of the Susquehanna,* 1823; *Lionel Lincoln: Or, The Leaguer of Boston,* 1825; *The Last of the Mohicans: A Narrative of 1757,* 1826; *The Prairie: A Tale,* 1827; *The Red Rover: A Tale,* 1827; *The Wept of Wish-Ton-Wish: A Tale,* 1829; *The Water-Witch: Or, The Skimmer of the Seas,* 1830; *The Bravo: A Tale,* 1831; *The Heidenmauer: Or, The Benedictines—A Tale of the Rhine,* 1832; *The Headsman: Or, The Abbaye des Vignerons,* 1833; *The Monikens,* 1835; *Home as Found,* 1838; *Homeward Bound: Or, The Chase,* 1838; *Mercedes of Castile: Or, The Voyage to Cathay,* 1840; *The Pathfinder: Or, The Inland Sea,* 1840; *The Deerslayer: Or, The First War-Path,* 1841; *The Two Admirals: A Tale,* 1842; *The Wing-and-Wing: Or, Le Feu-Follet,* 1842; *Le Mouchoir: An Autobiographical Romance,* 1843 (also known as *Autobiography of a Pocket Handkerchief*); *Wyandotté: Or, The Hutted Knoll,* 1843; *Afloat and Ashore: A Sea Tale,* 1844; *Miles Wallingford: Sequel to Afloat and Ashore,* 1844; *Satanstoe: Or, The Littlepage Manuscripts, a Tale of the Colony,* 1845; *The Chainbearer: Or, The Littlepage Manuscripts,* 1845; *The Redskins: Or, Indian and Injin, Being the Conclusion of the Littlepage Manuscripts,* 1846; *The Crater: Or, Vulcan's Peak, a Tale of the Pacific,* 1847; *Jack Tier: Or, The Florida Reef,* 1848; *The Oak Openings: Or, The Bee Hunter,* 1848; *The Sea Lions: Or, The Lost Sealers,* 1849; *The Ways of the Hour,* 1850.

Other literary forms • Although James Fenimore Cooper was primarily a novelist, he also tried his hand at short stories, biographies, and a play. Among these works, only the biographies are considered significant. He also wrote accounts of his European travels, history, and essays on politics and society. Among his political writings, *The American Democrat* (1838) retains its appeal as an analysis of contemporary political and social issues and as an expression of Cooper's mature political and social thought. His *The History of the Navy of the United States of America* (1839, two volumes) is still considered a definitive work. Cooper was an active correspondent. Many of his letters and journals have been published, but large quantities of material remain in the hands of private collectors.

Achievements • Though he is best known as the author of the Leatherstocking Tales, Cooper has come to be recognized as America's first great social historian. The Leatherstocking Tales—*The Pioneers, The Last of the Mohicans, The Prairie, The Pathfinder,* and *The Deerslayer*—are those novels in which the frontier hunter and scout, Natty Bumppo, is a central character. Along with *The Spy* and *The Pilot,* two novels of the American Revolution, the Leatherstocking Tales are familiar to modern readers, and critics agree that these are Cooper's best novels. Less well known are the novels he began writing during his seven-year residence in Europe, his problem and society novels. In these books, he works out and expresses a complex social and political theory and a social history of America seen within the context of the major modern developments of European civilization. Because his problem and society novels often are marred by overstatement and repetition, they are rarely read for pleasure, but they remain, as Robert Spiller argues, among the most detailed and accurate pictures available of major aspects of American society and thought in the early nineteenth century.

Cooper achieved international reputation with *The Spy*, his second novel, which was translated into most European languages soon after its publication. With this work, he also invented a popular genre, the spy novel. He is credited with having invented the Western in the Leatherstocking Tales and the sea adventure with *The Pilot*, another popular success. His ability to tell tales of romance and adventure in convincingly and often beautifully described settings won for him a devoted readership and earned a title he came eventually to resent, "The American Scott." His reputation began to decline when he turned to concerned criticism of American society. Though his goal in criticism was always amelioration through the affirmation of basic principles, Cooper's aristocratic manner and his frequent opposition to popular ideas made him increasingly unpopular with the public. The political and social atmosphere was not favorable to his opinions, and his works routinely received scathing reviews as pretentious and aristocratic, also as politically motivated and self-serving. As Spiller argues, Cooper was too much a man of principle to use consciously his public position for personal ends. His suits against the press to establish a definition of libel, his exploration of the principles of democracy in his novels and essays, and his careful and objective research in his naval histories and biographies reveal a man who passionately sought truth and justice regardless of the effect on his popularity.

Though his popularity declined after 1833, Cooper continued writing with energy. In his thirty-year writing career, he wrote more than thirty novels, the naval history, several significant social works, and many other works as well. Howard Mumford Jones credits Cooper with early American developments of the international theme, the theme of the Puritan conscience, the family saga, the utopian and dystopian novel, and the series novel. By general agreement, Cooper stands at the headwaters of the American tradition of fiction; he contributed significantly to the themes and forms of the American novel.

Biography • James Cooper was born in Burlington, New Jersey, on September 15, 1789, the twelfth of thirteen children of William and Elizabeth Cooper. He added "Fenimore" in 1826 in memory of his mother's family. Elizabeth Fenimore was an heir whose wealth contributed to William Cooper's success in buying and developing a large tract of land on which he founded Cooperstown, New York. Cooper's father, descended from English Quakers, expressed enlightened ideas about developing wilderness lands in his *A Guide in the Wilderness* (1810). William Cooper and Cooperstown became models for Judge Temple and Templeton in *The Pioneers*. The Coopers moved to Cooperstown in 1790, and Cooper grew up there as the son of the community's developer and benefactor, a gentleman who eventually became a judge and a Federalist congressman. Cooper's conservative Enlightenment views of the frontier, of American culture, and of democracy had their roots in his Cooperstown youth.

Like many sons of the wealthy gentry, Cooper had some difficulty deciding what to do with his life. In his third year at Yale, he was dismissed for misconduct. In 1806, he began a naval career that led to a commission in the U.S. Navy in 1808, and he served on Lake Ontario, scene of *The Pathfinder*. In 1809, his father died from a blow delivered from behind by a political opponent, and Cooper came into a large inheritance. In 1811, he married Susan Augusta DeLancey, of an old and respectable Tory family, and he resigned from the Navy. For eight years he lived the life of a country gentleman, eventually fathering seven children. By 1819, however, because of the financial failures and deaths of all his brothers, which left him responsible for some of their families, Cooper found himself in financial difficulty. Cooper began writing at this time, not with the hope of making money—there was no precedent for achieving a living as an author—but in response to a challenge from his wife to write a better novel than one he happened to be reading to her. After he began, Cooper found in various ways the energy and motivation to make writing his career. Susan's support and the family's continued domestic tranquility inspired Cooper's writing and protected him from what he came to see as an increasingly hostile public.

Courtesy, New York State Historical Association

The success of *The Spy* and of his next four novels made him secure enough in 1826 to take his family to Europe, where he hoped to educate his children and to improve the foreign income from his books. While living in Paris and London and traveling at a leisurely pace through most of Europe, Cooper involved himself in French and Polish politics and published several works. Before his return to the United States in 1833, he met Sir Walter Scott, became intimate with Marie de La Fayette, aided the sculptor Horatio Greenough in beginning his career, and cultivated his lifelong friendship with Samuel Morse. This period of travel was another turning point in his life. In *Notions of the Americans* (1828), Cooper wrote an idealized defense of American democracy that offended both his intended audiences, the Americans and the English. When he went on to publish a series of novels set in Europe (1831-1833), Cooper provided American reviewers with more reasons to see him as an apostate. Upon his return to America, he tended to confirm this characterization by announcing his retirement as a novelist and publishing a group of travel books, satires, and finally a primer on republican democracy, *The American Democrat.* When he returned to writing novels with *Homeward Bound* and *Home as Found* in 1838, he indicated that he had found America much decayed on his return from Europe. The promises of a democratic republic he had expressed in *Notions of the Americans* were fading before the abuse of the Constitution by demagogues and the increasing tyranny of the majority. *The American Democrat* was, in part, a call to return to the original principles of the republic.

Having resettled in Cooperstown in 1833, Cooper soon found himself embroiled in controversies over land title and libel, controversies that the press used to foster the image of Cooper as a self-styled aristocrat. He is credited with establishing important legal precedents in the libel cases he won against editors such as Thurlow Weed and Horace Greeley. By 1843, Cooper's life had become more tranquil. He had settled down to the most productive period of his life, producing sixteen novels between 1840 and 1851; among them are many marred by obtrusive discussions of political and social issues, but also several that are considered American classics, such as *The Pathfinder* and *The Deerslayer*, the last two of the Leatherstocking Tales. His last five novels show evidence of increasing interest in religious ideas. Though Cooper had been active in religious institutions all his life, and though all his novels express Christian beliefs, he was not confirmed as an Episcopalian until the last year of his life. He died at Cooperstown on September 14, 1851.

Analysis • James Fenimore Cooper was a historian of America. His novels span American history, dramatizing central events from Columbus's discovery (*Mercedes of Castile*) through the French and Indian Wars and the early settlement (the Leatherstocking Tales) to the Revolution (*The Spy* and *The Pilot*) and the contemporary events of the Littlepage and the Miles Wallingford novels. In some of his European novels, he examined major intellectual developments, such as the Reformation, which he thought important to American history, and in many of his novels, he reviewed the whole of American history, attempting to complete his particular vision of America by inventing a tradition for the new nation. Modern criticism is divided concerning the meaning and nature of Cooper's tradition. Following the lead of D. H. Lawrence, a group of myth critics have concentrated on unconscious elements in Cooper's works, while Robert Spiller and a group of social and historical critics have concentrated more on his conscious opinions.

In his *Studies in Classic American Literature* (1923), Lawrence argued that Cooper's myth of America is centered in the friendship between Natty Bumppo and his American Indian friend, Chingachgook, and in the order of composition of the Leatherstocking Tales. Of the friendship, Lawrence says, Cooper "dreamed a new human relationship deeper than the deeps of sex. Deeper than property, deeper than fatherhood, deeper than marriage, deeper than love. . . . This is the nucleus of a new society, the clue to a new epoch." Of the order of writing, he says that the novels "go backwards, from old age to golden youth. That is the true myth of America. She starts old, old and wrinkled in an old skin. And there is a gradual sloughing of the old skin, towards a new youth." These insightful statements have been elaborated by critics who have looked deeply into Cooper's works but who have concentrated most of their attention on the Leatherstocking Tales in order to find in Cooper affinities with Herman Melville, Mark Twain, and others who seem to find it necessary, like Natty Bumppo, to remain apart from social institutions to preserve their integrity. Because these critics tend to focus on Leatherstocking and mythic elements in the tales, they may be better guides to American myth than to Cooper. Although Cooper contributes images and forms to what became myths in the hands of others, his own mind seems to have been occupied more with making American society than with escaping it.

Another more traditional mythic pattern pervades all of his works, including the Leatherstocking Tales. Several critics have called attention to a key passage in *The Last of the Mohicans* when Natty describes the waterfall where the scout and his party take refuge from hostile Native Americans. The pattern of a unified flow falling into disorder and rebellion only to be gathered back again by the hand of Providence into a new order not only is descriptive of the plot of this novel but also suggests other levels of meaning that are reflected throughout Cooper's work, for it defines Cooper's essentially Christian and Enlightenment worldview, a view that he found expressed, though with too monarchical a flavor, in Alexander Pope's *Essay on Man* (1733-1734).

In *Home as Found*, Cooper sees the same pattern in the development of frontier settlements. They begin with a pastoral stage in which people of all kinds cooperate freely and easily to make a new land support them. The second stage is anarchic, for when freed of the demanding laws of necessity, society begins to divide as interests consolidate into factions and as families struggle for power and position. Though it appears painful and disorderly, this phase is the natural, providential reordering process toward a mature society. In the final phase, established, mutually respecting, and interdependent classes make possible a high civilization. In *The American Democrat*, Cooper often echoes Pope's *Essay on Man* as he explains that human life in this world is a fall into disorder where the trials exceed the pleasures; this apparent disorder, however, is a merciful preparation for a higher life to come. Many of Cooper's novels reflect this pattern; characters leave or are snatched out of their reasonably ordered world to be educated in a dangerous and seemingly disordered one, only to be returned after an educational probation into a more familiarly ordered world, there to contribute to its improvement. This pattern of order, separation, and reintegration pervades Cooper's thought and gives form to his conscious dream of America. He came to see America as moving through the anarchic and purifying phase of the Revolution toward a new society that would allow the best that is in fallen humankind to be realized. This dream is expressed, in part, in *The Pioneers*.

The Pioneers • *The Pioneers* is Cooper's first great novel, the first he composed primarily to satisfy himself. The popular success of *The Spy* increased both his freedom and his confidence, encouraging him to turn to what proved to be his richest source of material, the frontier life of New York State. This first novel in the Leatherstocking series has a complex double organization which is an experimental response to what Robert Spiller sees as Cooper's main artistic problem, the adaptation of forms developed in aristocratic civilized Europe to his democratic frontier material. On one hand, *The Pioneers* describes daily life in the new village of Templeton on Otsego Lake and is ordered within a frame of seasonal change from Christmas, 1793, until the following autumn. Behind this organization, on the other hand, stands a hidden order that gradually reveals itself as the story unfolds; central to this plot is the transfer of title of the largest portion of land in the district from Judge Marmaduke Temple to Edward Oliver Effingham. These two structures interact to underline the providential inevitability and significance of this transfer.

The seasonal ordering of events brings out the nature of the community at Templeton at this particular point in its development. Templeton is shown to be suspended between two forms of order. Representing the old order are the seventy-year-old Natty Bumppo, the Leatherstocking, and his aged Indian friend, John Mohegan, whose actual name is Chingachgook. The forest is their home and their mediator with divine law. Natty, through his contact with Chingachgook and his life in the forest, has become the best man that such a life can produce. He combines true Christian principles with the skills and knowledge of the best of American Indian civilization. Natty and the Indian live an ideal kind of life, given the material circumstances of their environment, but that environment is changing. Otsego Lake is becoming settled and civilized. Chingachgook remains because he wishes to live where his ancestors once dwelt. Natty stays with his friend. Their presence becomes a source of conflict.

The new order is represented at first by Judge Temple, but the form of that order remains somewhat obscure until the revealing of motives and identities at the end of the novel. Temple's main function in the community is moral. He is important as the owner and developer of the land. He has brought settlers to the land, helped them through troubled times, and, largely at his own expense, built the public buildings and established the institutions of Templeton. During the transition to civilization, Temple is a center of order, organization, and—most important—restraint. In part through his efforts, the legislature is enacting laws to restrain the settlers in the state. Restraint on two kinds of behavior is necessary. On one hand, there are characters such as Billy Kirby, whose wasteful use of community resources stems primarily from the inability to understand the needs of a settled country. These individuals live in the old forest world but without the old forest values. On the other hand, there are the settlers themselves: Some, such as Richard Jones and Hiram Doolittle, tend toward cupidity, while others, such as the community's poor, are so unaccustomed to having plenty that they waste it when they have it. These attitudes are shown in the famous scenes of pigeon shooting and lake fishing, and they are pointedly contrasted with the old values practiced by Natty and Chingachgook. The settlers need restraint; Judge Temple feels in himself the desire to overharvest the plentiful natural resources of Templeton and knows at first hand the importance of restraining laws that will force the settlers to live by an approximation of the divine law by which Natty lives.

The central conflict in the seasonal ordering of the novel is between Natty, who lives by the old law, the natural law of the forest that reflects the divine law, and the settlers, who are comparatively lawless. This conflict is complicated as the new restraining civil laws come into effect and the lawless members of the community exploit and abuse those laws in order to harass Natty. Hiram Doolittle, a justice of the peace, and Richard Jones, the sheriff, become convinced that Natty is secretly mining silver on Judge Temple's land. In reality, Natty is concealing the aged and senile original white owner of this land, Major Effingham, helping to care for the old man until his grandson, Oliver Effingham, is able to move him to better circumstances. Doolittle succeeds at maneuvering the law and its institutions so that Judge Temple must fine and jail Natty for resisting an officer of the law. Thus, Natty becomes a victim of the very laws designed to enforce his own highest values, underlining the weakness of human nature and illustrating the cyclical pattern of anarchy, order, and repression and abuse of the law. When Doolittle's machinations are revealed and Natty is freed, he announces his intent to move west into the wilderness that is his proper home.

The conflict between the old order and the new is resolved only in part by Natty's apparent capitulation and retreat into the wilderness. Before Natty leaves, he performs a central function in the land transfer plot, a function which infuses the values of the old order into the new order. The land to which Judge Temple holds title was given to Major Effingham by a council of the Delaware chiefs at the time of the French and Indian Wars. In recognition of his qualities as a faithful and brave warrior, Effingham was adopted into the tribe as a son of Chingachgook. In this exchange, the best of Native American civilization recognized its own qualities in a superior form in Effingham, a representative of the best of European Christian civilization. This method of transfer is crucial because it amounts to a gentleman's agreement ratified by family ties; the transfer is a voluntary expression of values and seems providentially ordained. The history of the land, as it passes from the Major to his son, illustrates these same values. The Major confidently gives his son control over his estates, knowing that his son will care for them as a gentleman should. Generosity and honor, rather than greed and violence, characterize these transfers.

For the transfer to be complete, the owners must be Americanized by means of the American Revolution. This process is a purification which brings to culmination in Oliver the traditions of American democracy and European and American Indian aristocracy. The Effinghams are a Tory family. Oliver's father and Judge Temple are brothers in honor, a civilized reflection of Natty and Chingachgook. Temple is an example of Americanized aristocracy. His aristocratic family had declined in the New World, but beginning with his father, they reemerged as democratic "aristocrats," what Cooper referred to as gentlemen. A gentleman is one whose superior talents are favored by education and comparative leisure to fit him as a moral leader of the community. The gentleman differs from the Old World aristocrat in that he has no hereditary title to political power. In the ideal republic, the gentleman is recognized for his attainments by the common people, who may be expected to choose freely their political leaders from among the gentry. The Effinghams have not undergone this Americanizing process. The process is portrayed in the novel in Oliver Effingham's resentful efforts to restore his grandfather to his accustomed way of life.

Oliver labors under the mistaken idea that Temple has usurped his family's land, but as the final revelations show, the Americanized gentleman has remained faithful, holding the land in trust for the Effinghams to take once they have become American. Oliver's deprivation, the military defeat of his family, and his working in disguise for Judge Temple are lessons in humility that reveal to him the moral equality between himself and the Temples. Without such an experience, he might well consider himself above the Judge's daughter, Elizabeth, unable to marry her and unable to bring together the two parts of the estate. The other main component of Oliver's transformation comes under the tutelage of Natty and Chingachgook, who attempt to impress upon Oliver, as well as upon Elizabeth, their obligations to the land and to its previous owners. Through this two-pronged education, the aristocrat becomes a gentleman, and the breach caused by the American Revolution is healed. This healing is manifested most clearly in the marriage of Oliver and Elizabeth. The best of the Old World is recognized by the best of New World Indians and, by means of the Revolution, is purified of its antidemocratic prejudices; the aristocrat becomes a gentleman worthy to rule in America.

The transfer of title takes place within the context of inevitable seasonal change; its rhythm of tension and crisis reflects similar events within the seasons. The transition from the old order of Native American occupation to the new order of white democratic civilization is shown, despite local tensions and conflicts, to be providentially ordered when viewed from a sufficient distance. Within the seasons as well as in the human actions, the central theme of displacement underlines and elaborates the meaning of the overall movement.

The novel is filled with displaced persons. Remarkable Pettibone is displaced as mistress of the Temple mansion by Elizabeth. Natty and Chingachgook are displaced by white civilization. Oliver is displaced by the American Revolution, Le Quoi by the French Revolution. Finally, Judge Temple is displaced as the first power in the community. Within this thematic pattern, two general kinds of resolution occur. Oliver, Chingachgook, and Le Quoi are variously restored to their proper places, though Chingachgook must die in order to rejoin his tribe. Pettibone and

Temple come to accept their displacement by their superiors. Natty is unique. His displacement seems destined for repetition until Providence finally civilizes the continent and no place is left that is really his home. For him, as for Chingachgook, only death seems to offer an end to displacement. Natty's legacy must live on, however, in those gentlemen who combine "nature and refinement," and there is some hope that in a mature American society, Natty as well as good American Indians might find a home.

Critics tend to see Natty as an idealized epic hero who is too good for any society he encounters, but this is not quite true. In each of the books in which he appears, he acts as a conserver of essential values. This role is clearest when he teaches Elizabeth the ethics of fishing for one's food and when he saves her and Oliver from a fire on the mountain. His complaints about the "wasty ways" of civilization and about the laws that ought to be unnecessary are a part of this function. Though he fails to understand the weaknesses of civilized people and their need for the civil law, he still functions to further the best interests of civilization, not only by taming the wild but also by performing a role like that of the Old Testament prophets. He constantly calls people's attention back to the first principles of civilized life. In this respect, Natty is much like Cooper.

The Pioneers is a hopeful novel, for in it Cooper reveals a confidence in a providential ordering of history that will lead to the fulfillment of his ideas of a rational republic. This novel resolves the central anarchic displacements of the native inhabitants and of the traditional European ruling class by asserting that the American republic is the fruition of these two traditions. Though far from perfect, the American experiment seems, in this novel, to be destined for a unique success.

The Last of the Mohicans • *The Last of the Mohicans* is the best known of the Leatherstocking Tales, probably because it combines Cooper's most interesting characters and the relatively fast-paced adventure of *The Spy* and *The Pilot.* Set in the French and Indian Wars, this novel presents Natty and Chingachgook in their prime. Chingachgook's son, Uncas, is the last of the Mohican chiefs, the last of the line from which the Delaware nation is said to trace its origins. Although the novel moves straightforwardly through two adventures, it brings into these adventures a number of suggestive thematic elements.

The two main adventures are quests, with filial piety as their motive. Major Duncan Heyward attempts to escort Cora and Alice Munro to their father, commander of Fort William Henry on Horican Lake (Lake George). Led astray by Magua, an American Indian who seeks revenge against Munro, the party, which comes to include a comic psalmodist, David Gamut, encounters and enlists the help of Natty and his Indian companions. This quest is fully successful. Magua joins the Hurons who are leagued with the besieging French forces at William Henry and captures the original party, which is then rescued by Natty and his friends to be delivered safely to the doomed fort. This adventure is followed by an interlude at the fort in which Heyward obtains Munro's permission to court Alice and learns, to his own secret pain, that Cora has black blood. Also in this interlude, Munro learns he will get no support from nearby British troops and realizes that he must surrender his position. Montcalm allows him to remove his men and equipment from the fort before it is destroyed, but the discontented Native Americans, provoked by Magua, break the truce and massacre the retreating and exposed people for booty and scalps. Magua precipitates the next quest by capturing Alice and Cora and taking them, along with

David Gamut, north toward Canada. The second quest is the rescue mission of Natty, Chingachgook, Uncas, Heyward, and Munro. This attempt is only partly successful, for both Cora and Uncas are killed.

Cooper heightens the interest of these quests in part through a double love plot. During the first movement, Duncan and Alice come to love each other, and Uncas is attracted to Cora. Though thematically important, the first couple is not very interesting. Except for the slight misunderstanding with Munro that reveals the secret of Cora's ancestry, the barriers between Heyward and Alice are physical and temporal. More complicated and puzzling is the relationship between Cora and Uncas. Although Alice seems to spend most of the two quests calling on her father, weeping, and fainting, Cora shows a spirit and courage that make her an interesting character and that attract the admiration of Uncas. Magua is also interested in Cora, proposing in the first capture that if she will become his wife, he will cease his persecution of the rest of the family. Magua is primarily intent on revenge against Munro, but it seems clear that his interest in Cora as a woman grows until it may even supplant his revenge motive. Near the end of the novel, Natty offers himself in exchange for Cora, but even though Natty is a much more valuable prisoner, Magua prefers to keep Cora. When the hunted Magua's last remaining comrade kills Cora, Magua turns on him. Though there is no indication that Magua's is more than a physical passion, he seems strongly attracted to Cora, perhaps in part because of her courageous refusal to fear or to submit to him.

Critics have made much of the relationship between Cora, Uncas, and Magua, suggesting that Cooper gives Cora black blood to "sanitize" her potential relationship with Uncas and the heavenly marriage between them suggested in the final funeral service of the Indians. Cora becomes an early example of "the tragic mulatto" who has no place in the world where racial purity is highly valued. Natty insistently declares that even though he has adopted American Indian ways, he is "a man without a cross"; his blood is pure white. On the other hand, the three-part pattern that seems to dominate Cooper's historical vision might imply a real fulfillment in the Indian funeral that is intended to bring Cora and Uncas together in the next life. This incident may be as close as Cooper came to a vision of a new America such as Lawrence hints at, in which even the races are drawn together into a new unity. The division between races is a symptom of a fallen and perverse world. Natty more than once asserts that there is one God over all and, perhaps, one afterlife for all.

The first meeting of Heyward's party with Natty's party in the forest has an allegorical quality that looks forward to the best of Nathaniel Hawthorne and begins the development of the theme of evil, which—in Cooper's vision—can enjoy only a temporary triumph. Lost in the forest, misled by the false guide, Magua, this party from civilization has entered a seemingly anarchic world in which they are babes "without the knowledge of men." This meeting introduces two major themes: the conception of the wilderness as a book one must know how to read if one is to survive, and the conception of Magua and his Hurons as devils who have tempted Heyward's party into this world in order to work their destruction. Though Magua is represented in Miltonic terms as Satan, he is not so much a rebel angel as a product of "the colonial wars of North America." Magua's home is the "neutral territory" that the rival forces must cross in order to fight each other; he desires revenge on Munro for an imprudent act, an act that symbolizes the whites' disturbance of Magua's way of life. As Magua asserts, Munro provided the alcohol that unbalanced him, then whipped him for succumbing to that alcohol. Magua has most of the qualities of the good men:

courage, cunning, the ability to organize harmoniously talent and authority, and highly developed skills at reading the book of nature. He differs from Natty and his Native American companions, however, in that he allows himself to be governed by the evil passion of revenge rather than by unselfish rationality. Of his kind, the unselfishly rational men must be constantly suspicious. Montcalm's failure to control his Indian forces demonstrates that only the most concerted efforts can prevent great evil. The novel's end shows that ultimately only divine Providence can fully right the inevitable wrongs of this world.

Within this thematic context, a crucial event is David's response to Natty's promise to avenge his death if the Hurons dare to kill him. David will have no vengeance, only Christian forgiveness. Natty acknowledges the truth and beauty of the idea, but it is clear that his struggle is on another level. Those he fights are devils, the dark side of himself, of Chingachgook and Cora and Uncas—in fact, of all the main characters—for Magua is doubled with each of the main characters at some point in the novel. Magua comes to represent the evil in each character. In this forest world, the dark self takes shape in passionate savages who must be exterminated absolutely, like those who first capture Heyward's party. To show them pity is to endanger oneself; to neglect killing them is to open one to further jeopardy, such as the "descent into hell" to rescue the captured maidens, which is one element of the second quest. Only under the rule of civil law in civilization does human evil become a forgivable weakness rather than a metaphysical absolute.

The Prairie • Critics have noted the improbable plot of *The Prairie* while acknowledging its powerful and moving episodes. Ishmael Bush, an opponent of land ownership and of the civil law, has led onto the vast western prairie his considerable family, including a wife, seven sons, and an unspecified number of daughters; his brother-in-law, Abiram White; a well-educated and distantly related orphan, Ellen Wade; Obed Battius, a comic naturalist and doctor; and Inez Middleton, whom Abiram has kidnapped for ransom. Bush's ostensible motive is to escape the various restraining regulations of civilization and, particularly, to set up his farm far from the irksome property law. It is never made clear why he has consented to join the kidnapping or how anyone expects to collect a ransom. This expedition draws in its wake Paul Hover, a secret suitor of Ellen, and a party of soldiers led by Duncan Uncas Middleton, who seeks to recover his bride, who was snatched between the ceremony and the consummation. On the prairie, they all meet the eighty-seven-year-old Natty, who has forsaken human-made clearings in order to avoid the sound of the axe and to die in a clearing made by God. The situation is complicated by the presence of feuding American Indian bands: the bad Indians, the Hurons of the plains, are the Sioux, led by the treacherous Mahtoree; the good Indians are the Pawnee, led by the faithful Hard Heart. With these melodramatic materials, Cooper forges a moving tale that he makes significant in part by bringing into play issues of law and morality.

During the captivities and escapes that advance the novel's action, the white characters divide into two alliances that are then associated with the two Native American tribes. Both alliances are patriarchal, but their characters are significantly different. Bush is the patriarch of physical power. He lives by the "natural law" that "might makes right," establishing his dominance over his family through physicial strength and his conviction of his own power and rectitude. This alliance is beset by internal danger and contradiction. The second alliance is a patriarchy of wisdom and virtue.

Bound together by the faith of its members, it grows under the leadership of Natty to include Paul, Duncan, Ellen, Inez, and Dr. Battius. The conflict between these two groups is prefigured in the first confrontation between Natty and Ishmael. Ishmael is represented in the opening of the novel as being out of place on the prairie, for he is a farmer who has left the best farmland to take the route of those who, "deluded by their wishes," are "seeking for the Eldorado of the West." In one of the many great tableaux of this novel, Ishmael's group first sees Natty as a gigantic shadow cast toward them by the setting sun. He is a revelation who suggests to them the supernatural. Bush has come to the prairie in the pride of moral self-sufficiency, but Natty is an example of humble dependency on the wisdom of God. In part, through Natty's example, Ishmael finally leads his "wild brood" back to civilization at the novel's end.

Pride on the prairie, as in the wilderness of New York, leads to the subjection of reason to passion, to precipitate actions and death, whereas humility, though it may not save one from death, leads to the control of passion, to patience and probable survival. Natty teaches this lesson repeatedly to the group of which he becomes father and leader. Ishmael and the Sioux, "the Ishmaelites of the American deserts," learn the lesson through more bitter experience. The narrator implies that both Ishmael and Mahtoree, in attempting to be laws unto themselves, are playing God. In the central dialogue of the novel, Natty tells Dr. Battius in terms that echo *Essay on Man* that humankind's

> gifts are not equal to his wishes . . . he would mount into the heavens with all his deformities about him if he only knew the road. . . . If his power is not equal to his will, it is because the wisdom of the Lord hath set bounds to his evil workings.

Mahtoree, unrestrained by the traditional laws of his tribe, seeks through demagoguery to manipulate his people to effect his selfish desire for Inez. He and his band are destroyed in consequence. Bush's lesson comes when he discovers that Natty is not actually the murderer of Bush's eldest son, Asa.

The lesson Bush learns is always present to him. When his sons learn the well-kept secret that Ishmael is assisting Abiram in a kidnapping, they become indignant and rebellious. Cooper uses this conflict to demonstrate the precariousness of arbitrary power. Bush knows that he deserted his parents when he felt strong enough, and he is aware that only his strength keeps his sons with him in the present danger from American Indians. This knowledge of instability becomes complete when he learns that Abiram has returned the blow he received from Asa by shooting the boy in the back. It is difficult to determine how fully Bush understands this revelation. He feels his dilemma, for he admits that while he suspected Natty, he had no doubt that the murderer deserved execution, but when he learned of his brother-in-law's guilt, he became unsure. The wound to his family can hardly be cured by killing another of its members. For the first time in his life, Bush feels the waste and solitude of the wilderness. He turns to his wife and to her Bible for authority. He feels the extent to which Abiram has carried out Ishmael's own desire to punish his rebellious son, and thus he himself suffers as he carries out the execution of Abiram. This bitter lesson humbles him and sends him back to settled country and the restraints of civil law.

For Natty's informal family, there are gentler lessons. Paul and Duncan learn to be humble about their youthful strength, to realize their dependency on others, and to become better bridegrooms. Battius learns a little intellectual humility from

Natty's practical knowledge of the wilderness. The center of Natty's teaching is that the legitimate use of power is for service rather than for self. This lesson arises out of the relationship between Natty and Hard Heart. Natty and the faithful Pawnee chief adopt each other when it appears the Sioux will kill Hard Heart. Natty later asserts that he became Hard Heart's father only to serve him, just as he becomes the figurative father of the more civilized fugitives in order to serve them. After their relationship is established, it endures. Natty lives the last year of his life as a respected elder of the Pawnee and dies honored in their village. Having learned their lesson on the humble use of power in God's wilderness, Paul and Duncan carry their wisdom back to the high councils of the republic, where they become respected family men, property owners, and legislators. Like the Effinghams at Otsego Lake, the Hovers and the Middletons—the latter descending from the Heywards of *The Last of the Mohicans*—infuse the wisdom of the wilderness into the social order of America.

Cooper believed he had ended his Leatherstocking Tales when he completed *The Prairie.* Probably for this reason, he brought together his themes and characters and clarified the importance of Natty Bumppo to American civilization. Most critics have agreed that Cooper was drawn toward two ideals, the ability to exist in the wilderness and the ideal of a "natural aristocracy" of social and political order. It may be, however, that the first three of the Leatherstocking Tales are intended in part to create a history of America in which the wisdom of the wilderness is transferred to the social and political structure of the republic. Natty distrusts written tradition because "mankind twist and turn the rules of the Lord to suit their own wickedness when their devilish cunning has had too much time to trifle with his commands." Natty's experience provides a fresh revelation which renews the best of the Christian tradition and that calls people back to basic Christian principles. That revelation consists essentially of a humble recognition of human limitations, justifying Cooper's vision of a republic where rulers are chosen for wisdom and faithfulness, where the tradition is not rigidly controlled by a hereditary elite but is constantly renewed by the unfettered ascendancy of the good and wise.

Throughout his career, Cooper worked within a general understanding of human history as a disordered phase of existence between two orders, and a particular vision of contemporary America as a disordered phase between the old aristocratic order and the new order to be dominated by the American gentleman. In the first three of the Leatherstocking Tales, Cooper reveals a desire to naturalize the aristocratic tradition through exposure to the wilderness and its prophet, the man who reads God's word in the landscape. The result of this process would be a mature natural order that, though far from divine perfection, would promise as much happiness as is possible for fallen humankind. In his later novels, Cooper gave increasing attention to the ways in which American society failed to understand and to actualize this purified tradition. He looked back often, especially in *The Deerslayer,* to the purity and goodness of those basic values. Although they are rarely read today, novels such as *Satanstoe* and *The Oak Openings* among his later works are well worth reading, as is *The Bravo* from among his problem novels. In all these works, Cooper continues to express his faith in the possibility of a high American civilization.

Terry Heller

Other major works

NONFICTION: *Notions of the Americans*, 1828; *A Letter to His Countrymen*, 1834; *Sketches of Switzerland*, 1836; *Gleanings in Europe: England*, 1837; *Gleanings in Europe: France*, 1837; *Chronicles of Cooperstown*, 1838; *Gleanings in Europe: Italy*, 1838; *The American Democrat*, 1838; *The History of the Navy of the United States of America*, 1839 (2 volumes); *Ned Meyers: Or, A Life Before the Mast*, 1843; *Lives of Distinguished American Naval Officers*, 1845; *New York*, 1851; *The Letters and Journals of James Fenimore Cooper*, 1960-1968 (6 volumes; J. F. Beard, editor).

Bibliography

Barker, Martin, and Roger Sabin. *The Lasting of the Mohicans: History of an American Myth.* Jackson: University Press of Mississippi, 1995. From the series Studies in Popular Culture. Includes bibliographical references and an index.

Clark, Robert, ed. *James Fenimore Cooper: New Critical Essays.* Totowa, N.J.: Barnes & Noble Books, 1985. Each of the eight essays in this collection covers a different aspect of Cooper's fiction; most focus on a specific novel. A complete index helps the student find references to a particular work or theme.

Darnell, Donald. *James Fenimore Cooper: Novelist of Manners.* Newark: University of Delaware Press, 1993. Explores manners and customs in literature. Includes bibliographical references and an index.

Dyer, Alan Frank, comp. *James Fenimore Cooper: An Annotated Bibliography of Criticism.* New York: Greenwood Press, 1991. A good starting point for research.

Fields, W., ed. *James Fenimore Cooper: A Collection of Critical Essays.* Boston: G. K. Hall, 1979. The collection of new essays at the end of this book offers much of value to beginning students of Cooper, though the essays are not indexed. The first section of the book is a selection of nineteenth century reviews of Cooper's novels.

Franklin, Wayne. *The New World of James Fenimore Cooper.* Chicago: University of Chicago Press, 1982. Through a close reading of five of Cooper's novels—*The Pioneers*, *The Wept of Wish-ton-Wish* (1829), *Wyandotté* (1843), *The Crater* (1847), and *The Last of the Mohicans*—Franklin examines Cooper's attitude toward the frontier. Maintains that for Cooper, the wilderness begins as a place of hope and promise but ends as the source of tragedy.

Frye, Steven. *Historiography and Narrative Design in the American Romance: A Study of Four Authors.* Lewiston, N.Y.: Edwin Mellen Press, 2001. Comparative study of four nineteenth century American writers: James Fenimore Cooper, William Gilmore Simms, Lydia Maria Child, and Nathaniel Hawthorne.

Long, Robert Emmett. *James Fenimore Cooper.* New York: Continuum, 1990. This general study of Cooper and his fiction touches on all the major works. The five-page bibliography lists the most important studies of Cooper up to the 1990's.

McWilliams, John. *The Last of the Mohicans: Civil Savagery and Savage Civility.* New York: Twayne, 1995. Part of the Twayne Masterworks Series, this volume provides a general introduction to Cooper's most widely read novel as well as a particular approach to it. Divided into two sections, the first of which explores the literary and historical context of *The Last of the Mohicans*, followed by a section devoted to analysis of the style of the novel, as well as what Cooper was attempting to say about race, gender, history, and imperialism.

Newman, Russell T. *The Gentleman in the Garden: The Influential Landscape in the Works of James Fenimore Cooper.* Lanham, Md.: Lexington Books, 2003. Study of relationships between landscapes and social standing in Cooper's fiction.

Peck, H. Daniel, ed. *New Essays on "The Last of the Mohicans."* New York: Cambridge University Press, 1992. The introduction by Peck provides information about the composition, publication, and contemporary reception of the novel, as well as the evolution of critical opinion concerning *The Last of the Mohicans.* Each of the five original essays that follow—such as Nina Baym's "How Men and Women Write Indian Stories"—places the novel in a particular context, thus providing readers with an array of interesting perspectives from which to view Cooper's masterpiece.

Verhoeven, W. M., ed. *James Fenimore Cooper: New Historical and Literary Contexts.* Atlanta: Rodopi, 1993. An interesting collection. Includes bibliographical references.

Waples, Dorothy. *The Whig Myth of James Fenimore Cooper.* New Haven, Conn.: Yale University Press, 1938. Claims that many of the attacks on Cooper during his lifetime came from Whigs who distorted his character. Stresses Cooper's political views.

Robert Coover

Born: Charles City, Iowa; February 4, 1932

Principal long fiction • *The Origin of the Brunists*, 1966; *The Universal Baseball Association, Inc., J. Henry Waugh, Prop.*, 1968; *Whatever Happened to Gloomy Gus of the Chicago Bears?*, 1975 (expanded, 1987); *The Public Burning*, 1977; *Hair o' the Chine*, 1979 (novella/screenplay); *A Political Fable*, 1980 (novella); *Spanking the Maid*, 1981 (novella); *Gerald's Party*, 1985; *Pinocchio in Venice*, 1991; *Briar Rose*, 1996 (novella); *John's Wife*, 1996; *Ghost Town*, 1998; *The Adventures of Lucky Pierre: Directors' Cut*, 2002.

Other literary forms • In addition to his novels and novellas, Robert Coover has published numerous, usually experimental short fictions, most of which have been collected in *Pricksongs and Descants* (1969), *In Bed One Night and Other Brief Encounters* (1983), *A Night at the Movies: Or, You Must Remember This* (1987), and *A Child Again* (2005). His reviews and essays, while few in number, are exceptional in quality; his studies of Samuel Beckett ("The Last Quixote," in *New American Review*, 1970) and Gabriel García Márquez ("The Master's Voice," in *New American Review*, 1977) are, in addition to being important critical works in their own right, useful for the light they shed on Coover's interests and intentions in his own fiction. His plays, *The Kid* (1972), *Love Scene* (1972), *Rip Awake* (1972), and *A Theological Position* (1972), have been successfully staged in Paris and Los Angeles, and the New York production of *The Kid* at the American Place Theater in November, 1972, won for its director, Jack Gelber, an Obie award. Coover, who finds some relief from the fiction-writer's necessary isolation in the communal aspect of theater and motion-picture production, has also written, directed, and produced one film, *On a Confrontation in Iowa City* (1969), and published others, including the novella/screenplay *Hair o' the Chine* (1979, written some twenty years earlier). His poetry and one translation have appeared in various "little magazines."

Achievements • Coover's preeminent place among innovative contemporary writers has already been firmly established by academic critics. His various honors include the William Faulkner Foundation Award for best first novel (1966), a Rockefeller Foundation grant (1969), two Guggenheim Fellowships (1971, 1974), a citation in fiction from Brandeis University (1971), an Academy of Arts and Letters award (1975), the Rea Award for the short story (1987), and a National Book Award nomination for *The Public Burning*. Even before its publication by The Viking Press, *The Public Burning* became a succès de scandale when Alfred A. Knopf, which had originally contracted for the novel, refused to publish it. The ensuing literary gossip undoubtedly fueled sales (including copies of the book club edition), though not to the extent expected, and had the unfortunate result of bringing to both the book and its author the kind of notoriety neither deserved. The short-lived paperback editions of *The Public Burning* and *The Origin of the Brunists* (the latter novel had long been out of print) seemed to confirm that, except for *The Universal Baseball Association, Inc., J. Henry Waugh, Prop.*, which has attracted a diversified readership, Coover's works appeal to a fairly specialized audience.

National Archives

Biography • Robert Lowell Coover was born in Charles City, Iowa, on February 4, 1932. His family later moved to Indiana and then to Herrin, Illinois, where his father, Grant Marion Coover, managed the town newspaper. (Both the newspaper and a local mining disaster figure prominently in Coover's first novel.) Small-town life as the son of a newspaperman gave Coover both an interest in journalism and a desire to travel. After beginning his college education at nearby Southern Illinois University (1949-1951), he transferred to Indiana University, where he received a bachelor's degree in 1953, at which time he enlisted in the United States Naval Reserve, attaining the rank of lieutenant. While serving in Europe, he met Marie del Pilar San-Mallafre, whom he married on June 13, 1959. Coover's serious interest in fiction dates from the period immediately prior to his marriage, and his novel-writing followed the favorable response to his first published story, "Blackdamp" (1961), which he reworked and expanded into *The Origin of the Brunists*. Unable to make a living as a fiction writer, Coover left Spain, his wife's native country, and began teaching in the United States; he held positions at Bard College (1966-1967), the University of Iowa (1967-1969), Columbia University (1972), Princeton (1972-1973), Virginia Military Institute (1976), and Brown University (beginning in 1979), and has served as writer-in-residence at Wisconsin State University-Superior (1968) and Washington University (1969).

Coover has remained on the Brown University faculty as an adjunct professor in the graduate program in literary arts. He has taught workshops in standard writing, hypertext writing, and writing and mixed media. He has also organized festivals and conferences on literature, including "Unspeakable Practices" (1988), which assembled postmodernist writers; "Unspeakable Practices II" (1993), which highlighted the early days of hypertext fiction; and "Unspeakable Practices III" (1996), which attracted print and hypertext writers from around the world.

Coover's attitude toward the university is similar to his attitude toward his native country. Contending that residence abroad stirs the memory and frees the imagination, Coover has, since 1953, spent more than half of his time and done most of his writing in Guatemala, Spain, and England. At a time when much of American literature no longer seems distinctly American, Coover has written plays and fiction about some of his country's most characteristic myths, traits, events, and institutions, including baseball, millenarianism, the West, Dr. Seuss, the Rosenberg spy case, and

Rip Van Winkle. By the 1990's, he was living in Providence, Rhode Island, teaching a film and writing course at Brown University and continuing to explore the relations between narrative possibilities and American popular culture, including film, pornography, and detective fiction.

On June 21, 1992, Coover published an article in *The New York Times Book Review* titled "The End of Books." In this article, he discusses some of his observations and conclusions drawn from an experimental course he had been teaching at Brown University on hypertext. Coover borrows his definition of hypertext from a computer populist named Ted Nelson, saying that hypertext is "writing done in the nonlinear or nonsequential space made possible by the computer. Moreover, unlike print text, hypertext provides multiple paths between text segments, now often called 'lexias'"—a term borrowed from the poststructuralist critic Roland Barthes. Coover's point seems to be that computers have made possible the deconstructionist's ideal of navigation through "networks of alternate routes" of textual meaning "as opposed to print's fixed unidirectional page-turning."

This argument for the death of the printed novel is different from John Barth's earlier declaration of the novel's death in his 1963 essay "The Literature of Exhaustion," because, where Barth lamented that the possibilities of the novel as a genre had been exhausted, Coover's essay opines that computer technology has made the author-controlled, printed mode of textual transmission passé. Coover argues that fictions of the future will be created for the computer so that the hypertext reader will become a cowriter and fellow traveler with the creator of the text, coinvolved with the "mapping and remapping of textual (and visual, kinetic and aural) components, not all of which are provided by what used to be called the author." In a subsequent article titled "Hyperfiction: Novels for the Computer," he offers an examination of some early forays into the hypertext genre.

Analysis • In Robert Coover's work, humanity is presented not as the center of the universe, the purpose of creation, but, instead, as the center of the fictions it itself creates to explain its existence. Only when people learn the crucial difference between these opposing viewpoints will they understand their possibilities and limitations; only then will they be free to use their imaginations to live life fully and in all its perplexing variety.

Coover strongly distrusts humankind's reasoning faculty and, more particularly, the Enlightenment concept of human progress. As he explains in the prologue to *Pricksongs and Descants*, Coover finds himself in the same position that Miguel de Cervantes was four hundred years before: at the end of one literary tradition and the beginning of another, where the culture's traditional way of perceiving the world is breaking down. Reading the classic Greek poet Ovid, Coover came to understand that humanity's basic and continual struggle is to resist these and other changes, to struggle "against giving in to the inevitability of process." Accordingly, his stories depict a constantly shifting or metamorphosizing world, one in which the sheer abundance of material implies the abundance of life and where the straight linear plot of conventional realistic fiction no longer suffices. In these works, the active imagination battles the deadening influence of various systems of thought—religious, political, literary—that are, as Larry McCaffery has pointed out, ideological rather than ontological in nature. Understanding this difference brings people to the edge of the abyss, from which they then recoil, seeking safety and comfort in various rituals and explanatory sytems that are necessary and, to some degree, related to the artistic process itself. These rituals and systems, however, are dangerous insofar as people allow themselves to believe in them as other than self-generated imaginative constructs.

Coover urges his readers both to live in a more direct relationship to unmediated experience and to create fictions that will relieve them of their burden of anxiety in the indeterminate world. This balance of self-conscious fiction-making and unself-conscious participation in life is, however, not always achieved by Coover's characters. Even the best of them, the pattern-breakers, are often guilty of the same rigidity of the imagination that typifies their antagonists, the pattern-keepers. Refusing to accept their own mortality or that of their systems and beliefs, they venture forth on a spurious quest after immortality and platonic absolutes. Their terror of the void is real enough, but because their responses to it are ludicrous and absurd, the terror is rendered comically, fears turning into pratfalls, as in the misadventures of the Chaplinesque "Charlie in the House of Rue." If, as Coover believes, existence does not have an ontological status, then life necessarily becomes not the serious business his characters make it but a kind of play, to which social historian Johan Huizinga, author of *Homo Ludens: A Study of the Play Element in Culture* (1949), is the appropriate guide.

Coover is a fiction writer who distrusts fiction, not because it is "exhausted," as Barth claimed, but because he feels that writers' various fictions—not only their stories and novels, but also their histories and religions—are always in danger of being confused with reality. He parodies myths, history, literary formulas, and elements of popular culture in an effort to expose their artifice. He imposes order on his fictions, both as structure and as subject, to undermine that order effectively, to prove its arbitrariness, and thus to lay bare the indeterminacy of the world. In place of the inadequate, narrowly conceived systems that some of his characters devise or even the more expansive but eventually imprisoning fantasies of others, Coover writes what one critic has called "cubist fictions," inviting the reader's participation in a work that is less a product than a process, a revelation of the instability and uncertainty of modern existence.

The parallels between Coover's fiction and process-oriented abstract expressionist art, modern physics, and postexistentialist philosophy mark Coover as a distinctly modern writer. His works are often discussed as leading examples of metafiction, a formally experimental, highly reflexive literary mode that, as critic Robert Scholes has explained, "assimilates all the perspectives of criticism into the fiction itself." Although many of Coover's shorter works are clearly metafictional in nature, in the novels and novellas formal inventiveness gives way to an interest in traditional narrative, in telling a good story. What results is a tension between contemporary and traditional narrative modes that is analogous to Coover's notion of the artist-audience relationship (dramatized in his story "The Hat Act"). In Coover's view, the fiction-maker is at once an anarchist and a priest: "He's the one who tears apart the old story, speaks the unspeakable, makes the ground shake, then shuffles the pieces back together into a new story." Coover's power to disturb is clearly evident in reviews of his work. More important, however, is the fact that these relationships between Coover and his readers, artist and audience, innovation and tradition, bear a striking similarity to the plight of his characters.

The Origin of the Brunists • Coover's first novel, *The Origin of the Brunists,* is not "a vicious and dirty piece of writing," as one reviewer claimed; rather, it is a work in which

Coover pays his dues (as he has said) to the naturalistic novel and exhaustively details the various ways in which people imaginatively respond to the randomness and variety of their world. Briefly stated, the story concerns a mining disaster that kills ninety-seven men, the formation of a millenarian cult around the sole survivor, Giovanni Bruno, and the reactions of the townspeople, especially Justin "Tiger" Miller, editor of the local newspaper, to the Brunists. An odd assortment of immigrant Italians, Protestant fundamentalists, a composer of folk songs, a numerologist, and a theosophist, the Brunists are drawn together by their desire to live meaningful lives in a comprehensible, cause-and-effect world, one in which they misinterpret random events as providential signs. Many of those who do not join the cult find a sense of purpose and a release from the frustrations (often sexual) of living in a small, dying town by forming a Common Sense Committee. By accepting their roles as generally passive participants in these groups, the Brunists and their opponents gain the social approval, the feeling of power and significance, and the sense of communal purpose that make their unimaginative lives bearable.

Miller suffers from the lack of purpose and sense of frustration that afflict the others—perhaps more so because he is able to articulate these feelings to a degree that they are not. This same consciousness, however, also frees Miller from delusions concerning the truth of the fictions they accept without question. Unlike the others, who read his headline "Miracle in West Condon" literally, Miller, the ironist, distinguishes between experience, on one hand, and history and journalism, on the other, which he knows are not unmediated, factual accounts but imaginative constructions. The Brunists commit themselves to their version of reality and as a result become trapped within it. Miller, who is vaguely troubled by his own lack of commitment, joins the cult only to meet Bruno's attractive sister, relieve his boredom, and work up material for his paper. He does not serve the Brunists in the way his namesake, the apologist Justin, did the early Christians, for Miller only pretends to be a believer. In fact, as the movement's chronicler, he creates the cult and its members the way a novelist creates story and characters. Miller's problem, one that recurs throughout Coover's work, begins when his creation slips out of his control and takes on a life of its own, forcing its creator to assume an unwanted role: part antichrist, part blood sacrifice.

Life does not conform to the Brunist view. Yet, even though the world does not end on the date predicted and despite the fact that their vigil on the Mount of Redemption turns into a Roman circus, the Brunists survive and prosper in their delusion. Growing into a worldwide religion with their own ecclesiastical hierarchy, the Brunists find a mass audience for their apocalyptic gospel. Miller also survives, resurrected by his author and comforted by his nurse, Happy Bottom, and it is their lusty, playful, and imaginative relationship, their finding the "living space between the two," that Coover holds forth as the alternative to Brunism and the denial of life it represents.

The Universal Baseball Association, Inc., J. Henry Waugh, Prop. • Coover is not the only modern American author to have written a novel about baseball and myth, but unlike Philip Roth's *The Great American Novel* (1973), which is played chiefly for laughs, or Bernard Malamud's *The Natural* (1952), in which mythic parallels seem forced, *The Universal Baseball Association, Inc., J. Henry Waugh, Prop.* successfully incorporates its various elements into a unified but complex and richly ambiguous work of narrative art. More than its baseball lore, mythic resonance, theological probings, stylistic virtuosity, or wordplay, it is the novel's blend of realism and fantasy and the elaborate development of its simple main idea or conceit that mark its achievement.

The novel focuses on a fifty-six-year-old bachelor named J. Henry Waugh and the tabletop baseball game he invents: not only dice and charts but also eight teams, players with full biographies, and fifty-five years of league records and history. Henry's fantasizing is not so much childish as necessary, given his environment, the urban equivalent of Miller's West Condon. Whereas the real world oppresses Henry with "a vague and somber sense of fatality and closed circuits," his fantasy liberates and fulfills him in several ways. For the meaningless routine of accounting, Henry substitutes the meaningful rituals of baseball and in this way finds the continuity, pastoral wholeness, and heroic purpose that his everyday existence lacks. In his association, Henry directs and chronicles the course of history; outside it he is merely a loner, an anonymous clerk.

The advantages of his association are not without their risks, however, for at the same time that Henry uses his imagination to enliven his moribund world, he also reduces it to the narrow confines of his league: the USA miniaturized in the UBA, with its own "closed circuits." What is needed, Henry understands, is a balance of fact and fantasy, but in his attempt to right the imbalance that characterizes his life as an accountant, Henry goes to the opposite extreme, withdrawing into his fantasized realm. When a chance throw of the dice "kills" his rookie hero, Damon Rutherford ("His own man, yet at home in the world, part of it, involved, every inch of him a participant"), Henry despairs, choosing to exert that "unjustifiable control" that destroys the necessary balance of chance (dice) and order (imagination) and transforms his useful fiction into a version of the Brunists' providential universe. No longer a free, voluntary activity (according to Huizinga, a defining characteristic of true play), the Universal Baseball Association becomes repetitive work. Although the novel concludes with an unambiguous affirmation of the play spirit, the ending is itself ironic, for Henry, the godlike creator of his fiction (Jahweh), is no longer in control; having disappeared into the intricate mechanism of his association, he is now controlled by it.

Henry's fate, which is very nearly Miller's in *The Origin of the Brunists*, represents for Coover the danger all writers face. As he has explained, *The Universal Baseball Association*, "as I wrote it, not necessarily as it ought to be read, is an act of exemplary writing, a book about the art of writing." In the light of Coover's belief that all people are fiction-makers insofar as they create systems to explain their world, the novel serves the related purpose of pointing out to the reader how difficult—and how necessary—is the task of distinguishing the real from the imaginary if one is to avoid Henry's fate. The need to make this distinction is the explicit subject of *The Universal Baseball Association*; the difficulty of making it is implicit in Coover's method. In the novel's opening pages, for example, Coover forces the reader to share Henry's predicament in the parallel act of reading about it. At first, the reader assumes Henry is actually at the ballpark where rookie pitcher Damon Rutherford is a few outs away from a no-hitter, but when Henry takes advantage of the seventh-inning stretch to grab a sandwich at Diskin's delicatessen, one floor below, the reader corrects his mistake, perhaps unconsciously, now assuming that the game is being watched on television.

Even when it becomes clear that the game is being played in Henry's mind and that Henry is himself having trouble separating fact from fiction, the reader does not stop his reading to consider what this means because, thanks to Coover's pacing, he, like Henry, is completely caught up in being "*in* there, *with* them." After the game is over, he does have the opportunity to consider Henry's state of mind, but by the end of the first of the novel's eight chapters (seven for the days of creation plus one for the apocalypse), the reader again becomes lost in Coover's exuberant fantasy, as Henry, now in the guise of his imaginary hero Damon Rutherford, and local B-girl Hettie Irden (earth mother) play a ribald game of sexual baseball. Throughout the novel, the reader not only reads about Henry's dilemma but is also made to experience it.

Tiger Miller understands that it is better to undertake numerous short "projects" than to commit himself to any one, as J. Henry Waugh does. Similarly, Coover has explained that the writing of short plays or stories involves very little commitment on the author's part—at most a few weeks, after which the work is either complete or discarded—whereas a novel requires not only a greater expenditure of time and energy but a certain risk as well. The starting point for each of Coover's works is not a character or plot but a metaphor, the "hidden complexities" of which he develops by means of some appropriate structural device, as in the play *The Kid* or the short stories "The Babysitter" and "The Elevator." At times, the demands of the metaphor exceed the limits of structural devices appropriate to these short forms, and here Coover turns to the novel; thus, the two early stories, "Blackdamp" and "The Second Son" were transformed and expanded into *The Origin of the Brunists* and *The Universal Baseball Association*, respectively.

The Public Burning • The composition of Coover's third novel, *The Public Burning*, followed a similar but longer and more involved course, going from play to novella to novel over a difficult ten-year period during which Coover often questioned whether the expanding work would ever be completed.

One reason the novel took so long to write is that its main character, Richard Nixon, began taking real-life pratfalls in the Watergate scandal of 1973-1974, outstripping the ones that Coover had imagined for him in *The Public Burning*. A second reason lies in the nature of the work Coover chose to write: a densely textured compendium of American politics and popular culture in which literally thousands of details, quotations, names, and allusive echoes had to be painstakingly stitched together so as to suggest a communal work written by an entire nation. Against this incredible variety (or repetitive overabundance, as many reviewers complained) is the novel's tight and self-conscious structure: four parts of seven chapters each (traditionally, magical numbers), framed by a prologue and epilogue and divided by three intermezzos. Using two alternating narrators—Vice President Richard Nixon and the sometimes reverent, sometimes befuddled, even frantic voice of America—Coover retells the familiar story of Ethel and Julius Rosenberg, specifically the three days leading up to their execution, which Coover sardonically moves from Sing Sing Prison to Times Square. Although it is clear that Coover is distressed by the injustice done the Rosenbergs, his aim is not to vindicate them; rather, he uses their case to expose American history as American fantasy.

Originally titled "an historical romance," *The Public Burning* interweaves ostensible "facts," such as newspaper and magazine articles, courtroom transcripts, presidential speeches, personal letters, and obvious fantasy, including the superhero Uncle Sam and a ludicrous deathhouse love scene involving Nixon and Ethel Rosenberg. By creating "a mosaic of history," Coover provides the reader with a self-consciously fictive version of the Rosenberg case designed to compete with the supposedly historical view (as reiterated, for example, in Louis Nizer's *The Implosion Conspiracy*, 1973, which Coover reviewed in the February 11, 1973, issue of *The New York Times Book Review*). Coover's point is that, more often than not, humanity does not see experience directly (and therefore cannot presume to know its truth value) because it places that experience—or has it placed for it—in a context, an aesthetic frame, that determines its meaning. *The New York Times*, for example, is not shown printing "all the news that's fit to print"; rather, it selects and arranges the news on its pages ("tablets") in ways that, intentionally or not, determine the reader's ("pilgrim's") perception of what he or she assumes to be objective reality.

In sifting through the plethora of materials related to the Rosenberg case, Nixon comes very close to accepting Coover's view of history as essentially literary romance, or myth. He realizes that the Rosenberg conspiracy trial may actually be a government conspiracy against the accused (ritual scapegoats), depending chiefly on fabricated evidence, or stage props, and dress rehearsals for the prosecution; indeed, American life itself may be a kind of nationwide theatrical performance in which individuals play the roles assigned to them in the national scripts: manifest destiny, the Cold War, Westerns, and the Horatio Alger rags-to-riches plot. Nixon, however, is too much a believer in the American myths to break entirely free of them. Moreover, suffering from the same loneliness that afflicts Miller and Waugh, but being much less imaginative than they, Nixon desperately craves approval, and that requires his playing his part as it is written: "no ad-libbing," as the stage directions in *The Kid* make clear. To have a role in the Great American Plot, to be a part of the recorded "History" that he carefully distinguishes from merely personal "history," are the limited goals Nixon sets for himself because he is either unwilling or unable to imagine any other projects as equally workable and fulfilling. As a result, he plays the role Coover has appropriately assigned him: chief clown in the national farce.

The Public Burning is not a piece of easy political satire of the sort that Philip Roth dashed off in his Nixon book, *Our Gang* (1971); in fact, Coover's Nixon is a surprisingly sympathetic character. It is not "a cowardly lie" that defames a nation and exonerates criminals, as one reviewer claimed. Coover's third novel, like all of his major works, is a warning to the reader concerning the uses and the dangers of the imagination: Humankind must accept its role as fiction-maker and its responsibility for its fictions, or it will pay the penalty for confusing its facts with its fables.

Gerald's Party • After 1978, Coover continued to explore literary and "mythic" forms and to stretch generic classifications, revising or recycling a number of short fictions as "novels"—"A Working Day" (1979) as *Spanking the Maid* (1981), "The Cat in the Hat for President" (1968) as *A Political Fable* (1980), and "Whatever Happened to Gloomy Gus of the Chicago Bears?" (1968; novel, 1987)—and in an intertextual triple feature of film parodies titled *A Night at the Movies*, including previews, weekly serial episode, shorts, intermission, cartoon, travelogue, and musical interlude. All these texts manage to subvert the disclaimer that appears at the beginning of *A Night at the Movies*—"Ladies and Gentlemen May safely visit this Theatre as no Offensive Films are ever Shown Here"—but none so flagrantly as *Gerald's Party* (1985). Harking back to Coover's two "Lucky Pierre" stories about an aging pornographer, *Gerald's Party* constitutes a full-scale narrative onslaught, a playfully sadistic attack on its clownishly masochistic reader, and a vast recycling project that reverses the centrifugal reach of *The Public Burning*, moving centripetally in on itself to form Coover's fullest and most claustrophobic exploration of a single narrative metaphor.

Considered reductively, *Gerald's Party* parodies the English parlor mystery, but the parody here serves as little more than a vehicle for Coover's Rabelaisian exploitation in which John Barth's "literature of exhaustion" meets Roland Barthes's "plural text." The result is at once exhilarating and exhausting, freely combining murder mystery, pornography, film, theater, video, sex, puns, jokes, rituals, slapstick, clichés, fairy tales, party chatter, memory, desire, and aesthetic and philosophical speculation, all in one thickly embedded, endlessly interrupted yet unstoppable, ribald whole. The narrative is at once abundant (like the food and drink), full of holes (like the one in the victim Ros's breast), clogged (like Gerald's upstairs toilet), and stuck (as Gerald becomes in one sex scene). Plots proliferate but do not progress in any conventional way. As Inspector Pardew tries to solve the murder mystery, Gerald pursues Alison; Sally Ann pursues Gerald; Jim, a doctor, attends to the dying; Steve, a plumber, fixes everything but the toilet; Gerald's wife continues to prepare food, vacuum, and make wondrously inappropriate remarks ("I wish people wouldn't use guns in the house," she says after one guest has been fatally shot); and Gerald's mother-in-law, trying to put her grandson Mark to bed, looks on disapprovingly. These are but a few of the novel's myriad plots.

Gerald's efforts to understand what is happening, along with his inability to order the chaos, parallel the reader's. The novel in fact anticipates and thus short-circuits the reader's own efforts to understand Coover's bewildering but brilliant text, which seems to question its own purpose and seriousness and whose structure follows that of an all-night party, including the almost inevitable winding down to its anticlimactic end, or death. Not surprisingly, Pardew's solution resolves little and interests the reader not at all. Moreover, the most serious and philosophical comments in the novel—the ones upon which the conventional reader would like to seize for their power to explain and control the rest of the text—seem to be nothing more than additional false clues. Clearly, here as in all Coover's novels, stories, and plays, the reader can survive and in fact enjoy this narrative assault on his or her abilities and sensibilities only by resisting the Inspector's obsession with patterns and "holistic criminalistics." However, even if the reader takes a pratfall or two, Coover's parodic range and supercharged narrative energy make the ride worth the risk.

John's Wife • *John's Wife* is Coover's postmodern version of small-town life in middle America, much as *Winesburg, Ohio* (1919) was Sherwood Anderson's modernist take on the subject. Coover continues and expands the modernist angst expressed in *Winesburg, Ohio* and other fin de siècle works by focusing on the clichéd sexual repression and personal alienation of the characters until the corruption of the American Dream becomes mythic parody. Coover presents a plethora of characters whose lives revolve around the most powerful man in town, a late twentieth century "mover and shaker," a builder and businessman whose power to transform the small town and the lives of the people who live in it is matched only by his amorality. John, the builder, rewards personal loyalty from those who work for him with business promotions and upward social mobility, while destroying those who get in his way, including his own father-in-law.

John becomes the archetype of the late twentieth century materialist who will stop at nothing in his own rise to power. Concepts such as culture and tradition become palimpsest commodities to be bought and sold and ultimately transformed into consumer goods. John's wife, the titular character, is seen only through the impressions of the other characters. In fact, John's wife becomes an ironic archetypal exemplar of the feminist concept of the woman as "other" in much putatively patriarchal fiction. She is the focus of desire, both sexual and artistic, for the male characters of the book, while she is the friend and confidant of most of the female characters, yet, as one character states, she is "a thereness that was not there." She seems to fade out of existence even while people are talking to her. The theme of the book seems to be that we are born into stories made by others.

Ghost Town • *Ghost Town* is a fabulation (to use a term coined by Robert Scholes) of the trope of the American Western, first introduced in the dime novels of the late nineteenth century and then popularized by the films and television of the twentieth. *Ghost Town* transmogrifies the clichéd elements of the genre (character, plot, and setting) in the "play space" of the fiction, allowing the author's imagination to explore the ironic possibilities inherent in the form. The main character, for example, is at times both good and bad. He is the archetypal hero, innocent yet tempered by experience. He is "leathery and sunburnt and old as the hills. Yet just kid. Won't be anything else." Instead of riding into the town from a Beckettian nonplace, the town "glides up under his horse's hoofs from behind." Thus, in this ghost town, the hero can become the sheriff as well as a gunslinger and a train robber. The officious schoolteacher can also be the saloon chanteuse in disguise. The hackneyed plots (the hanging, the train robbery, the shoot-out, the rescue of the schoolteacher from her bondage to the train tracks) and the setting itself (the saloon, the jail, the rough-hewn church, the hideout) all become available for parody and ironic paradigmatic substitutions.

Robert A. Morace
Updated by Gary P. Walton

Other major works

SHORT FICTION: *Pricksongs and Descants*, 1969; *The Water Pourer*, 1972 (a deleted chapter from *The Origin of the Brunists*); *Charlie in the House of Rue*, 1980; *The Convention*, 1981; *In Bed One Night and Other Brief Encounters*, 1983; *Aesop's Forest*, 1986; *A Night at the Movies: Or, You Must Remember This*, 1987; *The Grand Hotels (of Joseph Cornell)*, 2002 (vignettes); *A Child Again*, 2005.

PLAYS: *A Theological Position*, pb. 1972; *Love Scene*, pb. 1972; *Rip Awake*, pr. 1972; *The Kid*, pr., pb. 1972; *Bridge Hound*, pr. 1981.

SCREENPLAYS: *On a Confrontation in Iowa City*, 1969; *After Lazarus*, 1980.

Bibliography

Andersen, Richard. *Robert Coover.* Boston: Twayne, 1981. A useful and accessible introduction to Coover's production up to 1981. Andersen combines plot summary with commentary, helping the reader to make an initial acquaintance with Coover's work. Notes, select bibliography, and index.

Coover, Robert. "As Guilty as the Rest of Them: An Interview with Robert Coover." Interview by Larry McCaffery. *Critique* 42, no. 1 (Fall, 2000): 115-125. Incisive interview with Coover between his publication of *Ghost Town* and his publication of *The Adventures of Lucky Pierre: Directors' Cut.*

____________. "Interview." *Short Story*, n.s. 1 (Fall, 1993): 89-94. Coover comments on the difference between the short story and the novel, the writing of *Pricksongs and Descants*, his use of sexuality in his fiction, his iconoclastic streak, postmodernism, and his use of the short story to test narrative forms.

____________. Interview by Amanda Smith. *Publishers Weekly* 230 (December 26, 1986): 44-45. Coover discusses the motivations that lie behind his experimental fiction; states he believes that the artist finds his metaphors for the world in the most vulnerable areas of human outreach; he insists that he is in pursuit of the mainstream. What many people consider experimental, Coover argues, is actually traditional in the sense that it has gone back to old forms to find its new form.

Cope, Jackson I. *Robert Coover's Fictions.* Baltimore: The Johns Hopkins University Press, 1986. Cope's readings of selected texts are as provocative as they are unfocused; Cope considers the various ways in which Coover extends the literary forms within and against which he writes. The densely written chapter on *Gerald's Party* and the Bakhtinian reading of *The Public Burning* are especially noteworthy.

Couturier, Maurice, ed. *Delta* 28 (June, 1989). Special issue on Coover. Includes an introduction, a chronology, a bibliography, a previously unpublished Coover story and brief essay on why he writes, and critical essays on a wide variety of topics and fictions, including *Gerald's Party.*

Critique, 23, no. 1 (1982). Special issue devoted to essays on *The Public Burning*: Tom LeClair's (reprinted in expanded form in *The Art of Excess*; see below); Raymond Mazurek's on history, the novel, and metafiction; Louis Gallo's on a key scene in which a viewer exits from a three-dimensional film; and John Ramage's on myth and monomyth.

Evenson, Brian K. *Understanding Robert Coover.* Columbia: University of South Carolina Press, 2003. Evenson explains the particularly dense style of Coover's metafiction (his writing about writing) in a comprehensive survey that is part of the Understanding Contemporary American Literature series. Evenson guides readers through Coover's postmodern fiction, which deals with myth- and story-making and their power to shape collective, community action, which often turns violent.

Gordon, Lois. *Robert Coover: The Universal Fictionmaking Process.* Carbondale: Southern Illinois University Press, 1983. Like Richard Andersen's book, this volume provides a friendly introduction and overview of Coover's work, placing him in the context of metafictional or postmodernist literature. Notes, select bibliography, and index.

LeClair, Tom. *The Art of Excess: Mastery in Contemporary American Fiction.* Urbana: University of Illinois Press, 1989. LeClair discusses *The Public Burning* in terms of systems theory and the author's mastery of world, of reader, and of narrative technique. Like the rest of his book, the Coover chapter is intelligent and provocative despite, at times, the arbitrariness and obfuscations of the book's thesis.

McCaffery, Larry. *The Metafictional Muse: The Works of Robert Coover, Donald Barthelme, and William H. Gass.* Pittsburgh: University of Pittsburgh Press, 1982. After describing what he considers a major current in contemporary American fiction, McCaffery discusses the metafictional traits of Coover's work and relates him to other important contemporary American writers.

____________. "Robert Coover on His Own and Other Fictions." *Genre* 14 (Spring, 1981): 45-84. A lively discussion in which Coover examines, among other things, the importance of stories about storytelling, the function of the writer in a world threatened by nuclear apocalypse, the fiction that has influenced his work, and popular culture.

Maltby, Paul. *Dissident Postmodernists: Barthelme, Coover, Pynchon.* Philadelphia: University of Pennsylvania Press, 1991. A comparative look at these three writers and their fictions. Includes a bibliography and an index.

"The Pleasures of the (Hyper)text." *The New Yorker* 70 (June/July, 1994): 43-44. Discusses Coover's Hypertext Hotel, the country's first online writing space dedicated to the computer-generated mode of literature known as hypertext; describes Coover's writing class at Brown University and its use of hypertext.

Stephen Crane

Born: Newark, New Jersey; November 1, 1871
Died: Badenweiler, Germany; June 5, 1900

Principal long fiction • *Maggie: A Girl of the Streets,* 1893; *The Red Badge of Courage: An Episode of the American Civil War,* 1895; *George's Mother,* 1896; *The Third Violet,* 1897; *The Monster,* 1898 (serial), 1899 (novella; pb. in *The Monster, and Other Stories*); *Active Service,* 1899; *The O'Ruddy: A Romance,* 1903 (with Robert Barr).

Other literary forms • Stephen Crane was an accomplished poet, short-story writer, and journalist as well as a novelist. His first collection of poems, *The Black Riders and Other Lines,* appeared in 1895; in 1896, a collection of seven poems and a sketch was published as *A Souvenir and a Medley*; and *War Is Kind,* another collection of poetry, was published in 1899. Crane's uncollected poems form part of the tenth volume of *The University Press of Virginia Edition of the Works of Stephen Crane* (1970). *The Blood of the Martyr,* a closet drama believed to have been written in 1898, was not published until 1940. One other play, *The Ghost* (1899), written for a Christmas party at Crane's home in England by Crane and others, has not survived in toto. Crane's short stories and sketches, of which there are many, began appearing in 1892 and have been discovered from time to time. His journalistic pieces occasionally have literary value.

Achievements • Crane's major achievement, both as a fiction writer and as a poet, was that he unflinchingly fought his way through established assumptions about the nature of life, eventually overcoming them. His perceptions were the logical end to the ideas of a long line of American Puritans and transcendentalists who believed in the individual pursuit of truth. The great and perhaps fitting irony of that logic is that Crane repudiated the truths in which his predecessors believed.

Rejecting much that was conventional about fiction in his day—elaborate plots, numerous and usually middle-or upper-class characters, romantic settings, moralizing narrators—Crane also denied values of much greater significance: nationalism, patriotism, the greatness of individual and collective man, and the existence of supernatural powers that care, protect, and guide.

In his best fiction, as in his life, Crane squarely faced the horror of a meaningless universe by exposing the blindness and egotism of concepts that deny that meaninglessness. He was unable to build a new and positive vision on the rubble of the old; he died at the age of twenty-eight, his accomplishments genuinely astounding.

Biography • Born on November 1, 1871, in the Methodist parsonage in Newark, New Jersey, Stephen Crane was the fourteenth and last child of Mary Peck Crane and Reverend Jonathan Crane, whose family dated back more than two centuries on the American continent. On the Peck side, almost every male was a minister; one became a bishop. By the time his father died in 1880, Crane had lived in several places in New York and New Jersey and had been thoroughly indoctrinated in the faith he was soon to reject. Also around this time, he wrote his first poem, "I'd Rather Have." His first short story, "Uncle Jake and the Bell Handle," was written in 1885, and the same year he enrolled in Pennington Seminary, where he stayed until 1887. Between 1888 and 1891, he attended Claverack College, Hudson River Institute, Lafayette College, and Syracuse University. He was never graduated from any of these, preferring baseball to study. In 1892, the New York *Tribune* published many of his New York City sketches and more than a dozen Sullivan County tales. Having apparently forgotten Miss Helen Trent, his first love, he fell in love with Mrs. Lily Brandon Munroe. During that same year, the mechanics union took exception to his article on their annual fete, which resulted in Crane's brother Townley being fired from the *Tribune.*

In 1893, Crane published, at his own expense, an early version of *Maggie: A Girl of the Streets.* William Dean Howells introduced him to Emily Dickinson's poetry, and in the next year he met Hamlin Garland. Also in 1894, the Philadelphia *Press* published an abridged version of *The Red Badge of Courage.*

During the first half of 1895, Crane traveled in the West, where he met Willa Cather, and in Mexico for the Bachellor Syndicate; *The Black Riders and Other Lines* was published in May; and *The Red Badge of Courage* appeared in October. By December, he was famous, having just turned twenty-four. In 1896, he published *George's Mother* and *The Little Regiment and Other Episodes of the American Civil War,* and fell in love with Cora Stewart (Howarth), whom he never married but with whom he lived for the rest of his life.

In January, 1897, on the way to report the insurgency in Cuba, Crane was shipwrecked off the Florida coast. Four months later, he was in Greece, reporting on the Greco-Turkish War. Moving back to England, he became friends with Joseph Conrad, Henry James, Harold Frederic, H. G. Wells, and others. During that year, he wrote most of his great short stories: "The Open Boat," "The Bride Comes to Yellow Sky," and "The Blue Hotel."

Never very healthy, Crane began to weaken in 1898 as a result of malaria contracted in Cuba while he was reporting on the Spanish-American War. By 1899, Crane was back in England and living well above his means. Although he published *War Is Kind, Active Service,* and *The Monster, and Other Stories,* he continued to fall more deeply in debt. By 1900, he was hopelessly debt-ridden and fatally ill. Exhausted from overwork, intestinal tuberculosis, malaria, and the experiences of an intense life, Crane died at the early age of twenty-eight, leaving works that fill ten sizable volumes.

Analysis • As one of the Impressionist writers—Conrad called him "The Impressionist"—Crane was among the first to express in writing a new way of looking at the world. A pivotal movement in the history of ideas, Impressionism grew out of scientific discoveries that showed how human physiology, particularly that of the eye, determines the way everything in the universe and everything outside the individual body and mind is perceived. People do not see the world as it is; the mind and the eye collaborate to interpret a chaotic universe as fundamentally unified, coherent, and explainable. The delusion is compounded when human beings agglomerate, for then they tend to create grander fabrications such as religion and history. Although Crane is also seen as one of the first American naturalistic writers, a Symbolist, an imagist, and even a nihilist, the achievements designated by these labels all derive from his impressionistic worldview.

Maggie • Stephen Crane's first novel, *Maggie: A Girl of the Streets,* was written before Crane had any intimate knowledge of the Bowery slums where the novel is set. It is the first American novel to portray realistically the chaos of the slums without either

Library of Congress

providing the protagonist with a "way out" or moralizing on the subject of social injustice. It obeys Aristotle's dictum that art imitates life and the more modern notion that art is simply a mirror held up to life. *Maggie* is the story of a young Irish American girl who grows up in the slums of New York. The novel seems to belong to the tradition of the *Bildungsroman,* but its greatness lies in the irony that in this harsh environment, no one's quest is fulfilled, no one learns anything: The novel swings from chaos on the one side to complete illusion on the other.

By the time Maggie reaches physical maturity, her father and young brother have died, leaving only her mother, Mary—a marauding drunken woman, and another brother, Jimmie, a young truck driver who scratches out a place for himself in the tenements. Living with an alcoholic and a bully, Maggie is faced with a series of choices that tragically lead her to self-destruction. First, she must choose between working long hours for little pay in the sweatshops or becoming a prostitute. She chooses the former, but the chaotic reality of home and work are so harsh that she succumbs to her own illusions about Pete, the bullying neighborhood bartender, and allows herself to be seduced by him. When this happens, Mary drives Maggie out of their home. For a short time, Maggie enjoys her life, but Pete soon abandons her to chase another woman. Driven from home and now a "fallen woman," Maggie must choose between prostitution and suicide. Deciding on the life of a prostitute, Maggie survives for a time but ultimately is unable to make a living. She commits suicide by jumping into the East River.

The form of the novel is that of a classical tragedy overlaid by nihilism that prevents the final optimism of tragedy from surfacing. The tragic "mistake," what the Greeks called *hamartia,* derives from a naturalistic credo: Maggie was unlucky enough to have been born a pretty girl in an environment she was unable to escape. Although she tries to make the best of her limited choices, she is inexorably driven to make choices that lead her to ruin and death. The novel's other characters are similarly trapped by their environment. Mary drinks herself into insensibility, drives her daughter into the street, and then, when Maggie kills herself, exclaims "I fergive her!" The irony of this line, the novel's last, is nihilistic. Classical tragedy ends on an optimistic note. Purged of sin by the sacrifice of the protagonist, humankind is given a reprieve by the gods, and life looks a little better for everyone. In *Maggie: A Girl of the Streets* there is no optimism. Mary has nothing upon which to base any forgiveness. It is Maggie who should forgive Mary. Jimmie is so egocentric that he cannot see that he owed his sister some help. At one point he wonders about the girls he has "ruined," but he quickly renounces any responsibility for them. Pete is a blind fool who is destroyed by his own illusions and the chaos of his environment.

For the first time in American fiction, a novel had appeared in which there clearly was no better world, no "nice" existence, no heaven on earth. There was only the world of the stinking tenements, only the chaos of sweat and alcohol and seduction, only hell. Also for the first time, everything was accomplished impressionistically. Maggie's sordid career as a prostitute would have required an earlier writer several chapters to describe. In *Maggie: A Girl of the Streets,* the description requires only a paragraph or two.

George's Mother • *George's Mother,* originally titled *A Woman Without Weapons* and Crane's only other Bowery novel, is a companion piece to *Maggie: A Girl of the Streets.* Mrs. Keasy and her son George live in the same tenement as Mary Johnson, Maggie's mother. The story is more sentimental than that of the Maggie novel and therefore less effective. George gradually succumbs to the destructive elements of the Bowery—drink and a subsequent inability to work—in spite of the valiant efforts of his mother to forestall and warn him. As Maggie has her "dream gardens" in the air above sordid reality, so young George has dreams of great feats while he actually lives in the midst of drunkenness and squalor. As drink provides a way out of reality for George, so the Church provides his mother with her escape. Both in *Maggie* and in *George's Mother,* illusions simultaneously provide the only way out of reality and a way to hasten the worsening of reality.

The Red Badge of Courage • In his most famous novel, *The Red Badge of Courage,* Crane takes his themes of illusion and reality and his impressionistic method from the Bowery to a battlefield of the Civil War, usually considered to be the Battle of Chancellorsville. A young farm boy named Henry Fleming hears tales of great battles, dreams of "Homeric" glory, and joins the Union Army. Published in 1895, the story of Henry Fleming's various trials took the literary world by storm, first in England and then in the United States. Crane became an immediate sensation, perhaps one of America's first media darlings. *The Red Badge of Courage* became a classic in its own time because it combined literary merit with a subject that captured the popular imagination. Never again did Crane reach the height of popularity that he achieved with *The Red Badge of Courage.*

Structurally, the novel is divided into two parts. In the first half, Henry's illusions disappear when confronted by the reality of battle. During the first skirmish, he sees vague figures before him, but they are driven away. In the next skirmish, he becomes so frightened that he runs away, becoming one of the first heroes in literature actually to desert his fellow soldiers in the field. Although Achilles had done something similar in the *Iliad* (c. 800 B.C.E.), in the intervening millennia, few heroes had imitated him.

Separated from his regiment, Henry wanders through the forest behind the lines. There he experiences the kinds of illusions that predominate in all of Crane's writing. First, he convinces himself that nature is benevolent, that she does not blame him for running. Next, he finds himself in a part of the woods that he interprets as a kind of religious place—the insects are praying, and the forest has the appearance of a chapel. Comforted by this, Henry becomes satisfied with himself until he discovers a dead soldier in the very heart of the "chapel." In a beautiful passage—beautiful in the sense of conveying great emotion through minute detail—Henry sees an ant carrying a bundle across the face of the dead man. Shifting to a belief in nature as malevolent or indifferent, Henry moves back toward the front. He soon encounters a line of wounded soldiers, among whom is his friend Jim Conklin and another man called simply "the tattered man." Conklin, badly wounded, is dying. Trying to expiate his crime of desertion, Henry attempts to help Conklin but is rebuffed. After Conklin dies, the tattered man probes deeply into Henry's conscience by repeatedly asking the youth "where ya hit?" The tattered man himself appears to be wounded, but Henry cannot abide his questions. He deserts the tattered man as well.

When Henry tries to stop another Union soldier to ask the novel's ubiquitous question "Why?," he is clubbed on the head for causing trouble. Ironically, this wound becomes his "red badge of courage." Guided back to his regiment by a "Cheery Soldier," who performs the same function as the ancient gods and goddesses who helped wandering heroes, Henry embarks on the novel's second half. Between receiving the lump on his head and returning to his regiment, Henry's internal wanderings are over. Not until the last chapter does Henry ask questions of the universe. Most of the repudiations are complete: Heroes do not always act like heroes; no one understands the purpose of life or death; nature may be malevolent, probably indifferent, but is certainly not the benevolent, pantheistic realm of the transcendentalists; and God, at least the traditional Christian God, is simply nowhere to be found.

In the second half of the novel, Henry becomes a "war devil," the very Homeric hero he originally wanted to be. Wilson, his young friend, who was formally called "the loud soldier," has become a group leader, quiet, helpful, and utterly devoted to the regiment. He becomes, in short, what Henry would have become had he not run from the battle. The idea of "Brotherhood," so prevalent in Crane's works, is embodied by Wilson. Henry is another kind of hero, an individual owing allegiance to no group; he leads a successful charge against the enemy with the spirit of a primitive warrior.

When the battle is over, however, all that Henry has accomplished is negated. Many critics have found the last chapter confused and muddled, for Henry's feelings range from remorse for the "sin" for which he is not responsible to pride in his valor as a great and glorious hero. Finally, he feels that "the world was a world for him," and he looks forward to "a soft and eternal peace." The beautiful lyricism of the novel's last paragraphs is, like that of many of Crane's conclusions, completely ironic. No one lives "eternally peacefully"; the world is not a world for Henry. As John Berryman says, Crane's "sole illusion was the heroic one, and not even that escaped his irony."

Thus, the novel's conclusion is not at all inconsistent. During the course of his experiences, Henry learns at first hand of the indifference of the universe, the chaos of the world, and the illusory nature of religion and patriotism and heroism, but he learns these lessons in the heat of the moment, when recognition is virtually forced on him. When the memory has an opportunity to apply itself to past experience, that experience is changed into what humanity wants it to be, not what it was. Henry, then, becomes representative of humankind. The individual memory becomes a metaphor for collective memory, history. Everything is a lie. Not even heroism can last.

The Third Violet • Crane was only twenty-two when he began working on *The Third Violet*, and before it was published he had already written *Maggie: A Girl of the Streets*, *The Red Badge of Courage*, and *George's Mother*. Of the four, *The Third Violet* is by far the least successful. In Crane's attempt to portray middle-class manners, his best portraits, as well as his most admirable characters, are the simple farmer and the heir, whereas the others, who actually fall within the middle class, are more or less insipid.

The protagonist of *The Third Violet*, Billie Hawker, is a young New York artist who returns to his family's farm for a summer vacation. While there, he falls in love with Grace Fanhall, a young heir vacationing at a nearby resort hotel called the Hemlock Inn. The remainder of the novel recounts Hawker's anxieties as he botches repeated attempts to declare his love and win the fair maiden at the hotel, during summer picnics, in New York studios, and in mansions. Aside from portraits of Hawker's father and the heir, the most rewarding portraits are of a little boy and his dog. A memorable scene occurs when Grace Fanhall and Billie's father ride together in a farm wagon, their disparate social standings apparently freeing them from rigid middle-class stiffness. Equally worthwhile is the scene in the New York bohemian studio where Hawker's friends "Great Grief," "Wrinkles," and Pennoyer manage to divert the landlord and concoct a meal in a manner reminiscent of the opening scenes of Giacomo Puccini's opera *La Bohème* (1896). There is even a beautiful young model named "Splutter" O'Conner, whose easy and gay love for Hawker provides a contrast to his own doleful courtship of Fanhall.

The reality behind the mask of convention in *The Third Violet* is never sufficiently revealed. Reality in *The Third Violet* seems to be that love would predominate if only Hawker could free himself of his inferiority complex at having been born poor. Although others might make great fiction from such a feeling, Crane could not.

Active Service • The only great piece of fiction Crane produced from his experience of reporting the Greco-Turkish War of April and May, 1897, was "Death and the Child." By contrast, his Greek novel, *Active Service*, is lamentably bad. Following a creakingly conventional plot, *Active Service* relates the story of a boy and a girl in love: The girl's parents object; the boy pursues the girl and overcomes her parents' objections by rescuing the family from danger and by manfully escaping the snares of another woman.

Crane's protagonist, Rufus Coleman, Sunday editor of the New York *Eclipse*, is in love with Marjory Wainright, the demure and lovely daughter of a classics professor at Washurst University. Disapproving of the match on the rather solid evidence that Coleman is "a gambler and a drunkard," Professor Wainright decides to include his daughter in a student tour of Greece, a tour the professor himself is to lead. While touring ruins near Arta in Epirus, the group is trapped between the Greek and Turkish lines. Meanwhile, back in the offices of the *Eclipse*, the not so mild-mannered reporter, Coleman, is discovering that he cannot exist without Marjory. Arranging to become the *Eclipse*'s correspondent in Greece, he heads for Europe. Temporarily distracted while traveling to Greece by a beautiful British actor and dancer, Nora Black, Coleman finally arrives in Athens and discovers that the Wainright party is in danger. He jauntily sets out to rescue them and equally as jauntily succeeds. So heroic and noble is Coleman that the professor is quite won over. The novel finishes like hundreds of turn-of-the-century love adventures, with the hero and heroine sitting with the Aegean Sea in the background while they declare their love for each other in the most adolescent manner.

Indeed, Crane intended to write a parody of love adventures. The hero is too offhandedly heroic; the rival is too mean and nasty. The "other woman" wears too much perfume; the parents are too inept. The novel is banal and trite, however, because the characters lack interest, and the parody cannot sustain the reader's interest in the absence of a substantial form worthy of parody. The novel is probably bad for extraliterary reasons: Crane's poor health and finances. Crane began the book late in 1897, when he was still fairly healthy and when his finances were not yet completely chaotic. The effects of the malaria and the tuberculosis, however, were becoming increasingly debilitating and began to take their toll long before *The Third Violet* was finished in May, 1899. By then, too, his finances were depleted. Crane had the intellectual and cultural resources to write a first-rate book on this subject, but not the health and good fortune. One must agree with Crane: "May heaven help it for being so bad."

The Monster • *The Monster* was Crane's last great work. A short book even when compared to his notably short novels, *The Monster* is often regarded as a novella rather than as a novel. Like *The Red Badge of Courage*, it is divided into twenty-four episodes, is divided in half structurally, and concerns a man caught in a straitjacket of fate. Like Maggie, Dr. Trescott, the hero, is led down a road that gradually leaves behind all side trails until his only choice is essentially made for him by his circumstances. Trescott is more intelligent and educated than Maggie, and he is certainly more conscious of his choices, but the most crucial difference lies in the intensity of the tragedy. Although *Maggie: A Girl of the Streets* is about the individual facing chaos without the mediating power of a civilized group, *The Monster* concerns the conflict between individual ethics and the values of the group. For Crane, small towns in America exist to mediate between the individual and chaos. Ordered society blocks out reality, providing security.

Henry Johnson, the Trescotts' black hostler, is badly burned while rescuing Jimmy, the doctor's young son, from the Trescotts' burning house. This heroic act creates Trescott's tragic dilemma: Personal ethics dictate that he care for the now horrific looking and simpleminded Henry; public security requires that Henry be "put away" or allowed to die, for civilization does not like to see reminders of what humankind would be like without the thin veneer of order. Although Trescott faces his responsibility toward Henry, he fails to reckon with the task of forcing the community to face it as well. When he does, he consciously sets himself on a collision course with that society. Unlike Henry Fleming, Trescott cannot win even a temporary victory. The community defeats him utterly.

Trescott at first tries to avoid conflict by paying Alex Williams, a local black man who lives on the outskirts of town, to care for Henry. When Henry escapes into town and, although harmless, frightens little children, the community demands that Trescott do something. Standing by his obligation to Henry, Trescott is quickly ostracized by the community. At the novel's end, Trescott recognizes that he has lost. He cannot retain his moral and ethical stance toward Henry Johnson and remain within the community. He cannot concede defeat to the community without doing irrevocable damage to his own honor. The dilemma is a classical tragic one that must be faced by each individual. Ralph Ellison called *The Monster* a metaphor for America's treatment of the black minority, but the greatness of the work lies in the fact that it is a larger metaphor for the human community's treatment of the individual.

The O'Ruddy • *The O'Ruddy* is a parodic picaresque romance about English and Irish manners. Its humor belies the fact that Crane was writing on his deathbed, in great anguish and pain. Crane's only first-person novel, *The O'Ruddy* exposes the "dullness of the great mass of people, the frivolity of the gentry, the arrogance and wickedness of the court," and celebrates the notion that "real talent was usually engaged in some form of rascality." Similar to *Active Service* in that it recounts the story of an adventure-loving hero who overcomes the objections of a stuffy father and vehement mother for the hand of a somewhat demure but beautiful young lady, *The O'Ruddy* is similarly unable to sustain greatness. Although sketchy as to the date of the events, *The O'Ruddy* seems to be set in late eighteenth century England, where young Tom O'Ruddy, a poor but noble Irishman, has come to return to the earl of Wesport some papers given to Tom by his father. The reader learns more than halfway through the novel that the papers give title to certain lands in Sussex. Smitten by Lady Mary, the earl's daughter, Tom eventually trades the papers for her hand in marriage. Before the novel's conclusion, in which Tom and Mary are married, there are many duels, robberies, journeys through secret passages, and portraits of literary meetings and turnings at Kensington Gardens, all of which are parodied. Crane disliked the manners of many of the English, saying at one point that western New York farmers had better manners.

The parody is occasionally amusing, but since parody must mock form as well as content to be great, the novel fails. Understandably, given Crane's illness and the reluctance of Robert Barr to finish the novel after Crane's death, there are numerous discrepancies, among which is a confusion as to whether Tom O'Ruddy can read and write. All in all, Crane's intensity is lacking in this slight novel, his freshness, his impressionistic insights, his accustomed power gone. The last words he wrote in the novel before dying are lamentably apropos of the book itself: "This is no nice thing."

Chester L. Wolford

Other major works

SHORT FICTION: *The Little Regiment and Other Episodes of the American Civil War,* 1896; *The Open Boat, and Other Tales of Adventure,* 1898; *The Monster, and Other Stories,* 1899; *Whilomville Stories,* 1900; *Wounds in the Rain: War Stories,* 1900; *Last Words,* 1902.

PLAYS: *The Blood of the Martyr,* wr. 1898?, pb. 1940; *The Ghost,* pr. 1899 (with Henry James; fragment).

POETRY: *The Black Riders and Other Lines,* 1895; *A Souvenir and a Medley,* 1896; *War Is Kind,* 1899; *The University Press of Virginia Edition of the Works of Stephen Crane,* 1970 (volume 10).

NONFICTION: *The Great Battles of the World,* 1901; *The War Dispatches of Stephen Crane,* 1964.

Bibliography

Benfey, Christopher E. G. *The Double Life of Stephen Crane.* New York: Alfred A. Knopf, 1992. A narrative of Crane's life and literary work that argues that the writer attempted to live the life his works portrayed. Includes bibliography and index.

Berryman, John. *Stephen Crane: A Critical Biography.* New York: Cooper Square Press, 2001. A reissue of the first major biography of the author, which Berryman published in 1950. Still valuable for its detail and insight as an absorbing Freudian reading of Crane's life and work. Berryman, himself a major American poet, eloquently explains the patterns of family conflict that appear in Crane's fiction. Furthermore, Berryman's wide-ranging interests allow him to tackle such large topics as Crane's influence on the birth of the short story.

Colvert, James B. *Stephen Crane.* New York: Harcourt Brace Jovanovich, 1984. This biography, aimed specifically at the nonspecialist, is highly readable and is enhanced by numerous illustrations. Its bibliography is limited but well selected. The author's research is impeccable.

____________. "Stephen Crane and Postmodern Theory." *American Literary Realism* 28 (Fall, 1995): 4-22. A survey of postmodern approaches to Crane's fiction. Summarizes the basic premises of postmodern interpretation, examining how these premises have been applied to such Crane stories as "The Open Boat," "The Upturned Face," and "Maggie"; balances such interpretive strategies against critics who affirm more traditional, humanistic approaches.

Davis, Linda H. *Badge of Courage: The Life of Stephen Crane.* Boston: Houghton Mifflin, 1998. This biography of Crane depicts him as a perpetual adolescent who was very much an enigma.

Halliburton, David. *The Color of the Sky: A Study of Stephen Crane.* New York: Cambridge University Press, 1989. Though somewhat thematically disorganized, the author's philosophical grounding and ability to look at Crane's works from unusual angles make for many provocative readings. In his discussion of "The Blue Hotel," for example, he finds much more aggression directed against the Swede than may at first appear, coming not only from seemingly benign characters but also from the layout of the town. Notes, index.

Johnson, Claudia D. *Understanding "The Red Badge of Courage": A Student Casebook to Issues, Sources, and Historical Documents.* Westport, Conn.: Greenwood Press, 1998. An excellent accompaniment to the novel. Essential for students.

Knapp, Bettina L. *Stephen Crane.* New York: Frederick Ungar, 1987. A succinct introduction to Crane's life and career, with a separate chapter on his biography, several chapters on his fiction, and an extensive discussion of two poetry collections, *The Black Riders and Other Lines,* and *War Is Kind.* Includes a detailed chronology, a bibliography of primary and secondary sources, and an index.

Monteiro, George. *Stephen Crane's Blue Badge of Courage.* Baton Rouge: Louisiana State University Press, 2000. A demonstration of the ironic role of temperance propaganda, in which Crane was emersed as a child, in the imagery and language of his darkest work.

Nagel, James. *Stephen Crane and Literary Impressionism.* University Park: Pennsylvania State University Press, 1980. Nagel carefully delineates what he considers Crane's application of impressionist concepts of painting to fiction, which involved Crane's "awareness that the apprehension of reality is limited to empirical data interpreted by a single human intelligence." This led the writer to a stress on the flawed visions of men and women and a depiction of the dangers of this natural one-sidedness in works such as *Maggie: A Girl of the Streets,* as well as depictions of characters who transcended this weakness through an acceptance of human inadequacies in such works as "The Open Boat." Notes, index.

Weatherford, Richard M., ed. *Stephen Crane: The Critical Heritage.* Boston: Routledge & Kegan Paul, 1973. Divided into sections that provide contemporary British and American reviews of Crane's work as it was published. Similarly, the introduction charts Crane's career in terms of each published text, noting the critical reception of his work and the details of his publishing career. Includes a brief annotated bibliography and an index.

Wertheim, Stanley. *A Stephen Crane Encyclopedia.* Westport, Conn.: Greenwood Press, 1997. A very thorough volume of Crane information. Includes bibliographical references and an index.

Wertheim, Stanley, and Paul Sorrentino. *The Crane Log: A Documentary Life of Stephen Crane, 1871-1900.* New York: G. K. Hall, 1994. Stanley and Sorrentino, editors of *The Correspondence of Stephen Crane* (1988), have attempted to counter many of the falsehoods that have bedeviled analyses of Crane's life and work by providing a documentary record of the author's life. Opening with biographical notes on persons mentioned in the text and lavishly sourced, *The Crane Log* is divided into seven chapters, beginning with the notation in Crane's father's diary of the birth of his fourteenth child, Stephen, and ending with a newspaper report of Crane's funeral, written by Wallace Stevens.

Wolford, Chester L. *The Anger of Stephen Crane.* Lincoln: University of Nebraska Press, 1983. Walford considers Crane a semiliterate genius and presents his work as a repudiation of the epic tradition and of conventional religion. Although the book is not always convincing, it is engaging and original in its approach.

Robertson Davies

Born: Thamesville, Ontario, Canada; August 28, 1913
Died: Toronto, Ontario, Canada; December 2, 1995

Principal long fiction • *Tempest-Tost*, 1951 (with *Leaven of Malice* and *A Mixture of Frailties* known as the Salterton trilogy); *Leaven of Malice*, 1954; *A Mixture of Frailties*, 1958; *Fifth Business*, 1970 (with *The Manticore* and *World of Wonders* known as the Deptford trilogy); *The Manticore*, 1972; *World of Wonders*, 1975; *The Rebel Angels*, 1981 (with *What's Bred in the Bone* and *The Lyre of Orpheus* known as the Cornish trilogy); *What's Bred in the Bone*, 1985; *The Lyre of Orpheus*, 1988; *Murther and Walking Spirits*, 1991; *The Cunning Man*, 1994.

Other literary forms • Dramatist, journalist, and essayist, Robertson Davies wrote plays such as *Fortune, My Foe* (1948), *A Jig for the Gypsy* (1954), *Hunting Stuart* (1955), and dramatizations of some of his novels; histories (notably *Shakespeare's Boy Actors*, 1939); numerous newspaper commentaries and columns (often for the *Peterborough Examiner* and the *Toronto Star*); and essays of all kinds, including many for volume 6 (covering the years 1750-1880) of *The Revels History of Drama in English*. Other occasional writings are collected in *The Merry Heart: Reflections on Reading, Writing, and the World of Books* (1997).

Achievements • Perhaps the foremost Canadian man of letters of his generation, Davies achieved virtually every literary distinction his country offers, including the Governor-General's Award for Fiction and fellowship in the Royal Society of Literature. He was the first Canadian honorary member of the American Academy and Institute of Arts and Letters. Professor of English at the University of Toronto, he held the Edgar Stone Lecturership in Dramatic Literature (as its first recipient); he was also the founding master of Massey College.

Biography • Born into a family of enterprising and individualistic Canadian entrepreneurs and newspaper publishers, the third child of Rupert and Florence MacKay Davies was to inherit the verbal skills and high-energy work ethic of his parents, along with their Welsh temperament. Receiving a cultural education that included frequent visits to the opera and theater, balanced with regular exposure to church music, Davies learned to love words very early from the family habit of reading aloud. He learned to read at the age of six and promptly began consuming the classics as well as popular newspaper and magazine fare.

When his family moved to Renfrew, young Davies was forced to attend a country grade school, where ruffians and jealous peers made his quiet, bookish life miserable. These times were to be recalled in some of his best fiction. Travel with his father, in Europe as well as throughout Canada, convinced him of the importance of a British education; after undergraduate work at Upper Canada College, he spent 1932 to 1938 at Queen's College and Oxford University, reading literature, drama, and history. A predilection for acting led him to the Old Vic (1938-1939), until the war sent him back to Canada, to begin a journalistic career, following his father's finan-

©Jerry Bauer

cial interests. By 1942 he was editor of the *Peterborough Examiner*, a man of great interests and broad education trapped by circumstance in a fairly provincial town in Canada, forced to deal daily with the pedestrian affairs of journalism. Far from fading into the woods, however, he found his creative voice and energy in the contradiction and began a fruitful writing career.

At the center of Davies' strange reconciliation of apparent opposites was his ability to live moderately, sanely, while expressing his outrageous imagination in writing. He took on the journalistic persona of Samuel Marchbanks, an outspoken man of letters, at once the antithesis and the complement of Davies the man. So successful was his ability to generate a reality for Marchbanks that for eleven years the Marchbanks columns of the *Peterborough Examiner* were syndicated in Canadian papers.

Responding to his love of theater, Davies wrote several plays as well during this period, notably *Eros at Breakfast* (1948) and *Fortune, My Foe.* He was also instrumental in founding, with Sir Tyrone Guthrie, the Shakespeare Festival in Stratford, Ontario. Although his plays were only modestly successful outside Canada, in his homeland he is highly respected for his original stagework and his adaptations of classics such as Ben Jonson's *Bartholomew Fair* (1614).

Davies underwent a major career change in 1962, when he joined the faculty of Trinity College, University of Toronto, first as a visiting professor and, in 1967, as founding master of Massey College, a nonteaching graduate college in the University of Toronto. Although his new duties meant giving up his editorship (his father died in 1967, and the business was sold), the change of career gave him time to begin a long and full fiction-writing career, while continuing his stage and essay work. He had become disenchanted with theater as a full-bodied medium when his stage adaptation of *Leaven of Malice* failed to enjoy a long run on Broadway in 1960. He turned to the novel form as more independent of outside interference and the uncertain financial fortunes of the stage. A trilogy, sometimes called the Salterton novels, demonstrated the transition in Davies' own life by concentrating on the backstage events, mostly humorous, of amateur and professional acting companies trying to put on classic and modern plays. However successful these novels were, it remained for Davies to find in his next trilogy a more suitable setting and cast of characters to inform his novels.

Davies' most interesting and, according to many critics, long-lasting writing began with his 1970 publication of the novel *Fifth Business*, the first of the so-called Deptford trilogy, to be continued with *The Manticore* in 1972 and concluded with *World of Wonders* in 1975. These novels combined Davies' previous experiences in rural Canada and cosmopolitan Europe, his familiarity with academic circles, and his love of the world of theater to bring to life a series of characters that would appear repeatedly in his subsequent fiction.

Davies retired from his post at Massey College in 1981, continuing to live and write in Toronto. During the next ten years of Davies' academic life, a second trilogy appeared, examining in depth a Canadian family so similar to his own that some early critics considered it an autobiographical series. *The Rebel Angels* (1981) and *What's Bred in the Bone* (1985) were followed by *The Lyre of Orpheus* in 1988. These works continued in fresh perspective the lives and adventures of characters very like those in the previous trilogy. Many readers of Davies' work enjoy his habit of moving his characters from peripheral to central positions in a retrospective reintroduction of their favorite narratives, sometimes serving support roles and sometimes taking center stage in exciting, humorous, and erudite stories that can be read separately, in any order, or enjoyed in their entirety.

Analysis • At the core of Robertson Davies' novels is a sense of humor that reduces pompous institutional values to a refreshing individuality. Interplays of the formal with the specific—officious academia versus lovable satyr-professor, self-important charitable foundation versus reclusive forger-artist, elaborately constructed "magic" paraphernalia versus truly gifted magician, Viennese Jungian psychology versus painfully intimate self-exploration—are the pairings that make the novels come alive. The theatrical metaphors from his early work come forward whenever Davies' novels are to be described: Behind the scenes, his cast of characters perform their roles even more effectively than on the stage of their professional lives, but Davies, often in his fictive personas of Dunstan Ramsay and, in the later trilogy, Simon Darcourt, is there to unmask them and make them laugh at themselves.

Davies perceives a basic duality in human nature and exploits the tensions between the two sides to produce novelistic excitement and philosophical insight. Another way to clarify the duality of Davies' view is to make use of the central "grid" in *The Manticore*: reason versus feeling. Giving both of the main characters' human impulses their proper due, Davies finds the fissure in their marriage and wedges his humor into the gap, penetrating the surface of their union to reveal the weakness of one and the domination of the other. The "gypsy" in each individual (a subject at the center of *The Rebel Angels*) must be answered to, or else an imbalance will turn life sour. For David Staunton in *The Manticore*, reason has overpowered his ability to feel; for Parlabane in *The Rebel Angels*, feelings and emotions have made his intellectual life a hollow pretense. Davies finds and repairs the imbalances, giving to each novel a closure of reconciliation between feeling and reason. Thus, despite the intertwining of characters and incidents, providing a "perspectivist," kaleidoscopic view of both, each novel stands apart, complete, while at the same time the richness of the situations promises more.

Coupled with Davies' vast erudition and education (he was called a "polymath" by more than one critic) is a fine sense of how the English language works; these qualities combined provide both the broad stroke and the marvelous attention to detail that make his novels successful. One unusual feature of all of his work is the very high level of education enjoyed by virtually all the characters, an intellectual *mise-en-scène* that allows the reader and Davies to share all kinds of sophisticated observations. The title *Rebel Angels* subtly suggests its subject, François Rabelais; *What's Bred in the Bone* echoes the "paleopsychology" of a character in *The Rebel Angels*; and the character Magnus prepares the reader for the fact that another character, Pargetter, will be called a "Magus" in a subsequent novel. The puns and plays on words are polylingual and are never spelled out (the character names "Parlabane," "Cruikshank," and "Magnus Eisengrim" are examples ready to hand); Davies does not patronize his readers. Ramsay lost his leg in World War II; he may be David Staunton's biological father, having been in love with Leola Cruikshank Staunton (her maiden name means "crooked leg"). These few examples point to a general trend: metaphor before bald statement, reflected heat before direct blast, euphemism before naked statement. When Dr. von Haller refers to a person's age as "a psalmist's span," she makes no apologies. To appreciate fully what Davies is getting at in his work, a fairly comprehensive cultural literacy is required of the reader.

The earthiness of real life is never lost among the intellectual conceits: A plot line of one whole novel deals with the quality of dung to improve the tonal qualities of stringed instruments. When the time is right for describing sexual aberrations or cadaverish details, Davies is ready. It is true that Ramsay's vast knowledge of arts and letters (Davies himself was famous among his colleagues for extemporaneous but highly informative lectures on obscure subjects of every kind) gives glimpses, if not insights, into such a broad range of cultures and historical periods that Davies' full canon can almost serve as a checklist of gaps in the reader's erudition. As Ramsay himself points out while speaking of his own book in *World of Wonders*, Davies' novels are "readable by the educated, but not rebuffing to somebody who simply wanted a lively, spicy tale."

The Deptford trilogy • Dunstan Ramsay is clearly the authorial persona in the Deptford novels, as actor and audience; whether taking part in the plot directly, as in *Fifth Business*, or as observer and narrator in *World of Wonders*, or as a coincidental facilitator in *The Manticore*, Ramsay emerges as having the closest to Davies' own fine sense of the observably ridiculous, along with a forgiving spirit that makes Davies' work uplifting and lighthearted, despite its relentless examination and criticism of everything spurious and mediocre in the human spirit. Simon Darcourt, a priest and academician in the later novels, is yet another Davies persona, recognizable by his penetration into (and forgiveness of) the foibles of the rest of the characters.

Fifth Business • *Fifth Business*, the first novel of what has become known as the Deptford trilogy, has been cited by many critics as the real beginning of Davies' major work, a "miracle of art." The novel marks Davies' first real "thickening" of plots and details, and a list of the subjects dealt with reads like a tally sheet of Western civilization's accomplishments to date: saints' lives, psychology, mythology, folk art, place-names and family lineages, magic arts, medieval brazen heads and other tricks of the trade, and the complex workings of nineteenth century theater. It is the autobiography of Dunstan Ramsay himself, at the age of seventy, looking backward at the impulses that formed his life and character, beginning with an accident in a winter snowball fight, in which a passerby, Mary Dempster, was injured, causing the premature birth of her son. The "friend/enemy" relationship between Ramsay and Boy Staunton (intended target and careless launcher, respectively) is the singular metaphor for Davies' pursuit of the dichotomy in every person: a drive for worldly success foiled by a need for spiritual or aesthetic grace. For Ramsay, the reverse is true: His life is so affected by the snowball-throwing incident that he never succumbs to merely material reward but spends his life in self-examination. In this novel, all the major characters for the next two are introduced in some form or another: David Staunton (Boy's son) is the central figure in *The Manticore*; the stunted child of Mary Dempster, now Magnus Eisengrim, centers the third novel, *World of Wonders*.

The Manticore • *The Manticore*, an examination of Jungian psychology, serves as *dramatis personae* for all Davies' novels: The archetypes appear again and again in various disguises, from the shadow figure to the father figure to the hero, from the anima to all of its component parts. David Staunton's analyst, Dr. von Haller, a woman truly balanced between reason and feelings, helps him find the missing part of his life and represents the Davies character that appears in every novel: the grown woman, wise, often not beautiful but very attractive nevertheless, who leads the central figure past his conventional assumptions about all women into a deeper, more substantive appreciation of the Eternally Feminine. As Staunton describes the death of his "swordsman" father, Boy Staunton (the name's significance becomes clearer as the analysis progresses), he learns to recognize all sorts of shadows in his past that have led to his celibacy, his indifference to feelings, and his essential loneliness. Ramsay was one of David's tutors, and their reunion at the novel's end, also in the presence of Magnus Eisengrim and Liesl Naegeli, an "ogress," is another example of the sense of reconciliation and closure that each novel offers, despite the interrelatioship of the trilogies themselves. The reader is treated to a full-length portrait of the major characters and then finds them, like old friends, reappearing in other places, other novels, so that the reader is in fact dwelling in the same regions as the heroes of the books. It is a reassuring and comforting realization that, once a book is finished, the characters will be back to reacquaint themselves with the reader in future volumes.

World of Wonders • *World of Wonders* follows Magnus's career up to the point at which Ramsay is asked to write a fictional autobiography of Magnus, as part of a large commercial enterprise that includes a film on the life of Harry Houdini, with Magnus in the title role. The central metaphor is once again a duality, the division of illusion and reality, for Magnus's real genius lies not in the tricks of the trade but in a spiritual gift, given to him at his unusual birth. Now the story of Ramsay and Boy Staunton and Mary Dempster is told from yet another perspective, that of the putative victim, enriched beyond measure by the accident of the stone-filled snowball. The stone inside the snowball, like the knives of Spanish literature, is almost alive, with a mind and a direction all its own; Boy Staunton's body will be found in the river with the stone in his mouth; at the end of *The Manticore*, Ramsay had tossed the stone down a mountain, remarking almost in passing, "I hope it didn't hit anybody." In this way Davies looks at the cause-effect duality apparently at work on the plane of reality, reflecting a larger karmic cause-effect relationship on the spiritual plane. Magnus's life and success, unforeseen at his birth, tell the listeners (they gather each night to continue the story) that human beings can neither foresee nor alter the future by conscious acts, but they affect the future nevertheless by their own facticity. That is the "world of wonders" the book's title introduces.

The Rebel Angels • A special and very important motif for Davies is the mentor-protégé relationship, dealt with in every novel in some form or another. *The Rebel Angels*, beginning a new trilogy, is an example. The protagonists are three professors who have been asked to oversee the distribution of a vast collection of art and manuscripts, left to a charitable foundation by Francis Cornish (the subject of the next novel in the trilogy, *What's Bred in the Bone*). Their contentions and agreements form the framework for a deeper discussion of the nature of human achievement. Simon Darcourt is one of the executors, the kindest and broadest in his interests; he shares the narration with his gifted student Maria Magdalena Theotoky, a young student about to venture on the same academic, "reasoned" path as her tutors. Her Gypsy mother insists, however, on a larger image of her life, and in the reexamination of her values, she discovers the Rabelaisian side of her, in the person of Parlabane, a dissolute, perverted, and most warmhearted individual, a murderer and a suicide, who gives her a great gift in his dying wish.

At least three plots join and part as the book progresses, even the two narrative voices alternating as the story unfolds. Parlabane is a modern manifestation of the seventeenth century Rabelais, Maria's dissertation topic and the author of three valuable letters stolen by one of the three executors. A thoroughly unlikable character named McVarish serves as a foil to the larger, more humanitarian lives of the other professors and the idealized free-enterprise benefactor, Arthur Cornish. Cornish eventually marries Maria, but not before her idol, Clement Hollier, almost absent-mindedly has his way with her on the office couch (a false start in the mentor-protégé relationship). In the process of telling four or five stories at once, Davies manages to give the reader a tour of dozens of cultural worlds, including the care and feeding of rare violins, the cataloging of art collections, the literary secrets of seventeenth century letter-writers, the habits of obscure monastic cults, and the fine points of academic infighting.

What's Bred in the Bone • The second novel in the trilogy, *What's Bred in the Bone*, moves backward one generation, to Canada and Europe just before World War II. Francis Cornish, a member of the Cornish clan, recognizably similar to but different from the Staunton clan, is the scion of a rich Canadian entrepreneur. Brought up both Roman Catholic and Protestant (like Davies), Francis combines a quiet talent for drawing with an uncanny ability to imitate the brushstrokes of the masters. A series of circumstances finds him forging paintings in a German castle, painting his own personal life story into large canvases (a metaphor for Davies' own work), and spying for the British government by counting the clacks of the passing Nazi trains on their way to concentration camps. This mild form of spying is inherited from his military father, in the mold of Boy Staunton, a great diplomatic success but something of a failure as a nurturing parent and an aesthetic model.

Most valuable to scholars seeking biographical references are Davies' descriptions of Francis's childhood in rural Canada, especially his gradual, painful understanding about class differences and the sexual indiscretions of adults (a theme examined more fully in *The Manticore*). Simon Darcourt, academic-priest, has been commissioned to write a biography of Francis Cornish but has turned up some questionable material about his European experiences: He may have forged some drawings, now in the possession of a prestigious public museum. Davies uses the device of splitting the narration (as he does in *Rebel Angels*) between two supernatural beings, one Zadkiel, the "angel of biography," and the other the Daimon Maimas, a dark but energetic manifestation of the artistic conscience. Their otherworldly debate as Cornish's story unfolds allows Davies to investigate once again the necessity of balancing human dualities for sanity and satisfaction.

The Lyre of Orpheus • *The Lyre of Orpheus* finds a musical theme for Davies, a lost and incomplete musical treatment of the Arthurian legend by E. T. A. Hoffmann. The music student Hulda, indirectly under Simon Darcourt's tutelage, decides to complete the opera, and Darcourt is asked to supply a text—his choice of Sir Walter Scott's poetic rendition of the legend makes for an excellent example of how Davies winds the arts around themselves into a whole act of achievement. Here the mentor-protégé relation is developed fully, not only between the narrator and Hulda but also between the student and a visiting composer/conductor, Gunilla, one of Davies's strong, ugly (but attractive), mature women. The "ominous" Professor Pfeiffer, called in as external examiner to Hulda's examination, provides Davies with an opportunity to lampoon all that is disagreeable about certain academics of his acquaintance.

Murther and Walking Spirits • Two final novels complete Davies' oeuvre. Both are set in present-day Toronto; each story is complete and unrelated to the other, though the main character in the first is the son of a friend of characters in the second, and a third novel could have conceivably united them into a trilogy. *Murther and Walking Spirits* is a technical rarity in that the point-of-view character, Conor Gilmartin, is dead before the story begins, murdered by his wife's lover. He stalks the murderer to the Toronto Film Festival, where he views all the films in the annual competition but sees a series that is uniquely his: film after film showing the story of his family from their Welsh roots to their arrival in Canada after the American Revolution through the integration into the new society. After his "personal film festival" is over, Gilmartin has the satisfaction of watching his murderer exposed by the priest from whom he seeks absolution. The priest, a Roman Catholic on the faculty of the University of Toronto, belongs to a group of intermediaries between the physical and spiritual worlds who appear in all of Davies' novels. It is fitting, then, that his last novel, *The Cunning Man*, concerns the mysteries of faith.

The Cunning Man • *The Cunning Man* tells the story of Jonathan Hullah, a doctor who witnessed the death, possibly the murder, of an Anglican priest at an Easter service in 1951. As the doctor discusses the events with a journalist, he reflects on his long life. He remembers the medicine woman who saved his life when he was deathly ill as a child in a remote wilderness outpost, and who inspired his love of medicine. He recalls his education and his first years in the city, when he became involved in the parish where the strange events took place. His "cunning" is the semisupernatural knowledge that enables him to participate in the real world of money-grubbing, fame-seeking people while serving as a force for good.

Thomas J. Taylor
Updated by Thomas Willard

Other major works

SHORT FICTION: *High Spirits*, 1982.

PLAYS: *Overlaid*, pr. 1947, pb. 1949 (one act); *At the Gates of the Righteous*, pr. 1948, pb. 1949; *Eros at Breakfast*, pr. 1948, pb. 1949; *Fortune, My Foe*, pr. 1948, pb. 1949; *Hope Deferred*, pr. 1948, pb. 1949; *The Voice of the People*, pr. 1948, pb. 1949; *Eros at Breakfast, and Other Plays*, pb. 1949 (includes *Hope Deferred, Overlaid, At the Gates of the Righteous, The Voice of the People*); *At My Heart's Core*, pr., pb. 1950; *King Phoenix*, pr. 1950, pb.

1972; *A Masque of Aesop,* pr., pb. 1952; *A Jig for the Gypsy,* pr. 1954 ([broadcast and staged], pb. 1954); *Hunting Stuart,* pr. 1955, pb. 1972; *Love and Libel: Or, The Ogre of the Provincial World,* pr., pb. 1960 (adaptation of his novel *Leaven of Malice*); *A Masque of Mr. Punch,* pr. 1962, pb. 1963; *Hunting Stuart, and Other Plays,* pb. 1972 (includes *King Phoenix* and *General Confession*); *Question Time,* pr., pb. 1975.

TELEPLAY: *Fortune, My Foe,* 1953 (adaptation of his play).

NONFICTION: *Shakespeare's Boy Actors,* 1939; *Shakespeare for Younger Players: A Junior Course,* 1942; *The Diary of Samuel Marchbanks,* 1947; *The Table Talk of Samuel Marchbanks,* 1949; *Renown at Stratford: A Record of the Shakespeare Festival in Canada, 1953,* 1953 (with Tyrone Guthrie); *Twice Have the Trumpets Sounded: A Record of the Stratford Shakespearean Festival in Canada, 1954,* 1954 (with Guthrie); *Thrice the Brinded Cat Hath Mew'd: A Record of the Stratford Shakespearean Festival in Canada, 1955,* 1955 (with Guthrie); *A Voice from the Attic,* 1960; *The Personal Art: Reading to Good Purpose,* 1961; *Marchbanks' Almanack,* 1967; *Stephen Leacock: Feast of Stephen,* 1970; *One Half of Robertson Davies,* 1977; *The Enthusiasms of Robertson Davies,* 1979; *The Well-Tempered Critic,* 1981; *Reading and Writing,* 1993; *The Merry Heart: Reflections on Reading, Writing, and the World of Books,* 1997; *"For Your Eyes Alone": Letters, 1976-1995,* 1999.

Bibliography

Cameron, Elspeth, ed. *Robertson Davies: An Appreciation.* New York: Broadview Press, 1991. Provides criticism and interpretations of Davies' life and works. Bibliography.

Cheaney, J. B. "Bred in the Bone: The Fiction of Canadian Author Robertson Davies." *The World & I* 16, no. 8 (August, 2001): 247-255. Profiles the life and works of Davies.

Davies, Robertson. *Conversations with Robertson Davies.* Edited by J. Madison Davis. Jackson: University Press of Mississippi, 1989. Collection of interviews with Davies.

_____________. *The Well-Tempered Critic: One Man's View of Theatre and Letters in Canada.* Toronto: McClelland and Stewart, 1981. The first half of this volume is a collection of essays on the theater, spiced with Davies' own acerbic wit but revealing his benevolent attitude toward traditional, even medieval, dramatic forms. Contains many reviews of the festival seasons at Stratford, Ontario.

Grant, Judith Skelton. *Robertson Davies: Man of Myth.* New York: Viking, 1994. The authorized biography, covering all but the last year of Davies' life. Provides critical commentary on his novels as well as information on his dealings with publishers.

Heintzman, Ralph H., ed. *Journal of Canadian Studies* 12 (February, 1977). A special issue of Davies criticism; much of the scholarly work on Davies appears only in Canadian publications. This special edition includes a valuable Davies log of writing and important events, with six other essays examining the Deptford trilogy.

La Bossière, Camille R., and Linda Morra, eds. *Robertson Davies: A Mingling of Contrarieties.* Ottawa: University of Ottawa Press, 2001. Examines, among other topics, Davies' humor, "masks," and postmodern elements in his works. Bibliography.

Lawrence, Robert G., and Samuel L. Macey, eds. *Studies in Robertson Davies' Deptford Trilogy.* Victoria, B.C.: English Literary Studies, University of Victoria, 1980. Davies introduces this collection with a personal retrospective of the creative impulses that resulted in the Deptford trilogy. The studies range from traditional historical criticism to folklore backgrounds to Jungian analysis to examinations of law. An opening article surveying the Salterton novels brings the reader up to the Deptford novels.

Little, Dave. *Catching the Wind: The Religious Vision of Robertson Davies.* Toronto: ECW Press, 1996. Discusses an important theme in Davies' fiction: "the search for the self as a religious journey." Includes a helpful list of biblical allusions in the novels through *Murther and Walking Spirits.*

MacLulich, T. D. *Between Europe and America: The Canadian Tradition in Fiction.* Toronto: ECW Press, 1988. Despite its title, this study deals with Davies' earliest plays, *Hope Deferred* and *Overlaid,* before a brief synopsis of *Fortune, My Foe* and *At My Heart's Core.* Much on Davies' prose work as well. Helpful index.

Monk, Patricia. *The Smaller Infinity: The Jungian Self in the Novels of Robertson Davies.* Toronto: University of Toronto Press, 1982. The most thorough book-length study of Jungian influences in all of Davies' writing, especially concentrating on *The Manticore.* Monk finds the archetypal constructions of the characters a more overpowering leitmotif than Davies' own autobiographical renditions, and she systematizes the Deptford trilogy's characters around the traditional figures of Jungian psychology. This study was begun in her essay "Davies and the Drachenloch," in Lawrence and Macey, above.

Peterman, Michael. *Robertson Davies.* Boston: Twayne, 1986. The first four chapters deal with Davies' journalistic and dramatic careers; the last chapters discuss the Salterton novels, the Deptford trilogy, and *The Rebel Angels.* Peterman explains well the importance of Davies' Canadian birth and childhood. Valuable bibliography (to 1985) and index.

Steinberg, M. W. "Don Quixote and the Puppets: Theme and Structure in Robertson Davies' Drama." In *Dramatists in Canada: Selected Essays,* edited by William H. New. Vancouver: University of British Columbia Press, 1972. Offers a structural analysis of Davies' early plays, notably *Fortune, My Foe; At My Heart's Core*; and *A Jig for the Gypsy.* "Eminently stageworthy and . . . a valuable contribution to a genre that Canadian talent has unfortunately neglected," Steinberg notes.

Woodcock, George. "A Cycle Completed: The Nine Novels of Robertson Davies." *Canadian Literature: A Quarterly of Criticism and Review* 126 (Autumn, 1990): 33-48. A good overview of Davies' major literary contribution, as a backdrop for his dramatic output. Woodcock sees Davies' "traditional" forms as "calming and comforting" in an otherwise "permissive" literary world.

Samuel R. Delany

Born: New York, New York; April 1, 1942

Principal long fiction • *The Jewels of Aptor,* 1962; *Captives of the Flame,* 1963 (revised, 1968, as *Out of the Dead City*); *The Towers of Toron,* 1964; *City of a Thousand Suns,* 1965; *The Ballad of Beta-2,* 1965; *Babel-17,* 1966; *Empire Star,* 1966; *The Einstein Intersection,* 1967; *Nova,* 1968; *The Fall of the Towers,* 1970 (includes revised versions of *Out of the Dead City, The Towers of Toron,* and *City of a Thousand Suns*); *The Tides of Lust,* 1973 (also known as *Equinox*); *Dhalgren,* 1975; *Triton,* 1976 (also known as *Trouble on Triton*); *Empire,* 1978; *Tales of Nevèrÿon,* 1979; *Nevèrÿona: Or, The Tale of Signs and Cities,* 1983; *Stars in My Pocket Like Grains of Sand,* 1984; *Flight from Nevèrÿon,* 1985; *The Bridge of Lost Desire,* 1987 (also known as *Return to Nevèrÿon*); *Hogg,* 1993; *They Fly at Çiron,* 1993; *The Mad Man,* 1994.

Other literary forms • Samuel R. Delany is known for his work in a number of other literary forms, including those of the short story, autobiography, and, most notably, literary criticism and theory. Delany's short stories have been collected in *Driftglass: Ten Tales of Speculative Fiction* (1971), and some have been reprinted along with new stories in *Distant Stars* (1981). *Heavenly Breakfast: An Essay on the Winter of Love* (1979) is a memoir describing Delany's experiences as a member of a commune in New York. *The Motion of Light in Water: Sex and Science-Fiction Writing in the East Village, 1957-1965* (1988) is an autobiography covering Delany's youth and the early part of his writing career. Delany also published a number of important essays on science fiction, some of which have been collected in *The Jewel-Hinged Jaw* (1977), *Starboard Wine* (1984), *The Straits of Messina* (1987), and *Longer Views* (1996). In addition to other, uncollected essays, introductions, and speeches, Delany wrote *The American Shore: Meditations on a Tale of Science Fiction by Thomas M. Disch* (1978), a structuralist-semiotic study of Disch's short story "Angouleme," and *Silent Interviews* (1994), a collection of what Delany calls "written interviews." Delany worked in other forms as well: With his then-wife, Marilyn Hacker, he coedited the speculative-fiction journal *Quark* from 1970 to 1971; he wrote for comic books, including a large-format "visual novel," *Empire* (1978); and he made two experimental films, *Tiresias* (1970) and *The Orchid* (1971).

Achievements • Delany is one of a handful of science-fiction writers to have been recognized by the academic community as well as by authors and fans of the genre (he won both the Hugo and Nebula Awards). Delany studied and taught at the State University of New York at Buffalo and the University of Wisconsin at Milwaukee and served as a contributing editor to the scholarly journal *Science-Fiction Studies.* Unlike mainstream (or "mundane," as Delany prefers) authors such as Walker Percy and John Barth who have dabbled in science fiction, or science-fiction writers such as Kurt Vonnegut, who would reject that label, Delany is known as a vigorous defender and promoter of the equality of science fiction with other genres. In his criticism as well as in his practice, he has continually stressed the importance of care, thought, and craft in writing. His own work, like that of those writers he most consistently praises (including especially Joanna Russ, Thomas Disch, and Roger Zelazny), is marked by its attention to language and its concern with issues beyond "hard science" and technology, particularly with the roles of language and myth in society and the potential of and constraints on human behavior within different social constructs.

Delany's own background informs these social concerns: One of a handful of black science-fiction writers, he also became known as a committed feminist and a gay writer and parent. His graphic depictions of sex and violence often exceed the usual limits of his genre (he even published several explicitly pornographic novels). On the other hand, his criticism and his writing converged over the years, as Delany sought to popularize his theoretical interests by publishing them in formats accessible to science-fiction fans and by incorporating them into the very structures of his fiction. Although Delany's theoretical stance sometimes alienates those very fans, he must be seen as one of the foremost modern writers and critics of science fiction or, indeed, of any type of fiction.

Biography • Samuel Ray Delany, Jr., was born in Harlem in New York City on April 1, 1942, to an upper-middle-class black family. His father was a prominent Harlem funeral director and was active in the National Association for the Advancement of Colored People (NAACP). Delany attended grade school at the prestigious Dalton School, noted for its progressive curriculum and eccentric teachers and staff. Tensions with his father and a learning disability that would later be diagnosed as dyslexia kept Delany's childhood and teen years from being particularly happy. In turn, though, he was attracted to theater, science, gymnastics (all of which figure in his novels), and especially writing.

Toward the end of his Dalton years, Delany began to write short stories. He also began reading science fiction, including the works of such writers as Theodore Sturgeon, Alfred Bester, and Robert Heinlein. After being graduated from Dalton in 1956, Delany attended the Bronx High School of Science, where he was encouraged in his writing by some of his teachers and by a fellow student and aspiring poet, Marilyn Hacker. After high school graduation in 1960, Delany received a fellowship to the Breadloaf Writers' Conference in Vermont, where he met Robert Frost and other professional writers.

In 1960, Delany enrolled in City College of New York but dropped out in 1961. He continued to write, supporting himself as a folksinger in Greenwich Village clubs and cafés. On August 24, 1961, he and Hacker were married. Although their marriage of more than thirteen years was open and loosely structured (the couple often lived apart), Hacker and Delany were highly influential on each other as he developed his fiction and she her poetry (Hacker's influence is especially strong in *Babel-17*). Delany submitted his first published book, *The Jewels of Aptor*, to Ace Books, where Hacker worked, at her suggestion. Hacker herself is the model for Rydra Wong, the heroine of *Babel-17*.

Delany's life in New York over the next several years, including his personal relationships and a near nervous breakdown in 1964, figures in a number of his works from *Empire Star* to *Dhalgren*. After *The Jewels of Aptor*, he completed a trilogy, *The Fall of the Towers*, and in 1964 reenrolled at City College of New York, where he edited the campus poetry magazine, *The Promethean*. He soon dropped out again and in 1965, after completing *The Ballad of Beta-2*, went with a friend to work on shrimp boats in the Gulf of Mexico.

At this point, Delany's writing was beginning to return enough to help support him, and, after completing *Babel-17* and *Empire Star*, he used the advance money to

Linda Koolish/Courtesy, University Press of Mississippi

tour Europe and Turkey during 1965 and 1966, an experience that influenced both *The Einstein Intersection* and *Nova.* When he returned to the United States, Delany became more involved in the science-fiction community, which was beginning to take notice of his work. He attended conferences and workshops and met both established science-fiction writers and younger authors, including Joanna Russ and Thomas Disch, who would both become good friends. In 1967, The Science Fiction Writers of America awarded *Babel-17* the Nebula Award for best novel (shared with *Flowers for Algernon* by Daniel Keyes), and in 1968 the award again went to Delany, this time for both *The Einstein Intersection* and the short story "Ave, and Gomorrah. . . . "

During the winter of 1967, while Hacker was living in San Francisco, Delany moved in with a New York rock group called The Heavenly Breakfast, who lived communally. This experiment in living, recorded in *Heavenly Breakfast,* is reflected in *Dhalgren.* By 1968, Delany was becoming firmly established as an important science-fiction writer. He had won three Nebulas; had a new book, *Nova,* published in hardcover; had begun to receive critical acclaim from outside science-fiction circles; and had spoken at the Modern Language Association's annual meeting in New York. During the next few years, while working on *Dhalgren,* he devoted himself to a number of other projects, including reviewing and filmmaking. He received the Hugo Award in 1970 for his short story "Time Considered as a Helix of SemiPrecious Stones" and in the same year began coediting, with Hacker, *Quark: A Quarterly of Speculative Fiction.* The journal—which published writers such as Russ, Disch, R. A. Lafferty, and others who experimented with both form and content in the genre—ceased publication in 1971 after four issues.

In 1972, Delany worked for DC Comics, writing the stories for two issues of *Wonder Woman* and the introduction of an anthology of *Green Lantern/Green Arrow* comics. In 1973, he joined Hacker in London, where he continued to work on *Dhalgren* and sat in at the University of London on classes in language and philosophy that profoundly influenced his later writing. Completing *Dhalgren,* Delany began work on his next novel, *Triton,* which was published in 1976.

On January 14, 1974, Hacker gave birth to a daughter, Iva Hacker-Delany, in London. Delany, with his family, returned to the United States late in 1974 to take the position of Visiting Butler Chair Professor of English at the State University of New York at Buffalo, a post offered to him by Leslie Fiedler. At this time, Hacker and Delany agreed to a separation, and Hacker returned to London (they were divorced in 1980). Delany completed *Triton* and in September, 1976, accepted a fellowship at the

University of Wisconsin at Milwaukee's Center for Twentieth Century Studies. In 1977, he collected some of his critical essays in *The Jewel-Hinged Jaw* and in 1978 published *The American Shore*, a book-length study of a Disch short story.

During the 1980's, Delany spent much of his time in New York, writing, looking after Iva, and attending conferences and conventions. His major project in that decade was the creation of a "sword-and-sorcery" fantasy series, comprising *Tales of Nevèrÿon*, *Neveryóna*, *Flight from Nevèrÿon*, and *The Bridge of Lost Desire*. The impact of the acquired immunodeficiency syndrome (AIDS) crisis is seen in the latter two books, especially *Flight from Nevèrÿon*. In 1984, Delany collected more of his criticism in *Starboard Wine* and also received the Pilgrim Award for achievement in science-fiction criticism from the Science Fiction Research Association. Delany's only science-fiction work in that decade was *Stars in My Pocket Like Grains of Sand*, the first part of a planned "dyptich." In 1988, he published his autobiographical recollections about his earlier years in *The Motion of Light in Water*, and he became a professor of comparative literature at the University of Massachusetts, Amherst.

During the 1990's Delany produced a great deal of writing and gained the recognition of being, in the words of critic and author James Sallis, "among our finest and most important writers." The most controversial of Delany's 1990's publications are his erotic novels—*Equinox*, *Hogg*, and *The Mad Man*—and his 1998 comic-book-format erotic autobiography, *Bread and Wine*. *Equinox* appeared briefly in 1973, and *Hogg*'s scheduled publication that same year was canceled. Both went back into print in the mid-1990's, along with the release of *The Mad Man*, the only one of the three erotic novels composed during the 1990's. Although these books have disturbed and challenged many readers and scholars of Delany's work, a number of critics, most notably Norman Mailer, have defended them as examples of Delany's belief in pushing the boundaries of literature and of dealing with sexual subjects with absolute openness.

Delany also published two important nonfiction works during the 1990's: *Silent Interviews*, a collection of Delany's written interviews with subjects ranging from racism to aesthetic theory; and *Longer Views*, a collection of Delany's major essays on art, literature, and culture. Finally, there were two new works of fiction: *Atlantis*, a collection of three mainstream stories set during the 1920's; and *They Fly at Çiron*, a fantasy novel that appeared in 1993 but became widely available two years later. Delany also won the Bill Whitehead Award for Lifetime Achievement in Gay Literature in 1993 and was the Guest of Honor at the World Science-Fiction Convention at London, England, in 1995. During that same year, he was also a distinguished visiting writer at the University of Idaho. In 1997, he was a master artist-in-residence at the Atlantic Center for the Arts. In 1999, he began teaching at the University of Buffalo. Since then, he has remained active in the field of science fiction, attending conventions and teaching at the Clarion Science Fiction Writers' Workshops. In 2001, he taught comparative literature at Philadephia's Temple University.

Analysis • The great twentieth century poet T. S. Eliot remarked that a poet's criticism of other writers often reveals as much or more about that poet's own work as about that of the writers being discussed. This observation certainly holds true for Samuel R. Delany, perhaps the most vocal and certainly among the most intellectual of science-fiction author-critics. All too often, science fiction has been regarded by mainstream critics as an adolescent subgenre, a form to be lumped with mysteries, Westerns, and gothic romances, barely literate and hardly deserving of serious attention. The genre does have its apologists, whose defense takes many forms. Some treat science fiction thematically and historically, as the latest manifestation of a great tradition of heroic and mock-heroic fantasy and utopian literature, running in a line from the epic of Gilgamesh through Homer's *Odyssey* (c. 800 B.C.E.) and Ludovico Ariosto's *Orlando furioso* (1516) and including the works of Thomas More, Jonathan Swift, François Rabelais, and Edward Bellamy.

Others take a more pragmatic approach, centered on science fiction as a predictive form, able to explore the implications of new technologies and new social forms, as in the works of Jules Verne, H. G. Wells, George Orwell, and Aldous Huxley. Still others point to the literary merits of an elite handful of science-fiction writers from Wells to Ursula K. Le Guin.

What all these approaches have in common is an assumption that science fiction is a form that can and occasionally does live up to the standards of "true" literature. Delany, though, turns the premises of such critics upside down. Rather than seeking the meaning and value of science fiction by detecting the presence of "literary" elements and properties, Delany insists, the reader and critic must employ a set of "reading protocols" as a methodology for tapping the richness and complexity of science fiction. The protocols one applies to reading science fiction of necessity must be different from the protocols one applies to "mundane" literature, if only in how the reader must constitute whole worlds and universes as background for any narrative.

As an example, first noted by Harlan Ellison, Delany frequently cites a sentence from a Robert Heinlein novel: "The door dilated." Given only these three words, one can make a wealth of suppositions about a culture that needs doors that dilate rather than swing or slide open and shut and that has the technology to manufacture and operate them. The more profound implications of the "protocol of reading" that science fiction necessitates can be seen in another example often mentioned by Delany. In another Heinlein novel, *Starship Troopers* (1959), it is casually revealed two-thirds of the way through the book that the first-person narrator is Hispanic, not Anglo. Placed so casually in the narrative and read in the context of American society during the 1950's—when Delany himself read it—such a revelation must have been disruptive, all the more so for a reader such as Delany, who is black. The fact that a society can be imagined in which race is no longer a major factor in determining social position opens to question the social fabric of the society in which the book is read and thereby generates potentials for change. Indeed, it may come as a surprise that requires such a shift in understanding for some of Delany's readers to realize that virtually none of his major protagonists are white.

Such a protocol of reading has the power to affect the reader's reaction to the language itself; Delany's own writing virtually confronts the reader with the need to watch for cues and read carefully for complexity and variety. Mollya, a character in *Babel-17*, explains her desire to aid the heroine, Rydra Wong, by stating, "I was dead. She made me alive." In a mainstream novel, such a statement would be merely a clichéd metaphor. In *Babel-17*, though, Mollya means what she says quite literally: She had been "discorporate" before she was revitalized by Rydra, who needed a new crew member. With this new weight of literal meaning, the cliché is refreshed and itself given new life as a metaphor as well as existing as a factual statement. It is through such potential to refresh the language, Delany suggests, that science fiction is the form of prose that is closest to poetry, even, through its popularity, coming to usurp some of poetry's traditional social functions.

Delany's critical comments and theoretical observations have three effects. First, they are an incitement to the literary critic to accept science fiction as a serious genre. (His essay "Letter to a Critic" was prompted by his offense at Leslie Fiedler's expressed hope that science fiction would not lose its "sloppiness" or "vulgarity.") Second, he has insisted that science-fiction writers give greater care to their art, in the texture of their prose as well as in the precision with which they render their imagined worlds. (His attack on Ursula K. Le Guin's highly praised novel in "To Read *The Dispossessed*" takes the author to task precisely for the book's weaknesses on both counts.) Finally, these observations are above all a comment on the standards that Delany has set for himself.

To read through Delany's novels is to trace the growth and coming to maturity of a literary artist as well as to see the development and mutation of prevalent themes and images. Up through *Dhalgren*, his works usually center on a quest for identity undertaken or observed by a young man (*Babel-17*, with its female hero, is a notable exception). More often than not, the novel's center of consciousness is an artist, usually a writer or musician. These characters themselves are in varying stages of development, and their quest usually culminates in their reaching a new level of awareness. In *The Ballad of Beta-2*, the young scholar-protagonist not only discovers behind an apparently trivial piece of space folklore a meaning that will alter humanity's future and knowledge of the universe but also discovers the dangers of glib preconceptions and the value of dedicated work. In *Empire Star*, the young Comet Jo advances from "simplex" to "multiplex" levels of thought in a tale that is also a neat twist on the paradoxes of time travel.

A major concern throughout Delany's career up through *Tales of Nevèrÿon* has been the function of language and myth. The power of language in shaping awareness is the major thematic concern of *Babel-17*. Its heroine, the poet and space captain Rydra Wong (fluent in many languages, including those of body movements) is sent to interpret and discover the source of an enemy alien language, Babel-17. In so doing, she discovers a way of thinking that is highly analytical and marvelously efficient and compact but that is also dangerous—having no concept of "I" or "you," the language can induce psychotic and sociopathic behavior in those who use it.

Myth is employed to varying degrees in Delany's novels, most heavily in *The Einstein Intersection*, *Nova*, and *Dhalgren*—so much so that the three almost form a trilogy of meditations on the subject. In *The Einstein Intersection*, aliens have populated a ruined earth deserted by human beings. Before these new inhabitants can create their own culture, though, they must first act through the myths—from those of Orpheus and Jesus to those of Billy the Kid and Jean Harlow—that they have inherited from humanity. In *Nova*, space captain Lorq von Ray self-consciously sets out on a Grail-like quest for Illyrion, an element found at the heart of exploding stars, in order to change the social and economic structure of the entire universe. In *Dhalgren*, media and rumor elevate characters to legendary status almost overnight. The book effectively examines the disjuncture between myth and experience without denying the reality or validity of either.

Myth reappears in a different form in the Nevèrÿon cycle. Although three of the books—*Tales of Nevèrÿon*, *Flight from Nevèrÿon*, and *The Bridge of Lost Desire* (in addition to *Neveryóna*)—are collections of "tales," they have to be read as complete fictions whose individual parts create a greater whole. In fact, the tetralogy can be considered one complete text in itself; however, in keeping with Delany's insistence on the importance of the provisional, the random, and the contradictory as features to be accepted in life and in literature, the parts do not always cohere and may be read in different orders. Myth is the very subject of these writings, inspired in part by Robert Howard's Conan the Barbarian books but also playing with numerous utopian concepts. (The name Nevèrÿon itself—"never/there"—is a play on the word utopia—"no place.") The books themselves are further framed within the context of an ongoing mock-scholarly analysis, "Some Informal Remarks Toward the Modular Calculus" (which actually began as part of *Triton*), suggesting that Nevèrÿon is an extrapolation of an ancient text, possibly the beginning and source of all writing.

In his mature works, from *Babel-17* on, Delany became increasingly "multiplex" as his characterizations took on new levels of depth and complexity. Delany has moved increasingly to the realization that neither the individual nor society is a stable, unitary entity and that meaning is not to be derived from either or both of these forces in themselves but from the relationships and interactions between them. This realization is manifested in two images that recur throughout Delany's fiction and criticism. The first is the palimpsest—the inscribed sheet that has been imperfectly erased and reinscribed several times, creating a rich and difficult multilayered text whose meanings may be incomplete and can never be reduced to any one reading. The Nevèrÿon cycle, as an extreme instance, is a densely layered text that comments on its own narrative, its generic counterparts and origins, and its own composition.

The second image is that of the web, which is multidirectional rather than linear and in which the individual points are no more important than the connections between them. To recognize the web is to understand its structure and learn how to use it or at least work within it, possibly even to break or reshape it. On the literal level, such understanding allows Rydra Wong to break free of a web that straps her down; on the figurative level, recognition of the web allows one to understand and function within a culture. Katin, the protonovelist of *Nova*, comes to realize that his society, far from being impoverished and lacking a necessary center of tradition (a common complaint of modern artists), is actually rich and overdetermined, multilayered, when one looks at the interrelationships of points within the culture rather than at any single point. The fatal mistake of Bron Helstrom, the protagonist of *Triton*, is his inability to recognize the web, his attempt to seek a sense of unitary being that is increasingly elusive instead of accepting the flux and flow that characterize Triton's society. In *Stars in My Pocket Like Grains of Sand*, the Web is the name of the information and communication network that spans the universe, affecting its operations in mysterious ways.

In these images of palimpsest and web, Delany echoes modern thought in many disciplines. Some psychiatrists assert that the individual ego is illusory, a construct to give the semblance of unity to the multiple and conflicting layers of desire and repression which constitute the subject. Anthropologists and sociologists define society by the interactions within its patterns and structures rather than as a unitary and seamless "culture" or even a collection of such cultures. Linguists stipulate that the meanings of individual utterances cannot be determined by isolating individual parts of speech, that in fact the concepts "noun" and "verb" have no individual meaning except in relation to whole statements and the context within which they occur. Finally, post-Einsteinian physics has demonstrated that matter itself is not composed of stable, unitary particles but that atoms and their components are actually "energy packets" whose characteristics and behavior depend upon the expectations of observers and the contexts in which they are observed. Delany is aware of all these intellectual currents and is in fact a part of this "web" of thought himself; within this pattern of relationships he has set a standard for all writers, whether fantastic or mainstream. Two of the novels that explore the implications of these assumptions are *Dhalgren* and *Triton.*

Dhalgren • *Dhalgren* begins with an archetypal scenario: A young man, wearing only one sandal and unable to remember his name, wanders into Bellona, a midwestern city that has suffered some nameless catastrophe. In the course of the novel's 880 pages, he encounters the city's remaining residents; goes through mental, physical, and sexual adventures; becomes a local legend; and leaves. In its complexity and its ambitious scope, *Dhalgren* invites comparison with a handful of contemporary novels, including Vladimir Nabokov's *Ada or Ardor* (1969) and Thomas Pynchon's *Gravity's Rainbow* (1973), which make Joycean demands of the reader. Unlike many other science-fiction novels set in a post-holocaust society, *Dhalgren* is not concerned with the causes of the breakdown, nor does it tell of an attempt to create a new society out of the ashes of the old. There is no need for such a reconstruction. Bellona's catastrophe was unique; the rest of the country and the world are unaffected. Separated from outside electronic communication and simply abandoned by the larger society, Bellona has become a center of attraction for outcasts and drifters of all descriptions as well as remaining a home to its own disenfranchised, notably the city's black population. The city has become a place of absolute freedom, where all can do and be whatever they choose, yet it is not in a state of anarchy. There are rules and laws that govern the city, but they are not recorded or codified.

To the newcomer (and to a first reader of the book), these "rules" seem random and unpredictable. Clouds obscure the sky, so that time of day has little meaning, and the days themselves are named arbitrarily. Direction in this city seems constantly to shift, in part because people change the street signs at whim. Fires burn throughout the city, but listlessly and without pattern. When the clouds do part, they might reveal two moons in the night sky or a sun that covers half the sky. The protagonist (who comes to be known simply as The Kid) must define his identity in terms of these shifting relationships, coping with the ever-fluid patterns Bellona offers.

The price of failing to work within the web and to accommodate reality—even an unreal reality—is exemplified by the Richards family, white middle-class citizens who try to maintain a semblance of the life they had known and are going mad as a result. The Kid begins his stay in Bellona by working for the Richards, helping them to move upstairs in their apartment complex, away from a "nest" of "Scorpions," the mostly black street gangs who wander through the city. (The Scorpions themselves are almost as annoyed and bothered by the Richardses.) The move is futile—the Richardses are no happier or saner in their new apartment, and their son accidentally dies during the move; The Kid is not paid his promised wages (in any case, money is useless in Bellona). Nevertheless, the job has helped The Kid to adjust to Bellona's society, and he has begun to write poetry in a notebook he has found. As he nears the end of his job, he finds himself becoming, almost by accident, a Scorpion and eventually the leader of a "nest." His poetry is published, and he becomes, within the city, famous.

The characters and events of *Dhalgren* are rich and detailed enough in themselves to make the book notable. It is Delany's attention to form, though, that makes the book so complex and the act of reading it so disruptive. Not only are the city and its events seemingly random, but the plot and characterization are likewise unpredictable. Questions remain unanswered, few elements are fully resolved, and the answers and resolutions that are given are tentative and possibly misleading. Near the end of the novel, The Kid believes that he has discovered his name, but this is never confirmed. He leaves Bellona at the end of the book, but his fate is left obscure. The Kid is, moreover, an unreliable center of consciousness. He was once in a mental institution, so the reader must doubt his perceptions (he unaccountably loses stretches of time; after his first sexual encounter early in the book, he sees the woman he was with turn into a tree). He is also ambidextrous and possibly dyslexic, so that the random ways in which Bellona seems to rearrange itself may be the result of The Kid's own confusion. At the same time, though, Delany gives the reader reason to believe The Kid's perception; others, for example, also witness the impossible double moons and giant sun.

Dhalgren is not a book that will explain itself. A palimpsest, it offers new explanations on each reading. The Kid's notebook contains observations by an unknown author that tempt the reader to think that they are notes for the novel *Dhalgren*; there are minor but significant differences, however, between notes and text. The last phrase of the novel, ". . . I have come to," runs into the first, "to wound the autumnal city," recalling the circular construction of *Finnegans Wake* (1939). Unlike the riverrun of James Joyce's dream book, though, *Dhalgren* does not offer the solace of such a unitary construction. The two phrases do not, after all, cohere, but overlap on the word "to." If anything, the construction of the book echoes the "optical chain" made of mirrors, prisms, and lenses that The Kid and other characters wear. Events and phrases within the book do not exactly repeat, but imprecisely mirror, one another. Certain events and phenomena, such as the giant sun, are magnified as if by a lens; others are fragmented and dispersed, as a prism fragments light into the visible spectrum.

Ultimately, Delany's Bellona is a paradigm of contemporary society. Within this seeming wasteland, though, the author finds not solace and refuge in art and love, as so many modern authors have, but the very source and taproot of art and love. Delany's epigraph reads, "You have confused the true and the real." Whatever the "reality" of the city, the book's events, or The Kid's ultimate fate, "truth" has been discovered. The Kid no longer needs the city, and his place is taken by a young woman entering Bellona in a scene that mirrors The Kid's own entrance. Even the "reality" of this scene is not assured, as The Kid's speech fragments into the unfinished sentences of the notebook. "Truth," finally, is provisional, whatever is sufficient for one's needs, and requires to be actively sought and separated from the "real."

Triton • Delany's next novel, *Triton*, has some similarities to *Dhalgren* but turns the premises of the earlier novel inside out. Once again, a protagonist is introduced into a society of near-total freedom. This time, however, the setting is an established, deliberately and elaborately planned society on Neptune's moon Triton in the year 2112, and the protagonist, Bron Helstrom, is a worker in "metalogics" for a company (termed a "hegemony") on that moon. Triton is at least as free a society as Bellona—indeed, more so, since people are not only free to behave and live in almost any social, sexual, or religious pattern but also may change their residences, their physical sex, and their psychological sexual orientation almost at will.

In the novel's course, Triton joins with the other Outer Satellites of the worlds beyond Jupiter in a war against Mars and Earth, but Delany subverts one's expectations in his treatment of this conflict. The war involves no soldiers, causes the deaths of millions, and is over quickly; it is also peripheral to the book's main focus, a psychological study of Bron Helstrom. Helstrom, a seemingly normal individual and a recent emigrant from Mars, is out of place on this moon which has a place for everybody. He meets a roaming actor and theatrical producer called The Spike and becomes romantically obsessed with her, but she ultimately rejects him. This rejection, caused by and coupled with Helstrom's narcissism and obsession with correct responses to codes, conventions, and patterns of behavior, drives him deeper into himself. Unable, as he thinks, to find a woman who will suit his ideal, he has a sex-change operation to become that ideal himself, one who will then be available for a man like himself. His (or now her) rules of conduct, though, require complete passivity. Helstrom must wait for the right man and can make no sign to him, so she must wait forever, all the more so because she has falsely idealized a code of "correct" male and female behavior. The end reveals a total solipsism: The one man who could meet Bron Helstrom's standards is himself, just as she is the one woman who could meet his.

Triton is, in its way, an illustration of Gödel's theorem: No logical system is sufficient to explain itself, and thus every system is incomplete and open to paradox. Triton's social system, designed to accommodate everyone (one of its rules even requires a place where no rules apply) still cannot accommodate someone such as Helstrom who, coming from Mars, does not share the presuppositions on which that system is founded. Helstrom's logic of male-female relationships, on the other hand, stems from his failure to operate on Triton's terms and is paradoxical and incomplete within itself too.

Triton, subtitled *An Ambiguous Heterotopia,* is in some ways a reply to Ursula K. Le Guin's *The Dispossessed* (1974, subtitled *An Ambiguous Utopia*). Although Triton's society is in certain aspects utopian, offering a nearly ideal model of a future society, that model—like all utopias, including Le Guin's—is insufficient. Thus Delany alludes to the notion of the "heterotopia" advanced by the French philosopher Michel Foucault. In contrast to utopias, which provide consolation, heterotopias disturb and disrupt, refusing to allow things to hold together. Triton can not "hold together" metaphorically or literally. It cannot anticipate a Helstrom; it also may lose its artificial gravity by a random coherence of the subatomic particles in its energy field.

The contradictions of modern American society—tending toward libertarianism on one hand and repression on the other—are extrapolated into the future interplanetary society of *Triton.* Triton itself is an idealized extension of aspects of Delany's experiences in New York's East Village, San Francisco, and elsewhere during the 1960's and early 1970's. Earth, however, remains mired in its dominant hierarchical, patriarchal culture. Helstrom, from Mars, is sufficiently distant from Earth's culture to be shocked at its brutality and bemused by its adherence to money. Helstrom, though, patterns his own models of sex role behavior on sexist and patriarchal assumptions about the supposedly innate natures of men and women, behavior that is rendered ridiculous by a society in which "male" and "female" are simply categories of choice. It should be noted that in its depictions of Helstrom's behavior, *Triton* is often richly comic.

Delany's probing goes even further. He reminds the reader that *he* is presenting models too. The novel includes two appendices, one a collection of notes and omitted segments from the novel and the other a segment of lectures by a Martian scholar, Ashima Slade, titled "Some Informal Remarks Toward the Modular Calculus, Part Two." These additions are integral to the novel. They serve to remind the reader that the book is a made object, subject to work and revision, and they also comment on the method of the models provided in the "novel" itself. They also give hints of possible answers to some of the questions raised by the text while raising new ones in turn.

Stars in My Pocket Like Grains of Sand • As noted above, the Nevèrÿon series continues Delany's radical examination of narrative formats, in this case the sword-and-sorcery fantasy narrative, through the various tales and plot lines within the four books of the series and through a continuation of the "Informal Remarks Toward the Modular Calculus." In the category of science fiction itself, *Stars in My Pocket Like Grains of Sand* continually tests readers' assumptions. The two major protagonists, Rat Korga and Marq Dyeth—the former an illiterate slave who has become filled with knowledge thanks to technological information devices and the latter a descendant of an ancient family and "industrial diplomat"—become lovers. The reader is uncertain, though, of their genders until well into the novel; both are male, but in this future universe people are usually classed as "women" and referred to as "she" regardless of actual sex, as in English (until the late twentieth century) "man" has been assumed to refer to humanity in general and "he" could refer generically to men or women. One paradox the book presents is that travel and communication can cut across vast distances between planets and galaxies, thus making the universe a smaller place, while the social complexities and contradictions among differing groups on one planet can make a world a very large place. Marq Dyeth travels to and communicates with different interstellar planets with relative ease; it is much harder, though, for social and practical reasons to travel on his own home planet. Marq's family grouping (and the word "family" is a richly complex term) includes Evelmi, the planet's aboriginal insectoid beings, who are enslaved on the same planet's other hemisphere.

The love between Marq and Rat is complicated by the social and political structures within which they exist. Throughout the inhabited worlds there is a power struggle between two factions, the Family and the Sygn. The Family seeks dominance to impose what a contemporary person might call "traditional moral values"—a restrictive, authoritarian system of beliefs and behaviors. The Sygn is a looser, almost ideally anarchic force; if it gains power, it will avoid the use of power in any social sense. Complicating this contention of forces are the roles of the Web, the information link that connects the planets, and the Xlv, a nonhuman species that is capable of space travel and may have destroyed Rat's home planet. At the novel's end, little is resolved; Marq and Rat have been forcibly separated, the Xlv threaten Marq's planet, and the social issues have yet to reach a peak. Thus, *Stars in My Pocket Like Grains of Sand* leaves room for many explorations of the rich and dazzling cultures that Delany presents or hints at in addition to the novel's complex narrative threads.

They Fly at Çiron • With *They Fly at Çiron*, Delany returns to some of the themes and motifs he explored in the Nevèrÿon series. He also returns to his creative origins, for *They Fly at Çiron* is an expanded version of a short story Delany wrote in 1962, just after completing his first novel, *The Jewels of Aptor.* Therefore, in a sense, the novel is a collaboration between the young Delany and Delany at midlife.

The novel takes place, like *Tales of Nevèrÿon*, in a fantasy realm where the basic inventions of civilization are just dawning. Çiron is a peaceful, pastoral realm where the people spend their time growing food, playing games, and singing songs. They do not even know what a weapon is. However, there is tension in this utopia—the Çironians distrust the Winged Ones, flying humans who inhabit the nearby mountains of Hi-Vator.

The Çironian peace comes to a shocking end when soldiers from the empire of Myetra, led by Prince Nactor, slam into Çiron, ending its innocence by introducing brutality, weaponry, and slavery. Under the pressures of the invasion, the Çironians join with the Winged Ones in resistance to the Myetra invasion, as personified by the friendship between Rahm, a Çironian, and Vortcir, a Winged One.

The turning point comes with Kire, a Myetra officer who has become disturbed by Prince Nactor's cruelty. When Nactor sentences Kire to death for refusing to rape and kill a Çironian girl, Kire abandons the Myetra Empire and joins Rahm and Vortcir in defending Çiron and Hi-Vator. Ultimately the Çironians and the Winged Ones are victorious, but they lose their innocence forever. Like William S. Burroughs's concept of the virus of language infecting humankind, the virus of civilization has infected the Çironians and the Winged Ones, who, at the novel's close, are committing acts of revenge against the soldiers of Myetra that echo Prince Nactor's earlier atrocities.

Delany has been referred to in jest by some as the "ultimate marginal writer"—a black, gay, poststructuralist writing in a marginal literary form—but those very margins serve to offer a critique of what is missing in the center and a vision of what could be found there instead. Increasingly, Delany's work has come to stand for openness, diversity, randomness, and the provisional; it opposes closedness and stagnation, hierarchies and fixities. Delany's fiction is a continuing challenge to assumptions about sex, race, and social roles as well as to assumptions about what fiction is and how it should be read.

Atlantis: Three Tales • Semiautobiographical in nature, this collection of three novellas begins with *Atlantis: Model 1924*, in which a young man, Sam, travels from North Carolina to New York in order to find his family. In the six months after his arrival, he has an encounter with a poetic stranger, in a complex and allusive narrative, as well as encountering historical figures such as Paul Robeson, Hart Crane, and Jean Toomer, and finally rejoins his older siblings.

In *Erik, Gwen, and D. H. Lawrence's Esthetic of Unrectified Feeling*, a second Sam, an artistic young boy in the 1950's, is taught both by his formalist art teacher and by a farmhand and gradually is awakened to his feelings about art as well as his own burgeoning sexuality. Sam muses on what art really is, how its definition has changed over the history, and its importance to both himself and the world.

In the final *Citre et Trans*, the third of the Sams, a twenty-something bisexual American writer in Greece in the 1960's, confronts the impact of rape after his roommate brings home a pair of Greek sailors. The darkest of the three stories, including both a homosexual rape and a dog's owner being forced to kill it, the story is still told with the finesse Delany brings to the entirety of his work.

All three of the novellas contained in *Atlantis: Three Tales* focus less on external action than on changes in the main character's consciousness. The work itself is highly experimental, playing with typography, splitting the work into columns to convey concurrent narration, marginal notes, surrealism, and stream of consciousness, in order to juxtapose time, memory, and fact. While they trace the interdepency of memory, experience, and the self, the book met with mixed reviews, many critics feeling that the experimental nature of the text made it overly difficult to extract the story.

Donald F. Larsson
Updated by John Nizalowski and Catherine Rambo

Other major works

SHORT FICTION: *Driftglass: Ten Tales of Speculative Fiction*, 1971 (revised and expanded, 2003, as *Aye and Gomorrah*); *Distant Stars*, 1981; *Atlantis: Three Tales*, 1995.

NONFICTION: *The Jewel-Hinged Jaw: Notes on the Language of Science Fiction*, 1977; *The American Shore: Meditations on a Tale of Science Fiction by Thomas M. Disch*, 1978; *Heavenly Breakfast: An Essay on the Winter of Love*, 1979; *Starboard Wine: More Notes on the Language of Science Fiction*, 1984; *The Straits of Messina*, 1987; *The Motion of Light in Water: Sex and Science-Fiction Writing in the East Village, 1957-1965*, 1988 (memoir); *Silent Interviews*, 1994; *Longer Views*, 1996; *Bread and Wine: An Erotic Tale of New York City, an Autobiographical Account*, 1998; *Shorter Views: Queer Thoughts and the Politics of the Paraliterary*, 1999; *Times Square Red, Times Square Blue*, 1999; *Nineteen Eighty-Four: Selected Letters*, 2000; *About Writing: Seven Essays, Four Letters, and Five Interviews*, 2005.

EDITED TEXTS: *Quark: A Quarterly of Speculative Fiction*, 1970-1971 (with Marilyn Hacker).

Bibliography

Barbour, Douglas. *Worlds Out of Words: The SF Novels of Samuel R. Delany*. London: Bran's Head Books, 1979. This fairly early critique of Delany's works gives a brief biography of Delany and a general discussion of his works, before concentrating on different aspects such as cultural, literary, and mythological allusions and some individual works. Includes notes and primary bibliography.

Dery, Mark. "Black to the Future: Interviews with Samuel R. Delany, Greg Tate, and Tricia Rose." *The South Atlantic Quarterly* 92 (Fall, 1993): 735-778. Examines why so few African Americans write science fiction, since it is a genre in which encounters with the Other are central; discusses these matters with Delany and others.

Fox, Robert Elliot. *Conscientious Sorcerers: The Black Postmodernist Fiction of LeRoi Jones/Amiri Baraka, Ishmael Reed, and Samuel R. Delany*. New York: Greenwood Press, 1987. Fox's text is useful for comparing and contrasting Delany's writing with that of his contemporaries in black fiction. Despite the gulf between their genres, Fox manages to find some similarity in the styles and subjects of these writers. Contains bibliographical information and an index.

Freedman, Carl. *Critical Theory and Science Fiction*. Hanover, N.H.: Wesleyan University Press, 2000. One chapter is devoted to a reading of *Stars in My Pocket Like Grains of Sand*.

Gawron, Jean Mark. Introduction to *Dhalgren*, by Samuel R. Delany. Reprint. Boston: Gregg Press, 1977. Gawron's forty-three-page introduction to this edition is an excellent starting point for readers wishing to deal with the complexities of Delany's longest single work. The Gregg Press reprint series includes textually accurate hardbound editions of Delany's major works through *Triton*. The introductions by various critics and scholars are especially helpful.

Kelso, Sylvia. "'Across Never': Postmodern Theory and Narrative Praxis in Samuel R. Delany's Nevèrÿon Cycle." *Science-Fiction Studies* 24 (July, 1997): 289-301. Argues that Derridean theory supplies the "Symbolic Order" of the blurred margins and centerless structure of Delany's Nevèrÿon cycle and that Michel Foucault's use of sadomasochistic experience is imaged in the cycle's "homoerotic Imaginary."

McEvoy, Seth. *Samuel R. Delany*. New York: Frederick Ungar, 1984. Much of the information in this text comes from personal interviews that McEvoy did with Delany. The book covers biographical information and interpretation of individual works, including short fiction as well as long fiction. Complemented by notes to the chapters and an index.

Peplow, Michael W., and Robert S. Bravard. *Samuel R. Delany: A Primary Bibliography, 1962-1979.* Boston: G. K. Hall, 1980. This exhaustive bibliography is the best starting reference book about Delany's early life and career. The introduction includes a lengthy biographical sketch, and the primary and secondary bibliographies list virtually all writings by and about Delany up to 1979.

Reid-Pharr, Robert F. "Disseminating Heterotopia" *African American Review* 28 (Fall, 1994): 347-357. Discusses how Delany confronts traditional ideas of proper identity and community politics, deconstructing lines between black and white communities and homosexual and heterosexual communities.

Review of Contemporary Fiction 16 (Fall, 1996). Special issue on Delany with essays on his novels and his science-fiction theory and criticism. Features an essay on his tales and an interview with Delany in which he discusses his theory of science fiction and his ideas about science fiction as a genre and a way of reading.

Sallis, James, ed. *Ash of Stars: On the Writing of Samuel R. Delany.* Jackson: University Press of Mississippi, 1996. An excellent source for information on Delany's life and work. Includes a bibliography and an index.

Slusser, George Edgar. *The Delany Intersection: Samuel R. Delany Considered as a Writer of Semi-Precious Words.* San Bernardino, Calif.: Borgo Press, 1977. This text sets out the structuralist interpretation of Delany's works, using Delany's literary criticism pieces to judge his own writing. Also traces the evolution of Delany's work from heroic epics to psychological fiction and beyond. Brief biographical and bibliographical notes.

Tucker, Jeffrey Allen. *A Sense of Wonder: Samuel R. Delany, Race, Identity, and Difference.* Middletown, Conn.: Wesleyan University Press, 2004. Study of Delany's use of racial themes and motifs in his fiction.

Don DeLillo

Born: New York, New York; November 20, 1936

Principal long fiction • *Americana,* 1971; *End Zone,* 1972; *Great Jones Street,* 1973; *Ratner's Star,* 1976; *Players,* 1977; *Running Dog,* 1978; *The Names,* 1982; *White Noise,* 1985; *Libra,* 1988; *Mao II,* 1991; *Underworld,* 1997; *The Body Artist,* 2001; *Cosmopolis,* 2003.

Other literary forms • Although Don DeLillo's major literary efforts center on the novel, he has contributed short stories to periodicals, including *The New Yorker, Esquire, Sports Illustrated,* and *The Atlantic Monthly,* and has written several plays.

Achievements • The publication in 1971 of DeLillo's first novel, *Americana,* launched the career of one of America's most innovative and intriguing writers. DeLillo produced satirical novels that drill into and hammer at the chaos of modern society, the lack of coherence and order in institutions, the breakdown of personal relationships, and particularly the failure of language. His driving, mercurial, upbeat prose at times smacks of an idiosyncratic pedantry yet abounds in lyricism and musicality. Some readers have labeled his prose "mandarin," after the fashion of Donald Barthelme and Thomas Pynchon. Pynchon definitely influenced him, but DeLillo pushed far beyond the limits of imitation or even derivation and asserted a truly independent voice. The promise of prodigious talent inherent in his first novel flowered in later works. Although DeLillo's novels are often criticized as plotless disquisitions that never produce anything but comic-strip characters, they nevertheless stimulate and excite readers and critics with their musicality, their rhetorical rigor, and their philosophical depth.

In 1984, the American Academy and the National Institute of Arts and Letters presented to DeLillo their Award in Literature. *White Noise* won the 1985 National Book Award, *Libra* won the 1989 *Irish Times*'s Aer Lingus International Fiction Prize, *Mao II* won the 1991 PEN/Faulkner Award. DeLillo was also one of two fiction writers to receive the 1995 Lila Wallace-Reader's Digest Award, which provides three years of financial support. His *Underworld* was nominated for the 1997 National Book Award and received the 2000 William Dean Howells Medal, which the American Academy of Arts and Letters awards every five years to the outstanding work of American fiction. In 1999, DeLillo became the first American to be awarded the prestigious Jerusalem Prize, which has been awarded every two years since 1963 to an international writer whose body of work best expresses the dignity of the individual.

Biography • Don DeLillo was born in New York City on November 20, 1936. A member of an immigrant Italian family, he was raised in Roman Catholicism in Pennsylvania and in New York City's South Bronx. After graduating in communication arts from Fordham University in 1958, he worked in advertising for several years, then quit to devote himself to writing. After earning a Guggenheim Fellowship, he spent time in Greece, which later served as the setting for *The Names.*

DeLillo published his first novel, *Americana,* in 1971. It was followed by *End Zone* (1972), *Great Jones Street* (1973), *Ratner's Star* (1976), *Players* (1977), *Running

Thomas Victor

Dog (1978), *The Names* (1982), *White Noise* (1985), *Libra* (1989), *Underworld* (1997), *The Body Artist* (2001), and *Cosmopolis* (2003). Although his books generally received positive reviews, his first breakthrough did not come until *White Noise*, which won the 1986 American Book Award. His novel about the John F. Kennedy's assassination, *Libra*, elevated him to the select group of writers who enjoy commercial success, critical praise, and academic attention.

Never open about his private life, DeLillo prefers to let his novels to speak for themselves. He has responded openly to interviews, however, thereby yielding a sense of how he feels about his work. As his career has progressed, DeLillo has learned to process his experience in the crucible of his imagination. With the success of *Libra* and after more than thirty years as something of a writer's writer, DeLillo began to emerge into the national cultural spotlight. To promote *Libra*, DeLillo agreed to undertake his first book tour, during which he encountered the realities of media attention at first hand. Perhaps reflecting that experience, 1991's *Mao II* uses the character of a J. D. Salinger-like reclusive writer to explore the implications of celebrity.

Analysis • What little there is of traditional narrative structure in a DeLillo novel appears to serve principally as a vehicle for introspective meanderings, a thin framework for the knotting together of the author's preoccupations about life and the world. Thematically, each novel is a profound reworking of the familiar precepts that make up the core of his literary belief system. This basic set of ideas includes the function (misfunction) of language as it relates to being, the absurdity of death and the meaning of apocalypse, the complications and chaotic workings of societies (particularly governments and institutions), the ontological purity of women and children, the notion of sacred spaces, and the interrelatedness of time, history, and myth. DeLillo's great facility with a language perfectly tuned for irony and satire allows him to range the breadth and depth of these themes.

Americana • All these thematic strains are present in *Americana*. The problem of language and meaning finds a penetrating focus in the conversation between the protagonist, David Bell, a dissatisfied minor network executive who seizes upon a documentary assignment to make a cross-country odyssey of self-discovery, and Carol Deming, a distracted yet aggressive young woman actor who reads a part for David's film: The encounter is set up to be sexual but proves to be nothing more than a bizarre verbal tryst, a duel of wacky hyperbole laced with sarcasm. Beneath the words fired rapidly back and forth between David and Carol, there are the levels of behavior and intensity normally associated with seduction. In this case, words appear to substitute for the great diversity of emotional responses associated with the sex act. The reader, however, knows that verbal intercourse is no substitute for sexual intercourse and commiserates with David on his lack of fulfillment; words are false images that can be made to disguise the multilayered nature of reality. In the end, however, the word is destroyed by the meaning it tries to mask.

This verbal affair takes place in the middle of America, in a town called Fort Curtis, the designated location for the filming of David's documentary. He has been commissioned to film the Navajo Indians but decides that the town will be the backdrop for a film about the central moment of his own childhood, the moment he learned that his mother, for him the bastion of health and security, would soon face disintegration and death. Each stop on his "sacred journey" out West holds a numinous attraction for him: the starting point, the chaotic craziness of the network office with its mad memo writer; the garage of Bobby Brand (a friend who uses his van for the trip); Fort Curtis; and ultimately Rooster, Texas, where David's pilgrimage of self-exploration ends in a boozy orgy in the dust. In Fort Curtis, David hires local people to read absurd lines and then has traveling companion Sullivan, an enigmatic sculptor, play the part of his mother on the day he learned, in the pantry of his parents' home, the tragic truth that women were not what he expected and wanted them to be: They cannot be held as an anodyne against the fear of death. In David's hands, the camera has the power to create from the union of a special place and a particular moment an image that is again an illusion of reality. When he later tries to make a created image real (that is, make Sullivan a real mother figure by having her tell him a precoital bedtime story), he is again instructed in the misalignment between images and the world. DeLillo, by constantly emphasizing the impossibility of the world's true representation in time and place via the word (history), mythologizes his characters and frees them from the bounds of historicity.

End Zone • One of DeLillo's mythic characters, Myna Corbett, appears in *End Zone*, the one novel that most of the author's critics agree is a brilliant piece. Myna, a student at Logos College in West Texas, is typical of DeLillo's female characters: She is big, carrying 165 pounds, which she refuses to shed because of her desire not to have the "responsibility" of being beautiful; she fills her mind with trivial matter (she reads science-fiction novels); and she has large breasts in which Gary Harkness, the protagonist, hopes to find solace from the world.

Gary is a talented but eccentric footballer at Logos College who, because of his strange behavior, has been cut from the team rosters of larger institutions such as Penn State and Syracuse. He does not change his ways at Logos, walking off the field during the last game, high on marijuana and very hungry. He has a fascination with war and audits the Reserve Officers' Training Corps classes that have to do with mass killing strategy. When Colonel Staley asks him to become a cadet, Gary refuses, saying that he wants only to fantasize about nuclear war. He enjoys playing nuclear destruction games with the colonel, but he will not prepare himself to become an Air Force officer: He will not drop real bombs.

When not engaged in his graphic war daydreams, Gary is either playing football, an abstraction of war, or having picnics with Myna. If war is organized, palpable death, then Myna must be its opposite, an image of life and a defense against the fear of death. The tension between women (as the word or image of antideath) and harsh reality finds expression in the scene in which Gary undresses Myna in the library stacks. He says to himself that it is important to have her completely nude in the midst of the books containing millions of words. He must see her as the word (the image of harmless, uncomplicated femaleness) made flesh. He wants to see Myna, as the embodiment of the illusion of safety that words give, appear to belie the truth behind the image, the truth that women are not immune from the dread of death and therefore cannot offer the security that he seeks. He does not want to confront the mystery and lure of feminine beauty: He is upset when Myna loses weight. When she returns from vacation slender, it is he who does not want the responsibility of Myna's beauty. Women's love can lead to death, and words can have deadly connotations.

Great Jones Street • DeLillo further explores his themes dealing with language, death, women, and time in *Great Jones Street*, the story of a rock star, Bucky, who grows tired of the business, leaves his band in Houston, and returns to a hovel of an apartment in New York City. There his seclusion is destroyed when Skippy, a hippie girl, leaves with him a box full of a special kind of dope that is untested but is thought to be extremely powerful, and therefore of great interest to the drug people. The rest of the novel focuses on the many people who want to get the drugs. One of the agents sent for the drugs is Opel, who eventually dies in Bucky's bed. She is only an image of a living woman as she lies in the bed; the anti-image, death, is the reality of her being there. When she dies, Bucky can contemplate only her dead self; once people leave one extreme of being, they must become the other.

Bucky tries to make his apartment a refuge from the relentless roll of time and the world. He talks into a dead phone, stifling any possibility that words can reach their destination and complete the communication process. He refuses to wind the clock, hoping to arrest time, that hard reality that lies beneath the illusory image of stasis. Opel, although safe in bed in Bucky's timeless, wordless (telephoneless) world of the apartment, dies nevertheless.

The song that has made Bucky famous, "Pee-Pee-Maw-Maw," provides grist for another favorite DeLillo theme, that children, because of their few years, have no thoughts or fears of dying and therefore are immune from death. Bucky sings in the simple, life-giving syllables of children. The Mountain Tapes, traded for the drugs by a boy named Hanes, bring the same release as do the drugs in the box: They reduce language to nonmeaning. Later, when Bucky is injected against his will with the drug, he loses the power of speech; he is silent. Childish babble and wordlessness are equated with a loss of the fear of death and consequently, a loss of humanity. Only humans fear death, says Bucky.

Ratner's Star • A child is the central character in *Ratner's Star*, a dense and overly long novel about the shortcomings of modern science. Billy, a fourteen-year-old mathematical genius who has just won the first Nobel Prize for Mathematics, is called to a futuristic think tank to help decipher a signal presumed to be a communication from Ratner's Star. The boy eventually finds the answer: The pulses of the message are really from the earth as it existed long ago. The meaning of the mathematical "words," the exact time of day as Billy looks at the clock on the wall (and coincidentally the exact time as an unscheduled eclipse of the sun), is that the secret of all knowledge is what one has at a particular place at the present time. All the supposed power of the modern scientific community can be reduced to the utter simplicity of the time of day in a child's room on our own planet in our own time. When a spontaneous heavenly movement takes place, it is announced first to the child's mind.

The adult scientists with whom Billy is obliged to interact by their utter egregiousness offer DeLillo myriad openings for the insertion of his biting satirical barbs. Endor, for example, the world's greatest mathematician, has given up solving the mystery of the pulses and has gone to live in a mud hole, living off worms and roots that he digs from the ground. Fitzroy-Tapps, the rat-talk scholar, hails from Crutchly-on-Podge, pronounced Croaking-on-Pidgett. Hoy Hing Toy, the obstetrician who once ate a newborn placenta; Grbk, who has to be officially reprimanded for showing his nipples to young children; and Armand Verbene, S.J., a practitioner of red-ant metaphysics, are representative of the resident staff. Of these bizarre characters, one in particular provides DeLillo with an excellent opportunity to hold forth on the meaning of language. Young Billy, a Nobel laureate by virtue of his having conceived the mathematical notion of the zorg (an entity reduced as far as it can be—that is, to nothing), confronts the astronomical mind of Lazarus Ratner. It is necessary to say that Billy confronts the "mind" of Ratner, because that is practically all that is left of the man. He is kept from collapsing in on himself by constant silicone injections, and his bodily functions are kept going mechanically inside a protective bubble. Billy sits astride the biotank, talks to Ratner (who will speak to nobody but the child), and translates what the great scientist says for those who stand near.

DeLillo uses this conversation between the old man and the boy to explore provocative notions about language, knowledge, and God. Ratner tells the boy about the Kabbala: The hidden and unknowable name of God is a literal contraction of the superdivinity. The contraction of divine anti-or other-being, *en sof,* makes possible the existence of the world. Being (God) is somewhere on a spectrum between light and darkness, something and nothing, between an integer and a zorg, in Billy's mathematical code. Divinity (pure being) is revealed in the expansion of matter. As the universe expands, human beings, as part of that expansion, come into existence. Existence, then, is like the birth and death of stars, says Ratner: It is manifested with the expansion and perishes with the contraction of its mass. Thus, as elements, or *sephiroth* of the primal being, humans are like tiny sparks of Ratner's Star. Human names, the words that equate with human existence, are merely artificial and abstract images of a constant expansion and contraction. Real being consists of the flux and levels of being behind the image.

Billy puts this theory into simple, incomplete terminology that, complains Ratner, is not fully expressive of the reality of that which is being communicated. Here again is the old problem: Words, as images of reality, cannot possibly convey the entire dimension of the meaning of the world. Those who listen to Billy as he interprets Ratner are able to glean only a small portion of the content of Ratner's words.

The Names • Of the later novels, *The Names* and *White Noise* offer the most moving and powerful treatment of DeLillo's recurring themes. *The Names* features the decay of the typical American marriage. James and Kathryn are married, have a son named Tap, and live happily for a time on an island in the eastern United States. They live peacefully until the bright image of marital bliss splinters, broken into a multileveled subset of hard problems, the first of which is separation. Kathryn, yielding to the fascination for digging in the ground in search of lost messages, commits herself to a life of archaeological digging; she joins an excavation site on an island in Greece. James, wanting to be near his fractured family, gets a job in Greece as a so-called risk analyst. Even though this bit of darkness has tarnished the core of the little family, they live on a reasonably even keel until archaeologist Owen Brademas begins an investigation of a cult of hammer killers.

These cultists occasionally pound to death a chosen victim who happens to wander into a town, the initials of which match the initials of the victim's name: For example, they kill Michaelis Kalliambestos as he enters Mikro Kamini. Brademas, whose profession it is to find and translate ancient script written in stone, really is more interested in the cabalistic power of the alphabet as it is combined and recombined to reveal the hidden names of God. He finds the Names, as the members of the hammer cult refer to themselves, becomes one of them in spirit, witnesses a ritual hammer murder (death comes to him who finds, even if by accident, correspondence in letters and reality), and then retires to read stones and live unmolested in his final sacred place, a hotel room in Bombay. Owen Brademas seems to be merely a mythic extension of an innocent, babbling language spoken by Kathryn and her sister as children, and used by Kathryn and her son: The language inserts the syllable "ob" among the syllables of real words to create a special code. The initials of wordmonger Owen Brademas's name happen to be "O. B." He seeks the meaning of alphabetic combinations even when they lead to death: He is the one who figures out the workings of the Names. In many ways, he is the shadow image of Kathryn's husband, a writer, who lives by the combinations of words and who follows Brademas in search of the cult. James finds his place of revelation in a Roman ruin just as Brademas finds his in a hotel room. Brademas is also an alter ego of Kathryn, who seeks hidden wisdom by a kind of mindless digging at the site, yet he takes archaeological inquiry to the ultimate degree and ends in a room with nothing but ordered space, a perfect stasis, a state much like death.

In the same way, James's job is nothing but a cover for an operation conducted by the Central Intelligence Agency (CIA). His image of a harmless and rather pleasant way of life in Greece is destroyed: He experiences a dark underside of intrigue and deception. It seems that the surface of daily life can never remain innocuously in place; there is always a seepage of antilife. His wife and profession appear to be entities resting on shifting sands; only his son, the child, who writes away at a nonfiction novel, can be counted on for authenticity.

White Noise • *White Noise* is a thematic duplicate of *The Names.* The characters are cartoons. Babette is the physically large wife to whom Jack Gladney, her husband, looks for a peaceful domestic life totally removed from danger. Babette, also called Baba, appears to be very capable of fulfilling her husband's needs: She is the perfect image of easygoing housewifery. She volunteers for community service, she shops constantly in the supermarket, and she lovingly cares for the children. The children are precocious and serious-minded. Heinrich, the oldest boy, seems to know much more than his father, a college professor, about the real world. The girls, especially Denise, are concerned about Babette's health, hiding her drugs and looking for hidden habits that might bring her danger or death. Husband and wife, lost in triviality, make inconsequential or erroneous statements, while the children speak with precision and maturity. There is a reversal in the parent-child roles; these children, therefore, are not as innocent as the typical DeLillo child figure. Only Wilder, the baby, embodies the ideal of the deathless child hero: At the end of the novel, he rides his tricycle into the street, across a four-lane street teeming with speeding vehicles, into the grass of the opposite shoulder, miraculously escaping death.

Babette crumbles as the symbolic shield against fear; she is exposed as a woman so terrified of death that she trades sex for a special kind of drug that causes one to forget about the fact that one must die. She takes these pills on the sly and is finally found out by her snooping family. Jack has been happy with Babette because she is open and guileless, unlike his previous wives, who were mysterious, complicated secret agents who worked for the CIA. His illusion is destroyed when he finds out about her pills. Her complicity in this kind of intrigue reinforces his recently discovered vulnerability to death (a physical examination has revealed that his exposure to a toxic chemical spill may leave him only a short time to live). Even Baba, the large, comfortable, unbeautiful, unmysterious, faithful wife, who has consoled Jack as he has lain with his face between her large breasts, proves to be full of duplicity and treachery.

This complication leads Jack to reflect on what Murray Siskind, a fellow faculty member, has told him regarding death: Death, says Siskind, can be purged only by killing. Jack has already intuited this precept on his own: His success as a professor of "Hitler studies" (which he established as a full-fledged academic discipline) depends in part on his awareness of the peculiar fascination of the Nazis. Ultimately, Jack shoots Willie Mink, a seedy drug dealer who dispenses death-forgetting pills to women in exchange for sex. He enjoys the bleeding of his wife's seducer for a while but then has pity on the mindless Mink, a victim of his own pills, and drags him by the foot to a hospital. The nuns who attend the wounded man destroy the last great image of security that Jack has left: Jack learns that those whom he had always thought of as sainted women, women firm in their faith that death's dominion has been crushed by the resurrection of Christ, have no more faith in salvation than he, his wife, or anybody else. The white noise of death silences any voice that would offer human beings a verbal sanctuary from its assault.

Libra • DeLillo followed *White Noise* with *Libra*, a novel about the assassination of President John F. Kennedy; atypically for DeLillo, the novel enjoyed a run on the national best-seller lists while winning critical acclaim. *Libra* is, in a sense, two novels in one. It is, first, a fictional re-creation of the assassination and the events leading up to it. In the book's opening pages, and at intervals throughout, the reader shares the consciousness of Lee Harvey Oswald. From Oswald's point of view and many others as well, DeLillo constructs his scenario of this still-enigmatic and much-disputed moment in American history. Although DeLillo's version departs from the conclusions of the Warren Report (he posits a second gunman and a fortuitous confluence of conspirators, including rogue CIA agents and Cuban exiles who want Fidel Castro overthrown), much of the speculation is grounded in the public record.

At the same time, *Libra* is a novel about the making of fiction and, more broadly, about the way in which people make sense of their lives. The novelist's alter ego is Nicholas Branch, a retired senior analyst for the CIA, hired by the agency during the 1980's to write the "secret history" of the assassination. This device allows DeLillo to sketch for the reader the process he went through in order to re-create happenings of the 1960's: sifting through the incredible profusion of evidence (he describes the twenty-six-volume Warren Report as "the Joycean Book of America, . . . the novel in which nothing is left out"), discovering strange patterns of coincidence. Novelists and conspiracy theorists, DeLillo suggests, are in the same business.

Mao II • Continuing this preoccupation with the making of fictions, *Mao II* juxtaposes writers, terrorists, and crowds. Narratively similar to *Libra*, the novel interweaves scenes of reclusive novelist Bill Gray; Scott Martineau, his assistant; Brita Nilsson, the photographer assigned to take Gray's photograph as part of the publicity for his new book; and a Swiss United Nations worker and poet, Jean-Claude Julien, who is held hostage in Beirut by a Palestinian group so shadowy that the only knowledge that exists about them is that they have taken him hostage. The first half of the novel gives an intimate view of the writer, the different machinations and rationalizations that sustain his work, and the attempts made by his publishers to get Gray to finish his novel and allow his image to be publicized. Continually rewriting and withholding his last book, the image of the writer in modern, media-saturated society, solitary and alone, is contrasted to crowds: China, the Moonies, mass marriages, terrorist movements.

It is terrorism that undoes Bill Gray in the second half of the novel. When Gray is asked to help in the attempt to get Julien released, he goes to London and then to Beirut, where he dies of untreated injuries sustained in a random automobile accident in London. Along the way, on this journey of unmaking, he has cut off all contact with Martineau, who in his absence goes about the process of organizing all of Gray's papers, taking the reader backward in time, via a lifetime's worth of detritus. Accompanying this deconstruction of the archetypal writer is the rise of scenes of terrorism, which take away from the novelist's ability to influence people. Faceless groups displace the writer's power to make societal change possible. Replacing Bill Gray in the narrative's coda is the terrorist leader, Abu Rashid, and the "rising movement" he represents. Ironically, the final scene in the novel is Nilsson's interviewing and photographing of Rashid. *Mao II* draws a desolate picture of life at the end of the twentieth century. Where there had once been the importance of solitary individuals struggling to present their understanding of the world, what is left at the end of the novel is faceless violence, mass influence in the form of religiously or ideologically inspired movements, and the hypermediated publicity machine that broadcasts these images to the world.

Underworld • Perhaps because of the bleakness at the end of *Mao II*, DeLillo's next novel seems to be attempting to understand the world after World War II. A synthesis of many of the concerns in the previous ten novels, *Underworld* may possibly be seen as DeLillo's magnum opus. Beginning with the simultaneous events of October 3, 1951—Bobby Thompson's home run, "The Shot Heard 'Round the World," and the Soviet Union's conducting of a second nuclear bomb test—the novel jumps back and forth from the early 1950's to the late 1990's. This process repeatedly grounds the language and institutions of the Cold War in a diverse range of contexts, including 1950's schoolchildren huddling under their desks during practice responses to nuclear attack, the week of the Cuban Missile Crisis (October, 1962), the compartmentalized world of the 1970's bomb makers, the 1980's construction of waste storage, and 1990's post-Cold War Russia's elimination of nuclear waste via nuclear explosions. Simultaneously, *Underworld* is also a story of degrees of separation, mingling together the lives of brothers Nick and Matt Shay, the former running a waste-management company, the latter a designer of nuclear weapons; Klara Sax, a found-object artist and their childhood Brooklyn neighbor; Albert Bronzini, her ex-husband and Matt's chess teacher; and Sister Edgar, a nun in the slums of New York and the brothers' former teacher. Additionally, the novel is the tale of Thompson's home-run baseball and its journey from owner to owner, particularly the crucial first day after the game, when the African American child who caught the ball, Cotter Martin, has it stolen from him and sold by his father, Manx Martin.

What is revealed again and again in the novel is the underworld of modern life:

never-mentioned family stories of an absent father; the charity work done by nuns in America's forgotten inner cities; the inner life of the director of the Federal Bureau of Investigation (FBI), J. Edgar Hoover; the transformation of stockpiled and rusting B-52 bombers into acres-long pieces of artwork; the creation of landfills for America's ever-increasing garbage; and the waste that results from fifty years of nuclear stockpiling. Like DeLillo's previous novels, *Underworld* offers a picture of life at the end of twentieth century that is extremely conflicted, with resolution an impossibility. Yet, through it all, the underworld of civilization's forgotten garbage continues to increase, revealing what sustains peoples' lives.

Watson Holloway
Updated by Joshua Stein

Other major works

SHORT FICTION: "Pafko at the Wall," 1992.

PLAYS: *The Engineer of Moonlight*, pb. 1979; *The Day Room*, pr. 1986; *The Rapture of the Athlete Assumed into Heaven*, pb. 1990; *Valparaiso: A Play in Two Acts*, pb. 1999; *Love-Lies-Bleeding*, pb. 2005.

NONFICTION: *Conversations with Don DeLillo* (Thomas DePietro, editor).

Bibliography

Bilton, Alan. "Don DeLillo." In *An Introduction to Contemporary American Fiction.* New York: New York University Press, 2002. Brief appreciation of DeLillo's place in modern American literature.

Bizzini, Silvia Caporale. "Can the Intellectual Still Speak? The Example of Don DeLillo's *Mao II.*" *Critical Quarterly* 37, no. 2 (Summer, 1995): 104-117. Bizzini discusses the "transformation" of the writer in *Mao II* using the theories of Roland Barthes and Michel Foucault. An interesting examination of the writer in postmodern society and a helpful introduction to the uses of both critics' ideas within textual criticism.

Bloom, Harold, ed. *Don DeLillo's "White Noise."* New York: Chelsea House, 2002. Part of the Modern Critical Interpretations series edited by Bloom. A wide range of essays are presented to give an overview of critical reactions to DeLillo's novel.

Bryant, Paula. "Discussing the Untellable: Don DeLillo's *The Names.*" *Critique: Studies in Modern Fiction* 29 (Fall, 1987): 16-29. Discusses DeLillo's avocation of language in his novel *The Names.* Bryant cites DeLillo as a writer who uses "idiosyncratic expression within the existing language system." Well worth reading; Bryant writes with knowledge and confidence.

Carmichael, Thomas. "Lee Harvey Oswald and the Postmodern Subject: History and Intertextuality in Don DeLillo's *Libra, The Names, and Mao II.*" *Contemporary Literature* 34, no. 2 (Summer, 1993): 204-218. An intertextual reading of three of DeLillo's novels within the context of critical debates over the "subject." Using the theories of Jean Baudrillard and Fredric Jameson, Carmichael argues the importance of Oswald's presence in DeLillo's novels and the "inescapable subversion" of history that results. For those familiar with critical theory.

Dewey, Joseph, Steven G. Kellman, and Irving Mallen, eds. *Underwords: Perspectives on Don DeLillo's "Underworld."* Newark: University of Delaware Press, 2002. Collection of essays focused on DeLillo's award-winning novel.

LeClair, Tom. *In the Loop: Don DeLillo and the Systems Novel.* Urbana: University of Illinois Press, 1987. LeClair argues for placing DeLillo in the genre of what he calls the "systems novel." LeClair's lively study contains a bibliographical checklist, including a useful list of titles on systems theory.

Mullen, Bill. "No There There: Cultural Criticism as Lost Object in Don DeLillo's *Players* and *Running Dog.*" In *Powerless Fictions? Ethics, Cultural Critique, and American Fiction in the Age of Postmodernism,* edited by Ricardo Miguel Alfonso. Amsterdam: Rodopi, 1996. An intense, close reading of connections between two of DeLillo's novels. A thought-provoking discussion of DeLillo's uses and abuses of official history.

Osteen, Mark. *American Magic and Dread: Don DeLillo's Dialogue with Culture.* Philadelphia: University of Pennsylvania Press, 2000. Eight essay-like chapters dissect DeLillo's engagement with American culture and institutions, both respecting their power and integrity and denouncing the dangerous repercussions of their acts.

Ruppersburg, Hugh, and Tim Engles, eds. *Critical Essays on Don DeLillo.* New York: G. K. Hall, 2000. Part of the Critical Essays on American Literature series, this volume collects a number of fine essays on the novelists.

Philip K. Dick

Born: Chicago, Illinois; December 16, 1928
Died: Santa Ana, California; March 2, 1982

Principal long fiction • *Solar Lottery*, 1955 (pb. in England as *World of Chance*, 1956); *The Man Who Japed*, 1956; *The World Jones Made*, 1956; *Eye in the Sky*, 1957; *Time Out of Joint*, 1959; *Dr. Futurity*, 1960; *Vulcan's Hammer*, 1960; *The Man in the High Castle*, 1962; *The Game-Players of Titan*, 1963; *Clans of the Alphane Moon*, 1964; *Martian Time-Slip*, 1964; *The Penultimate Truth*, 1964; *The Simulacra*, 1964; *The Three Stigmata of Palmer Eldritch*, 1964; *Dr. Bloodmoney: Or, How We Got Along After the Bomb*, 1965; *Now Wait for Last Year*, 1966; *The Crack in Space (Cantata 140)*, 1966; *The Unteleported Man*, 1966 (pb. in England as *Lies, Inc.*, 1984); *Counter-Clock World*, 1967; *The Ganymede Takeover*, 1967 (with Ray Nelson); *The Zap Gun*, 1967; *Do Androids Dream of Electric Sheep?*, 1968 (reissued as *Blade Runner*, 1982); *Galactic Pot-Healer*, 1969; *Ubik*, 1969; *A Maze of Death*, 1970; *Our Friends from Frolix 8*, 1970; *The Philip K. Dick Omnibus*, 1970; *We Can Build You*, 1972; *Flow My Tears, the Policeman Said*, 1974; *Confessions of a Crap Artist*, 1975; *Deus Irae*, 1976 (with Roger Zelazny); *A Scanner Darkly*, 1977; *The Divine Invasion*, 1981; *Valis*, 1981; *The Transmigration of Timothy Archer*, 1982; *The Man Whose Teeth Were All Exactly Alike*, 1984; *In Milton Lumky Territory*, 1985; *Puttering About in a Small Land*, 1985; *Radio Free Albemuth*, 1985; *Humpty Dumpty in Oakland*, 1986; *Mary and the Giant*, 1987; *The Broken Bubble*, 1988.

Other literary forms • Before he began writing long fiction, in 1955, Philip K. Dick went through an extraordinarily prolific period as a short-story writer. His first story, "Beyond Lies the Wub," appeared in 1952. In both 1953 and 1954 Dick published twenty-eight short stories per year. His total output in this genre is more than one hundred stories, most of which he wrote early in his career. Many have been reprinted in his collections *A Handful of Darkness* (1955), *The Variable Man, and Other Stories* (1957), *The Preserving Machine, and Other Stories* (1969), *I Hope I Shall Arrive Soon* (1985), and elsewhere. A five-volume collection, *The Collected Stories of Philip K. Dick*, was published in 1987. He has also collaborated on novels, including *The Ganymede Takeover* (with Ray Nelson) and *Deus Irae* (with Roger Zelazny).

Achievements • In all histories of science fiction, Dick is hailed as one of the greatest and most distinctive exponents of the genre. Literary awards, however, came his way surprisingly rarely. He received the Hugo Award (which is decided by vote of science-fiction fans attending the World Science Fiction Convention) for the best novel of the year 1962, for *The Man in the High Castle*. He received the John W. Campbell Award (decided by a panel of writers and critics, and also administered by the World Science Fiction Convention) for *Flow My Tears, the Policeman Said*, in 1975. More recognition might have been expected, and would surely have been forthcoming, if it were not for two things. One is that Dick was, for a while, an amazingly prolific author (five novels were published, for example, in 1964), yet one who wrote very few evidently weak or minor novels. His high level of productivity and consistency have accordingly made it difficult for single novels to be chosen as superior to others. Probably few critics would agree even on which are the best ten of his nearly forty novels. A further point is that Dick, while a writer of amazing power and fertility, is also prone to convolution and to the pursuit of personal obsessions.

Biography • Philip Kindred Dick was born in Chicago in 1928, but he lived most of his life in California. He studied for one year at the University of California at Berkeley, but he did not take a degree. Dick held several jobs for short periods, then began writing science fiction with great speed and immediate success, first short stories and then novels. His output slowed markedly at the beginning of the 1970's, as a result of personal problems, involvement with drugs, strong discontent with American society in the Vietnam War era, and a sequence of failed relationships. When he resumed writing, his books were significantly more personal and more propagandist. He died on March 2, 1982, following a stroke.

Analysis • Philip K. Dick's novels are, without exception, distinctive in style and theme. Their style may be characterized relatively easily: Dick writes clearly and plainly and is a master of realistic dialogue. He is, however, also a master of the art of "cutting." Frequently a chapter or a scene will end with a short summary statement, often of doubt, bewilderment, or unease, only to be followed in the next chapter by a longish sentence introducing a new character going about his daily concerns in a manner that seems—but only seems—to have no connection with the foregoing. For all of his plainness, Dick furthermore makes considerable use of words of his own coinage—for example, "flapple," "quibble" (a kind of vehicle), "thungly," "gubbish," or "kipple." The latter has even achieved a certain currency outside its novel, *Do Androids Dream of Electric Sheep?*, to mean the morass of useless objects, such as gum wrappers or junk mail, which seems to reproduce by itself in any modern dwelling. The overall effect of Dick's style is to give an impression of plainness and superficial normality, but to suggest strongly that beneath this surface things are going on which are ominous, disastrous, inexplicable.

This preoccupation is clearly mirrored in Dick's characteristic themes, many of which are shared with the body of science fiction at large. He often writes of androids, simulacra, and mechanical men. He bases several plots on consciousness-raising drugs. His later works in particular tend toward the dystopian, presenting visions of a future America as a vast gulag or a slave-labor state. The notions of alternate worlds and of post-Holocaust societies are often exploited. Where Dick differs from other users of these themes is in the strange insecurity that he generates while handling them. Androids are common in science fiction, and so are plots in which androids cannot be told from people. Only Dick produces plots in which the test to distinguish human from android is so deeply infected with the bureaucratic mentality that even people are likely to fail and be eliminated. Only Dick has a hero giving himself his own test, having come (for good reason) to doubt his own humanity.

Similarly, Dick is capable of writing a story that appears to be set in an alternate world but then begins to suggest that the real world never existed and is merely a drug-induced hallucination—only to switch back again, deny its own hypothesis, and leave the reader quite unsure even of the bases of judgment. Dick is fascinated by forgeries and by coincidences. In scene after scene, he presents a hero doubting even his own identity, and doing so with total rationality on the basis of all the evidence in the world around him. Most readers soon realize that the common concern that binds Dick's repeated themes and plot elements is the very nature of reality it-

self and that Dick doubts common notions of reality more sincerely and more corrosively than almost any writer in any genre. Dick could be described as the poet of paranoia, yet his cool and sensible style enables him to present horrifying alienations in a way with which even the sanest reader can sympathize.

Solar Lottery • Dick's overriding concerns are quite apparent in even his earliest novels. *Solar Lottery*, his first novel, presents a future society that is dedicated entirely to chance, as a result of "extrapolation," first of the then-new phenomenon of television quiz shows, and second (as one might have expected) of the "Uncertainty Principle" as a basic rule of the universe. In this world, all authority devolves on "the Quizmaster," but the Quizmaster may be deposed at any moment from his position by a "twitch of the bottle," an event determined by the intrinsically unpredictable forces of submolecular physics. The bottle twitches. Reese Verrick the Quizmaster is deposed. His place goes to an unknown fanatic called Cartwright, whose only interest is the search for a (mythical?) tenth planet. Caught up in all these events is a hero who has had the colossal bad luck to swear irrevocable fealty to Verrick just before he fell from power. Already the sense of an unpredictable world where anything can go wrong is very marked.

Eye in the Sky • Even more revealing is *Eye in the Sky*, in which eight characters caught up in a scientific accident find themselves exploring what they slowly realize are the worlds of one another's minds: first that of a total believer in an obscure fundamentalist sect, then that of an inhibited housewife, a borderline paranoid, a fanatical communist, and so on. The worlds themselves are presented with great verve. In the first, for example, a man going for a job asks not about pay but about credits for salvation, and if he presses is told that in his position the God of this world, "Tetragrammaton," will probably grant his prayers to the extent of four hundred (dollars?) a week. The job may be constructing a grace reservoir, or improving the wire to Heaven. There is in fact an "eye in the sky," belonging to the unnameable (Tetragrammaton). Underlying the structure of the whole novel, though, is the notion that each person's individual universe is not only private but unreachable; most people are mad. In view of Dick's later development it is also interesting that the novel is strongly anti-McCarthyite, even though one of the characters (ironically a security chief) is indeed a communist agent.

Time Out of Joint • The novel that best sums up Dick's earliest phase as a novelist, however, is *Time Out of Joint*. This appears for quite some time not to be science fiction at all. It reads instead as a pleasantly pastoral, perhaps rather dull, account of life in a small American town of the 1950's. The only odd feature is that the hero, Ragle Gumm, makes his living by continually winning a newspaper contest "Where Will the Little Green Man Be Next?" Slowly, however, this idyllic setting begins to drift by quarter-tones to nightmare. Gumm does not recognize a picture of Marilyn Monroe (something unthinkable if he were really of that time and place). An old phone book found in some ruins has his name in it, with eight phone numbers for all hours of the day and night. A boy's crystal radio picks up voices saying in effect "That's *him* down there, Ragle Gumm." It transpires that the small town with its idealized families is a total deception, all created to shield Ragle Gumm and maintain him in his stress-free delusion while he performs his real job—using extrasensory powers to predict the fall of enemy rockets on Earth, under the fiction of the newspaper contest.

The Man in the High Castle • In *Time Out of Joint,* Ragle Gumm is mad at the start. When he thinks he is going mad, he is learning the truth. There is no way to prove that reality is not a perfectly rehearsed plot. This latter is a classic Dick conclusion. In *The Man in the High Castle*—Dick's most famous but not most characteristic work—the reader is plunged into an alternate reality in which the Allies have lost World War II, California is occupied by the Japanese, and the inhabitants rather like the situation. The hero here, Robert Childan, is a seller of "ethnic" American curios, such as Mickey Mouse watches and Civil War handguns, for which the conquerors have an insatiable appetite. His problem is that some of the guns are fakes. The problem of the man who made the fake guns, Frank Frink, is that he is a Jew and could be deported to German-controlled areas. Nevertheless, the predictable theme of resistance, triumph, and escape to the real universe where the right side won hardly materializes. Instead, the reader is presented with a complex argument in favor of Japanese sensitivity, with strong underlying hints that even the "alternate worlds" of this "alternate world" would not be the same as our world. The novel suggests powerfully that history is chance, merely one possibility among a potential infinity of realities.

The Penultimate Truth • By 1964 Dick was at the height of his power as a writer, and almost any of the fifteen novels published between this year and 1969, including *The Simulacra, Dr. Bloodmoney, Counter-Clock World,* or *Galactic Pot-Healer,* would find admirers. Some especially significant themes emerge, however, from five novels in this group: *The Penultimate Truth, Martian Time-Slip, The Three Stigmata of Palmer Eldritch, Do Androids Dream of Electric Sheep?,* and *Ubik.* The first of these returns to the theme of total, deliberate illusion. In the future imagined in this novel, most of the inhabitants of Earth live underground, in ant-tanks, under the conviction that World War III is still going on and that if they emerge from hiding they will die from the Bag Plague, the Stink of Shrink, Raw-Claw-Paw, or one of a multitude of human-made viruses. In reality, though, the war stopped long ago, and the earth is a park, divided up into the demesnes of the ruling classes. Like Ragle Gumm, one character digs his way out to discover the truth and to try to lead these latter-day Morlocks up to the light. The particular point that Dick wishes to rub in here, though, is that even outside science fiction, people are genuinely at the mercy of their television screens. They cannot tell whether they are watching truth or a construct. They usually have no way of telling true history from the false varieties that Dick makes up. The end of the novel declares that what is essential—and not only in the novel—is a ferocious skepticism. People are too gullible, too easily deceived.

Martian Time-Slip • There is no such overt political thesis in *Martian Time-Slip*, of the same year, but in this Dick creates one of his most likable sets of characters, in Jack Bohlen, the Martian repairman, and Arnie Kott, senior member of the Waterworkers' Union—naturally a privileged body on arid Mars, though no one had previously been mundane enough to say so. Dick also brings into the novel what seems to be a personal image of the "Tomb World," a world in which everything is rotten and decaying, with buildings sliding to ruin and bodies to corruption. This world is perceived only by an autistic child, but that child's perceptions seem stronger than the grandiose claims of governments and land speculators. Still another route into horror is via drugs.

The Three Stigmata of Palmer Eldritch • *The Three Stigmata of Palmer Eldritch* moves rapidly from a protagonist who has the seemingly harmless job of guessing fashion for dolls and dollhouses to the notion of exploitation—for these "Perky Pat Layouts," as they are called, can be experienced only by people who take the drug Can-D to let them into the doll-world—to menace and terror. Can-D is about to be superseded by Chew-Z, a drug allegedly harmless, nonaddictive, and government sponsored. This drug, however, puts its users (as in *Eye in the Sky*) in the world of Palmer Eldritch, a demon-figure with steel teeth, an artificial hand, and mechanical eyes. They cannot return from it. Chew-Z takes one into a variant, one might say, of the "Tomb World."

Ubik • The hero of *Ubik*, Joe Chip, finds the "Tomb World" happening around him, as it were. Cigarettes he touches fall into dust; cream turns sour; mold grows on his coffee; even his coins turn out of date. Then he himself starts to age. The only thing that can cure him is a spray of "Ubik," a material that halts the race to corruption and obsolescence. In a memorable scene near the end, Joe Chip reaches a drugstore just before it closes, to demand Ubik, only to find that the store is closing, the stock is out, and spray cans too have aged, becoming cardboard packets. What force is doing all this? Are the characters in fact already dead, now existing only in a bizarre afterlife? For whose benefit is the spectacle being played out? Once again, Dick creates a happy ending, but more strongly than usual, one believes that this ending is demanded by the conventions of the field rather than by the logic of the plot.

Do Androids Dream of Electric Sheep? • For depth of paranoia, the prize should go to *Do Androids Dream of Electric Sheep?* This novel is best known as the original of the 1982 film *Blade Runner*, both book and film centering on a bounty hunter whose job is to kill androids. What the film could not do is show the depth of devotion that the characters in the book—who live in a world so radioactive that almost all unprotected creatures have died—give to their pets. Deckard the bounty hunter has a counterfeit electric sheep because he is too poor to afford a real one, but like everyone in the book he consistently consults the manual of animal prices. If he kills three more androids, could he buy a goat? If he spares one, will they give him an owl (thought to be extinct)? Would it be an artificial owl? The pitiless slaughter of androids is balanced against the extraordinary cosseting of every nonartificial creature, down to spiders. What, however, is the basis of the division? In a heartrending scene, after Deckard has wiped out his androids, another android comes and kills his goat. Before then, though, Deckard himself has been accused of being an android, been taken to the Hall of Justice, and been quite unable to prove his own identity—because, as soon becomes clear, all the authorities are themselves androids. The notions of undetectable forgery, total illusion, and unanimous conspiracy combine to make the central scenes of this novel as disorienting as any in Dick's work.

Somewhere near this point, Dick's development was cut off. He wrote most movingly on the subject in the author's note to *A Scanner Darkly*. This novel, he says, is "about some people who were punished entirely too much for what they did." They were real people, the author's friends. They took drugs, like children playing; it was not a disease, it was an error of judgment, called a "life-style." He then lists seven of his friends who have died, three more with permanent brain damage, two with permanent psychosis, one with permanent pancreatic damage . . . the list goes on. How deeply Dick himself was involved in late 1960's California "drug culture," one cannot say. He himself insists this was exaggerated. However, for whatever cause, Dick wrote less, and his mood became angrier, less playful.

Flow My Tears, the Policeman Said • The great surprise of *Flow My Tears, the Policeman Said* is its ending. In this world—a dystopia based on Nixon-era America—students are persecuted, the "nats" and the "pols" run identification checks in the streets, a quota is taken off daily to slave camps, and civil liberties have vanished. Through the world wanders Jason Taverner, in the first chapter a rich and fantastically successful entertainer, who finds himself suddenly (in dream? psychosis? alternate reality?) in a place where everything is familiar, but no one knows him. His hunter is Police General Felix Buckman, as it were the arch-bogey of the liberal conscience, the policy maker for the police-state. However, at the end, with his sister dead and Taverner arrested, Buckman, weeping, finds himself at an all-night garage. He climbs out of his "quibble" and goes over to hug a lonely black—one of the very few black people in this world to have got through the sterilization programs. The moral is totally unexpected, as a reaction to incidents such as the Kent State University shootings. It is that even policemen can love. Even men who are systematically evil can abandon the system. The ending of this novel comes over as an extraordinarily generous gesture from an embittered man. As with the very strongly antidrug stance of *A Scanner Darkly*, this scene shows that Dick, for all of his liberalism, is not prepared to accept the complete "anti-Establishment" package.

Nevertheless, from this point his works grow weirder and more connected. Some of his later novels, such as the posthumously issued *Radio Free Albemuth*, were either not submitted or not accepted for publication. This group also includes the best of Dick's non-science-fiction novels, *Humpty Dumpty in Oakland*, a book most easily described as a sequel to John Steinbeck's *The Grapes of Wrath* (1939), recounting what happened after the "Okies" got to California: They settled down, lost their way, ran used-car lots, and became "humpty dumpties"—passive spectators of the American Dream. The central idea of the last set of Dick's science-fiction novels, however, is a form of Gnosticism, the ancient Christian heresy that insists that the world contains two forces, of good and evil, in eternal conflict, with only a remote or absent God trying occasionally to get through. Dick writes variations on this theme in *Valis*, *The Divine Invasion*, *The Transmigration of Timothy Archer*, and *Radio Free Albemuth*, mentioned above.

Valis • *Valis*, at least, makes a direct assault on the reader by including the character Horselover Fat, a transparent translation of Philip K. Dick. He hears voices, very like the characters from Berkeley in *Radio Free Albemuth*, who believe they are being contacted by a sort of divine transmission satellite. What the voices say are variations on the view that the world is ruled by a Black Iron Empire, by secret fraternities in Rome or the United States; that the president of the United States, Ferris F. Fremont, has "the number of the beast" in his name; that true believers are exiles from another world. Is this mere madness? Horselover Fat remarks himself that the simplest explanation is that the drugs he took during the 1970's have addled his mind during the 1980's. Nevertheless, he has to believe his voices. One might say that Dick's corrosive skepticism has finally developed a blind spot, or alternatively, that the novelist has become a sadder and a wiser man. Whatever the decision, Dick's last novels could be characterized not as science fiction but as theological fiction.

Dick's work as a whole shows clear evidence of his deep social concerns, reacting against Senator Joseph McCarthy and President Richard Nixon, first praising and then condemning drugs, testing one notion after another concerning the limits of government. However, it also remained solidly consistent in its private and personal quest for a definition of reality that will stand any trial. It could be said that Dick's work is obsessive, introspective, even paranoid. It has also to be said that it very rarely loses gentleness, kindness, even a rather wistful humor. Dick has certainly contributed more first-class novels to science fiction than anyone else in the field, and he has convinced many also of the genre's ability to cope with serious reflections on the nature of humanity and of perception.

T. A. Shippey

Other major works

SHORT FICTION: *A Handful of Darkness*, 1955; *The Variable Man, and Other Stories*, 1957; *The Preserving Machine, and Other Stories*, 1969; *The Book of Philip K. Dick*, 1973 (pb. in England as *The Turning Wheel, and Other Stories*, 1977); *The Best of Philip K. Dick*, 1977; *The Golden Man*, 1980; *I Hope I Shall Arrive Soon*, 1985; *Robots, Androids, and Mechanical Oddities: The Science Fiction of Philip K. Dick*, 1985; *The Collected Stories of Philip K. Dick*, 1987 (5 volumes); *Selected Stories of Philip K. Dick*, 2002 (Jonathan Lethem, editor).

NONFICTION: *In Pursuit of Valis: Selections from the Exegesis*, 1991 (Lawrence Sutin, editor); *The Selected Letters of Philip K. Dick*, 1991-1993 (Don Herron, editor); *The Shifting Realities of Philip K. Dick: Selected Literary and Philosophical Writings*, 1995 (Lawrence Sutin, editor); *What If Our World Is Their Heaven: The Final Conversations of Philip K. Dick*, 2000 (Gwen Lee and Elaine Sauter, editors).

MISCELLANEOUS: *The Dark Haired Girl*, 1988.

Bibliography

Aldiss, Brian W., and David Wingrove. *Trillion Year Spree: The History of Science Fiction*. London: Victor Gollancz, 1986. Aldiss's work is useful as an overall survey of themes and writers of science fiction, and he allots several pages to Dick's work. His focus is on Dick's novels, but his comments are useful for looking at the short stories as well.

Carrère, Emmanuel. *I Am Alive and You Are Dead: The Strange Life and Times of Philip K. Dick*. Translated by Timothy Bent. New York: Metropolitan Books, 2003. Interesting study of Dick by a noted French author and film director.

Dick, Anne R. *Search for Philip K. Dick, 1928-1982: A Memoir and Biography of the Science*

Fiction Writer. Lewiston, N.Y.: Edwin Mellen Press, 1995. An important documentation of Dick's life, told in candid detail by his wife.

Dick, Philip K. *What If Our World Is Their Heaven: The Final Conversations of Philip K. Dick.* Edited by Gwen Lee and Elaine Sauter. Woodstock, N.Y.: Overlook TP, 2002. This collection of virtually unedited transcriptions of extensive interviews that Dick gave shortly before he died provides unique insights into his mind.

DiTommaso, Lorenzo. "Redemption in Philip K. Dick's *The Man in the High Castle.*" *Science-Fiction Studies* 26 (March, 1999): 91-119. Discusses the role of Christian theology in Dick's fiction, particularly Gnostic Christian dualism and fundamental Pauline theology. Discusses *The Man in the High Castle* as an important stage in the development of Dick's thought.

Gillespie, Bruce, ed. *Philip K. Dick: Electric Shepherd.* Melbourne, Australia: Norstrilia Press, 1975. This collection of essays on Dick's work includes an article by Dick himself called "The Android and the Human."

Golumbia, David. "Resisting 'The World': Philip K. Dick, Cultural Studies, and Metaphysical Realism." *Science-Fiction Studies* 23 (March, 1996): 83-102. A discussion of reality and appearance and metaphysics and politics in Dick's work and thought; comments on the relationship of his thought to culture studies.

Greenberg, Martin Henry, and Joseph D. Olander, eds. *Philip K. Dick.* New York: Taplinger, 1983. Contains excellent essays, one by Dick himself, supplemented by notes on the essays, a biographical note, a comprehensive bibliography of primary sources, a selected bibliography of criticism, notes on the contributors, and an index.

Lee Zoreda, Margaret. "Bakhtin, Blobels, and Philip Dick." *Journal of Popular Culture* 28 (Winter, 1994): 55-61. A discussion of the story "Oh, to Be a Blobel" from a Bakhtinian perspective; argues the story demonstrates the complexities in the presence/absence of dialogism. Discusses how the story demonstrates the misery, suffering, and irreversible injury created by the military-capitalist complex.

Levack, Daniel J. H., comp. *PKD: A Philip K. Dick Bibliography.* Rev. ed. Westport, Conn.: Meckler, 1988. A useful research tool.

Mackey, Douglas A. *Philip K. Dick.* Boston: Twayne, 1988. A book-length study of Dick. After a sketch of Dick's life, Mackey provides a comprehensive survey of his fiction from the 1950's through the 1980's. Supplemented by a chronology, notes, an extensive bibliography of primary sources, an annotated list of selected secondary sources, and an index.

Mason, Daryl. *The Biography of Philip K. Dick.* London: Gollancz, 2006. A British view of Dick's life.

Palmer, Christopher. *Philip K. Dick: Exhilaration and Terror of the Postmodern.* Liverpool, England: Liverpool University Press, 2003. Another British view of Dick's life that attempts to reconcile Dick's postmodern views of the possible with his humanist views.

Robinson, Kim Stanley. *The Novels of Philip K. Dick.* Ann Arbor, Mich.: UMI Research Press, 1984. A survey of Dick's narrative structures and fictional techniques by a highly respected science-fiction writer.

Science-Fiction Studies 2, no. 1 (March, 1975). This issue of the journal is devoted to the work of Dick and contains essays by writers eminent in the field of science-fiction criticism.

Sutin, Lawrence. *Divine Invasions: A Life of Philip K. Dick.* New York: Harmony Books, 1989. Sutin has written a well-researched biography that includes some discussion of Dick's work.

Umland, Samuel J., ed. *Philip K. Dick: Contemporary Critical Interpretations.* Westport, Conn.: Greenwood Press, 1995. An indispensable collection of essays on Dick's varied body of work. Umland has compiled extremely valuable primary and second bibliographies. Like Umland's introduction, the essays take careful note of the body of critical literature already published on Dick.

Warrick, Patricia S. *Mind in Motion: The Fiction of Philip K. Dick.* Carbondale: Southern Illinois University Press, 1987. Contains excellent studies of eight of Dick's major novels.

James Dickey

Born: Atlanta, Georgia; February 2, 1923
Died: Columbia, South Carolina; January 19, 1997

Principal long fiction • *Deliverance,* 1970; *Alnilam,* 1987; *To the White Sea,* 1993.

Other literary forms • James Dickey's early fame as a writer was based on several volumes of poetry. He also published books of criticism and of children's poetry.

Achievements • At the age of thirty-eight, while Dickey was in the midst of a successful career as an advertising executive, he became a full-time poet. Five years later, in 1966, he won the National Book Award for a collection of poems titled *Buckdancer's Choice* (1965), and he was appointed Poetry Consultant to the Library of Congress. In 1967, his collection *Poems, 1957-1967* won him critical praise. He published his first novel, *Deliverance,* in 1970 and saw it become a best-seller. His second novel, *Alnilam,* appeared in 1987 after a seventeen-year gestation period, and his final novel, *To the White Sea,* was published in 1993—four years before he died.

Biography • Born and reared in Atlanta, Georgia, James Dickey attended public schools and experienced a typical twentieth century boyhood and adolescence. He excelled in sports and became a notable football player at Clemson University. During World War II and the Korean War, he flew more than one hundred night combat missions. After he returned to the United States at the end of World War II, he enrolled at Vanderbilt University. There the subjects of his compositions for a writing course, based on his war experiences, made Dickey stand out from other students, who were writing about their summer vacations. At Vanderbilt, Dickey absorbed the literary tradition established by the Fugitive poets, such as John Crowe Ransom, Allen Tate, and Robert Penn Warren, and discovered himself to be a poet. He graduated with honors and went on to finish a master's degree before taking a job teaching English in college.

Dickey left teaching for immediate success in advertising, first in New York and later in Atlanta. A grant allowed him to retire from advertising in his mid-thirties and pursue writing full-time. He became convinced of the absolute necessity and worth of writing, of writing as a calling demanding total commitment and absorption. His poems were the narration of intense experiences both imaginary and real, whether the dreamlike falling of an airline stewardess into a midwestern cornfield or the shark-fishing experience of young boys. As he wrote his poems as extended narratives, it was natural for Dickey also to write novels. Like his poems, his novels deal with human intensities on a visceral level, where the limits of human vulnerability and endurance are explored.

Dickey published two poetry collections and a novel during the early 1990's and died in Columbia, South Carolina, on January 19, 1997.

Analysis • James Dickey's novels *Deliverance* and *Alnilam* were published seventeen years apart, and the chronological separation parallels the levels of difference in their content and style. *Deliverance*, written by Dickey when he was in his forties, is more conventional in form and more accessible to a popular readership. The reader is quickly plunged into the equivalent of an adventure story, as four middle-aged men take a canoe trip in North Georgia and a malevolent pair of mountain men force them into a primal life-or-death encounter. *Alnilam*, a formidably physical book of 682 pages, defies the reader in many ways, including the intermittent use of experimental double-column pages where the simultaneous narration of the blind character's perception and the seeing narrator is developed. The blind man, Frank Cahill, is physically incapable of the more conventionally heroic feats performed by the narrator of *Deliverance*. This limitation of the main character seems a deliberate aim of Dickey, as he is writing a book about the delusions human beings sustain in their assumed youth and strength. However, Dickey is also concerned with physical reality, and the task of characterizing the blind Cahill gives Dickey's imagination a broad field of sensations to explore.

Though different in many ways, the novels share a concern with men struggling to survive. *Deliverance* considers the angst of middle-aged suburban men and the efforts they make to escape their civilized imprisonment while dreading the alternative of survival in the wild. *Alnilam* takes the he-man Cahill—a carpenter and lover of boards and nails—and, by making him become blind, places him in a wilderness of greater darkness than the North Georgia forests of *Deliverance*; the normal world becomes as mysterious and untrustworthy as wild nature. Both novels consider the questions quoted from David Hume in an epigraph to *Alnilam*: "Where am I, or what? From what causes do I derive my existence, and to what condition do I return? Whose favour shall I court, and whose anger must I dread? What beings surround me?"

Deliverance • *Deliverance* conjures the world of modern America in the commercial South of the 1960's. The four male characters have jobs that are typical of this world: bottle distribution, mutual fund sales, advertising, and apartment rental. The main character, Ed Gentry, becomes increasingly aware that running an advertising agency is death in life. He admires the survivalist Lewis, who has honed his body to a muscular perfection through constant exercise and is devoted to a hypothetical future fantasy in which his physical superiority will keep him alive. Dickey is both critical and supportive of Lewis's point of view. He suggests there is in men a need to be tested, to be physically pitted against stress, as a daily fact of life. The modern world has eliminated this part of what it means to be human, and the restlessness of men such as Ed and Lewis to polish their survival skills and instincts indicates a real human need. The modern world has replaced the world where such skills were practiced, however, and men look ridiculous if they believe and behave as sincerely as Lewis. Thus, Lewis must manufacture his own wilderness, must find it before it is buried by developers.

Lewis discovers his dangerous place in North Georgia: a river to explore by canoe. Ed and Lewis are joined by Bobby and Drew, who are less avid but ready for a change of scene. Though the river has treacherous places and does damage to the novice canoers, it is human ugliness that is revealed to be the main danger. Two hillbillies appear to Bobby and Ed on the second day. They are repulsive, lacking teeth and manners, and they sodomize Bobby and prepare to do worse to Ed before Lewis kills one of the mountain men with an arrow through his chest. The four suburbanites are faced with a decision: Do what civilization dictates and face the local authorities, or bury "the evidence" and hope to escape. Lewis argues that survival dictates the latter, and Bobby and Ed agree. After burying the attacker and continuing down the river, Drew is shot and killed by the other hillbilly, the two canoes capsize, and the three survivors are battered by water and stones before landing in a gorge. With Lewis's broken leg and Bobby's general cowardice, Ed is left to scale the gorge walls and kill the sniper with his bow and arrow. The three make it to a town, ultimately escape the local law, and live to savor the next year's damming of the river, creating a recreational lake that hides all evidence of their experience.

Courtesy, The Augusta Chronicle

Ed has been tested—a good thing, as implied by the title of the novel, but horrible. Ed has taken the blood and life of another man who had wanted his own. Had he not, he and his friends would have perished. He has also been delivered into an understanding of something disturbing about being human, about what humans carry inside them. This knowledge is good because it is truth, and nothing more. Dickey is aware that men in World War II learned to kill thousands from bombers without seeing their faces or hearing their screams. *Deliverance* presents its main character with an enemy who must be killed face to face, as men killed one another before modern warfare. There is a kind of joy for Ed in this combat, but he must return to Atlanta for a lifetime of remembering while he pursues the art of advertising. Dickey intimates that, after such a deliverance experience, the spiritual corrosions of civilization—designing ads for women's underwear—will not so completely dampen Ed Gentry's spirit, as they had before.

Alnilam • *Deliverance* is an unabashedly self-reflective book. At the time that he wrote it, Dickey's passions for archery and the guitar, which Drew plays in the novel, were well documented in magazine articles. Ed Gentry, the narrator, works in the field of advertising, where Dickey spent many successful years. With *Alnilam*, however, Dickey projects a persona whose similarities to himself are more metaphorical than literal. Frank Cahill is an Atlanta carpenter with a high school education who loves to build things, look at blueprints, construct an amusement park labyrinth with his bare hands, and run a swimming pool for the public. Then, in middle age, he becomes blind from diabetes. Suddenly, a man who had loved to be in the visible world, making new things appear with hammer, wood, and nails, is now closed off permanently from being that man. Cahill does not complain and listens to the doctor, who suggests that blindness, rather than killing him, can make Cahill alive in a new way. Another epigraph from David Hume suggests how this might occur: "May I not clearly and distinctly conceive that a body, falling from the clouds, and that, in all other respects, resembles snow, has yet the taste of salt or feeling of fire?"

The reader senses the test Dickey is giving himself as a writer. All characterization demands empathy, but it is more difficult to imagine what one is not than what one is. Also, Dickey is passionate about the world, and a blind narrator forces him to view it through a new dimension. Blindness, while closing off the visible, sharpens touch, smell, hearing, and, most satisfying to Cahill, memory. Cahill's memory, whether of roller skating all day on Atlanta streets, watching a boy fly a rubber band airplane in a park, or coming upon a waterfall during a picnic hike, becomes an etched message that repeatedly appears and a measure for all the unseeableness of his present world. Cahill in his blindness is a metaphor for the private consciousness to which everyone is confined, and the replays of memory allow Dickey to emphasize this point. Cahill, divorced, having never seen his son, and regretting neither the divorce nor the sonlessness, has unashamedly accepted his privacy and distance. Blinded, however, he makes a pilgrimage into the land of other selves.

With Cahill drawn in such a manner that he cannot be easily identified with the author, Dickey places him in a world very familiar to the younger Dickey: a training base for World War II pilots. Cahill's son, Joel, a pilot trainee, has died in a crash during a forest fire in the North Carolina hills. Cahill comes to the base in his new blindness accompanied by his version of a Seeing Eye dog. Zack is not a graduate from a training school for guide dogs but part shepherd and part wolf; Cahill and a friend trained him before Cahill went blind. Zack possesses a blend of viciousness and loyalty that Cahill adores.

Mystery surrounds the death of Joel, and initially Cahill suspects foul play. Joel had been an inspiration to his fellow trainees, and a secret society developed, with Joel as the leader. Cahill's conversations with Joel's friends reveal the society's name, Alnilam (the middle star of the constellation Orion's belt), and intention: the mystical union with other young pilots across the nation leading to a destruction of all war and the means to wage war.

By novel's end, this scheme will be revealed for what it is—high-minded but naïve youthful rebellion against authority. However, Joel was an extraordinary young man. He innately grasped the subtleties of flying and developed a hypnotic training called "Death's Baby Machine," which struggling young pilots received sitting in an ordinary chair. In his mind, Cahill is able to create a psychological and physical portrait of Joel from questioning those who knew him on the base, and he realizes that giftedness mixed with unwillingness to obey rules constituted Joel's essence. Cahill, who never saw Joel alive or made any effort to that end, can now clutch the few personal remnants of his son in his coat pockets: the pilot's broken goggles, a burned zipper from his boot found near the crash, a piece of wire from the airplane. Cahill steadily contemplates the tangible remains while absorbing the memory fragments from the other pilots. His boy is alive in his head. Cahill, in this blitz of story and memorabilia, is learning to love, but the word does little to indicate the combination of physical impressions and the straining for meaning that come to make up Joel in Cahill's consciousness.

Dickey's creation of a blind character allows him to exploit his bias toward the physical. The world has never been so mediated as felt. Even when the seeing, right-hand column is being read, the experience is emphatically visceral. A bus drives away at the novel's end: "The gears gathered, smashed and crowded, found each other; the bus straightened onto the highway. . . . The highway came to exist in the bodies of the passengers, as the driver brought it into himself, and with it made the engine hoarse and large."

Dickey shows that Cahill, while now blind, has never been so fully *in* the world, and a dead son has never been more alive for him. Joel's Alnilam brothers show a film of their group's arrival at the base. Cahill, privy to their secrets because of their perception of his own arrival as part of Joel's master plan, is present at the showing and asks for a description of Joel when the projector sends out his image. Hearing of a curl of hair across the forehead, Cahill strains out of his chair in an effort to see his son. Later, taking a bath and speaking aloud of the wondrous good things there are in the world, such as a hot bath to soak in and a bottle of gin to swallow, Cahill hears Joel speak. Zack hears him as well and tears up the room. A ghost is as real and sensible as hot water. The world is full of marvels, and human beings are rich creatures both to be and to know.

This message might be a summation of what Dickey wrote fiction about. He would not leave disenchanted suburbanites amid unmitigated ennui. *Deliverance* claims that a man has things to prove to himself. *Alnilam* claims that a man is composed of more than he knows and lives in a world of presences and forces that he tends to ignore or disbelieve. In Cahill, Dickey creates a primal character, a sort of caveman, through whom Dickey as a writer can imagine all sensations anew, from the feeling of snowflakes to the taste of water. Dickey wants to go back to humanity before it was dulled by civilization, and in *Deliverance* and *Alnilam* he imagines characters who experience their basic vitality as living creatures.

To the White Sea • Parts of *To the White Sea* are good and original. However, what is original can not be considered among the best of Dickey's prose, and what is good is not terribly original, leaning heavily on *Deliverance* and its survivalist ethos. In the opening section, Dickey reaches back into his own experience as an airman who took part in the 1945 firebombing of Japan. Later on he will smoothly segue into imagined, mystical passages of immersion in animal world and nature, scenes of hunting, stalking, and killing. Halfway through the novel, during the long train ride episode, his language will become even more poetic and associative. Overall, it is not inaccurate to describe the novel as a sustained internal monologue interlaced with curt, matter-of-fact, explosive sequences of action and violence. The mixture of these disparate styles may jar readers, but it is entirely deliberate. As a 1988 letter to Gore Vidal reveals, Dickey made no real distinction between fact, fiction, history, reminiscence, and fantasy because, as he put it, imagination inhabits them all.

Color imagery dominates the protagonist's progression from Tokyo to the northern tip of the island of Honshu and across the strait to Hokkaido. The dominant hue changes from the fire red during the bombing raid to the whiteness of the polar landscape at the end. In between, the author strives to emphasize the imagistic play of other hues and shades, but the overall effect is often contrived and detracting from the protagonist's progress—and, in some way, regress. Dickey's favorite structural device is to strip the plot and his characters to the barest essentials and then intimate emotionally laden questions about this cubist tableau. In *To the White Sea*, these questions seem to be aimed at the survivalist ethic in the days of human-made holocaust. Yet filtered through the mind of the American airman, Muldrow, whom the author himself characterized as a sociopath and a conscienceless murderer much like the infamous serial killer Ted Bundy, they seem shallow at best, self-justifying the senseless killing.

Preaching and living the mantra of being ever-ready for the veneer of civilization to fall away, leaving everyone at the mercy of their survival skills, Muldrow instinctively—but also with full deliberation—seeks to leave the war behind and get to the wastelands of northern Japan. His separate peace has little to do, however, with the rituals of valor and respect. Its only trace is when the killer honors the fallen Japanese sword-master. For most of the journey, Muldrow is not so much apart from the human society as a part of a force of nature, almost amoral in his basic survivalist drives. His ultimate death at the hands of the Japanese is not an act of victory by the superior enemy but an act of supreme indifference to death from a man who has finally found his place in the nature-driven scheme of things—one that transcends human warfare, loyalty, and perhaps civilization as a whole.

Bruce Wiebe
Updated by Peter Swirski

Other major works

SHORT FICTION: *Telling Stories,* 1978.

SCREENPLAY: *Deliverance,* 1972 (adaptation of his novel).

TELEPLAY: *The Call of the Wild,* 1976 (adaptation of Jack London's novel).

POETRY: *Into the Stone, and Other Poems,* 1960; *Drowning with Others,* 1962; *Helmets,* 1964; *Two Poems of the Air,* 1964; *Buckdancer's Choice,* 1965; *Poems, 1957-1967,* 1967; *The Eye-Beaters, Blood, Victory, Madness, Buckhead, and Mercy,* 1970; *The Zodiac,* 1976; *The Strength of Fields,* 1977; *Head-Deep in Strange Sounds: Free-Flight Improvisations from the UnEnglish,* 1979; *Falling, May Day Sermon, and Other Poems,* 1981; *The Early Motion,* 1981; *Puella,* 1982; *The Central Motion: Poems, 1968-1979,* 1983; *The Eagle's Mile,* 1990; *The Whole Motion: Collected Poems, 1945-1992,* 1992.

NONFICTION: *The Suspect in Poetry,* 1964; *A Private Brinkmanship,* 1965 (address); *Spinning the Crystal Ball,* 1967; *From Babel to Byzantium,* 1968; *Metaphor as Pure Adventure,* 1968; *Self-Interviews,* 1970; *Sorties,* 1971; *In Pursuit of the Grey Soul,* 1978; *The Enemy from Eden,* 1978; *The Starry Place Between the Antlers: Why I Live in South Carolina,* 1981; *The Poet Turns on Himself,* 1982; *The Voiced Connections of James Dickey,* 1989; *Striking In: the Early Notebooks of James Dickey,* 1996 (Gordon Van Ness, editor); *Crux: The Letters of James Dickey,* 1999; *The One Voice of James Dickey: His Letters and Life, 1942-1969,* 2003 (Gordon Van Ness, editor); *Classes on Modern Poets and the Art of Poetry,* 2004 (Donald J. Greiner, editor); *The One Voice of James Dickey: His Letters and Life, 1970-1997,* 2005 (Gordon Van Ness, editor).

CHILDREN'S LITERATURE: *Tucky the Hunter,* 1978.

MISCELLANEOUS: *Night Hurdling: Poems, Essays, Conversations, Commencements, and Afterwords,* 1983; *The James Dickey Reader,* 1999.

Bibliography

Bowers, Neal. *James Dickey: The Poet as Pitchman.* Columbia: University of Missouri Press, 1985. Focuses on Dickey as a public figure who was not only a successful poet but also a successful promoter of his work and of poetry in general. Bowers's analysis of individual poems is sometimes thin, and his assessment of Dickey as "pitchman" for poetry is overly simplistic, but the study serves as a good introductory overview of Dickey as a media phenomenon.

Bruccoli, Matthew J., and Judith S. Baughman, eds. *Crux: The Letters of James Dickey.* New York: Alfred A. Knopf, 1999. Collection of Dickey's personal correspondence.

Calhoun, Richard J., and Robert W. Hill. *James Dickey.* Boston: Twayne, 1983. The first book-length study of Dickey's work, this study covers his writing from *Into the Stone, and Other Poems* to *Puella.* The authors attempt to analyze virtually everything Dickey wrote during a twenty-two-year period, so that at times the discussions are rather sketchy. Nevertheless, this book provides a solid introduction to Dickey.

Dickey, Christopher. *Summer of Deliverance: A Memoir of Father and Son.* New York: Simon & Schuster, 1998. A biography of Dickey written by his son. Includes bibliographical references and an index.

Dickey, James. *The Voiced Connections of James Dickey.* Edited by Ronald Baughman. Columbia: University of South Carolina Press, 1990. This collection of interviews covers Dickey's career from the mid-1960's to the late 1980's. Baughman, who taught at the University of South Carolina with Dickey, has selected important and lively interviews. A useful chronology and a helpful index are included.

Hart, Henry. *James Dickey: The World as a Lie.* New York: Picador USA, 2000. A narrative biography detailing the rise and self-destruction of a literary reputation. Little of Dickey's prose or verse is quoted for analysis, and the book relies on Dickey's interviews and those held by the power of his personality.

Kirschten, Robert. *James Dickey and the Gentle Ecstasy of Earth: A Reading of the Poems.* Baton Rouge: Louisiana State University Press, 1988. Provides one of the best readings of Dickey's poems. Employs four hypotheses—mysticism, neoplatonism, romanticism, and primitivism—to identify Dickey's characteristic techniques and thematic concerns. When a poem is analyzed extensively, long sections of it are reprinted so readers can follow the critic's insights.

___________, ed. *Critical Essays on James Dickey.* New York: Maxwell Macmillan International, 1994. Provides early reviews and a selection of more modern scholarship. Authors include Robert Bly, Paul Carroll, James Wright, and Wendell Berry. Bibliography and index.

Suarez, Ernest. "Emerson in Vietnam: Dickey, Bly, and the New Left." *Southern Literary Journal,* Spring, 1991, 100-112. Examines controversial elements in Dickey's poems and the adverse critical reaction to Dickey's work. His complex metaphysics collided with the politics of a historic particular, the Vietnam War, generating a New Left critical agenda that could not accommodate the philosophical underpinnings of his poetry. The result was widespread misinterpretations of Dickey's work.

___________. "The Uncollected Dickey: Pound, New Criticism, and the Narrative Image." *American Poetry* 7 (Fall, 1990): 127-145. By examining Dickey's early uncollected poems and his correspondence with Ezra Pound, Suarez documents Dickey's struggle to move out from under modernism's domination and arrive at his mature poetic aesthetic.

Weigl, Bruce, and T. R. Hummer, eds. *The Imagination as Glory: The Poetry of James Dickey.* Urbana: University of Illinois Press, 1984. The best articles on Dickey up to 1984. Especially noteworthy is Joyce Carol Oates's "Out of the Stone and into the Flesh," which argues that Dickey is a relentlessly honest writer who explores the human condition in a world of violence and chaos.

Joan Didion

Born: Sacramento, California; December 5, 1934

Principal long fiction • *Run River*, 1963; *Play It as It Lays*, 1970; *A Book of Common Prayer*, 1977; *Democracy*, 1984; *The Last Thing He Wanted*, 1996.

Other literary forms • Joan Didion is respected as a novelist, but she is even more highly acclaimed as an essayist. Her career as a writer was launched by a piece of nonfiction; in 1956, during her senior year at the University of California at Berkeley, her article on the San Francisco architect William Wilson Wurster won *Vogue*'s Prix de Paris contest for young writers, and she was awarded a job with that magazine. Although she resigned her position at *Vogue* in 1963 to devote more time to her fiction, she continued as a film critic for the magazine and began publishing regularly in *The Saturday Evening Post*. She also wrote articles for periodicals such as *The American Scholar*, *The New York Times Magazine*, *National Review*, *Esquire*, *New West*, and *The New York Review of Books*. Didion also collaborated with her husband, John Gregory Dunne, on several screenplays.

Didion achieved national recognition with her first collection of essays, *Slouching Towards Bethlehem* (1968); her second collection, *The White Album* (1979), was a bestseller. Her books *Salvador* (1983) and *Miami* (1987) are overtly political and aroused considerable controversy. *After Henry* (1992), her third essay collection, largely concerns California subjects. This return to her original source of topics was well received by many critics. Most of her later books have been nonfiction, such as the collection of essays titled *Political Fictions* (2001).

Achievements • Didion's achievements are somewhat paradoxical. Despite her claims that she speaks only for herself, she became a spokesperson for the anxiety-ridden generation of the late 1960's and early 1970's. As surely as F. Scott Fitzgerald became the chronicler of the Jazz Age, Didion became the chronicler of a generation living, in her terms, "close to the edge." Didion developed a reputation for cool, detached observation and for her syncopated but elegant style. Poet James Dickey called her "the finest woman prose stylist writing in English today," and even some who dismiss her as intellectually shallow respect her craftsmanship. Her accomplishments were formally recognized in 1996 when she was awarded the Edward MacDowell Medal for outstanding contributions to the arts. Previous recipients included Robert Frost, Lillian Hellman, and Mary McCarthy.

Biography • Joan Didion was born to Frank Reese and Eduene Jerrett Didion on December 5, 1934, in Sacramento, California. Both the date and the place are significant. Though Didion had just turned seven when Pearl Harbor was attacked, she is not, strictly speaking, a child of the postwar generation. This fact might explain some of her detachment from the 1960's and some of the nostalgia she evidently feels even when she is pointing out the shortcomings of the more traditional and more orderly values of pre-World War II America.

Didion's place of birth is even more important. Didion is a child of the West—not the West of Los Angeles, but of the more pastoral Sacramento Valley. The land on which Didion lived had been in her family for five generations, and as a child, she was expected to absorb the myth that America was a new Eden. In *Slouching Towards Bethlehem,* Didion reports that her Episcopal Sunday school teacher used to ask the children, "In what ways does the Holy Land resemble the Sacramento Valley?" Didion explores—and largely explodes—the myth of the Sacramento Valley as Eden in her first novel, *Run River.* Eden, however, is not lost—or rejected—without some sense of regret, and Didion's novel reflects a nostalgia for the lost paradise and the passing of innocence.

Didion's intellectual break from a more traditional world may have begun in high school, when she discovered literature, and it must have been accelerated by her studies at the University of California at Berkeley, where she majored in literature, read Ernest Hemingway, Joseph Conrad, Henry James, and Albert Camus, moved out of her sorority house, and did not, as she points out with some regret, make Phi Beta Kappa. She did, however, win first prize in *Vogue*'s Prix de Paris contest. Given as an award the choice of a trip to Paris or a job on the magazine, Didion chose the more practical option and moved to New York.

At *Vogue,* Didion learned to write for the general public, and she began writing for several other magazines as well. She also seriously began writing fiction, and *Run River* was published in 1963. Her time in New York, then, was important for her development as a writer, and, judging from her essay "Good-bye to All That," she enjoyed her first few years there. However, as the essay continues, she began to believe that "it is distinctly possible to stay too long at the fair." Disenchantment turned to depression. In January, 1964, in lieu of seeing a psychiatrist, she married John Gregory Dunne, also a writer, and the couple moved to Los Angeles. They adopted a daughter, Quintana Roo, in 1966.

In Los Angeles, Didion's writing continued to go well—she published *Slouching Towards Bethlehem* in 1968, and she and Dunne wrote the screenplay for *The Panic in Needle Park* (1971)—but for some time, she continued to suffer from the depression and sense of disorientation she describes in *The White Album.* Her marital problems were publicized in her own essays and in Dunne's. During the 1970's, however, both her marriage and her emotional state improved, and her literary success continued to grow: *Play It as It Lays, The White Album,* and *A Book of Common Prayer* were all best-sellers. Financial success also came, not so much from the books as from Didion and Dunne's collaboration on screenplays, many of which were never filmed. Besides *The Panic in Needle Park* and the film adaptation of Dunne's novel *True Confessions,* the couple worked on the script for *A Star Is Born* (1976). According to Dunne, that motion picture "made us a fortune." Didion and Dunne have also written scripts for cable television films. Their work on the theatrical release *Up Close and Personal* (1996) was highly publicized and became the subject of Dunne's book *Monster: Living off the Big Screen* (1997), a less-than-fond look at filmmaking.

Didion's journalism has also remained an important part of her career. She reported on the 1988 and 1992 presidential campaigns, a detail of her life that resurfaced in her novel *The Last Thing He Wanted*; the novel's protagonist, Elena McMahon, begins the story as a reporter for *The Washington Post* who is covering the 1984 presidential election. Praise for Didion's journalism was particularly effusive after she published "Trouble in Lakewood" (a Los Angeles suburb beset by social problems after the defense industry in Southern California drastically contracted) in *The New Yorker* (July 16, 1993).

Quintana Roo Dunne

Didion and Dunne continued to live in greater Los Angeles until 1988, when they returned to Manhattan to be closer to their business interests and friends. Nevertheless, Didion continued to write about California while managing to avoid being labeled a regional writer. Despite the atmosphere of angst and dread that pervades much of Didion's writing, Dunne wrote in the June, 1990, issue of *Esquire* magazine that his and his wife's epitaph could well read, "They had a good time."

In late 2003, Didion entered a difficult period in her personal life. Shortly before Christmas, her recently married daughter, Quintana Dunne Michael, fell ill and went into a medically induced coma. On December 30, Didion's husband suffered a fatal heart attack, thus ending the productive writing partnership that he and Didion had enjoyed for forty years. In late 2005, Didion published *The Year of Magical Thinking*, a book that describes her efforts to make her husband come back through what she called "magical thinking." The book also discusses her concerns for her daughter, who died shortly after Didion's book was released. The book earned Didion a National Book Award.

Analysis • Almost all of Joan Didion's works are concerned with similar themes, and there is an interesting complementary relationship between her essays and her novels. Her essays generally seem intended to force the reader to strip away illusions about contemporary life and accept realities, even if they are bleak. The novels are generally explorations of characters crippled by illusions. To some extent, in each novel, the heroine is disabused of her illusions. The fragile hope that each novel holds out, however, is not offered in terms of this disillusionment but in terms of new illusions and almost meaningless gestures. Each novel ends with the heroine learning to care for others—for a husband, for a lover, for children, for friends—and yet this caring is generally based on illusion and seems doomed to failure. Didion's final implication, then, seems to be that people need to strip away all illusions, except those that help them to care for others. Such illusions—even though they are doomed to lead to failure—are sacred. These sacred illusions might be fictional, as stories are fictional, but, as Didion has said, "We tell ourselves stories in order to live . . . or at least we do for a while."

Run River • Although Didion's first novel, *Run River*, is not autobiographical, it does explore the myth she absorbed in her childhood, the myth of America as the new

Eden, the new Promised Land. This myth was brought to the New World by the earliest settlers of Virginia and Massachusetts, but it took special form with the westward expansion. Lily Knight, the heroine of *Run River,* expresses her faith directly: "She believed that it was America's mission to make manifest to the world the wishes of an Episcopal God, [and] that her father would one day be Governor of California." The novel can be quickly summarized. It begins—and finally ends—on the night that Everett McClellan, Lily's husband, kills Ryder Channing, Lily's lover, and then himself. The novel backtracks to trace the lives of the main characters and returns full circle to the murder and suicide. Along the way, it suggests that Lily, Everett, and Everett's sister Martha have been shattered because of a misplaced faith in traditional, romantic notions about their lives and about their home, the Sacramento Valley.

Lily, after she admits to herself that she probably will not be offered the lead role in *Gone with the Wind,* accepts a traditional, passive woman's role. After passively "accepting" Everett twenty-seven times, she agrees to marry him: "It seemed as inescapable as the ripening of the pears, as fated as the exile from Eden." However, she finds the role of river matron less than satisfactory, and she continues to accept men—first Joe Templeton and later Ryder Channing—for little more reason than that they desire her. Through it all, Lily fails to come to terms with who she is and what she really wants.

The traditional dream of ranch and family no longer works for Everett, either. Ironically, he seems happy only when he runs away from the ranch, his wife, and his sister, to join the army during World War II. When his father dies, however, he feels bound by duty to return to the ranch, to try to make it work, and to take care of his wife and sister. It does not work; his wife is unfaithful, his sister is destroyed by the "lack of honor" in the world, and his son obviously intends to abandon the homestead.

Martha, Everett's sister, is perhaps the most utterly destroyed character in the novel. She cannot act out her incestuous feelings for her brother, and the man she does accept for a lover, Ryder Channing, is no gentleman. After he marries another woman and their affair ends, he almost brutally "seduces" her again. Martha is forced to admit that she is not a "lady"—their affair had not been a great romantic passion, but what advice columnist Ann Landers might describe as "chemistry." Stripped of her illusions, she cannot live. Her brother cannot protect her—a fact that will make him, a romantic gallant, feel even more guilty—and she kills herself.

All of the romantic illusions of the traditional world come crashing down when Everett kills Ryder Channing and then himself. It could be argued that it is not the traditional world that has failed these characters; it is rather that they have failed it. After all, a good river matron should not have an affair while her husband is serving his country; Everett should have been stronger; and Martha should have had more self-respect than to take up with a man such as Ryder. Such an argument, however, would simply ignore too much of the characters' background. Lily's father, Walter Knight, was not so shining as Lily had thought. He does not become governor of California. He is a near alcoholic, and he carries on an adulterous relationship with Rita Blanchard, another "good spinster" who proves no better and no worse than Martha. Walter is no more a rancher than Everett; his Mexican foreman Gomez is the one who keeps the place going. Finally, he can no more protect his Rita than Everett can protect Martha; both he and Rita drown when he accidentally drives into the Sacramento River.

The novel, then, shows the myth of the Sacramento Valley as a second Eden to be a second-generation failure. The book might seem to imply that it is World War II that renders this idyllic world "gone with the wind," but it is doubtful that Didion believes that things were really better in the old days. Her vision of the settling of the West seems centered on the Donner-Reed party; her great-great-great grandmother had been part of that party originally, but she left it before they were stranded by winter snows and forced to eat their own dead to survive. In her essay "On Morality," Didion equates morality with not leaving the dead to the coyotes, and she writes of the Donner-Reed party: "We were taught instead that they had somewhere abdicated their responsibilities, somehow breached their primal loyalties or they would not have found themselves helpless in the mountain winter . . . would not have failed." At the end of *Run River*, all three major characters have failed to live up to their primal loyalties of wife to husband, husband to wife, brother to sister, sister to sister-in-law. They have been "immoral," not because of their sexual misconduct but because they have failed to take care of one another.

There is, perhaps, some hope for Lily at the end. She has survived, not by virtue but by luck, and she may have learned. Looking at Everett's body, she finally—perhaps for the first time—tries to talk to him. She recalls the good times and realizes the importance of their love: "She hoped that . . . he would rise thinking of her, *we were each other, we were each other, not that it mattered much in the long run but what else mattered as much.*" "Not that it mattered much" is vintage Didion, but the "what else mattered as much" seems heartfelt. The hope that lovers will rise thinking of each other "through all eternity" has the ring of romantic illusion, but at this point, such a hope constitutes the only possible relationship left for Lily and Everett. At the end of the novel, she is left thinking about what she will say to her children. To sustain them, she will probably be compelled to sustain an illusion about the man she has come to love too late: "She did not know what she could tell anyone except that he had been a good man. She was not certain that he had been but it was what she would have wished for him, if they gave her one wish."

The ease with which *Run River* can be explained as an explosion of traditional American myths probably suggests why the novel is generally considered Didion's most modest achievement. So many people have exploded traditional American myths since 1963 that it does not seem necessary to reread *Run River* to see it done again. In *Play It as It Lays*, however, Didion does something few writers have done as well as she; she turns the tables and explodes the myths and illusions of the contemporary sensibility.

Play It as It Lays • Perhaps no setting could be more appropriate for an illusion-hunter than Los Angeles. In *Play It as It Lays*, Didion places her heroine Maria (pronounced "Mar-eye-ah," like the west wind in the musical *Paint Your Wagon*) squarely in the fast lane of life in Southern California. The novel opens with Maria in a psychiatric ward. She has been placed there, presumably, for her failure to attempt to stop a friend from committing suicide in her presence. As the novel unfolds (like *Run River*) backward into the past, however, the reader comes to realize that if Maria has become unhinged, it is probably a result of the cumulative effect of her abortion, her divorce, and the miscellaneous acts of casual sex, drugs, and other perversities one might expect in a novel about Hollywood.

Didion does not condemn the fast lane from a traditional moral perspective; that would have been too easy, and probably not very convincing or interesting. Besides,

Didion's target is not simply the sexual mores of contemporary culture. Rather, she explores the popular "philosophy" or worldview that so many have accepted since the collapse of the traditional morality—a "philosophy" that might be called sloppy existentialism, extreme relativism, or simply nihilism. Maria states the key tenet of this philosophy on the second page of the novel: "NOTHING APPLIES."

Maria herself was not reared with the traditional American values. Instead of the Puritan work ethic ("God helps those who help themselves"), she was taught the gambler's code: "My father advised me that life itself was a crap game." That view was infused with a faith in good luck: "I was raised to believe that what came in on the next roll would always be better than what went on the last." For a long time, Maria was content to wait for the rolls, to go with the flow, and to "play it as it lays."

However, Maria's luck runs out. The bad roll is an unwanted pregnancy. She thinks, but is not sure, that Carter, her husband, is not the father. He demands that she have an abortion and threatens to take away Kate, their brain-damaged daughter, if she refuses. Maria acquiesces, and her mental deterioration begins.

If Maria could completely accept the mores of her set, she would have no problem; for them, neither abortion nor divorce is anything to lose one's composure over. Maria, however, does cling to one traditional dream; she wants a family. She fantasizes about living a simple life with Kate and some man—in almost identical fantasies, the man is either Ivan or Les, two of her steadier lovers. Abortion—the termination of another possible child—is almost more than Maria can contemplate, yet she undergoes the procedure.

Maria's reaction to the abortion is not philosophical, moral, or religious; it is emotional, physical, and psychological. She cries; she hemorrhages; she reaches a point where she cannot easily use plumbing because she imagines pipes clogged with chopped-up pieces of flesh.

Didion does not attempt to make an abstract moral issue out of abortion. Maria's reaction is almost primitive, in the sense of being immediate and unreflecting. In a real sense, however, to return to Didion's essay "On Morality," abortion is a denial of the most basic social responsibility, that of mother to child (it is hard here not to recall Didion's own traumatic miscarriage and her devotion to her adopted daughter). In *Play It as It Lays*, even more emphatically than in *Run River*, characters fail to fulfill their primal social responsibilities. Carter, Les (even Les's wife), Maria's friends, Helene and BZ, and a number of others all say that they are "seriously worried" about Maria as she slips more and more into self-destructive behavior; they say that they care, but none of them can reach her, none of them can take care of her. Some of their protestations are hard to take seriously; Carter humiliates Maria on a number of occasions, and Helene and BZ use her—while she is drunk and only half-conscious—for obscure and unpleasant sexual purposes.

Most of these characters profess not to be concerned with the sexual conduct of their spouses. When Helene, BZ's wife, drifts into an affair with Carter, BZ asks Maria if she cares. For a time, Maria tries to insist that she does care, but as the novel draws to a conclusion, BZ forces her more and more to a nihilistic position: "'Tell me what matters,' BZ said. 'Nothing,' Maria said." The "nothing" here is Ernest Hemingway's "nada," and at the end of the novel, BZ, like Hemingway, kills himself. BZ, however, does not use a gun. He goes out with a bottle of vodka and a grain-and-a-half of Seconal. When Helene and Carter force their way into the room, BZ is dead and Maria is asleep next to him, holding his hand.

On the last page of the novel, Maria, from the psychiatric ward, affirms BZ's nihilism, if not his suicide: “I know what ‘nothing’ means, and keep on playing. Why, BZ would say. Why not, I say.” That, however, is not all there is to it. Maria has already made it clear that she is playing for Kate. She wants to take Kate away from the hospital; she wants them to have a home by the sea where they can live a simple life. Given Kate’s condition—to say nothing of Maria’s—this future does not sound very likely. Despite her acceptance of nihilism, Maria holds on to one last romantic notion. Perhaps she realizes how illusory her hope is, but, like Lily’s hope that Everett will rise thinking of her, the illusion and the hope are necessary. They keep her in the game and away from the Seconal.

***A Book of Common Prayer* •** *Run River* and *Play It as It Lays* demonstrate the failures both of traditional American myths and of more current nihilistic lifestyles. Lily Knight McClellan and Maria Wyeth both survive, but both are sustained by hopes that seem largely based on illusion. In Didion’s third novel, *A Book of Common Prayer,* the reader is told on the first page that the protagonist, Charlotte Douglas, does not survive. The narrator, however, comments that “she died, hopeful.” Whether Charlotte’s hope is also illusory is a central question of the novel.

It is the question that the narrator, Grace Strasser-Mendana, née Tabor, is trying to answer throughout the novel. Grace, originally from the United States, “married into one of the three or four solvent families in Boca Grande,” the small Central American republic in which Charlotte Douglas is finally killed (or murdered; as Grace says, neither word seems to work). The death of Grace’s husband has left her “in putative control of fifty-nine-point-eight percent of the arable land and about the same percentage of the decisionmaking process in La Repűblica.” From this position of power, Grace observes the political scheming of her family. She also watches Charlotte walk barefooted into the scene and become caught up in it. Grace leaves the country before Charlotte dies, and the novel is her attempt to understand Charlotte. As she says, “Call it my witness to Charlotte Douglas.”

At the very beginning of her witness, Grace comments that Charlotte “dreamed her life,” and much of what Grace says makes Charlotte seem a woman even more given to illusion than was Lily Knight McClellan or Maria Wyeth. Grace insists that Charlotte was the “usual child of comfortable family in the temperate zone.” She had been supplied with all the material benefits and easy optimism of an affluent American. As a child, she was given a carved Austrian angel that listened to her bedside prayers: “In these prayers the child Charlotte routinely asked that ‘it’ turn out all right, ‘it’ being unspecified and all-inclusive, and she had been an adult for some years before the possibility occurred to her that ‘it’ might not.”

Like Maria, Charlotte loses some of the optimism; her luck runs out. The more traditional lifestyle fails her. Her first husband, Warren Bogart (perhaps the name is meant to be halfway between Warren Beatty and Humphrey Bogart), had been “raised to believe not in ‘hard work’ or ‘self reliance’ but in the infinite power of the personal appeal.” He is also sadistic, sexually perverse, and alcoholic. Charlotte is not perfect, either; one Easter, while their child Marin is still a baby, she gets drunk and sleeps with a man she does not even like (she later conveniently forgets the episode). Warren hits her, and she finally walks away from the marriage.

Her second marriage is not unlike Maria’s life in the fast lane, except that the game is no longer motion pictures but radical politics. Her husband is not a director but a radical chic lawyer who flies from one center of revolution to another. Leonard does seem genuinely to care for Charlotte, but there are complications. Marin, Charlotte's child by Warren, turns revolutionary; she and her friends hijack a jetliner, burn it in the desert, and join the underground.

Charlotte's main illusion, like Maria's, is centered around her daughter. She later tells Grace that she and Marin were "inseparable" (a term she also uses to describe her relationship with Warren), and she spins out fantastic accounts of their visit to the Tivoli Gardens. As might be expected, the revolutionary Marin claims to have little use for her bourgeois mother.

After a disastrous reunion with Warren and after the birth and almost immediate death of her child by Leonard, Charlotte drifts to Boca Grande, where she meets Grace. At first, Charlotte gives Grace every reason to think that she is dreaming her life; for quite a while, she goes to the airport every day, on the offhand chance that Marin will pass through Central America; she drifts aimlessly into sexual relations with Victor, Grace's brother-in-law, and then with Gerardo, Grace's son; she seems not to notice the growing signs of revolution; she refuses the attempts of Gerardo, Leonard, and Grace to persuade her to leave; finally, the revolution begins, and she is arrested and killed. Her body is dumped on the lawn of the American embassy.

All this does seem to add up to a life of dreams and illusions, yet throughout the novel, Charlotte proves herself to be capable of very practical behavior. She kills a chicken with her bare hands; she skins an iguana for stew; she performs an emergency tracheotomy with a penknife; and she inoculates people against an epidemic of cholera for thirty-four hours without a break. Although Charlotte often seems not to notice what is going on around her, she corrects people who claim to know what is happening; she reminds a reporter that Marin's comrade killed himself in Arizona, not Mexico, and she later corrects Gerardo on a technical point: "'Carmen wasn't using an M-3.' Charlotte said. She leaned forward slightly and her face was entirely grave. 'Antonio was. Carmen was using an M-16.'"

If Charlotte is not as out of touch as she seems, why then does she stay in Boca Grande and risk her life? In her last conversation with Leonard, she says very simply, "I walked away from places all my life and I'm not going to walk away from here." In another context, one could imagine John Wayne speaking those lines. In this context, however, there is no sense of the heroic. For a moment, Leonard seems to misunderstand this, and he warns her, "You don't get any real points for staying here, Charlotte." Charlotte understands perfectly: "'I can't seem to tell what you do get the real points for,' Charlotte said. 'So I guess I'll stick around for a while.'" Didion does not glorify Charlotte's decision to stay; it is not a self-defining existential act. She simply returns to her work at a birth-control clinic (an ironic job for a woman whose passport lists her occupation as *madre*). Her work is not particularly meaningful, since Charlotte routinely advises women to use the diaphragm while the clinic stocks only intrauterine devices (IUD's). In any event, no clients come on Charlotte's last day of work, the last day of her life. In deciding to stay, Charlotte maintains something of her integrity, what Didion would call "character," but Didion allows the reader no illusions about the act; it is the integrity of a cardplayer playing out a losing hand.

Charlotte's integrity can only be appreciated in comparison to the values of the other characters, particularly Grace. Even though Grace has been trying to understand Charlotte throughout the novel, she is as much a victim of delusion as Charlotte is. For some time, Grace has realized the difficulty in understanding things, in trying to get the story straight. She had abandoned her first discipline before the beginning of the novel: "I am an anthropologist who lost faith in her own method, who stopped believing that observable activity defined anthros." She turned to biochemistry, but that, too, failed: "Give me the molecular structure of the protein that defined Charlotte Douglas." When Leonard reveals to her that her husband Edgar had been involved with the guerrillas himself, Grace is finally forced to realize that her life, as much as Charlotte's, has been one of delusion.

Grace's statement, "We all remember what we need to remember," is one of the lessons of the novel; all people prefer to believe their own versions of the stories in which they are trapped; all people accept delusions. Grace finally realizes that, "I am more like Charlotte Douglas than I thought I was." Perhaps Charlotte's death was something of a meaningless gesture, but beside her coffin, Grace can only make a small meaningless gesture of love; she places a T-shirt painted like an American flag on the casket. By way of comment, she borrows a phrase from Charlotte and Leonard: "There were no real points in that either."

Neither Grace nor Charlotte—perhaps none of Didion's characters in any of her novels—scores any real points in the end. They try to take care of one another, but they fail. Grace and Leonard try to take care of Charlotte, but they fail. Charlotte would like to take care of Marin, but she cannot. Warren wants Charlotte to take care of him, but it does not work. As cynical as Warren is, he may have the final judgment in the novel: "It doesn't matter whether you take care of somebody or somebody takes care of you. . . . It's all the same in the end. It's all the same." Warren dies alone; Charlotte dies alone. Grace will die—as she says—very soon, and she will be alone. It is all the same in the end. At least Charlotte does to some degree shape her own life toward the end. The night she was arrested, she was, Grace imagines, "walking very deliberately."

Democracy • The protagonist of Didion's fourth novel, *Democracy*, is Inez Christian Victor, the daughter of a prominent Honolulu family and the wife of a liberal California senator who narrowly lost the Democratic nomination for president in 1972. The love of her life, however, is a shadowy soldier of fortune named Jack Lovett. She follows him to Southeast Asia on the eve of the fall of Vietnam (to retrieve her daughter—a heroin addict who has drifted to Saigon because she hears that employment opportunities are good there) and sees him drown in a hotel pool in Jakarta. She brings the body back to Hawaii to be buried under a jacaranda tree at Schofield Barracks and returns to Kuala Lumpur to work with refugees.

In *Democracy*, one finds evidence of two of Didion's most prominent characteristics as a writer—her acute sense of place and her fascination with the American West. Although these twin aspects of her muse have always been evident in her writings about California, she has occasionally cast her glance farther westward to Hawaii. In *Slouching Towards Bethlehem*, she wrote: "I sat as a child on California beaches and imagined that I saw Hawaii, a certain shimmer in the sunset, a barely perceptible irregularity glimpsed intermittently through squinted eyes." In a column for *New West* magazine, written more than a decade later, she revealed that she kept a clock in her bedroom in Los Angeles, set at Honolulu time.

When Didion, however, tried to write a novel about feudal Hawaii (originally titled *Pacific Distances*), she produced a book that is only marginally about that subject. In *Democracy*, Hawaii is less important as a society in transition than as a way station between the Mainland and America's ultimate western frontier, Southeast Asia. (In *Slouching Towards Bethlehem*, she speaks of sailors who got drunk in Honolulu because "they were no longer in Des Moines and not yet in Da Nang.") As Walt Whitman proclaimed more than a century earlier in his poem "Passage to India" (1871), the roundness of the earth leads not to some apocalyptic West but back east whence we came. America's manifest destiny, however, has not even produced a mystical passage to India, but rather helicopters lifting off the roof of the American embassy in Saigon during the final days of the only war the United States has ever lost.

In this imagistic, elliptical novel, much is left to conjecture. More than in any of her previous works, Didion has helped fuel this conjecture by an almost compulsive literary allusiveness. Certainly the most significant allusion is to Henry Adams, who in 1880 published a novel titled *Democracy*. Although in her review of Didion's novel Mary McCarthy made nothing of the novels having the same name, Thomas R. Edwards saw both Didion and Adams as displaced aristocrats who with "irony and subtlety confront a chaotic new reality that shatters the orderings of simpler, older ways."

From a purely technical standpoint, the most controversial and problematic aspect of *Democracy* is its point of view. Departing from the more conventional narrative techniques of her earlier novels, Didion inserts herself into *Democracy* and claims to have been acquainted personally with her characters. Although this device may appear to make Didion's tale a postmodernist novel about novel writing, it also places her in the decidedly premodernist company of George Eliot and William Makepeace Thackeray, who both inserted themselves into their fiction.

By revealing her problems in writing this book and by treating her characters as if they were as real as the figures in her journalism, Didion may be trying to collapse the distinction between fiction and nonfiction narrative. If the new journalism brings the techniques of fiction to the writing of fact, this novel brings the illusion of fact to the writing of fiction. Such a device is for *Democracy* what the title *A Book of Common Prayer* was for Didion's earlier novel—a reason for telling the story.

The Last Thing He Wanted • In *The Last Thing He Wanted*, Didion's technique of writing fiction as though it were fact becomes much more assured. She creates a journalist narrator who claims not only to be the novel's author but also to have written about one of the story's characters for *The New York Times Magazine*, the type of high-profile periodical in which readers would expect to find an article by the real Joan Didion. In contrast to *Democracy*, however, Didion does not identify herself as the narrator. "For the record," she writes, "this is me talking. You know me, or you think you do. The not quite omniscient author." Readers may be tempted to think that the "me" refers to Didion herself, but the novel's characters are clearly fictional, and the narrator belongs to the same created world as the characters. Instead, the "me" seems to refer more to the idea of the narrator as "not quite omniscient author." Unlike true omniscient authors, who know everything that goes on in their stories, this narrator-author has a limited view. She must piece together the story of Elena McMahon, the novel's heroine, from transcripts of tape recordings, news articles, diplomatic reports, and interviews with not always truthful sources.

Out of these fragments the narrator-author constructs a story that explains Elena's mysterious death. After she walks away from her job covering the 1984 presidential campaign for *The Washington Post*, her seriously ill father, who is an arranger of ambiguous "deals," asks her to fly to the Caribbean to deliver something for him. The plane does not land exactly where Elena expects it to, and the something turns out to be illegal arms for the Contras, a counterrevolutionary group that opposed the Sandinista government of Nicaragua during the 1980's. After Elena reads in a U.S. paper that her father has suddenly died, she (along with the reader) realizes that her life is in extraordinary danger. Ultimately, she is framed for an assassination attempt on Treat Morrison, a U.S. operative with whom Elena has a fleeting romance. The attempt ends with Elena shot dead and Morrison gravely wounded. The novel itself ends two brief chapters later, as the narrator-author tries to reshape the story so that it ends with Elena and Morrison still together, a form the story's narrator-author finds more pleasing than the "actual" one.

Perhaps Didion's greatest achievement in this novel is the complexity that she wrings out of its lean, deceptively easy-to-read prose. Although several critics during the 1990's noted that her fiction was becoming ever more spare and her nonfiction was growing in length and density, *The Last Thing He Wanted* merges both characteristics. The novel's language makes it seem simple on its surface, but keeping track of the story requires the reader to maneuver through murky, difficult-to-follow conspiracies involving rival government factions, just as did the actual 1980's news coverage of alleged (and illegal) U.S. government support of the Contras. Although not all critics believed that the novel broke new ground for Didion, its reviews were mostly positive—atribute to Didion's position as one of the most highly regarded writers of her generation.

James Reynolds Kinzey
Updated by Kelly Fuller

Other major works

SHORT FICTION: *The Panic in Needle Park*, 1971 (with John Gregory Dunne); *Play It as It Lays*, 1972 (with Dunne); *A Star Is Born*, 1976 (with Dunne and Frank Pierson); *True Confessions*, 1981 (with Dunne); *Up Close and Personal*, 1996 (with Dunne).

TELEPLAYS: *Hills Like White Elephants*, 1990 (with John Gregory Dunne); *Broken Trust*, 1995 (with Dunne).

NONFICTION: *Slouching Towards Bethlehem*, 1968; *The White Album*, 1979; *Salvador*, 1983; *Joan Didion: Essays and Conversations*, 1984 (Ellen G. Friedman, editor); *Miami*, 1987; *After Henry*, 1992 (also known as *Sentimental Journeys*, 1993); *Political Fictions*, 2001; *Fixed Ideas: America Since 9-11*, 2003; *Where I Was From*, 2003; *Vintage Didion*, 2004; *The Year of Magical Thinking*, 2005; *We Tell Ourselves Stories in Order to Live: Collected Nonfiction*, 2006.

Bibliography

Didion, Joan. "Dave Eggers Talks with Joan Didion." Interview by Dave Eggers. *The Believer Book of Writers Talking to Writers*, edited by Vendela Vida. San Francisco: Believer, 2005. Revealing interview with Didion by the noted novelist.

Felton, Sharon, ed. *The Critical Response to Joan Didion*. Westport, Conn.: Greenwood Press, 1994. This useful collection of reviews and scholarly essays covers Didion's work through *After Henry*.

Friedman, Ellen G., ed. *Joan Didion: Essays and Conversations*. Princeton, N.J.: Ontario Review Press, 1984. Collects essays on various themes and deals with works through *Salvador*.

Gagné, Laurie Brands. "The Child and the Mother: Joan Didion, Mary Gordon, Virginia Woolf." In *The Uses of Darkness: Women's Underworld Journeys, Ancient and Modern*. Notre Dame, Ind.: University of Notre Dame Press, 2000. Comparative study of mother-child relationships in the fiction of Didion, the younger American novelist Mary Gordon, and the early twentieth century British writer Virginia Woolf.

Hall, Linda. "The Writer Who Came in from the Cold." *New York* 29 (September, 1996): 28-33, 57. Published shortly after the release of *The Last Thing He Wanted,* this profile is particularly strong on Didion's early career and the influence of her former mentor Noel Parmentel.

Hanley, Lynne. *Writing War: Fiction, Gender, and Memory.* Amherst: University of Massachusetts Press, 1991. Two chapters of this elegantly written study discuss Didion's depictions of war in *A Book of Common Prayer, El Salvador,* and *Democracy.*

Henderson, Katherine Usher. *Joan Didion.* New York: Ungar, 1981. A brief but helpful introductory study of Didion's life and work up through *The White Album,* this book is written for a general audience of nonspecialists.

Loris, Michelle Carbone. *Innocence, Loss, and Recovery in the Art of Joan Didion.* New York: Peter Lang, 1989. Explores psychological aspects of Didion's fiction. Includes bibliographical references.

Winchell, Mark Royden. *Joan Didion.* Rev. ed. Boston: Twayne, 1989. A revised and updated version of the first book written on Didion, this study follows its subject's career up through *Miami.* Although his work is accessible to the general reader, Winchell writes for a scholarly audience.

E. L. Doctorow

Born: New York, New York; January 6, 1931

Principal long fiction • *Welcome to Hard Times,* 1960; *Big as Life,* 1966; *The Book of Daniel,* 1971; *Ragtime,* 1975; *Loon Lake,* 1980; *World's Fair,* 1985; *Billy Bathgate,* 1989; *The Waterworks,* 1994; *City of God,* 2000; *The March,* 2005.

Other literary forms • E. L. Doctorow seldom ventured outside the novel genre. However, he wrote a play, *Drinks Before Dinner* (1978), a collection of short stories, *Lives of the Poets* (1984), and a collection of essays, *Jack London, Hemingway, and the Constitution* (1993).

Achievements • *Ragtime,* a popular and critical success, catapulted E. L. Doctorow into prominence as one of the finest and most exciting novelists of his generation. With *Welcome to Hard Times* and *The Book of Daniel,* he had already established a solid reputation, but the rave reviews of *Ragtime* and the subsequent film and Broadway musical adaptations of the novel secured his place in the contemporary culture. *Ragtime* won the National Book Critics Circle Award in 1976, *World's Fair* won the American Book Award in 1986, and *Billy Bathgate*—nearly as successful as *Ragtime*—won the 1990 National Book Critics Circle Award and the PEN/Faulkner Award for fiction the same year. Among the awards Doctorow has received for lifetime achievement are the 1996 Medal of Honor for Literature from the National Arts Club and the 1998 National Humanities Medal.

Doctorow's novels are noted for their blendings of fact and fiction and of history and literature. His 2000 novel, *City of God,* suggests a renewed interest in philosophical studies. *The March* (2005) establishes Doctorow as a master at portraying historical events, while at the same time demonstrating their effect on the lives of everyday citizens.

Biography • Edgar Laurence Doctorow was born in the Bronx in 1931, and his fiction returns again and again to urban themes, particularly to the life of New York City at the turn of the twentieth century and during the 1920's and 1930's. He graduated from Kenyon College with a major in philosophy, and after serving in the Army he worked for publishers in New York City, editing the works of important writers such as Norman Mailer. His philosophical training is evident in his novels, in which he tries to infuse serious ideas into popular genres such as the Western (*Welcome to Hard Times*), science fiction (*Big as Life*), and detective fiction (*The Waterworks*).

Identifying with the downtrodden, with immigrants, criminals, and political protesters, he fashioned fiction with a leftist orientation, and on occasion he joined his voice to public protests against government censorship and other forms of tyranny. With residences in New York City and New Rochelle, New York, he divided his time between the city and the suburbs, teaching at Sarah Lawrence College and New York University as Glucksman Professor of American and English Letters.

Analysis • E. L. Doctorow's work is concerned with those stories, myths, public figures, and literary and historical forms that have shaped public and political consciousness. Even when his subject is not overtly political—as in his first novel, *Welcome to Hard Times*—he chooses the genre of the Western to comment upon the American sense of crime and justice. Knowing that the Western has often been the vehicle for the celebration of American individualism and morality, Doctorow purposely writes a fablelike novel in which he questions American faith in fairness and democracy. At the same time, he writes from within the genre by maintaining the customary strong opposition between good and evil, between the "bad guys" and the "good guys," and by fashioning a simple but compelling plot line.

©Barbara Walz

Welcome to Hard Times • The struggle in *Welcome to Hard Times* is between the Man from Bodie, who in a fit of rage destroys a town in a single day, and Blue, the tragic old man who almost singlehandedly tries to rebuild it. The plot and characters echo classic Western films such as *High Noon* (1952) with their solitary heroes who oppose villains' tyrannizing of a community. Doctorow's vision, however, is much bleaker than that of the traditional Western and cannot be encompassed by the usual shootout or confrontation between the sheriff and the outlaw. In fact, Doctorow's novel implies the West was chaotic and demonic, and order was not usually restored in the fashion of a Hollywood Western. The reality of American history has been much grimmer than its literature or its popular entertainment has ever acknowledged. Indeed, Doctorow's fiction shows again and again an America whose myths do not square with its history.

It is a paradoxical aspect of Doctorow's success that his parodies of popular genres are themselves usually best-sellers. Perhaps the reason is that alongside his ironic use of popular genres runs a deep affection for the literary forms he burlesques. The title of the novel, for example, is a kind of genial welcome, an invitation to have some fun with the pieties and clichés of the Western. Doctorow is deadly serious about the "hard times" and grave flaws in American culture, but he usually finds a way to present his criticism in a comic vein.

The Book of Daniel • Doctorow's fiction is often set in the past, during an identifiable historical period—the 1870's, the 1920's, the 1930's Depression, the 1950's, or the 1960's. Characteristic of Doctorow's deft handling of important political themes and historical periods is *The Book of Daniel*, a major political novel about the Cold War period of the 1950's. Centering on a couple (who bear a striking resemblance to spies Ethel and Julius Rosenberg) who were executed for espionage (supposedly for stealing the "secret" of the atomic bomb for the Soviet Union), the story is narrated by one of their children, Daniel. He sets out to investigate what happened to his parents while trying to come to terms with his own 1960's brand of radicalism. Concerned less with whether the couple was actually guilty of spying than with uncovering his own identity, Daniel tracks down and interviews those who had been closest to his parents. Through this personal story, Doctorow conducts an analysis of the failure of American radicalism, of one generation to speak to another. By and large, 1960's radicals did not know much about the history of the Left, and the traditional Left has done little to pass on its past, so that young men like Daniel feel isolated, bereft, and angry about their lack of connection to a heritage of social protest.

Daniel mourns the loss of his family. Unable to cope with his parents' sacrifice of themselves to a political movement, he allows his own marriage to deteriorate as he is racked by memories of what it was like for his parents to be constantly harassed for their political beliefs. The human costs of political activism are what embitter Daniel, but those costs are also what make him fiercely determined to gain some truth out of what happened to his parents and to confront those relatives who seem to have collaborated in his parents' execution.

From the point of view of 1960's radicalism, Daniel has a certain contempt for his parents and their attorney, who tried scrupulously to accommodate themselves to the American judicial system rather than challenging that system outright by calling the trial political and acting in court—as protesters did during the 1960's—as defiant political prisoners. Politics serves as the metaphor for the divisions in family life. In other words, there is a merging between the private and public realms, between individuals and political movements, just as the narrative swings between Daniel's first-person (intimate) and third-person (impersonal) points of view. In his great trilogy, *U.S.A.* (1937), John Dos Passos separated elements of history and fiction by creating discrete sections called "Camera Eye" and "Newsreel." It is Doctorow's achievement to have fused the personal and the public, the fictional and the historical, into one narrative voice, suggesting the indivisibility of history and the individual's perceptions of it. There is no "history" out there, he implies; there is only the "history" within the minds of the people who live it and recreate it.

Near the end of *The Book of Daniel* there is a brilliant set-piece description of Disneyland, which comes to stand for the forces in American life that threaten any complex sense of history. On the Disneyland lot, which resembles a film set, are arranged figures and artifacts of American history, the symbols and the tokens of the national heritage, wrenched from their social and historical context, abstracted into a series of entertainments for customers who do not have to analyze what is presented to them. This spectacle of history substitutes for the real thing, demeaning the past and replacing it with a comfortable, pacific, and convenient product that need only be enjoyed and consumed.

Ragtime • In *Ragtime*, Doctorow goes even further in suggesting that much of American history has been turned into a myth. In this novel historical figures have the same status as fictional creations. The novelist's Sigmund Freud, who appears in *Ragtime* going through the Tunnel of Love with Carl Jung, one of his disciples (later a rival), and the historical Freud are equally products of the imagination, of the language that is used to invent both history and fiction. So convincing is Doctorow in inserting famous people such as J. P. Morgan, Henry Ford, and Emma Goldman into his narrative that he has caused many people to wonder that incidents in the novel are "true." Doctorow has implied in interviews that in a sense it is all "true," since the imagination has such power to reconfigure history. *Ragtime* is surely one of the most subversive novels ever written by an American, for it suggests that history can be viewed as a consummate fiction.

Like *The Book of Daniel, Ragtime* is anchored in the story of a family—this time of a boy who grows up in New Rochelle, New York, at the turn of the twentieth century during the time of polar exploration, the development of great inventions such as motion pictures, and political upheavals led by radicals such as Emma Goldman. From his naïve viewpoint, the small boy observes the explosive changes and the stresses of a society that does not know how to handle its own dissenting elements. One of these is Coalhouse Walker, a proud black man who is insulted by a group of white firemen and who resorts to violence and hostage-taking, demanding that society recognize his rights after his wife, Sarah, is killed while trying to petition a politician on Coalhouse's behalf. Although the boy sees his society falling apart, it is also reconstructing itself. He sees his mother take into their home Sarah and the child she had with Coalhouse, and the boy later sees his uncle join the Coalhouse gang.

A third family important to the novel is the immigrant family of Eastern European Jews: Tateh, Mameh, and their little girl. After their financial crisis causes Mameh to resort to prostitution, Tateh expels her from the family, becomes increasingly desperate in his attempts to get money, and finally, after leaving his past behind, manages in Horatio Alger fashion to make a fortune as a film director. The final interweaving of the novel's families occurs when the mother of the New Rochelle family marries Tateh and they move to California with their two children and the black child they have adopted, the son of Coalhouse and Sarah.

If the actions of Coalhouse Walker seem more appropriate to the 1960's than to turn-of-the-century America, it is Doctorow's way of exaggerating those elements of the future that inhere in the past. The rage that Walker feels is both a personal and a historical rage; the insult is to him and to his race. If a black man in the age of J. P. Morgan would not in fact take over the financier's library full of art treasures, the truth is (Doctorow implies) that the conditions for such terrorism were brewing for a long time in the United States. Such an act could almost have happened then. The fact that the seemingly stable world before World War I was on the verge of cataclysm is suggested at the end of the novel's first chapter, when the boy exclaims, "Warn the duke"—referring to the assassination of the Archduke Ferdinand, the event that precipitated World War I.

Ragtime is similar to *Welcome to Hard Times* in that it has a fairy-tale quality. The prose is quite simple, descriptive, and declarative: Doctorow could almost begin with the phrase "once upon a time." It is clear, however, that his point is to link the past and the present, to show that the craving for mass entertainment at the turn of the century naturally had its outlet in the invention of motion pictures, just as the urge of Robert Peary and other explorers to roam the world had its counterpart in the mass production of the automobile. Repeatedly, Doctorow links the innovations in domestic life with great public adventures and events, fusing public and private affairs in an almost magical, uncanny manner.

The very title of the novel, *Ragtime*, refers not merely to the syncopated, accented music of the time but also to the quality of the period, with its fragmented, volatile changes that transformed the character of the country. This was the beat, the rhythm of the period, Doctorow implies. Time was being given a different tempo by the inventions, innovations, and struggles of the immigrants, the underclass, and the black people, even as Americans of an earlier generation took refuge in patriotism and public displays that excluded these new groups.

Loon Lake • The class distinctions that play an important role in *Ragtime* become the focal element of *Loon Lake*, which, like *The Book of Daniel*, contains a double narrative perspective. *Loon Lake* shifts between the experience of a poet on a rich man's isolated estate and a poor man's picaresque adventures across 1930's America. Somehow the power of the materialist, the millionaire capitalist, is meant to be balanced by the imagination of the poet, but the novel fails to measure up to *Ragtime*'s astonishing feat of fusing the different realms of fiction and history.

The poetic interludes in *Loon Lake* are reminiscent of the stream-of-consciousness "Camera Eye" sections of Dos Passos's *U.S.A.* trilogy. *Loon Lake* also has a haunting, ineffable quality, evoking a metaphorical but almost tangible sense of history that is akin to the novel's image of the lake: a dazzling surface of ever-shifting and widening perspectives and hinted-at depths. History as mirror—refracting, distorting, highlighting, and obscuring human actions—is a palpable presence. A great social novelist, Doctorow describes every level and grouping of society in the soup kitchens, mansions, and assembly lines in the United States between the two world wars.

World's Fair • In comparison to Doctorow's earlier novels, *World's Fair* seems remarkably straightforward. It resembles a work of conventional nonfiction, and like a memoir it is largely bound by a chronological structure. Although a few sections resemble oral history accounts from other characters' perspectives, much of the action is seen through the consciousness of a young boy, Edgar, growing up in the Bronx during the 1939-1940 World's Fair. Given the main character's name and background, it is difficult not to conclude that Doctorow has himself and his family in mind. He had already used his New Rochelle house as a model for the house in *Ragtime* and the mind of a young boy as the intuitive medium through which many of the domestic, private events of that novel would be filtered. Doctorow's interest in the way the fictional and factual impinge upon each other would naturally lead to this exercise in quasi-autobiography, in which the materials from his own background underpin the plot. The World's Fair becomes a metaphor for the boy's growing up and for the country's maturation.

Unlike many American novelists, Doctorow does not merely criticize American materialism, seeing in the emphasis on things a soul-deadening culture that is antithetical to the artist's imagination. On the contrary, he enjoys playing with the materiality of America, decrying, to be sure, the way in which the culture often turns its important figures and events into toys and commercials for capitalism, but also capturing—and honoring—the American delight in inventiveness and machinery. In *World's Fair*, he triumphantly combines the personal and familial aspects of life with the way a society celebrates itself. In doing so, he recovers the synthesis of history and literature that made *Ragtime* such a resounding success.

Billy Bathgate • In most of Doctorow's work there is a tension between a naïve, childlike point of view, often fresh with perception, and an older, ironic, detached perspective. Sometimes this split gets expressed in terms of first-and third-person narration, as in *The Book of Daniel*. In *Ragtime*, the narrator seems to be simultaneously the little boy and his older self, both observing for the first time and remembering the past. Like *World's Fair*, *Billy Bathgate* seems more conventional than earlier novels, for it is told from the standpoint of its main character, a mature man reviewing his past. However, the novel unfolds with such immediacy that it appears to be taking place as the narrator tells it.

The first long sentence of *Billy Bathgate* launches right into a scene in which Dutch Schultz is disposing of a disloyal associate, Bo Weinberg. The setting is described by fifteen-year-old Billy Bathgate, the novel's narrator, who is impressed with the smooth running of the Dutchman's criminal enterprise. A car drives up to a dark dock, and without using any light or making a sound, Dutch's crew gets on the boat with Bo and his girl, Drew Preston. Dutch's control over the situation is inspiring for the young boy, who has been given the honor of running errands and performing other chores for the famous gang.

Doctorow exquisitely handles the feeling of an adult remembering his adolescent self and the sheer excitement of being privy to the most secret counsels of criminals. Billy describes, in fascinating detail, the process by which Bo's feet are encased in concrete. Facing the torture of drowning, Bo taunts Dutch, hoping to provoke his famous temper so that Dutch will shoot him quickly rather than make him suffer the agony of a slow death. Dutch keeps calm, however, while Bo retails instances of Dutch's violent and ungiving nature. Dutch takes his revenge by appropriating Bo's mistress, Drew.

Billy fears but is also fascinated by Dutch's violence, for Dutch cuts a great figure in the world, with minions to serve him and women to fawn over him. Billy's Irish mother has occasional periods of dementia (pushing around a baby carriage full of garbage), and his Jewish father long ago abandoned his family. Dutch provides a glamorous alternative to this grim life, and the gang a surrogate family for the neglected boy. The Dutchman sees him juggling on the street and takes a shine to him, eventually calling Billy his "pro-to-jay." Billy is, in Dutch's words, "a capable boy."

Dutch has a way of utterly changing the face of things, and for a long time working for him has a fairy-tale quality. No sooner is Bo Weinberg overboard with his cement overshoes than Dutch is making love to Drew Preston—a socialite who is fascinated, for a while, by his presence and energy. She even accompanies him to Onondaga in upstate New York, where Dutch takes over a town, plying the locals with gifts and setting up a cozy atmosphere in preparation for what he rightly expects will be a favorable jury verdict in the case brought against him for tax evasion.

Dutch has the power to create his own world, staying for days at a time in his hotel room with Drew. There is something engaging and down-to-earth in his crude, raw energy, which is perhaps why Drew finds herself attracted to a man so unlike her husband and his rich cronies. Drew's involvement with Dutch is reminiscent of Evelyn Nesbit's fascination with Tateh, the Jewish immigrant, and his daughter in *Ragtime*, for they represent a life of the streets, a flavor of what is going on in the lower orders, that is at once alien and appealing to those living a highly stylized and often repressed life in the upper classes.

Dutch's great strength is also his great weakness. By making all of his business revolve around himself, he fails to see how crime is becoming organized and corporate. His way of doing business is almost feudal—depending on violence and on the loyalty of subordinates—and he has no grasp of how to put together an organization that can compete with the government or his rival, Lucky Luciano. Dutch wants to personalize everything, so that it all evolves out of his own ego. However, that ego is unstable. On an impulse, he kills an uncooperative colleague in an Onondaga hotel, one of many instances when he goes berserk against his opponents.

Members of Dutch's gang—particularly his accountant, Abbadabba Berman—sense that the old ways of doing things are nearly finished. Bo's defection is only the beginning of events that put Dutch on the defensive and that culminate in his gangland murder. Abbadabba tries to persuade Dutch to recognize that he is part of a larger crime network, but Dutch can think only in terms of his own ambitions and calls off plans to join with Lucky Luciano and other gangsters. In compensation, perhaps, for Dutch's inability to adapt to new times, Abbadabba turns to Billy, making him an apprentice and lavishing attention on the boy.

Through Abbadabba and Drew, Billy gains perspective on Dutch. Drew, Billy finds, has her own sort of power and sense of ease. When she tires of Dutch, she simply leaves him, conveying to Billy the impression that Dutch's charisma has its limits. Billy never dares to think of actually leaving the gang, but he keeps his own counsel and is prepared to take care of himself when Dutch is murdered. At the death scene, in which Dutch, Abbadabba, Lulu, and Irving have been shot, Billy learns from Abbadabba the combination of the safe where Dutch has stashed much of his loot. Evasive about his subsequent career, Billy intimates at the end of the novel that he has indeed gained the Dutchman's fortune, but he does not explain what he will do with it.

Billy's reticence is a perfect foil to the Dutchman's very public career: Even Dutch's last delirious words are taken down by a stenographer and published in the papers. Dutch never learns to be circumspect and even plans to assassinate Thomas E. Dewey, the district attorney who made it his mission to put Dutch in prison. By the end of his career, not only has Dutch alienated his gangland associates, but he has also made it impossible for corrupt Tammany politicians to accept his bribes. He is a relic of an earlier age of unbridled individualism. Billy, on the other hand, hides Dutch's fortune, goes back to school, graduates from an Ivy League college, and becomes an Army officer in World War II and then a business entrepreneur—an inconceivable career in Dutch Schultz's world.

Billy Bathgate is a combination of Huck Finn, Tom Sawyer, and Horatio Alger. He is a hero who is prudent, yet an adventurer who risks making love to Drew Preston, even though he knows that it means certain death if the Dutchman finds out. He keeps a cool head even when the Dutchman is punishing him for not having provided a piece of vital information sooner. Billy is a romantic, melting at the sight of Drew and hardly believing that they have been sexual partners. He is also a rationalist, realizing that his best chance of survival is to play the role of the loyal Bronx kid.

As Billy prospers and gets to know the different worlds to which he has been introduced, he finds it impossible to return as he was to his old neighborhood. He dresses differently, carries himself differently, and has a consciousness of a world that extends far beyond the Bathgate Avenue from which he has derived his assumed name. Billy becomes, in other words, a self-invented figure, transcending his origins not only in the actions he narrates but also in his very language, a blend of popular and sophisticated vocabulary that precisely captures the boy and the man who has become the narrator of this novel.

The Waterworks • The possibility that even a child like Billy Bathgate may be destroyed by adults is suggested by *The Waterworks*, in which the industrialism and politics of 1870's New York threaten all children. In some ways Doctorow's bleakest novel, *The Waterworks* has elements of a detective tale by Edgar Allan Poe. Unlike Doctorow's novels in which a young man's viewpoint is central, *The Waterworks* is narrated by a mature journalist, McIlvaine, who sees the victimization not only of the masses of homeless, abandoned children wandering New York, but also of youth at the top of the social scale. McIlvaine's young freelance writer Martin Pemberton, son of the corrupt businessman Augustus Pemberton, finds himself first disinherited by his father and eventually made a subject for experiments by the novel's mad scientist, Dr. Wrede Sartorius.

When Martin abandons his fiancé, Emily Tisdale, disappearing after announcing that he has seen his supposedly dead father still alive and riding through the streets in an omnibus, McIlvaine joins with an honest policeman (a rare creature in this time of the Tweed Ring) to solve the mystery. They discover that old men are faking their deaths, abandoning their wives and children, and turning their wealth over to Sartorius, who will keep them alive as long as possible by injecting them with bodily fluids taken from children. The casket August Pemberton's wife and sons thought they had buried him in is discovered to hold a child's body. Although the conspiracies against children are apparently defeated by the novel's end and two marriages appear to give the novel a happy ending, McIlvaine concludes his tale with little faith that children (or adult women, for that matter) can do anything to defend themselves against preying men.

McIlvaine comments on the difficulty of pinning down the source of evil in his story. Sartorius can be given alibis, much of the evil activity is learned about through rumor, evil characters are glimpsed rather than caught in spotlights. It is as if the city itself is evil, or as if evil is in the water. Even more troubling is McIlvaine's similarities to his supposed villains, for he too takes advantage of young people in order to produce his book. *The Waterworks* shares with several other novels a thematic concern for the role of the writer in society, and like Blue in *Welcome to Hard Times*, McIlvaine may create evils in the course of trying too hard to cover up horror. Insofar as *The Waterworks* is read as a prologue to Doctorow's other New York novels, it casts a pall over them. This novel allows the reader less ability to accept what looks like a loophole for optimism in another book, because it instructs the reader on the ways civilization ignores or forgets its errors, the ways civilization chooses to remember what supports its illusions.

Doctorow's work contains acute perceptions of the way the public makes its selections about what it will remember about the past, aided by the film industry and Disneylands of the culture. Gangsters, film stars, cowboys—all have a certain glamour in Doctorow's fiction, because they have that glamour in the popular genres he mimics. As models for a rational, democratic society, these stock types fail, and Doctorow is fully aware of that reality. However, he cannot abandon them, for these amusements reflect the core of the American psyche, the overwhelming urge to mythologize history, to make it amenable to human desires and hopes.

City of God • Doctorow's underlying theme in *City of God* is humanity's quest for meaning. Everett, the story's writer-narrator, is compiling a nonfiction account of the way his friend Pem (Thomas Pemberton) is dealing with loss of religious conviction. The son of a clergyman, Pem has repeatedly been disillusioned by his own ethical failures, especially his failure to discover a rational basis for Christian faith. He is considering a complete break with the Church—a literal rejection of Christianity and a symbolic rejection of his father.

A seemingly random street crime then brings Pem into contact with Joshua Green, his wife, Sarah Blumenthal, and their Synagogue of Evolutionary Judaism. A large brass cross stolen from the wall of St. Timothy's is found on the synagogue's roof. The cross seems symbolic of Pem's diminished religious conviction: Beneath its brass veneer, it is steel, and it can easily be dismantled because it consists of two parts held together with screws. Pem never discovers the identity or motives of the thieves, but he sees the theft as a sign leading him to Joshua and Sarah, rabbis whose search for the City of God parallels his own. Complicating their quest, though, are stories of the Holocaust told by Sarah's father, who is sinking into dementia. For Joshua especially, modern society seems overwhelmed by what Saint Augustine called "the City of the World," and he is martyred as he tries to reveal the ghetto horrors, thus ending humanity's apparent indifference to the Holocaust.

Everett becomes obsessed with the ghetto stories, which become the new focus of his book. Recording those stories brings him into closer contact with his own heritage, as he explores his father's World War I exploits and those of his brother in World War II.

First Joshua and later Pem search for the long-lost ghetto records. In effect, Pem avenges his friend's death by locating the trunk of records written by ghetto leaders, smuggled out by Sarah's father and preserved by an anti-Nazi Roman Catholic priest. Sarah gives the originals to the government to be used as evidence against war criminals, and Everett uses her photocopies to complete his book.

Near the end of the novel is another symbolic film scenario. Obsessed with a war criminal living in the United States, a writer stalks the old man, considering ways to execute him, then accidentally kills him in a bike accident. Although the writer escapes capture, newspaper accounts portray him as the villain, and the old man is honored instead of dishonored. In contrast, even though the ghetto accounts are located too late to prosecute the local commandant, using contemporary accounts to authenticate his atrocities proves a more effective revenge.

As the novel ends, Pem converts to Judaism and, with Sarah, continues his quest to establish meaningful religious traditions. Soon they are married—a symbolic union of Jewish and Christian traditions prefigured early in the novel when Everett observes a great blue heron and a snowy white egret perched back to back, sharing a New York City pier. Near the novel's end, another ecumenical symbol appears as Everett describes the City of Birds, near Madrid, where many species of birds peaceably pick over a huge garbage dump.

Carl Rollyson
Updated by Marshall Bruce Gentry and Charmaine Allmon Mosby

Other major works

SHORT FICTION: *Lives of the Poets*, 1984; *Sweet Land Stories*, 2004.

PLAY: *Drinks Before Dinner*, pr. 1978.

SCREENPLAYS: *Three Screenplays*, 2003.

NONFICTION: *Jack London, Hemingway, and the Constitution: Selected Essays, 1977-1992*, 1993; *Poets and Presidents*, 1993; *Conversations with E. L. Doctorow*, 1999; *Reporting the Universe*, 2003; *Creationists: Selected Essays, 1993-2006*, 2006.

EDITED TEXTS: *Best American Short Stories, 2000*, 2000.

Bibliography

Bloom, Harold, ed. *E. L. Doctorow.* New York: Chelsea House, 2001. A collection of essays offering an overview of Doctorow's career and works from a variety of perspectives. Intended as a starting point for students first reading the author.

____________. *E. L. Doctorow's "Ragtime."* New York: Chelsea House, 2002. A collection of essays illuminating the historical context of Doctorow's work as well as offering literary analysis.

Doctorow, E. L. *Conversations with E. L. Doctorow.* Edited by Christopher D. Morris. Jackson: University Press of Mississippi, 1999. Part of the Literary Conversations series, this collection of interviews reveals Doctorow's thoughts and goals.

Fowler, Douglas. *Understanding E. L. Doctorow.* Columbia: University of South Carolina Press, 1992. Introduces the reader to Doctorow and his works on a basic level, surveying arguments of other critics and noting Doctorow's links to other writers. This book emphasizes the extent to which family life is Doctorow's most enduring thematic concern.

Friedl, Herwig, and Dieter Schulz, eds. *E. L. Doctorow: A Democracy of Perception.* Essen, Germany: Blaue Eule, 1988. Primarily essays by German and American writers from a 1985 symposium held in Heidelberg, Germany. Features the transcript of a question-and-answer session Doctorow held with students while attending the symposium.

Harter, Carol, and James R. Thompson. *E. L. Doctorow.* Boston: Twayne, 1990. Emphasizes Doctorow as an artist rather than as a politician or experimental historian. More than other books, this study sees significant differences among Doctorow's works and sees Doctorow himself moving toward autobiography over the course of his career.

Levine, Paul. *E. L. Doctorow.* London: Methuen, 1985. The first major study. Levine provides sound readings of individual novels as well as discussions of themes in the fiction: politics, the nature of fiction and history, and Doctorow's critique of the American Dream.

____________. *Models of Misrepresentation: On the Fiction of E. L. Doctorow.* Jackson: University Press of Mississippi, 1991. The most theoretically sophisticated of the book-length studies of Doctorow's works. This book relays very original and controversial readings of both Doctorow's novels and his essays by emphasizing the ways in which readers are forced to use literary texts to maintain their illusions.

Parks, John G. *E. L. Doctorow.* New York: Continuum, 1991. Emphasizes the study of Doctorow through the theories of Mikhail Bakhtin, for whom the job of an author is to bring the conflicting voices within a novel into harmony. Probably the best introduction to Doctorow's works, this book considers Doctorow to value society over the individual.

Tokarczyk, Michelle M. *E. L. Doctorow's Skeptical Commitment.* New York: P. Lang, 2000. A political literary analysis of Doctorow's works. Covers all the novels up to *The Waterworks.*

Trenner, Richard. *E. L. Doctorow: Essays and Conversations.* Princeton, N.J.: Ontario Review Press, 1983. Includes several of Doctorow's important essays as well as articles by others. The pieces reflect the range of critical opinion on Doctorow, the variety of his themes and techniques, and the historical background required to read his novels.

Williams, John. *Fiction as False Document: The Reception of E. L. Doctorow in the Postmodern Age.* Columbia, S.C.: Camden House, 1996. Reviews and analyzes all the important criticism on Doctorow, including major reviews, especially in relation to how criticism has promoted Doctorow's reputation, used postmodernism to understand Doctorow, and used Doctorow's texts to promote postmodern critical theories.

J. P. Donleavy

Born: Brooklyn, New York; April 23, 1926

Principal long fiction • *The Ginger Man*, 1955, 1965; *A Singular Man*, 1963; *The Saddest Summer of Samuel S*, 1966; *The Beastly Beatitudes of Balthazar B*, 1968; *The Onion Eaters*, 1971; *A Fairy Tale of New York*, 1973; *The Destinies of Darcy Dancer, Gentleman*, 1977; *Schultz*, 1979; *Leila: Further in the Destinies of Darcy Dancer, Gentleman*, 1983; *De Alfonce Tennis, the Superlative Game of Eccentric Champions: Its History, Accoutrements, Rules, Conduct, and Regimen*, 1984; *Are You Listening, Rabbi Löw?*, 1987; *That Darcy, That Dancer, That Gentleman*, 1990; *The Lady Who Liked Clean Rest Rooms: The Chronicle of One of the Strangest Stories Ever to Be Rumoured About Around New York*, 1995; *Wrong Information Is Being Given out at Princeton*, 1998.

Other literary forms • All of J. P. Donleavy's principal works are novels, but some of the protagonists and central situations of these novels are explored in other literary forms. *A Fairy Tale of New York* is derived from the play *Fairy Tales of New York* (1961) and the short story, "A Fairy Tale of New York" (1961), later collected in Donleavy's collection of short stories *Meet My Maker the Mad Molecule* (1964). Donleavy adapted several published novels for the stage: *The Ginger Man* (1961), *A Singular Man* (1965), *The Saddest Summer of Samuel S* (1972), and *The Beastly Beatitudes of Balthazar B* (1981). He also wrote a book of satirical nonfiction, *The Unexpurgated Code: A Complete Manual of Survival and Manners* (1975). Among Donleavy's limited production of occasional pieces are two important autobiographical essays: "What They Did in Dublin with *The Ginger Man*," an introduction to that play, and "An Expatriate Looks at America," which appeared in *The Atlantic Monthly* in 1976. He explored his Irish heritage in *J. P. Donleavy's Ireland: In All of Her Sins and Some of Her Graces* (1986), *A Singular Country* (1990), and *The History of the Ginger Man* (1994).

Achievements • The prevailing literary image of Donleavy is that of the one-book author: He gained celebrity status of a notorious sort with his first novel, *The Ginger Man*, but his subsequent novels failed to generate equal interest. Reactions to *The Ginger Man*, a book that only appeared in an unexpurgated American edition ten years after first publication, ranged from outraged condemnations of it as obscene in language and immoral in content to later appreciations of it as a comic masterpiece. The later novels have been received with moderate praise for their style and humor and with slight dismay for their lack of structure or apparent intent. Donleavy himself remained confidently aloof from all critical condemnation, exaltation, and condescension. He continued to pursue his private interests in fiction, to discourage academic interest in his work, and to express, when pressed, bemusement at literary frays of any sort. His work is difficult to place in standard literary traditions: His residency in Ireland and fondness for Irish settings seem to place his work outside American literature, but his birth and use of American protagonists seem to place it outside Anglo-Irish literature as well.

Biography • James Patrick Donleavy was born of Irish parents in Brooklyn, New York, on April 23, 1926. After being educated at private schools, he served in the

United States Navy during World War II. He saw no combat action in the service, but he did encounter the work of James Joyce through an English instructor at the Naval Preparatory School in Maryland. This combination of family background and reading interests led to his enrollment in Dublin's Trinity College from 1946 to 1949, on funds provided by the American G.I. Bill. There he was registered to read natural sciences, but he readily admits that most of his energies were devoted to pub crawls with fellow American students such as Gainor Crist, the model for Sebastian Dangerfield in *The Ginger Man*, and A. K. O'Donoghue, the model for O'Keefe in the same novel.

Donleavy married Valerie Heron after leaving Trinity and briefly considered pursuing a career as a painter. He returned to the United States, where he finished *The Ginger Man* in 1951, but the novel was rejected by one publisher after another on the basis of its supposed obscenity. On his return to Dublin in 1954, he became friends with playwright and man-about-town Brendan Behan. Through Behan's efforts, *The Ginger Man*, having been refused by some thirty-five American and British publishers, was accepted for publication in 1955 by the Olympia Press of Paris, a house whose main list of pornography titles enabled it to gamble on unusual literary properties such as Behan's works and Samuel Beckett's novel *Watt* (1953). Donleavy's book was greeted rudely by the British press and by its courts, where it was prosecuted for censorship violations, but the ensuing publicity, combined with the enthusiasm of early critics and readers, led to the publication of expurgated English (1956) and American (1958) editions that brought Donleavy financial stability and an enviable literary reputation for a first novelist. These editions also marked the beginning of a series of lawsuits filed against Donleavy by Olympia Press over the rights to republish the novel. The litigation ended with appropriate irony when Donleavy acquired the ownership of Olympia Press after decades of legal maneuvering, a story told in his *The History of the Ginger Man.* After that time, he made his home in Ireland, on Lough Owel in Westmeath, in rather baronial circumstances that resembled the affluence of his later characters rather than the student poverty of *The Ginger Man.*

After his marriage to Valerie Heron ended in divorce in 1969, Donleavy married Mary Wilson Price. Each of his marriages produced one son and one daughter. He became an Irish citizen in 1967 and settled in a twenty-five-room mansion on a 180-acre estate in Mullingar, about sixty miles from Dublin. Fittingly, descriptions of his house appear in James Joyce's early *Stephen Hero* (1944), providing yet another link to the writer with whom Donleavy is most frequently compared. Donleavy is also known as a serious artist whose numerous paintings have appeared at many exhibitions.

Analysis • In his *Journal of Irish Literature* interview published in 1979, Donleavy said: "I suppose one has been influenced by people like Joyce. But also possibly—and this is not too apparent in my work—by Henry Miller who was then literally a private god." Appreciation of Donleavy's work is indeed improved by cognizance of these two acknowledged predecessors, and it is entirely appropriate that the former is Irish and the latter American and that all three expatriates have been subject to censorship litigation.

The influence of James Joyce is most apparent in Donleavy's style, and it should be noted that the Ireland of Donleavy's work scarcely overlaps with that of Joyce's work. Joyce made self-conscious and even self-indulgent style a necessity for the serious modern novelist, and Donleavy creates his own evocation of Dublin and other Irish environs in an intricate prose style characterized by minimal punctuation, strings of sentence fragments, frequent shifts of tense, and lapses from standard third-person

Library of Congress

narration into first-person stream of consciousness. The single most obvious indication of Donleavy's stylistic ambitions is his habit of ending his chapters with brief poems.

The influence of Miller is most apparent in the fact that Donleavy's novels, for all their supposedly "graphic" language and sexual encounters, create a world that is a patent fantasy. As in Miller's case, the primary aspect of the fantasy is a distinctly male fabrication based on unending sexual potency and invariably satisfying liaisons with uniformly passionate and voluptuous women. To this, Donleavy adds fantasies about immense wealth, requited infantile eroticism, Dionysian thirst, and spectacular barroom brawls. Because of this comic freedom from actual contingencies, his work satirizes absurd caricatures of recognizable social evils.

The central concern of all of Donleavy's novels is the fortune of a single male protagonist isolated from family and country and pursuing a lifestyle that is improvised and erratic. The great exemplar of this essential situation is *The Ginger Man*, a novel that weighs the joys of decadent drunkenness and ecstatic sex against spiritual fears of loneliness and death. After that first novel, which left the future of its protagonist ambiguous, Donleavy went through a period of bleak despair over the viability of a free lifestyle and emerged from it into a period of wholehearted endorsement of its pleasures. In the process, his view of the world changed from a belief in its essential malevolence to an assertion of its essential benevolence. He thus confronted the problem of the value of independence from social conformity from two wholly different perspectives.

The Ginger Man • *The Ginger Man*, Donleavy's famous first novel, opens with a pair of subordinate clauses; the first celebrates the spring sun, and the second laments Dublin's workaday horse carts and wretched child beggars. It is between these two emotional poles that the Ginger Man, Sebastian Dangerfield, vacillates throughout the novel. He will be exalted by visions of freedom and possibility, but he will also be crushed by fears and depressions. In *The Ginger Man*, freedom is revolt against the forces of social conformity and rigidity, a casting over of the bulwark virtues of thrift, reverence, and self-discipline. The fear, however, is of the ultimate victory of those same forces and values. The novel refuses to resolve neatly these oppositions. Dangerfield, subject to reckless extremes throughout, finally remains both the Ginger Man, an alias suggestive of spirit and mettle, and Sebastian, the namesake of a betrayed and martyred saint.

One of the novel's achievements is its candid admission of the most deplorable aspects of a quest for freedom such as Dangerfield's. It is appropriate and commonplace in contemporary fiction that an alienated protagonist should court his wife for her dowry and run into debt with landlords, shopkeepers, and other pillars of middle-class society. Donleavy, however, proceeds beyond this comfortable degree of roguery to a proposal of a more complete anarchy that is the novel's most compelling and disturbing quality. Dangerfield also beats his wife, abuses his child, senselessly vandalizes the property of strangers, and is otherwise selfishly destructive because of a self-proclaimed natural aristocracy, a phrase crucial to Donleavy's later novels. In this respect, he sins far more than he is sinned against, and one measure of the novel's complexity is the fact that its most sympathetic character is a matronly Miss Frost, who is devoted to Sebastian but is abandoned by him when her finances have been consumed. *The Ginger Man* is superior to many contemporary novels contemptuous of society because of this admission of the sheer egotism and selfishness underlying such contempt.

Dangerfield's redeeming features, which make him an antihero rather than a villain, are his invigorating bohemian bravura and his true appreciation of life's quiet beauties. The novel is appropriately set in Dublin, mirroring a fine appetite for great talk and plentiful drink. On one level, the novel is about the meeting of the vital New World with the stagnant Old World, for Dangerfield and his Irish American cronies flamboyantly outtalk and outdrink the Irish, who are portrayed as a mean and frugal people who can only be bettered by insult. Dangerfield's appreciation of subtler sensual delights, however, is as essential to his character as those more raucous tastes. His love of the smell of freshly ground coffee wafting from Bewley's in Grafton Street is as important to this novel as its more notorious adventures with whiskey and women. In these aesthetic moments, including the appreciation of the rising sun in the opening of the novel, Sebastian provisionally justifies his sense of aristocracy and demonstrates a kind of moral purity not shared by the novel's other characters.

In conjunction with the picaresque comedy and titillation of Dangerfield's more preposterous adventures, there remains the essentially naïve and ultimately unfulfilled desire for a simpler, solitary bliss. *The Ginger Man* is Donleavy's salient novel because it manages this balance between frivolity and remorse, between freedom and surrender, an opposition resolved in different ways in all of his subsequent novels.

A Singular Man • Donleavy's second novel, *A Singular Man*, was also held up by worries about censorship, and it was published only after Donleavy threatened to sue his own publisher. Donleavy left the bohemian lifestyle that gave Sebastian Dangerfield vitality for the opulent but gloomy existence of George Smith, whose freedoms have been lost to the encroachments of great wealth. The premise of the novel has obvious autobiographical relevance to the success of *The Ginger Man*; George Smith is accused by his estranged wife of sneaking into society, and he is in fact bewildered by his inexplicable attainment of sudden wealth and fame. The novel frustrates autobiographical interpretation, however, because it represents the emergence in Donleavy's work of the caricatured environment common in his later novels. The nature of Smith's industrial empire is mysterious, but he travels through surroundings with names such as Dynamo House, Electricity Street, and Cinder Village, and makes his home in Merry Mansions.

Smith's only obvious claim to singularity is his solitary appreciation of the hollowness of material wealth, and the novel records his increasing disillusionment and despair. The only satisfying one of his several love affairs is with the sassy Sally Thompson, doomed by the sorrowful machinations of the plot to death in an automobile accident. Smith's only respite from the responsibilities of his financial empire is the construction of a fabulous mausoleum under the pseudonym "Doctor Fear." *A Singular Man* is controlled completely by the obsession with death that was always counterpointed in *The Ginger Man* with a potential for sudden joy, and its style reflects this severe introversion in its reliance on more extended passages of stream-of-consciousness narration than is common in Donleavy's novels.

The Saddest Summer of Samuel S • Although *A Singular Man* explored the despair of wealth, *The Saddest Summer of Samuel S* broadened the gloom of Donleavy's post-*Ginger Man* novels by exploring the despair of a vagrant lifestyle. An expatriate American living in Vienna, Samuel S is an overage Ginger Man whose misery is caused by the stubborn isolation from society that was at least a mixed virtue in Donleavy's first novel. In this novel, the only humor is provided by Samuel's bleak confessions to his shocked psychoanalyst Herr S, who functions as a socially acclimated if complacent foil to the alienated but determined Samuel S. The comedy is, however, completely overwhelmed by Samuel's inability to accept the apparent happiness of a relationship with an invigorating American student named Abigail. It is as if Donleavy set out to correct simplistic praise for *The Ginger Man* as an unambiguous paean to rootlessness by stressing in *The Saddest Summer of Samuel S* the costs of bohemian disregard for domestic and social comforts. The novel presents no acceptable alternative to Samuel's self-destructive insistence on alienation for its own sake, none of the moments of happy appreciation of life that redeemed Sebastian Dangerfield.

The Beastly Beatitudes of Balthazar B • Balthazar B is Donleavy's most withdrawn and morbid protagonist, and the novel named for him represents the author's most consistent use of religious resignation as a metaphor for a passive secular disengagement from a malevolent world. The presence of his prep school and college classmate Beefy adds a raucous dimension reminiscent of *The Ginger Man*, however, and *The Beastly Beatitudes of Balthazar B* resuscitates the power of outrageous farce in Donleavy's work. Balthazar, another Donleavy protagonist who is fatherless and without a surname, progresses only from childhood fantasies about African pythons to more adult but equally futile ones about sex in aristocratic surroundings. Throughout the novel, he provides naïve perspective that enables Donleavy to satirize social pretensions and rampant materialism. The beatitudes that govern most of the novel are Beefy's, which bless the beastly virtues of complete decadence and joyful carnality but prove inadequate in the face of repressive social conformity. The ultimate beatitudes of the novel, however, are Balthazar's, which emerge late in the work and resemble those delivered in the sermon on the mount. Having accompanied Beefy on his salacious adventures and seen his companion undone, Balthazar—who, like Donleavy's other early protagonists, identifies with martyrs—is left only with a saintly hope for later rewards such as those in the beatitudes recorded in Matthew's gospel.

The Onion Eaters • Like Balthazar B, Clementine of *The Onion Eaters* is a protagonist plagued by lonely remorse and surrounded by a dynamism in others that he is unable to emulate. He is a young American heir to a medieval British estate, a situation whose effect is that of placing an introspective and morose modern sensibility in the raucous world of the eighteenth century novel. As in most of Donleavy's novels, the central theme is the vicissitudes of a natural aristocracy, here represented by the fortunes of Clementine of the Three Glands in a chaotic world of eccentric hangers-on and orgiastic British nobility. The emotional tension of the novel is based on a deep desire for the freedom of complete decadence in conflict with a more romantic yearning for quieter satisfactions. That conflict enables Donleavy, as in parts of *The Ginger Man*, to create a titillating fantasy while concurrently insisting on a sort of innocence, for Clementine survives his picaresque adventures with his essential purity intact. The significant contemporary revision of an older morality, however, lies in the fact that in Donleavy's fiction such virtue goes unrewarded.

A Fairy Tale of New York • In Donleavy's later work, fantasy is allowed to prevail over remorse, and this new direction emerges first in *A Fairy Tale of New York*, in which a protagonist named Christian is tempted by the evils of the modern metropolis much as the traveler Christian is tempted in John Bunyan's *The Pilgrim's Progress* (1678, 1684). This novel has a special interest within Donleavy's work for its description of a return from Ireland to New York City, which is characterized in the novel by gross consumerism. In *A Fairy Tale of New York*, Christian is more a protector of real virtues than a seeker of them, and the novel ends with a comment on life's minor and earthy beauties rather than the plea for mercy that is common in Donleavy's earlier works. A brief vignette of the same title published a decade earlier provided the opening of *A Fairy Tale of New York*, and the intervening years saw a change in Donleavy's literary interests that enabled him to pursue a fulfilling fantasy beyond the limits of vignette. The result, however it may finally be judged, is a sacrifice of the emotional tension of his finest earlier work in favor of the pleasure of unconstrained fabrication, a surrender of psychological depth for a freer play of literary imagination.

The Destinies of Darcy Dancer, Gentleman • Returning to the spirit of the eighteenth century novel that animated *The Onion Eaters*, *The Destinies of Darcy Dancer, Gentleman* evokes a world of baronial splendor, earthy servants, seductive governesses, and naïve tutors without apparent concern for the forces of modern technology and consequential social ills common to the contemporary novel. It is a stylish and literate entertainment without moral pretensions, a vein of fiction entirely appropriate to the alliance with freedom of imagination arduously explored in the course of Donleavy's work.

There are allusions to a darker world beyond the novel's immediate environs, such as housekeeper Miss von B.'s wartime experiences in Europe, but these serve only to stress the value of the free lifestyle pursued by Darcy Dancer without guilt and without controls beyond a decent sense of chivalry. One indication of the shift from morbidity to frivolity apparent in Donleavy's work is the fact that the setting here is Andromeda Park, named for a goddess whose miseries were relieved rather than for a saint who was martyred. However, *Leila*, sequel to *The Destinies of Darcy Dancer, Gentleman*, retains the tone of upper-class superficiality while reintroducing a darker view: In this novel, Dancer becomes enamored of a woman but is left helpless when she marries another man.

Schultz • *Schultz* is similar to *The Ginger Man* but expresses no remorse or recrimination. Its operative assumption and central motif is a concept of the world as a pointless Jewish joke, and this permits the London theatrical impresario Sigmund Schultz to exploit materialism without moral doubts and Donleavy to create a world in which even the sinfully rich prove ultimately benevolent. Class consciousness and privilege are a matter for comedy rather than bitterness in this novel, and the foul-mouthed American social climber Schultz is accepted with amusement rather than repelled with horror by English royalty.

The perspective of the novel is so completely comic that venereal diseases are presented as mere inconveniences, the political world is represented by the monarch of an African nation named Buggybooiamcheesetoo, and the romantic liaisons are unabashed and masturbatory fantasies. The most important distinction between *The Ginger Man* and *Schultz* is that in Donleavy's first novel the world was seen as malevolent and in the latter it is seen as benign. In accordance with this movement, the author has shifted from a celebration of gallant but doomed improvised lifestyles to a forthright assertion of their superiority to accepted and inherited modes of behavior.

The style and structure of Donleavy's work continued to evolve: *De Alfonce Tennis, the Superlative Game of Eccentric Champions*, for example, is such a mishmash of story, satire, and whimsy that the reader is hard-pressed to categorize it. Despite the negative critical response to *Schultz*, Donleavy's public proved loyal, justifying an even less distinguished sequel, *Are You Listening, Rabbi Löw?* Donleavy's fiction of this period deliberately deprives itself of the emotional conflicts central to his earlier, saintlier protagonists. It represents as well an insolent abrogation of the traditional concerns of "serious" fiction. By contrast, *The Ginger Man* was superior to the bulk of postwar novels about bohemian expatriates in Europe because of its sense of the limitations of that lifestyle as well as its potential. His nonfiction of the same period includes two books about his adoptive country, the largely autobiographical *J. P. Donleavy's Ireland* and *A Singular Country*.

That Darcy, That Dancer, That Gentleman • *That Darcy, That Dancer, That Gentleman* completes the trilogy of Darcy novels, which collectively provide the high point of Donleavy's later work as a novelist. Although ostensibly set in twentieth century Ireland, the focus is on traditional, even anachronistic Irish rural life and values, which impelled Donleavy to make important stylistic modifications to fit the leisurely milieu, particularly in slowing the pace of events and descriptions to mirror the setting. This well-integrated juxtaposition of plot and characters drawn from the tradition of the eighteenth century novel with Donleavy's distinctively modernist style accounts for much of the freshness of the three works.

Darcy's battle to keep Andromeda Park afloat as his resources run out depends upon finding a wealthy wife, but the only woman he can imagine truly loving, Leila, is lost beyond hope of recovery as a marchioness in Paris. Among the unsuitable matches he considers are his neighbor Felicity Veronica Durrow-Mountmellon and two American women heirs from Bronxville, Florida, and Virginia. Rashers Ronald plays a large role in the book as Darcy's virtually permanent houseguest and best, though most unreliable, friend. The novel's climax is a chaotic grand ball at Darcy's estate, at which virtually every character to have been featured in the trilogy makes an appearance. At the end of the book, Ronald is engaged to Durrow-Mountmellon and Darcy is finally reunited with Leila, providing unusually traditional closure for a Donleavy novel, perhaps by way of winding up the trilogy.

Wrong Information Is Being Given out at Princeton • Donleavy's next full-length novel, *Wrong Information Is Being Given out at Princeton*, presents the first-person narrative of

Alfonso Stephen O'Kelly'O, in some ways a typical Donleavy hero. He is a social outsider with no money and expensive tastes, a problem he thinks he has solved in marrying the daughter of a wealthy family. Stephen differs from most of his predecessors, however, in that he is a dedicated musician, composer of a minuet that has been offered a prestigious opening performance by the book's end. Although most of Donleavy's protagonists have artistic sensibilities, Stephen is one of the few who manages to be genuinely productive. His devotion to his work provides him with a moral and ethical center that often outweighs his hedonistic impulses, making him to some extent a principled rebel rather than just another of Donleavy's failed would-be conformists.

John P. Harrington
Updated by William Nelles

Other major works

SHORT FICTION: *Meet My Maker the Mad Molecule*, 1964.

PLAYS: *The Ginger Man*, pr. 1959 (adaptation of his novel; also known as *What They Did in Dublin, with The Ginger Man: A Play*); *Fairy Tales of New York*, pb. 1961 (adaptation of his novel *A Fairy Tale of New York*); *A Singular Man*, pb. 1965; *The Plays of J. P. Donleavy: With a Preface by the Author*, pb. 1972; *The Saddest Summer of Samuel S*, pb. 1972 (adaptation of his novel); *The Beastly Beatitudes of Balthazar B*, pr. 1981 (adaptation of his novel).

NONFICTION: *The Unexpurgated Code: A Complete Manual of Survival and Manners*, 1975; *J. P. Donleavy's Ireland: In All Her Sins and Some of Her Graces*, 1986; *A Singular Country*, 1990; *The History of the Ginger Man*, 1994; *An Author and His Image: The Collected Shorter Pieces*, 1997.

Bibliography

Donleavy, J. P. "The Art of Fiction LIII: J. P. Donleavy." Interview by Molly McKaughan. *Paris Review* 16 (Fall, 1975): 122-166. In this lengthiest of interviews with Donleavy, he discusses the complex publishing history of *The Ginger Man*, the painful process of writing, the differences between his characters and himself, his preference for reading newspapers and magazines rather than novels, his life on his Irish farm, and his attitudes toward critics, New York, and death.

____________. "An Interview with J. P. Donleavy." Interview by Kurt Jacobson. *Journal of Irish Literature* 8 (January, 1979): 39-48. Donleavy explains how he evolved from student of natural science to painter to writer and discusses the origins of some of the characters and events in *The Ginger Man* and that novel's controversial reception.

____________. "Only for the Moment Am I Saying Nothing: An Interview with J. P. Donleavy." Interview by Thomas E. Kennedy. *Literary Review* 40 (1997): 655-671. A wide-ranging interview at Donleavy's mansion in Ireland, addressing issues from all periods of his literary career and personal life. Particular attention is afforded to the details of his methods of writing and the status of his manuscripts. Contains a bibliography of books by Donleavy.

Lawrence, Seymour. "Adventures with J. P. Donleavy: Or, How I Lost My Job and Made My Way to Greater Glory." *Paris Review* 32 (1990): 187-201. Donleavy's first American editor reveals the inside story behind the complicated negotiations, fueled by fears of obscenity prosecution, that plagued the first two novels, *The Ginger*

Man and *A Singular Man.* Lawrence eventually had to publish under his own imprint the first unexpurgated American edition of *The Ginger Man,* followed by eleven subsequent Donleavy books.

LeClair, Thomas. "A Case of Death: The Fiction of J. P. Donleavy." *Contemporary Literature* 12 (Summer, 1971): 329-344. Shows how Donleavy's protagonists are both classical rogues in the tradition of Henry Fielding's Tom Jones and modern victims resembling Franz Kafka's Joseph K. Perhaps the best analysis of Donleavy's obsession with death, identified as the controlling element in his fiction.

Masinton, Charles G. *J. P. Donleavy: The Style of His Sadness and Humor.* Bowling Green, Ohio: Bowling Green State University Press, 1975. This pamphlet-length study of Donleavy's fiction through *A Fairy Tale of New York* places him in the American black humor tradition. Explains that while Donleavy's characters become increasingly morose and withdrawn, his fiction is most notable for its humor and irony. This most complete interpretation of Donleavy includes a brief bibliography.

Morse, Donald E. "American Readings of J. P. Donleavy's *The Ginger Man.*" *Eire-Ireland: A Journal of Irish Studies* 26 (Fall, 1991): 128-138. Morse explores the treatment of the novel in American criticism and discusses the American reaction to the use of slang, myth, and Irish values depicted in the novel.

Norstedt, Johann A. "Irishmen and Irish-Americans in the Fiction of J. P. Donleavy." In *Irish-American Fiction: Essays in Criticism,* edited by Daniel J. Casey and Robert E. Rhodes. New York: AMS Press, 1979. Donleavy's attitudes toward his native and adopted countries in *The Ginger Man, The Beastly Beatitudes of Balthazar B,* and other works are examined with the conclusion that he has grown more hostile toward America while gradually accepting a romanticized view of Ireland. The best consideration of Donleavy's use of Ireland. A bibliography is included.

John Dos Passos

Born: Chicago, Illinois; January 14, 1896
Died: Baltimore, Maryland; September 28, 1970

Principal long fiction • *One Man's Initiation—1917*, 1920; *Three Soldiers*, 1921; *Streets of Night*, 1923; *Manhattan Transfer*, 1925; *The 42nd Parallel*, 1930; *1919*, 1932; *The Big Money*, 1936; *U.S.A.*, 1937 (includes previous 3 novels); *Adventures of a Young Man*, 1939; *Number One*, 1943; *The Grand Design*, 1949; *Chosen Country*, 1951; *District of Columbia*, 1952 (includes *Adventures of a Young Man*, *Number One*, and *The Grand Design*); *Most Likely to Succeed*, 1954; *The Great Days*, 1958; *Midcentury*, 1961; *World in a Glass*, 1966; *Century's Ebb: The Thirteenth Chronicle*, 1975 (posthumous).

Other literary forms • John Dos Passos published only one collection of poetry, *A Pushcart at the Curb* (1922), which re-creates a journey through crowded streets and countrysides of Spain and the Near East. He also published a collection of plays, *Three Plays* (1934), written and produced during the author's experimentation with the expressionistic techniques of the New Playwright's Theatre group.

In addition to Dos Passos's many long fictions, which he called contemporary chronicles, he also published many volumes of historical narratives, essays, and reportage. Among his books of travel and reportage, which spanned his entire career, were *Rosinante to the Road Again* (1922), *Orient Express* (1927), *In All Countries* (1934), *Journeys Between Wars* (1938), *State of the Nation* (1944), *Tour of Duty* (1946), *The Prospect Before Us* (1950), *Brazil on the Move* (1963), *The Portugal Story* (1969), and *Easter Island: Island of Enigmas* (1971).

Most of Dos Passos's historical narratives were written in his later years and reflect the shift in his political stance; they include *The Ground We Stand On: Some Examples from the History of a Political Creed* (1941), *The Head and Heart of Thomas Jefferson* (1954), *The Men Who Made the Nation* (1957), *Mr. Wilson's War* (1962), *Thomas Jefferson: The Making of a President* (1964), and *The Shackles of Power: Three Jeffersonian Decades* (1966).

Achievements • Dos Passos's importance can neither be highlighted with one literary accomplishment nor summarized with a list of singular achievements. Rather, he offered a constant but integrated response to the nation and to the new. Throughout his writing career of fifty years, Dos Passos was committed to exploring individual freedom and utilized every literary means to that end. Combining his interest in history with his experience as a journalist and as an artist, Dos Passos produced a remarkable number of novels, poems, plays, essays, and various nonfictional pieces. They are important for their intrinsic merit as well as for their great documentary value. In addition to his extensive list of publications, Dos Passos was a loyal and impassioned correspondent; his letters to significant literary figures and friends also serve as chronicles of the age.

Finally, and unknown to many of his readers, Dos Passos was a talented painter. His sketchbooks, watercolors, and drawings—which date from his youth to his last days—are evidence of Dos Passos's fascination with the visual innovations and artistic movements of his lifetime. His painting had a significant influence on his methods as a writer.

Although Dos Passos experienced a decline in popularity when the critics believed he had abruptly shifted his political views to the right, there is now a revived interest in his best works, which are acknowledged as among the most inventive pieces of the twentieth century.

Biography • From the start of his life, John Roderigo Dos Passos was the victim of circumstances that would set him on an isolated course. In 1896, he was illegitimately born in a Chicago hospital. His father, John R. Dos Passos, Sr., was a famous defense lawyer and stock-market expert. He was also a writer of brokerage texts. His mother, Lucy Addison Sprigg, was of a fine southern stock. Apparently, his birth was never recorded: This would have meant a scandal for Dos Passos, senior, whose Roman Catholic wife, Mary Dyckman Hays Dos Passos, was an invalid.

For the most part, Dos Passos's childhood was spent with his mother in Brussels, London, or on the Continent, where reunions with his father were possible. From time to time, he was able to visit his father along the New Jersey shore or in New York, but only in a formal gathering where the affections of the boy for his "guardian" were repressed. Dos Passos's own account of his father's rare presence and peculiar hold are captured poignantly in *The Best Times* (1966).

Dos Passos's father, however, managed to shape the boy's intellect and attitudes, not through fatherly attentions, but with books and clear opinions about politics and through his son's elitist schooling. Dos Passos attended Peterborough Lodge, outside London, and the Choate School after returning to the United States. In 1910, Mary Dos Passos died; the boy's mother and father were married, and Dos Passos was given his actual surname. This new life and early schooling culminated in a grand tour of Europe and the Near and Middle East, complete with a mentor—Virgil Jones, a Dominican candidate. At this point, Dos Passos's great interest in art, architecture, and history was kindled. Ironically, he returned home to find that his mother, like Mary, had become an invalid.

The following autumn, Dos Passos entered Harvard, and the great avenues were opened for the nurturing of his writing, his political and social tendencies, and his artistic abilities. He ardently read both the classics and the moderns, as well as *Insurgent Mexico* (1914) by John Reed, an activist and a Harvard contemporary. Outside Harvard's walls, Dos Passos and his friends absorbed such artistic events as the Boston Opera, Sergei Diaghilev's ballet, the sensational Armory Show of modernist paintings, and the approach of world war.

Dos Passos's final year in school was somewhat sad, for his mother died, deepening his sense of isolation. It was also a springboard for his literary career, since it afforded the opportunity to collect and edit material and negotiate funds from his father for *Eight Harvard Poets*. He wrote for various Harvard publications, especially *The Harvard Monthly*, for which he was secretary and editor.

In 1916, Dos Passos studied architecture in Spain—an experience that would color his perspective on the civil war there and alienate him from his friend, Ernest Hemingway. It was at this time, too, that Dos Passos's father died of pneumonia; his subsequent feeling of abandonment can be traced through correspondence with friends in *The Fourteenth Chronicle* (1973).

During "Mr. Wilson's War," as he dubbed it, Dos Passos, like many writer friends, joined the selective Norton-Harjes Ambulance Unit, serving France and Italy. Following the war, he was considered to be a member of the so-called lost generation, but always remained somewhat apart. Dos Passos immersed himself in and contributed to the artistic excitement in Paris. Designing and painting sets for the ballet and writing consistently for the first time, Dos Passos also observed the Peace Conference and the postwar unrest.

National Portrait Gallery, Smithsonian Institution

Travels took Dos Passos to the Basque country, to New York, and to the Near East on the trans-Siberian Railroad. There, the danger of the desert, the stench of the cities, and the exotic activity greatly affected Dos Passos's creative notions. Back in New York by 1924, Dos Passos rode on the wave of socialism, jazz, and the fragmentation of the postwar period—precisely the right mixture for his highly stylized work, *Manhattan Transfer.* Simultaneously, he directed the New Playwright's Theatre group, which produced his dazzling, expressionistic productions on labor issues: *The Moon Is a Gong* (1926); *Airways, Inc.* (1928); and *Fortune Heights* (1933).

In 1928, Dos Passos met and married Katy Smith, a writer and friend of the Hemingways. Her temperament, wit, and goodness seemed to be the perfect match for Dos Passos's solitary nature and restless spirit. The couple enjoyed years of extensive travel and literary success before Katy was killed in a tragic automobile accident, in which her husband was driving. As for his political development during these years, Dos Passos supported the labor cause and the more universal cause for justice and individual freedom. When the Spanish Civil War broke out, however, and the making of a film rallied writers to Spain, Dos Passos's reaction to the execution of his friend, the poet José Robles, caused a serious rift with Hemingway.

The 1940's and 1950's marked a transition away from the political left: For Dos Passos, it was a natural shift to maintain his defense of freedom; for others, it remained a puzzling and outrageous movement to the right. During this period, Dos Passos was a war correspondent in the Pacific; after the war, he married a widow, Elizabeth Holdridge, and fathered a daughter, Lucy. He spent his remaining years traveling widely—particularly to South American countries such as Chile, Argentina, Brazil, and also around the United States. Discomfort due to a serious heart condition plagued him.

On September 28, 1970, John Dos Passos died of a heart attack in an apartment near Baltimore. He is buried near Spence's Point, his family's home in the northern neck of Virginia.

Analysis • Readers of Dos Passos's unusual novels have attempted to define the writer as a chronicler, a historian, or a critic of twentieth century America. To these titles, Dos Passos added another dimension by calling himself "an architect of history." Indeed, his works move in skillfully drawn directions—horizontally across continents, vertically through socioeconomic strata, temporally to the deepest places of memory. Considering further Dos Passos's training in architecture and painting, it is not solely by conventional literary means that students can come to grips with his novels; the reader must also be a good viewer. In fact, in the best of his long fiction—Three Soldiers, *Manhattan Transfer*, and the *U.S.A.* trilogy—the image and the word are often synonymous.

Three Soldiers • *Three Soldiers* emerged from Dos Passos's post-World War I travels through Italy, Portugal, and Spain. Published in 1921, it was not the writer's first novel, but it refined an artistic process he had begun during his ambulance service, a process that yielded his first novel, *One Man's Initiation*, in 1920. Both this novel and *Three Soldiers* were drawn from sketchbooks of notes, highly descriptive entries, diagrams and sketches of landscapes, characters, and confrontations. Although they are both antiwar books, *Three Soldiers* is clearly a better experiment in realism. Recalling Stephen Crane's *The Red Badge of Courage* (1895), the novel presents war through the eyes of the common soldier in France. Widening the range, Dos Passos poignantly captures the disillusionment and dehumanization of war for all soldiers.

True to his architectural design, Dos Passos allows for three geographical and individual perspectives—that of Dan Fuselli, a Californian; that of Chrisfield, a restless Indiana farmer boy; and that of Andrews, a Virginian and a composer. Through a thick buildup of violent encounters, he vividly portrays the army's destruction of the individual. Each responds to the regimentation and absurd conformity in different ways. Dan accepts the fantasy that conforming will result in promotion and the ultimate possession of his girl. Chrisfield plans to avenge himself on the hated sergeant. Andrews, the artist, struggles to find his creative place. In a series of violent confrontations, each soldier fails miserably to achieve his personal goals. Dan is promoted to corporal, but only after total exploitation by his superiors; Mabe, his girl, has married another man. Chrisfield vows to murder the sergeant. Having practiced on a solitary German in an abandoned house, he throws his last two grenades at the wounded sergeant in the woods. Dos Passos focuses on the artist, Andrews, who has managed to study legitimately in Paris and meet a sympathizer, Geneviève. Finally, he decides to go absent without leave (AWOL) and is discovered and beaten by the military police. As Andrews is dramatically removed from his hiding place, a gust of wind scatters his unfinished composition titled "John Brown," an homage to the liberator of slaves.

Although simplistic when compared to the later works, *Three Soldiers* is an exercise in an important visual process. First, he planned his novel from collected verbal and visual sketches. Second, his strong sense of painterly composition allowed for three diverse perspectives in Chrisfield, Fuselli, and Andrews. The reader will discover this geographical interest later in the *U.S.A.* trilogy, as well. Finally, he positioned images of violent confrontations against serene French landscapes. The violent action is shockingly portrayed while the images of the countryside are almost nostagically impressionistic. The effect is similar to the anxiety created in cubist paintings, where familiar objects and spaces are reshaped and limited. In the juxtaposition of images, the reader will sense Dos Passos's extreme personal disdain for war and his appreciation of a lost world.

Manhattan Transfer • The writing that followed *Three Soldiers* was not so much a futher refinement as it was a sudden explosion of artistic innovation, yet the germination of *Manhattan Transfer* was like that which produced Dos Passos's first two novels: a rich collage of images, impressions, notes, and sketches. Just as *Three Soldiers* is critical of war, so *Manhattan Transfer* focuses on the dehumanizing effects of the city, particularly on immigrants or outsiders. To convey his theme, Dos Passos transformed the conventional components of character, setting, and plot in much the same way that cubist painters distorted familiar objects and transformed the viewer's perception of them. New York, for example, is not really a setting or a backdrop, to use a visual term, but a major and monstrous character. Similarly, while there are approximately twelve identifiable characters out of the masses, they are important only as facets of the portrait of the real antagonist, the city. Finally, while there is a complicated network of overlapping and chaotic activities among and between the characters, there is no single plot. Instead, the novel is like a roller coaster or rapid transit ride; the reader experiences flashes of sense, sound, color, and conflict. It is, then, a collective novel—a compilation of the notes and pictures created while Dos Passos himself was in motion as a traveler.

The novel is divided into three sections, demarcated not by logical, literary closures but by highly visual introductory commentaries. Each section also contains several divisions, the headings of which allude to the metals and myths of great cities: "Ferryslip," "Tracks," "Rollercoaster," "Steamroller," "Revolving Doors," "Skyscrapers," and "The Burthen of Nineveh." What occurs within each division is not an unfolding of ideas or action, but an envelopment of the reader into a frenzy of lives colliding in the city's mainstream.

To create this collage, Dos Passos welds fragments of dialogue, action, newspaper clippings, signs, city sights, and time. In "Ferryslip," a child is born to an uncertain father, Ed Thatcher, and a hysterical mother, Susie. The child suddenly becomes Ellie, Ellen, or Elaine, depending upon the fortunes and fame of the gentlemen she lures. In "Tracks," the reader meets Jimmy Herf, an immigrant newspaper reporter who is the only figure eventually to escape the city's grasp. There is George Baldwin, a manipulative attorney who turns politician; Congo and Emile, two Frenchmen who represent the extremes of survival in a new land—one marries and conforms while the other returns to sea. Joe O'Keefe, a labor organizer, is juxtaposed with a successful Broadway producer, Harry Goldweiser. Almost all the characters collide with one another or else their adventures are butted against one another's in the same section of the novel. Herf provides the final view as he waits for a ferry to take him from Manhattan. Broken by every component of life in New York, he decides to hitchhike out of the city on a furniture truck, glistening and yellow. He provides the reader with an uncertain perspective; when asked how far he is going, Herf replies aimlessly that he wants to go far away.

Recalling the collective portrayal of the army in *Three Soldiers, Manhattan Transfer* captures the entirety and enormity of the city. The realism of *Three Soldiers*, however, was brilliantly and vividly transformed into a masterful expressionistic style. Instead of a conventional linear narrative about the dehumanization of the modern city, Dos Passos chose to re-create the eclectic experience of Manhattan. He verbally reproduced the rhythms, forms, plasticity, and chaotic activity of the city without the traditional literary processes of describing, developing, or narrating. The novel initially shocks the reader, forces a complicated sensual experience, and convinces the reader of the city's power by its sheer visual frenzy. The innovative techniques of Manhattan Transfer won for Dos Passos the praise of eminent contemporaries: Sinclair Lewis compared the novel to the modernist masterpieces of Gertrude Stein, Marcel Proust, and James Joyce. Certainly, Dos Passos had concocted a work in which the mass of the image and the word were of equal weight.

***U.S.A.* trilogy** • If *Manhattan Transfer* represented a heightened style and structure in comparison to *Three Soldiers*, then the *U.S.A.* trilogy was the apex of Dos Passos's expressionistic novels; generally acknowledged as his masterpiece, it is on this work that his reputation rests. The trilogy is a panoramic fictional history of America in the first three decades of the twentieth century. The title of the first novel in the trilogy, *The 42nd Parallel*, suggests the sweep of the work, across the United States from Plymouth, Massachusetts, through the industrial centers of Detroit and Chicago, over to the gold coast of northern California. Along the way, history is not remembered or narrated, but reproduced by a series of modernist devices.

Dos Passos composed his trilogy with fragments of American life—newsreels, headlines, songs, letters, placards, colloquialisms, and biographical pieces of fictional and nonfictional figures. These fragments click away like an early film or newsreel itself, which captures the reader's attention for the narrative that follows. Dos Passos embellished this superstructure, more elaborate in scope than the divisions of *Manhattan Transfer*, with illustrations and with the ingenious and provocative device of the "Camera Eye." Interspersed and intruding into the narrative, the Camera Eye is composed of images in such a way as to reproduce memory, probably the writer's memory. The voice seems both deterministic and vulnerable to all that happens around it. Its focus set, the epic catalog of characters, real and imagined, is called to action.

The 42nd Parallel • The characters in the trilogy are representative figures intended to form a composite of the American soul. In *The 42nd Parallel*, there is Mac McCreary, a printer who eventually joins the revolutionary movement in Mexico, following disillusionment with marriage. J. Ward Moorehouse, a charismatic and powerful figure, is then introduced; the reader follows him throughout the trilogy as he is transformed from a public relations man and government servant in France to a wealthy advertising executive. Among the female characters is Eleanor Stoddard, an artsy interior decorator at Marshall Field's in Chicago; she eventually makes the acquaintance of Moorehouse. There is also Charley Anderson, an opportunist whose mechanical inventiveness leads him to become an airplane manufacturer. The reader observes his steady decline through the trilogy. These are but a few of the many contrasting characters sketched throughout the trilogy.

The historical portraits are of eloquent and eccentric figures of the period: Eugene V. Debs, the labor organizer jailed by President Woodrow Wilson; William Jennings Bryan, the silver-tongued midwestern orator and frequent presidential candidate; the socialist mathematician Charles Proteus Steinmetz, who, as the property of General Electric, developed the law of hysteresis that produced electrical transformers for the world. The novel is a portrait collection of real and imagined people. Some are creative, cunning, impassioned; most are naïve. To link them, Dos Passos develops a kind of self-portrait through the Camera Eye series. The reader traces the

Eye's consciousness from young and constant traveler in Europe and feisty adolescent to observer of labor rallies. The very last Camera Eye in *The 42nd Parallel* parallels the final sequence of Charley Anderson's crossing to war-torn France. The Eye pans out on the *Espagne*, dangerously crossing the Atlantic, its passengers caught in ironic responses to the great fear of destruction. The Eye moves quickly to death in the trenches, to the prosperity of vinegrowers, to a town in France unpleasantly interrupted by agents searching bags in well-known hotels. Through one Eye, then, and through the other biographies, the reader views rather than reviews the transition of Americans from naïveté to anticipation of some inevitable doom.

1919 • If *The 42nd Parallel* finishes in fearful anticipation, then *1919* fills the void with the thunder of World War I and the frightened inner voices of the characters. Far more tragic and total a portrayal of war than *Three Soldiers*, *1919* unmasks the entire absurdity, debauchery, and waste of "Mr. Wilson's War" at home and abroad. This second volume in the trilogy opens with a grimly ironic headline concerning the "great" battle of Verdun. The horror implicit in this headline is counterpointed by domestic suffering, by scenes of an America in which the wealthy few prosper at the expense of the masses.

Against this panorama of war and an industrializing nation, Dos Passos paints his imaginary portraits. There is Dick Savage, a literary Harvard graduate who resembles the author in several ways. He serves in the ambulance corps, caring for the mutilated and deranged. His horror is juxtaposed with a farcical censuring and punishment by the army for his mild criticism of war in a letter to a friend. (In a similar incident, Dos Passos himself had been expelled from the Red Cross.) Dick eventually finds his way into J. Ward Moorehouse's association after the war. There is also Ben Compton, the son of a Jewish immigrant, who travels north, south, east, and west as a political agitator at home. He is jailed, persecuted, and finally broken by the forces of law and order. Eleanor Stoddard begins her climb to the top through a series of affairs ultimately leading to J. Ward Moorehouse in Paris. Together, they exploit all around them to buy into the power of "Big Business" back home.

The historical figures expand Dos Passos's portrayal of this contradictory world at war. There is Jack Reed, the Harvard man who spoke and wrote revolution. Theodore Roosevelt is portrayed by a series of vivid anecdotes. He was, for Dos Passos, the last major figure of everything American, what Teddy characterized as "bully." The great J. P. Morgan is last. His family's empire built upon warmongering, Morgan's portrait prepares the reader for the monsters to come in *The Big Money*.

Just as in *The 42nd Parallel*, the Camera Eye moves the reader's view from the dying and dead in ambulance vans, to harlots, to soldiers running for cover in city streets, and finally to civilians collecting scrap iron at the war's end. Moreover, Dos Passos adds to the collage scraps of headlines of suicides and murders at home, news of an uprising of the workers, and bits of melancholy American and French war songs. These grim scraps are collected for the future recycling of postwar industrial and political figures in *The Big Money*. The reader experiences the change in American consciousness from innocent anticipation to horror.

The end of *1919* is quite poignant both in technique and in meaning. Dos Passos blends the essence of the "newsreels," the Camera Eye, and the biographies to create a moving elegiac portrait of the Unknown Soldier. From the almost flippant choosing among pieces of bodies in France, to the imagined home and youth of the anonymous man, to the placing of Wilson's bouquet of poppies at the Tomb, Dos Passos movingly portrays the common dehumanizing experience of all soldiers and the unique and sacred individuality of every human being.

The Big Money • Following the brilliant design of the first two volumes of the trilogy, *The Big Money* picks up the pace of *1919* and brings the author's rather cynical perspective into perfect focus. Against the scenes of war's end and the anticipation of the Great Depression, Dos Passos draws his ultimate conclusion—that the simple individual, as an American ideal, was not strong enough to confront the new powers of the modern world. It is not so much the individual against the world that is of importance here, however, as it is the composite view of America as one character after all, a collection of all the victims and aggressors of the early twentieth century. America is both protagonist and antagonist in *The Big Money*; both Dos Passos's subject and his means of painting it are unsettling.

Exploiting the technical innovations of the previous volumes, Dos Passos paints a pessimistic picture of Americans coming to terms with the twentieth century. Charley Anderson, corrupted by money, booze, and sexual affairs, drives south and dies in a car crash in Florida. Eveline Johnson, reaching her lowest point of boredom with Moorehouse and company, takes her life with sleeping pills. Margo Dowling, the ultimate plastic Hollywood starlet, is created and controlled by her powerful producer-husband, Sam Mongolies. In contrast, Mary French remains honest, constant, and determined in her work for the Communist Party, particularly in her protest against the executions of Nicola Sacco and Bartolomeo Vanzetti. Among the real biographies, there is Isadora Duncan, who danced for the sake of art, accidentally drowned her children, and died in a joyride when her neck scarf caught in the wheel of an automobile. There is Frank Lloyd Wright, whose functional designs for the rich were not beauty enough to disguise his ugly family squabbles, bankruptcy, and scandalous affairs. Even the Wright brothers, whose flying machine becomes a new war machine, present no triumph for the common person—at least, not at first—but they are admiringly portrayed.

The Camera Eye seems surer, more direct than before, more focused as it captures the Great Depression era. The man behind the camera was older, more experienced. The Eye in *The Big Money* is not reminiscent, as in *The 42nd Parallel*, or horrified, as in *1919*, but strong and clear about the plight of the social worker, the immigrant, and the laborer; about the triumph of the rich, the powerful, and the political. In fact, one of the last Camera Eyes of the trilogy forces the reader to view finally two nations in one, two languages, two experiences—that of the poor and that of the wealthy. Somehow, nevertheless, through Dos Passos's concentration on the common American, the nation seems on the brink of renewal.

The use of the now-familiar experimental tools of newsreels and cultural fragments is also sharper in *The Big Money*, especially in Dos Passos's juxtapositions of realities and absurdities, a technique begun in *1919*. One newsreel, for example, proclaims in archaic speech and images that the steel corporation is a marvelous colossus, while bomb scares, suicides, and Georgia's new controversial dance, Shake That Thing, are stated matter of factly. Another announces America's air supremacy and a boom year ahead while it simultaneously lists a massacre of six hundred in Canton, the production of gas for warfare, the use of machine guns and steamrollers on strikers. The musical fragments come from the blues and from poetic choruses written for the unemployed. What seems hidden in the portrayal of America as shaken, explosive, and cruelly challenged is a wishful portrait of America as diversified, creative, and positively evolving.

Although Dos Passos continued to explore the themes of his great trilogy in seven subsequent novels, none of them was as provocative, as innovative in visual techniques, or as critically acclaimed as his masterpiece, *U.S.A.*

Mary Ellen Stumpf

Other major works

PLAYS: *The Garbage Man*, pr., pb. 1926 (pr. as *The Moon Is a Gong*, pr. 1925); *Three Plays*, pb. 1934.

POETRY: *A Pushcart at the Curb*, 1922.

NONFICTION: *Rosinante to the Road Again*, 1922; *Orient Express*, 1927; *In All Countries*, 1934; *Journeys Between Wars*, 1938; *The Ground We Stand On: Some Examples from the History of a Political Creed*, 1941; *State of the Nation*, 1944; *Tour of Duty*, 1946; *The General*, 1949; *The Prospect Before Us*, 1950; *The Head and Heart of Thomas Jefferson*, 1954; *The Theme Is Freedom*, 1956; *The Men Who Made the Nation*, 1957; *Prospects of a Golden Age*, 1959; *Mr. Wilson's War*, 1962; *Brazil on the Move*, 1963; *Lincoln and the Gettysburg Address*, 1964; *Occasions and Protests*, 1964; *Thomas Jefferson: The Making of a President*, 1964; *The Best Times: An Informal Memoir*, 1966; *The Shackles of Power: Three Jeffersonian Decades*, 1966; *The Portugal Story*, 1969; *Easter Island: Island of Enigmas*, 1971; *The Fourteenth Chronicle*, 1973.

Bibliography

Becker, George J. *John Dos Passos*. New York: Frederick Ungar, 1974. A critical biography, this short book links Dos Passos's major works, his artistic observations, and his treatment of American social institutions.

Carr, Virginia Spencer. *Dos Passos: A Life*. Garden City, N.Y.: Doubleday, 1984. Presents a detailed biography with critical insights into the personal and political influences on Dos Passos's fiction.

Casey, Janet Galligani. *Dos Passos and the Ideology of the Feminine*. New York: Cambridge University Press, 1998. Discusses Dos Passos's female characters. Includes bibliographical references and an index.

Colley, Lain. *Dos Passos and the Fiction of Despair*. Totowa, N.J.: Rowman & Littlefield, 1978. One of the most frequently cited texts in Dos Passos scholarship.

Koch, Stephen. *The Breaking Point: Hemingway, Dos Passos, and the Murder of José Robles*. New York: Counterpoint, 2005. Study of the split that occurred between Ernest Hemingway and Dos Passos after Dos Passos's poet friend José Robles was executed during the Spanish Civil War.

Ludington, Townsend. *John Dos Passos: A Twentieth Century Odyssey*. Rev. ed. New York: Carroll & Graf, 1998. A standard biography first published in 1980; updated introduction.

McGlamery, Tom. *Protest and the Body in Melville, Dos Passos, and Hurston*. New York: Routledge, 2004. Comparative study of common motifs in the writings of American novelists Herman Melville, John Dos Passos, and Zora Neale Hurston.

Maine, Barry, ed. *Dos Passos: The Critical Heritage*. London: Routledge, 1988. Devoted to the contemporary critical reception of Dos Passos's individual novels. Divided into twelve sections, each covering a major work. These chapters contain between two (*Number One, The Grand Design*) and twelve (*The Big Money*) different reviews, taken from publications ranging from *American Mercury* to the *Daily Worker.*

____________. "*U.S.A.*: Dos Passos and the Rhetoric of History." *South Atlantic Review* 50, no. 1 (1985): 75-86. This important article treats the role of narrative in conveying history in the first of Dos Passos's trilogy, with attention to the relationship between narrative and film.

Nanney, Lisa. *John Dos Passos.* New York: Twayne, 1998. An excellent introductory study of Dos Passos and his works.

Sanders, David. *John Dos Passos: A Comprehensive Bibliography.* New York: Garland, 1987. Includes an index.

Strychacz, Thomas. *Modernism, Mass Culture, and Professionalism.* New York: Cambridge University Press, 1993. Places the *U.S.A.* trilogy in historical context.

Wagner, Linda W. *Dos Passos: Artist as American.* Austin: University of Texas Press, 1979. A comprehensive (624-page) study of Dos Passos's development as artist/observer, treating his quest for an American hero through his major works.

Theodore Dreiser

Born: Terre Haute, Indiana; August 27, 1871
Died: Hollywood, California; December 28, 1945

Principal long fiction • *Sister Carrie*, 1900; *Jennie Gerhardt*, 1911; *The Financier*, 1912, 1927; *The Titan*, 1914; *The "Genius,"* 1915; *An American Tragedy*, 1925; *The Bulwark*, 1946; *The Stoic*, 1947.

Other literary forms • The scope of Theodore Dreiser's literary accomplishment includes attempts in every major literary form, including autobiography and philosophy. His poetry is generally of poor quality; his plays have been produced on occasion, but drama was not his métier. His sketches, such as those included in *The Color of a Great City* (1923), are vivid and accurate, but seem to be only workmanlike vignettes that Dreiser developed for the practice or for later inclusion in one of his many novels. His short stories are, like the sketches, preparation for the novels, but the compression of scene, character, and idea necessary for the short story lend these pieces a life of their own, distinct from the monolithic qualities of the novels. Dreiser's philosophical works, such as *Hey, Rub-a-Dub-Dub!* (1920), and his autobiographical forays are the product of an obsession for explaining himself; the philosophy is often obscure and arcane and the autobiography is not always reliable. Dreiser's letters have been collected and offer further understanding of the man, as do the massive manuscript collections, which are the product of his tortuous composition and editing processes.

Achievements • The enigma that is Dreiser divides the critical world into two clearly identifiable camps: those who despise Dreiser and those who honor him just short of adulation—there is no middle ground. With the publication of *Sister Carrie* in 1900, Dreiser committed his literary force to opening the new ground of American naturalism. His heroes and heroines, his settings, his frank discussion, celebration, and humanization of sex, his clear dissection of the mechanistic brutality of American society—all were new and shocking to a reading public reared on genteel romances and adventure narratives. *Jennie Gerhardt*, the Cowperwood trilogy (at least the first two volumes), and *An American Tragedy* expand and clarify those themes introduced in *Sister Carrie*. Dreiser's genius was recognized and applauded by H. L. Mencken, who encouraged him, praised his works publicly, and was always a valued editorial confidant, but the general reaction to Dreiser has always been negative.

Dreiser has been called a "crag of basalt," "solemn and ponderous" and "the world's worst great writer," but his influence is evident in the works of Sherwood Anderson, Sinclair Lewis, Ernest Hemingway, and James T. Farrell, among others. Lewis refused the 1925 Pulitzer Prize, which probably should have gone to Dreiser for *An American Tragedy*, and in 1930 took the Nobel Prize committee to task for choosing him as the first American Nobelist for literature instead of Dreiser. Dreiser's political and social activism during the long hiatus between *An American Tragedy* and *The Bulwark*, and his never-ending battle against censors and censorship, kept him in the public eye, and the failure of *The Bulwark* and *The Stoic* consigned him to years of ne-

Library of Congress

glect after his death. His technical and stylistic faults have often obscured his real value, but the effects of Dreiser's work are still rippling through American fiction. He was the first to point out the fragile vulnerability of the facade that was understood to be the American Dream and to depict the awful but beautiful reality that supported the facade.

Biography • Theodore Herman Albert Dreiser was born in Terre Haute, Indiana, on August 27, 1871, into a family of German Americans. His father, John Paul Dreiser, was a weaver by trade, and from the time of his entry into the United States (in 1846), he had worked westward in an attempt to establish himself. He induced Sarah Schanab (later shortened to Shnepp), the daughter of an Ohio Moravian, to elope with him and they settled near Fort Wayne. John Paul became the manager in a woolen mill and soon amassed enough funds to build his own mill in Sullivan, Indiana. In 1870, the year before Theodore's birth, the mill burned, John Paul was seriously injured, Sarah was cheated out of the family property by unscrupulous "yankee trickery," and the family was forced to move to Terre Haute, where Theodore was born the eleventh of twelve children, ten of whom survived to adulthood.

After the family misfortunes, John Paul never recovered physically and sank into a pattern of paternal despotism and narrow religious fervor, against which Theodore and the rest of the children could only express contempt and revolt and from which their only haven was the open, loving character of their mother.

In 1879, with the family teetering on the edge between poverty and penury, Sarah took Theodore and the youngest children to Vincennes, Indiana, and the girls stayed with John Paul in Terre Haute in an attempt to economize. There then followed a series of moves that took the two parts of the family, in succeeding moves, from Vincennes back to Sullivan, to Evansville to live with Theodore's brother Paul (who had succeeded in the vaudeville circuit), to Chicago, and finally to Warsaw, Indiana. This nomadic life could only deepen the destitution of the family and heighten the children's craving for the material part of life they never had. In 1887, after the move to Warsaw, sixteen-year-old Theodore announced that he was going back to Chicago; his mother, characteristically, gave him six dollars of her savings and her blessing, and Theodore went on his way back to the most wonderful city he had ever seen.

As a sixteen-year-old, alone in Chicago, Dreiser, like Carrie Meeber, could find only menial labor, first as a dishwasher, later working for a hardware company. In 1889, however, a former teacher who believed in his latent abilities encouraged him to enroll at Indiana University and subsidized his enrollment. After a year of frustrated attempts to break into the fraternity social life of Bloomington, Dreiser left Indiana University and returned to Chicago.

After another series of menial jobs, including driving a laundry delivery wagon, Dreiser managed to land a job with the Chicago *Globe* as a reporter. After a few months, he was invited to take a position on the St. Louis *Globe-Democrat* and *Republic* staff and he moved to St. Louis. In St. Louis, he covered the usual types of news events and met Sara (Sallie) White, to whom he found himself unaccountably attracted. In 1895, after brief periods on newspaper staffs in St. Louis, Toledo, Cleveland, and Pittsburgh, Dreiser took up residence in New York City. Even after his newspaper success in St. Louis and Chicago, however, Dreiser could only find freelance work in New York City until his brother Paul, by then a successful songwriter and publisher, persuaded his publishers to make Dreiser the editor of their newly established music periodical, *Ev'ry Month*, for which he wrote monthly editorial columns. This forum for Dreiser's talents was the beginning of a long editorial career that led him to editorships of *Smith's Magazine*, *Broadway Magazine*, and editorial positions with Street and Smith and Butterick. During this period he published *Sister Carrie*, separated from his wife, Sallie White, whom he had married in 1898, suffered the death of his brother Paul, began work on *Jennie Gerhardt*, and quit his position at Butterick's to avoid scandal and to devote his time to fiction.

After his publication of *Jennie Gerhardt*, Dreiser's career is the story of one laboriously prepared publication after another. Even at the end, he was working on *The Stoic*, the last of the Cowperwood trilogy, almost as if it were unfinished business. He died in Hollywood on December 28, 1945.

Analysis • Literary historians have shown, by identifying sources and characters, that Dreiser, even in his fiction, was a capable investigative reporter. His reliance on research for setting, character, and plot lines is evident in *The Financier* and *The Titan* and, most important, in *An American Tragedy*, but Dreiser was not bound by his investigative method. He went often to his own memories for material. Only when Dreiser combines autobiographical material with his research and reportage does his fiction come alive.

Dreiser's youth and early manhood prepared him for the themes he developed. His unstable home life; the dichotomy established between a loving, permissive mother and a narrow, bigoted, dogmatic, penurious father; abject poverty; and his own desires for affluence, acceptance, sexual satisfaction, and recognition were all parts of his fictional commonplace book. His sisters' sexual promiscuity was reflected in Carrie and Jennie, and his own frustrations and desires found voice in, among others, Clyde Griffiths. The character of Frank Cowperwood was shaped in Dreiser's lengthy research into the life of C. T. Yerkes, but Cowperwood was also the incarnation of everything that Dreiser wanted to be—handsome, powerful, accepted, wealthy, and capable. Dreiser projected his own dreams on characters such as Griffiths and Cowperwood only to show that human dreams are never ultimately fulfilled. No matter for what man (or woman) contested, "his feet are in the trap of circumstances; his eyes are on an illusion." Dreiser did not condemn the effort; he chronicled the fragile nature of the pursued and the pursuer.

Sister Carrie • The genesis of *Sister Carrie*, Dreiser's first novel, was as fantastic as its appearance in Victorian America. In Dreiser's own account, he started the novel at the insistence of his friend Arthur Henry, and then only to appease him. In order to end Henry's wheedlings and annoyances, Dreiser sat down and wrote the title of the novel at the top of a page. With no idea of a program for the novel or who the basic characters were to be, Dreiser began the book that did more to change modern American fiction than any since.

The amatory adventures of Dreiser's sisters in Indiana and his own experiences in Chicago and in New York were the perfect materials for the story of a poor country girl who comes to the city to seek whatever she can find. The one thing she is certain of is that she does not wish to remain poor. With this kind of material, it is surprising that Dreiser escaped writing a maudlin tale of a fallen girl rescued at the end or an Algeresque tale of her rise from rags. *Sister Carrie* is neither of these. Carrie does rise, but she does so by the means of a male stepladder. She is not a simple gold digger; she is much more complex than that. Her goals are clothes, money, and fame, and the means by which she achieves them are relatively unimportant. More important, however, is that Carrie is a seeker and a lover. She cannot be satisfied. There must always be a new world to conquer, new goals to achieve. In New York, when she has finally acquired all that she has sought, Ames shows her that there is a world beyond the material—a world of literature and philosophy; it is an aesthetic world of which Carrie has not dreamed and that she recognizes as a new peak to conquer and a new level to achieve. There is a hint that this new level is more satisfying than any she has reached, just as Ames seems more interesting and satisfying than either of her previous lovers, Drouet and Hurstwood, but the novel ends with Carrie still contemplating her attack on this new world.

Carrie subordinates everything to her consuming ambition. She comes to understand the usefulness of sex, but she also understands the emotional commitment necessary to love, and she refuses to make that commitment. In the pursuit of the fullest expression and fulfillment of life she can achieve, human attachments are only transitory at best, and Drouet and Hurstwood are only means to an end for Carrie.

Drouet, the traveling salesman Carrie meets on the train to Chicago, becomes her first lover after she has had time to discover the frustration of joblessness and sweatshop employment and the despair of the poverty in which the relatives with whom she is staying live. Drouet ingratiates himself with Carrie by buying her dinner and then by slipping two ten-dollar bills into her hand. Not long thereafter, Drouet outfits a flat for her, and they set up housekeeping together. Drouet is, for Carrie, an escape. She does not love him, but his means are a source of amazement, and she recognizes that the relative opulence of his chambers and of the apartment he procures for her are the signs of that for which she is striving. She recognizes very early that Drouet is static, a dead end, but he is only an intermediary in her movement from poverty to affluence.

Hurstwood is the bartender and manager of a prominent Chicago tavern. As he watches Carrie perform in a cheap theatrical, he is smitten by her youth and her vitality. A middle-aged, married man, possessed of a virago of a wife, he is naturally attracted to Carrie. Carrie in turn recognizes the quality of Hurstwood's clothes, his style, and his bearing as distinct improvements on Drouet and makes it clear she will accept his advances. Hurstwood's wife uncovers the subsequent affair, a messy divorce threatens Hurstwood's stability and prestige in his job, fortuity brings him to embezzle ten thousand dollars from the bar safe, and he flees with Carrie first to

Montreal and then to New York. After they reach New York, the chronicle becomes the tale of Hurstwood's steady degeneration and Carrie's alternatively steady rise to stardom on the stage.

Hurstwood does not carry his status with him from Chicago to New York. In New York, he is merely another man who either cannot hold or cannot find a job. His funds are seriously depleted in the failure of an attempt to open his own saloon, and the more he fails the further he withdraws from life and from Carrie, until he becomes completely dependent on her. When Carrie leaves him because she cannot support both of them and buy the clothes necessary to her profession, he drifts deeper and deeper into New York's netherworld until he commits suicide by turning on the gas in a Bowery flophouse. Typically, Carrie never knows or cares that Hurstwood is dead. If Drouet is a dead end, Hurstwood is a weak man trapped by circumstance and by his unwillingness or inability to cope with situations he recognizes as potentially disastrous. His liaison with Carrie is based on mutual attraction, but he is also enamored of his daily routine and of the prestige that accompanies it. Only when his wife threatens him with exposure is he forced to make the final commitment to Carrie and, eventually, to the gas jet.

Carrie's desertion of Hurstwood can be interpreted as cold and cruel, but she stays with him until it is clear that there is nothing anyone can do to save him. To try to save him would only mire her in his downward spiral. The counterpoint of Carrie's rise and Hurstwood's fall is the final irony of the novel. Carrie and Hurstwood reach their final disappointments in almost the same basic terms. Hurstwood dies tired of the struggle and Carrie realizes that she has finally arrived and there is nothing more to conquer or achieve. Only the promise of an aesthetic world beyond material affluence offers hope for Carrie, and that hope seems illusory. The ubiquitous rocking chair is the perfect symbol for *Sister Carrie.* It is an instrument that forever moves but never goes anywhere and never truly achieves anything. Carrie's every success is ultimately unsatisfying and every new horizon offers only a hollow promise.

Sister Carrie was stillborn in the first edition. Published but suppressed by the publisher, it did not reach the public until seven years later, when it was given to a new publisher. The novel contains the seeds of most of Dreiser's themes.

Jennie Gerhardt • The protagonist of *Jennie Gerhardt,* Dreiser's second novel, is Carrie's natural sister or, perhaps, her alter ego. Jennie is also the product of Dreiser's early family life, of his sisters' fatal attraction to men and the natural result. When Dreiser turned to *Jennie Gerhardt* while still embroiled in the publication problems of *Sister Carrie,* he drew upon the events in the life of his sister Mame, who was seduced, abandoned, and ended up living successfully with another man in New York City. From this basic material, Dreiser created a girl much like Carrie in origin, who has the same desires for material ease, but who has none of the instincts Carrie possesses or who has the same instincts channeled into a different mode of expression.

Jennie Gerhardt is divided into two parts. In the first part, as the daughter of a poor washerwoman, Jennie is noticed by Senator George Sylvester Brander, another older man attracted by youth and vitality; he is kind, tips her heavily for delivering his laundry, and eventually seduces her. Brander is, however, more than a stereotype. He has a real need for Jennie and a fatherly attachment to her. Jennie, who is more than the "fallen angel" as some have seen her, responds in kind. Surrounded by conventional morality and religious prohibitions, represented by Old Gerhardt and others, Jennie, unlike Carrie, has a desperate need to give in order to fulfill herself. Despite the veneer of indebtedness Jennie brings to her seduction by Brander (he arranges the release of her brother from jail, among other things), there is a surprisingly wholesome atmosphere to the affair. Brander is solicitous and protective, and Jennie is loving and tender. When Jennie becomes pregnant, Brander plans to marry her, put her parents in a more comfortable situation, and, in short, do the right thing. Brander, however, dies, and Jennie gives birth to his illegitimate child; she is condemned by her parents and society, and her previous joy and prospects dissolve before her eyes.

Dreiser's portrayal of Jennie does not allow the reader to feel sorry for her. Vesta, Jennie's child, is not the product of sin, but the offspring of an all-suffering, all-giving earth mother. Dreiser's depiction of Jennie as a child of nature verifies this impression. Despite society and its narrow views, Jennie is not destroyed or even dismayed. She is delighted with her child and thus snatches her joy and fulfillment from a seeming disaster. As long as she can give, be it to child or lover, she is unassailable.

The second seduction occurs when the Gerhardts, except for Old Gerhardt, move to Cleveland at the behest of brother Bass and supposedly at his expense. Bass is expansive and generous for a while, but then begins to demand more and more until Jennie must take a position as a chambermaid at the Bracebridge house, where she meets Lester Kane. Once again, as with Brander, the seduction wears the facade of obligation—this time because Lester Kane helps the family when Old Gerhardt suffers debilitating burns, which deprive him of his glassblowing trade, his sole means of support. Lester has pursued Jennie and his help fosters the ensuing affair. Like the first seduction, however, the second is not the simple matter it seems.

Lester Kane is Dreiser's portrayal of the enlightened man—the man who has serious doubts about religion, morality, societal restrictions, and mores. He serves the basic needs of Jennie's character; he also understands his own needs for the devotion, care, and understanding that Jennie is able and willing to give. With his willingness to make a more-or-less permanent commitment to Jennie, he seems to be a match, but Lester also understands the restrictions of class that forbid him to marry Jennie and feels the strong pull of family duty, which requires that he play a vital part in shaping the family's considerable enterprises. Lester, then, is caught with Jennie, as Dreiser puts it, between the "upper and nether millstones of society."

When Jennie and Lester set up their clandestine apartment in Chicago, they are enormously happy until they are discovered by Lester's family; the newspapers make front-page news of the discovery, and Jennie reveals to Lester that she has hidden the existence of her daughter, Vesta, from him. Amazingly, Lester weathers all these shocks and even brings Vesta and Old Gerhardt to share the apartment with them, but Lester's "indiscretions" have allowed his less heroically inclined brother to take control of the family business, and when his father dies, his will decrees that Lester must make a choice. If he marries Jennie, he gets a pittance; if he leaves her, he gets a normal portion. At this point, Letty, an old flame of Lester—of the "right" class—surfaces, and Jennie, fully recognizing the mutual sacrifices she and Lester will have to make whether he leaves or stays, encourages him to leave her. Lester eventually marries Letty and claims his inheritance. Jennie sacrifices Lester and in rapid succession sees Old Gerhardt and Vesta die. Deprived of her family, she manufactures one by taking in orphans. The device is not satisfying and the worldly refinement she has assimilated in her life with Lester is not enough to succor her, yet she survives to be called to Lester's death bed. Lester tells her that he has never forgotten her and that he loves her still, and Jennie reciprocates. The scene brings together a man and a woman who have given away or had taken away everything they loved through no particular fault of their own.

Lester is a weak man, like Hurstwood, but unlike Hurstwood he does not give up; he is beaten until he can no longer resist. Unlike Carrie, Jennie is not brought to the point of emptiness by achievements, but by losses. Her nature has betrayed her, and when one sees her hidden in the church at Lester's funeral, unrecognized by his family, one senses the totality of her loss. One also senses, however, that she has emerged a spiritual victor. She seems to have grown more expansive and more generous with each loss. Her stature grows until she looms over the novel as the archetypal survivor. She has been bruised, battered, and pushed down, but she has not been destroyed. She cannot be destroyed so long as she can give.

The Financier • In *The Financier,* the first of the three volumes of the Cowperwood *Trilogy of Desire,* which also includes *The Titan* and *The Stoic,* perhaps more than in any other of his works, Dreiser relied on research for character, setting, plot, and theme. The characters are not drawn from memories of his family or his beloved Chicago, at least not exclusively nor primarily; the themes are most clearly the result of Dreiser's enormous reading.

"Genus Financierus Americanus," or the great financial wizards of turn-of-the-century America, fascinated Dreiser, and in their world of amorality, power, money, and materialism, he saw the mechanism that led America. Frank Cowperwood is a fictional representation of Charles T. Yerkes, a relatively obscure name but one of the movers in American finance. Dreiser encountered Yerkes in Chicago and New York and watched his machinations from a reporter's and an editor's vantage. Yerkes was no worse or better than the Rockefellers or Goulds, but by the time Dreiser started the trilogy, Yerkes was dead and his career could be studied in its totality. In addition, Yerkes's career was extensively documented in newspaper accounts, a fact that facilitated Dreiser's research, and that career had the advantage of a wife and a mistress and the final breaking up of Yerkes's empire by his creditors—all of which fit nicely into Dreiser's plan. The failure by one of the "titans of industry" to leave an indelible mark on humanity or on his immediate surroundings is the key to Dreiser's "equation inevitable," a concept first clearly worked out in *The Financier.*

Dreiser's readings of Arthur Schopenhauer, Friedrich Nietzsche, Karl Marx, Herbert Spencer, Jacques Loeb, and others confirmed his idea that the strong are meant to fulfill their course, to alter the pattern of life, and to "be a Colossus and bestride the world." At the same time, other strong individuals or groups (the "masses" were a real but troublesome entity for Dreiser) appear with equal strength but opposite intentions specifically intended by nature to maintain an equilibrium—a sort of cosmic check and balance. For Dreiser, "no thing is fixed, all tendencies are permitted, apparently. Only a balance is maintained." All people, significant and insignificant, are tools of nature and all are, in some way, a part of the equation. From Cowperwood's youth, the equation is seen in action. His victory in a boyhood fight confirms his trust in strength and resolution (or the first lick), and the now-famous lobster/squid narrative clarifies his understanding of the operation of nature. If the squid is prey for the lobster and the lobster prey for man, then man must also be prey, but only to man. These early insights are borne out in Cowperwood's Philadelphia life.

Cowperwood's early successes and his dealings with Colonel Butler are built on his philosophy of prey, but they are also founded on his realization that form and substance are separate. In order to succeed, one must maintain the semblance of propriety while carrying on normal business, which is ruthless and unfeeling. When he is jailed, he does not consider it a defeat, only a setback. Cowperwood is basically a pragmatist who does what is necessary to please himself. Besides this pragmatic nature, however, Cowperwood has another side that seems anomalous in his quest for power.

The other side of Cowperwood is epitomized by his simultaneous lust for and pride in his women and his art collection. Often styled by his quest for the beautiful, Cowperwood's desire for women and art, no matter which woman or which masterpiece, is still a facet of his acquisitive nature, but it is a facet that reflects the hidden recesses of his spirit. Inside the ruthless, conniving, buccaneering entrepreneur is a man seeking to outdo even nature by acquiring or controlling the best of her handiwork, but there is also a closely guarded, solidly confined sensibility. This artistic sensibility is confined because it is the antithesis of strength and power and because Cowperwood understands that if he yields to it, he will no longer be in control of his life, his fortune, and his world.

Morality has no relevance in Cowperwood's understanding of the equation. He and his desires are all that exist. His desires are completely carnal in relationships with women. Even with Aileen, who understands him best, there is only lust, never love, because love is a part of that hidden Cowperwood, which he knows he must suppress. The implication is that if he ever loved, Cowperwood would no longer be the financier, but would become simply human.

Aside from the development of the equation and its workings in Cowperwood's world, *The Financier* is a faintly realized novel when set against *Sister Carrie* or *An American Tragedy*. Cowperwood's motto, "I satisfy myself," is the prevailing motto and his failure to satisfy himself, his wife, his competitors, and anyone or anything, provides the answer to the motto's arrogance.

An American Tragedy • *An American Tragedy* is Dreiser's acknowledged masterpiece; of all his novels, it most successfully blends autobiography with the fruits of his painstaking research. In the work, Dreiser was interested in exposing the flaws in the seamless fabric of the American Dream. He had seen the destructive nature of the untempered drive for success and he understood that such a drive was an unavoidable result of the social temperament of the times. He also understood that the victims of that destructive urge were those who strove, not fully understanding why they struggled nor why they failed. Thus, his criticism is aimed at both those who struggle for an unattainable dream and at the society that urges them on and laughs when they fall. His research led Dreiser to the case of Chester Gillette and the narrative skeleton for *An American Tragedy*.

The events leading to Gillette's murder of Grace Brown in 1906 and the circumstances of his early life were amply documented in the sensational, yellow-press coverage of the Gillette trial, and they provide a circumstantial sketch of the events of Clyde Griffiths's life and times. Gillette and Griffiths also bear the marks of a common background with Dreiser. The poverty-stricken youth, the desire for success and material things, the sexual frustrations, and the attraction to beautiful, well-placed women are all parts of Dreiser's youth and young manhood. If one adds Dreiser's later unhappy marriage, his philandering, and his tense relationship with Helen Richardson, one has all the pieces that produced Dreiser's empathy for and attraction to Chester Gillette and, ultimately, Clyde Griffiths. Thus, in addition to the dramatic possibilities of the Gillette case, Dreiser felt a kinship with his protagonist that allowed him to portray him as a pitiable, arresting, trapped creature.

Clyde Griffiths, in Dreiser's vision, is trapped by forces over which he has little or no control. The "chemisms" of Clyde's life trap him: He no more has control over his desires for success, sex, and material goods than he has over the voice that urges him during the accident/murder that kills Roberta. In short, Clyde has no control over the irresistible American Dream. Writing of the Gillette case, Dreiser observes that Chester Gillette, if he had not committed murder, "was really doing the kind of thing that Americans should and would have said was the wise and moral thing to do" by trying to better his social standing through a good marriage. Gillette did, however, commit murder; Clyde Griffiths, on the other hand, intends to commit murder but loses his nerve in the boat with Roberta. When she falls into the water after he accidentally hits her with the camera, she drowns only because of Clyde's inaction. Faced with the decision to save her or not, Clyde cannot or will not make the decision, and his inaction damns him. The evidence against him is circumstantial at best and objective examination allows doubt as to his guilt. That doubt intensifies Clyde's entrapment. It is a trap of his own making, but the reader is never sure if he deserves his fate.

In the trial scenes and the events surrounding the trial, Dreiser shows all the external forces that work against Clyde to seal that fate. Political pressures on the defense attorneys and the prosecutors, the prejudice of the rural jury impaneled to try Clyde, the haste with which his wealthy cousins disavow him in order to save their social standing, and Clyde's own ineptitude as a liar form a second box around him, enclosing the first box of his own desires and failures.

Clyde's almost inevitable conviction and death sentence place him in the final box—his prison cell. This final enclosure is the ultimate circumstance over which Clyde has no control. There is no exit after the governor is convinced of Clyde's guilt by Clyde's mother and his clergyman. When Clyde is finally executed, his inexorable fall is complete.

Clyde's doom is sealed in his tawdry youth, first as a member of an itinerant evangelist's family, later in his work at the Green-Davidson, and ultimately in his fatal liaison with his wealthy Lycurgus cousins. He is not clever enough to help himself, is not wealthy enough to pay anyone to help him (especially during Roberta's pregnancy), and his "chemisms" drive him on in spite of his limitations. When he has his goal of wealth and success in sight, the only obstacle in his path, the pregnant Roberta, must be discarded at any cost without a thought of the consequences. His dreams are the driving force and those dreams are the product of forces over which he has not a shred of control. When he attempts to force his dreams to fruition, he further commits himself into the hands of those forces, and they lead him to his death.

Clyde lacks Carrie's inherent sense for survival and success, Jennie's selflessness and resilience, and Cowperwood's intelligence and wealth, but for all of that, he is a reflection of all of them and of the society in which they function. Clyde commits the crime and is punished, but Dreiser indicts all of society in Clyde's execution. Clyde's death sounds the knell for the romance of success and heralds the vacuum that takes its place. Clyde is not strong and falls; Cowperwood is strong and falls anyway. Carrie finds there is no fulfillment in success and feels the emptiness of her discovery; Jennie is beaten down again and again until she finds that she is living in a void that cannot be filled even with her abundant love. Thus, Clyde is not only the natural product of all these characters and of Dreiser's development but is also the symbol of Dreiser's worldview: a relentless vision which permanently altered American literature.

Clarence O. Johnson

Other major works

SHORT FICTION: *Free, and Other Stories,* 1918; *Chains: Lesser Novels and Stories,* 1927; *Fine Furniture,* 1930; *The Best Stories of Theodore Dreiser,* 1947 (Howard Fast, editor); *Best Short Stories,* 1956 (James T. Farrell, editor).

PLAYS: *Plays of the Natural and Supernatural,* pb. 1916; *The Girl in the Coffin,* pr. 1917; *The Hand of the Potter: A Tragedy in Four Acts,* pb. 1919; *The Collected Plays of Theodore Dreiser,* pb. 2000.

POETRY: *Moods: Cadenced and Declaimed,* 1926, 1928; *Epitaph: A Poem,* 1929; *The Aspirant,* 1929.

NONFICTION: *A Traveler at Forty,* 1913; *A Hoosier Holiday,* 1916; *Twelve Men,* 1919; *Hey, Rub-a-Dub-Dub!,* 1920; *A Book About Myself,* 1922 (revised as *Newspaper Days,* 1931); *The Color of a Great City,* 1923; *Dreiser Looks at Russia,* 1928; *My City,* 1929; *Dawn,* 1931 (autobiography); *Tragic America,* 1931; *America Is Worth Saving,* 1941; *Letters of Theodore Dreiser,* 1959; *Letters to Louise,* 1959; *Notes on Life,* 1974 (Marguerite Tjader and John J. McAleer, editors); *American Diaries, 1902-1926,* 1982; *An Amateur Laborer,* 1983; *Selected Magazine Articles of Theodore Dreiser,* 1985; *Dreiser's Russian Diary,* 1996 (Thomas P. Riggio and James L. W. West, editors); *Theodore Dreiser's Ev'ry Month,* 1996 (magazine articles; Nancy Warner Barrineau, editor); *Art, Music, and Literature, 1897-1902,* 2001 (Yoshinobu Hakutani, editor); *Theodore Dreiser's Uncollected Magazine Articles, 1897-1902,* 2003 (Hakutani, editor).

Bibliography

Cassuto, Leonard, and Clare Virginia Eby, eds. *The Cambridge Companion to Theodore Dreiser.* New York: Cambridge University Press, 2004. A collection of twelve essays discusses the novelist's examination of (then) new American conflicts between materialistic longings and traditional values.

Gerber, Philip. *Theodore Dreiser Revisited.* New York: Twayne, 1992. Includes chapters on all Dreiser's major works, three chapters on the development of Dreiser studies, a chronology, notes and references, and an annotated bibliography.

Gogol, Miriam, ed. *Theodore Dreiser: Beyond Naturalism.* New York: New York University Press, 1995. Divided into sections on gender studies, psychoanalysis, philosophy, film studies, and popular literature. Gogol's introduction advances the argument that Dreiser was much more than a naturalist and deserves to be treated as a major author.

Lingeman, Richard. *At the Gates of the City, 1871-1907.* Vol. 1 in *Theodore Dreiser.* New York: Putnam, 1986. First part of two-volume biography of Dreiser.

____________. *An American Journey, 1908-1945.* Vol. 2 in *Theodore Dreiser.* New York: Putnam, 1990. One of the most ambitious and thorough biographies of Dreiser yet published.

Loving, Jerome. *The Last Titan: A Life of Theodore Dreiser.* Berkeley: University of California Press, 2005. Written by a distinguished biographer, this engrossing survey of the author's life and work is a welcome addition to Dreiser scholarship.

Lydon, Michael. "Justice to Theodore Dreiser." *The Atlantic* 272 (August, 1993): 98-101. Argues that Dreiser should be seen without reservation as a giant of American letters who stood at the vanguard of modernism; argues that the incongruities and eccentricities of Dreiser's life have always affected the critical reception of his writing.

McAleer, John J. *Theodore Dreiser: An Introduction and Interpretation.* New York: Barnes & Noble Books, 1968. This volume studies the artist with the aim of helping the reader grasp the whole of Dreiser's fiction. Includes a lengthy chronology and a bibliography.

Pizer, Donald. *The Novels of Theodore Dreiser: A Critical Study.* Minneapolis: University of Minnesota Press, 1976. A solid study and introduction to Dreiser's eight published novels. Pizer examines each work as a separate unit and points out their respective merits and flaws.

____________, comp. *Critical Essays on Theodore Dreiser.* Boston: G. K. Hall, 1981. An excellent compilation of articles and essays. The criticism is arranged around Dreiser's works and ideas in general. A second section is reserved for individual novels.

Riggio, Thomas P. "Following Dreiser, Seventy Years Later." *The American Scholar* 65 (Autumn, 1996): 569-577. A biographical sketch that focuses on Dreiser as the most famous American to be invited to Moscow for the tenth anniversary of the Russian Revolution in 1927; describes a visit to Russia to research an edition of a diary kept by Dreiser during the late 1920's during his three months' stay in the Soviet Union.

Zayani, Mohamed. *Reading the Symptom: Frank Norris, Theodore Dreiser, and the Dynamics of Capitalism.* New York: Peter Lang, 1999. Examines the theme of capitalism in *Sister Carrie.*

Ralph Ellison

Born: Oklahoma City, Oklahoma; March 1, 1914
Died: New York, New York; April 16, 1994

Principal long fiction • *Invisible Man,* 1952; *Juneteenth,* 1999 (John F. Callahan, editor).

Other literary forms • Ralph Ellison's reputation rests primarily on *Invisible Man,* but *Shadow and Act* (1964), a collection of nonfiction prose, established him as a major force in the critical theory of pluralism and in African American aesthetics. Arranged in three thematically unified sections, the essays, most of which appeared originally in journals such as *Antioch Review, Partisan Review,* and *The New Republic,* emphasize the importance of folk and popular (especially musical) contributions to the mainstream of American culture. Several of the essays from *Shadow and Act* are recognized as classics, notably "Richard Wright's Blues," "Change the Joke and Slip the Yoke," and "The World and the Jug." In addition, Ellison published several excellent short stories, including "Flying Home" and "Did You Ever Dream Lucky?" A collection of essays, *Going to the Territory,* was published in 1986.

Achievements • Ellison occupied a central position in the development of African American literature and of contemporary American fiction. Equally comfortable with the influences of Fyodor Dostoevski, Mark Twain, Louis Armstrong, Igor Stravinsky, James Joyce, and Richard Wright, Ellison was the first African American writer to attain recognition as a full-fledged artist rather than as an intriguing exotic. Whereas Caucasian critics had previously, and unjustly, condescended to African American writers such as Langston Hughes, Zora Neale Hurston, and Richard Wright, most granted Ellison the respect given Euro-American contemporaries such as Norman Mailer and Saul Bellow. A 1965 *Book World* poll identifying *Invisible Man* as the most distinguished postwar American novel simply verified a consensus already reflected in the recurrence of the metaphor of invisibility in countless works by both Caucasians and African Americans during the 1950's and 1960's.

Within the African American tradition itself, Ellison occupies a similarly prominent position, although his mainstream acceptance generates occasional reservations among some African American critics, particularly those committed to cultural nationalism. A *Black World* poll, reflecting these reservations, identified Wright rather than Ellison as the most important black writer. The discrepancy stems in part from the critical image during the late 1960's of Ellison and James Baldwin as leading figures in an anti-Wright "universalist" movement in African American culture, a movement that some critics viewed as a sellout to Euro-American aesthetics. In the late twentieth century, however, both Euro-American and African American critics recognized Ellison's synthesis of the oral traditions of black culture and the literary traditions of both his black and his white predecessors. The consensus of that time viewed Ellison as clearly more sympathetic than Wright to the African American tradition. As a result, Ellison seems to have joined Wright as a major influence on younger black fiction writers such as James Alan McPherson, Leon Forrest,

Toni Morrison, and David Bradley.

Ellison's most profound achievement, his synthesis of modernist aesthetics, American Romanticism, and African American folk culture, embodies the aspirations of democratic pluralists such as Walt Whitman, Mark Twain, and Langston Hughes. His vernacular modernism earned Ellison an international reputation while exerting a major influence on the contemporary mainstream. With a reputation resting almost entirely on his first novel, Ellison's career is among the most intriguing in American literary history.

National Archives

Biography • Despite Ralph Ellison's steadfast denial of the autobiographical elements of *Invisible Man* and his insistence on the autonomy of the individual imagination, both the specific details and the general sensibility of his work clearly derive from his experience of growing up in a southern family in Oklahoma City, attending college in Alabama, and residing in New York City during most of his adult life. Ellison's parents, whose decision to name their son after Ralph Waldo Emerson reflects their commitment to literacy and education, moved from South Carolina to the comparatively progressive Oklahoma capital several years before their son's birth. Reflecting on his childhood, which was characterized by economic hardship following his father's death in 1917, Ellison emphasizes the unusual psychological freedom provided by a social structure that allowed him to interact relatively freely with both white and black people. Encouraged by his mother Ida, who was active in socialist politics, Ellison developed a frontier sense of a world of limitless possibility rather than the more typically southern vision of an environment filled with dangerous oppressive forces.

During his teenage years, Ellison developed a serious interest in music, both as a trumpet player and as a composer-conductor. Oklahoma City offered access both to formal classical training and to jazz, which was a major element of the city's nightlife. The combination of Euro-American and African American influences appears to have played a major role in shaping Ellison's pluralistic sensibility. After he graduated from high school in 1933, Ellison accepted a scholarship to the Tuskegee Institute, founded by Booker T. Washington, where he remained for three years, studying music and literature, until financial problems forced him to drop out. Although he originally planned to finish his studies, his subsequent relocation to New York City marked a permanent departure from the South.

Arriving in the North in 1936, Ellison established contacts with African American literary figures, including Hughes and Wright, who encouraged him to develop his knowledge of both the African American literary world and Euro-American modernism, especially that of T. S. Eliot and James Joyce. Never as deeply involved with leftist politics as Wright, Ellison nevertheless began developing his literary ideas in reviews and stories published in radical magazines such as *New Masses*. In 1938, Ellison, who had previously supported himself largely as a manual laborer, worked for the Federal Writers' Project, which assigned him to collect urban folklore, providing direct contact with northern folk culture to complement his previous knowledge of southern folkways. Ellison's short fiction began appearing in print during the late 1930's and early 1940's. After a short term as managing editor of *Negro Quarterly* in 1942, he briefly left New York, serving in the merchant marine from 1943 to 1945. Awarded a Rosenwald Fellowship to write a novel, Ellison returned to New York and married Fanny McConnell in 1946.

Invisible Man, which took Ellison nearly seven years to write, was published in 1952, bringing him nearly instantaneous recognition as a major young writer. The novel won the National Book Award in 1953, and its reputation has continued to grow. Starting in 1952, Ellison taught at Bard College, Rutgers University, New York University, and other institutions. In addition, he delivered public lectures, wrote essays, and worked on a second novel. Less inclined to direct political involvement than contemporaries such as Amiri Baraka and James Baldwin, Ellison participated in the Civil Rights movement in a relatively quiet manner. He nevertheless attracted political controversy during the rise of the African American nationalist movements in the mid-1960's. Refusing to endorse any form of cultural or political separatism, Ellison was attacked as an aesthetic European and a political reactionary, especially after accepting appointments to the American Institute of Arts and Letters (1964) and to the National Council on the Arts and Humanities, acts that were interpreted as support for the Johnson administration's Vietnam War policy. During the mid-1970's, however, these attacks abated as nationalist critics such as Larry Neal rose to Ellison's defense and a new generation of African American writers turned to him for aesthetic inspiration. Retired from full-time teaching, during the 1980's Ellison continued to work on his second novel, *Juneteenth*, which was delayed both by his own perfectionism and by events such as a house fire that destroyed much of the manuscript during the 1960's. The novel was incomplete at the time of his death on April 16, 1994, in New York.

Analysis • A masterwork of American pluralism, Ellison's *Invisible Man* insists on the integrity of individual vocabulary and racial heritage while encouraging a radically democratic acceptance of diverse experiences. Ellison asserts this vision through the voice of an unnamed first-person narrator who is at once heir to the rich African American oral culture and a self-conscious artist who, like T. S. Eliot and James Joyce, exploits the full potential of his written medium. Intimating the potential cooperation between folk and artistic consciousness, Ellison confronts the pressures that discourage both individual integrity and cultural pluralism.

Invisible Man • The narrator of *Invisible Man* introduces Ellison's central metaphor for the situation of the individual in Western culture in the first paragraph: "I am invisible, understand, simply because people refuse to see me." As the novel develops, Ellison extends this metaphor: Just as people can be rendered invisible by the willful failure of others to acknowledge their presence, so by taking refuge in the seductive but ultimately specious security of socially acceptable roles they can fail to see *themselves*, fail to define their own identities. Ellison envisions the escape from this dilemma as a multifaceted quest demanding heightened social, psychological, and cultural awareness.

The style of *Invisible Man* reflects both the complexity of the problem and Ellison's pluralistic ideal. Drawing on sources such as the blindness motif from *King Lear* (1605), the underground man motif from Fyodor Dostoevski, and the complex stereotyping of Richard Wright's *Native Son* (1940), Ellison carefully balances the realistic and the symbolic dimensions of *Invisible Man.* In many ways a classic *Künstlerroman,* the main body of the novel traces the protagonist from his childhood in the deep South through a brief stay at college and then to the North, where he confronts the American economic, political, and racial systems. This movement parallels what Robert B. Stepto in *From Behind the Veil* (1979) calls the "narrative of ascent," a constituting pattern of African American culture. With roots in the fugitive slave narratives of the nineteenth century, the narrative of ascent follows its protagonist from physical or psychological bondage in the South through a sequence of symbolic confrontations with social structures to a limited freedom, usually in the North.

This freedom demands from the protagonist a "literacy" that enables him or her to create and understand both written and social experiences in the terms of the dominant Euro-American culture. Merging the narrative of ascent with the *Künstlerroman,* which also culminates with the hero's mastery of literacy (seen in creative terms), *Invisible Man* focuses on writing as an act of both personal and cultural significance. Similarly, Ellison employs what Stepto calls the "narrative of immersion" to stress the realistic sources and implications of his hero's imaginative development. The narrative of immersion returns the "literate" hero or heroine to an understanding of the culture he or she symbolically left behind during the ascent. Incorporating this pattern in *Invisible Man,* Ellison emphasizes the protagonist's links with the African American community and the rich folk traditions that provide him with much of his sensibility and establish his potential as a conscious artist.

The overall structure of *Invisible Man,* however, involves cyclical as well as directional patterns. Framing the main body with a prologue and epilogue set in an underground burrow, Ellison emphasizes the novel's symbolic dimension. Safely removed from direct participation in his social environment, the invisible man reassesses the literacy gained through his ascent, ponders his immersion in the cultural art forms of spirituals, blues, and jazz, and finally attempts to forge a pluralistic vision transforming these constitutive elements. The prologue and epilogue also evoke the heroic patterns and archetypal cycles described by Joseph Campbell in *Hero with a Thousand Faces* (1949). After undergoing tests of his spiritual and physical qualities, the hero of Campbell's "monomyth"—usually a person of mysterious birth who receives aid from a cryptic helper—gains a reward, usually of a symbolic nature involving the union of opposites. Overcoming forces that would seize the reward, the hero returns to transform the life of the community through application of the knowledge connected with the symbolic reward. To some degree, the narratives of ascent and immersion recast this heroic cycle in specifically African American terms: The protagonist first leaves, then returns to his or her community bearing a knowledge of Euro-American society potentially capable of motivating a group ascent. Although it emphasizes the cyclic nature of the protagonist's quest, the frame of *Invisible Man* simultaneously subverts the heroic pattern by removing him from his community. The protagonist promises a return, but the implications of the return for the life of the community remain ambiguous.

This ambiguity superficially connects Ellison's novel with the classic American romance that Richard Chase characterizes in *The American Novel and Its Tradition* (1975) as incapable of reconciling symbolic perceptions with social realities. The connection, however, reflects Ellison's awareness of the problem more than his acceptance of the irresolution. Although the invisible man's underground burrow recalls the isolation of the heroes of the American romance, he promises a rebirth that is at once mythic, psychological, and social:

> The hibernation is over. I must shake off my old skin and come up for breath. . . . And I suppose it's damn well time. Even hibernations can be overdone, come to think of it. Perhaps that's my greatest social crime, I've overstayed my hibernation, since there's a possibility that even an invisible man has a socially responsible role to play.

Despite the qualifications typical of Ellison's style, the invisible man clearly intends to return to the social world rather than light out for the territories of symbolic freedom.

The invisible man's ultimate conception of the form of this return develops out of two interrelated progressions, one social and the other psychological. The social pattern, essentially that of the narrative of ascent, closely reflects the historical experience of the African American community as it shifts from rural southern to urban northern settings. Starting in the deep South, the invisible man first experiences invisibility as a result of casual but vicious racial oppression. His unwilling participation in the "battle royal" underscores the psychological and physical humiliation visited upon black southerners. Ostensibly present to deliver a speech to a white community group, the invisible man is instead forced to engage in a massive free-for-all with other African Americans, to scramble for money on an electrified rug, and to confront a naked white dancer who, like the boys, has been rendered invisible by the white men's blindness. Escaping his hometown to attend a black college, the invisible man again experiences humiliation when he violates the unstated rules of the southern system—this time imposed by black people, rather than white people—by showing the college's liberal northern benefactor, Mr. Norton, the poverty of the black community. As a result, the black college president, Dr. Bledsoe, expels the invisible man. Having experienced invisibility in relation to both black and white people and still essentially illiterate in social terms, the invisible man travels north, following the countless black southerners involved in the "Great Migration."

Arriving in New York, the invisible man first feels a sense of exhilaration resulting from the absence of overt southern pressures. Ellison reveals the emptiness of this freedom, however, stressing the indirect and insidious nature of social power in the North. The invisible man's experience at Liberty Paints, clearly intended as a parable of African American involvement in the American economic system, emphasizes the underlying similarity of northern and southern social structures. On arrival at Liberty Paints, the invisible man is assigned to mix a white paint used for government monuments. Labeled "optic white," the grayish paint turns white only when the invisible man adds a drop of black liquid. The scene suggests the relationship between government and industry, which relies on black labor. More important, however, it points to the underlying source of racial blindness/invisibility: the white need for a black "other" to support a sense of identity. White becomes white only when compared to black.

The symbolic indirection of the scene encourages the reader, like the invisible man, to realize that social oppression in the North operates less directly than that in the South; government buildings replace rednecks at the battle royal. Unable to mix the paint properly, a desirable "failure" intimating his future as a subversive artist, the invisible man discovers that the underlying structure of the economic system differs little from that of slavery. The invisible man's second job at Liberty Paints is to assist Lucius Brockway, an old man who supervises the operations of the basement machinery on which the factory depends. Essentially a slave to the modern owner/master Mr. Sparland, Brockway, like the good "darkies" of the Plantation Tradition, takes pride in his master and will fight to maintain his own servitude. Brockway's hatred of the invisible man, whom he perceives as a threat to his position, leads to a physical struggle culminating in an explosion caused by neglect of the machinery. Ellison's multifaceted allegory suggests a vicious circle in which black people uphold an economic system that supports the political system that keeps black people fighting to protect their neoslavery. The forms alter but the battle royal continues. The image of the final explosion from the basement warns against passive acceptance of the social structure that sows the seeds of its own destruction.

Although the implications of this allegory in some ways parallel the Marxist analysis of capitalist culture, Ellison creates a much more complex political vision when the invisible man moves to Harlem following his release from the hospital after the explosion. The political alternatives available in Harlem range from the Marxism of the "Brotherhood" (loosely based on the American Communist Party of the late 1930's) to the black nationalism of Ras the Exhorter (loosely based on Marcus Garvey's pan-Africanist movement of the 1920's). The Brotherhood promises complete equality for black people and at first encourages the invisible man to develop the oratorical talent ridiculed at the battle royal. As his effectiveness increases, however, the invisible man finds the Brotherhood demanding that his speeches conform to its "scientific analysis" of the black community's needs. When he fails to fall in line, the leadership of the Brotherhood orders the invisible man to leave Harlem and turn his attention to the "woman question." Without the invisible man's ability to place radical politics in the emotional context of African American culture, the Brotherhood's Harlem branch flounders. Recalled to Harlem, the invisible man witnesses the death of Tod Clifton, a talented coworker driven to despair by his perception that the Brotherhood amounts to little more than a new version of the power structure underlying both Liberty Paints and the battle royal. Clearly a double for the invisible man, Clifton leaves the organization and dies in a suicidal confrontation with a white policeman. Just before Clifton's death, the invisible man sees him selling Sambo dolls, a symbolic comment on the fact that black people involved in leftist politics in some sense remain stereotyped slaves dancing at the demand of unseen masters.

Separating himself from the Brotherhood after delivering an extremely unscientific funeral sermon, the invisible man finds few political options. Ras's black nationalism exploits the emotions the Brotherhood denies. Ultimately, however, Ras demands that his followers submit to an analogous oversimplification of their human reality. Where the Brotherhood elevates the scientific and rational, Ras focuses entirely on the emotional commitment to blackness. Neither alternative recognizes the complexity of either the political situation or the individual psyche; both reinforce the invisible man's feelings of invisibility by refusing to see basic aspects of his character. As he did in the Liberty Paints scene, Ellison emphasizes the destructive, perhaps apocalyptic, potential of this encompassing blindness. A riot breaks out in Harlem, and the invisible man watches as DuPree, an apolitical Harlem resident recalling a number of African American folk heroes, determines to burn down his own tenement, preferring to start again from scratch rather than even attempt to work for social change within the existing framework. Unable to accept the realistic implications of such an action apart from its symbolic justification, the invisible man, pursued by Ras, who seems intent on destroying the very blackness he praises, tumbles into the underground burrow. Separated from the social structures, which have changed their facade but not their nature, the invisible man begins the arduous process of reconstructing his vision of America while symbolically subverting the social system by stealing electricity to light the 1,369 light bulbs on the walls of the burrow and to power the record players blasting out the pluralistic jazz of Louis Armstrong.

As his frequent allusions to Armstrong indicate, Ellison by no means excludes the positive aspects from his portrayal of the African American social experience. The invisible man reacts strongly to the spirituals he hears at college, the blues story of Trueblood, the singing of Mary Rambro after she takes him in off the streets of Harlem. Similarly, he recognizes the strength wrested from resistance and suffering, a strength asserted by the broken link of chain saved by Brother Tarp.

These figures, however, have relatively little power to alter the encompassing social system. They assume their full significance in relation to the second major progression in *Invisible Man*, that focusing on the narrator's psychological development. As he gradually gains an understanding of the social forces that oppress him, the invisible man simultaneously discovers the complexity of his own personality. Throughout the central narrative, he accepts various definitions of himself, mostly from external sources. Ultimately, however, all definitions that demand he repress or deny aspects of himself simply reinforce his sense of invisibility. Only by abandoning limiting definitions altogether, Ellison implies, can the invisible man attain the psychological integrity necessary for any effective social action.

Ellison emphasizes the insufficiency of limiting definitions in the prologue when the invisible man has a dream-vision while listening to an Armstrong record. After descending through four symbolically rich levels of the dream, the invisible man hears a sermon on the "Blackness of Blackness," which recasts the "Whiteness of the Whale" chapter from Herman Melville's *Moby Dick* (1851). The sermon begins with a cascade of apparent contradictions, forcing the invisible man to question his comfortable assumptions concerning the nature of freedom, hatred, and love. No simple resolution emerges from the sermon, other than an insistence on the essentially ambiguous nature of experience. The dream-vision culminates in the protagonist's confrontation with the mulatto sons of an old black woman torn between love and hatred for their father. Although their own heritage merges the "opposites" of white and black, the sons act in accord with social definitions and repudiate their white father, an act that unconsciously but unavoidably repudiates a large part of themselves. The hostile sons, the confused old woman, and the preacher who delivers the sermon embody aspects of the narrator's own complexity. When one of the sons tells the invisible man to stop asking his mother disturbing questions, his words sound a leitmotif for the novel: "Next time you got questions like that ask yourself."

Before he can ask, or even locate, himself, however, the invisible man must directly experience the problems generated by a fragmented sense of self and a reliance on others. Frequently, he accepts external definitions, internalizing the fragmentation dominating his social context. For example, he accepts a letter of introduction from Bledsoe on the assumption that it testifies to his ability. Instead, it creates an image of him as a slightly dangerous rebel. By delivering the letter to potential employers, the invisible man participates directly in his own oppression. Similarly, he accepts a new name from the Brotherhood, again revealing his willingness to simplify himself in an attempt to gain social acceptance from the educational, economic, and political systems. As long as he accepts external definitions, the invisible man lacks the essential element of literacy: an understanding of the relationship between context and self.

Ellison's reluctance to reject the external definitions and attain literacy reflects both a tendency to see social experience as more "real" than psychological experience and a fear that the abandonment of definitions will lead to total chaos. The invisible man's meeting with Trueblood, a sharecropper and blues singer who has fathered a child by his own daughter, highlights this fear. Watching Mr. Norton's fascination with Trueblood, the invisible man perceives that even the dominant members of the Euro-American society feel stifled by the restrictions of "respectability." Ellison refuses to abandon all social codes, portraying Trueblood in part as a hustler whose behavior reinforces white stereotypes concerning black immorality. If Trueblood's acceptance of his situation (and of his human complexity) seems in part heroic, it is a heroism grounded in victimization. Nevertheless, the invisible man eventually experiments with repudiation of all strict definitions when, after his disillusionment with the Brotherhood, he adopts the identity of Rinehart, a protean street figure who combines the roles of pimp and preacher, shifting identities with context. After a brief period of exhilaration, the invisible man discovers that "Rinehart's" very fluidity guarantees that he will remain locked within social definitions. Far from increasing his freedom at any moment, his multiplicity forces him to act in whatever role his "audience" casts him. Ellison stresses the serious consequences of this lack of center when the invisible man nearly becomes involved in a knife fight with Brother Maceo, a friend who sees only the Rinehartian exterior. The persona of "Rinehart," then, helps increase the invisible man's sense of possibility, but lacks the internal coherence necessary for psychological, and perhaps even physical, survival.

Ellison rejects both acceptance of external definitions and abandonment of all definitions as workable means of attaining literacy. Ultimately, he endorses the full recognition and measured acceptance of the experience, historical and personal, that shapes the individual. In addition, he recommends the careful use of masks as a survival strategy in the social world. The crucial problem with this approach, derived in large part from African American folk culture, involves the difficulty of maintaining the distinction between external mask and internal identity. As Bledsoe demonstrates, a protective mask threatens to implicate the wearer in the very system he or she attempts to manipulate.

Before confronting these intricacies, however, the invisible man must accept his African American heritage, the primary imperative of the narrative of immersion. Initially, he attempts to repudiate or to distance himself from the aspects of the heritage associated with stereotyped roles. He shatters and attempts to throw away the "darky bank" he finds in his room at Mary Rambro's. His failure to lose the pieces of the bank reflects Ellison's conviction that the stereotypes, major aspects of the African American social experience, cannot simply be ignored or forgotten. As an element shaping individual consciousness, they must be incorporated into, without being allowed to dominate, the integrated individual identity. Symbolically, in a scene in which the invisible man meets a yam vendor shortly after his arrival in Harlem, Ellison warns that one's racial heritage alone cannot provide a full sense of identity. After first recoiling from yams as a stereotypic southern food, the invisible man eats one, sparking a momentary epiphany of racial pride. When he indulges the feelings and buys another yam, however, he finds it frost-bitten at the center.

The invisible man's heritage, placed in proper perspective, provides the crucial hints concerning social literacy and psychological identity that allow him to come provisionally to terms with his environment. Speaking on his deathbed, the invisible man's grandfather offers cryptic advice that lies near the essence of Ellison's overall vision: "Live with your head in the lion's mouth. I want you to overcome 'em with yeses, undermine 'em with grins, agree 'em to death and destruction, let 'em swoller you till they vomit or bust wide open." Similarly, an ostensibly insane veteran echoes the grandfather's advice, adding an explicit endorsement of the Machiavellian potential of masking:

> Play the game, but don't believe in it—that much you owe yourself. Even if it lands you in a straitjacket or a padded cell. Play the game, but play it your own way—part of the time at least. Play the game, but raise the ante, my boy. Learn how it operates, learn how *you* operate. . . . that game has been analyzed, put down in books. But down here they've forgotten to take care of the books and that's your opportunity. You're hidden right out in the open—that is, you would be if you only realized it. They wouldn't see you because they don't expect you to know anything.

The vet understands the "game" of Euro-American culture, while the grandfather directly expresses the internally focused wisdom of the African American community.

The invisible man's quest leads him to a synthesis of these forms of literacy in his ultimate pluralistic vision. Although he at first fails to comprehend the subversive potential of his position, the invisible man gradually learns the rules of the game and accepts the necessity of the indirect action recommended by his grandfather. Following his escape into the underground burrow, he contemplates his grandfather's advice from a position of increased experience and self-knowledge. Contemplating his own individual situation in relation to the surrounding society, he concludes that his grandfather "*must* have meant the principle, that we were to affirm the principle on which the country was built but not the men." Extending this affirmation to the psychological level, the invisible man embraces the internal complexity he has previously repressed or denied: "So it is that now I denounce and defend, or feel prepared to defend. I condemn and affirm, say no and say yes, say yes and say no. I denounce because though implicated and partially responsible, I have been hurt to the point of abysmal pain, hurt to the point of invisibility. And I defend because in spite of all I find that I love. In order to get some of it down I *have* to love."

"Getting some of it down," then, emerges as the crucial link between Ellison's social and psychological visions. In order to play a socially responsible role—and to transform the words "social responsibility" from the segregationist catch phrase used by the man at the battle royal into a term responding to Louis Armstrong's artistic call for change—the invisible man forges from his complex experience a pluralistic art that subverts the social lion by taking its principles seriously. The artist becomes a revolutionary wearing a mask. Ellison's revolution seeks to realize a pluralist ideal, a true democracy recognizing the complex experience and human potential of every individual. Far from presenting his protagonist as a member of an intrinsically superior cultural elite, Ellison underscores his shared humanity in the concluding line: "Who knows but that, on the lower frequencies, I speak for you?" Manipulating the aesthetic and social rules of the Euro-American "game," Ellison sticks his head in the lion's mouth, asserting a blackness of blackness fully as ambiguous, as individual, and as rich as the whiteness of Herman Melville's whale.

Juneteenth • Forty-seven years after the release of *Invisible Man*, Ellison's second novel was published. Ellison began working on *Juneteenth* in 1954, but his constant revisions delayed its publication. Although it was unfinished at the time of his death, only minor edits and revisions were necessary to publish the book.

Juneteenth is about a black minister, Hickman, who takes in and raises a little boy as black, even though the child looks white. The boy soon runs away to New England and later becomes a race-baiting senator. After he is shot on the Senate floor, he sends for Hickman. Their past is revealed through their ensuing conversation.

The title of the novel, appropriately, refers to a day of liberation for African Americans. Juneteenth historically represents June 19, 1865, the day Union forces announced emancipation of slaves in Texas; that state considers Juneteenth an official holiday. The title applies to the novel's themes of evasion and discovery of identity, which Ellison explored so masterfully in *Invisible Man*.

Craig Werner

Other major works

SHORT FICTION: *Flying Home, and Other Stories*, 1996.

NONFICTION: *Shadow and Act*, 1964; *The Writer's Experience*, 1964 (with Karl Shapiro); *Going to the Territory*, 1986; *Conversations with Ralph Ellison*, 1995 (Maryemma Graham and Amritjit Singh, editors); *The Collected Essays of Ralph Ellison*, 1995 (John F. Callahan, editor); *Trading Twelves: The Selected Letters of Ralph Ellison and Albert Murray*, 2000; *Living with Music: Ralph Ellison's Jazz Writings*, 2001 (Robert O'Meally, editor).

Bibliography

Applebome, Peter. "From Ellison, a Posthumous Novel, with Additions Still to Come." *The New York Times*, February 11, 1999. This article gives information on the origins of *Juneteenth*, both historical and personal to Ellison.

Benston, Kimberly, ed. *Speaking for You: The Vision of Ralph Ellison.* Washington, D.C.: Howard University Press, 1987. A useful resource of responses to Ellison's fiction and essays. Also includes an extensive bibliography of his writings.

Bloom, Harold, ed. *Modern Critical Views: Ralph Ellison.* New York: Chelsea House, 1986. Though this widely available collection of essays focuses mainly on *Invisible Man*, it provides insights from which any reader of Ralph Ellison may profit, and Berndt Ostendor's essay, "Anthropology, Modernism, and Jazz," offers much to the reader of "Flying Home."

Busby, Mark. *Ralph Ellison.* Boston: Twayne, 1991. An excellent introduction to Ellison's life and work.

De Santis, Christopher C. "'Some Cord of Kinship Stronger and Deeper than Blood': An Interview with John F. Callahan, Editor of Ralph Ellison's *Juneteenth*." *African American Review* 34, no. 4 (2000): 601-621. Revealing interview with the scholar who edited a collection of Ellison's essays and Ellison's unfinished novel for publication.

Jackson, Lawrence. *Ralph Ellison: Emergence of Genius.* New York: Wiley, 2001. The first book-length study of Ellison's life. A good background source for the novelist's early life and career. Jackson, however, ends his study in 1953, shortly after the publication of *Invisible Man.*

Nadel, Alan. *Invisible Criticism: Ralph Ellison and the American Canon.* Iowa City: University of Iowa Press, 1988. A look at Ellison's place in the study of American literature.

O'Meally, Robert G. *The Craft of Ralph Ellison.* Cambridge, Mass.: Harvard University Press, 1980. Traces Ellison's development as a writer and includes considerations of his fiction published after *Invisible Man.*

___________, ed. *New Essays on "Invisible Man."* New York: Cambridge University Press, 1988. A collection of essays that includes many responses to questions raised by earlier critics.

Porter, Horace A. *Jazz Country: Ralph Ellison in America.* Iowa City: University of Iowa Press, 2001. Study of Ellison in the larger context of American culture.

Schor, Edith. *Visible Ellison: A Study of Ralph Ellison's Fiction.* Westport, Conn.: Greenwood Press, 1993. Published a year before Ellison's death, this is an excellent full-length study of the fiction that was generally available at the time, including his short fiction, which had not yet been collected in book form. This is probably the best place for the serious scholar of Ralph Ellison to begin.

Warren, Kenneth W. *So Black and Blue: Ralph Ellison and the Occasion of Criticism.* Chicago: University of Chicago Press, 2003. Study of Ellison that attempts to balance its consideration of him as an author, critic, and intellectual.

Watts, Jerry Gafio. *Heroism and the Black Intellectual: Ralph Ellison, Politics, and Afro-American Intellectual Life.* Chapel Hill: University of North Carolina Press, 1994. Chapters explore critic Harold Cruse's influential interpretation of black intellectuals, the biographical background to *Invisible Man,* the relationship between the novel and black music, and the responsibilities of the black writer. Includes notes and a bibliography.

Louise Erdrich

Born: Little Falls, Minnesota; June 7, 1954

Principal long fiction • *Love Medicine*, 1984 (revised and expanded, 1993); *The Beet Queen*, 1986; *Tracks*, 1988; *The Crown of Columbus*, 1991 (with Michael Dorris); *The Bingo Palace*, 1994; *Tales of Burning Love*, 1996; *The Antelope Wife*, 1998; *The Last Report on the Miracles at Little No Horse*, 2001; *The Master Butchers Singing Club*, 2003; *Four Souls*, 2004; *The Painted Drum*, 2005.

Other literary forms • *Jacklight* (1984) and *Baptism of Desire* (1989) are books of poetry (along with a few folktales) which present vivid North Dakota vignettes, as well as personal reflections on Louise Erdrich's relationships to her husband and children. Her memoir of her daughter's birth, *The Blue Jay's Dance: A Birth Year*, was published in 1995.

Achievements • A poet and poetic novelist, Erdrich learned to draw on her Ojibwa (also known as Chippewa) and German-immigrant heritage to create a wide-ranging chronicle of American Indian and white experience in twentieth century North Dakota and Minnesota. She received fellowships from the MacDowell Colony in 1980 and from Dartmouth College and Yaddo Colony in 1981. Since she began to publish her fiction and poetry during the early 1980's, her works have garnered high critical praise, and her novels have been best-sellers as well. *Love Medicine*, Erdrich's first novel, won the National Book Critics Circle Award in 1984, and three of the stories gathered in that book were also honored: "The World's Greatest Fishermen" won the five-thousand-dollar first prize in the 1982 Nelson Algren fiction competition, "Scales" appeared in *Best American Short Stories, 1983* (1983), and "Saint Marie" was chosen for *Prize Stories 1985: The O. Henry Awards* (1985). Two of the stories included in the novel *Tracks* also appeared in honorary anthologies: "Fleur" in *Prize Stories 1987: The O. Henry Awards* (1987) and "Snares" in *Best American Short Stories, 1988* (1988). In addition, Erdrich was awarded a National Endowment for the Arts Fellowship in 1982, the Pushcart Prize in 1983, and a Guggenheim Fellowship in 1985-1986.

Erdrich's works often focus on the struggle of Native Americans for personal, familial, and cultural survival. However, her treatment of white and mixed-blood characters also reveals an empathic understanding of the ways in which people of all races long for closer connection with one another and the land.

Biography • Louise Erdrich, whose grandfather was tribal chair of the Turtle Mountain Band of the Ojibwa Nation, grew up in Wahpeton, a small town in southeastern North Dakota. Her father, Ralph Erdrich, is a German immigrant who taught in Wahpeton at the American Indian boarding school. Her mother, Rita Gourneau Erdrich, is a three-quarters Ojibwa who also worked at the school. Erdrich's mixed religious and cultural background provided a rich foundation for her later poetry and fiction.

Erdrich earned two degrees in creative writing, a bachelor's degree from Dart-

Michael Dorris

mouth College in 1976 and a master's degree from Johns Hopkins University in 1979. In 1981, she married Michael Dorris, a professor of anthropologyand head of the Native American studies program at Dartmouth. Erdrich and Dorris devoted much of their married life to ambitious family, literary, and humanitarian goals. Dorris, who was three-eighths Modoc Indian, had previously adopted three Lakota Sioux children; together Erdrich and Dorris had three daughters. Professionally, they collaborated on virtually all the works that either one published—whether fiction, poetry, or nonfiction. Thus, Erdrich has acknowledged Dorris's important contribution to her fiction; similarly, she collaborated with him on his first novel, *A Yellow Raft in Blue Water* (1987), and on his study of fetal alcohol syndrome (FAS), *The Broken Cord* (1989). Erdrich and Dorris donated money and campaigned for legislation to combat FAS, which afflicts the lives of many American Indian children born to alcoholic mothers.

However, their private lives became difficult. All of their adopted children were permanently affected by the alcoholism of their mothers and led troubled lives after adolescence. One son attempted to extort money from his parents, and their daughter became estranged. The oldest adopted child, Abel (renamed "Adam" in *The Broken Cord*), was struck by a car and killed in 1991, an event that deeply affected the marriage.

Erdrich and Dorris eventually moved from New Hampshire to Minneapolis and later separated after fifteen years of marriage. During subsequent divorce proceedings, Dorris, who had been profoundly depressed since the second year of their marriage, attempted suicide twice. He succeeded on April 11, 1997. Despite these personal traumas, Erdrich continued to be productive as a novelist, In 1998, she published *The Antelope Wife*. She followed it with *The Last Report on the Miracles at Little No Horse* (2001), *The Master Butchers Singing Club* (2003), *Four Souls* (2004), and *The Painted Drum* (2005). Through these years, she also continued to publish nonfiction and children's literature.

Analysis • In a 1985 essay titled "Where I Ought to Be: A Writer's Sense of Place," Erdrich states that the essence of her writing emerges from her attachment to her North Dakota locale. The ways in which Erdrich brought this region to literary life have been favorably compared by critics to the methods and style of William Faulkner, who created the mythical Yoknapatawpha County out of his rich sense of rural Mississippi. Like Faulkner, Erdrich created a gallery of diverse characters spanning several generations, using multiple points of view and shifting time frames. Erdrich's fiction further resembles Faulkner's in that the experience of her characters includes a broad spectrum of experience "from the mundane to the miraculous," as one critic put it. Erdrich's stories generally begin with a realistic base of ordinary people, settings, and actions. As her tales develop, however, these people become involved in events and perceptions that strike the reader as quite extraordinary—as exaggerated or heightened in ways that may seem deluded or mystical, grotesque or magical, comic or tragic, or some strange mixture of these. Thus, one critic has described Erdrich as "a sorceress with language" whose lyrical style intensifies some of the most memorable scenes in contemporary American fiction.

Love Medicine • Erdrich's first novel, *Love Medicine,* spans the years 1934-1984 in presenting members of five Chippewa and mixed-blood families, all struggling in different ways to attain a sense of belonging through love, religion, home, and family. The novel includes fourteen interwoven stories; though the title refers specifically to traditional Ojibwa magic in one story, in a broader sense "love medicine" refers to the different kinds of spiritual power that enable Erdrich's Native American and mixed-blood characters to transcend—however momentarily—the grim circumstances of their lives. Trapped on their shrinking reservation by racism and poverty, plagued by alcoholism, disintegrating families, and violence, some of Erdrich's characters nevertheless discover a form of "love medicine" that helps to sustain them.

The opening story, "The World's Greatest Fishermen," begins with an episode of "love medicine" corrupted and thwarted. Though June Kashpaw was once a woman of striking beauty and feisty spirit, by 1981 she has sunk to the level of picking up men in an oil boomtown. However, June fails in her last attempts to attain two goals that other characters will also seek throughout the novel: love and home. However, though she appears only briefly in this and one other story, June Kashpaw is a central character in the novel, for she embodies the potential power of spirit and love in ways that impress and haunt the other characters.

Part 2 of "The World's Greatest Fishermen" introduces many of the other major characters of *Love Medicine,* as June's relatives gather several months after her death. On one hand, several characters seem sympathetic because of their closeness to June and their kind treatment of one another. Albertine Johnson, who narrates the story and remembers her Aunt June lovingly, has gone through a wild phase of her own and is now a nursing student. Eli Kashpaw, Albertine's granduncle, who was largely responsible for rearing June, is a tough and sharp-minded old man who has maintained a traditional Chippewa existence as a hunter and fisherman. Lipsha Morrissey, who, though he seems not to know it, is June's illegitimate son, is a sensitive, self-educated young man who acts warmly toward Albertine. In contrast to these characters are others who are flawed or unsympathetic when seen through the eyes of Albertine, who would like to feel that her family is pulling together after June's death. These less sympathetic characters include Zelda and Aurelia (Albertine's gossipy mother and aunt), Nector Kashpaw (Albertine's senile grandfather), and Gordon Kashpaw (the husband whom June left, a hapless drunk). Worst of all is June's legitimate son King, a volatile bully. King's horrifying acts of violence—abusing his wife Lynette, battering his new car, and smashing the pies prepared for the family dinner—leave Albertine in dismay with a family in shambles.

Love Medicine then shifts back in time from 1981, and its thirteen remaining stories proceed in chronological order from 1934 to 1984. "Saint Marie" concerns a mixed-blood girl, Marie Lazarre, who in 1934 enters Sacred Heart Convent and embarks on a violent love-hate relationship with Sister Leopolda. In "Wild Geese," also set in 1934, Nector Kashpaw is infatuated with Lulu Nanapush, but his affections swerve unexpectedly when he encounters Marie Lazarre on the road outside her convent. By 1948, the time of "The Beads," Marie has married Nector, had three children (Aurelia, Zelda, and Gordie), and agreed to rear her niece June. Nector, however, is drinking and philandering, and June, after almost committing suicide in a children's hanging game, leaves to be brought up by Eli in the woods. "Lulu's Boys," set in 1957, reveals that the amorous Lulu Lamartine (née Nanapush) had married Henry Lamartine but bore eight sons by different fathers. Meanwhile, in "The Plunge of the Brave," also set in 1957, Nector recalls the development of his five-year affair with Lulu and tries to leave his wife Marie for her, but the result is that he accidentally burns Lulu's house to the ground.

The offspring of these Kashpaws and Lamartines also have their problems in later *Love Medicine* stories. In "A Bridge," set in 1973, Albertine runs away from home and becomes the lover of Henry Lamartine, Jr., one of Lulu's sons, a troubled Vietnam War veteran. "The Red Convertible," set in 1974, also involves Henry, Jr., as Lyman Lamartine tries unsuccessfully to bring his brother out of the dark personality changes that Vietnam has wrought in him. On a lighter note, "Scales," set in 1980, is a hilarious account of the romance between Dot Adare, an obese clerk at a truck weighing station, and Gerry Nanapush, one of Lulu's sons who is a most unusual convict: enormously fat, amazingly proficient at escaping from jail, but totally inept at avoiding recapture. "A Crown of Thorns," which overlaps with the time of "The World's Greatest Fishermen" in 1981, traces the harrowing and bizarre decline of Gordie Kashpaw into alcoholism after June's death.

Though in these earlier *Love Medicine* stories the positive powers of love and spirit are more often frustrated than fulfilled, in the last three stories several characters achieve breakthroughs that bring members of the different families together in moving and hopeful ways. In "Love Medicine," set in 1982, Lipsha Morrissey reaches out lovingly to his grandmother Marie and to the ghosts of Nector and June. In "The Good Tears," set in 1983, Lulu undergoes a serious eye operation and is cared for by Marie, who forgives her for being Nector's longtime extramarital lover. Finally, in "Crossing the Water," set in 1984, Lipsha helps his father, Gerry Nanapush, escape to Canada and comes to appreciate the rich heritage of love, spirit, and wiliness that he has inherited from his diverse patchwork of Chippewa relatives—especially from his grandmother Lulu, his great-aunt Marie, and his parents, June and Gerry.

The Beet Queen • In *The Beet Queen*, her second novel, Erdrich shifts her main focus from the American Indian to the European-immigrant side of her background, and she creates in impressive detail the mythical town of Argus (modeled on Wahpeton, where she was reared, but located closer to the Ojibwa reservation) in the years 1932-1972.

The opening scene of *The Beet Queen*, "The Branch," dramatizes two contrasting approaches to life that many characters will enact throughout the novel. On a cold spring day in 1932, two orphans, Mary and Karl Adare, arrive by freight train in Argus. As they seek the way to the butcher shop owned by their Aunt Fritzie and Uncle Pete Kozka, Mary "trudge[s] solidly forward," while Karl stops to embrace a tree that already has its spring blossoms. When they are attacked by a dog, Mary runs ahead, continuing her search for the butcher shop, while Karl runs back to hop the train once again. As the archetypal plodder of the novel, Mary continues to "trudge solidly forward" throughout; she is careful, determined, and self-reliant in pursuit of her goals. On the other hand, Karl is the principal dreamer—impressionable, prone to escapist impulses, and dependent on others to catch him when he falls.

The Adare family history shows how Karl is following a pattern set by his mother, Adelaide, while Mary grows in reaction against this pattern. Like Karl, Adelaide is physically beautiful but self-indulgent and impulsive. Driven to desperation by her hard luck in the early years of the Great Depression, Adelaide startles a fairground crowd by abandoning her three children (Mary, Karl, and an unnamed newborn son) to fly away with the Great Omar, an airplane stunt pilot.

In Argus, Mary tangles with yet another beautiful, self-centered dreamer: her cousin Sita Kozka, who resents the attention that her parents, Pete and Fritzie, and her best friend, the mixed-blood Celestine James, pay to Mary. However, Mary prevails and carves a solid niche for herself among Pete, Fritzie, and Celestine, who, like Mary, believe in a strong work ethic and lack Sita's pretentious airs.

A number of episodes gratify the reader with triumphs for Mary and comeuppances for the less sympathetic characters Karl, Adelaide, and Sita. Mary becomes famous for a miracle at her school (she falls and cracks the ice in the image of Jesus), gains Celestine as a close friend, and in time becomes manager of the Kozka butcher shop. By contrast, Karl becomes a drifter who finds only sordid momentary pleasure in his numerous affairs. Meanwhile, Adelaide marries Omar and settles in Florida, but she becomes moody and subject to violent rages. Similarly, Sita fails in her vainglorious attempts to become a model and to establish a fashionable French restaurant; she escapes her first marriage through divorce and becomes insane and suicidal during her second.

However, even as Erdrich charts the strange and sometimes grotesque downfalls of her flighty characters, she develops her more sympathetic ones in ways that suggest that the opposite approach to life does not guarantee happiness either. Mary is unsuccessful in her attempt to attract Russell Kashpaw (the half-brother of Celestine), and she develops into an exotically dressed eccentric who is obsessed with predicting the future and controlling others. Like Mary, Celestine James and Wallace Pfef are hardworking and successful in business, but their loneliness drives each of them to an ill-advised affair with Karl, and he causes each of them considerable grief. In addition, the union of Celestine and Karl results in the birth of Dot Adare (who grows up to be the ill-tempered lover of Gerry Nanapush in the *Love Medicine* story "Scales"); since Celestine, Mary, and Wallace all spoil the child, Dot turns out, in Wallace's words, to have "all of her family's worst qualities." As a teenager, Dot herself comes to grief when she is mortified to learn that the well-meaning Wallace has rigged the election for Queen of the Argus Beet Festival so that she, an unpopular and ludicrously unlikely candidate, will win.

However, in addition to the defeats and disappointments that all the characters bear, Erdrich dramatizes the joy that they derive from life. The compensations of family and friendship—ephemeral and vulnerable as these may be—prove to be significant for all the characters at various times in the story, particularly at the end. The irrepressible vitality of these people, troublesome as they often are to one another, keeps the reader involved and entertained throughout the novel.

Tracks • Erdrich's third novel, *Tracks*, is concentrated, intense, and mystical. It is the shortest, covers a time span of only twelve years, and alternates between only two first-person narrators. This compression serves the story well, for the human stakes are high. At first, and periodically throughout the novel, the Chippewa characters fear for their very survival, as smallpox, tuberculosis, severe winters, starvation, and feuds with mixed-blood families bring them close to extinction. Later in the novel, government taxes and political chicanery threaten the Chippewas' ownership of family and tribal land. In response, Erdrich's Chippewa characters use all the powers at their command—including the traditional mystical powers of the old ways—to try to survive and maintain their control over the land.

Nanapush, one of the novel's two narrators, is an old Chippewa whom Erdrich names for the trickster rabbit in tribal mythology who repeatedly delivers the people from threatening monsters. In *Tracks*, Erdrich's Nanapush often does credit to his mythological model, Nanabozho, by wielding the trickster rabbit's powers of deliverance, wiliness, and humor. He saves Fleur Pillager, a seventeen-year-old girl who is the last but one of the Pillager clan, from starvation. Later he delivers young Eli Kashpaw from the sufferings of love by advising him how to win Fleur's heart. Also, Nanapush is instrumental in saving the extended family that forms around Fleur, Eli, and himself. This family grows to five when Fleur gives birth to a daughter, Lulu, and Eli's mother, Margaret Kashpaw, becomes Nanapush's bedmate. As these five come close to starvation, Nanapush sends Eli out to hunt an elk; in one of the most extraordinary passages of the novel, Nanapush summons a power vision of Eli hunting that the old man imagines is guiding Eli to the kill. Nanapush also demonstrates the humor associated with his mythological model in his wry tone as a narrator, his sharp wit in conversation, and the tricks that he plays on his family's mixed-blood antagonists: the Pukwans, Morrisseys, and Lazarres.

Foremost among these antagonists is the novel's other narrator, Pauline Pukwan. A "skinny big-nosed girl with staring eyes," Pauline circulates in Argus from the Kozkas' butcher shop to the Sacred Heart Convent, and on the reservation from the Nanapush-Pillager-Kashpaw group to the Morrissey and Lazarre clans. At first attracted to Fleur by the beauty and sexual power that she herself lacks, Pauline later takes an envious revenge by concocting a love potion that seems to drive Fleur's husband, Eli, and Sophie Morrissey to become lovers. Ironically, though one side of her believes in a Roman Catholic denial of her body, Pauline later gives birth out of wedlock to a girl named Marie, and at the end of her narrative Pauline enters the convent to become Sister Leopolda—the cruel nun who later torments her own daughter, Marie Lazarre, in *Love Medicine.*

Though Erdrich clearly feels passionately about the sufferings visited on her Chippewa characters in *Tracks*, she treats this politically charged material with her usual disciplined restraint. Her dispassionate, deadpan use of first-person narrators (never broken by authorial commentary) matches the understated, stoic attitude that Nanapush adopts toward the numerous waves of hardship and betrayal that the Chippewas must endure.

If in some ways *Tracks* seems to conclude with a feeling of fragmentation and defeat, in other ways it strikes positive notes of solidarity and survival, especially when considered in relation to *Love Medicine* and *The Beet Queen.* Fleur disappears, leaving her husband and daughter, but Nanapush uses his wiliness to become tribal chairman and then to retrieve Lulu from a distant boarding school. At the end, the reader is reminded that Nanapush has addressed his entire narrative to Lulu: The old man hopes that his story will persuade Lulu to embrace the memory of Fleur, "the one you will not call mother." Further, the reader familiar with *Love Medicine* will realize how this young girl, who becomes Lulu Lamartine, carries on the supernaturally powerful sexuality of her mother Fleur and the wily talent for survival of Nanapush, the old man who gave her his name and reared her.

The Bingo Palace • *The Bingo Palace* takes place roughly ten years after the end of *Love Medicine* and follows several characters who were introduced in the first three novels. Primary among these is June Kashpaw's luckless son Lipsha Morrissey, back on the reservation after a series of failed jobs. His uncle, shrewd businessman Lyman Lamartine, offers him a job at his bingo parlor as a part-time bartender and night watchman. After his dead mother June appears with bingo tickets that are destined to change his luck significantly, gentle Lipsha not only wins a prize van but also pockets more of Lyman's money by continuing to win. A further complication in their relationship is Shawnee Ray Toose (Miss Little Shell), champion jingle-dress dancer, with whom Lipsha is promptly smitten, even though she has had a son by Lyman.

This loosely structured novel recounts Lipsha's sweet but faltering courtship of Shawnee, who rebuffs both of her suitors; Lyman's schemes to erect a splendid bingo palace on the last bit of Pillager land; and a joint vision quest that is serious for Lyman but comic for Lipsha, whose vision animal turns out to be a skunk that really sprays him. Lipsha has another abortive reunion with his father, escaped convict Gerry Nanapush, and is left stranded in a stolen car in a blizzard until his great-grandmother Fleur Pillager steps in. Erdrich employs techniques of Magical Realism, as the dead speak and the lake monster Misshepeshu continues to strike terror into the hearts of all except the dauntless Fleur.

The Antelope Wife • Erdrich's seventh novel, *The Antelope Wife,* shifts to a new set of characters and a new locale, Minnesota. A young cavalry private, Scranton Roy, is sent to quell an American Indian uprising but mistakenly attacks a neutral Ojibwa village. Realizing his error, he manages to rescue a baby whom he then nurses with his own miraculous milk and raises to adulthood. In this way the white Roy family begins a relationship that spans five generations with two Ojibwa families.

The infant's grieving mother marries a man named Showano and bears twin girls. Her twin granddaughters Zosie and Mary Showano figure prominently as the wife and the lover of Scranton Roy's grandson and as the two mothers of Rozina Roy Whiteheart Reads, herself the mother of twin daughters. Rozina wants to leave her husband Richard for a Minneapolis baker, Frank Showano. Although this novel was completed just before Michael Dorris's death, it is uncomfortably prescient in its account of the unhappy marriage between Rozina and her suicidal husband.

This is a novel of repeated family patterns (lost mothers, lost daughters), emphasized by the linking imagery of the archetypal headings that introduce each section. In this subtle and seamless blending of Ojibwa myth with contemporary life, Magical Realism becomes even more pronounced. Frank Showano's brother Klaus is nearly destroyed by his infatuation with a seductive, shape-shifting antelope woman. The windigo, a cannibal hunger spirit, is a very real presence and threat, while some chapters are narrated by a talking dog named Almost Soup. *The Antelope Wife* affirms the vitality of Ojibwa culture on and off the reservation.

If Louise Erdrich had been born two hundred years earlier, she might have become a traditional Ojibwa storyteller, whose tales would have reminded her listeners of their unchanging relationship to the land and to the mythic and legendary characters who inhabited it. Several generations removed from such a stable and undamaged culture, Erdrich nevertheless was able to create a richly neotribal view of people and place. Her novels testify to the profound interrelatedness of her characters—American Indian and white, contemporaries and ancestors—both with one another and with their midwestern homeland.

The Last Report on the Miracles at Little No Horse • This 2001 novel plunges readers into the lifetime saga of Father Damien and his work among the Ojibwas on the Little No Horse reservation. A prologue, containing a 1996 letter to the pope from Father Damien, begins the book's four-part narration by returning to 1910-1912. As in all Erdrich's work, landscape plays a major role. "Eighty-some years previous, through a town that was to flourish and past a farm that would disappear, the river slid—all that happened began with that flow of water." Novitiate Sister Cecelia, the former Agnes De Witt, is introduced as a young nun whose piano playing contains such emotion it disturbs her community and prompts her leaving. The arrangements she makes to live on a nearby farm catapult her into an adventure that will engulf her life. An accidental brush with petty criminals causes her common-law husband's death and sets the stage for the rest of the novel. Themes of passionate devotion, religious life, individual will, and survival in the face of overwhelming odds are set in motion in part 1, "The Transfiguration of Agnes." After a disastrous flood washes her out of her home, Agnes takes the role of Father Damien Modeste, a drowned priest whose body she finds. She walks onto Ojibwa land, and the novel's main conceit is in place.

Throughout part 2, "The Deadly Conversions," and part 3, "Memory and Suspicion," Erdrich continues the technique of interspersing chapters about the aged priest's daily routine and life in his parish with chapters about the past. In these sections Father Jude, an emissary from the Vatican, interacts with Father Damien and the parishioners that he has come to know and accept over the years. As Father Jude Miller investigates Sister Leopolda's life and the miracles reported at Little No Horse, the novel incorporates earlier episodes between Father Damien, Nanapush, and Fleur Pillager as well as revealing the history of the Puyat clan and the tale of the Kashpaw wives, the drama of Mary Kashpaw in the convent kitchen and Lulu Pillager's struggle with her mother, Fleur. Lulu's hatred for Fleur takes root in these sections when she is sent to Indian Boarding School. To further complicate life, another priest arrives to help Father Damien, and this means sharing a living space—a huge difficulty for "Father" Damien. The two of them discover each other with a passion that cannot be contained.

Part 4, "The Passions," gives both report and prophecy concerning Lulu Pillager, returned as a woman to the reservation. It contains Sister Leopolda's final confession of a murder and her threat to unmask "Father" Damien to the authorities when they quarrel. Father Jude Miller begins his account of Leopolda's passion and finds himself spending equal time thinking about Father Damien's life as he writes. Father Damien, unwilling to be indefensible in death, plans his disappearance, and Mary Kashpaw helps him carry it out. Finally, it is the love that Father Damien shared with his Ojibwa flock that they and readers remember.

The Master Butchers Singing Club • This 2003 novel adds another family saga to those of the residents of Argus, North Dakota, whom Erdrich's readers have been getting to know since the 1980's. Fidelis Waldvogel's return from World War I in 1918 and his emigration from Germany in 1922 begin a narrative that moves through the development of small-town culture in the upper Midwest at the twentieth century's beginning to the Great Depression; it culminates nine years after the end of World War II.

Erdrich's genius for metaphor is employed in her creation of chapter titles. For example, chapter three, "The Bones," begins with Argus's structure as a town; the framework of Fidelis's life shifts when Eva arrives with "their" son; Fidelis opens a butcher shop which schedules his life through work; Cyprian and Delphine establish a fake marriage to mollify the townspeople; and Roy is found wallowing in filth and confusion. The chapter's events allude to bones' functions as support, and other chapter titles suggest metaphors for memory, time, and patterns of connection in human lives.

Early in the novel, Fidelis founds a singing club like the one he remembers in his German home, Ludwigsruhe, and the men begin weekly meetings to harmonize and socialize. Delphine struggles to negotiate the early childhood loss of her mother and the alcoholic incompetence of her father. Cyprian struggles with his homosexual desires. Confronting Cyprian after she discovers him in an encounter with a man, Delphine means to remind him of their one night of passion, but instead she asks, "How do you balance?" Delphine and Cyprian tour successfully with a vaudeville group and traveling circus until Delphine needs to return to Argus and quiet her worries about her father, Roy Watzka. Argus then becomes the backdrop for how the two couples struggle for equilibrium.

The couples' lives mingle when Delphine begins to help out in the butcher shop. She is drawn into Eva's kitchen for coffee the first day that she comes to the shop as a customer, and in that room, she senses the domestic tranquillity she had longed for. Eva becomes fatally stricken with cancer, and Delphine nurses her friend through a painful death. All the while she and Cyprian maintain the charade of marriage while they live nearly platonically. Erdrich introduces two eccentrics: Tante Maria Waldvogel, Fidelis's embittered spinster sister, and Step-and-a-Half, a wandering collector of junk. Gradually the plot becomes more about how the women manage to maintain order and live than how the men prosper.

Finally, Fidelis proposes to Delphine, and she is free to accept him. She has been a surrogate mother for his sons and has achieved a respected place in Argus through her economic ways, her efficient way of meeting her responsibilities, her steady presence, and her wide reading. The novel is weighted with the vision of what it means to survive and achieve balance in the world as one finds it, not as one wishes it.

Terry L. Andrews
Updated by Joanne McCarthy and Karen L. Arnold

Other major works

SHORT FICTION: "The Red Convertible," 1981; "Scales," 1982; "The World's Greatest Fisherman," 1982; "American Horse," 1983; "Destiny," 1985; "Saint Marie," 1985; "Fleur," 1987; "Snares," 1987; "Matchimanito," 1988.

POETRY: *Jacklight*, 1984; *Baptism of Desire*, 1989; *Original Fire: Selected and New Poems*, 2003.

NONFICTION: *The Blue Jay's Dance: A Birth Year*, 1995; *Books and Islands in Ojibwe Country*, 2003.

CHILDREN'S LITERATURE: *Grandmother's Pigeon*, 1996 (illustrated by Jim LaMarche); *The Birchbark House*, 1999; *The Range Eternal*, 2002; *The Game of Silence*, 2004.

Bibliography

Beidler, Peter G., and Gay Barton. *A Reader's Guide to the Novels of Louise Erdrich.* Columbia: University of Missouri Press, 1999. A comprehensive and informative handbook for students of Erdrich's long fiction.

Brehm, Victoria. "The Metamorphoses of an Ojibwa *Manido.*" *American Literature* 68 (December, 1996): 677-706. This article traces the evolution of the legendary Ojibwa water monster Micipijiu (Misshepeshu), with a fascinating section on the symbolism and significance of the monster in Erdrich's *Love Medicine, Tracks,* and *The Bingo Palace.*

Bruchac, Joseph. "Whatever Is Really Yours: An Interview with Louise Erdrich." In *Survival This Way: Interviews with American Indian Poets.* Tucson: University of Arizona Press, 1987. Erdrich discusses her poetry in particular but also her inspirations for her stories and her philosophy on what makes a good story. She explains how the characters and their stories are formed as well.

Chavkin, Allan, ed. *The Chippewa Landscape of Louise Erdrich.* Tuscaloosa: University of Alabama Press, 1998. Collects original essays focusing on Erdrich's writings that are rooted in the Chippewa experience. Premier scholars of Native American literature investigate narrative structure, signs of ethnicity, the notions of luck and chance in Erdrich's narrative cosmology, and her use of comedy in exploring American Indians' tragic past.

Erdrich, Louise. *Conversations with Louise Erdrich and Michael Dorris.* Edited by Allan Chavkin and Nancy Feyl Chavkin. Jackson: University Press of Mississippi, 1994. Collection of twenty-five interviews over a number of years in which Erdrich discusses her work.

Hafen, P. Jane. *Reading Louise Erdrich's "Love Medicine."* Boise, Idaho: Boise State University Press, 2003. A Taos Pueblo Indian, Hafen explores approaches to understanding Erdrich's first novel. Hafen also examines Erdrich's poetry in "Sacramental Language: Ritual in the Poetry of Louise Erdrich," an article she published in *Great Plains Quarterly* in 1996. Hafen finds in Erdrich's writings evidence of the oral culture and a blending of rituals from the Chippewa and European American religious traditions.

Ludlow, Jeannie. "Working (in) the In-Between: Poetry, Criticism, Interrogation, and Interruption." *Studies in American Indian Literature* 6 (Spring, 1994): 24-42. Ludlow writes a sophisticated literary analysis of Joy Harjo's "The Woman Hanging from the Thirteenth Floor Window" and Erdrich's "Lady in the Pink Mustang" from *Jacklight.* She finds Erdrich's poem potentially more empowering.

Rebein, Robert. *Hicks, Tribes and Dirty Realists: American Fiction After Postmodernism.* Lexington: University Press of Kentucky, 2001. An assertion that gritty realism has gained ascendancy over metafiction in American writing. Examines the works of Dorothy Allison, Annie Proulx, Thomas McGuane, Cormac McCarthy, Larry McMurtry, and Louise Erdrich.

Sarris, Greg, et al., eds. *Approaches to Teaching the Works of Louise Erdrich.* New York: Modern Language Association of America, 2004. Very useful handbook for teachers of high school and undergraduate literature courses.

Scott, Steven D. *The Gamefulness of American Postmodernism: John Barth and Louise Erdrich.* New York: Peter Lang, 2000. Comparative study of Erdrich and novelist John Barth as postmodernist writers.

Smith, Jeanne Rosier. *Writing Tricksters: Mythic Gambols in American Ethnic Literature.* Berkeley: University of California Press, 1997. A thorough examination of ethnic trickster figures as they appear in the work of Erdrich, Maxine Hong Kingston, and Toni Morrison. Chapter 3 explores the trickster characteristics of Old Nanapush, Gerry Nanapush, Lipsha Morrissey, Fleur Pillager, and others.

Stone, Brad. "Scenes from a Marriage: Louise Erdrich's New Novel—and Her Life." *Newsweek* 131, no. 12 (March 23, 1998): 69. Discusses Erdrich's *The Antelope Wife* and the suicide of her husband Michael Dorris.

Stookey, Lorena Laura. *Louise Erdrich: A Critical Companion.* Westport, Conn.: Greenwood Press, 1999. A good study of Erdrich's works. Includes bibliographical references and an index.

Wong, Hertha D. Sweet, ed. *Louise Erdrich's "Love Medicine": A Casebook.* London: Oxford University Press, 2000. Presents documents relating to the historical importance of *Love Medicine*, representative critical essays, and excerpts from several interviews with Erdrich and Michael Dorris.

James T. Farrell

Born: Chicago, Illinois; February 27, 1904
Died: New York, New York; August 22, 1979

Principal long fiction • *Young Lonigan: A Boyhood in Chicago Streets*, 1932; *Gas-House McGinty*, 1933; *The Young Manhood of Studs Lonigan*, 1934; *Judgment Day*, 1935; *Studs Lonigan: A Trilogy*, 1935 (collective title for *Young Lonigan, The Young Manhood of Studs Lonigan*, and *Judgment Day*); *A World I Never Made*, 1936; *No Star Is Lost*, 1938; *Tommy Gallagher's Crusade*, 1939; *Father and Son*, 1940; *Ellen Rogers*, 1941; *My Days of Anger*, 1943; *Bernard Clare*, 1946; *The Road Between*, 1949; *This Man and This Woman*, 1951; *Yet Other Waters*, 1952; *The Face of Time*, 1953; *Boarding House Blues*, 1961; *The Silence of History*, 1963; *What Time Collects*, 1964; *Lonely for the Future*, 1966; *When Time Was Born*, 1966; *New Year's Eve/1929*, 1967; *A Brand New Life*, 1968; *Judith*, 1969; *Invisible Swords*, 1971; *The Dunne Family*, 1976; *The Death of Nora Ryan*, 1978.

Other literary forms • James T. Farrell began his career, as so many other novelists have done, by writing short stories, and his more than two hundred tales are an integral part of the vast world he portrays. Most of his stories have been gathered in collections such as *Calico Shoes, and Other Stories* (1934) and *$1,000 a Week, and Other Stories* (1942), but there are several stories and manuscript works that remain unpublished. His poetry, collected by Farrell himself in a 1965 edition, seems to be the product of early and late speculations—the early poetry probably coming from the period of *Studs Lonigan* and the later poetry seemingly produced during the early 1960's when he was beginning his "second career" with *A Universe of Time*, an unfinished multicycled series of novels, stories, and poems. All the poetry is uneven in quality and, despite some remarkable effects, is not memorable. Farrell also published volumes of literary criticism, cultural criticism, and essays on a wide range of subjects. *The Mowbray Family* (1946), a play written with Hortense Alden Farrell, is a dramatic treatment of the same material that he treats brilliantly in his fiction. The drama, however, lacks the vitality of his novels and seems lifeless alongside a work such as *My Days of Anger*. His letters remain to be collected, and his biography has yet to be completed.

Achievements • Farrell's career encompassed many diverse literary movements and trends. He was active to the end of a long life, publishing his last novel in the year before his death. On the evidence of his three major complete works, the *Studs Lonigan* trilogy, the Danny O'Neill series (or the O'Neill-O'Flaherty series, as Farrell preferred to call it), and the Bernard Carr trilogy, Farrell presented urban America and the people who sprang from it with a brutal candor rarely equaled in American literature.

Farrell's youth, spent in Irish Catholic, lower-and middle-class Chicago, gave him the milieu from which a whole society could be examined and explained. His career began with his conscious decision to quit a steady job and become a writer and survived despite indifference, shock, bad reviews, prejudice, and ignorance. Farrell's social activism led him into and out of Marxist circles, sustained him through attacks by the Marxist critics who accused him of abandoning the cause, and gave him the focus necessary to show Americans an entire society that survived and prospered in spite of its environment.

Farrell never achieved great popularity; his style was deemed too flat and brusque, his language profane, and his methods inartistic. His fiction was considered basically plotless or merely photographic, and he was condemned, especially by the Marxists, for failing to be didactic. In the years following his death, however, the scope of his urban vision has been recognized; Farrell's fictional world has the breadth of conception associated with greatness and has been compared favorably to that of William Faulkner. Much like Theodore Dreiser, whom he admired, Farrell went his own way when it was extremely unpopular to do so, and his impact on modern fiction remains to be assessed.

Library of Congress

Biography • James Thomas Farrell was born on February 27, 1904, in Chicago, where he lived until 1931, except for a short sojourn in New York City during the 1920's. The son of a family of Irish teamsters and domestics, he was the product of a curious dual lifestyle in his youth. One of fifteen children, Farrell was taken, when he was three, to live with his maternal grandparents as the result of his own family's impoverished condition. His grandparents, John and Julia Daly, were of the same poor, hard-working stock as his father and mother, but they were somewhat more financially stable and lived a different, more affluent life. The difference in these two families was important in Farrell's development.

Living with the Dalys, Farrell found himself in a neighborhood of modern brick buildings that were a sharp contrast to the poor, wooden-shack neighborhood where his parents lived with the rest of their children. The personal confusion and divisions of loyalties caused by this unusual arrangement were only a part of Farrell's childhood problems. Living in one household and coming from another made Farrell the center of many family tensions and involved him in most of the family's disagreements.

Farrell entered Corpus Christi Parochial Grammar School in 1911, and through the course of his education was a loner and a dreamer. He became an excellent athlete, taking seven letters in sports at St. Cyril High School. He attended St. Cyril after giving up early plans to attend a seminary to become a priest. He excelled in his studies and was active on the St. Cyril *Oriflamme*, the school's monthly magazine, in addition to being an active member of the high school fraternity, Alpha Eta Beta. He was desperately in need of acceptance, but his classmates sensed that he was different and his social incapacity was another influence on his later life.

After high school, Farrell went to work full-time for the Amalgamated Express Company, where he had worked summers while in school. After nearly two years with the express company, Farrell felt trapped by the routine and, in 1924, enrolled in night classes at De Paul University as a prelaw student. He first encountered political and economic theory there and first read Theodore Dreiser. The financial and mental strain eventually became too much for Farrell, and he left De Paul and the express company in 1925. He then took a job as a gas station attendant for the Sinclair Oil and Refining Company and saved part of his wages for tuition at the University of Chicago.

In eight quarters at the University, completed between 1925 and 1929, Farrell became a voracious reader, enjoyed an intellectual awakening that has been compared to Herman Melville's similar awakening during the 1840's, and discovered that he wanted to become a writer. In 1927, he dropped out of school and hitchhiked to New York City, determined to succeed as a writer. He returned to Chicago in 1928, reentered the University, and began to write, placing critical articles and book reviews in campus publications and in Chicago and New York newspapers. By 1929, he had sold his first story, "Slob," to a little magazine, and his career was launched.

Farrell married Dorothy Patricia Butler secretly in 1931. (Farrell was to divorce Dorothy later, marry the actor Hortense Alden, whom he also divorced, and remarry Dorothy in 1955.) Farrell and Dorothy sailed for France immediately after their wedding. In France, Farrell discovered that he had little in common with the American expatriates in Paris and that he had important admirers and supporters such as Samuel Putnam, James Henle, and Ezra Pound. The publication of *Young Lonigan* and *Gas-House McGinty* by the Vanguard Press during this period established Farrell as a writer and confirmed his faith in his vision. He began to publish a great number of short stories, and by the time the Farrells returned to New York in 1932, his conceptions for the entire *Studs Lonigan* trilogy and the first Danny O'Neill novel, *A World I Never Made*, were outlined. He was prepared to become an integral part of American literary history. His contribution to American letters included stormy confrontations with Marxist critics and novelists and a staunch defense of the integrity of art and the artist as opposed to the socialist demands that fiction, and all art, serve the party.

The 1930's were the end of the personal experiences that Farrell used as the material for his major fiction; the *Studs Lonigan* trilogy, the Danny O'Neill series, and the Bernard Carr trilogy are all drawn from the same well. In describing that world, Farrell was determined to "shake the sack of reality" until it was empty. In 1957, he completed his original life plan for twenty-five volumes that were to be "panels of one work" and had begun a second lifework, called *A Universe of Time*, of which he had published seven volumes (*The Silence of History, What Time Collects, When Time Was Born, Lonely for the Future, A Brand New Life, Judith,* and *Invisible Swords*). Farrell died in New York on August 22, 1979, before this lifework was complete.

Analysis • An understanding of Farrell and his work on the basis of one novel, or even as many as three individual novels, is impossible. Farrell's vision was panoramic, however limited his subject matter may have been, and cannot be understood except in terms of large, homogeneous blocks of fiction. He did not write exclusively of Chicago or of Irish Catholics, but it was on this home "turf" that he most effectively showed the effects of indifference and disintegration on an independent, stubborn, often ignorant, urban subculture. He was at once appalled by and attracted to the spectacle of an entire people being strangled by the city and by their own incapacity to understand their position, and he was most successful when he embodied the society in the life and times of an archetypal individual.

Farrell's three major, complete works total eleven novels; each of the eleven creates another panel in the same essential experience. Although the *Studs Lonigan* trilogy, the five novels of the O'Neill-O'Flaherty series, and the Bernard Carr trilogy have different protagonists, they all share a common impulse and reflect Farrell's almost fanatical obsession with time, society, and the individual's response to both. Studs Lonigan, Danny O'Neill, and Bernard Carr are extensions or facets of Farrell's primal character, pitted against a hostile urban environment.

Studs Lonigan: A Trilogy • The *Studs Lonigan* trilogy, arguably Farrell's best and certainly his best-known work, is the story of the development and deterioration not only of the title character, but also of the Great Depression-era, Irish Catholic Chicago society from which he springs. In the fifteen-year span of *Young Lonigan, The Young Manhood of Studs Lonigan*, and *Judgment Day*, Farrell shows the total physical, moral, and spiritual degeneration of Studs Lonigan.

Studs is doomed from the moment he appears just prior to his graduation from grammar school. His announcement that he is "kissin' the old dump goodbye tonight" is ominously portentous. He drops out of high school, goes to work for his father, a painting contractor, and becomes a member and leading light of the gang that hangs out in Charlie Bathcellar's poolroom. The association with the gang is Studs's life—everything else is "plain crap." Through a swirl of "alky," "gang-shags," "craps," and "can-houses," Studs fights to prove himself to be the "real stuff" and ultimately finds himself a frail, thirty-year-old shell of the vigorous youth he once was. The physical ruin of Studs Lonigan, however, is only the result of larger deficiencies.

Studs is a sensitive, moral being who consciously rejects his innate morality as a weakness. He blindly accepts his Roman Catholic upbringing without believing it. There is never a present for Studs Lonigan—there is only a future and a past. In *Young Lonigan*, the future is the vision of Studs standing triumphantly astride the fireplug at 58th and Prairie proclaiming his ascendancy to the brotherhood of the gang. The past is his rejection of juvenile harassment he suffered as the result of his one moment of ecstasy with Lucy Scanlan in Washington Park. He proclaims himself the "real stuff" and flees from human emotions and the potentialities of those experiences with Lucy.

Studs consistently refuses to allow his emotional sensitivity to mature. The spiritual stagnation which results confines him to dreams of future aggrandizement or of past glories. The future dies, and Studs is left with memories of his degeneracy. His affair with Catherine Banahan awakens new sensibilities in Studs, but he is unable to nurture them, and they die stillborn. His heart attack at the beach, his dehumanizing odyssey through the business offices of Chicago looking for work, his shockingly prurient behavior at the burlesque show, and his final delirium are simply the payment of accounts receivable.

As Studs dies, his world is dying with him. His father's bank has collapsed, the mortgage on his building is due, Studs's fiancé is pregnant, and the gang has generally dispersed. These are not the causes of Studs's failures, however; they are reflections of that failure. Studs is the product and the producer. He is not a blind victim of his environment. He makes conscious choices—all bad. He is bankrupt of all the impulses that could save him. He batters and abuses his body, he strangles his emotions, and he clings to the stultifying spirituality of a provincial Catholicism. As Lucy

Scanlan dances through his final delirium and his family abuses his pregnant fiancé, Studs Lonigan's dying body becomes the prevailing metaphor for the empty world it created, abused, and in which it suffered.

The O'Neill-O'Flaherty series • Danny O'Neill, of the O'Neill-O'Flaherty series, is the product of the same environment, but recognizes that he controls his destiny in spite of overbearing environmental pressures and, by the end of the series, seems on the verge of success. If he succeeds, he does so because he refuses to fall into the trap that Studs builds for himself, and he thus escapes into the larger world that Studs never knows. In the five novels of the series, *A World I Never Made, No Star Is Lost, Father and Son, My Days of Anger,* and *The Face of Time,* Danny not only escapes the strictures of environment but also sloughs off the psychological and spiritual bondage of family and religion and creates his own freedom.

Farrell's most clearly autobiographical work, the O'Neill-O'Flaherty series, portrays Danny's growth from 1909 to 1927—from a five-year-old child to a man breaking from college and Chicago. Unlike the *Studs Lonigan* trilogy, the O'Neill series portrays a larger world and more diverse elements of that world. Although the Lonigan trilogy is dependent on the portrayal of its central character for action and meaning, Danny's story introduces more people and more settings and thus illustrates one of the major differences between Studs and Danny. Whereas Studs demands his personal image as a loner but actually depends heavily upon his gang as a prop, Danny begins as an atypical child—the result of his life in a bifurcated family much like Farrell's own—and learns the hypocrisy of the accepted values around him, which prompts him to formulate and depend on his own personal values.

The process by which Danny reaches this understanding is the contorted progress of a hybrid adolescence. Born to Jim and Lizz O'Neill, a poor, working-class Irish couple, he is taken to live with his grandparents, of the lace-curtain Irish variety, because his parents cannot support their already large family. He is accepted wholeheartedly by his grandmother, and he accepts her as a surrogate mother, but he has problems rationalizing his relatively opulent life while his natural siblings are dying of typhoid and neglect. He also refuses, violently, to return to his natural parents, to the poverty in which they live, and to the oppressive Roman Catholicism that his mother practices.

The tensions forged between the two families are the stuff of which Danny is made, but he is also affected by the lonely, drunken promiscuity of his Aunt Peg, the decorous commercialism of his Uncle Al, and the maternal tyranny of his grandmother, Mary O'Flaherty. Danny grows up alone in a world that he has difficulty understanding and that seems to engulf but reject him summarily. He is not a clear member of either of the families that are the heart of the story, he is rejected by Studs Lonigan's gang because of his youth and because he is considered a neighborhood "goof," and he cannot find the love he desperately seeks. Only late in the series does he understand Jim, his father, and come to accept him for what he is—a hardworking, decent, poor, Irish laborer, who loves his children desperately enough to thrust them into a better world than he can make for them.

By the time Danny understands his father, Jim is dying, Danny has discovered the importance of books, he has had a hint of love through a college affair, and he has realized that education may be his key to a broader world. In the course of his intellectual discoveries at the University of Chicago, he has rejected religion and become something of a socialist. He has also discovered that New York City is the hub of the world, and, after quitting his job and dropping out of college in order to pursue his dream, seems on the verge of simultaneously discovering himself and success by migrating to New York.

The O'Neill series, then, comes full circle—from Chicago back to Chicago both actually and metaphorically; the distinction is unimportant. For all his effort to escape what he views as mindless and oppressive, Danny finally seems to understand that his basic character is still that of the poor, hardworking Irishman that, with all its flaws, is at least pitiable rather than repugnant. As Danny prepares to escape from Chicago, he escapes with a fuller appreciation and self-preserving understanding of his heritage and an ability to progress beyond his previous angry rejections. He does not give up his new certainties, particularly in relation to the Church and religion (he has become an avowed atheist), but he displays a tolerance and acceptance of himself and his culture that are the foreground of promised success.

The Bernard Carr trilogy • Bernard Carr seems to take up the story where Danny leaves it. The trilogy of *Bernard Clare* (Farrell changed the name to Carr in the second novel after a man named Bernard Clare brought libel proceedings against him), *The Road Between*, and *Yet Other Waters*, is Farrell's attempt to represent the lives of a generation of artists in New York during the Great Depression era and in the circles of politically radical activism.

The trilogy, for the first time in Farrell's fiction, is largely set in New York. Bernard's life in New York, however, is highlighted with periodic flashbacks of Chicago; thus Farrell's integrity of vision is preserved, and Bernard's lower-class origins are discovered. Bernard is the last member of Farrell's Irish Catholic trinity—he is the embodiment of the whole man whom Studs could not become and Danny might well have become had his story been continued.

Bernard's New York is a world of struggling artists and communists. In the early New York years, Bernard becomes involved with communists and then rejects them as being little more than a gang—brutes who demand mindless adherence to the party propaganda, no matter what that adherence does to artistic integrity and vitality. He also recognizes that the dogma of communism is akin to that of Roman Catholicism—that they are both crutches for weak men.

Bernard's marriage introduces him to family life and the wonder of birth and rearing a child, and it is the spur in his attempt to recover and understand his family and his heritage. During all of these events, Bernard is achieving a limited success from his writing, and by the end of the trilogy he has brought all the pieces together and has found himself, his vocation, and an enlightened ability to see life for what it is and make the most of it.

The Bernard Carr trilogy does not carry the impact of the Lonigan saga, but the diffusion necessary to present Bernard's story precludes the grim concentration necessary to portray Studs and his life. The world expands for Danny and Bernard, and that expansion naturally admits the people, ideas, ideals, and philosophies that are the components of an expanded sensibility.

The dovetailing of the experiences and environments of his three major characters is what ultimately makes Farrell's work live. Their stories make up a tapestry that mirrors the world from which they sprang and rivals it for true pathos and vitality.

Clarence O. Johnson

Other major works

SHORT FICTION: *Calico Shoes, and Other Stories*, 1934; *Guillotine Party, and Other Stories*, 1935; *Can All This Grandeur Perish?, and Other Stories*, 1937; *Fellow Countrymen: Collected Stories*, 1937; *The Short Stories of James T. Farrell*, 1937; *$1,000 a Week, and Other Stories*, 1942; *Fifteen Selected Stories*, 1943; *To Whom It May Concern, and Other Stories*, 1944; *Twelve Great Stories*, 1945; *More Fellow Countrymen*, 1946; *More Stories*, 1946; *When Boyhood Dreams Come True*, 1946; *The Life Adventurous, and Other Stories*, 1947; *A Hell of a Good Time*, 1948; *An American Dream Girl*, 1950; *French Girls Are Vicious, and Other Stories*, 1955; *An Omnibus of Short Stories*, 1956; *A Dangerous Woman, and Other Stories*, 1957; *Saturday Night, and Other Stories*, 1958; *Side Street, and Other Stories*, 1961; *Sound of a City*, 1962; *Childhood Is Not Forever*, 1969; *Judith, and Other Stories*, 1973; *Olive and Mary Anne*, 1977.

PLAY: *The Mowbray Family*, pb. 1946 (with Hortense Alden Farrell).

POETRY: *The Collected Poems of James T. Farrell*, 1965.

NONFICTION: *A Note on Literary Criticism*, 1936; *The League of Frightened Philistines, and Other Papers*, 1945; *The Fate of Writing in America*, 1946; *Literature and Morality*, 1947; *The Name Is Fogarty: Private Papers on Public Matters*, 1950; *Reflections at Fifty, and Other Essays*, 1954; *My Baseball Diary*, 1957; *It Has Come To Pass*, 1958; *On Irish Themes*, 1982.

Bibliography

Branch, Edgar M. *James T. Farrell*. New York: Twayne, 1971. After tracing Farrell's "plebeian origin," Branch discusses major works including the Studs Lonigan trilogy, the O'Neill-O'Flaherty series, and the Bernard Carr trilogy. Essays on other works including the cycle of *A Universe of Time* follow. A chronology, notes, a selected bibliography, and an index complete the work.

____________. *Studs Lonigan's Neighborhood and the Making of James T. Farrell*. Newton, Mass.: Arts End Books, 1996. A look at the Chicago neighborhood of Farrell's youth and the inspiration for the Studs Lonigan series. Includes illustrations, maps, bibliographical references, and an index.

Fanning, Charles. "Death and Revery in James T. Farrell's O'Neill-O'Flaherty Novels." In *The Incarnate Imagination: Essays in Theology, the Arts, and Social Sciences in Honor of Andrew Greeley: A Festschrift*, edited by Ingrid H. Shafer. Bowling Green, Ohio: Bowling Green State University Press, 1988. Although Fanning is primarily concerned with Farrell's novels, he does identify themes that pervade all Farrell's fiction: the artist as an isolated being, the role of memory and dreaming in achieving the necessary isolation, and the relationship of the isolation to the experience of death.

Farrell, James T. *Selected Essays*. Edited by Lunor Wolf. New York: McGraw-Hill, 1967. This book, which contains an overview of Farrell's literary criticism, reprints many of Farrell's most significant essays, among them "On the Function of the Novel" and "The Writer and His Conscience." Also contains discussions of naturalism, Leo Tolstoy, and the American literary tradition.

Freedman, Samuel G. "Echoes of Lonigan, Fifty Years After." *The New York Times Book Review* 90 (March 17, 1985): 45. Argues that Farrell's *Studs Lonigan* trilogy still conveys the essence of Chicago life; states his portrayal of the Lonigans' bigotry still rings true; argues that the trilogy is valuable on aesthetic as well as sociological grounds and that Farrell deserves recognition as a prime influence on writers like Nelson Algren, Saul Bellow, Bette Howland, and David Mamet.

Fried, Lewis F. *Makers of the City.* Amherst: University of Massachusetts Press, 1990. Fried argues that Farrell portrays the city as a liberalizing and democratizing force. Fried does an excellent job of weaving together discussion of Farrell's life, career, and fiction. He also provides a helpful bibliographical essay on other studies of Farrell.

Landers, Robert K. *An Honest Writer: The Life and Times of James T. Farrell.* San Francisco: Encounter Books, 2004. A fresh look at the creator of Studs Lonigan, this biography argues for renewed appreciation for the American Naturalist, who has fallen out of popular and critical favor.

Pizer, Donald. "James T. Farrell and the 1930's." In *Literature at the Barricades: The American Writer in the 1930's,* edited by Ralph F. Bogardus and Fred Hobson. University: University of Alabama Press, 1982. Pizer argues convincingly that Farrell's literary roots are during the 1920's, that he owes as much to the Chicago school of philosophical pragmation as to naturalism, and that James Joyce and Sherwood Anderson also influenced Farrell's fiction. To demonstrate his theses, Pizer analyzes the *Studs Lonigan* trilogy.

Smith, Gene. "The Lonigan Curse." *American Heritage* 46 (April, 1995): 150-151. Claims that while the character of Studs Lonigan became Farrell's most popular creation, it was also his biggest personal albatross; notes that after killing Studs off, Farrell had trouble getting his work published and came to look back at his earlier work with loathing.

Wald, Alan M. *James T. Farrell: The Revolutionary Socialist Years.* New York: New York University Press, 1978. Wald's chapter "The Literary Record" demonstrates the intent of Leon Trotsky's influence on Farrell's fiction, and several short stories ("John Hitchcock," "The Dialectic," "The Renegade") receive extensive political readings. Wald identifies the real persons represented by Farrell's fictional characters and focuses on Farrell's treatment of the plight of the socialist writer. Contains an excellent bibliography with many political entries.

William Faulkner

Born: New Albany, Mississippi; September 25, 1897
Died: Byhalia, Mississippi; July 6, 1962

Principal long fiction • *Soldiers' Pay*, 1926; *Mosquitoes*, 1927; *Sartoris*, 1929; *The Sound and the Fury*, 1929; *As I Lay Dying*, 1930; *Sanctuary*, 1931; *Light in August*, 1932; *Pylon*, 1935; *Absalom, Absalom!*, 1936; *The Unvanquished*, 1938; *The Wild Palms*, 1939; *The Hamlet*, 1940; *Go Down, Moses*, 1942; *The Bear*, 1942 (novella); *Intruder in the Dust*, 1948; *Requiem for a Nun*, 1951; *A Fable*, 1954; *The Town*, 1957; *The Mansion*, 1959; *The Reivers*, 1962; *The Wishing Tree*, 1964 (fairy tale); *Flags in the Dust*, 1973 (original version of *Sartoris*); *Mayday*, 1976 (fable).

Other literary forms • William Faulkner published two volumes of poetry and several volumes of short stories. Most of his best stories appear in *Knight's Gambit* (1949), *Collected Short Stories of William Faulkner* (1950), and the posthumous *Uncollected Stories of William Faulkner* (1979). His early journalistic and prose pieces have been collected and published, as have his interviews and a number of his letters. New Faulkner material is steadily seeing print, much of it in the annual Faulkner issue of *Mississippi Quarterly*. Scholars are making public more information on Faulkner's screenwriting in Hollywood, where he collaborated on such major successes as *To Have and Have Not* (1945) and *The Big Sleep* (1946). Several of his works have been adapted for television and film; notably successful were film adaptations of *Intruder in the Dust* and *The Reivers*.

Achievements • When Faulkner received the Nobel Prize in Literature for 1949, he completed an emergence from comparative obscurity that had begun three years before. In 1946, when nearly all of Faulkner's books were out of print, Malcolm Cowley published *The Portable Faulkner*. Cowley's introduction and arrangement made clear "the scope and force and interdependence" of Faulkner's work up to 1945.

Even in 1945, Faulkner was reasonably well known to the readers of popular magazines, his stories having appeared with F. Scott Fitzgerald's and Ernest Hemingway's in publications such as the *Saturday Evening Post*, *Scribner's Magazine*, *Harper's Magazine*, and *The American Mercury*. Despite his success in selling short stories and as a Hollywood screenwriter, Faulkner's novels, except for the notorious *Sanctuary*, had little commercial success until after Cowley's volume and the Nobel Prize. The notoriety of *Sanctuary*, widely reviewed as salacious, brought him to the attention of the film industry; it was his screenwriting that sustained him financially during the years of comparative neglect when he produced the series of powerful novels that constitute one of the major achievements of world fiction. His first novel to appear on the big screen after Cowley's volume, *Intruder in the Dust* was filmed in Faulkner's hometown, Oxford, Mississippi, and released in 1949.

After the Nobel Prize, honors came steadily. He was made a member of the French Legion of Honor, received two National Book Awards for *A Fable* and *Collected Short Stories of William Faulkner*, and received two Pulitzer Prizes for *A Fable* and *The Reivers*. He traveled around the world for the U.S. State Department in 1954. During 1957, he was writer-in-residence at the University of Virginia. Recognition and financial security, while gratifying, neither diminished nor increased his output. He continued writing until his death.

Faulkner has achieved the status of a world author. His works have been painstakingly translated into many languages. Perhaps more critical books and articles were written about him in the late twentieth century than about any other writer with the exception of William Shakespeare. Critics and scholars from all over the world have contributed to the commentary. Faulkner's achievement has been compared favorably with that of Henry James, Honoré de Balzac, and Charles Dickens; many critics regard him as the preeminent novelist of the twentieth century.

Biography • William Cuthbert Faulkner was born in New Albany, Mississippi, on September 25, 1897. His ancestors had emigrated from Scotland in the eighteenth century. Faulkner's great-grandfather, William Clark Falkner, was a colonel in the Civil War; wrote *The White Rose of Memphis* (1881), a popular romance; and provided a model for the patriarch of the Sartoris clan in *The Unvanquished.* Faulkner's family was very important to him. The oldest son of Maud and Murry Falkner, William Cuthbert later became the head of the family. He took this responsibility seriously, struggling most of his life to care for those whom, whether by blood or moral commitment, he considered members of his family. In 1924, he changed the spelling of his family name to Faulkner.

Faulkner discovered his storytelling gifts as a child, but his writing career did not really begin until after his brief training for the Royal Air Force in Canada, shortly before the World War I armistice in 1918. He attended the University of Mississippi for one year, worked at odd jobs, and published a volume of poetry, *The Marble Faun* (1924). He took writing more seriously, with encouragement from Sherwood Anderson, while living in New Orleans in 1925. The influence of Anderson, especially his "The Book of the Grotesque" from *Winesburg, Ohio* (1919), seems to pervade Faulkner's work. During his apprenticeship he spent several months traveling in Europe. Out of his experiences in New Orleans and Europe came a number of journalistic sketches, most dealing with New Orleans, and a group of short stories set in Europe.

The early novels are interesting, but Faulkner began to show his powers as a prose stylist and as a creator of psychologically deep and interesting characters in *Sartoris,* which he had originally written as *Flags in the Dust.* Beginning with *The Sound and the Fury* through *Go Down, Moses,* Faulkner wrote the major novels and stories of his Yoknapatawpha series. Of the ten novels he published in these thirteen years, five are generally considered to be masterpieces: *The Sound and the Fury, As I Lay Dying, Light in August, Absalom, Absalom!,* and *Go Down, Moses.* At least two others, *Sanctuary* and *The Hamlet,* are widely studied and admired. The entire series of novels set in the mythical Yoknapatawpha County, Faulkner's "little postage stamp of native soil," is sometimes considered as a great work in its own right, especially when all of the Snopes trilogy (*The Hamlet, The Town, The Mansion*) is included with the above named masterpieces. Stories from his two collections of the 1929-1942 period regularly appear in anthologies; "Old Man" and "The Bear," which are parts of *The Wild Palms* and *Go Down, Moses,* are perhaps his best-known novellas.

Faulkner's personal life was difficult and has provoked much critical interest in tracing relationships between his life and his work. The family-arranged and unhappy marriage to Estelle Oldham in 1929 ended in divorce. Both Faulkner and his wife were subject to alcoholism. He carried on a virtually continuous struggle against debt, resentful and unhappy over the necessity of working in Hollywood in order to keep his family solvent. Though Faulkner was a fiercely loyal husband and father, he was also capable of philandering.

Although Faulkner preferred to work at home in Mississippi, he traveled a great deal, first for education, later to deal with publishers and to work in Hollywood, and finally as a goodwill ambassador for the United States. He met and formed acquaintances with several important contemporaries, notably Nathanael West, Sherwood Anderson, and Howard Hawkes.

Faulkner died of a heart attack on July 6, 1962, after entering the hospital to deal with one of his periodic drinking bouts.

Analysis • When Faulkner accepted the Nobel Prize in December, 1950, he made a speech that has become a justly famous statement of his perception of the modern world and of his particular place in it. In the address, Faulkner speaks of the modern tragedy of the spirit, the threat of instant physical annihilation, which seems to overshadow "the problems of the human heart in conflict with itself." He argues that all fiction should be universal and spiritually significant, "a pillar" to help humankind "endure and prevail." Literature can be such a pillar if it deals with "the old verities and truths of the heart, the universal truths lacking that any story is ephemeral and doomed—love and honor and pity and pride and compassion and sacrifice."

All of Faulkner's greatest works were written before the first explosion of the atomic bomb, yet in all of them there is an awareness of the threat of annihilation of which the bomb may be only a symptom: a kind of spiritual annihilation. One critic argues that Faulkner, like the greatest of his contemporaries, dramatizes in most of his novels some version of the central problem of modern man in the West, how to respond to the recognition that man has no certain knowledge of a stable transcendent power that assures the meaning of human history. Panthea Broughton makes this view of Faulkner more concrete: In Faulkner's world, characters struggle to find or make meaning, exposing themselves in various ways to the danger of spiritual self-destruction, of losing their own souls in the effort to find a way of living in a universe that does not provide meaning.

The immense quantity of critical commentary on Faulkner provides several satisfying ways of viewing and ordering the central concerns of his novels. Although the way into Faulkner suggested by Simpson and Broughton is only one of many, it seems particularly helpful to the reader who wishes to begin thinking about Faulkner's whole literary career. Broughton demonstrates that the Faulknerian universe is characterized essentially by motion. Human beings need meaning; they need to impose patterns on the motion of life. Out of this need spring human capacities for mature moral freedom as well as for tragic destructiveness. Closely related to this pattern that Broughton sees in Faulkner's stories are his tireless experimentation with form and his characteristic style.

In an essay published in 1960, Conrad Aiken notes the similarities between Faulkner's characteristic style and that of Henry James. The comparison is apt in some ways, for both in their greatest novels seem especially concerned with capturing in the sentence the complexity of experience and of reflection on experience. As Walter Slatoff, in the same volume, and others have shown, Faulkner seems especially drawn to paradox and oxymorons, kinds of verbal juxtaposition particularly suited to conveying the tension between the motion of life and the human need for pattern. When one notices these aspects of Faulkner's style in a complex novel such as

Absalom, Absalom!, in which Faulkner's characteristic style finds its ideal subject, much that initially seems obscure becomes clearer.

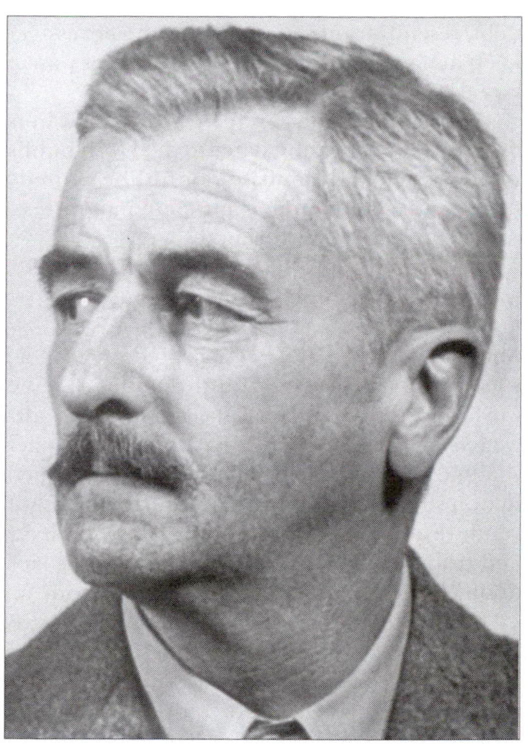

©The Nobel Foundation

Faulkner seems to have found most instructive the "loose" forms characteristic of the Victorian panoramic novel as it was developed, for example, by his favorite author, Charles Dickens. Faulkner's novels generally contain juxtapositions of attitudes, narrative lines, voices, modes of representation, and emotional tones. His more radical and probably less successful experiments in this vein include the alternation of chapters from two quite separate stories in *The Wild Palms* and the alternation of fictionalized historical narrative with dramatic acts in *Requiem for a Nun*, a kind of sequel to *Sanctuary*. *Light in August* is his most successful work in this direction.

Somewhat less radical and more successful experiments involved the incorporation of Faulkner's previously published stories into "collections" and sustained narratives in such a way as to produce the unity of a novel. Parts of *The Unvanquished*, the Snopes trilogy, and *A Fable* have led dual lives as stories and as parts of novels. *Go Down, Moses* is probably the most successful experiment in this direction. Faulkner was particularly interested in the juxtaposition of voices. His career as a novelist blossomed when he juxtaposed the voices and, therefore, the points of view of several characters in *The Sound and the Fury* and *As I Lay Dying*. In *Absalom, Absalom!*, the juxtaposition of voices also becomes the placing together of narrative lines, comparable episodes, points of view, modes of narration, attitudes, and emotional tones. This one novel brings together everything of which Faulkner was capable, demonstrating a technical virtuosity that in some ways is the fruit of the entire tradition of the novel. *Absalom, Absalom!* also realizes to some extent a special potential of Faulkner's interest in juxtaposition, the conception of his Yoknapatawpha novels as a saga that displays a unity of its own.

The technique of juxtaposition, like Faulkner's characteristic style, reflects his concern with the problems of living meaningfully within the apparently meaningless flow of time. Because life will not stand still or even move consistently according to patterns of meaning, it becomes necessary to use multiple points of view to avoid the complete falsification of his subject. Juxtaposition, the multileveled and open-ended sentence, and the oxymoronic style heighten the reader's awareness of the fluidity of the "reality" that the text attempts to portray. Faulkner's most tragic characters are those who feel driven to impose so rigid a pattern upon their lives and on the lives of others as to invite destruction from the overwhelming forces of motion and change.

These characters experience the heart in conflict with itself as the simultaneous need for living motion and meaningful pattern.

The Sound and the Fury • *The Sound and the Fury* is divided into four parts to which an appendix was later added. Faulkner repeated in interviews that the novel began as a short story that grew into the first section. He then found that the point of view he had chosen did not tell the whole story even though it closely approximated the flow of events before a nonjudgmental consciousness. Gradually, Faulkner found himself retelling the story four and, finally, five times. The effect of reading these juxtapositions may be described as similar to that of putting together a puzzle, the whole of which cannot be seen until the last piece is in place. Like several of Faulkner's novels, notably *Absalom, Absalom!, The Sound and the Fury* is not fully comprehendible upon a single reading. The first reading provides a general idea of the whole with subsequent readings allowing one to fill in the details and to see ever more deeply into this moving narrative.

The novel concerns the tragic dissolution of the Compson family. The decline dates decisively from the marriage of Candace (Caddy), the only daughter of Jason Compson III and Caroline Bascomb. Caddy's marriage is not the sole cause of the family's decline; rather, it becomes symbolic of a complex of internal and external forces that come to bear on this Mississippi family early in the twentieth century. Caddy becomes pregnant by Dalton Ames, a romantic, heroic, and apparently devoted outsider. Her mother then seeks out Sydney Herbert Head as a respectable husband for her. After the marriage, Herbert finds he has been gulled and divorces Caddy. These events deprive all the Compson men of their center of meaning. Quentin, the oldest son who loves Caddy not as a sister but as a woman, commits suicide. Jason III drinks himself to death, having lost the children upon whom his meaning depended. Jason IV seeks petty and impotent revenge on Caddy's daughter, also named Quentin, because he believes the failure of Caddy's marriage has deprived him of a chance to get ahead. Benjy, the youngest brother, who has a severe mental disability, suffers the absence of the only real mother he ever had. Control of the family passes to Jason IV, and the family ceases finally to be a place where love is sustained, becoming instead, despite the efforts of the heroic and loving black servant, Dilsey, a battleground of petty scheming, hatred, and revenge.

This general picture emerges from the internal monologues of Benjy, Quentin (male), and Jason IV, from a third-person narrative centering on Dilsey and Jason IV, and from the final appendix. Each of the four main sections is set on a particular day: Benjy's section on his thirty-third birthday, Easter Saturday, 1928; Jason's on Good Friday; and Dilsey's (the fourth section) on Easter Sunday of the same year. Quentin's section is on the day of his suicide, June 2, 1910. As the portrait of the family's decline emerges from these juxtaposed sections, their tragic significance becomes apparent.

Benjamin Compson's internal monologue consists of images, most of which are memories. At the center of his memory and of his stunted life is Caddy, whose "hair was like fire" and who "smelled like trees." Every experience of Benjy, which evokes these images or that resembles any experience he has had with Caddy, automatically triggers his memory. As a result, Benjy lives in a blending together of past and present in which memory and present experience are virtually indistinguishable. The spring of his suffering is that for him the experience of losing Caddy is continuous; the memory of her presence is perfect and the experience of her absence is constant.

This section proceeds by a series of juxtapositions that place Benjy's present, deprived condition starkly beside the richness of his memory. Though the pattern is difficult to see at first, repeated readings show that Faulkner works in this section primarily by pairing certain events: the funeral of Damuddy (Caroline's mother and Benjy's grandmother) and Caddy's wedding with all the attendant suggestions of meaning; Caddy with her boyfriends on the porch swing and Quentin (female) with her boyfriends; Benjy at the gate waiting for Caddy to come home from school one Christmas and Benjy waiting at the gate on the day Jason IV leaves it open. This last event, part of Jason's spitefulness against Caddy, leads to Benjy's castration after he grabs a school girl to ask about Caddy, though he cannot speak. Among the many pairings, the most pathetic appears at the end of the section. Benjy remembers his family long ago:

> Her hair was like fire, and little points of fire were in her eyes, and I went and Father lifted me into the chair too, and Caddy held me. She smelled like trees.
>
> *She smelled like trees. In the corner it was dark, but I could see the window. I squatted there, holding the slipper. I couldn't see it, but my hands saw it.*

The contrast between the firelight of the library, with its mirror and the loving people and the now barren and dark library with only one of Caddy's wedding slippers reveals much of the mood, the meaning, and the effectiveness of technique in Benjy's section.

Quentin's section also proceeds largely by the juxtaposition of memory and present experience. Quentin's memories are triggered by present events and he is sometimes unable to distinguish between memory and external reality. He commits suicide at the end of his first year at Harvard. As he carries out his plans to drown himself, he is caught up in various events that repeat aspects of his loss of Caddy, the last being a picnic with some college classmates during which he remembers his abortive attempt to be the brother who avenges a wronged sister. This memory is simultaneous with and is repeated in a fight with Gerald Bland, the kind of womanizer Quentin wishes Dalton Ames was.

Perhaps the major irony of Quentin's suicide is that the state of being that he desires is in many ways like the state in which his youngest brother suffers. Quentin wishes to be free of time, to end all motion. He gives as a motive his fear that grief over the loss of Caddy will attenuate, for when grief is gone, his sister will have become meaningless and his life utterly empty. However, his grief, of which every event reminds him, is unbearable. He wishes to keep Caddy as she was and to deny the repetitions that force him to remember her loss. Though he sees such a transcendent state in many images in his world, he can only *imagine* himself in that state, for it is impossible in life. Suicide seems his only alternative. In death, he can at least shirk everything, he can at least escape the *again* that to him is a sadder word than *was*.

Quentin's relationship with Caddy is highly problematic. One fairly simple way of understanding how his sister becomes so important to him that he must commit suicide when she marries is to observe Quentin's and Caddy's relationship with their parents: Jason III does not love Caroline. She believes that he has come to resent the fact that her family is socially inferior. In reality, she is a selfish and stupid woman who is completely inadequate as a mother and wife. Her husband is unable to deal with her. His growing unhappiness and cynicism magnify her weakness. The result is that these children have no real parents, and the responsibility falls on the gifted Caddy.

Despite her extraordinary capacity, Caddy is a girl. When she grows into a woman, she must, almost inevitably, betray the brothers who depend on her love. Even when she is with them, she cannot love them as an adult would; she cannot teach them to give. Her gifts lead her to another who is also capable of passion, Dalton Ames. This affair exaggerates the meaning of the betrayal by heightening the inadequacy of the family, including Quentin, to meet Caddy's needs. Caddy's sense of her parents' failure is captured in her memory of a picture in a book that made her think of her parents as keeping her from the light. Quentin needs Caddy not only as a mother, a source of pure affection, but also as a center of meaning. She embodies all the forms and traditions to which Quentin clings to escape the despair his father teaches him. Losing her, he loses his life.

Jason's section of the novel is much easier to read, for his interior life is more or less in the present. He neither desires nor even conceives of any transcendent reality; he desires power above all things, even money, though he is well aware that money is, in his world, the superior means to power. He delights in the power to be cruel, to make others fear him, yet he is remarkably impotent. His impotence stems from his inability to imagine in others any motives different from his own. In these respects, his character, as well as the mode in which it is presented, recalls the jealous monk in Robert Browning's "Soliloquy of the Spanish Cloister." Jason's interior monologue is the only one of the three that has all the marks of being spoken. It is as if Jason were two people, one constantly explaining and justifying himself to the other.

Jason tells primarily about his troubles bringing up Caddy's daughter, Quentin. The girl has been left in the care of the family while the divorced Caddy makes her way in the world. Quentin becomes the central instrument of Jason's revenge against Caddy for the failure of her marriage and the disappointment of his hope. Jason is so fixed on his need to exercise cruel power that he is unable to restrain himself sufficiently to keep the situation stable. He drives Quentin out of the family, losing the monthly checks from Caddy that he has been appropriating, the hoard he has collected in part from this theft, and the one person on whom he can effectively take his revenge.

"I've seed de first en de last," says Dilsey. She refers to the beginning and the end of the doom of the Compson family, to Caddy's wedding and Quentin's elopement. Each of these events suggests more meanings than can be detailed here, but the importance of Dilsey's section is that she sees a pattern of human meaning in the events that threaten an end to meaning for so many. Her part in these events has been a heroic struggle to bind the family together with her love and care, a doomed but not a meaningless struggle, for she can still see pattern, order, meaning in all of it. The events of Easter morning, in which Dilsey figures, suggest that at least one source of that power to mean and to love is her community at the African American church service, a community that, in the contemplation of the Christian symbols of transcendence, attains an experience of communion which partakes of the eternal even though it is temporary. Dilsey's church is a model of the family, and her experience there is not unlike Benjy's experience in Caddy's arms on Father's lap before the library fire. The Compson family has somehow lost this experience. As the appendix suggests, all the Compsons, except perhaps for Benjy, are damned, for they have all, in various ways, come to see themselves as "dolls stuffed with sawdust."

The Sound and the Fury is in part an exploration of the loss of the Christian world view. Temple and Popeye in *Sanctuary* respond in ways similar to Jason's. Addie in *As I Lay Dying* and Horace Benbow in *Sanctuary* play parts similar to Quentin's. Benbow attempts to prove the truth of the traditional view he has inherited from his family and class, the view that "God is a gentleman" and that Providence takes an active hand in human affairs. He is disastrously and blindly wrong and apparently suffers the loss of his faith. Addie Bundren's attempt to impose order on her world seems even more disastrous because Faulkner centers attention on the suffering she causes her family.

As I Lay Dying • In *As I Lay Dying*, Addie Bundren wants and fails to find a kind of transcendent communion with some other being. When she realizes the almost inevitable impermanence of such communion, she plans revenge against the people who have failed her, especially her husband, Anse. She makes him promise that he will bury her with her relations in Jefferson. This simple promise is a subtle revenge because it binds Anse with words for which he has too much respect and it becomes a terrible vengeance when Anse comes to fulfill that promise. Addie believes that a word is "a shape to fill a lack." By this she means that the communion she feels when she is pregnant with her firstborn is an essential experience for which words are unnecessary and inadequate. Not only are words inadequate to this experience, but they are also symbols of separation from this experience. At one point Addie reflects, "I would think how words go straight up in a thin line, quick and harmless, and how terribly doing goes along the earth." By making Anse "promise his word," Addie forces her husband to attempt a union of saying and doing, an attempt that sends Addie's entire family on a grotesque and tortured journey along the earth.

Addie imposes a verbal pattern on her family in revenge because pregnancy and passion are temporary. Each pregnancy ends in separation. Her one love affair is with the Reverend Whitfield, whom she describes as "the dark land talking the voiceless speech." When this affair ends in the birth of Jewel, her third son, her despair is complete. The promise she extracts from Anse elicits a catastrophic juggernaut, for she dies at the beginning of a storm that floods the area, making the wagon journey to Jefferson next to impossible.

The novel is presented in a series of monologues similar in depth and intensity to Quentin's in *The Sound and the Fury*. As the narrative emerges from these monologues so do the internal relationships of the family. The reader becomes intensely aware of the feelings and the needs of each family member. Anse is driven not only by his promise but also by the desire to regain the dignity he believes he loses by having no teeth. A sedentary man, he has needed this prod to set him in motion. He eventually returns, not only with teeth and dignity, but with several other new possessions as well, including a new wife. Cash, the oldest son, is the family's repository of technical skill. Almost without questioning, he solves the material problems of the journey. In crossing the flooded river, he breaks his leg, yet he finishes the journey in incredible pain. Darl, the son Addie has rejected, is the most sensitive of her children. He is seemingly capable of a kind of communion that might have fulfilled her, for he seems able to read minds and to know of events he does not see. He opposes the journey at every significant point, understanding that it is Addie's revenge and that it threatens to tear apart the family. Anse finally commits Darl to a mental hospital in order to escape financial responsibility for a barn that Darl ignites in an attempt to burn Addie and end the journey.

Jewel, product of the Whitfield affair, though he is barely articulate, comes to seem the living embodiment of Addie's wordless will to revenge. He saves the coffin from the flood when the wagon overturns in the river and from the fire in the barn.

He sacrifices his much prized pony in trade to replace the mules lost in the river crossing. Dewey Dell, the only daughter, is desperate to reach Jefferson where she believes she can get an abortion. She shares Darl's sensitivity and hates it because it makes her feel naked and vulnerable. She violently assists in the capture of Darl for she is glad to be rid of the kind of communion Addie so deeply desired. Vardaman, the youngest son, suffers loss. Drawn along on the journey by promises of bananas and a view of a toy train, he registers all the family's pain: the loss of a mother, the dislocations of the journey, the humiliation as Addie begins to smell, the shiftless poverty of Anse, the sufferings of the brothers, the vulnerability of Dewey Dell and, finally, the loss of Darl. Because the unity of the family is his identity, he suffers a kind of dismemberment.

This brief glimpse hardly conveys the richness and power of this novel. Nevertheless, it should make clear that part of the novel's meaning derives from Addie's attempt to impose a rigid pattern upon a significant part of her family's life and the extreme suffering her success brings about.

Sanctuary • Popeye and Temple in *Sanctuary* are lost children, victims of their moment in history, in that they are without souls. Their culture has failed to give them reasons for doing one thing rather than another. They do not have the natural acquisitiveness of Jason IV and the Snopeses, nor do they have a motive such as revenge to give direction to their lives. Popeye wears the mask of a gangster, though the mask slips occasionally. It is the role itself that gives Popeye substance and makes him appear somewhat like a normal human being. He also has a vague desire that he expresses in his abduction of Temple Drake. He desires to join the human community, to live a meaningful life. Just as he imitates gangsters in order to take possession of some identity, he also imitates the acts of men who reveal themselves to be under the power of a strong motive. He tries to desire and to possess Temple Drake because other men desire her. He fails even to desire her and apparently, as a result of this failure, he gives up his life. He has money, says the narrator, but there is nothing to buy with it.

Temple is perhaps the most fully developed example in early Faulkner of a character who simply flows, who seeks no meanings at all, but merely acts out her impulses. When she is abducted by Popeye, she is freed of the social restraints that have never been made important to her. Nothing in her experience has taught her to internalize social restraints as communal values. She is virtually without values, virtually unable to make moral choices; freed of external restraint, she seeks pointless and ultimately unsatisfying gratification of whatever impulses come to the fore. She becomes capable of killing in order to achieve sexual satisfaction. In her final act in the novel, she pointlessly condemns an innocent man to death as she begins to adopt Popeye's failed strategy, assuming a role to pass the time.

In Temple one sees that the utter surrender to motion is no solution to the search for meaning in Faulkner's world. Neither surrender nor rigid resistance to the flow of events will suffice. Faulkner's heroes, like Dilsey, are generally those who are able to find a balance between what Broughton calls the abstract and the actual, a balance that seems to answer the cry of the heart and to make loving possible. Faulkner's novels suggest that the modern tragedy of a lack of soul, of spiritual annihilation, results from some decisive break in the process by which one generation teaches the next how to love.

Light in August • The central juxtaposition in *Light in August* is between Lena Grove and Joe Christmas. Lena Grove, scandalously pregnant and deserted by Lucas Burch, alias Joe Brown, walks the dirt roads of Alabama, Mississippi, and finally Tennessee in tranquil search of a husband. She is a center of peace and faith and fertility, though all around her may be waste and catastrophe. She is like the peaceful center of Herman Melville's Grand Armada on the outer circles of which the stricken whales murder one another. Byron Bunch, who loves her at first sight even though she is nine months pregnant, tells his friend, the Reverend Gail Hightower, that Lena seems to have two persons inside her, one who *knows* that Lucas Burch is a scoundrel who will never marry her, and another who *believes* that God will see to it that her family will be together when the child is born. God somehow keeps these two persons within Lena from meeting and comparing notes.

When the child is born, there is a family indeed, for Lena seems to attract all the help she needs. Byron is camped outside her door. Gail is there to deliver the child. Joe Christmas's grandparents are present, reliving a past moment that promises them some small redemption. Even Lucas Burch makes a brief appearance before leaving the field open to Byron. Lena's tranquil faith, her trust in the world and its people, and her submission to her natural being make her into a kind of Faulknerian heroine. She is capable of finding meaning for herself in the flow of life, and this meaning attracts and vitalizes others. The images used to describe her are filled with the paradoxes of stillness in motion. This attitude gives her power, not a power that she often consciously uses, but still a real power to draw recluses such as Byron and Gail out of spiritual death and into the flow of living.

While Lena moves peacefully through the book, seeking a husband and bearing a child, Joe Christmas careens through the last days of his life, the culmination of more than thirty years of bigoted education. Joe's life story is the center of a novel that is composed largely of condensed biographies. Of the major characters, only Byron and Lena have relatively obscure pasts. Gail, Joanna Burden, and Joe are presented as the end products of three generations in their respective families. Even Percy Grimm, a relatively minor character, receives a fairly full biography. Each of these lives contrasts starkly with the life of Lena and, eventually, with Lena and Byron's relationship. Gail, Joanna, Joe, and Percy are, in the words of Gail, "lost children among the cold and terrible stars." They are the children of a generation that saw its world crumble and that adopted fanatic versions of Calvinism mixed with an inherited racism in order to resist the flow of history with its threat of meaninglessness. They are products of the failure of love. Although Lena, miraculously immunized against lovelessness, is capable of accepting the world and its lawful motion as her home, most of the other major characters resist and reject the world, living in alienation.

Joe's life reveals the sources and meanings of resistance and alienation. The story of his life comes in several blocks. After learning that Joe has murdered Joanna, the reader is plunged deeply into the suffering consciousness of the murderer during the twenty-four hours preceding the crime. Joe is seen as a driven man: He seems to be under the control of the voices that speak inside him, and he is unaware of the loving, caressing voices in his natural environment. This glimpse into his consciousness reveals ambivalent attitudes toward his racial background, a hatred of the feminine, a sense that Joanna has somehow betrayed him by praying over him, and a sense of being an abandoned child who wants to be able to say with conviction, "God loves me, too." The middle section of the novel separates into strands the inner voices that drive Joe to murder that, in his culture, is a suicide.

In an orphanage at the age of five, Joe accidentally provokes the dietician into speeding his placement with a family. His adoptive father, the Calvinist fanatic Simon McEachern, teaches Joe the skills of resistance to nature. He learns to cultivate a rocklike will and an indomitable body. He learns to relate to people impersonally. He grows up not only without love but also in resistance to love: To be a man is not to love. McEachern derives his hatred of the world from his Calvinist theology, while Joe learns to resist the world in defense of his selfhood. Joe is not a Calvinist; he resists the content of McEachern's teachings by mastering its forms. Inside Joe, the voice perhaps first awakened by a girl who mothered him in the orphanage continues to speak. Joe continues to desire to love, to belong, and ultimately to be free of the voices that drive him.

Of the forms Joe's rebellion against his culture takes, those involving sex and race seem most significant. Joe's desire to love and be loved is revealed and betrayed in his adolescent affair with Bobbie Allen, a local prostitute, a relationship that paradoxically combines intimacy with impersonality. In his adult life, his rebellion often takes the form of asserting his presumed black blood. In doing so, he provokes a ritual reaction which becomes the dominant pattern in his life, the pattern that is worked out in full when he kills Joanna and suffers the consequences.

Joe's affair with Joanna, his life and death in Jefferson, Mississippi, replay the patterns of his life in their full significance, bringing him again to the moment of rebellious protest in which he faces an authority figure in the fullness of his identity and strikes out in murderous self-defense. Joe and Joanna are virtually doubles. They proceed through tortured and perverse phases of sexual relations until they reach a kind of purged state of near normality, a point at which both seem seriously able to contemplate marriage, children, a normal human life. When Joanna enters menopause, however, she is simply unable to accept the natural flow of time. Her "sins" with Joe lose their meaning if they do not lead to marriage, motherhood, and "normal" feminine fulfillment. She reverts to her inherited Calvinism and racism, changing from Joe's double to McEachern's double. Betrayed herself, she betrays Joe, trying to form into a piece of her sick world. Joe responds to this change as he responded to McEachern's attempt to cast him into Hell.

During Joe's flight from the pursuing Jefferson authorities, he comes closer than ever before to the peace, freedom, and love he has desired. In his disorientation and physical suffering, for the first time in his life, he feels unity with the natural world. He partakes of "the peace and unhaste and quiet" that are characteristic of Lena's experience because for the first time he is really free of the compulsive voices of his culture, free to feel at home in his world.

Contrasted to this experience is the story of Joe's first five years as told to Gail by Joe's fanatical grandfather, Doc Hines, and by his grandmother. Doc Hines sees himself as the agent of a Calvinist deity avenging the lust after worldly pleasure symbolized by femininity and the inferior race ("God's abomination upon the earth"). Against these disembodied "voices of the land," Joe emerges as somewhat ambiguously victorious in his death. Joe's death is almost inevitable. Even though he seems to have found freedom from the internal compulsions that have driven him to self-destruction, he cannot escape the consequences of his actions in the world. He can only accept. The way in which Joe accepts the consequences of his acts suggests for him a kind of heroic status.

Joe's death appears to be inevitable because he has set in motion a deeply embedded social ritual, a fateful machine that cannot stop until it has completed its movement. The community's heritage of Calvinism and racism has produced that ritual machine. In a desperate need to assert control over the flow of history, the culture has embraced the Calvinist denial of all things in this world that might turn one's attention from God.

Among other elements that contribute to the view of Joe as a hero is his effect on Gail. Gail has been on the edges of all the events of these days in Jefferson. He has had several opportunities to mitigate suffering, but he has, on the whole, failed to act. He is afraid to leave his sanctuary in order to help those he could really help. Joe appears at Gail's door, moments before dying, like an avenging god to strike Gail down in a kind of judgment, even as Gail confesses part of his sin. Finally, Joe dies in Gail's house, another sacrifice to the very kinds of rituals and legalisms that Gail has used to buy what he calls peace, the right to sit unmolested in his house dreaming of his grandfather's absurdly heroic death. Gail learns from this experience. He goes on to make, to himself at least, a full confession of his sins. He faces the fact that what he has wanted, a sterile stasis in a dead past moment, was selfish, that this desire has led him to bring about his wife's death, to welcome being ostracized by the town, ultimately to serve his small need at the cost of abandoning those he promised to serve when he became a minister.

The juxtaposition of lives tragically ruined by a heritage of racism and fanatical Calvinism with Lena's life creates an unforgettable and moving work. One of the easily overlooked effects of the whole is the impression it gives of a community whose heart is basically good, which responds, albeit sometimes grudgingly, with sympathy to those in need and with kindness to those in trouble. Lena brings out this side of the community. On the lunatic fringe of the community are those who express the deep compulsions that thrive in the insecurity of modern life. Joe is brought up to evoke this underside of the community that it would like to forget. They are not to forget. The images of horror pass from one generation to the next. The uncertainties of life, especially in a world that seems to have lost the easy comfort of religious consensus, continue to produce personalities such as those of Doc Hines and Percy Grimm, who cannot deal with or bear an indifferent universe. Their rigid imposition of abstraction upon the flow of life forces them ever backward to the legalism of their secret rituals. Society is tragically in the grip of the past despite its great desire to be finally free of these compulsions.

Absalom, Absalom! • *Absalom, Absalom!* juxtaposes differing accounts of the same events. In *The Sound and the Fury*, Faulkner thought of himself as trying to tell the whole story and finding that he had to multiply points of view in order to do so. In *Absalom, Absalom!*, as Gary Stonum argues, "the labor of representation is . . . made a part of the text." The story is only partly known; it is a collection of facts, not all of which are certain, which seem to those who know them profoundly and stubbornly meaningful. The various characters who try their formulae for bringing those facts together into a meaningful whole are the historians of the novel. Faulkner has written a novel about writing novels, about giving meaning to the flow of events. *Absalom, Absalom!* dramatizes so effectively the processes and obstacles to creating a satisfying structure for events and offers such an ideal wedding of structure, content, technique, and style, that many critics regard it as Faulkner's greatest achievement. With *The Sound and the Fury* this novel shares characters from the Compson family and a degree of difficulty that may require multiple readings.

The central concern of the narrative is the life of Thomas Sutpen and his family.

Sutpen has appeared out of nowhere to build a vast plantation near Jefferson, Mississippi, in the early nineteenth century. Apparently without much wealth, he nevertheless puts together the greatest establishment in the area, marries Ellen Coldfield, a highly respectable though not a wealthy woman, and fathers two children by her. When Sutpen's son, Henry, goes to college, he meets and befriends Charles Bon. Charles and Sutpen's daughter, Judith, fall in love and plan to marry. For no apparent reason, Sutpen forbids the marriage and Henry leaves his home with Charles. During the Civil War, Ellen dies. Near the end of the war, Henry and Charles appear one day at the plantation, Sutpen's Hundred, and Henry kills Charles. After the war, Sutpen becomes engaged to Rosa Coldfield, Ellen's much younger sister, but that engagement is suddenly broken off. A few years later, Sutpen fathers a daughter with Milly Jones, the teenage daughter of his handyman, Wash Jones. When Sutpen refuses to marry Milly, Jones kills him. Then Sutpen's daughter, Judith, and his slave daughter, Clytie, live together and, somewhat mysteriously, care for the descendants of Charles Bon by his "marriage" to an octoroon.

Though not all the known facts, these constitute the outline of the story as it is generally known in Jefferson. The major mysteries stand out in this outline. Why did Sutpen forbid the marriage? Why did Henry side with Charles and then kill him? Why did Rosa agree to marry Sutpen and then refuse? Why did Sutpen get a squatter's daughter pregnant and abandon her, bringing about his own death? Why did Judith take responsibility for Bon's family? These are the questions to which Rosa Coldfield, Jason Compson III and his father General Compson, and Quentin Compson and his Harvard roommate Shreve McCannon address themselves. A rough chapter outline will give an idea of the novel's structure while suggesting how the various accounts interrelate.

The setting in chapters 1 through 5 is day one of time present, early September, 1909, before Quentin Compson leaves for Harvard. (1) Afternoon, Rosa tells Quentin about Sutpen in summary, painting him as a destructive demon of heroic proportions. (2) Evening, Jason III repeats his father's description of how Sutpen built his empire of one hundred square miles and married Ellen. (3) Evening, Jason III gives the public version, with some inside information, of Rosa's relationship with Sutpen, centering on her involvement with the Judith-Charles relationship and her eventual refusal to marry Sutpen. (4) Evening, Jason attempts to explain why Sutpen forbade the marriage and why Henry killed Charles. He argues that Bon intended to keep his octoroon mistress/wife when he married Judith. Jason offers this explanation as plausible but does not really feel it is adequate. (5) Later that same evening, Rosa tries to explain why she refused to marry Sutpen, giving her own version of how she came to be on the scene and describing the death of Bon and its effect on the family. She ends this part by revealing her belief that the Sutpen mansion contains some secret that she intends to discover that evening.

Chapters 6 through 9 are set in day two of time present, January of 1910; Quentin and Shreve spend an evening in their Harvard dormitory working out their version of the Sutpen story. (6) Quentin has a letter saying that Rosa is dead. The story is recapitulated with more details coming to light and completing the story of the Sutpen line in outline. (7) Quentin and Shreve concentrate on Sutpen's youth, retelling his story up to his death in the light of information Quentin received directly from his grandfather. (8) The boys work out the story of Charles Bon's and Henry Sutpen's relationship, constructing a new answer to the question of why Henry killed Charles. Not only was Charles Henry's half brother, but he also had black blood. (9) Quentin recalls his trip with Rosa to Sutpen's house on the September night and his brief meeting with the returned Henry. They finish Jason III's letter and contemplate the whole story.

The novel's climax comes in chapter 8 when Shreve and Quentin construct their explanation. They "discover" through intense imaginative identification with Henry and Charles a meaning latent in the facts they have gathered. Their discovery implies that Sutpen prevented the marriage and alienated Henry by revealing that Charles and Henry were half brothers. The substance of their discovery is that the first wife whom Sutpen put aside, the mother of Charles, was a mulatto. Sutpen reserves this information as his trump card in case Henry comes to accept an incestuous marriage. Only this revelation could have brought Henry to kill Charles rather than allow him to marry Judith. The means by which the boys arrive at this conclusion reveal much about the meanings of the novel. Not least among these meanings is the revelation of a sickness at the "prime foundation" of the South, the sickness of a planter society that prevents one from loving one's own children.

There is no way for the boys to *prove* this solution. Their discovery is above all an imaginative act, yet it has the ring of truth. No one who is alive, except Henry, knows what passed between Sutpen and Henry in the conversations that broke off the marriage and led to the murder, and Henry tells no one before his own death. The truth is utterly hidden in the past. The materials that make up this truth are fragmentary, scattered in distance, time, and memory. Only through the most laborious process do Quentin and Shreve gather the facts together from the narratives of their elders and a few documents. Informants such as Rosa and Jason III are Sherwood Anderson grotesques; they have chosen simple truths to which they make all their experiences conform. Rosa's portrait of Sutpen grows almost entirely out of Sutpen's proposal that they produce a child before they marry. Jason III's portrait of Charles Bon is an idealized self-portrait. Even eyewitnesses such as General Compson and Rosa have faulty memories and biased points of view. In the world of this novel, the truth is difficult to know because the facts on which it is based are hard to assemble.

When the facts are assembled, they are even harder to explain. Jason realizes that he has "just the words, the symbols, the shapes themselves." Quentin and Shreve are able to explain, not because they find the facts, but because they use their imaginations so effectively as to find themselves in the tent with Sutpen and Henry in 1865 and in the camp when Charles tells Henry that even though they are brothers, Charles is the "nigger" who is going to marry his sister. Quentin and Shreve have felt Thomas Sutpen's motives, his reasons for opposing the marriage. They have felt Charles's reasons for insisting on the marriage and Henry's victimization as an instrument of his father. They have entered into the heart's blood, the central symbolic image of the novel, the symbol of the old verities that touch the heart and to which the heart holds as truth. Sutpen's honor is embodied in the design that will crumble if he accepts Charles as his son or allows the marriage. The love of sons for fathers and of brothers for sisters becomes a tragic trap within that design. If love, honor, courage, compassion, and pride are found at the center of these inexplicable events, then the boys have discovered "what must be true." As Cass Edmonds says to young Ike McCaslin in *Go Down, Moses,* "what the heart holds to becomes truth, as far as we know truth."

In order for Quentin and Shreve to complete this act of imagination, they must come to understand Sutpen more fully than anyone does. The key to understanding Sutpen comes in chapter 6, when Quentin repeats what he has learned from General

Compson, to whom Sutpen has confided much of his life story. Sutpen is the child of an independent mountain family who have fallen on hard times and have become tenant farmers. His ambition springs into being on the day he discovers that in the eyes of the plantation owner's black doorman he is insignificant "white trash." On that day, he determines to right this injustice by becoming a planter himself. He dreams that when he is a planter, he will not turn away the boy messenger from his door. He becomes a planter in Haiti, then abandons everything to go to Mississippi. Having built a second plantation there and begun his dynasty again, he sacrifices his son to cancel the son by the first marriage. As General Compson sees it, Sutpen's great weakness is his innocence. Sutpen is never able to understand how history betrays him. By becoming a planter, Sutpen almost inevitably adopts the material forms that determine the morality of the planter, and he lacks the imagination to circumvent those forms. In fact, Sutpen is so literal, rigid, and puritanical in his adoption of the design that he becomes a grotesque of a planter. The messenger boy who comes to his door is his own mulatto son, yet Sutpen can only turn away without even so much as an "I know you are my son though I cannot say so publicly."

Sutpen's innocence and the rigidity of his design account for many of the mysteries of his life. As General Compson says, Sutpen seems to think of morality, even of life as a whole, as like a cake; if one includes the ingredients and follows the recipe, only cake can result. Supten's design is so abstract that he is utterly blind to the feelings of others. He fails to anticipate Rosa's probable reaction to the second proposal. He never thinks of how Wash will react to his treatment of Milly. He never expects that Charles Bon will be the boy at his door. When Sutpen tells his story to General Compson, he is seeking the missing ingredient that has twice prevented him from completing his design and his revenge. Sutpen's boyhood experience has cut him off from the truth of the heart. He has, instead, rigidly grasped a single truth and has made it into a falsehood in his Olympian effort to make the world conform to the shape of that truth.

Because of Sutpen's failure, many children stand before doors that they cannot pass. Only an act of sympathetic imagination can get one past the symbolic doors of this novel, but most of the children are so victimized that they are incapable of imaginative sympathy. Even Quentin would not be able to pass his door, the subjects of incest and a sister's honor, without help from Shreve. Without Quentin's passion and knowledge, Shreve would never have seen the door. Their brotherhood is a key "ingredient" in their imaginative power.

Many significant elements of this complex novel must remain untouched in any brief analysis. One other aspect of the novel, however, is of particular interest: In *Absalom, Absalom!*, Faulkner suggests the possibility of seeing the Yoknapatawpha novels as a saga, a unified group of works from which another level of significance emerges. He chooses to end *Absalom, Absalom!* with a map of Yoknapatawpha County. This map locates the events of all the preceding Yoknapatawpha novels and some that were not yet written, though the relevant Snopes stories had appeared in magazines. Reintroducing the Compson family also suggests that Faulkner was thinking of a unity among his novels in addition to the unity of the individual works. It seems especially significant that Shreve McCannon, an outsider, neither a Compson nor a southerner nor an American, makes the final imaginative leap that inspirits Sutpen's story with the heart's truth. In this way, that truth flows out of its narrow regional circumstances to a world that shares in the same heart's blood. With *Absalom, Absalom!*, Faulkner may have seen more clearly than before how his novels could be pillars to help men "endure and prevail" by reminding them of those "old verities," the central motives that bind humankind and the Yoknapatawpha novels together.

Go Down, Moses • In *Go Down, Moses,* Faulkner juxtaposes two sides of the McCaslin family. This contrast comes to center on Lucas Beauchamp, a black descendant, and Isaac McCaslin, a white descendant of L. Q. C. McCaslin, the founder of the McCaslin plantation. Although the novel divides roughly in two and has the appearance of a collection of stories, it is unified as an explanation of the opening phrases that summarize Isaac's life. Ike is distinguished by his refusals to inherit the family plantation or to own any other land because he believes the earth belongs to no man, by his love for the woods, and by the fact that though he has married and is uncle to half a county, he has no children.

"Was," "The Fire and the Hearth," and "Pantaloon in Black" deal primarily with the black McCaslins. Taken together, these stories dramatize the suffering of basically good people, black and white, as they struggle to make and preserve their marriages and to honor their blood ties despite the barrier of racism.

"Was" tells how Tomey's Turl and Tennie arrange their marriage. Turl and Tennie are slaves on neighboring plantations in the days when such farms were half a day's travel apart. In this comic interlude, remembered from before Isaac's birth, Hubert Beauchamp, owner of the neighboring farm, tries without success to marry his sister, Sophonsiba, to Isaac's father, Buck McCaslin. It becomes clear that the plot to land Buck is a cooperative effort among the slave couple and the Beauchamps. The plot ends with a poker game in which Buck's twin, Uncle Buddy, nearly outmaneuvers Hubert. The fact that Turl is the dealer persuades Hubert to settle for the advantages he has gained rather than chance losing everything to Buddy. Buck escapes for the time being, though he eventually marries Sophonsiba, and Tennie and Turl achieve their marriage. These two marriages generate the two main characters of the novel, Lucas and Isaac. From this point of view the tale is funny and almost heartwarming, but it has a tragic undertone, for Turl, it turns out, is half brother to the twins. Even though Buck and Buddy are reluctant and enlightened slaveholders, they try to prevent their brother's marriage and must be tricked into permitting it.

This barrier of race that separates brothers and threatens marriages is the center of "The Fire and the Hearth." This long story dramatizes two pairs of conflicts. In the present, Lucas Beauchamp discovers a gold piece buried on Roth Edmonds's plantation. The Edmonds have become inheritors of the McCaslin land because of Isaac's repudiation. In his mad search for "the rest of the gold," Lucas becomes a barrier to the marriage of his daughter with George Wilkins, a rival moonshiner. To get rid of Wilkins, Lucas uses the very racist rituals that have caused him suffering; he appeals to Roth's paternalistic dominance of his black tenants. This conflict reminds Lucas of his previous conflict with Roth's father, Zack. In this conflict, Zack and Lucas, who were reared as brothers, nearly kill each other because as a black, Lucas simply cannot believe Zack's statement that though he had the opportunity, he has not cuckolded Lucas.

The second present conflict arises when Lucas's wife, Mollie, decides she will divorce her husband because he has become obsessed with finding gold. When she announces this plan to Roth, Roth remembers his own relationship with Lucas and Mollie, especially that Mollie is the only mother he ever had. His childhood memories prominently include the shame he felt when racism came between him and his "family." Now, when he most needs to, he cannot talk with them heart to heart.

In "Was" and "The Fire and the Hearth," the wall of racism divides lovers, brothers, parents, and children. All suffer because what their hearts yearn for is forbidden by their racial experience. Familial love is blocked by racism. "Pantaloon in Black" completes this picture of tragic suffering with a powerful image of what whites, especially, lose by inherited racist attitudes. Rider and Mannie, tenants on Edmonds land, love passionately. When Mannie dies, Rider cannot contain his grief. He moves magnificently toward a complex love-death. Juxtaposed to this image is the marriage of a local deputy that contains no passion or compassion. They live separate lives, the wife's emotional needs satisfied by card parties and motion pictures. Their brief discussion of Rider's grief and death reveals that because they are unable to see their black brothers as human, they are cut off from imagining their feelings, cut off from sympathy and, finally, cut off from their own humanity.

"The Old People," "The Bear," and "Delta Autumn" tell the story of Isaac: of his education for life in the woods, his consecration to that life, the resulting decision to repudiate his inheritance and the consequence of that decision, including his wife's refusal to bear his children.

Isaac's education begins with Sam Fathers. Sam contains the blood of all three races that share in the founding of America. In him the wilderness ideal of brotherhood is made visible. On the other hand, Sam contains the sins of the American Indians who sold land not theirs to sell and then went on to buy and sell men, including Sam, who was sold as a slave by his own father. Sam is the last of the old people and, therefore, figures in both the origins and the victimizations of the races. When Isaac perceives these meanings in Sam's life, his spontaneous response is, "Let him go!" However, this Mosaic wish is futile, Ike is told. There is no simple cage that can be unlocked to free Sam. From that moment, Ike tries to discover some effective way to set some of God's lowly people free.

By means of the stories of the old people, Sam teaches Ike that, in the wilderness, all people are guests on the earth. In the wilderness, the hunt becomes a ritual by which man, in taking the gifts of the land for his sustenance, participates in the immortal life processes of the cosmos. Here even the barriers between life and death lack significance. Opposed to this view is the civilization represented by the divided fields outside the wall of the big woods. In this outer world, land ownership divides the haves and the have-nots. Conceiving of the land as dead matter to be bought and sold leads to conceiving of people as beasts to be bought and sold. Ike comes to see this decline in humanity in his own family history as contained in the ledgers of the plantation commissary.

In part 4 of "The Bear," having seen the death of Old Ben, the bear that stands for the life of the old wilderness, Ike explains to his older cousin, Cass Edmonds, why he will not accept his inheritance, the McCaslin plantation. Though quite complex, his argument is mainly that if owning land leads directly to the exploitation of God's lowly people, then refusing to own the land may help end such exploitation. He takes on the responsibility of attempting to realize in civilization the values of the wilderness to which he has consecrated himself. Among the reasons for his choice is the pattern he sees in his family history.

Ike's grandfather, L. Q. C. McCaslin, seems almost incomprehensible to Ike because he bought a beautiful slave, fathered a daughter with her, and then fathered a son, Tomey's Turl, with that daughter. To Ike, these acts represent the worst of the violations that arise from arrogant proprietorship. In his grandfather's will, in the subsequent actions of Buck and Buddy in freeing slaves, in the Civil War and in his own education, Ike sees a pattern that leads him to think his family may have a responsibility to help bring an end to these wrongs. By repudiating his inheritance, he hopes humbly to participate in making love possible between the races.

Critics disagree about whether readers are to see Ike as heroic in the tradition of saintliness or as a fool who hides his light under a bushel by refusing to risk the exercise of power in behalf of his beliefs. Although Ike does not fall into Sutpen's trap, largely because he conceives of his mission as acting for others rather than for himself, he may choose too passive a means to his end. It may be that Faulkner intended a suspension between these alternatives that would heighten the tragic dimensions of moral choice in the complex welter of human events. It is difficult to fault Ike's motives or his perception of the situation, but when assessing the effectivenes of his actions, one finds roughly equal evidence for and against his choice.

In "Delta Autumn," Ike is a respected teacher. He speaks with a wisdom and authority that command attention, if not full understanding, from his companions and that speak directly to Roth Edmonds's shame at his inability to marry the mulatto woman he loves and to claim his son by her. Although Ike has nothing of which to be ashamed, his refusal of the land has helped to corrupt the weaker Roth. Ike has known that he would probably never see the amelioration for which he has worked and, more than any of his companions, Ike understands that something sacred, which he can call God, comes into being when people love one another. Nevertheless, he must suffer seeing the sins of his grandfather mirrored by Roth, for Roth's mistress is a descendant of Tomey's Turl. Ike must tell that woman to accept the repudiation of her love, and he must accept her accusation that he knows nothing about love. Whether Ike is a saint or a fool seems endlessly arguable. The fact that he is to some extent aware of this dilemma may be part of the tragic significance of his life. He cannot learn whether his example will contribute to ending the shame of denied love that results from racism and that perpetuates it. He can only believe.

"Go Down, Moses," the last story, reemphasizes the desire for spiritual unity between the races and the apparently insuperable barriers that remain. Mollie Beauchamp's grandson, Samuel Worsham Beauchamp, is executed for murdering a Chicago policeman. Sam is the opposite of Sam Fathers. He is the youngest son, sold into the slavery of making money too fast, which devalues human life. Mollie's grieving chant that Roth Edmonds sold her Benjamin into Egypt echoes the imagined grief of the biblical Jacob whom his sons claim will die if they return from Egypt without their youngest brother. Roth has taken responsibility for this young relation and then has repudiated him. Mollie's accusation is fundamentally correct. The sympathetic but paternalistic white community of Jefferson cannot see this connection and so, despite its good heart, it cannot cross the barrier between races and truly enter into Mollie's grief. Gavin Stevens, the community's representative, feels driven from the scene of grief before the fire on the hearth by the intense passion of Mollie's grieving. Ike's sacrifice has changed nothing yet, but whether it was a bad choice remains hard to decide.

Faulkner wrote many fine novels that cannot be discussed here. The Snopes trilogy and *The Reivers* are often included among his masterpieces, in part because they reveal especially well Faulkner's great but sometimes overlooked comic gifts.

Faulkner's reputation has grown steadily since his Nobel Prize. Some critics are ready to argue that he is America's greatest novelist. They base their claim on the power of his novels to fascinate a generation of readers, to provoke serious and profound discussion about the modern human condition while engaging significant emotions, and to give the pleasures of all great storytelling, the pleasures of seeing, knowing, believing in and caring for characters like oneself at crucial moments in their lives. The quantity and quality of his work, as well as the worthy unity of purpose that emerges from analysis of his career, tend to confirm the highest estimate of Faulkner's accomplishment.

Terry Heller

Other major works

SHORT FICTION: *These Thirteen*, 1931; *Doctor Martino, and Other Stories*, 1934; *The Portable Faulkner*, 1946, 1967; *Knight's Gambit*, 1949; *Collected Short Stories of William Faulkner*, 1950; *Big Woods*, 1955; *Three Famous Short Novels*, 1958; *Uncollected Stories of William Faulkner*, 1979.

SCREENPLAYS: *Today We Live*, 1933; *To Have and Have Not*, 1945; *The Big Sleep*, 1946; *Faulkner's MGM Screenplays*, 1982.

POETRY: *The Marble Faun*, 1924; *A Green Bough*, 1933.

NONFICTION: *New Orleans Sketches*, 1958; *Faulkner in the University*, 1959; *Faulkner at West Point*, 1964; *Essays, Speeches and Public Letters*, 1965; *The Faulkner-Cowley File: Letters and Memories, 1944-1962*, 1966 (Malcolm Cowley, editor); *Lion in the Garden*, 1968; *Selected Letters*, 1977.

MISCELLANEOUS: *The Faulkner Reader*, 1954; *William Faulkner: Early Prose and Poetry*, 1962.

Bibliography

Bleikasten, André. *The Ink of Melancholy: Faulkner's Novels from "The Sound and the Fury" to "Light in August."* Bloomington: Indiana University Press, 1990. Concentrating on four of William Faulkner's finest novels, Bleikasten offers a wide-ranging study of the writer and the limits of authorship.

Broughton, Panthea. *William Faulkner: The Abstract and the Actual.* Baton Rouge: Louisiana State University Press, 1974. Of several fine critical studies that attempt to see Faulkner whole and understand his worldview, this is one of the best, especially for readers just beginning to know Faulkner. Broughton sees the tension between the ideal and the actual as central to understanding the internal and external conflicts about which Faulkner most often writes.

Fargnoli, A. Nicholas, and Michael Golay. *William Faulkner A to Z: The Essential Reference to His Life and Work.* New York: Facts On File, 2001. Wide-ranging reference source with alphabetically arranged entries on aspects of Faulkner's life and writings.

Gray, Richard. *The Life of William Faulkner: A Critical Biography.* Oxford, England: Blackwell, 1994. A noted Faulkner scholar, Gray closely integrates the life and work. Part 1 suggests a method of approaching Faulkner's life; part 2 concentrates on his apprentice years; part 3 explains his discovery of Yoknapatawpha and the transformation of his region into his fiction; part 4 deals with his treatment of past and present; part 5 addresses his exploration of place; and part 6 analyzes his final novels, reflecting on his creation of Yoknapatawpha. Includes family trees, chronology, notes, and a bibliography.

Inge, M. Thomas, ed. *Conversations with William Faulkner.* Jackson: University Press of Mississippi, 1999. Part of the Literary Conversations series, this volume gives insight into Faulkner the person. Includes bibliographical references and index.

Karl, Frederick Robert. *William Faulkner: American Writer.* New York: Weidenfeld & Nicolson, 1989. Full-scale biography of Faulkner that focuses on his literary career.

McHaney, Thomas. *William Faulkner: A Reference Guide.* Boston: G. K. Hall, 1976. Though somewhat difficult to use, this guide provides an admirably complete annotated listing of writing about Faulkner through 1973. Because Faulkner is a world-class author, a tremendous amount has been written since 1973. A good source of information about later writing is *American Literary Scholarship: An Annual.*

The Mississippi Quarterly 50 (Summer, 1997). A special issue on Faulkner, including articles that discuss displaced meaning, dispossessed sons, the wilderness and consciousness, and subjectivity in *Go Down, Moses.*

Parini, Jay. *One Matchless Time: A Life of William Faulkner.* New York: HarperCollins, 2004. Appreciative biography of Faulkner that pays close attention to the content of novels and the critical receptions that they received.

Peek, Charles A., and Robert W. Hamblin, eds. *A Companion to Faulkner Studies.* Westport, Conn.: Greenwood Press, 2004. Student-friendly handbook to the writings of Faulkner.

Singal, Daniel J. *William Faulkner: The Making of a Modernist.* Chapel Hill: University of North Carolina Press, 1997. A study of the thought and art of Faulkner, charting the development of his ideas from their source in his reading to their embodiment in his writing. Depicts two Faulkners: the country gentleman and the intellectual man of letters.

Volpe, Edmond L. *A Reader's Guide to William Faulkner: The Novels.* Syracuse, N.Y.: Syracuse University Press, 2003. Very handy novel-by-novel guide to Faulkner's long fiction. Volpe has also written a similar volume on Faulkner's short stories.

Wagner-Martin, Linda, ed. *New Essays on "Go Down, Moses."* Cambridge, England: Cambridge University Press, 1996. After an introduction that summarizes contemporary reception and critical analysis of *Go Down, Moses,* Wagner-Martin collects essays that approach the work from the perspective of race, environment, gender, and ideology.

Edna Ferber

Born: Kalamazoo, Michigan; August 15, 1885
Died: New York, New York; April 16, 1968

Principal long fiction • *Dawn O'Hara: The Girl Who Laughed,* 1911; *Fanny Herself,* 1917; *The Girls,* 1921; *So Big,* 1924; *Show Boat,* 1926; *Cimarron,* 1930; *American Beauty,* 1931; *Come and Get It,* 1935; *Saratoga Trunk,* 1941; *Great Son,* 1945; *Giant,* 1952; *Ice Palace,* 1958.

Other literary forms • In addition to twelve novels, Edna Ferber wrote eight plays, two novellas, eighty-three short stories, and two autobiographies. Although her novels have perhaps been the most enduring part of her work, her short stories and plays were equally or more important during her lifetime. Almost all her work, except drama, first appeared serially in magazines. In addition, she wrote numerous short articles and commentaries. Twenty-two Emma McChesney stories made Ferber a best-selling writer. These were first published in *The American Magazine* or *Cosmopolitan* between 1911 and 1915 and later were collected in *Roast Beef Medium* (1913), *Personality Plus* (1914), and *Emma McChesney and Co.* (1915). Emma McChesney also was the heroine of *Our Mrs. McChesney* (1915), Ferber's first play written with George V. Hobart. The McChesney character was a significant innovation—the first successful businesswoman depicted in popular American literature. Finally, however, Ferber declined *Cosmopolitan*'s proffered contract for as many McChesney stories as she wished to write at a price she could name. Ferber saw herself, instead, as a novelist and dramatist. The plays she wrote with George S. Kaufman, especially *Dinner at Eight* (1932), *The Royal Family* (1927), and *Stage Door* (1936), enjoyed long Broadway runs and secured her fame as a dramatist. Her autobiographies, *A Peculiar Treasure* (1939, 1960) and *A Kind of Magic* (1963), explain her motivations and detail her writing techniques. The books also are intensely personal and revealing. The second, written after her health began to deteriorate, is rambling and repetitive but essentially completes the story of her active life.

Achievements • Ferber maintained herself as a best-selling author and a popular celebrity from the appearance of the Emma McChesney stories in 1911 to the publication of *Ice Palace* in 1958. During this period, she was cited several times as America's best woman novelist, and literary notables, such as William Allen Wright, Rudyard Kipling, and James M. Barrie, praised her work. Her reputation, however, abruptly declined during the late 1960's. Resurgence began during the 1980's, fueled mostly by interest in her various social crusades. Advocacy of social and political causes in her fiction significantly influenced public opinion and policy. Ernest Gruening, territorial senator elect of Alaska, for example, cited Ferber's *Ice Palace* as important in winning Alaska's statehood. Explication of regional history and culture in her novels also played a prominent part in raising pride in American culture after World War I. Her short story *Half Portions* received the O. Henry Award in 1919. In 1924, her novel *So Big* won the Pulitzer Prize for fiction. Jerome Kern and Oscar Hammerstein II's classic musical play *Show Boat* (1927), based on Ferber's novel, was the first American musical with a serious plot derived from a literary source. The story also was used in a successful radio serial program and four films; it made so much money that Ferber referred to it as her "oil well." She associated with many prominent theatrical, literary, and political figures, including members of the Algonquin Round Table, the literary circle that met for lunch at New York's Algonquin Hotel. At least twenty-seven films are based on her works.

Biography • Edna Jessica Ferber was the second daughter of a Hungarian Jewish immigrant storekeeper, Jacob Charles Ferber, and Julia Neuman Ferber, daughter of a prosperous, cultured German Jewish family. She was named Edna because the family, hoping for a male child, had already selected the name Edward. When she was born in Kalamazoo, Michigan, her father owned and operated a general store. Soon the business faltered, and they moved in with Julia's parents in Chicago. After moving to Ottumwa, Iowa, then back to Chicago, then to Appleton, Wisconsin, the store still failed to prosper. Jacob Ferber, though intelligent, kindly and cultured, never acquired business skills and soon lost his sight. Thus, Julia assumed management of the business and became the head of the family. With great personal effort and the active assistance of Edna, she stabilized the business, paid off debts, and maintained the family's independence.

Edna described Ottumwa as narrow-minded and sordid. There she experienced anti-Semitism and witnessed a lynching. During her high school years at Appleton, however, she enjoyed pleasant, tolerant, midwestern small-town life. Unable to afford college tuition in 1902, she began her professional writing career as a reporter for the *Appleton Daily Crescent.* Eighteen months later the editor, who had hired her on the strength of her reportorial writing in her high school paper, left, and Ferber was fired. The most credible reason given for her dismissal was her imaginative "embroidering" of news reports. She then became a reporter on the *Milwaukee Journal.* Exhausted by overwork and anemia, she returned home in 1905 and began writing fiction. High school and about five years of newspaper writing constituted Ferber's entire preparation for her literary career.

After her father's death in 1909, her mother sold the store and took her two daughters to Chicago. There, while her mother and sister earned their living, Edna continued writing. In 1912, after selling some of her work, she moved to New York but remained closely attached to her mother. Thereafter, she and her mother resided in hotels or apartments in New York, Chicago, and elsewhere but considered themselves New Yorkers. Though they did not always actually live together, their lives were closely intertwined. In 1938, Edna built a house for herself in suburban Connecticut, pointedly leaving her mother in a New York apartment. After Julia died, Edna sold her house and returned to a New York apartment. During her last ten years, a painful nervous disorder impaired her writing. Never married, she died of stomach cancer in New York City on April 16, 1968.

Analysis • Ferber was a feminist, a conservationist, a crusader for minorities and immigrants, and a staunch believer in the work ethic and American culture. Strong women characters rising above the limitations of birth and gender dominate her novels; most men in her works are weak, and many desert their women and children. She describes and condemns mistreatment of African Americans, Jews, Latinos, and Native Americans. Results of unrestrained capitalism and wasteful exploitation of natural resources are decried. Her novels celebrate regional culture and history

Library of Congress

in an effective and pleasing style that clearly reflects her journalistic background. Characterization, however, is less effective and plots tend toward melodrama and coincidence.

All of Ferber's novels were commercial successes, and many remained in print for decades after publication. Her first novels, *Dawn O'Hara: The Girl Who Laughed* and *Fanny Herself*, are strongly autobiographical. They remain interesting because they show Ferber's literary growth. Background material in *Great Son* is sketchy, characters are stereotypic, and the plot is contrived. At the time of its writing, Ferber was preoccupied writing World War II propaganda. Her final novel, *Ice Palace*, is a political tract of little literary merit; Ferber was ill at the time of its writing.

The Girls • Ferber expected this book to be a best-seller and considered it her best novel. The story recounts six decades of Chicago middle-class history and intergenerational conflict. Charlotte Thrift, forbidden to marry an unsuitable boy, loses him to death in the Civil War. She never marries. Her unmarried niece, Lottie, under her mother's domination, keeps house for her mother and aunt. Lottie finally rebels, joins the Red Cross during World War I, has a brief affair, and returns with her illegitimate daugher, whom she passes off as a French orphan. Charly (Charlotte), Lottie's niece, falls in love with a poet, who is killed in World War I, and moves in with her aunt and great-aunt. All three are strong personalities, while their men are either incompetent boors or scoundrels.

So Big • Ferber's first best-seller effectively contrasts humble life in the Halstead Street Market with that of pretentious Chicago society. A genteelly reared orphan, Selina Peake, goes to teach school in a community of Dutch market gardeners, where she must adjust to a brutal existence. Her only intellectual companion is thirteen-year-old Roelf, the artistically talented son of the family with whom she lives. After a year, she marries kindly Pervus DeJong, an unimaginative, unenterprising widower. They have a son, Dirk, nicknamed So Big. After Pervus's death, Selina makes their farm a thriving success. She sacrifices all for So Big, who, after a few years as a struggling architect, shifts to a banking career and high society. In contrast, Selina's first protégé, Roelf, becomes a famous sculptor. At the end So Big finally realizes that his life is empty. Although the novel was critically acclaimed, characterization barely develops beyond stereotypes, and many anecdotes are clichés.

Show Boat • *Show Boat* describes life aboard late nineteenth and early twentieth century Mississippi River showboats and their cultural significance. Magnolia Hawkes, daughter of Captain Andy and Parthenia Hawkes of the showboat Cotton Blossom, marries Gaylord Ravenal, a charming professional gambler. After Captain Andy's death, Magnolia, Gaylord, and their daughter Kim move to Chicago, where they squander Magnolia's inheritance. Magnolia, deserted by her wastrel husband, becomes a successful singer and raises Kim to become a successful serious actor. Parthenia inherits and successfully operates the showboat. Parthenia, Magnolia, and Kim are all protofeminist career women. Captain Andy, though competent and wise, defers to Parthenia in almost everything. African Americans are presented as patient, upright, and hardworking people. A tragic incident of miscegenation and the injustice of southern law balance the romanticized account of the showboat life, which is charming.

Cimarron • *Cimarron* is set in Oklahoma between the 1889 land rush and the 1920's oil boom. Sabra Cravat begins life as a genteel, impoverished southern girl but ends up an assured newspaperwoman and congresswoman. Her husband, Yancey Cravat, a flamboyant lawyer-newspaperman of dubious background, starts grandiose projects, performs heroic acts, and upholds high ideals, but he accomplishes little. Desertion of his family clears the way for Sabra's rise. These characters exemplify the tension between those who "won" Oklahoma and those who "civilized" it. Also, interaction between Native and Euro-Americans is perceptively treated.

American Beauty • Ferber rhapsodically describes the Connecticut landscape in this novel, in which abuse of land and resources is chronicled. Polish immigrant culture is sympathetically presented, and the indigenous New Englanders are depicted as played-out aristocrats. Judy Oakes and her niece, Tamar Pring, are strong, stubborn women devoted to their aristocratic background and ancestral home. Their hired man, Ondy Olszak, a kindhearted, hard-working, unimaginative Polish immigrant, maintains the farm at just above subsistence level. Tamar seduces and marries Ondy, and their son Orrange combines Ondy's peasant vigor and Tamar's cultural sensibilities. Although Orrange inherits the farm, Ondy's family forces him to sell. Millionaire True Baldwin, who, as an impoverished farm lad, had aspired to marry Judy Oakes, buys it. Baldwin's architect daughter, Candace (Candy) Baldwin, sexually attracted to Orrange, then hires him to manage the farm.

Come and Get It • Ferber draws heavily on her own background in this story of resource exploitation, unrestrained capitalism, and social contrast. After lumberjack Barney Glasgow fights his way up to a managerial position at the mill, he marries his boss's spinsterish daughter. Timbering and papermaking thrive under his direction, until he is fatally attracted to Lotta Lindaback, granddaughter of his longtime lumberjack pal, Swan Bostrom. Barney's daughter, frustrated by unacknowledged desire for her father, marries a dull young businessman. Bernard, Barney's son, pursues Lotta when Barney restrains his own passion for her. Barney then fights with Bernard and expels him from the house. Immediately afterward, Barney and his family are killed in an explosion. Bernard marries Lotta and builds an industrial empire in steel and paper. Lotta, meanwhile, enters international high society. The Great Depression forces Lotta's return to Wisconsin, where her twins come under the influence of Tom Melendy, an idealistic young man of a mill-hand family. Rejecting their parent's materialism, they return to the simple Bostrom ways.

Saratoga Trunk • In this story, Ferber decries the evils of unrestrained capitalism and the decadent snobbery of New Orleans high society. She also promotes women's causes and natural resource conservation. Illegitimate Clio Dulain and Texas cowboy-gambler Clint Maroon join forces to extort money from Clio's aristocratic father. Then they move to Saratoga, New York, where Clio sets out to snare a rich husband. Although she entraps railroad millionaire Van Steed, she drops him for Clint when Clint is injured fighting for Van Steed's railroad, the Saratoga Trunk. Thereafter Clio and Clint become railroad millionaires but idealistically give their wealth to charity. Clio subtlely manipulates Clint in all important matters.

Giant • Ferber's flamboyant version of Texas history and culture exemplified the Texas mythology and earned violent protests from Texans. Ferber's typical strong female central character, Leslie Lynnton, daughter of a world-famous doctor living in genteel shabbiness, is swept off her feet by a visiting Texas rancher. Transported to his gigantic ranch, she finds her husband ruled by his spinster sister, Luz. Luz dies violently, and, with great skill and wisdom, Leslie guides her man through repeated crises as the great cattle and cotton "empires" are hemmed in by vulgar oil billionaires. The original Texans, Mexican Americans, are shown as deeply wronged, patient, dignified, and noble. However, the book's end leaves ongoing problems unsolved.

Ralph L. Langenheim, Jr.

Other major works

SHORT FICTION: *Buttered Side Down*, 1912; *Roast Beef Medium*, 1913; *Personality Plus*, 1914; *Emma McChesney and Co.*, 1915; *Cheerful—By Request*, 1918; *Half Portions*, 1919; *Mother Knows Best*, 1927; *They Brought Their Women*, 1933; *Nobody's in Town*, 1938 (includes *Nobody's in Town* and *Trees Die at the Top*); *One Basket*, 1947.

PLAYS: *Our Mrs. McChesney*, pr., pb. 1915 (with George V. Hobart); *$1200 a Year*, pr., pb. 1920 (with Newman A. Levy); *Minick*, pr., pb. 1924 (with George S. Kaufman); *The Royal Family*, pr. 1927, pb. 1928 (with Kaufman); *Dinner at Eight*, pr., pb. 1932 (with Kaufman); *Stage Door*, pr., pb. 1936 (with Kaufman); *The Land Is Bright*, pr., pb. 1941 (with Kaufman); *Bravo!*, pr. 1948, pb. 1949 (with Kaufman).

NONFICTION: *A Peculiar Treasure*, 1939 (revised 1960; with new introduction); *A Kind of Magic*, 1963.

Bibliography

Antler, Joyce. *The Journey Home: Jewish Women and the American Century*. New York: Free Press, 1997. This overview of the lives of a selection of American Jewish women beginning in 1890 contains a portrait of Ferber.

Batker, Carol. "Literary Reformers: Crossing Class and Ethnic Boundaries in Jewish Women's Fiction of the 1920's." *MELUS* 25, no.1 (Spring, 2000): 81-104. Ferber's work is examined in the context of Jewish women's fiction, along with that of Anzia Yezierska and Fannie Hurst.

Bloom, Harold, ed. *Jewish Women Fiction Writers.* New York: Chelsea House, 1998. Provides biographical information, a wide selection of critical excerpts, and complete bibliographies of ten Jewish-American fiction authors, including Ferber.

Gaines, James R. *Wits End, Days and Nights of the Algonquin Round Table.* New York: Harcourt Brace Jovanovich, 1977. An anecdotal history illuminating Ferber's association with the Algonquin group.

Gilbert, Julie Goldsmith. *Ferber: Edna Ferber and Her Circle, A Biography.* New York: Applause, 1999. A good biography of Ferber. Gilbert calls Ferber a romantic realist, not opposed to working with the system, yet creating her own unique niche within it. Includes an index.

Kenaga, Heidi. "Edna Ferber's *Cimarron*, Cultural Authority, and 1920's Western Historical Narratives." In *Middlebrow Moderns: Popular American Writers of the 1920's*, edited by Lisa Botshon and Meredith Goldsmith. Boston: Northeastern University Press, 2003. Modern reconsideration of Ferber's classic Western tale.

Shaughnessy, Mary Rose. *Women and Success in American Society in the Works of Edna Ferber.* New York: Gordon Press, 1977. Discusses Ferber's place in the women's movement.

F. Scott Fitzgerald

Born: St. Paul, Minnesota; September 24, 1896
Died: Hollywood, California; December 21, 1940

Principal long fiction • *This Side of Paradise,* 1920; *The Beautiful and Damned,* 1922; *The Great Gatsby,* 1925; *Tender Is the Night,* 1934; *The Last Tycoon,* 1941.

Other literary forms • Charles Scribner's Sons published nine books by F. Scott Fitzgerald during Fitzgerald's lifetime. In addition to the first four novels, there were four volumes of short stories, *Flappers and Philosophers* (1920), *Tales of the Jazz Age* (1922), *All the Sad Young Men* (1926), and *Taps at Reveille* (1935); and one play, *The Vegetable: Or, From President to Postman* (1923). The story collections published by Charles Scribner's Sons contained fewer than a third of the 165 stories that appeared in major periodicals during his lifetime; now, virtually all of Fitzgerald's stories are available in hardcover collections. Fitzgerald also wrote essays and autobiographical pieces, many of which appeared during the late 1930's in *Esquire* and are now collected, among other places, in *The Crack-Up* (1945). Fitzgerald's Hollywood writing consisted mainly of collaborative efforts on scripts for films such as *Gone with the Wind* (1939) and others, although during his life and since his death there have been various screen adaptations of his novels and stories. Fitzgerald's notebooks, scrapbooks, and letters have also been published, and the record of his literary achievement is nearly complete.

Achievements • Curiously, Fitzgerald has appealed to two diverse audiences since the beginning of his career: the popular magazine audience and the elite of the literary establishment. His work appeared regularly during the 1920's and 1930's in such mass circulation magazines as the *Saturday Evening Post, Hearst's, International, Collier's,* and *Redbook.* The readers of these magazines came to ask for Fitzgerald's flapper stories by name, expecting to find in them rich, young, and glamorous heroes and heroines involved in exciting adventures. Popular magazines during the 1920's billed Fitzgerald stories on the cover, often using them inside as lead stories. Long after Fitzgerald lost the knack of writing the kind of popular stories that made him famous as the creator of the flapper in fiction and as the poet laureate of the jazz age, magazine headnotes to his stories identified him as such. Those who recognized the more serious side of his talent, as it was evidenced particularly in his best stories and novels, included Edmund Wilson, George Jean Nathan, H. L. Mencken, Gertrude Stein, Edith Wharton, and T. S. Eliot, who offered criticism as well as praise. Fitzgerald was generous with advice to other writers, most notably to Ring Lardner, Ernest Hemingway, and Thomas Wolfe, but also to struggling unknowns, who wrote to him asking advice and received it.

Many of Fitzgerald's critical opinions went into the public domain when he published essays in *Esquire* during the late 1930's, his dark night of the soul. Regarded by some in Fitzgerald's time as self-pitying, these essays are now often anthologized and widely quoted for the ideas and theories about literature and life that they contain. At the time of his death, Fitzgerald seemed nearly forgotten by his popular readers and greatly neglected by literary critics. After his death and the posthumous publication of his incomplete *The Last Tycoon*, a Fitzgerald revival began. With this revival, Fitzgerald's reputation as a novelist (principally on the strength of *The Great Gatsby* and *Tender Is the Night*), short-story writer, and essayist has been solidly established.

Library of Congress

Biography • Francis Scott Key Fitzgerald was born in St. Paul, Minnesota, on September 24, 1896. His mother's side of the family (the McQuillan side) was what Fitzgerald referred to as "straight 1850 potato famine Irish," but by the time of his maternal grandfather's death at the age of forty-four, the McQuillan fortune, earned in the grocery business, was in excess of $300,000. Fitzgerald's father was a poor but well-bred descendant of the old Maryland Scott and Key families. Always an ineffectual businessman, Edward Fitzgerald had met Mary McQuillan when he had come to St. Paul to open a wicker furniture business, which shortly went out of business. In search of a job by which he could support the family, Edward Fitzgerald moved his family from St. Paul to Buffalo, New York, in 1898, then to Syracuse and back to Buffalo. When Fitzgerald was eleven, the family returned to St. Paul and the security of the McQuillan wealth.

With McQuillan money Fitzgerald was sent (for two painfully lonely years) to private school, the Newman School in Hackensack, New Jersey. Discovering there a flair for writing musical comedy, Fitzgerald decided that he would attend Princeton, whose Triangle Club produced a musical comedy each year. At Princeton, Fitzgerald compensated for his feelings of social inferiority by excelling in the thing he did best, writing for the Triangle Club and the *Nassau Literary Magazine*. During a Christmas vacation spent in St. Paul, Fitzgerald met Ginevra King, a wealthy Chicago debutante whose initial acceptance of Fitzgerald was a supreme social triumph; her later rejection of him became one of the most devastating blows of his life. He kept her letters, which he had typed and bound and that ran to over two hundred pages, until his death.

In 1917, Fitzgerald left Princeton without a degree, accepted a commission in the army, and wrote the first draft of what was to become his first novel, *This Side of Paradise*. During the summer of 1918, Fitzgerald met Zelda Sayre while he was stationed near Montgomery, Alabama, and having recently received word of King's engagement, he fell in love with Zelda. Zelda, however, although willing to become engaged to Fitzgerald, did not finally agree to marry him until he could demonstrate his ability to support her. Fitzgerald returned to New York, worked for an advertising firm, and revised his novel, including in it details from his courtship with Zelda. When Charles Scribner's Sons agreed in September, 1919, to publish the novel, Fitzgerald was able to claim Zelda, and they were married in April of the following year.

The first two years of their marriage were marked by wild parties, the self-destructive mood of which formed the basis for some of the scenes in Fitzgerald's second novel, *The Beautiful and Damned.* After a trip to Europe, the Fitzgeralds returned first to St. Paul and then to Great Neck, New York, where they lived among the Astors and Vanderbilts while Fitzgerald accumulated material that would figure in *The Great Gatsby.*

In the decade that followed the publication of that novel, the Fitzgeralds lived, among other places, on the French Riviera, which would provide the background for *Tender Is the Night.* Zelda headed toward a mental collapse, a fictionalized version of which appears in the novel; Fitzgerald sank into alcoholism. In 1930, Zelda was institutionalized for treatment of her mental condition. The rest of Fitzgerald's life was spent writing stories and screenplays that would pay for her treatment, both in and out of institutions. In 1937, Fitzgerald went to Hollywood, met Sheila Graham, worked under contract for MGM Studios, and accumulated material for his last novel, while Zelda remained in the East. Fitzgerald died of a heart attack on December 21, 1940, while working on his unfinished novel, *The Last Tycoon.*

Analysis • "The test of a first-rate intelligence," Fitzgerald remarked during the late 1930's, "is the ability to hold two opposed ideas in the mind at the same time, and still retain the ability to function." At his best—in *The Great Gatsby,* in parts of *Tender Is the Night,* in the unfinished *The Last Tycoon,* and in parts of his first two novels, *This Side of Paradise* and *The Beautiful and Damned*—Fitzgerald demonstrates the kind of intelligence he describes, an intelligence characterized by the aesthetic principle of "double vision." An understanding of this phrase (coined and first applied to Fitzgerald's art by Malcolm Cowley) is central to any discussion of Fitzgerald's novels. "Double vision" denotes two ways of seeing. It implies the tension involved when Fitzgerald sets things in opposition such that the reader can, on one hand, sensually experience the event about which Fitzgerald is writing, becoming emotionally immersed in it, and yet at the same time retain the objectivity to stand back and intellectually criticize it. The foundation of double vision is polarity, the setting of extremes against each other; the result in a novel is dramatic tension. By following the changes in Fitzgerald's narrative technique from *This Side of Paradise* to *The Beautiful and Damned* to *The Great Gatsby* and finally into *Tender Is the Night,* one can trace the growth of his double vision, which is, in effect, to study his development as a literary artist.

The major themes of Fitzgerald's novels derive from the resolution of tension when one idea (usually embodied in a character) triumphs over another. Amory Blaine, the protagonist of Fitzgerald's first novel, *This Side of Paradise,* is a questing hero armed with youth, intelligence, and good looks. Anthony Patch in *The Beautiful and Damned* has a multimillionaire grandfather, a beautiful wife, and youth. Jay Gatsby in *The Great Gatsby* possesses power, newly made money, and good looks. Finally, Dick Diver in *Tender Is the Night* has a medical degree, an overabundance of charm, and a wealthy wife.

The common denominators here are the subjects with which Fitzgerald deals in all of his novels: youth, physical beauty, wealth, and potential or "romantic readiness"—all of which are ideals to Fitzgerald. Set against these subjects are their polar opposites: age, ugliness, poverty, squandered potential. Such conflict and resulting tension is the stuff of which all fiction is made. With Fitzgerald's characters, however, partly because of the themes with which he deals and partly because of his skillful handling of point of view, the choices are rarely as obvious or as clear-cut to the main characters at the time as they may be to a detached observer, or as they may seem in retrospect to have been. Daisy, for example, so enchants Gatsby and the reader who identifies with him that only in retrospect (if at all) or through the detached observer, Nick, does it become clear that she and the other careless, moneyed people in the novel are villains of the highest order. It is Fitzgerald's main gift that he can draw the reader into a web of emotional attachment to a character, as he does to Daisy through Gatsby, while simultaneously allowing him to inspect the complexity of the web, as he does through Nick. That is what Fitzgerald's double vision at its best is finally about.

For the origins of Fitzgerald's double vision, it is helpful to look at several ingredients of his early life, particularly at those facets of it that presented him with the polarities and ambiguities that would later furnish the subjects and themes of his art. "In a house below the average on a block above the average" is the way that Fitzgerald described his boyhood home. A block above the average, indeed. At the end of the "block" on Summit Avenue in St. Paul lived James J. Hill, the multimillionaire empire builder referred to by Gatsby's father in the last chapter of *The Great Gatsby*. The Fitzgerald family, however, nearly in sight of such wealth, lived moderately on the interest from his mother's inheritance, taking pains not to disturb the capital; Fitzgerald's father, in spite of his idealistic gentility and distinguished ancestral line, was unable to hold a good job. One of Fitzgerald's most devastating memories was of his father's loss of a job with Procter and Gamble, which left the older Fitzgerald, then beyond middle age, broken and defeated. When Fitzgerald was sent East to boarding school and then to Princeton, it was with his mother's money, less than a generation earned, and with considerably less of it than stood behind most of his classmates. Early, then, Fitzgerald, a child with sensitivity, intelligence, and good looks—qualities possessed by most of his heroes and heroines—was impressed with the importance of money, at least with the lifestyle of the moneyed class. However, Fitzgerald's participation in that lifestyle, like that of many of his fictional creations, was limited by something beyond his control: the fixed income of his family. In addition, he watched his father, an idealist unable to compete in a materialistic world, defeated.

With this kind of early life, Fitzgerald was prepared, or more accurately left totally unprepared, for the series of events in his life that formed the basis of much of his later fiction. Two of these stand out: his romantic attachment to Ginevra King, a wealthy Chicago debutante who in his words "ended up by throwing me over with the most supreme boredom and indifference"; and his relationship with Zelda Sayre, who broke their engagement (because Fitzgerald was neither rich enough nor famous enough for her) before finally marrying him after his first novel was accepted for publication by Charles Scribner's Sons. Fitzgerald emphasizes the importance of the King episode in particular and of biographical material in general in his essay "One Hundred False Starts": "We have two or three great and moving experiences in our lives. . . . Then we learn our trade, well or less well, and we tell our two or three stories—each time in a new disguise—maybe ten times, maybe a hundred, as long as people will listen." The subjects and themes from those experiences formed what Fitzgerald called "my material."

Through King, Fitzgerald saw the opportunity to be accepted into the wealth that the King family represented. Her father, however, did not conceal his "poor boys shouldn't think of marrying rich girls" attitude, recorded in Fitzgerald's notebooks, and when Fitzgerald was "thrown over" in favor of an acceptable suitor with money and social position, he saw the rejection not only as a personal one but also as evidence that the emergence of an upper caste in American society had rendered the American Dream an empty promise. Curiously though, Fitzgerald's infatuation with wealth and the wealthy, symbolized by the Kings, stayed with him for the rest of his life. As he wrote to his daughter during the late 1930's on the eve of seeing King for the first time since she had rejected him nearly twenty years earlier, "She was the first girl I ever loved and I have faithfully avoided seeing her up to this moment to keep that illusion perfect." It was this experience, then, coupled with the near-loss of Zelda and their subsequent, complex relationship that would provide his "material." Fitzgerald also describes an attitude that grows out of these experiences of enchantment and loss and that he identifies variously as his "solid gold bar" or his "stamp": "Taking things hard—from Ginevra to Joe Mank. That's the stamp that goes into my books so that people can read it blind like Braille."

Fitzgerald's achievements rest on three obsessions that characterized him as an artist and as a man. The first of these was "his material." It included the subjects of youth, wealth, and beauty and was an outgrowth of his social background. The second was his "solid gold bar" or his "stamp," which he defined as "taking things hard," an attitude that grew out of his background and was partly rooted in his feelings of social inferiority. The third was his "double vision," an artistic perspective that remained his goal until the end. This double vision matured as he gained objectivity toward his material. With these cornerstones, Fitzgerald constructed a set of novels that document the development of one of the most complex and fascinating literary personalities of modern times, which chronicle a time of unparalleled frivolity and subsequent national despondency in America, and that speak with authenticity about an international wasteland almost beyond reclaiming. "The evidence is in," wrote Stephen Vincent Benét regarding the body of Fitzgerald's work in a review of the incomplete *The Last Tycoon*. "This is not a legend, this is a reputation—and seen in perspective, it may well be one of the most secure reputations of our time."

This Side of Paradise • Writing in 1938 about the subject matter of his first novel, Fitzgerald alludes to its origins in his experience: "In 'This Side of Paradise' I wrote about a love affair that was still bleeding as fresh as the skin wound on a haemophile." The love affair that he refers to is his relationship with King, and it is but one of many episodes from Fitzgerald's life—his courtship with Zelda is another—that are loosely tied together in *This Side of Paradise* to form a *Bildungsroman*. Unlike the novel of "selected incident," the *Bildungsroman* is a novel of "saturation"—that is, a novel in which the hero takes on experiences until he reaches a saturation point; by virtue of his coming to this point he reaches a higher level of self-awareness. In *This Side of Paradise*, Amory Blaine, the hero and thinly veiled Fitzgerald persona, reaches this point when, at the end of the novel, he rejects all of the values that have been instilled in him, embraces socialism, and yells to the world, "I know myself . . . but that is all."

The route that Amory follows to arrive at this pinnacle of self-knowledge is more a meandering process of trial and error than it is a systematic journey with a clearly defined purpose. His mother, whom Amory quaintly calls by her first name, Beatrice, and whom he relates to as a peer, instills in Amory an egotism (almost unbearable to his own peers as well as to the reader) and a respect for wealth and social position.

These qualities make Amory an object of ridicule when he goes away to an eastern boarding school. His years at St. Regis are spent in isolation, and there he finally makes the emotional break with his mother that frees the "fundamental Amory" to become, in Fitzgerald's words, a "personage." The landmarks of this becoming process are, for the most part, encounters with individuals who teach Amory about himself: "The Romantic Egotist," as he is referred to in book 1 of the novel, is too solipsistic to go beyond himself even at the end of the novel. After learning from these individuals, Amory either leaves or is left by them. From Clara, a cousin whose beauty and intelligence he admires, he learns that he follows his imagination too freely; he learns from his affair with Rosalind, who almost marries him but refuses because Amory lacks the money to support her, that money determines the direction of love. Through Monsignor Darcy, he learns that the Church of Rome is too confining for him; and from half a dozen of his classmates at Princeton, he discovers the restlessness and rebelliousness that lead him to reject all that he had been brought up to believe, reaching out toward socialism as one of the few gods he has not tried.

Readers may wonder how Amory, whose path has zigzagged through many experiences, none of which has brought him closely in contact with socialism, has arrived at a point of almost evangelical, anticapitalistic zeal. It is worth noting, however, that, in addition to its interest to literary historians as an example of the *Bildungsroman*, *This Side of Paradise* also has value to social historians as an enlightening account of jazz age manners and morals. One contemporary observer labeled the novel "a gesture of indefinite revolt," a comment intended as a criticism of the novel's lack of focus. The social historian, however, would see the phrase as a key to the novel's value, which view would cast Amory in the role of spokesman for the vague rebelliousness of the "lost generation," a generation, in Amory's words, "grown up to find all gods dead, all wars fought, all faiths in man shaken." As Malcolm Cowley has noted,

> More than any other writer of these times, Fitzgerald had the sense of living in history. He tried hard to catch the color of every passing year, its distinctive slang, its dance steps, its songs . . . its favorite quarterbacks, and the sort of clothes and emotions its people wore.

John O'Hara, for one, recalls the impact of *This Side of Paradise* on his generation: "A little matter of twenty-five years ago I, along with half a million other men and women between fifteen and thirty, fell in love with a book. . . . I took the book to bed with me, and I still do, which is more than I can say of any girl I knew in 1920." By Fitzgerald's own account, the novel made him something of an "oracle" to his college readers, and largely on the strength of *This Side of Paradise*, Fitzgerald became the unofficial poet laureate of the jazz age.

For those interested in Fitzgerald's development as a novelist, the value of *This Side of Paradise* goes beyond its worth as a novel of growth or its importance as a social document. In it are contained early versions in rough form of most of the novels that Fitzgerald later wrote. By the time of its completion, Fitzgerald's major subjects were cast and marked with his "stamp": "taking things hard." Amory "takes hard" the breakup with the young, wealthy, and beautiful Isabel, modeled on Ginevra King. Amory "takes hard" his rejection by Rosalind by going on an extended drunk, similar to Fitzgerald's response when Zelda refused to marry him until he demonstrated that he could support her. Event after event in the novel shows Fitzgerald, through Amory, "taking hard" the absence of wealth, the loss of youth, and the ephemerality of beauty. Even in the characterization of Amory, who is born moneyed and aristocratic, Fitzgerald seems to be creating his ideal conception of himself, much the way Gatsby later springs from his own platonic conception of himself. With his subject matter, his themes, and his distinctive stamp already formed, Fitzgerald needed only to find a point of view by which he could distance himself, more than he had through Amory, from his material. He had yet, as T. S. Eliot would have phrased it, to find an "objective correlative," which is to say that he had not yet acquired the double vision so evident in *The Great Gatsby.*

The Beautiful and Damned • Although *The Beautiful and Damned,* Fitzgerald's second novel, is usually considered his weakest, largely because of its improbable and melodramatic ending, there is evidence in it of Fitzgerald's growth as a writer. Unlike *This Side of Paradise,* which is a subjective rendering through a thinly disguised persona and that includes nearly everything from Fitzgerald's life and work through 1920 (one critic called it "the collected works of F. Scott Fitzgerald"), *The Beautiful and Damned* moved toward the novel of selected incident. Written in the third person, it shows Fitzgerald dealing in a more objective fashion with biographical material that was close to him, in this instance the early married life of the Fitzgeralds. Whereas *This Side of Paradise* was largely a retrospective, nostalgic recounting of Fitzgerald's recently lost youth, *The Beautiful and Damned* projects imaginatively into the future of a life based on the belief that nothing is worth doing.

In spite of the differences between the two novels, however, particularly in narrative perspective, it is clear that the characters and subjects in *The Beautiful and Damned* are logical extensions, more objectively rendered, of those introduced in *This Side of Paradise,* making the former a sequel, in a sense, to the latter. With slight modifications, Anthony Patch, the hero of *The Beautiful and Damned,* is Amory Blaine grown older and more cynical. Add to Amory a heritage that links him to Anthony Comstock, a mother and father who died in his youth, a multimillionaire grandfather, and half a dozen years, and the result is a reasonable facsimile of Patch. To Amory's Rosalind (a composite of Ginevra and Zelda), add a few years, a "coast-to-coast reputation for irresponsibility and beauty," and a bit more cleverness, and the result is strikingly similar to Gloria Gilbert, the heroine of *The Beautiful and Damned,* who will, unlike Rosalind, marry the hero.

When Fitzgerald created Rosalind, Zelda had for the time being rejected him. Her reappearance in *The Beautiful and Damned* as the hero's wife reflects Fitzgerald's change in fortune, since he and Zelda had been married for two years when *The Beautiful and Damned* was published. Their life together provided the basis for many of the experiences in the novel, and there is good reason to believe that the mutual self-destructiveness evident on nearly every page of the novel reflects Fitzgerald's fears of what he and Zelda might do to each other and to themselves. In *This Side of Paradise* Amory knows himself, "but that is all." Anthony carries this knowledge two years into the future and cynically applies it to life: He will prove that life is meaningless and that "there's nothing I can do that's worth doing." His task is to demonstrate that it is possible for an American to be gracefully idle. Gloria's goal is to avoid responsibility forever, which was essentially Rosalind's goal in *This Side of Paradise.* The kind of life that Gloria and Anthony desire is dependent on the possession of wealth, of which Anthony has promise through the estate of his grandfather, a virtual guarantee until the social-reformer grandfather happens into one of the Patches' parties and disinherits Anthony.

The novel could logically end there, but it does not. Instead, its long conclusion leads the reader through a maze of melodramatic circumstances and improbabilities. Gloria and Anthony contest the will and, with dwindling funds, sink into despair and self-destructiveness. Gloria auditions for a part in a motion picture and is told that she is too old; Anthony remains drunk, tries unsuccessfully to borrow money from friends, and finally gets into a senseless fight with the film producer who has given Gloria the news that she is too old for the part she wants. On the day of the trial that will determine whether the will is to be broken, Anthony loses his mind and is capable only of babbling incoherently when Gloria brings him the news that they are rich.

The major flaw in the novel is this long, melodramatic ending and the thematic conclusions it presents. On one hand, Fitzgerald posits the theory that life is meaningless, yet Anthony's life is given meaning by his quest for money, not to mention that the philosophy itself can be practiced only when there is enough money to support it. Certainly Gloria, who is sane and happy at the novel's end, does not seem much impressed by life's meaninglessness, and the reader is left with the feeling that Anthony, when the advantages that his inheritance can offer him are evident, will recover from his "on-cue" flight into insanity. The effect of the ending is to leave the reader with the impression that Fitzgerald had not thought the theme carefully through; or, as Edmund Wilson hints, that Fitzgerald himself had not taken the ideas in either of his first two novels seriously:

> In college he had supposed that the thing to do was to write biographical novels with a burst of energy toward the close; since his advent into the literary world, he has discovered that another genre has recently come into favor: the kind which makes much of tragedy and what Mencken has called "the meaninglessness of life."

The greater truth suggested by Wilson here is that through 1922 Fitzgerald was writing, in part, what he thought he should write. With the completion of *The Beautiful and Damned*, his apprenticeship was over, and with an artistic leap he moved into his own as an original prose stylist, writing in *The Great Gatsby* what Eliot called "the first step that American fiction has taken since Henry James."

The Great Gatsby • For Amory Blaine in *This Side of Paradise*, there are four golden moments, as many perhaps as there are new and exciting women to meet; for Anthony Patch in *The Beautiful and Damned*, the moment is his meeting with Gloria Gilbert. For Jay Gatsby, the golden moment is the time when "his unutterable vision" meets Daisy's "perishable breath." For Fitzgerald, the artistic golden moment was the creation of *The Great Gatsby*. Critics have marveled that the author of *This Side of Paradise* and *The Beautiful and Damned* could in fewer than two years after the publication of the latter produce a novel of the stature of *The Great Gatsby*. Clearly, the writer of *This Side of Paradise* did not blossom overnight into the author of *The Great Gatsby*. The process by which Fitzgerald came to create *The Great Gatsby* is a logical one. From the beginning of his career as a novelist, Fitzgerald stayed with the subjects and themes that he knew well and that were close to him: wealth, youth, and beauty. What did change between the creation of *This Side of Paradise* and *The Great Gatsby* was Fitzgerald's perspective on his material and his ability to objectify his attitudes toward it. In 1925, Fitzgerald was more than five years removed from his affair with Ginevra, which gave him the distance to be Nick Carraway, the novel's "objective" narrator. However, he was also near enough in memory that he could recall, even relive, the seductiveness of her world; that is, he was still able to be the romantic hero, Jay Gatsby. In effect, he had reached the pivotal point in his life that allowed him to see clearly through the eyes of both Gatsby and Nick; for the time of the creation of *The Great Gatsby*, he possessed double vision.

The success of the novel depends on Fitzgerald's ability to transfer to the reader the same kind of vision that he himself had: the ability to believe in the possibilities of several opposite ideas at various levels of abstraction. On the most concrete level, the reader must believe that Gatsby will and will not win Daisy, the novel's heroine and symbol of the American ideal. On a more general level, the reader must believe that anyone in America, through hard work and perseverance, can and cannot gain access to the best that America has to offer. Until Daisy's final rejection of Gatsby in the penultimate chapter of the novel, the reader can, indeed, believe in both alternatives because both have been seen, from the perspective of Gatsby (who believes) and from the point of view of Nick (who wants to believe but intellectually cannot).

The central scene in *The Great Gatsby* nicely illustrates how Fitzgerald is able to present his material in such a way as to create dramatic tension through the use of double vision. This scene, which occupies the first part of chapter 5, is built around the reunion of Gatsby and Daisy after a five-year separation. The years, for Gatsby, have been devoted to the obsessive pursuit of wealth, which he wants only because he believes it will win Daisy for him. Daisy, who has married Tom Buchanan, seems to have given little thought to Gatsby since her marriage. The moment of their reunion, then, means everything to Gatsby and very little to Daisy, except as a diversion from the luxurious idling of her daily existence. In this meeting scene, as Gatsby stands nervously talking to Daisy and Nick, Fitzgerald calls the reader's attention to a defunct clock on Nick's mantelpiece. When Gatsby leans against the mantel, the clock teeters on the edge, deciding finally not to fall. The three stare at the floor as if the clock has, in fact, shattered to pieces in front of them. Gatsby apologizes and Nick replies, "It's an old clock."

On the level of plot, this scene is the dramatic high point of the novel; the first four chapters have been devoted to preparing the reader for it. The image of Daisy's desirability as she is seen through Nick's eyes in chapter 1 has been followed with an image at the chapter's end of Gatsby standing, arms outstretched, toward the green light across the bay at the end of Daisy's dock; the image of the emptiness of the Buchanans' world in chapter 1 has been followed with the image in chapter 2 of the valley of ashes, a huge dumping ground in which lives the mistress of Daisy's husband Tom; the open public gathering of Gatsby's lavish parties in chapter 3 has been set against the mysterious privacy of Gatsby's life. All of these scenes have come to the reader through the central intelligence, Nick, who has learned from Jordan Baker a truth that, at this point, only Gatsby, Jordan, and Nick know: Gatsby wants to turn time backward and renew his relationship with Daisy as if the five years since he has seen her have not gone by. Nick, Daisy's cousin and Gatsby's neighbor, is the natural link that will reconnect Daisy and Gatsby. To the tension inherent in the reunion itself, then, is added the ambivalence of Nick, who, on one hand, despises Gatsby's gaudiness but admires his romantic readiness; and who is captivated by Daisy's charm but also, by the time of the meeting in chapter 5, contemptuous of her moral emptiness.

On coming into the meeting scene, the reader is interested, first on the level of plot, to see whether Gatsby and Daisy can renew their love of five years before. In addition, he is interested in the reaction of Nick, on whose moral and intellectual judgment he has come to depend. At a deeper level, he is ready for the confrontation of abstract ideas that will occur in the clock scene. The clock itself, a focal point of the room in which Gatsby and Daisy meet, represents the past time that Gatsby wants to repeat in order to recapture Daisy's love for him. The fact that this clock, which has stopped at some past moment, can be suspended on a mantelpiece in front of them affirms the possibility of bringing the past into the present. Yet, the fact that they all envision the clock shattered on the floor suggests that all three are aware of the fragility of this past moment brought into the present. The fact that the clock does not work hints at the underlying flaw in Gatsby's dream of a relationship with Daisy.

The scene is a foreshadowing of what the rest of the novel will present dramatically: the brief and intense renewal of a courtship that takes place behind the closed doors of Gatsby's mansion, a courtship that will end abruptly behind the closed doors of a Plaza Hotel room after a confrontation between Gatsby and Tom persuades Daisy finally to reject Gatsby. The death of Myrtle, Tom's mistress; Gatsby's murder by Myrtle's husband; Daisy and Tom's "vacation" until the confusion dies down; Gatsby's funeral, whose arrangements are handled by Nick—all follow with an unquestionable inevitability in the last two chapters of the novel. Nick alone is left to tell the story of the dreamer whose dreams were corrupted by the "foul dust" that floated in their wake and of the reckless rich who "smashed up things and people and then retreated back into their vast carelessness, or whatever it was that kept them together, and let other people clean up the mess they had made."

At this endpoint, the reader will recall the ominous foreshadowing of the broken clock: Gatsby cannot, as Nick has told him, repeat the past. He cannot have Daisy, because as Nick knows, "poor guys shouldn't think of marrying rich girls." Gatsby cannot have what he imagined to be the best America had to offer, which Nick realizes is *not* Daisy. Yet, the fault does not lie in Gatsby's capacity to dream, only in "the foul dust" that floated in the wake of his dreams—a belief in the money-god, for example—which makes him mistake a counterfeit (Daisy) for the true romantic vision. "No—Gatsby turned out all right at the end," Nick says in a kind of preface to the novel, a statement that keeps Fitzgerald's double vision intact in spite of Gatsby's loss of Daisy and his life. At the highest level of abstraction, the novel suggests that an idealist unwilling to compromise can and cannot survive in a materialistic world, an ambivalent point of view that Fitzgerald held until his death. No longer did he need to write what he thought he should write; he was writing from the vantage point of one who saw that he had endowed the world of King with a sanctity it did not deserve. Part of him, like Gatsby, died with the realization. The other part, like Nick, lived on to make sense of what he had lost and to find a better dream.

Tender Is the Night • For the nine years that followed the publication of *The Great Gatsby* (sometimes referred to as "the barren years"), Fitzgerald published no novels. During the first five of these years, the Fitzgeralds made four trips to Europe, where they met Ernest Hemingway in 1925 and where they lived for a time on the French Riviera, near Gerald and Sara Murphy, prototypes for Dick and Nicole Diver in Fitzgerald's last complete novel, *Tender Is the Night.* In 1930, Zelda had her first mental breakdown and was hospitalized in Switzerland. Two years later she had a second one. For Fitzgerald, the years from 1930 to 1933 were years during which he was compelled to write short stories for popular magazines, primarily the *Saturday Evening Post,* to enable Zelda to be treated in expensive mental institutions. All of these years were devoted to developing a perspective on his experiences: his feelings about Zelda's affair with a French aviator, Edouard Jozan; his own retaliatory relationship with a young film star, Lois Moran; his attraction to the lifestyle of the Murphys; Zelda's mental illness; his own alcoholism and emotional bankruptcy. He carried the perspective he gained through seventeen complete drafts, fully documented by Matthew J. Bruccoli in *The Composition of Tender Is the Night* (1963), to its completion in his novel.

Partly because it attempts to bring together so many subjects, partly because it deals with so complex a theme as the decline of Western civilization, and partly because of its experimentation with multiple points of view, *Tender Is the Night* is usually regarded as Fitzgerald's most ambitious novel. The story line of the novel is straightforward and has the recognizable Fitzgerald stamp. Its hero, Dick Diver, is a gifted young American in Europe who studies psychiatry with Sigmund Freud, writes a textbook for psychiatrists, marries a wealthy American mental patient, and over a period of years makes her well, while sinking himself into an emotional and physical decline that leads him away from Europe to wander aimlessly in an obscure part of upper New York state. The plot rendered chronologically can be represented as two *v*'s placed point-to-point to form an *X*. The lower *v* is Dick's story, which follows him from a relatively low social and economic position to a high one as a doctor and scientist and back again to the low point of emotional bankruptcy. The story of his wife Nicole can be represented by the upper *v*, since Nicole starts life in America's upper class, falls into mental illness (caused by an incestuous relationship with her father), and then rises again to a height of stability and self-sufficiency.

Fitzgerald, however, does not choose to tell the story in chronological sequence, electing instead to focus first on Dick Diver at the high point of his career, following him through his training in a flashback, and ending the novel with his collapse into anonymity. Nicole's story, secondary to Dick's, is woven into that of Dick's decline, with the implication that she has helped to speed it along. Fitzgerald does not select for the novel a single focus of narration, as he does in *The Great Gatsby*. Instead, book 1 of the novel shows Dick in June and July of 1925 at the high point of his life, just before the beginning of his decline, from the viewpoint of Rosemary Hoyt, an innocent eighteen-year-old film star whose innocence Dick will finally betray at his low point by making love to her. Book 2 contains four chronological shifts covering more than a decade, beginning in 1917, and is presented variously from Dick's and then Nicole's perspective. Book 3 brings the story forward one and a half years from the close of book 2 to Dick's departure from the Riviera and Nicole's marriage to Tommy Barban, and it is from the point of view of the survivor, Nicole.

The complicated shifts in viewpoint and chronological sequence are grounded in the complexity of Fitzgerald's purposes. First, he is attempting to document both the external and internal forces that bring about the decline of a gifted individual. In Dick Diver's case, the inward flaw is rooted in an excess of charm and in a self-destructive need to be used, which the reader can best see from Dick's own perspective. From without, Nicole's money weakens his resistance and serves as a catalyst for the breaking down of his will power, a process more clearly observable in the sections from Nicole's point of view. The value of seeing Dick at a high point early in book 1 through Rosemary's eyes is that it emphasizes how attractive and desirable he could be; by contrast, the fact of his emotional bankruptcy at the end of the novel gains power. Fitzgerald, however, is also attempting to equate Dick's decline with the decline of Western society, a subject that had come to him primarily through his reading of Oswald Spengler's *The Decline of the West* (1918-1922). As Fitzgerald wrote to Maxwell Perkins: "I read him the same summer I was writing *The Great Gatsby* and I don't think I ever quite recovered from him." The moral invalids of the international set, who gather on "the little prayer rug of a beach" in *Tender Is the Night*, are, like the characters in Eliot's wasteland, hopelessly cut off from the regenerative powers of nature. There is evidence that even Nicole, whose strength seems assured at the novel's end, may soon be in danger of being overcome by Barban, whose name hints at the barbarian takeover of Western culture predicted by Spengler.

At first glance, *Tender Is the Night* may appear far removed in theme and narrative technique from *The Great Gatsby*, even farther from the two apprenticeship novels, *This Side of Paradise* and *The Beautiful and Damned*. Yet, it does not represent a radical departure from what would seem a predictable pattern of Fitzgerald's growth as a novelist. In *Tender Is the Night*, as in all of his earlier work, Fitzgerald remains close to biographical material, particularly in his drawing on actual people for fictional characters and parts of composite characters. Dick and Nicole Diver are patterned, in part, on Gerald and Sara Murphy, whose "living well" Fitzgerald admired and to whom he dedicated the novel.

The Divers are also the Fitzgeralds, plagued during the 1930's by mental illness and emotional bankruptcy. Similarly, Rosemary Hoyt, whose innocent and admiring viewpoint sets up the first book of the novel, is patterned after the young actor Lois Moran, and Tommy Barban is a fictional representation of Zelda's aviator, Jozan. Also, in drawing on subjects and themes that had characterized even his earliest work, especially wealth and its corrosive influence, Fitzgerald was extending his past concerns from as far back as *This Side of Paradise* into the present, most notably in Baby Warren in *Tender Is the Night*, who callously "buys" Nicole a doctor. Finally, the multiple viewpoint of the novel is a logical extension of the narrator-observer in *The Great Gatsby*, an attempt to carry objectivity even further than he does in that novel. Only perhaps in his reaching into historical prophecy does Fitzgerald go beyond his earlier concerns. However, even *The Great Gatsby*, which Nick calls "a story of the West," appears on one level to address the moral decay of society on an international level. What *Tender Is the Night* finally reflects, then, is a novelist who has gained philosophical insight and technical skill and has added them onto the existing foundation of his craftsmanship.

Bryant Mangum

Other major works

SHORT FICTION: *Flappers and Philosophers*, 1920; *Tales of the Jazz Age*, 1922; *All the Sad Young Men*, 1926; *Taps at Reveille*, 1935; *The Stories of F. Scott Fitzgerald*, 1951; *Babylon Revisited, and Other Stories*, 1960; *The Pat Hobby Stories*, 1962; *The Apprentice Fiction of F. Scott Fitzgerald, 1907-1917*, 1965; *The Basil and Josephine Stories*, 1973; *Bits of Paradise*, 1974; *The Price Was High: The Last Uncollected Stories of F. Scott Fitzgerald*, 1979; *Before Gatsby: The First Twenty-Six Stories*, 2001 (Matthew J. Bruccoli, editor).

PLAY: *The Vegetable: Or, From President to Postman*, pb. 1923.

NONFICTION: *The Crack-Up*, 1945; *The Letters of F. Scott Fitzgerald*, 1963; *Letters to His Daughter*, 1965; *Thoughtbook of Francis Scott Fitzgerald*, 1965; *Dear Scott/Dear Max: The Fitzgerald-Perkins Correspondence*, 1971; *As Ever, Scott Fitzgerald*, 1972; *F. Scott Fitzgerald's Ledger*, 1972; *The Notebooks of F. Scott Fitzgerald*, 1978; *A Life in Letters*, 1994 (Matthew J. Bruccoli, editor); *F. Scott Fitzgerald on Authorship*, 1996; *Dear Scott, Dearest Zelda: The Love Letters of F. Scott and Zelda Fitzgerald*, 2002 (Jackson R. Bryer and Cathy W. Barks, editors).

MISCELLANEOUS: *Afternoon of an Author: A Selection of Uncollected Stories and Essays*, 1958; *F. Scott Fitzgerald: The Princeton Years, Selected Writings, 1914-1920*, 1996 (Chip Deffaa, editor).

Bibliography

Berman, Ronald. *Fitzgerald, Hemingway, and the Twenties.* Tuscaloosa: University of Alabama Press, 2001. An explication of the cultural context of the era and how the works of these two American writers are imbued with the attitudes and icons of their day.

____________. *"The Great Gatsby" and Fitzgerald's World of Ideas.* Tuscaloosa: University of Alabama Press, 1997. Explores Fitzgerald's political and social views of his era and how he incorporated them into his seminal novel.

Bloom, Harold, ed. *F. Scott Fitzgerald: The Great Gatsby.* New Haven, Conn.: Chelsea House, 1986. A short but important collection of critical essays. This book provides an introductory overview of Fitzgerald scholarship (five pages), as well as readings from a variety of perspectives on Fitzgerald's fiction.

Conroy, Frank. "Great Scott." *Gentlemen's Quarterly* 66 (December, 1996): 240-245. A reconsideration of Fitzgerald on the centenary of his birth; Conroy argues that one of Fitzgerald's great strengths as a writer was his ability to make the metaphysical beauty of his female characters believable.

Curnutt, Kirk, ed. *A Historical Guide to F. Scott Fitzgerald.* New York: Oxford University Press, 2004. Collection of original articles by scholars on a wide variety of subjects pertaining to Fitzgerald; includes a bibliographical essay.

Gale, Robert L. *An F. Scott Fitzgerald Encyclopedia.* Westport, Conn.: Greenwood Press, 1998. Provides almost everything students should know about Fitzgerald's life and works. Indispensable.

Gross, Dalton, and MaryJean Gross. *Understanding "The Great Gatsby": A Student Casebook to Issues, Sources, and Historical Documents.* Westport, Conn.: Greenwood Press, 1998. Part of the Literature in Context series. An excellent study guide for students of the novel. Includes bibliographical references and an index.

Hook, Andrew. *F. Scott Fitzgerald: A Literary Life.* New York: St. Martin's, 2002. Part of the Literary Lives series. Concise rather than thorough, but with some interesting details.

Jefferson, Margo. "Still Timely, Yet a Writer of His Time." *The New York Times*, December 17, 1996, p. C17. A brief biography of Fitzgerald on the occasion of his centennial year; calls him one of those rare artists with a cultural radar system that is constantly picking up sensations, responses, and fresh thoughts.

Lee, A. Robert, ed. *Scott Fitzgerald: The Promises of Life.* New York: St. Martin's Press, 1989. An excellent collection of essays by Fitzgerald scholars, this book includes an introduction that surveys scholarship on the texts. Topics addressed include Fitzgerald's treatment of women, his notion of the decline of the West, his "ethics and ethnicity," and his use of "distortions" of the imagination.

Meyers, Jeffrey. *Scott Fitzgerald: A Biography.* New York: HarperCollins, 1994. In this biography, which makes use of previously unknown materials about Fitzgerald's life, Meyers discusses how such writers as Edgar Allan Poe, Ernest Hemingway, and Joseph Conrad influenced Fitzgerald's fiction.

Stanley, Linda C. *The Foreign Critical Reputation of F. Scott Fitzgerald, 1980-2000: An Analysis and Annotated Bibliography.* Westport, Conn.: Praeger, 2004. Very useful guide to international views of Fitzgerald that can also be useful to students looking for new perspectives.

Tate, Mary Jo. *F. Scott Fitzgerald A to Z: The Essential Reference to His Life and Work.* New York: Facts On File, 1998. A comprehensive study of the man and his oeuvre. Provides bibliographical references and an index.

Taylor, Kendall. *Sometimes Madness Is Wisdom: Zelda and Scott Fitzgerald, A Marriage.* New York: Ballantine, 2001. An examination of one of literature's most famous couples and their symbiotic marriage.

William Gaddis

Born: New York, New York; December 29, 1922
Died: East Hampton, New York; December 16, 1998

Principal long fiction • *The Recognitions,* 1955; *JR,* 1975; *Carpenter's Gothic,* 1985; *A Frolic of His Own,* 1994; *Agapé Agape,* 2002.

Other literary forms • William Gaddis's literary reputation is based upon his novels; he also contributed a number of essays and short stories to major magazines.

Achievements • Gaddis's writing is generally regarded as convoluted, confusing, and difficult—all qualities that have led some readers to criticize it. At the same time, however, his work is also sophisticated, multilayered, and technically innovative—qualities that have led other readers to consider Gaddis one of the most important American writers after World War II, and certainly one of the least appreciated and understood.

Gaddis's accomplishments began to receive greater attention during the late 1960's and early 1970's, during which time he was at work on his second monumental novel, *JR.* Between 1955 and 1970, only a single article on him appeared in the United States, but during the 1970's momentum started to build. The first doctoral dissertation on Gaddis was published in 1971, providing valuable information on *The Recognitions* and basic facts about Gaddis's life. The year 1982 saw the publication of new essays in a special issue of the *Review of Contemporary Fiction,* as well as a full-length guide by Steven Moore to *The Recognitions* and a prestigious MacArthur Prize fellowship.

Winning the 1976 National Book Award in fiction for *JR* confirmed Gaddis's success. Indeed, Gaddis responded by publishing his third novel only a decade later, down from the twenty years between his first two efforts. *Carpenter's Gothic* was widely hailed for its bitter yet readable satire of ethical vanity in American business, politics, and popular religion. The novel broadened the readership for a novelist accustomed to a comparatively small audience, and it confirmed him as one of the most gifted and serious writers of contemporary American fiction.

Gaddis's fourth novel, *A Frolic of His Own,* was published in 1994 to a mixed response similar to that given his earlier works. It won for him his second National Book Award and was praised for its savage wit. However, some reviewers raised the old complaints that it was difficult, long-winded, and all too faithful in its representation of the tedium of everyday conversation and legal minutiae.

Along with his National Book Awards, Gaddis was given a National Institute of Arts and Letters Award (1963), two National Endowment for the Arts grants (1963 and 1974), a MacArthur Foundation fellowship (1982), and a Lannan Foundation lifetime achievement award (1993).

Biography • After spending his early childhood in New York City and on Long Island, William Gaddis attended a private boarding school in Connecticut for nine years. He then returned to Long Island to attend public school from grade

©Marion Ettlinger

eight through high school. He was accepted by Harvard in 1941 and stayed there until 1945, when he took a job as reader for *The New Yorker.* Gaddis left this position after one year in order to travel. In the years that followed, he visited Central America, the Caribbean, North Africa, and parts of Europe, all of which became settings in his first novel. He continued to write after returning to the United States, and in 1955, with ten years of effort behind him, he published *The Recognitions.*

Within these broad outlines a few additional details about Gaddis's life are known, despite his extreme reluctance to discuss his private life. Although he was sometimes seen at writers' conferences and occasionally did some teaching, he guarded his privacy well. David Koenig and Steven Moore have made a number of important inferences about Gaddis's life. For example, the protagonist of *The Recognitions,* Wyatt, has a lonely and isolated childhood. His mother dies on an ocean voyage when he is very young, and his father gradually loses his sanity. When Wyatt is twelve, he suffers from a mysterious ailment that the doctors label *erythema grave.* They mutilate Wyatt's wasted body and send him home to die because they can find neither a cause nor a cure for his illness; unexpectedly, though, Wyatt recovers. Parallels to Gaddis's own childhood emerge. Apparently he was separated from his parents, at least while he attended a boarding school in Connecticut. He also contracted an illness that the doctors could not identify and therefore called *erythema grave.* Serious effects of the illness recurred in later years to cause further problems and to prevent the young Gaddis from being accepted into the U.S. Army during World War II. Forced to remain in college, he began to write pieces for the Harvard *Lampoon* that anticipated the satirical, humorous, and critical tone of his novels. He soon became president of the *Lampoon.*

Gaddis was involved in an incident during his final year at Harvard that required the intervention of local police. Although it was hardly a serious affair, the local newspapers covered it and created embarrassing publicity for the administration. Gaddis was asked to resign and did so. The end of traditional academic success did not prevent him from acquiring knowledge. Through his travels—and more so through many years of research—Gaddis constructed impressive works of fiction from a vast store of knowledge.

After the publication of *The Recognitions,* Gaddis supported himself by teaching and writing nonfiction. He spent four years working in public relations for the Pfizer Pharmaceutical Company. He was the father of two children. His daughter, Sarah Gaddis, is a novelist whose first book, *Swallow Hard* (1991), takes its title from a phrase in *JR* and features as protagonist an author of difficult, unpopular fiction. Gaddis's son, Matthew Hough Gaddis, is a filmmaker.

In late 1998, Gaddis died of prostate cancer at his New York home. An unconfirmed rumor reported at that time claimed that he left behind the completed manuscript of a book called *Agapé Agape*, dealing with the history of the player piano. That was the title and description of the book on which Jack Gibbs, in *JR*, was working. Sources did not agree as to whether the yet-to-be-discovered book was fiction or nonfiction. When the manuscript was eventually uncovered, it was found to be a semiautobiographical novella, which was published in 2002.

Analysis • Critics have placed William Gaddis in the tradition of experimental fiction, linking him closely to James Joyce and comparing him to contemporaries such as Thomas Pynchon. Gaddis himself also indicated the influence of T. S. Eliot on his work, and indeed his books contain both novelistic and poetic structures. The novels employ only vestiges of traditional plots, which go in and out of focus as they are blurred by endless conversations, overpowered by erudite allusions and a multitude of characters, conflicts, and ambiguities.

Like Joyce and Eliot, Gaddis uses myth to create a sense of timelessness—myths of Odysseus, the Grail Knight, the Fisher King, and Christ, along with parallels to the tales of Saint Clement, Faust, and Peer Gynt. Using devices of both modern poetic sequences and modern antirealistic fiction, Gaddis unifies the diversity of parts through recurring images, phrases, and locations; a common tone; historical and literary echoes; and other nonchronological and nonsequential modes of organization. In *The Recognitions*, point of view is alternated to create tension between the first-person and third-person voices, and there are complicated jokes and symbolism deriving from the unexpected use of "I," "you," "he," and "she." In *JR*, the first-person perspective dominates through incessant talk, with very little relief or explanation in traditional third-person passages. As one reviewer wrote: "[Gaddis] wires his characters for sound and sends his story out on a continuous wave of noise—truncated dialogue, distracted monologue, the racket of TV sets, radios, telephones—from which chaos action, of a sort, eventually emerges."

All of Gaddis's work is about cacophony and euphony, fragmentation and integration, art and business, chaos and order. To a casual reader, *Carpenter's Gothic*, *JR*, and *The Recognitions* may appear only cacophonous, fragmented, and chaotic, for their formal experimentation is so dominant. To the reader prepared for the challenge of brilliant fiction, these novels illustrate how very accurate Henry James was in predicting the "elasticity" of the novel and its changing nature in the hands of great writers.

The Recognitions • Considering the complexities of Gaddis's fiction, it is not surprising that the earliest reviews of *The Recognitions* were unenthusiastic. Although they gave Gaddis credit for his extensive knowledge of religion and aesthetics, of art, myth, and philosophy, they criticized the absence of clear chronology, the diffuseness of so many intersecting subplots and characters, the large number of references, and the supposed formlessness. In the decade following the publication of *The Recognitions*, very little was written about this allusive novel or its elusive author. Readers had difficulties with the book, and Gaddis did nothing to explain it. Few copies of the original edition were ever sold and the novel went out of print. In 1962, Meridian published a paperback edition under its policy to make available neglected but important literary works. Gradually, *The Recognitions* became an underground classic, although it again went out of circulation. Not until 1970 did another paperback edition appear. Throughout the precarious life of this novel, Gaddis was probably the person least surprised by its uncertain reception and reader resistance. During a party scene in *The Recognitions,* a poet questions a literary critic about a book he is carrying: "You reading that?" The critic answers, "No, I'm just reviewing it . . . all I need is the jacket blurb."

At its most fundamental level, *The Recognitions* is about every possible kind of recognition. The ultimate recognition is stated in the epigraph by Irenaeus, which translates as "Nothing empty nor without significance with God," but this ultimate recognition is nearly impossible to experience in a secular world where spiritual messages boom forth from the radio and television to become indistinguishable from commercials for soap powder and cereal.

The characters, major and minor, move toward, from, and around various recognitions. Some search for knowledge of how to perform their jobs, others search for knowledge of fraud, of ancestors, of love, self, truth, and sin. Wyatt, settling in New York City, moves sequentially through time and according to place to find his own recognition in Spain. His traditional path is crossed by the paths of many other characters who serve as his foils and reflections. Wyatt paints while Stanley composes music, Otto writes, and Esme loves. Wyatt, though, does more than paint; he forges the masterpieces of Fra Angelico and of Old Flemish painters such as Hugo van der Goes and Dirck Bouts. Thus, his fraudulent activity is reflected in others' fraudulent schemes. Frank Sinisterra, posing as a physician, is forced to operate on Wyatt's mother and inadvertently murders her. Frank is also a counterfeiter; Otto is a plagiarist; Benny is a liar; Big Anna masquerades as a woman, and Agnes Deigh, at a party, is unable to convince people that she is really a woman, not a man in drag; Herschel has no idea who he is (a "negative positivist," a "positive negativist," a "latent homosexual," or a "latent heterosexual"). In similar confusion, Wyatt is addressed as Stephen Asche, Estaban, the Reverend Gilbert Sullivan, and Christ arriving for the Second Coming.

As Wyatt matures from childhood to adulthood, his notions of emptiness and significance, of fraud and authenticity, undergo change. While his mother Camilla and his father are on an ocean voyage across the Atlantic, his mother has an appendicitis attack, is operated on by Sinisterra, and dies. Wyatt is reared by his father but essentially by his Aunt May. She is a fanatical Calvinist who teaches the talented boy that original sketches blaspheme God's original creation, so Wyatt eventually turns to copying from illustrated books. The distinctions between original work and forgery break down.

When he is a young man, Wyatt becomes a partner with Recktall Brown, a shrewd art dealer who finds unsuspecting buyers for the forgeries that Wyatt produces. Wyatt is so convinced that "perfect" forgery has nothing to do with sinning, much less with breaking the law, that he has only scorn for the nineteenth century Romantics who prized originality above all else, often, he thinks, at the expense of quality. It takes many years of disappointments and betrayals for Wyatt to recognize that perfection of line and execution are empty and without significance. The first and crucial step of any great work of art must be the conceptualization behind it, the idea from which the painting derives; there is otherwise no meaningful distinction between the work of the artist and that of the craftsman. Wyatt's abnegation of any original conception implies abnegation of self, which in turn affects his efforts to communicate and to share with his wife Esther and his model Esme. Wyatt's many failures are reflected—in bits and pieces—in the subplots of *The Recognitions.* Characters miss one another as their paths crisscross and they lose track of their appointments. They talk but no one listens, they make love but their partners do not remember, and finally, they are trapped within their useless and pretentious self-illusions.

The need for love, forgiveness, purification, and renewal emerges from this frantic activity motivated by greed and selfishness. Thus, Gaddis includes in the novel archetypal questers, priests, mourning women, arid settings, burials, dying and reviving figures, cathedrals, and keepers of the keys. These motifs bring to mind many mythic parallels, though it is hard not to think of specific parallels with Johann Wolfgang von Goethe's *Faust* (1808, 1833) and Eliot's *The Waste Land* (1922) and *Four Quartets* (1943). Toward the end of his pilgrimage, as well as the end of the novel, Wyatt achieves his recognition of love and authenticity, yet Gaddis does not succumb to the temptation to finish with a conventional denouement but keeps the novel going. In this way, the form of *The Recognitions* reflects its theme, that truth is immutable but exceptionally well hidden. After Wyatt's success follow chapters of others' failures. Anselm castrates himself and Esme dies; Sinisterra is killed by an assassin and Stanley, while playing his music in a cathedral, is killed as the walls collapse.

Just as *The Recognitions* is rich in meaning, so it is rich in form. The forward movement through chronological time is poised against other combinations of time, primarily the juxtaposition of past and present. The immediate effect of juxtaposition is to interrupt and suspend time while the ultimate effect is to make all time seem simultaneous. For example, in chapter 2, part 2, Wyatt looks out the window at the evening sky as Recktall Brown talks. Brown begins speaking about ancient Greece and Rome but is interrupted by a description of the constellation Orion, by an advertisement for phoney gems, by instructions for passengers riding a bus, by a passage about Alexander the Great, by a quotation from an English travel book of the fourteenth century. The result is that the reader temporarily loses his or her orientation, but the reader need not lose orientation completely. Unity for these disparate time periods is provided by a quality that is part of each passage—glittering beauty marred by a flaw or spurious detail. Thus, organization is based on concept, not on chronology.

Other nonchronological modes of organization include recurring patterns. Specific words become guides for the reader through difficult sections and also repeat the essential concepts of the novel. For example, "recognitions," "origin," "fished for," "design," "originality," and "fragment" can be found frequently. Larger anecdotes may also be repeated by different speakers, and opinions or metaphysical arguments may be repeated unknowingly or even stolen. The recurring images, words, and stories constitute an internal frame of reference that creates a unity apart from the plot.

In *The Recognitions,* it is possible, though not easy, to discover what activities Gaddis believes to be of enduring value. Deception and fraud are everywhere, but they cannot destroy the truth that is hidden beneath these layers of deception. A first-time reader of this novel will probably have an experience similar to that of first-time readers of Joyce's *Ulysses* (1922) in the years soon after its publication—before full-length guides extolled its merits and explained its obscurities. Like those readers of Joyce's masterpiece, readers of *The Recognitions* will be amply rewarded.

JR • Although *JR* may be even more difficult than Gaddis's first novel, it met with a more positive reception. Critics pointed to its imposing length, diffuse form, and lack of traditional narrative devices, but they believed that it was a novel that could not be ignored by people seriously interested in the future of literature. Reviewers included John Gardner, George Steiner, Earl Miner, and George Stade, further evidence of Gaddis's growing reputation.

Like *The Recognitions*, *JR* is concerned with distinguishing between significant and insignificant activities, all of which take place in a more circumscribed landscape than that of *The Recognitions*. There are no transatlantic crossings and no trips to Central America, only the alternating between a suburb on Long Island and the city of Manhattan. Gaddis shifts his satirical eye to contemporary education through the experience of his protagonist, JR, who attends sixth grade in a school on Long Island. Amy Joubert, JR's social studies teacher, takes the class to visit the stock exchange, and JR is sufficiently impressed by it to interpret the lesson literally. He is fascinated by money and uses the investment of his class in one share of stock to build a corporate empire. Although his immense profits are only on paper, the effects of his transactions on countless others are both concrete and devastating.

Despite the centrality of this obnoxious child, JR remains a shadowy figure. The events he triggers and the people he sucks into his moneymaking whirlwind are more visible. Edward Bast, JR's music teacher and composer, Jack Gibbs, Thomas Eigen, and Shepperman are all artists of some kind, and their realm of activity is quite different from JR's. Bast is forever trying to finish his piece of music, even as he works reluctantly for JR in the Manhattan office that is broken down, cluttered, and chaotic. Thomas Eigen has been writing a play, and Gibbs has tried for most of his life to write an ambitious book, but he is always losing pages he has written. Although some of Shepperman's paintings have been finished, they remain hidden from sight. The world of art is, however, at odds with the world of business. Bast wants nothing to do with his student's megalomania but proves to be no match for JR. The creative people cannot persuade others to leave them alone to their paper, oil paints, and canvases, and as a result they are used and manipulated by those who serve as their liaisons to others who buy, maintain, or publish their efforts.

The primary device for communication is not art but rather the telephone. The world that technology has created is efficient and mechanical since its purpose is to finish jobs so that money can be paid, at least symbolically on paper, and then be reinvested, again on paper. The artist is replaced by the businessman, and it is not even a flesh-and-blood businessman, but only his disembodied voice issuing orders out of a piece of plastic (JR disguises his voice so that he sounds older). The central "authority" is invisible, ubiquitous, and, at least while the conglomerate lasts, omniscient. The triumph of the telephone affords Gaddis endless opportunities for humor and irony, and the failure of art is accompanied by the failure of other means of communication—notably of love. As in *The Recognitions*, lovers miss each other, do not understand each other, and end their affairs or marriages unhappily.

The real tour de force of *JR* is its language. There is almost no third-person description to establish location and speaker and few authorial links or transitions between conversations or monologues. Originally, Gaddis did not even use quotation marks to set off one speaker from the next. *JR* is nearly one thousand pages of talk. The jargon, speech rhythms, and style of those in the educational establishment and in the stock market are perfectly re-created, but their language is a self-perpetuating system; regardless of their outpouring, the expressive power of words is obliterated by the sheer noise and verbiage. One early reviewer said of *JR* that "everything is insanely jammed together in this novel's closed atmosphere—there's no causality, no progression; and the frantic farcical momentum overlies the entropic unravelling of all 'systems.'" The words pile up as the structures of the culture collapse; the reader is faced with a formidable challenge in making his or her way through it all.

There can be no doubt that *JR*, probably even more than *The Recognitions*, poses serious difficulties for the reader. Despite them, and even perhaps because of them, *JR* is an extraordinary novel. Gaddis captures the dizzying pace, the language, and the absurdities of contemporary culture and mercilessly throws them back to his readers in a crazy, nonlinear kind of verisimilitude. The novel operates without causality, chronology, and the logical narrative devices upon which many readers depend. The cacophony of the characters and the lack of clarity are certainly meant to be disturbing.

Carpenter's Gothic • In *Carpenter's Gothic*, this cultural cacophony runs headlong toward a global apocalypse. Again, there is the confused eruption of voices into the narrative and the forward spinning blur of events common to Gaddis's earlier fictions. Gaddis's third novel, however, is not only more focused and brief, at 262 pages, but therefore the most readable of his works. Its story centers on Elizabeth Vorakers Booth and her husband Paul, renters of the ramshackle "Carpenter's Gothic" house, in which all of the action unfolds. Daughter of a minerals tycoon who committed suicide when his illegal business practices were exposed, Elizabeth married Paul Booth, a Vietnam War veteran and carrier of Vorakers's bribes, after Paul lied in testifying before Congress.

All the novel's complexities unfold from these tangled business dealings. The Vorakerses' estate is hopelessly ensnarled in lawsuits, manipulated by swarms of self-serving lawyers. Paul is suing or countersuing everyone in sight (including an airline, for an alleged loss of Liz's "marital services" after she was a passenger during a minor crash). Meanwhile, Paul's earlier testimony before Congress has landed him a job as "media consultant" for a Reverend Ude. Ude's fundamentalist television ministry, based in South Carolina, has mushroomed into an important political interest group, and Paul's meager pay from this group is the only thing keeping him and Liz from bankruptcy. Paul drunkenly schemes and rages at Liz, or at his morning newspaper; as in *JR*, the telephone intrudes with maddeningly insistent threats, deals, wrong numbers, and ads.

Events are intensified with the entry of McCandless, owner of the Carpenter's Gothic house. A sometime geologist, teacher, and writer, McCandless happens to have surveyed the same southeast African mineral fields on which the Vorakers company had built its fortunes. It also happens to be the same African territory in which Reverend Ude is now building his missions for a great "harvest of souls" expected during "the Rapture" or anticipated Second Coming of Christ. McCandless is being pursued by U.S. government agents for back taxes and for information about those African territories. He appears at the door one morning, a shambling and wary man, an incessant smoker and an alcoholic, but nevertheless an embodiment of romantic adventure to Liz, who promptly takes him to bed.

Events spin rapidly toward violence. During an unexpected visit, Liz's younger brother, Billy, hears McCandless's tirades against American foreign policy and promptly flies off to Africa—where he is killed when his airplane is gunned down by terrorists. The U.S. Congress has launched an investigation of Ude for bribing a senator to grant his ministry a coveted television license, a bribe that Paul carried. Ude has also managed to drown a young boy during baptismal rites in South Carolina's Pee Dee River. All of Liz and Paul's stored belongings, comprising her last links to family and tradition, have been auctioned off by a storage company in compensation for unpaid bills. Liz's behavior becomes increasingly erratic.

The apocalypse comes when all these events and forces collide. McCandless takes a payoff from the Central Intelligence Agency for his African papers and simply exits the novel, after Liz has refused to accompany him. She dies of a heart attack, the warning signs of which have been planted from the first chapter. Paul immediately files a claim to any of the Vorakerses' inheritance that might have been paid to Billy and Liz, and he too simply exits the novel—notably, after using the same seduction ploy on Liz's best friend as he had originally used on Liz herself. In Africa, though, events truly explode: U.S. forces mobilize to guard various "national interests," and a real apocalypse looms as newspapers proclaim the upcoming use of a "10 K 'DEMO' BOMB OFF AFRICA COAST."

Liz Booth's heart attack symbolizes the absolute loss of empathy and love in such a cynical and careless world. Indeed, her death is further ironized when it is misinterpreted, and also proclaimed in the newspapers, as having taken place during a burglary. As with his earlier works, Gaddis's message involves this seemingly total loss of charitable and compassionate love in a civilization obsessed by success, as well as by the technologies for realizing it. Once again, his satire targets the counterfeiting of values in American life, and the explosive force of mass society on feeling individuals.

The explosion of words that Gaddis re-creates is also a warning. As the efforts of painters, writers, musicians, and other artists are increasingly blocked, unappreciated, and exploited, those urges will be acknowledged by fewer and fewer people. Without an audience of listeners or viewers and without a segment of artists, there will be no possibilities for redemption from the chaos and mechanization. There will be neither sufficient introspection nor a medium through which any introspection can take concrete form. Gaddis's novels are humorous, clever, satiric, and innovative. They are also memorable and frightening reflections of contemporary culture and its values.

A Frolic of His Own • *A Frolic of His Own* could be seen as the culmination of Gaddis's career, applying to the world of law the same combination of acute detailed observation and merciless satirical invention that he gave the business world in *JR* and that of art in *The Recognitions.*

The protagonist, middle-aged college professor Oscar Crease, is suing film producer Constantine Kiester for theft of intellectual property, claiming that Kiester's film *The Blood in the Red, White and Blue* was plagiarized from Crease's unpublished and unproduced play, *Once at Antietam.* He is also suing himself (actually his insurance company) because he was run over by his own car while he was attempting to jump-start it.

Meanwhile Oscar's father, ninety-seven-year-old judge Thomas Crease, is deciding two even more bizarre cases, a wrongful-death suit against an evangelist (the Reverend Ude from *Carpenter's Gothic*) for the drowning of an infant he was attempting to baptize, and a case in which a dog has become trapped in a large nonrepresentational sculpture whose creator, R. Szyrk, is demanding an injunction to forestall any attempt to damage his work in order to free the dog.

Gaddis uses these cases to spotlight the increasingly Byzantine nature of the legal process, as well as some of the artistic issues dear to his heart. The intellectual property suit focuses attention on issues of plagiarism with the same thoroughness with which *The Recognitions* looked at counterfeiting. The heirs of American dramatist Eugene O'Neill, seeing similarities between *Once at Antietam* and O'Neill's *Mourning Becomes Electra* (1931), sue Oscar in turn, and elements of both are traced back to Plato, reminding us of the complexity of determining just what constitutes an original idea. The Szyrk case opposes artistic freedom to animal rights, among other issues, and both Szyrk and Oscar can be seen as somewhat ironic versions of that recurrent Gaddis character, the unappreciated "difficult" artist. In the end, as in most of Gaddis's work, the characters are ground down by the chaos and complexity of the modern world, granted only a few Pyrrhic victories. Oscar's winnings in the plagiarism suit are sharply reduced on appeal, and the father of the baptism victim is awarded fewer than twenty dollars.

With *A Frolic of His Own*, the creator of Recktall Brown now gives us the law firm of Swyne and Dour and the Japanese car brands Isuyu and Sosumi. The reader's already strained suspension of disbelief may stop altogether at a suit by the Episcopal Church against the makers of Pepsi-Cola for using a brand name that is an anagram of theirs. Again the dialogue is sparsely annotated and often as vague and garrulous as actual conversation. Trial transcripts and depositions are presented in all their verbosity and redundancy. At least enough of *Once at Antietam* is presented to convince us that it is a tedious play. Those who criticized Gaddis's previous works for being difficult and tedious can make the same charges against this one. Even more than his previous works, *A Frolic of His Own* displays the wit, inventiveness, and complexity of Gaddis at his best, but also the qualities to which readers have objected.

Agapé Agape • Surrounded by the documents and papers accumulated over the course of his life, the dying man who narrates *Agapé Agape* is desperate to convey what he can of his work. The title is a pun: *agapé* is a Greek word referring to unconditional brotherly love and community, now most commonly used by Christians. For such love to be agape may mean that it has been torn apart, or caught off-guard and surprised. Indeed, in tracing the history of the player piano to other developments in the modern world—including the rising use of binary (which in turn led to the computer age), as well as changing attitudes about the individual's relationship to art—the narrator is filled with frustration at how the significance of his work is not appreciated by the world at large.

There is a strong autobiographical element to the narrator, as Gaddis was also aware of his impending death and had decades of notes regarding his own history of the player piano. The writing is dense and intimidating. The syntax is more complex than any previous Gaddis harangue, with no paragraph breaks in the novella to help guide one's reading. There are frequent lapses into other languages, as well as a constant stream of historical and artistic allusions. As an example, the narrator returns again and again to the philosopher Jeremy Bentham's famous observation that pushpin (a pub game) is as good as poetry if the amount of pleasure is equal, and from there tends to link the word "pushpin" to Pushkin, referring to the Russian poet Alexander Pushkin.

The narrator compares himself to his own documents, his skin parchment thin from medicine and held together by staples. His only refuge is the work that he is trying to complete: "hallucinations took place in the head, in the mind, now everything out there is the hallucination and the mind where the work is done is the only reality." The novella ends much as it began, but the very act of communicating—the direct address to the reader, something Gaddis never attempted in his earlier novels—becomes its own message, its own grasp at hope and continuity in the face of bitter finality.

Miriam Fuchs
Updated by Arthur D. Hlavaty and Ray Mescallado

Other major works

NONFICTION: *The Rush for Second Place: Essays and Occasional Writings*, 2002 (Joseph Tabbi, editor).

Bibliography

Beer, John. "William Gaddis." *Review of Contemporary Fiction* 21 (Fall, 2001): 69-110. A very thorough overview article and a good introduction to Gaddis's body of work. Focuses on Gaddis's satirical style.

Bloom, Harold, ed. *William Gaddis: Bloom's Modern Critical Views*. Philadelphia: Chelsea House, 2003. Collection of critical essays about Gaddis that have been assembled for student use.

Gaddis, William. "The Art of Fiction, CI: William Gaddis." Interview by Zoltan Abadi-Nagy. *Paris Review* 105 (Winter, 1987): 54-89. An extensive interview with Gaddis, conducted during a 1986 visit to Budapest, Hungary. The author talks in detail about his sources, reputation, principal themes, and work in progress. He dispels a number of misconceptions, especially those linking his work to sources in Joyce, and discusses how the writer must ignore pressures of the literary marketplace.

Green, Jack. *Fire the Bastards!* Normal, Ill.: Dalkey Archive Press, 1992. A series of three essays originally published by the pseudonymous author in 1962, indignantly attacking the reviewers of *The Recognitions* for failing to appreciate its greatness. Green cites numerous factual errors in the reviews and excoriates the reviewers for being unwilling to make the effort to understand the book. In contrast to the academic tone of later studies, this book is written in tones of rage with eccentric syntax and capitalization.

Karl, Frederick R. *American Fictions, 1940-1980*. New York: Harper and Row, 1983. An important essay on Gaddis's place among contemporary writers such as Donald Barthelme and Thomas Pynchon, focusing in particular on Gaddis's satires of counterfeit art, fake sensibility, and empty values in American civilization. Includes useful discussions of Gaddis's narrative techniques, especially his development of scenes and characters in his first two novels.

Keuhl, John, and Steven Moore, eds. *In Recognition of William Gaddis*. Syracuse, N.Y.: Syracuse University Press, 1984. Gathers six previously published essays alongside seven new ones. Particularly useful is David Koenig's discussion of Gaddis's early career and his sources for *The Recognitions*, and other essays on Gaddis's satire of the monetization of art and love in contemporary culture.

Knight, Christopher J. *Hints and Guesses: William Gaddis's Fiction of Longing*. Madison: University of Wisconsin Press, 1997. A good study of Gaddis's oeuvre. Includes bibliographical references and an index.

Moore, Steven. *A Reader's Guide to William Gaddis's "The Recognitions."* Lincoln: University of Nebraska Press, 1982. An indispensable, line-by-line guidebook to Gaddis's difficult first novel, providing concise annotations of his extratextual allusions and quotations, as well as the novel's intratextual developments of character and events. Also includes a useful introductory essay and reprints three previously published but rare early pieces by Gaddis.

____________. *William Gaddis.* Boston: Twayne, 1989. The first full-length study of the writer's career and principal works, from *The Recognitions* through *Carpenter's Gothic.* An opening biographical chapter provides extensive information about his childhood, his education, his work, and his affiliations leading up to the first novel. A readable and critically incisive overview.

Review of Contemporary Fiction 2 (Summer, 1982). A special issue, one-half of which is devoted to Gaddis's work. Contains a rare though brief interview with the author, as well as seven original essays on *The Recognitions* and *JR.* Most of the essays concentrate on the bases of form in novels still regarded formless and sprawling.

Wolfe, Peter. *A Vision of His Own.* Madison, N.J.: Fairleigh Dickinson University Press, 1997. A thoroughgoing study of Gaddis's first four novels, emphasizing such themes as the role of the artist, language and law as efforts to assert meaning and order in the face of entropy, and the soul-destroying aspects of twentieth century American culture.

Ernest J. Gaines

Born: Oscar, Louisiana; January 15, 1933

Principal long fiction • *Catherine Carmier*, 1964; *Of Love and Dust*, 1967; *The Autobiography of Miss Jane Pittman*, 1971; *In My Father's House*, 1978; *A Gathering of Old Men*, 1983; *A Lesson Before Dying*, 1993.

Other literary forms • Ernest J. Gaines published a collection of short stories, *Bloodline*, in 1968. One story from that collection, *A Long Day in November*, was published separately in a children's edition in 1971.

Achievements • For more than thirty years, Gaines has been a serious and committed writer of fiction. He has always worked slowly, frustratingly slowly to his admirers, but that is because of his great devotion to and respect for the craft of fiction. The six novels he had written through 1999 are all set in rural Louisiana, north of Baton Rouge: Gaines, like William Faulkner, has created a single world in which his works are centered. Even though Gaines has written during a time of great racial turmoil and unrest, he has resisted becoming involved in political movements, feeling that he can best serve the cause of art and humanity by devoting himself to perfecting his craft. This does not mean that he has remained detached from political realities. Taken together, his novels cover the period of 1865 to 1980, reflecting the social movements that have affected black Americans during that time. Gaines has said again and again, however, that he is primarily interested in people; certainly it is in his depiction of people that his greatest strength lies. His focus is on the universals of life: love, pride, pity, hatred. He aspires thus not to have an immediate political impact with his writing but to move people emotionally. His supreme achievement in this regard is *The Autobiography of Miss Jane Pittman.* With its publication—and with the highly acclaimed television movie based on the novel—Gaines achieved the recognition he had long deserved.

Biography • From birth until age fifteen, Ernest J. Gaines lived in rural Louisiana with his parents. As a boy, he often worked in the plantation fields and spent much of his spare time with his aunt, Miss Augusteen Jefferson. He moved to Vallejo, California, in 1948 to live with his mother and stepfather, and he attended high school and junior college there before serving in the army. After his military service, he earned a bachelor's degree at San Francisco State College. On the basis of some stories written while he was a student there, he was awarded the Wallace Stegner Creative Writing Fellowship in 1958 for graduate study at Stanford University.

Gaines was a Guggenheim Fellow in 1971 and won an award from the Black Academy of Arts and Letters in 1972. In 1987 Gaines received a literary award from the American Academy and Institute of Arts and Letters, and in 1993 he was awarded a John D. and Catherine T. MacArthur Foundation fellowship. Also in that year, *A Lesson Before Dying* won the National Book Critics Circle Award.

Since 1958 Gaines has lived, impermanently, by his own testimony, in or near San Francisco, feeling that living elsewhere enables him to gain a perspective on his

©Jerry Bauer

southern material that would be unavailable were he to live in the South full time. By making yearly trips back to Louisiana, where in 1983 he became a visiting professor of creative writing at the University of Louisiana at Lafayette (formerly the University of Southwestern Louisiana). In 2003, he retired from active teaching with a lifetime appointment as writer-in-residence emeritus. He bought property in Oscar, near the plantation where he had grown up, and settled there. He continued to write. In 2005, his collection of essays and short fiction *Mozart and Leadbelly* was published. His work on what was to be his seventh novel *The Man Who Whipped Children* was interrupted by Hurricane Katrina in September, 2005, when he took in relatives from flood-stricken New Orleans.

Analysis • Before it became fashionable, Ernest J. Gaines was one southern black writer who wrote about his native area. Although he has lived much of his life in California, he has never been able to write adequately about that region. He has tried to write two novels about the West but has failed to finish either of them. Thus, while he has physically left the South, he has never left emotionally. His ties remain with the South, and his works remain rooted there. When he first began reading seriously, Gaines gravitated toward those writers who wrote about the soil and the people who lived close to it, among them William Faulkner, John Steinbeck, Willa Cather, and Ivan Turgenev. He was disappointed to discover that few black writers had dealt with the black rural southern experience. (Richard Wright had begun his career by doing so, and his work weakened as he moved further from the South.) Thus, Gaines began his career with the conscious desire to fill a void. He believed that no one had written fiction about his people.

This fact helps explain why his novels always concentrate on rural settings and on the "folk" who inhabit them. One of the great strengths of his work is voice; the sound of the voice telling the story is central to its meaning. Among his works, *Of Love and Dust*, *The Autobiography of Miss Jane Pittman*, and all the stories in *Bloodline* are told in the first person by rural black characters. The voices of the storytellers, especially Miss Jane's, express the perspective not only of the individual speakers but also in some sense of the entire black community, and it is the community on which Gaines most often focuses his attention.

Louisiana society, especially from a racial perspective, is complicated. Not only black and white people live there, but also Creoles and Cajuns. Thus there are competing communities, and some of Gaines's more interesting characters find themselves caught between groups, forced to weigh competing demands in order to devise a course of action.

Several themes recur in the Gaines canon, and together they create the total effect of his work. Generally, he deals with the relationship between past and present and the possibility of change, both individual and social. Using a broad historical canvas in his works, especially in *The Autobiography of Miss Jane Pittman,* Gaines treats the changes in race relations over time, but he is most interested in people, in whether and how they change as individuals. The issue of determinism and free will is therefore a central question in his work. Gaines has been very interested in and influenced by Greek tragedy, and in his fiction, a strain of environmental determinism is evident. In his works prior to and including *The Autobiography of Miss Jane Pittman,* a growing freedom on the part of his black characters can be seen, but the tension between fate and free will always underlies his works.

Some of Gaines's most admirable characters—for example, Marcus in *Of Love and Dust,* and Ned, Joe, and Jimmy in *The Autobiography of Miss Jane Pittman*—have the courage, pride, and dignity to fight for change. At the same time, however, Gaines reveres the old, who, while often resistant to change, embody the strength of the black people. In his work, one frequently finds tension between generations, a conflict between old and young that is reconciled only in the character of Miss Jane Pittman, who even in extreme old age retains the courage to fight for change.

Other recurring tensions and dichotomies are evident in Gaines's novels. Conflict often exists between men and women. Because of slavery, which denied them their manhood, black men feel forced to take extreme actions to attain or assert it, a theme most evident in *Of Love and Dust, The Autobiography of Miss Jane Pittman, A Gathering of Old Men* and the stories in *Bloodline.* Women, on the other hand, are often presented in Gaines's fiction as preservers and conservers. Each group embodies a strength, but Gaines suggests that wholeness comes about only when the peculiar strengths of the two sexes are united, again most clearly exemplified in Miss Jane and her relationship with the men in her life.

Among the male characters, a tension exists between fathers and sons. Treated explicitly in Gaines's fourth novel, *In My Father's House,* this theme is implicit throughout the canon. Though young men look to the older generation for models, there are few reliable examples for them to follow, and they find it difficult to take responsibility for their lives and for the lives of their loved ones.

Gaines's characters at their best seek freedom and dignity: Some succeed, and some fail in their attempts to overcome both outer and inner obstacles. Viewed in sequence, Gaines's first three novels move from the almost total bleakness and determinism of *Catherine Carmier* to the triumph of *The Autobiography of Miss Jane Pittman. In My Father's House,* however, reflects a falling away of hope in both individual and social terms, perhaps corresponding to the diminution of expectations experienced in America during the late 1970's and early 1980's.

Catherine Carmier • Gaines's first novel, *Catherine Carmier,* based on a work he wrote while an adolescent in Vallejo, has many of the characteristic weaknesses of a first novel and is more interesting for what it anticipates in Gaines's later career than for its intrinsic merits. Though it caused barely a ripple of interest when it was first published, the novel introduces many of the themes that Gaines treats more effectively in his mature fiction. The book is set in the country, near Bayonne, Louisiana, an area depicted as virtually a wasteland. Ownership of much of this region has devolved to the Cajuns, who appear throughout Gaines's novels as Snopes-like vermin, interested in owning the land only to exploit it. Like Faulkner, Gaines sees this kind of person as particularly modern, and the growing power of the Cajuns indicates a weakening of values and a loss of determination to live in right relationship to the land.

Onto the scene comes Jackson Bradley, a young black man born and reared in the area but (like Gaines himself) educated in California. Bradley is a hollow, rootless man, a man who does not know where he belongs. He has found the North and the West empty, with people living hurried, pointless lives, but he sees the South as equally empty. Feeling no link to a meaningful past and no hope for a productive future, Bradley is a deracinated modern man. He has returned to Louisiana to bid final farewell to his Aunt Charlotte, a representative of the older generation, and to her way of life.

While there and while trying to find a meaningful path for himself, Bradley meets and falls in love with Catherine Carmier. She, too, is living a blocked life, and he feels that if they can leave the area, they will be able to make a fulfilling life together. Catherine is the daughter of Raoul Carmier, in many ways the most interesting character in the novel. A Creole, he is caught between the races. Because of his black blood, he is not treated as the equal of whites, but because of his white blood, he considers black people to be beneath him. He has a near incestuous relationship with Catherine, since after her birth his wife was unfaithful to him and he considers none of their subsequent children his. Feeling close only to Catherine, he forbids her to associate with any men, but especially with black men. A man of great pride and love of the land, Raoul is virtually the only man in the region to resist the encroachment of the Cajuns. His attitude isolates him all the more, which in turn makes him fanatically determined to hold on to Catherine.

Despite her love for and loyalty to her father, Catherine senses the dead end her life has become and returns Bradley's love. Though she wants to leave with him, she is paralyzed by her love of her father and by her knowledge of what her leaving would do to him. This conflict climaxes with a brutal fight between Raoul and Bradley over Catherine, a fight that Bradley wins. Catherine, however, returns home to nurse her father. The novel ends ambiguously, with at least a hint that Catherine will return to Bradley, although the thrust of the book militates against that eventuality. Gaines implies that history and caste are a prison, a tomb. No change is possible for the characters because they cannot break out of the cages their lives have become. Love is the final victim. Catherine will continue living her narrow, unhealthy life, and Jackson Bradley will continue wandering the earth, searching for something to fill his inner void.

Of Love and Dust • Gaines's second novel, *Of Love and Dust,* was received much more enthusiastically than was *Catherine Carmier*; with it, he began to win the largely positive, respectful reviews that have continued to the present time. Like *Catherine Carmier, Of Love and Dust* is a story of frustrated love. The setting is the same: rural Louisiana, where the Cajuns are gradually assuming ownership and control of the land. *Of Love and Dust* is a substantial improvement over *Catherine Carmier,* however, in part because it is told in the first person by Jim Kelly, an observer of the central story. In this novel, one can see Gaines working toward the folk voice that became such an integral part of the achievement of *The Autobiography of Miss Jane Pittman.*

The plot of the novel concerns Marcus Payne, a young black man sentenced to prison for murder and then bonded out by a white plantation owner who wants him to work in his fields. Recognizing Marcus's rebelliousness and pride, the owner and his Cajun overseer, Sidney Bonbon, brutally attempt to break his spirit. This only makes Marcus more determined, and in revenge, he decides to seduce Louise, Bonbon's neglected wife. What begins, however, as simply a selfish and egocentric act of revenge on Marcus's part grows into a genuine though grotesque love. When he and Louise decide to run away together, Bonbon discovers them and kills Marcus. Even though he dies, Marcus, by resisting brutalizing circumstances, retains his pride and attempts to prove his manhood and dignity. His attempts begin in a self-centered way, but as his love for Louise grows, he grows in stature in the reader's eyes until he becomes a figure of heroic dimensions.

Through his use of a first-person narrator, Gaines creates a double perspective in the novel, including on one hand the exploits of Marcus and on the other the black community's reactions to them. The narrator, Jim Kelly, is the straw boss at the plantation, a member of the black community but also accepted and trusted by the whites because of his dependability and his unwillingness to cause any problems. His initial reaction to Marcus—resentment and dislike of him as a troublemaker—represents the reaction of the community at large. The older members of the community never move beyond that attitude because they are committed to the old ways, to submission and accommodation. To his credit, however, Jim's attitude undergoes a transformation. As he observes Marcus, his resentment changes to sympathy and respect, for he comes to see Marcus as an example of black manhood that others would do well to emulate.

Marcus's death gives evidence of the strain of fate and determinism in this novel as well, yet because he dies with his pride and dignity intact, *Of Love and Dust* is more hopeful than *Catherine Carmier.* Gaines indicates that resistance is possible and, through the character of Jim Kelly, that change can occur. Kelly leaves the plantation at the end of the novel, no longer passively accepting what fate brings him but believing that he can act and shape his own life. Though Marcus is an apolitical character, like Jackson Bradley, it is suggested that others will later build on his actions to force social change on the South. *Of Love and Dust* is a major step forward beyond *Catherine Carmier* both artistically and thematically. Through his use of the folk voice, Gaines vivifies his story, and the novel suggests the real possibility of free action by his characters.

The Autobiography of Miss Jane Pittman • Without a doubt, *The Autobiography of Miss Jane Pittman* is Gaines's major contribution to American literature. Except for an introduction written by "the editor," it is told entirely in the first person by Miss Jane and covers approximately one hundred years, from the Civil War to the Civil Rights movement of the 1960's. Basing the novel on stories he heard while a child around his aunt, Augusteen Jefferson, and using the format of oral history made popular in recent decades, Gaines created a "folk autobiography" that tells the story of people who are not in the history books. Although the work is the story of Miss Jane, she is merely an observer for a substantial portion of its length, and the story becomes that of black Americans from slavery to the present. Gaines's mastery of voice is especially important here, for Miss Jane's voice is the voice of her people.

From the very beginning of the novel, when Miss Jane is determined, even in the face of physical beatings, to keep the name a Union soldier gave her and refuses to be called Ticey, her slave name, to the end of the novel, when she leads her people to Bayonne in a demonstration against segregated facilities, she is courageous and in the best sense of the word "enduring," like Faulkner's Dilsey. In her character and story, many of the dichotomies that run through Gaines's work are unified. The differing roles of men and women are important elements in the book. Women preserve and sustain—a role symbolized by Miss Jane's longevity. Men, on the other hand, feel the need to assert their manhood in an active way. Three black men are especially important in Miss Jane's life, beginning with Ned, whom she rears from childhood after his mother is killed and who becomes in effect a "son" to her. Like Marcus Payne, Ned is a rebel, but his rebellion is concentrated in the political arena. Returning to Louisiana after the turn of the century, he attempts to lead his people to freedom. Though he is murdered by whites, his legacy and memory are carried on by Miss Jane and the people in the community.

Later, during the 1960's, Jimmy Aaron, another young man who tries to encourage his people to effective political action, appears. Again the members of the older generation hang back, fearful of change and danger, but after Jimmy is killed, Jane unites old and young, past and present by her determination to go to Bayonne and carry on Jimmy's work. Thus Marcus's apolitical rebellion in *Of Love and Dust* has been transformed into political action. The third man in Jane's life is Joe Pittman, her husband. A horse-breaker, he is committed to asserting and proving his manhood through his work. Although he too dies, killed by a wild horse he was determined to break, Jane in her understanding and love of him, as well as in her affection for all her men, bridges the gap between man and woman. In her character, the opposites of old and young, past and present, and man and woman are reconciled.

Miss Jane's strength is finally the strength of the past, but it is directed toward the future. When Jimmy returns, he tells the people that he is nothing without their strength, referring not only to their physical numbers but also to the strength of their character as it has been forged by all the hardships they have undergone through history. Even though the people seem weak and fearful, the example of Miss Jane shows that they need not be. They can shake off the chains of bondage and determinism, assert their free spirit through direct action, and effect change. The change has only begun by the conclusion of *The Autobiography of Miss Jane Pittman*, but the pride and dignity of Miss Jane and all those she represents suggest that ultimately they will prevail.

In My Father's House • Gaines's fourth novel, *In My Father's House*, was the first he had written in the third person since *Catherine Carmier*; the effect of its point of view is to distance the reader from the action and characters, creating an ironic perspective. Set during a dreary winter in 1970, in the period of disillusionment following the assassination of Martin Luther King, Jr., the novel suggests that the progress that was implicit in the ending of *The Autobiography of Miss Jane Pittman* was temporary at best, if not downright illusory. The atmosphere of the novel is one of frustration and stagnation.

Both the setting and the protagonist of *In My Father's House* are uncharacteristic for Gaines. Instead of using the rural settings so familiar from his other works, he sets his story in a small town. Rather than focusing on the common people, Gaines chooses as his protagonist Philip Martin, one of the leaders of the black community, a public figure, a minister who is considering running for Congress. A success by practically any measure and pridefully considering himself a *man*, Martin is brought low in the course of the novel. His illegitimate son, Robert X, a ghostlike man, appears and wordlessly accuses him. Robert is evidence that, by abandoning him, his siblings, and their mother many years previously, Martin in effect destroyed their lives. Having been a drinker and gambler, irresponsible, he tries to explain to his son that his earlier weakness was a legacy of slavery. Even though he seems to have surmounted that crippling legacy, his past rises up to haunt him and forces him to face his weakness. Martin wants to effect a reconciliation with his son and thus with his past, but Robert's suicide precludes that. *In My Father's House* makes explicit a concern that was only implicit in Gaines's earlier novels, the relationship between fathers and sons. No communication is possible here, and the failure is illustrative of a more general barrier between the generations. Although in the earlier novels the young people led in the struggle for change and the older characters held back, here the situation is reversed. Martin and members of his generation are the leaders, while the young are for the most part sunk in cynicism, apathy, and hopelessness, or devoted to anarchic violence. If the hope of a people is in the young, or in a reconciliation of old and young, hope does not exist in this novel.

A Gathering of Old Men • Hope does exist, however, in Gaines's *A Gathering of Old Men*, for which Gaines returns to his more characteristic rural setting. Here he returns as well to the optimism with which *The Autobiography of Miss Jane Pittman* ended. This time, as at the end of that novel and in *In My Father's House*, it is up to the old among the black community to lead the struggle for change, this time primarily because there are no young men left to lead. All of them have escaped to towns and cities that promise more of a future than does rural Louisiana.

In this small corner of Louisiana, however, as elsewhere in Gaines's fiction, Cajuns are encroaching on the land, replacing men with machines and even threatening to plow up the old graveyard where generations of black people have been buried. When Beau Boutan, son of the powerful Cajun Fix Boutan, is shot to death in the quarters of Marshall plantation, where Marshall black people have worked the land since the days of slavery, the old black men who have lived there all of their lives are faced with one last chance to stand up and be men. They stand up for the sake of Matthu, the only one of them who ever stood up before and thus the most logical suspect in the murder. They also stand up because of all the times in their past when they should have stood up but did not. They prove one last time that free action is possible when eighteen or more of them, all in their seventies and eighties, arm themselves with rifles of the same gauge used in the shooting and face down the white sheriff, Mapes, each in his turn claiming to be the killer.

As shut off as the quarters are from the rest of the world, it is easy to forget that the events of the novel take place as recently as the late 1970's. Beau Boutan's brother Gil, however, represents the change that has been taking place in the world outside Marshall. He has achieved gridiron fame at Louisiana State University by working side by side with Cal, a young black man. Youth confronts age when Gil returns home and tries to persuade his father not to ride in revenge against Beau's murderer, as everyone expects him to do. Gil represents the possibility of change from the white perspective. He persuades his father to let the law find and punish Beau's murderer, but he pays a heavy price when his father disowns him. He cannot stop other young Cajuns, led by Luke Will, who are not willing to change but would rather cling to the vigilantism of the old South.

In spite of their dignity and pride, the old men at Marshall risk looking rather silly because after all these years they stand ready for a battle that seems destined never to take place once Fix Boutan decides not to ride on Marshall. Sheriff Mapes taunts them with the knowledge that they have waited until too late to take a stand. Ironically, they are ultimately able to maintain their dignity and reveal their growth in freedom by standing up to the one person who has been most valiant in her efforts to help them: Candy Marshall, niece of the landowner. In her effort to protect Matthu, who was largely responsible for rearing her after her parents died, Candy has gone so far as to try to take credit for the murder herself. What she fails to realize is that the days are long past when black men need the protection of a white woman. She is stunned to realize that she too has been living in the past and has been guilty of treating grown black men like children.

The novel does eventually end with a gunfight, because Luke Will and his men refuse to let the murder of a white man by a black one go unavenged. It is fitting that the two men who fall in the battle are Luke Will, the one who was most resistant to change, and Charlie Biggs, the real murderer, who, at the age of fifty, finally proves his manhood by refusing to be beaten by Beau Boutan and then by returning to take the blame for the murder that he has committed. Charlie's body is treated like a sacred relic as each member of the black community, from the oldest to the youngest, touches it, hoping that some of the courage that Charlie found late in life will rub off. Apparently it already has.

With *A Gathering of Old Men*, Gaines returns to first-person narration, but this time the history is told one chapter at a time by various characters involved in or witnessing the action. His original plan was to have the narrator be the white newspaperman Lou Dimes, Candy's boyfriend. He found, however, that there was still much that a black man in Louisiana would not confide to a white man, even a sympathetic one, so he let the people tell their own story, with Dimes narrating an occasional chapter.

A Lesson Before Dying • *A Lesson Before Dying*, set in Gaines's fictional Bayonne during six months of 1948, reveals the horrors of Jim Crowism in the story of twenty-one-year-old Jefferson, a scarcely literate man-child who works the cane fields of Pichot Plantation. Jefferson hooks up with two criminals who are killed during the robbery of a liquor store, along with the store's white proprietor. Jefferson is left to stand trial before a jury of twelve white men who overlook his naïveté despite his lawyer's argument that he is a dumb animal, a "thing" that acts on command, no more deserving of the electric chair than a hog. When this description causes Jefferson to become practically catatonic, his grandmother enlists the local schoolteacher, Grant Wiggins, to help Jefferson gain his manhood before he is put to death. Thus, like *A Gathering of Old Men*, this novel questions the traditional devaluing of black men in the south.

Reluctantly, Wiggins agrees to help Jefferson by encouraging him to speak and to write, visiting him often and giving him a journal in which to record his thoughts. Finally, right before his execution, Jefferson has a breakthrough when he tells Wiggins to thank his students for the pecans they sent him in jail. Wiggins himself becomes the central character as he learns the real lesson of the novel, that all people are connected and responsible for each other. Wiggins comes to terms with his own role in the system that victimizes Jefferson, and the entire community learns from how Jefferson faces his execution. The novel pays a tribute to those who persevere in the face of injustice, and it also puts forward hope for better racial relationships, especially in the character of Paul, the young white jailer who is sympathetic to Jefferson and to Grant Wiggins's attempts to bring forth his humanity.

If *In My Father's House* represents a falling away of hope for human progress and perhaps also a falling away in artistry, one finds once again in *A Gathering of Old Men* and *A Lesson Before Dying* evidence of the same genuine strengths that Gaines exhibited in *The Autobiography of Miss Jane Pittman*: a mastery of the folk voice, a concern for common people, a reverence for the everyday, a love of the land, and a powerful evocation of the strength, pride, and dignity people can develop by working on and living close to the soil.

Frank W. Shelton
Updated by Rebecca G. Smith

Other major works

SHORT FICTION: *Bloodline*, 1968; *A Long Day in November*, 1971.

MISCELLANEOUS: *Porch Talk with Ernest Gaines*, 1990; *Mozart and Leadbelly: Stories and Essays*, 2005.

Bibliography

Auger, Philip. *Native Sons in No Man's Land: Rewriting Afro-American Manhood in the Novels of Baldwin, Walker, Wideman, and Gaines.* New York: Garland, 2000. Looks at Gaines's use of religious allegory in commenting upon and providing role models for manhood in his novels.

Babb, Valerie Melissa. *Ernest Gaines.* Boston: Twayne, 1991. A solid introduction to the author and his works. Includes a bibliography and an index.

Beavers, Herman. *Wrestling Angels into Song: The Fictions of Ernest J. Gaines and James Alan McPherson.* Philadelphia: University of Pennsylvania Press, 1995. This thoughtful analysis of the literary kinship of Gaines and McPherson with their precursor Ralph Ellison focuses on all three writers' characters' sense of community, storytelling, and self-recovery. While beginning with a look at their southernness, Beavers examines all three as American writers and discusses all Gaines's work through *A Lesson Before Dying.*

Carmean, Karen. *Ernest J. Gaines: A Critical Companion.* Westport, Conn.: Greenwood Press, 1998. An introductory overview of Gaines's work, with analysis of each of his novels and short-story collections and a thorough bibliography of primary and secondary sources.

Clark, Keith. *Black Manhood in James Baldwin, Ernest J. Gaines, and August Wilson.* Urbana: University of Illinois Press, 2002. The chapter on Gaines focuses on the "neo-masculinist literary imagination." The opening chapter of the book outlines the aesthetics of black masculinist protest discourse since 1940, contextualizing Clark's later discussion.

Doyle, Mary Ellen. *Voices from the Quarters: The Fiction of Ernest J. Gaines.* Baton Rouge: Louisiana State University Press, 2001. A celebration of Gaines's characters. Doyle examines the ways in which Louisiana's bayous and cane fields are peopled by Gaines with characters that exemplify their real life counterparts.

Estes, David E., ed. *Critical Reflections on the Fiction of Ernest J. Gaines.* Athens: University of Georgia Press, 1994. Fourteen essays that cover all six novels to 1994 and *Bloodline* as well as film adaptations of Gaines's work, offering detailed explications in addition to broad analyses of pastoralism, humor, race, and gender. An excellent introduction highlights important biographical facts, secondary sources, and literary themes in Gaines's work.

Gaines, Ernest J., Marcia G. Gaudet, and Carl Wooton. *Porch Talk with Ernest Gaines: Conversations on the Writer's Craft.* Baton Rouge: Louisiana State University Press, 1990. A transcription of an intimate interview conducted by colleagues of Gaines, this work offers an insightful look at how the author has transmuted his Louisiana heritage, familial experiences, literary influences, and strong folk tradition into fiction with a distinct voice.

Jones, Suzanne W. "New Narratives of Southern Manhood: Race, Masculinity, and Closure in Ernest Gaines's Fiction." *Critical Survey* 9 (1997): 15-42. Discusses Gaines's deconstruction of stereotypes and presentation of new models of black and white southern manhood. Asserts that Gaines suggests that in order to reconstruct the South, black and white men must reject the traditional Western model of manhood that links masculinity and violence.

Lowe, John, ed. *Conversations with Ernest Gaines.* Jackson: University Press of Mississippi, 1995. A selection of interviews in which Gaines speaks about his life, his themes, and his works. Includes an index and a chronology of his life.

Simpson, Anne K. *A Gathering of Gaines: The Man and the Writer.* Lafayette: Center for Louisiana Studies at the University of Southwestern Louisiana, 1991. Simpson's study, well documented with excerpts from Gaines's personal papers, offers a biographical sketch, an examination of his stylistic influences and characteristics, and a critical overview of his fiction. It includes an unannotated but thorough bibliography.